This is a volume in

THE UNIVERSITY OF MICHIGAN HISTORY OF THE MODERN WORLD

Upon completion, the series will consist of the following volumes:

The United States to 1865 *by Michael Kraus*

The United States since 1865 *by Foster Rhea Dulles*

Canada: A Modern History *by John Bartlet Brebner*

Latin America: A Modern History *by J. Fred Rippy*

Great Britain to 1688: A Modern History *by Maurice Ashley*

Great Britain since 1688: A Modern History *by K. B. Smellie*

France: A Modern History *by Albert Guérard*

Germany: A Modern History *by Marshall Dill, Jr.*

Italy: A Modern History *by Denis Mack Smith*

Russia and the Soviet Union: A Modern History *by Warren B. Walsh*

The Near East: A Modern History *by William Yale*

The Far East: A Modern History *by Nathaniel Peffer*

India: A Modern History *by Percival Spear*

The Southwest Pacific: A History *by C. Hartley Grattan*

Africa: A Modern History *by Ronald Robinson*

GREAT BRITAIN SINCE 1688

A Modern History

The University of Michigan History of the Modern World
Edited by Allan Nevins and Howard M. Ehrmann

GREAT BRITAIN SINCE 1688

A Modern History

BY K. B. SMELLIE

Ann Arbor: The University of Michigan Press

Contents

MAPS

GREAT BRITAIN SINCE 1688

A Modern History

CHAPTER I

The Economic Setting, 1688-1760

In 1689 the spirit of science had not yet transformed the outward and visible forms of Britain's economic and social life. She was quick with the thought of Newton, but had yet to be delivered of her industrial progeny. Although the age of statistics was in embryo—for Petty was its parent, and Charles Davenant applied statistical methods in his studies of the balance of trade, and John Gaunt examined bills of mortality in his study of the expectation of life in London—England was still agrarian and pastoral in her way of life. The cottage and not the factory was the center of her life. A vital part of her life was on the ocean wave, but while every Englishman had seen a sheep, many had never seen the sea. But in many hamlets and countinghouses interest was being directed to the things that could be measured and weighed and calculated. Fewer men were searching the Scriptures and bearing arms and more were studying trade and their accounts.[1] A census was not possible until 1801 because it was believed that it might incur divine displeasure, destroy the liberties of freemen, and give comfort and military secrets to her enemies. But if the government might not count its subjects, those subjects were coming to the opinion "that whoever could make two ears of corn or two blades of grass to grow upon a spot of ground where only one grew before, would deserve better of mankind, and do more essential service to his country than the whole race of politicians put together."

In 1688 Gregory King had made the first fairly accurate estimation of the population of England and Wales. It was about five and a half millions. Scotland had about a million and Ireland perhaps two million. The center of population in England was well to the South. More than half lived south of a line from Worcester to the Wash, and a quarter of the total was in and around London, which had a population of about 540,000 compared with the 488,000 of Paris and the 125,000 of Rome. Other cities and towns in England and Wales had about 876,000 and there were about 4,000,000 in villages and hamlets. People were more evenly spread than at any other time since. The most populous agricultural areas were those of the midland plain. There were concentrations outside London in Bristol and Exeter, and in other areas where there were ports with people engaged in shipping and shipbuilding, and in some areas where coal and tin or copper were mined. But the majority of workers, both in agriculture and in the various crafts or light industries which could be carried on in their own homes, were in the interior of the country. There was a scatter of small industries near London, in Essex and Kent, in Wiltshire and Somerset, in Yorkshire, Durham, and Cumberland, wherever iron, coal, or wool could be the basis of some industrial development. But England was predominantly a country of farmlands, of commons or moor and waste land. The south and southeast were preferred as places of residence by those who could make a choice.[2]

Since Cromwell's death, London had been changed from a medieval town built mainly of wood into a spacious and cosmopolitan city of brick and stone. The age of reason was first manifest in the elegance and order of some parts of Queen Anne's London. In the coffee houses of London, the ideas of a Swift, a Steele, and an Addison were discussed, and the lawyer could combine the financial advantage of practice in Westminster Hall with the opportunities for political advancement which might come from attendance in the House of Commons. Westminster was the physical home of the church, the crown, and the law. The English acropolis was not on a hill, but along a strand. London was becoming the Mecca of the political and economic ambitions of a country which was stirring to the breath of science and to the winds of change from India to the Mississippi. Country gentlemen arranged for a London solicitor to send them news from the capital. The marriage of the ancient monarchy to new movements of popular control was to produce strange and potent forms of political power such as a pamphlet literature, a periodical press, and party groups. London was already the metropolis of an imperial domain of island trading posts and coastal settlements scattered about the world. From London it was not a hyperbole to say that one could survey mankind from China to Peru—there was the fur trade of North America, the tea plantations of Ceylon, the trade in slaves and sugar, spices and textiles, coal and nails. The forest of masts in the port of London was growing thicker every day. In the center of London shops were displacing stalls. The theatre was a rival to the attraction of the lunatics at Bridewell, or to executions and bearbaiting. There were even beauty parlors staffed by gentlewomen who had attained "to great perfection preserving and improving beauty." [3]

Only in Edinburgh was there a culture comparable with that of London. It was said to have a population of about 30,000. The links between Scotland and France and Holland had given it a European outlook. But if Scotland had a continental air, her economic and social life was harsh even for that age. Glasgow in 1700 had a population of only 11,000. There were only two main streets, for the most part unpaved. House refuse was piled in the streets as there were no drains. The principal business was the importation of tobacco from Virginia. Only the commonsense and independence of the Scottish people saved them from suffocating in the antique dust of medievalism. Halifax said that in the administration of justice, personal motives were so strong that men were convicted on evidence which would not have hanged a dog in England. But religion and education were national ideals. The Scottish Kirk was almost a solitary instance of organized Christianity standing for the humble and obscure. The English regarded the Scots with dislike and contempt. Until the failure of the rebellion of 1745 they had reason to fear a savage northern border.

In Ireland there were about two million people of which only one-half million were Protestants. Here was a real frontier problem cursed with a tangle of religious, racial, and economic hates. It was a frontier problem England was never to solve. In 1700 Dublin was reputed to have a population of about 60,000. In a setting of squalor and destitution there was the most generous hospitality and some of the best conversation in Europe. Cork had a bare 35,000, Limerick 11,000, Waterford and Galway perhaps 6,000 each. Belfast was only a small port. The fertility of the land and the natural resources of fish and game which Ireland possessed led some contemporary economists to think that idleness was the curse of plenty.

Most Englishmen were husbandmen, graziers, shepherds, fishermen, miners, and quarrymen. Each country town had its miller, malster, brewer, tanner, and sawyer. Each village its baker, smith, and cobbler. These rural craftsmen engaged in primary production outnumbered the workers in more highly organized industries such as cotton, textiles, and mining. In domestic service the children of poor parents had opportunities for leisure, variety, educational advance, good food, and even promotion to positions of responsibility. The status of the housekeeper or confidential lady's maid was attractive to women. As Mandeville wrote: "The Variety of Services that are required to supply the luxurious and wanton desires as well as the real necessities of man, with all their subordinate callings, is in such a nation as ours prodigious." [4] The lot of the artisan in England compared well with that of many in other parts of Europe. At home it was often better than that of the small farmer. The artisan was often shod with boots and shoes. But at least half the population of England was poised on or much below the level of subsistence. In prosperous Exeter one-third of the cloth-workers were on the subsistence level and another third below it.[5] The workers varied from the highly skilled—the silversmith or cabinet makers with gild status—to the great mass of casual laborers who were kept off the poor rate by work. "Everybody knows that there is a vast number of Journey-men, weavers, taylors, clothworkers and twenty other handicrafts; who, if by four days labour in a week they can maintain themselves, will hardly be persuaded to work the fifth; and that there are thousands of labouring men of all sorts, who will, tho' they can hardly subsist, put themselves to fifty inconveniences, dis-oblige their masters, pinch their bellies, and run in debt, to make holi-days. When men show such an extraordinary proclivity to idleness and pleasure, what reason have we to think that they would ever work, unless they were obliged to it by immediate necessity?" [6] The witty Mandeville has a feel for some of the problems of an industrial society.

At least twenty of the total of twenty-seven million acres of England and Wales were in agricultural use. Three-fifths of the cultivated land was unenclosed by hedges or permanent fences. About one-third of the country was forest, heath, and fen. The richest farming areas were in the Midlands; the poorest in the north. Unenclosed land meant waste-ful farming, because the strips, annually allotted in the open fields, were too narrow to be ploughed economically. Enclosure made experiment and improvement possible. It also drew the hedges so characteristic of the English landscape. But near the towns land could not be en-closed by hedges or fences because the poor would pull them down for firewood. The great variety of soil and rainfall which in England is found within quite small areas made for mixed distribution of corn land, pasture, and forest. The cultivated land was almost evenly divided between arable and pasture. In mixed farms grass and grain provided food for livestock. Few areas were unable to produce the bread and milk they required.

While wheat, barley, oats, and rye were grown in most parts of England, there was a regional specialization in one or other of them. In northeast Norfolk water-borne transport made large-scale corn grow-ing possible. The river Severn with its tributaries, the Warwickshire

Avon and the Wye, formed a highway for a half a dozen counties in
the west of England, and several Welsh counties as well. Men thought
in terms of local autonomies, the creation of soil and climate. The
country was not a unity, but a collection of separate areas like the
lays of seventeenth-century France. Parliament which had a useful
procedure for passing local bills, often had to cut across local interests
which saw a new river or canal as a threat to an established order.
There was specialization in livestock as well as in crops. Defoe observed,
"tho' the feeding of cattle requires a rich soil, the breeding of them
does not, the mountains and moors being as proper for that purpose
as the richer lands." Store cattle bred in Scotland were fed in Norfolk
meadows. Others raised on the mountains of Brecknock and Radnor
were sent to the marshlands of Essex. The best race horses came from
Durham, the best coach or dray horses from Northampton, the best
plough horses from Suffolk. During the War of the Spanish Succession,
Durham changed from breeding horses suitable for hunting to a larger
breed fit for colonels of horse in battle. There were other specializations
—orchards and hop fields in Kent, cider in the west, geese and capons
raised in Sussex and Surrey. Turkeys and geese waddled from Norfolk
and Suffolk to London, feeding on the stubble from August to the end
of October, when the roads became too bad even for their webbed feet.
Market gardens were fertilized by the refuse of the towns. Haymakers
thronged the streets of London with fodder from the meadows round
it for the horses in it. The economics of the eighteenth-century stables
was almost as complex as that of the twentieth-century garage and
filling station.[7]

Although the ownership of land had almost a totem value for what
was still a feudal society, and although the estates were so nestled in
tradition, it could be said of the agricultural industry what Galileo
said of the earth itself *eppur si muove*. Agriculture employed more
resources than any other industry. It was Gregory King's guess that
in 1688 the great lord had an income of about £2,000 and cottagers
and paupers about £6.10s. About a quarter of the national income went
to 3.5 per cent of the families of England. At the apex of rural society
was the great titled landowner with a rent roll of nearly £3,000, a
citizen of the cosmopolitan world, but involved in local affairs where
lay the roots of political power and the control of vital administrative
actions. Next came the substantial squire with between £2,000 and
£800, the country gentleman who as justice of the peace and economic
overlord of his rural world was the representative there of the great
world of policy and power; next again was the smaller man with less

than £800. Below the squire and his relations were the freeholders, the copyholders, the tenants at will, and last but not least, the landless laborers.[8]

Fewer landowners than in the past were entirely dependent on land for their livelihood, for many had government office, directorships of trading companies, or profits from the legal profession. The larger landowners tended to live in the grand manner both at Court and on the Grand Tour. The smaller were becoming more provincial, harassed by the taxation for the great wars, jealous of their richer neighbors, and antagonistic to the official and financial classes. The small squires and the lower clergy were to form the strength of the Tory party that opposed Walpole.

The estates or family seats were most numerous in the home counties, but they were also sprinkled about in Durham and Lancashire and other counties remote from the pull of London. Some were owned by noble families, like the Talbots and the Howards; others by the gentry or squires. Others again by men of fortune from the growing trades and professions. The estates were units of ownership, not of production. The owner might have a home farm to supply the needs of his family and servants and not cultivate for a market. His function was to supply capital and general direction. To extend and consolidate their position the great landowners created entails for continuity and employed lawyers who were experts in property law and stewards who were specialists in farming practice. Money could be made in the intensive cultivation of land for a large and local market. Between 1680 and 1740 large-scale purchases of land were made by families which already had considerable estates. Smaller purchases were made by those who wanted a residential seat. The squire with a rental of less than £800 was in a weak position for he had few, if any, outside sources of income. The number of yeomen declined. They were not driven out, but there was a process of attrition because the idea that a holding should be sufficient to maintain a family, was giving place to the discovery of the economy of bigger units of production.

As in a slow-motion film of an industrial process, one can see, in the agricultural life of England, the action of the forces of the market. The advantages of division of labor and the principles of comparative costs were written into every detail of the landscape. Whether fields were open or enclosed depended on the lie of the land, the nature of the subsoil, its type of product, and the distance from centers of consumption. The open field system was unsuited to mountainous country or to pastoral farming. It might do for areas in which men raised grain for their own consumption, but it was not successful where production was for sale. The influence of the London market caused its early decline in Middlesex, Essex, and large parts of Suffolk. It could secure certain minimum standards, but it was obnoxious to individual experiment. It was difficult to drain. Nearly all the improvements in agricultural techniques were made on land which was enclosed or to be enclosed. By more intensive cultivation, improved rotation, and better management of the soil, England was to supply a growing population with a better standard of living. Enclosure increased the scope for sheep rearing and the production of wool. The sowing of root crops made it possible to provide winter feeding for the flocks. The average weight of sheep increased between 1710 and 1795 from twenty-eight to eighty pounds. Jethro Tull, by a device adapted from the mechanism of the church organ, developed a mechanical drill for the more regular sowing of seed.

In 1700 there was only a scatter of industries. Woolen manufacture, the most important, was dependent on the rural population spinning and weaving in their own homes. We still use the word spinster for an unmarried woman. Cloth was greatly valued. The "cloth" for the clergy recalls the respectability and durability of the old broadcloth. Wool was greatly valued because the rise and fall of rents was held to depend upon its price. There were three great areas of cloth production; East Anglia, the South West, and the West Riding of Yorkshire. In the cloth industry the middleman was attracting notice. There was also a nascent cotton industry. Cotton, originally called "Cyprus wool," was imported from the Levant and the West Indies, and although legislation intended to protect the woolen industry checked the manufacture of cotton goods, cloth was woven of cotton and wool and in Lancashire there were the foundations of a cotton industry. Cotton goods were a promise of wholesome change; they were the nylons of the eighteenth century, they could be washed more easily than wool, and a clean shirt—together with a disbelief in witches—came to be the characteristic of an eighteenth-century gentleman. The demands of the town and of the tropics encouraged the making of lighter fabrics. Oriental influence was strong throughout Europe's textile industry, and in England, Indian chintz was imitated by printing on white calico or linen. Between 1700 and 1750 the English came to equal the Dutch in the arts of dyeing and finishing cloth. The white cloth was still exported to Holland, but the final processes which were the key to the market passed into English hands.[9]

The prosperous woolen industry and the nascent cotton industry were incentives to the improvement of the processes of spinning and weaving—which are near the heart of the industrial revolution. In 1733 John Kay's flying shuttle made it possible for a weaver to operate a wider loom and doubled the pace of working. The spinning jenny of James Hargreaves in 1764 enabled a number of spindles to be worked simultaneously. The "water-frame" of Richard Arkwright in 1768 used rollers revolving at different speeds to draw out the twisted yarn and produced a stronger thread than the spinning jenny. In 1779 Samuel Crompton's mule combined the spinning jenny and the water frame, and made it possible to spin a finer yarn than any before produced in England. Arkwright's machine was driven by waterpower; Crompton's mule was at first worked by hand, but was later adapted to waterpower, and the first loom made by Cartwright was driven by a bull.

The development of industry would come from the interplay between wider markets made possible by improved communications and a growing population, improvements in the technical control of natural forces which would use the power of water not only as it flowed but as it boiled, and the properties of coal and iron as they were uncovered by the chemist. There was in 1700 a great diversity in the industrial pattern of England, slight as the pattern was. England was divided into industrial provinces. There were textiles in Lancashire and Yorkshire, metal in the west Midlands. The coal and iron districts of the Midlands and Gloucestershire were near the Severn River, which was a useful transport system. Each industrial region had at least one large town, which acted as a local capital. The more skilled workers would be there, and reputations in particular crafts could be made. At Sheffield there were the razors and knives, and the skilled artisan who worked at home or in a nearby shop was still very common. He might have one or two assistants. Even shipbuilding, except for ships built for the Royal Navy or the East India Company, was carried on in small yards. The houses of all but the rich were built by bricklayers or carpenters. Industrial production was often for local markets. But light and portable goods could be carried over bad roads and still pay their way, as gold and precious stones were worth their months of travel from the ancient East. Stockings came from Nottingham and Leicester, toys and nails from Birmingham, cutlery from Sheffield, and hats from many districts.[10]

The sea and navigable rivers had an all-pervading influence. London received her coal from Newcastle. A constant stream of colliers, built at Whitby and Yarmouth, plied between Newcastle and London. Grain from the east coast ports and building stone from Portland and other quarries near the sea could be sent to London. As most immigrants from Europe came first to London, industries based on their skills were to be found there, for example, papermaking and silk. London, too, made the high-quality consumer goods—the coaches, the furniture, silverware, and jewelry. She had everything for ships—anchormakers and sextantmakers. Other ports had their special interests and skills. Bristol built ships and specialized in sugar and tobacco. Newcastle had coal, ships, steel, and cutlery. Liverpool, ships, tools, and watches. Other places had their natural products: tin in Cornwall, rock salt in Cheshire, clay in Staffordshire, lead in Cumberland, and slate in north Wales. The most vital influence in the location of industry was the distribution of coal and water. Long before coal was used for industrial power it was used to heat the water needed for the textile industry. Local coal made possible the woolen industry of Yorkshire, and the cotton industry of Lancashire. It was used for pumping mines in Cornwall, for the sugar and glass industries of Bristol. Water made possible the papermaking of Hampshire, the tanning industry about London. Flowing water was power for the mines, for the bellows of the ironmasters, and the grindstones of Sheffield cutlers. Mill ponds, conduits, and water wheels were all fields of eighteenth-century investment.

The fact that there was a regional specialization, does not account for the "take off" of England from its agricultural past into its industrial future. The traditional diversities were informed by old and new forces which were to encourage mechanization and an insight into the forces of nature which would make possible its unforeseen acceleration. From the beginning of the sixteenth century there had been a process of standardization and an achievement in the precision by which cannon and other arms were made for military purposes. The demand for arms in general, and artillery in particular, stimulated the production of iron. The manufacture of large castings was carried on mainly in Sussex, which had the advantage of resources in fuel and ore near London. Until the eighteenth century wood charcoal was the only fuel used for smelting. The consumption of wood alarmed the government, because it was needed not only for iron, but also for shipbuilding. The use of wood in Sussex for making iron was, therefore, restricted. But the supplies of wood fuel throughout the country began to be scarce. Even as late as 1720 the total national output of bar iron was only about 20,000 tons. But in the 1690's the Quaker ironmasters had begun to emerge. They used small furnaces for smelting and forges for wire drawing and blacksmith's work. Abraham Darby early in the eighteenth century used coke and coal for smelting. In 1740 Benjamin Huntsman, a clock- and watchmaker, developed a process for making cast or crucible steel.

In 1766 the Cranege brothers invented the reverberatory furnace for converting pig iron into malleable or wrought iron bar. In printing, in the interests of accuracy and reduced costs, some of the features of factory enterprise had been developed. The process of printing involved, too, the manufacture of standardized and interchangeable parts for repetitive use. Clock mechanisms provided a basis for the development of gear-wheel transmissions. The watch trade had a high degree of division of labor. Long before Adam Smith and his pin, Mandeville had used the watch to illustrate the advantages of division of labor: "... I am persuaded, that even the Plenty we have of Clocks and Watches, as well as the Exactness and Beauty they may be made of, are chiefly owing to the Division that has been made of that Art into many Branches." [11] The clock perfected by John Harrison between 1728 and 1760 gave an accuracy in time measurement, which made possible the determination of longitude at sea and revolutionized navigation. So impressive was the subtlety and accuracy of watches and clocks that the Deity had the skill of a watchmaker attributed to him. "Look 'round the world: contemplate the whole and very part of it: You will find it to be nothing but one great machine, subdivided into an infinite number of lesser machines, which again admit of subdivisions, to a degree beyond what human senses and faculties can trace and explain. All these various machines, and even their most minute parts, are adjusted to each other with an accuracy, which ravishes into admiration, all men who have ever contemplated them." [12]

But machinery, however subtle, would not have transformed the world without a new source of power. Wind and water remained the principal power sources in the early eighteenth century. A prime mover more powerful, more efficient, and less restricted in application than wind and water was needed. Thomas Newcomen, a blacksmith, a native of Derbyshire, invented in 1708 a steam engine which was operated by atmospheric pressure acting on a piston in a vertical cylinder open at the top and closed at the bottom. Newcomen engines were to be installed in many parts of England, also in Russia, Sweden, France, and Hungary. About 1760 a Newcomen engine was erected at a mine in New Jersey. But the vital advance in the provision of a new source of power came when James Watt learned from Joseph Black the theory of latent heat. In the Newcomen engine a considerable amount of latent heat was lost without doing useful work. The solution of the problem was to add a separate condenser to the cylinder and piston of the Newcomen engines. It would not have been a practical success had it not been for a cannonmaking machine which could bore a truly cylindrical hole in iron. Cylinders made by John Wilkinson of Bersham were vital to the early steam engine. In 1776 the first steam engine was ready for the market in the English blast furnaces.

The history of the steam engine can be traced with some precision. Far less is known about the factors which were influencing the increase of manpower itself. When the first census was made in 1801 it gave about nine million population for England and Wales, which meant that in the eighteenth century it had increased by about two-thirds. In the nineteenth century it was to increase from nine to thirty-two million. The movement in the eighteenth century was small, particularly in the first half. The specific causes of the change are difficult to assess. There was no steady increase of births or steady decline in deaths. There were many causes to keep the birth rate low and the death rate high before 1750. The average expectation of life at birth was under thirty years. There were deficiency diseases such as rickets, smallpox, typhus, and tuberculosis, described by Bunyan as "captain of all the men of death." In the records "fever" covered all high temperatures, and "lethargy" covered terrifying things. As Donne had written: "It would overload and oppress any natural disorder and discompose any artificial memory, to deliver the names of several fevers." Of the total burials recorded in London in 1739, slightly more than half were those of children under eleven and 38 per cent were infants under three. Much harm was done by gin. The gin age did not end until 1751, when distillers were forbidden to sell by retail and when both spirit and licence duties were sharply raised. "Intoxicating Gin" wrote Mandeville, "was a Fiery Lake that sets the Brain in Flame, Burns up the Entrails, and scorches every part within; and at the same time a Lethe of Oblivion, in which the Wretch immersed drowns his most piercing cares, and with his Reason all anxious reflections of Bratts that cry for Food, hard Winters, Frosts, and horrid Empty Home." [13] Gin not only killed, it also reduced fertility. Custom also kept the birth rate down. Servants lived with their masters in the farmhouse and apprentices could not marry until they had completed their indentures. Unmarried women failed to get husbands not because there was a shortage of men, but because the men might not have the proper amount of cash. Marriage was inextricably bound up with the ownership of property. After 1750 improvements in agriculture and better transport made it possible to meet local food shortages. Vegetables reduced scurvy. The use of coal made the cottages less damp. Soap and washable clothes lengthened the life of the human and reduced the number of the verminous population. But even with these improvements, towns were still consumers of men. Before the development of sanitary science the more people were together the dirtier and the fewer they would be.

As the century went on the mobility of the population probably increased. People moved from places where wages were low to where they could get more. The agricultural laborer moved from parish to parish and from county to county, undeterred by the law of settlement. There were barriers to be overcome. The industrial revolution had not yet "entirely spoilt the faces of the north of England," but the north had even then a harsh and ugly look and feel for the softer southerner. It was not easy to change from wheaten bread, beef, and beer to oatmeal, bacon, potatoes, and buttermilk. But men did follow the jobs and the jobs did move—as for example, firearms from London to Birmingham, silk to Coventry and Cheshire. There was always the desire to be free from the frustrating traditions of the older towns. Apprenticeship decayed. Grocers were distinguished from apothecaries and distillers. Blacksmiths parted company from watch- and clockmakers. There was a subtle increase in the diversities of occupations, and with it increased mobility, and, with increased mobility, conditions favorable to increased fertility.

Students of the detailed records of the eighteenth century are impressed with the care with which domestic and family goods and chattels were administered. In the complexities of a changing rural order, enveloped in a cobweb of ancient legal forms, care was necessary. There were great contrasts. London was a gambler's paradise. "All classes betted on the turn of a coin, the throw of a dice, the result of an election, the sex of an unborn child." [14] In 1720 there was a craze for speculation and subscribers made a wild rush to invest in a number of preposterous "bubble" companies. But the resources were accumulating, and also the techniques for their use to improve production and distribution. There was an interest in the mechanism of finance to match the interest in the mechanism of nature. The marriage of thrift and reasonable risk helped to lay the foundation of new industries. While self-financing was a marked feature of the period there were new channels of finance, deep and widespread enough to support experiments and innovations. The century which saw the birth of modern economic theory was shot through and through with an increasing awareness of the economic facts of life. The mechanism of the market was examined with the same interest as the mechanism of a watch, a mill, or a loom. Changes in the structure of industry offered new chances to those who were skilled in the mechanism of the market for capital, as they also offered new chances for those who were skilled in the play of natural forces. The skilled artisan who worked at home or in a nearby shop was still very common. But a coal deposit or a spring of soft water might transform a nominal domestic industry into almost a factory form. When the machines used were large—as in the case of making broad-cloth—and the market distant, the merchant clothier from a convenient center would give out material and collect the finished or semifinished goods. Examples are the Norwich drapers, the Leeds clothiers, the Manchester warehousemen and the Nottingham hosiers.

Improvements in transport made possible improvements in production and marketing. With poor communications much of the energy of men and women was spent in fetching and carrying the materials they needed and the work they sold. In districts remote from rivers, coal was carried to hilly and outlying districts in small parcels by pack horse. In 1700 most of the retail trade of the large towns was done by hawkers: bread, gingerbread, apples, watercress, fish, rabbits, and cat's meat. There was much haggling—pleasant enough beneath the suns of Arabia, but tedious and wasteful in places which were sodden and un-kind. It was a discovery of the Quakers that honesty paid in business, because it simplified and speeded business. Haggling is so much friction in the wheels of commerce, which a little oil of honesty will reduce. The first price of the Quaker was his last. This was an improvement in com-munication among dealers and widened the market. The advantages of standardization in the parts of a machine or the quality of goods apply also to their price. It was a symptom of the age of enlightenment that the use of shop windows helped the buyer to see what was for sale. Markets from being in part a ceremony and in part a contest of wits were becoming machines for distribution.

Improvements in transport meant also that the factors of production were more easily assembled. Specialization was easier because capital was available and the market was widened. In 1722 Defoe pointed out that farmers once had to sell off their cattle in the autumn because the roads were impassable in bad weather. When the highways near Lon-don improved they could sell all the year round. With the development of more specialized production in industry, it was possible by trade marks and other devices to establish a direct relation between producers and retailers.

In the essentials of food England was self-supporting. She could export provisions and she could supplement her home produce with imports of butter, beef, and fish from Scotland and Ireland. Her cattle hides were of the best quality. Her leather goods were outstanding. Woolen goods were of almost infinite variety. She could pay with cloth for timber from the Baltic, Negroes from Africa, and wine from Europe. Contemporaries believed that a free and trading people like the English or the Dutch could in one year recover more strength than France in five. There was a theory of free trade before Adam Smith. Dudley North and Josiah Child held that no trade which was of advantage to the merchant would be detrimental to the state and that favor to one trade was an abuse as well as a prejudice to the economy of the nation. With the sense of security that constitutional government after 1689 was bringing, private investment was attracted to the expansion of trade, the purchase and improvement of land and domestic buildings. Influential men had a vested interest in stable government and in national expansion. They would have agreed with David Hume that security gives property, property plenty, plenty curiosity, and that curiosity makes possible civilization. A house did not have to be a fort. Even a ship might be as useful in the business of trade as in the business of war. This sense of security was a help to the finance of government. The state was able to use private savings for public purposes on a scale unknown in any other country. The National Debt rose from about one million pounds in 1688 to nearly eighty million in 1750; the rate of interest on government securities fell to 5 per cent in 1717 and 3 per cent in 1749.

But the nature of foreign trade was as difficult to lay bare as the secrets of the natural world itself. The changes which were taking place in the processes of production involved a growing subtlety in the web of trade. Compared with France the economy of Britain was more elastic and resilient. Her resources were more diversified. Internal communications were not impeded by tolls. The French mercantile marine was smaller than the British. France had a much shorter coast line and fewer ports. Her Mediterranean and oceanic trades were separated by the Spanish peninsula. She needed two navies. Britain had almost unlimited opportunities for the development of oceanic trade with the opening world. In her wars with the Dutch, Britain had two advantages: She lay across the Dutch communications and she had a strong and growing domestic industry upon which to base her foreign trade. She did not have to export in order barely to live. She had not begun to lend abroad. She could export surplus grain and textiles in order to buy naval stores from the Baltic, and the silk, coffee, and spices of the East. Exports would pay for mercenary troops and a surplus on overseas account would make possible an accumulation of precious metals as a source of national strength. For this purpose, too, there were the proceeds not only of exports, but of re-exports—West Indian sugar, the traffic in

African slaves, and the profits which would be brought home from India.

Eighteenth-century England greatly valued the benefits of foreign trade. There was a large volume of shipping and a powerful navy. Gregory King had put the number of common seamen at 50,000, and this could be increased by the press gang. In the spring of 1756 James Watt wrote to his father: "They now press anyone they can get, landsmen as well as seamen . . . and unless one be either a 'prentice or a creditable tradesman, there is scarce any getting off again." The ships were mostly small, but attention was being paid to stowage and convenience of handling. The reputation of English merchants was high. They were intelligent, resourceful, and honest. Marine insurance was rapidly developing and official marine statistics were collected. The underlying principle of foreign trade was being explored.

The century between 1660 and 1760 was the age of Mercantilism in action. The mercantile system was made up "of all the devices, legislative, administrative and regulatory, by which societies still predominantly agrarian sought to transform themselves into trading and industrial societies." [15] It was an attempt to control the political conditions on which the employment of citizens and the wealth of merchants depended. In the seventeenth century there had been a systematic attack on the vulnerable position held by the Dutch in the European economy —as middlemen, brokers, refiners, finishers. The Dutch occupying a small country with no natural resources, "not fully as big as two of our best shires," had shown what could be done by *artifice,* by "their continual industry in the trade of Merchandize." The Navigation Act of 1651 had aimed at cutting out the Dutch merchants and shipmasters from all the *import* trade into England. The whole trade between England and the Colonies was enclosed and protected and canalized in English shipping. The balance of trade this secured would give an income in precious metals. It was not that the mercantilists confused wealth with treasure. Some branches of foreign trade in 1700 did use large supplies of precious metal. The East India Company exported large quantities of silver to pay for the spices which it imported from the East. Merchants trading to the Baltic found it convenient to take coin and bullion with them for trading purposes. The expansion of the European economy into the peripheral areas of Asia, India, and America may have emphasized the traders' need for "capital in a solid and ponderable form." Adam Smith in the *Wealth of Nations* was to argue that there was no more occasion to be anxious over the supply of money than over the supply of any other commodity. It would be regulated by the laws of supply and demand. The emergencies of war, he thought, could be financed by the export of commodities and by the use of credit and paper money. The mercantile system was, he argued, a conspiracy contrived by a minority in their own interests. It professed so to regulate trade as to secure a favorable balance in the national interest, but its real object was to secure for manufacturers a monopoly of the home market. It sacrificed the interests of the consumer to those of the producer.[16]

It is possible that the obsession of the mercantilists with "treasure" had its roots in the political uncertainty and violence of the times, in the limited knowledge of more sophisticated conceptions of money and credit with which we are now blessed. Keynes has seen in the practice of the mercantilists "a contribution to statecraft" which was "concerned with the economic system as a whole and with securing the optimum employment of the system's entire resources." They wanted to kill two birds with one stone: to get rid of an unwelcome surplus of goods which was believed to be causing unemployment and to increase the total stock of money in the country. The ideal was national wealth and power based on abundant shipping, the supply of essential raw materials, and the control of employment and investment at home by indirect means. "At a time when the authorities had no direct control over the domestic rate of interest or the other inducements to home investment, measures to increase the favourable balance of trade were the only *direct* means at their disposal for increasing foreign investment; and, at the same time, the effect of a favourable balance of trade on the influx of the precious metals was their only *indirect* means of reducing the domestic rate of interest and so increasing the inducement to home investment." Monopolies in the hands of chartered companies like the East India Company or the Muscovy were justified by the extreme risk of the voyages and the need to supervise the conduct of traders and to facilitate the regulation of trade by the government. The object of colonization was to obtain goods which were complementary to the products of the mother country. A colony was to yield raw materials and to take English manufactures. The colonies were to confine themselves to agriculture and leave industry to the mother country.

CHAPTER II

The Revolution of 1689
and the World of Walpole

The Revolution of 1689 did not have the note of a call to a new age where all things could be bright and beautiful, which we hear in the American Revolution of 1776. There were few truths which seemed self-evident in 1689, and what there were supported the King who had fled over the water. The Revolution was the work of both Whigs and Tories, driven by the facts of the case to go where their theories would follow far behind them. As things fell out the Whigs were to make the revolution their property—and their professional skill lay in appropriating property. At the time the majority of the people were probably Tory in the sense that they believed that kings should rule and that they were by God appointed to the job.

About the nature of kingly authority there was no clear understanding, and the legal mist which surrounded the throne was, at the Revolution itself, only cleared to the extent of dispersing the fog about the dispensing power. Even today only a few people could explain with any precision what they understand by democracy. Kingly government had in 1689 a far longer history than any democratic form. Its divinity gave Claudius immunity from the wrath of Laertes. The more simple-minded in 1689, as yet untouched by the new science which was to dissolve their world, took the view that kings were by God appointed through the mysterious process of generation. That kings were the fathers of their people, as Adam had been the father of his smaller family, was a view to refuting which John Locke had devoted the first of his *Two Treatises of Government*. Others held that parliaments were as old as the nation, but their views about the pedigree of parliaments were as vague as the views of others about the pedigree of kings. Aeneas and Alfred were likely to be included in that dubious genealogical tree.

In the seventeenth century men appealed to history for the solution of political problems as they now appeal to psychology or statistics. The clue to political problems they sought in the past. But when history was in fable or in the Word of God, which it might be difficult to interpret, or in the tough and technical records of the common law, it was not easy to find a clue which would satisfy men living in a world already quick with the seed of Newtonian science. The past was often venerated for virtues which it had never had, and the future feared for dangers it would never see. No one could know that the English had seen their last civil war. Only the few who had read Locke or Harrington could look on institutions, even kingship itself, as a means to human happiness or consider that the roots of happiness could be pruned by using the tool of reason when cultivating the garden in which men must live.

The Revolution of 1689 produced a mutation in European political forms—the limited monarchy which was to suffer a sea change into the rich and strange systems of parliamentary government and, its cousin, presidential government, by which the free world now lives. It had to be limited monarchy because—although Charles II and James II and a majority of their subjects believed in the divine right of kings, and the most perfect form of monarchy then known was the *roi soleil* of France, center of the most glorious civilization of western Europe since the Antonines—the people of England were not prepared to subserve the foreign policy of France, nor were they prepared to accept the destruction of that Church of England which was the creation of their wisdom and experience in the world of religion. The Church of England was how the majority of Englishmen believed that God's word should be understood and how His church should be ordered. When James II had forced the Tories to choose between their church and their king they could but choose their church. It was a Protestant and reformed church, the spiritual center of a civilization to which the alternative was a Bourbon Stuart civilization, having as its agent the priest, the dragoon, and the hangman, and its threatening outpost on England's western flank in barbarous Ireland.

Although they were forced to resist their king, the Tories would have preferred a regency to a transfer of the Crown. As this was not possible they tried to say that he had abdicated, though clearly he had done nothing of the kind. But if he had not abdicated, then to say that he had done actions incompatible with his holding the Crown was to take the Whig view that the tenure of kings was in the nature of a trust. And if, hard pressed, a Tory said that James II had *de facto* ceased to be king and *de facto* someone else was now king, he had to decide who was the heir—for the whole point of monarchy for the relief of man's estate is that one can say "the king is dead; long live the king." The heir of James II was a Roman Catholic, and if you believed the tale that the alleged heir had been smuggled in a warming pan into the Queen's bedroom, then the heir was Mary the wife of William III, and she would not be Queen unless her husband were also King. William III would not accept the throne unless he were truly king—no mere consort he.[1]

Had James II not fled to France, a written constitution might have been imposed on him. As it was the Declaration of Rights solemnly presented to William and Mary before they accepted the Crown was almost an "instrument of government." Embodied in the Bill of Rights, it did not enunciate abstract principles of government, but it was designed to provide safeguards against royal wrongdoings, many of which were specified. While there was no reference to a social contract, the document implied some kind of contract between king and nation based on the "complete confidence" which Parliament professed in the two sovereigns. Using the well-known common law technique of changing existing law in the act of stating what it is, Parliament made important changes which limited the royal prerogative. Parliament had come to stay, and it was only a matter of time before the rule of a king in person would give place to the rule of the king in Parliament. The formidable trinitarian sovereign, King, Lords, and Commons, whose studied words no Briton could deny without rebellion, had been conceived.

As David Ogg said, there was not a word about democracy, about the economic betterment of the people, or about the extension of the franchise, but there was a great deal about those elementary legal rights of the subject, rights to which we are now so accustomed that we take them for granted and, therefore, assume that they have never been threatened. The Bill of Rights abolished "the pretended power of suspending of laws, or the execution of laws," by regal authority, without consent of Parliament. "It condemned the dispensing power, but only as it hath been assumed and exercised of late," and intended a statutory regulation of its exercise which was never carried out. It condemned the levying of taxation by pretense of prerogative, without grant of Parliament, but this was hardly more than a declaration of existing law. It declared that for "the amending, strengthening and preserving of the laws, parliament ought to be held frequently"; that elections of members of Parliament ought to be free. But it made no attempt to define the extent of the royal powers. The prerogative of mercy, the king's right to choose his ministers, to declare war, and to make peace were left untouched. Of all the powers unquestionably belonging to

ICELAND

ATLANTIC OCEAN

Faröe Is.

Shetland Is.

Orkney Is.

John o'Groats

SCOTLAND

NORTH SEA

NORWAY

DENMARK

Outer Hebrides

SCOTTISH
HIGHLANDS

Inner Hebrides

Tay R.
Forth R.

Edinburgh

NORTHERN IRELAND

Clyde R.

Tyne R.

Belfast

LAKE DISTRICT

Isle
of Man

Mersey R.

PENNINES

Anglesey

Humber R.

The Wash

IRELAND

IRISH SEA

WALES

ENGLAND

Cardiff

London

Thames R.

BRISTOL CHANNEL

Severn R.

Land's End

Scilly Isles

The Lizard

Isle of Wight

ENGLISH CHANNEL

FRANCE

The British Isles

Miles

0   40   80   120

the Crown in 1660, only one was destroyed—the raising or keeping a standing army within the kingdom in time of peace, unless with the consent of Parliament, was declared illegal. This power was henceforth based on the annual Mutiny Act, which fixed the size of the military establishment and authorized the maintenance of military discipline by courts-martial.[2]

After William and Mary had been declared king and queen, Parliament added to the laws of the constitution. The Triennial Act, 1694, obliged the king to summon Parliament at least every three years. The Act of Settlement, 1701 included rules which, had they not become a dead letter, would have made government chaotic and strangled cabinet government, as the British were to know it, in its cradle. No person who had an office or place of profit under the king could serve as a member of the House of Commons. All matters relating to the well governing of the kingdom which were the responsibility of the Privy Council were to be transacted there, and all resolutions taken thereupon were to be signed by the individuals responsible. This would have involved a subordination of the administration to the legislature which would have made impossible the development of a cabinet system by which the servants of the king exercise his prerogatives—the essential executive powers on which the life of the state depends—because they are members of the House of Commons and are supported by a majority of it in the implementation of a policy approved by the country, if necessary at a general election. The Septennial Act, 1715, increased the normal term of Parliament's existence from three to seven years and made it possible for the government in office to nurse the constituencies on which its power depended. Looking back, we can see that in Britain's tight little island, in the eighteenth century at least, collaboration between the king's ministers and the representatives of his people, even at the price of continuous comic and often scandalous, yet competent, corruption, was a better instrument of government than the uncontrolled power of a legislature or continuous friction between an independent royal executive and an irresponsible legislature.

One of the most radical innovations in British political life was the Union between England and Scotland, which was skillfully engineered in 1707. This was a union of parliaments: forty-five Scottish members were added to the 513 members of the English House of Commons and sixteen Scottish peers to the House of Lords. After 1689 the case for a union was very strong indeed. England had adopted the Hanoverian succession; she had involved herself in war with France and was fearful that there might be a Jacobite invasion through her northern back door.

By the union the English avoided the danger of a separate Scottish foreign policy. The Scots obtained access to the English colonies. Scotland had long been dissatisfied with English indifference to her economic aspirations—the miscarriage of the grandiose plan for a trading settlement on Panama had been blamed on the English. Scotland ceased to be "the wilderness to the English garden." From a country poor in national resources and rich in native talent trained in one of the best educational systems of the time, the Scots invaded the English colonies and England itself. They became customs officers in Jamaica, doctors in London, and district magistrates in British India. Even then there were others who became admirals in Russia. The basic principles of the Union were the Protestant succession to a united monarchy, the establishment of a single state with one parliament and one executive, a common economic and fiscal system. While the Scots parted with their parliament and separate executive they kept their separate legal system, separate church, and separate educational system.[3]

There were changes after 1689 far more fundamental than were made by acts of Parliament. Some Whigs liked to boast that they had turned James II out and would do the same again. But in a small island ruled by a king who, like William III, was used to real power and was determined to exercise it in protecting Europe from the domination of the French monarchy, there could be no policy of continuous revolution. The revolution of 1689 could be justified by necessity, but it could give no ground for a right of revolution in general. Kings might not be by God appointed, but the chaos of His fallen world was a warning that men could invite destruction by a pursuit of perfection.

The Whig party was a party of new men and new interests. Its leaders were drawn from the great landed families who had gathered territory and influence during the seventeenth century. They were for limited monarchy and the supremacy of Parliament, the Toleration Act and the Protestant succession, hostility to France, the development of commerce, and the security of property. Their political allies were the Dissenters—those rationalists of Christianity who did not accept the ornate complexities of the Church of England as the only possible house of God. Their religious organization was a standing criticism of a hierarchical society. They anticipated in the life of the spirit the methods which would later move through the industrial and commercial life of nineteenth-century England. They had a separate and often superior educational system, a trained ministry, and a belief that the Word of God could be read and understood by men of sense and substance without the help of an Establishment with its roots in the Middle Ages. The

Test and Corporation Acts had made them second-class citizens, but they had the right to vote, and, being small property owners often concentrated in the towns, their electoral influence was greater than their numbers. By 1714 a political alliance of the Dissenters and the greater landowners against the smaller landed gentry was the backbone of the Whig party.

It was from this Whig party that the new moneyed men who understood the growing importance of trade and industry had most support. Their case was put as follows by their ablest critic: ". . . the greatest Misfortune which can befall the Nation, are what would most answer their *Interest,* and their *Wishes;* a perpetual War increases their Money, breaks and beggars their *Landed Enemies.* The ruin of the Church would please the Dissenters, Deists, and Socinians, whereof the Body of their Party consists." [4] The landed enemies of the Whigs were described by a man of lesser genius than Swift: "For the honour of his Majesty, and the safety of his government, we cannot but observe that those who have appeared the greatest enemies to both, are of that rank of men who are commonly distinguished by the title of *Fox-hunters.* As several of these have had no part of their education in cities, camps, or courts, it is doubtful whether they are of greater ornament or use to the nation in which they live. It would be an everlasting reproach to politics, should such men be able to overturn an establishment which has been formed by the wisest laws, and is supported by the ablest heads." [5]

After the Revolution of 1689 it was impossible for the Tory party to support the Hanoverians without splitting their ranks and impossible also to support the Stuarts without denying their church. It might be said that the Whigs were to put the Crown in their pocket. But that is a simplification which ignores the drama of history and the realities of eighteenth-century politics. In the first place the Tories might have won, and, in the second, the Crown was far too potent a totem and much too vital a part of the mechanism of government to go into any pocket, capacious as were the pockets of the Whigs. In the course of William's reign the Tories abandoned for the most part the theories of divine right and nonresistance and "quietly appropriated the whig life belts which alone could ensure survival in the sea of royal iniquity." [6] To kill a king was a poor way of making him responsible for his policies. But so long as he had political initiative, his ministers could shelter themselves under the cloak of his royal command. The problem was solved by extending the lawyer's fiction—that the king could do no wrong—to matters of state. [7] A fictive innocence of the king was postulated in order to secure the responsibility of his ministers. As this responsibility could only be enforced by impeachment, this Whig doctrine implied the regular meeting of Parliament. The measure of royal innocence was the measure of ministerial guilt. In acts of state the kingly power could be thus sterilized. As the deadly passions of the bloody seventeenth century were stilled by the peace of the Augustans, it was realized that it might be as wasteful to behead a minister as to behead a king—and the use of the political wilderness was developed. Walpole went to the Tower, but he kept his head physically and mentally.

The Revolution was not really safe until the failure of the Jacobite rebellion of 1715. It was clear then that the sentiments of the past need not shed blood in the present, nor imperil the political order on which the future wealth of the nation would depend. Even more important than the failure of 1715 was the fact that the counterattack of the party of church and king had gone down in ruin in 1714. It was led by Henry St. John, Viscount Bolingbroke, described by Swift in a letter to Stella in 1711 as "the greatest young man I ever knew, wit, capacity, beauty, quickness of apprehension, good learning, and an excellent taste. The best orator in the House of Commons."

Bolingbroke is one of the most brilliant leaders any political party has ever had. In 1701–2 when he was only twenty-two he became a member of Parliament and made himself the spokesman of the inarticulate country gentry against the Whig settlement. In 1710 he became secretary of state, determined to make peace with France, to "break the body of the whigs" and to fill "the employments of the kingdom down to the meanest, with his own party among the tories." He took a leading part in the negotiations which led to the peace of Utrecht, 1713. That treaty put England in the foreground of the commercial and colonizing powers of Europe and left England and France, as Dutch and Spanish power declined, the two competitors for the control of the gorgeous East and the new West. To make that peace England had negotiated behind the backs of her allies, withdrawn British troops from the front, and betrayed military secrets to the enemy. Her allies were indignant. The Tories hoped for French support for a Stuart restoration. The Whigs saw that the Hanoverian succession was in danger. Marlborough, who had won the war, was dismissed. Walpole was sent to the Tower. But the Tories were divided between the Hanoverian Tories under Harley who saw the dangers of Jacobitism, and Bolingbroke, who, it was believed, was prepared to bring back the Pretender. The death of Queen Anne came before the Tory party could heal its divisions—and in principle they could not be healed, for the doctrine of divine right could not be acclimatized; like an old soldier it would never die, but merely fade away. On her deathbed Anne, on the unanimous advice of her Council, handed the treasurer's staff to Shrewsbury, who had been closely identified with the Revolution of 1689. The Tory party lost its opportunity. George I was proclaimed King of England; and the transmutation of limited monarchy into parliamentary government could begin.

The practice of limited monarchy could not be codified. The system of government which the British empirically developed has never been completely explained. Hume and Burke in their very different ways were to understand its necessity and interpret its spirit. An empire was lost because it was not understood. At the end of the eighteenth century it was to be transformed by the influence of utilitarian philosophy, an influence impeded by the exigencies of the war with the French Revolution, but aided by the steady pressure of the scientific spirit of the time. But in the first half of the eighteenth century when the new science of political arithmetic could illuminate the causes of the wealth of nations there was no comparable elucidation of the facts of political life. The British constitution might be the envy of Europe because it allowed a hitherto unknown political freedom, but its theory was incomprehensible, and its working was not as simple as a machine, but complex and comic as the life of a man. The more we learn about its actual working, the more we understand that the political arts are a matter of nerve and know-how.

The system was monarchical. When political decisions had to be made the king was the only person known to the law who could make them. "He makes Peace and War, makes Bishops, is the fountain of Honour, and has the sole power to bestow Titles and Dignities. He names all officers both Civil and Military, and the Coin bears his effigy. Leagues and Alliances with Foreign Princes, and the Political administration, and Management of Foreign Affairs, and the Interest of the Nation, in respect to other States and Potentates, are his Province. As to the Government of his subjects he has . . . the Superintendency over all the laws to render them effectual, and Justice is administered in his Name." [8]

William III by his moderate and reasonable use of his prerogative powers helped to secure for the Crown a permanent place in the British constitution. He was his own first minister. He had a much better knowledge of Europe and European affairs than any English statesman. But the Revolution of 1689 settlement implied a European war. William had accepted the English Crown the better to thwart Louis XIV. Moreover, the length and cost of his war caused both houses of Parliament to be much more critical of his right to make war and peace, and by the end of his reign that part of the prerogative was being tacitly surrendered. He had hardly recognized that he needed ministers who enjoyed the confidence of a majority in the Commons, but the impeachments of 1701 showed that it would be dangerous to sign treaties without the agreement of ministers who had the support of the House. The House of Commons, on edge with the anxieties of war and fearful of the Jacobites, had asked William III for information and accounts which no king had given before.

In the reign of Anne, Marlborough's campaigns needed administrative innovations and financial expedients of a wholly new range and skill. Much of the expenditure was met by loans which had to be repaid. Public finance ceased to be royal finance and became parliamentary finance. Parliament became the judge of the country's war effort and whoever has to watch the financial shadow cast by policy will seek to control that policy itself. The drabness, almost, of the period between the death of Anne and the opening of the Seven Years' War fostered conditions of economic change, rational speculation, and exuberant criticism in a multitudinous and scurrilous press. When George I came to the throne it was clear that the Crown must fall into dependence on Parliament in many ways which had nothing to do with written laws. "Dominion," wrote Mandeville, "always follows property and when great Fleets are to be equipped Armies rais'd and Maintain'd, General Officers are to get Estates, and Ministries to be enrich'd, when all this is to be done, and the purse of the Commons is to pay for it; when the very expenses of the Court, and all the various Pensions that belong to it are chiefly defray'd by them, it is no wonder, that they are often wanted, and have the Deference shown to them, which is due to the considerable share they have in the Sovereignty." [9]

That this system had in it the seeds of the later most subtle and powerful method of parliamentary government no one could foresee. In the early eighteenth century men of affairs and men of genius would have agreed with Plato that where there was change it would be most likely for the worse. Gulliver said of the Lilliputians: "I would only be understood to mean the original Institutions, and not the most scandalous corruptions into which these People are fallen by the degenerate Nature of Man." And Hume commented of the British constitutions: "If we have reason to be more jealous of monarchy because the danger is more imminent from that quarter; we have also more reason to be more jealous of popular government, because that danger is more terrible."

Before 1689, when parliaments were transient things dependent on the will of the king, men had been reluctant to invest time and money in a seat in the House of Commons. When it was clear that it would meet every year and that in it would be decided the issues that would determine the course of foreign trade, the conditions of internal economic life, and the distribution of the jobs and the honors which are the life blood of an old and hierarchical social order the competition for seats steadily increased. The character of the competition was determined by the very odd distribution of seats and of the right to vote and by the use which could be made of them.

Before the Union with Scotland, 1707, the House of Commons had 513 members. There were twenty-four Welsh members, eighty knights of the shire for the English counties, four university members, but the rest, the overwhelming majority, were returned by the boroughs. The southwest of England provided a quarter of the House. Cornwall, Devon, Somerset, and Wiltshire returned between them 142 members. East and West Looe, two halves of a tiny Cornish fishing village, returned as many members as the City of London. John Locke had written: "We see the bare name of a town of which there remains not so much as the ruins, where scarce so much housing as a sheepcot, or more inhabitants than a shepherd is to be found, sends as many representatives to the grand assembly of law-makers as a whole county numerous in people and powerful in riches." [10]

Locke did only bare justice to the complex and often fantastic reality. One small group of boroughs had universal male suffrage. In others the right to vote belonged either to the corporation or to those who paid poor rate or to the owners of particular bits of property. In one large group of about eighty boroughs the vote was the right of freemen of the town. Absolute control by a patron of the return of a borough member was rare. It was easiest if the right to vote was attached to a particular kind of property. The patron could buy the properties and fill them with men who would vote on his instructions. Those who had the right to vote naturally became adepts at trading their votes. Prices rocketed from a few pounds to a few thousands. Voters were influenced by a great variety of motives, ranging from the crude bribery by wealthy "carpetbaggers" to the traditional claims of a landed family in the neighborhood. There was a core of landed aristocracy in the House, for the younger member of a noble family might have a connection of long standing with a neighboring borough or boroughs. Where there were deeply entrenched local interests, loyalties, and passions, those who sought the seats might have to choose between a ruinous struggle and a compromise. Very few county seats were contested during the first half of the eighteenth century, most county members getting their seats by an understanding between local factions. Every borough is a study in itself.

Those who had seats in the Commons were expected to take an intelligent and financial interest in the provision of local amenities, such as a town hall, a grammar school, or a water supply. The membership of the Commons was varied. There were men of great distinction in the arts and sciences—Dryden, Newton, Wren, and Addison—there were great lawyers, men high in what we should now call the civil service, great city merchants, generals, and admirals. The House could distinguish between men who had ability and men who had estates. It had a wider cross section of national activities and achievements and a smaller proportion of professional politicians than the Commons of the present day. It had begun in medieval times as an assembly of those who could voice the opinion and state the needs of local areas. By the eighteenth century it had acquired a collective personality. The medieval conception of incorporation, the *persona ficta* had found its highest expression in a legislature which had more power than any other in the world.[11]

It was, of course, a House which represented property. It was thought right that this should be so. England was, as Mr. Justice Powell said in 1702, "a nation where property is better preserved than in any other government in the world. Here it is death for a man to take away anything, though never so small, by way of robbery." [12] "O Property! O Goddess, English-born!" wrote a minor poet. Property was a necessary condition of personality. The free were those who had some privilege— in the boroughs the freemen were those who had completed a period of regulated servitude in a craft and now had the freedom of their skill; while in the country the landed freeholder regarded himself as the unit in comparison with which the nature of other men might be assessed. In the seventeenth century the freeholder on the land and the freeman in the town were, each in his sphere, the accredited elements in society, in comparison with which other men were not rival classes, but mere adjuncts or even social dangers. They would have echoed Shakespeare's Ulysses: "Take but degree away; Untune that string and heark what discord follows." "Confined and pestered in this pinfold here," what reflection of heavenly order there might be was found in the ordered hierarchy of landed property. Trade, law, and government itself were visualized as ministering in different degrees to the sanctity of landed property. "If trade be lost, land will fall." The mystical view that a majority of mere individuals could determine fairly for all had not yet been developed—it would need Rousseau's conception of the general will and Bentham's utilitarian calculus to give us that. The House of

Commons in the eighteenth century represented the great landowners, the great trading interests, the universities, and the professions. If monarchy was limited it was because the influence of the landowners was far greater than that of the king.

The Crown was the center of what central government there was. Its antique mechanisms had to be geared to the new forces which were beginning to shape the new commercial and industrial order. We may be tempted to think that the economic forces were the reality and that the queer tangled and dusty legal and political forms were the appearance. But it was through those legal and political forms that the security and the unity of the social order had to be obtained. The economic loom of time had to be given some political stability.

Central administration had to be carried out through the Royal Household. The Household, like the constitution, was the child of time. It was like an unweeded garden, and things rank and gross may have possessed it. But nowhere else could be found the tools for the job. If limited monarchy was to work, the King's Household had to be related to the life of the country. Offices of great honor and small duties went to loyal noblemen of great wealth and territorial power. Offices with arduous administrative duties were given to active politicians. The master of the Great Wardrobe had only a few traditional duties to perform for the king personally. The chancellor of the Exchequer and first lord of the Treasury had heavy day to day business and, unlike a modern minister of finance, would do a great deal of their own computations. By tradition both types of official were the king's advisers.

Those who held Household offices and all who were responsible for the great departments of state met in the Privy Council. In William III's time it was still the central clearing house of the administration. It exercised a minute control over local administration by communications with the lord lieutenants. It gave effect to recommendations made by departments. It exercised a constant review over Irish and colonial legislation. As a body of about sixty members, it was too large for the discussion of policy. It would lack the relevant practical knowledge and it would develop factions. So there was a small inner cabinet which met frequently and consisted almost entirely of the political officers of the Household— the lord president, the lord privy seal, the chancellor of the Exchequer, the two secretaries of state and the lord chancellor. They could meet informally and when convenient. They could meet in their own homes where they could drink deep and talk to the point. This was known as the "efficient" cabinet. In the time of Anne it had not replaced the formal cabinet, but it eclipsed the latter under the Georges. When Walpole was in power he made it his business to dine with each of the chief ministers or spend a night with each of them at their country houses. Having prepared the ground in this way he would call a meeting of the efficient cabinet. When that had been squared, the formal cabinet could be summoned. But the King had to be persuaded to take the advice thus carefully prepared. And to persuade a George to take proffered advice was no mere matter of form. William III had made his own policies. He was prepared in the interest of his European strategy to adjust himself to English vagaries, though he said their Parliament used him like a dog. Dim as Anne might be, her views on policy and on appointments had to be respected. George I was stupid and ignorant, but he had the interests of his native Hanover at heart. When with the Hanoverians the king of England was king also of Hanover, the English lost in foreign policy some of the advantages of being an island. They had a frontier in the heart of Europe. George II had an astonishing knowledge of the complexities of European politics. Ministers knew that it was essential to have the support of their royal master. He was the head of the living constitution, and they had enough sense to know that constitutions are not made but grow. But if the constitution were to be preserved, ministers had to be brokers of political power who could tell the king what it was possible for him to do. There had to be at the head of affairs a man who was both the "Minister for the King in the House of Commons" and the "Minister for the House of Commons in the Closet."

The task of such a minister would have been impossible had not the sessions of Parliament lasted only four or five months in the year and if the work of Parliament had not been limited mainly to the discussion of foreign policy and its cost, with major legislation comparatively rare. For the other seven or eight months of the year the government could devote itself to diplomacy, patronage, and administration.

It has been said of Walpole that it would have seemed to him to be a crime against nature to diminish patronage.[13] Patronage was a technique by which private interest could be harnessed to serve the public good. It was not merely a question of a political realist seeing that there were jobs for the boys, but the art of using the only method by which the Court, the Commons, and the country could be brought into a working unity. An effective politician had to be able to lead the Commons and find favor with the king. He had to convince the king, his fellow ministers, and the Commons that his policy was right. He would have agreed with Hume that all government rests upon the opinion of the governed and that even a mameluke is dependent on the opinion of his janissaries. The eighteenth-century House of Commons was known to enjoy any "cunning mixture of principle and prejudice" which was presented with "grace and clarity." But the members were not there for the entertainment that was offered. It would have been pleasanter to curse the government at home than to listen to long speeches on the details of finance and frontiers in the stifling and often candle-lit gloom of the chapel of St. Stephens. It was hard work to get a House and keep a House, to get supporters to turn up with sufficient regularity. The party managers had to see that there were enough members present to get the work of government done.

Parties could not then be organized on a national scale. Communications were too poor. Mud and water in the eighteenth century were party hazards. Some little pigs might not get their grunts to market. But the Court and the countryside had to be kept in touch. The grass roots of political power were in the counties and the boroughs. The lord lieutenant was the greatest of all local officials. He controlled the distribution of the jobs which the government was able to give. The Duke of Newcastle was lord lieutenant of three counties—Sussex, Nottingham, and Middlesex. An eighteenth-century government saw to it that lord lieutenants were appointed on whom they could rely. The effective government of the country locally was in the hands of the justices of the peace. A man of great estate could expect to be justice of the peace whatever his politics might be, but the smaller fry were most carefully chosen. Walpole throughout his political life, even when he was the most powerful man in Britain, took his place as justice of the peace on the Norfolk bench whenever he could.

The number of men in any one county with political influence was small. But there were dozens of little oligarchies of power entrenched in the provincial towns and in the neighboring countryside. In the counties were families of ancient lineage, the Rolles of Devon, the Cartwrights of Northampton, and the Napiers of Dorset, for example, who were rich and powerful in their neighborhood. The lesser gentry lived on a modest scale and rarely visited outside their own counties. They associated with merchants, attorneys, and prosperous yeomen. The main source of their income was land, and they were the victims of all the ills that land is heir to: the vagaries of the harvest, the incidence of disease, and the temptations of attorneys and scriveners eager to offer mortgages. These smaller gentry were often men of culture. They had libraries of Latin and Greek classics. They read poetry and theology. They had heard of Hobbes and Locke. It was their representatives in Parliament who often acted decisively in the conflict between the factions. It was to them that Walpole looked when he was in power. It was they whom Bolingbroke deceived when he made his bid for power. Because the roots of their interests were

being cut by the forces of economic change and the climate of their beliefs
was feeling the chill wind of reason the country gentlemen tended to drift
into a politics of resentment.[14]

The key to the political struggle was in the boroughs of England and
Wales. They returned three-quarters of the members of the House of
Commons. In most of them power was in the hands of a small urban
oligarchy of attorneys, bankers, merchants, and brewers, entrenched in
self-electing corporations. A corporation in legal theory was a body politic, or an assembly into a fellowship and brotherhood, of which one is
chief and the others are the body. British pilots and lighthouses are to this
day managed by the master and brethren of the Blessed and Undivided
Trinity. Men still speak of the mayor and corporation. If there was a
divinity which hedged a king there was a dignity which encompassed a
mayor. All the commonwealth in respect of the king was said to be as
one corporation, and all other corporations might be thought of as limbs
of the greater body. Charles II and James II had attacked borough after
borough, forcing them to surrender their town charters, and giving them
new ones in which the election of members of Parliament was reserved
to the chief officials whose appointments were controlled by the king. It
was said that if corporations which sent members to Parliament could
be dissolved at the mandate of the Crown then "out of this leak may run
all the government of England." The fictive eternity of these corporations
was used to deny the power of prerogative to dissolve them. The Revolution of 1689 had brought a restoration of the old borough charters.

In London there was a different climate. Its bounding commercial life
was dominated by a small group of financiers. Some of them were directors of the Bank of England, in control of the East India Company, the
Africa Company, and the Levant Company. They were the Carnegies,
the Huntingtons, and Mellons of their age. Their daughters often married
into the aristocracy. Their natural allies in politics were the courtiers.
They would support any group of politicians who could give security
and competent administration. But in London also was the vigorous
radicalism of tradesmen and craftsmen. It was feared and hated by Walpole, who reduced the democratic privileges of the city. He secured the
disfranchisement of three thousand freemen.

In some other towns there were smaller oligarchies of wealth. Bristol
was controlled by its sugar and tobacco magnates and the princes of the
slave trade. Baltic and Dutch merchants flourished in Hull. Newcastle
rejoiced in the masters of the coal trade. Some of these monied men were
cautious and deplored the spirit of adventure which was to make England
great. Others were eager to exploit the opportunities which the disruption

of the French and Spanish empires would provide. Others again were imbued with the spirit of rational liberty and hated the luxury of the court and the corruption of government. In the towns, although the tide of literacy was rising, there was always the fear of the mob. The lean faces and hollow eyes of the poor stare at us from the prints of Hogarth. The horror of their poverty and disease is etched in Gulliver's vision of the giants in Brobdingnag. The rabble in action was the terror of all governments. The king's coach might be stoned and Walpole have to run like a highwayman from the anger of the mob. There was no police force, and the military could only be used in the last resort.

In the countryside the authority of the gentry and the parson was the basis of social order. Over the network of influence possessed by the country gentry in their counties and over the small oligarchies of the boroughs stretched the cousinage of the aristocracy which covered the whole country. There were never more than 150 really active aristocrats, including a few Scottish nobles, who played a decisive part in English political life. The country houses were the symbols of their greatness. They often had a style of living that a sovereign prince of Italy or Germany would have envied. The formal patterns of Hampton Court introduced by William and Mary had been copied so that England had become a country not only of great houses, but also of famous gardens.

George I and George II were so determined to protect the peerage from dilution that they ennobled only a few new men and the aristocracy hardly increased. An outstanding lawyer, soldier, or sailor might win a peerage. The politically active son of a nobleman might get a seat in the Lords, but the younger sons must do the best they could in the Army, the Church, or even trade. In the absence of the organized professions of the modern world, the need for lucrative jobs which a gentleman could perform without loss of caste was one of the roots of patronage. But jobs had to be managed with care—for unlike a modern currency they could not be depreciated by printing more—and everyone had to be made to bring in the maximum political dividend.[15]

Before 1720 the names "Whig" and "Tory" were something more than labels. There was a real distinction between the man who detested Marlborough's wars and who would give no toleration to dissenters—he was a Tory—and the man who was an out and out supporter of that war and favored religious toleration—he was a Whig. But the differences between them pressed too far would have meant civil war, so if life were not to be solitary, poor, nasty, brutish, and short some other alignment had to be made. A real Tory world would mean a Roman Catholic king and the supremacy of France. A Whig world might have had no king at all. One might perform the rites of a social contract in the backwoods of the New World, but not in the complex social order of an ancient feudal order undergoing a sea change into something commercial, rich, and strange. Between 1689 and 1714 the facts of political life were destructive of party warfare. The bread and butter business of the cost of contests for the available seats invited compromise. The names Whig and Tory became counters in the game of politics. Only the body of independent country gentlemen gave to the play a dramatic chorus.

The political realities of British life are revealed in the career of Robert Walpole. He was in the Commons for more than forty years of his life of sixty-nine; for more than thirty years he was in office, and for more than twenty he had supreme power. He was the earthy Pericles of a new political form—the British system of constitutional monarchy and parliamentary government. He knew that to secure the Hanoverian dynasty—and the alternative was Bourbon absolutism—the landed gentry must be conciliated, commerce fostered, the Church kept quiescent, and war avoided. He must let lie whole kennels of sleeping dogs. His policy of peace and prosperity, a contented king, and a contented Parliament was only possible because he knew how to manage the Court, how to master the Commons, and how to use every shred of patronage, while in the actual work of government he had administrative skill of the highest order.

In 1705 he had been a member of Prince George's council—Prince George was the lord high admiral and the undistinguished husband of Queen Anne. The council had to consider the state of the fleet and Walpole early showed his skill in business. In 1708 he was secretary at war, responsible for all aspects of military life in England and Scotland, troop movements, supply, discipline, and promotions. It was the alarm and disorder created by the South Sea Bubble—when the unfamiliar monster of credit had run wild—that gave him real power. The South Sea Company was a finance company organized to take over a part of the national debt in order to strengthen public credit. Walpole himself accepted it as part of the financial order. When the crisis broke he decided that even at the cost of protecting cheats and swindlers the court and the ministry must be saved from the ruin which would follow a Tory exploitation of the disaster. He did not foresee the bursting of the bubble, and he did not restore financial stability. The economic order righted itself, but Walpole saved the government from being wrecked. Once he had won the full confidence of the King, a combination of royal favor and control of the House of Commons mutually strengthening one another gave his government a strength unknown since the Tudors.[16]

Walpole's world was that of a small prosperous nation which had got rid of monarchical despotism—on the eve of the age of enlightened despots—and was developing a system of limited monarchy and parliamentary power which those who were making it did not themselves understand. Walpole knew that he must have the support of the Court. Without the loyal support of George I and George II he could not have lasted a month. Therefore, he was tireless in the assiduity with which he explained his policy and his appointments to the King. Under George II he was equally attentive to Queen Caroline, making sure in hours of informal talk that she understood the policies he pursued.

Before Walpole's time politicians had had to try to make patronage pay, to secure support from jobs and favors given. But they were in and out of power so often that the dividends they had earned were often collected by their successors. Walpole made a monopoly of the patronage the government could control. Nine-tenths of the jottings which he made in note form for his consultations with George II were about patronage. Before his time there had been independent dispensers of patronage—the customs and excise commissioners, the lord chancellor, the commander in chief and the master general of ordnance had their own use for the favors they could confer. Walpole set out to control the whole field and to use it to control the Commons and the elections on which such control would depend. The appointment of every bishop was so closely studied that Walpole could count on the steady support of twenty-four of the twenty-six bishops in the Lords. By tireless attention to patronage he created the Treasury party which was one of the most reliable groups supporting the government in the Commons. Because the Dissenters were loyal Whigs and had votes, he made it easier for Quakers to affirm, and he interested himself in the necessities of the widows of dissenting clergymen.

While Court favor and patronage were necessary, they would not have been sufficient to give Walpole power had he not had a superb knowledge of the House of Commons and great skill in administration. In his day it was not obvious that the head of a government would find it a great advantage to be in the House of Commons. The House of Lords played an active part in government, and a peerage was a supreme prize of political life. It was part of Walpole's political genius that he should have understood so well the real source of his power. He had a superb mastery in debate, a subtle sense of the moods of the House, and a thorough knowledge of its procedure. He knew how to woo the independent members. He would discourse on the mixed nature of the constitution, the danger of strengthening the democratic part of it, the need for a government to have security of tenure for more than three years. He would frankly admit the need for bribery, saying that the fact that it could be used was evidence that passion was ceasing to divide the nation. To give a man his price was better than shedding his blood—to put money in his purse better than cutting his throat. In the House of Commons Walpole was as gross as a Minotaur and subtle as a serpent.

In administration his power was in the Treasury. It was then the only department with a complete organization and more than a handful of civil servants. From the Treasury Walpole could control the financial business of the country. He made it efficient. He was attracted by the mathematical side of its work.[17] Since the Revolution of 1689 political arithmetic had been taken up with some enthusiasm by administrators. Walpole took an interest in the work of civil servants like Charles Davenant, William Lowndes, and Henry Martin. With their help he fostered trade, increased the revenue, and simplified the fiscal system.

Walpole was confronted with a brilliant opposition. This was based not on the influence of the Court alone, but also on an appeal to the House of Commons and the new vitality of public opinion nourished by a brilliant political journalism. After 1726 it was led by Bolingbroke and William Pulteney. Bolingbroke had learned his politics in the reign of Anne, when by backstair intrigue—"a chambermaid may slip a banknote into a gripping paw as well as the most subtle demon of hell"—a violent press campaign, and a bitter struggle in the Commons even Godolphin and Marlborough had been defeated. Walpole could not be dislodged in the same way. In the fight over the Treaty of Utrecht the pen in a pamphlet and a tongue in the cheek had been mightier than the sword. But in the 1730's neither the pen of a Swift nor the tongue of a Bolingbroke was a match for Walpole's tireless attention to the details of patronage and the hard work of administration. Opposition in the Commons was not easy to organize. The country gentlemen would not always stay on in London to press an attack in the Commons. They had their own divisions. There was a small group of Jacobites who lived in a dream world of pre-1689. There were rugged individualists and urban radicals. There was a group of self-righteous Hanoverian Tories suspicious of Jacobites, Whigs, and radicals. Last and most important was the group of place-hungry men and angry ardent young men who said that a worthless politician was forcing a minority policy through the Commons by means of corruption. Bolingbroke may have sensed the danger of corruption in an elected assembly and the chasm which might grow between an oligarchy and public opinion. Far more than Walpole he realized the dangers of isolation for Britain and the opportunities for empire in a struggle with France. But Bolingbroke did not understand the new political system which Walpole was fostering—a system in which Parliament would be the most important tool for political work and a tool which had its cutting edge from the presence in it of ministers of the Crown who had the support of their royal master and of the Commons too. A workable alternative to enlightened despotism would not be found in essays on poiltics, however witty and brilliant, but in the dust, heat, and dirt of empirical party politics.

After Walpole's resignation in 1742 it was clearly shown that the problem of English politics was something more than "the craving for power of a minister capable of wielding it." Walpole had shown great political insight.[18] He had had one serious defeat—in 1733—when he was compelled to drop a sensible proposal for helping the re-export trade and perhaps abolishing the land tax by extension of the excise system of allowing certain colonial imports to remain in bond without payment of customs duty but with payment of excise when released for home consumption. The opposition stirred up a frenzy of scurrilous pamphleteering, representing the scheme as a prelude to further taxation enforced by an army of excise men. Against his better judgment he had agreed in October 1739 to a declaration of war on Spain and had at the King's request continued in office, though he was not in spirit or in technique a good war minister. When he went to the House of Lords in 1742 as Lord Orford, there was a period of political instability until the Pelhams re-established stability in 1746.

The heart of the matter was that a government needed the support of the king, but it was essential that they had also the support of the Commons. During Walpole's time the men whom the Duke of Newcastle termed the "old corps of Whigs" had made themselves indispensable to any government. Newcastle and Hardwicke skillfully detached fragments of the opposition or "new Whigs" and side-stepped the attempt to bring Walpole to book for his alleged transgressions. William Pitt, Earl of Chatham, who was at the beginning of his great career, led the attack and was highly indignant at the negative result. In later years he admitted that Walpole had often been right. John Carteret became the real director of the new government's policy. He was a richly gifted man at home with the Greek and Latin classics and at home, too, with the bottle. He had the confidence of the King, whose heart he warmed by his fluent German and by his foreign policy in the European war then being waged. George II, as elector of Hanover, was suspected of furthering German politics, German measures, and German manners. It did not help that at the head of an army of British and Hanoverians he had defeated the French at Dettingen. The English did not like the cost of the mercenaries used. Pitt in the Commons thundered that England had been degraded to "a province to a despicable electorate." Carteret in the Lords could not directly reply to Pitt's attacks. More serious was the failure of Carteret to support his favor with the King by the arts of political management. "What is it to me, who is a judge or who a bishop? It is my business to make kings and emperors and to maintain the balance of Europe."

In 1744 his colleagues, Newcastle and his brother Henry Pelham, the Earl of Hardwicke, the lord chancellor, and others compelled the King to choose between Carteret and them. The King had said to Newcastle, "Surely when ministers disagree, it is hard if I may not determine amongst you." The Duke had replied, "To be sure, Sir, your Majesty ought must and does, but then, as is the Constitution, your Majesty will have the goodness to excuse those from executing what they think wrong, or not for your service." Each individual officeholder regarded himself as responsible primarily to the King, and his loyalty to his political associates was a secondary consideration. But both the administration and the opposition came to see the value of some group organization and discipline. In 1744 the Pelhams had simply made it clear that they could no longer continue to serve in an administration which was dominated by Carteret. The King's hand was forced, because Carteret was unable to find support in the House of Commons. But while Carteret could be forced to resign it was for the King to decide whom to appoint in his place. Henry Pelham, brother of Newcastle, became principal minister as first lord of the Treasury. He was a good House of Commons man and an able financier of the school of Walpole.

George II had found that he was hemmed in by the facts of political life. A solid core of placemen was indispensable if the Commons were to do the job of government. But this core was not sufficient. A coherent policy, debating strength, and administrative talent, too, were necessary. When Henry Pelham died in 1754, his brother Newcastle had little notion of how to use his power. He was compelled to make a deal with Henry Fox, who became secretary of state. When in 1756 the Seven Years' War began, Newcastle sought the support of Pitt. Pitt refused unless he were made head of the government, and in November 1756 George II was compelled to accept Pitt as head of his government, though he bitterly resented Pitt's attack on Hanover and distrusted his rhetorical appeals to popular emotion. Pitt in office, with a hostile king and without consistent support from the old corps of Whigs, was in a weak position. In April 1757 he was abruptly dismissed by the King, and after three months of crisis "a solution was found in an alliance between Pitt and Newcastle with the former in sole charge of the war and the latter as first lord of the Treasury." [19]

CHAPTER III

Britain and the World, 1688-1763

It has been said that the Europe of the early eighteenth century was closer to the Europe of the fifteenth century than to our own. Its basic structure was still feudal. The social prestige of the aristocracy was still very great. The aristocrat had the right to display armorial bearings and all descendants of aristocrats (England was an exception) had the hereditary use of a title. The position of the aristocrats varied from that of the politically powerful nobles of Poland, Sweden, Hungary, and England to the politically impotent nobles of France, Denmark, or Spain. The conditions of the peasantry and the bulk of the population varied from the free villages of England, Sweden, and some parts of France to the serfs of many parts of central, eastern, and southern Europe.

The central administrative institutions of most European monarchies were showing some degree of specialization. But in most countries high office in the army, at court, and in the diplomatic services was still filled almost exclusively by members of the aristocracy. In many parts of continental Europe nobles were exempt from taxation, could exercise jurisdiction over their tenants, and were entitled to various feudal payments and often to services. It was a world of fine gentlemen. What in Proust's Monsieur Charlus is to us near to madness was but common sense to them. "Take but degree away and hark what discord follows." The principle of inheritance had given Europe what order it had. The principle which determined the rise and fall of families and estates was also the shaping force of frontiers and political power. The problems of politics were largely dynastic. Wars were wars of succession (Spanish, Polish, Austrian).[1] In pedigree was, if not perfect peace, what peace is possible here below. Hobbes's Leviathans were multitudinous, and they could compose their differences only in the marriage bed and through its issue in the cradle. We do not yet know that the spirit of nationality will produce a more ordered world.

If the government of Europe was largely in the hands of its nobility its problems were created by its middle class. The sentiments of a Fortinbras were being modified by the interests of a Defoe. The feudal arras was shaking in the winds of change, one of them a freshening wind of trade. There was a growing merchant class. Some of its members had, as in Venice and the Netherlands and the free cities of the Empire, acquired freedom to build societies and governments based on their own values. Those values were a rational interest in cash in place of a passionate interest in blood. The glories of the blood and state were to them shadows, not substantial things. Merchants, especially in England and France, increased in numbers and in wealth as overseas trade expanded. In the first half of the eighteenth century there was a great increase in international trade, particularly in trade between countries in Europe and settlements in America, Africa, and Asia. The Atlantic trade, notably that with the islands of the Caribbean, the trade with India and Southeast Asia, and even the trade with Africa for slaves were causes of friction between the European powers bemused as they were about the relation between trade and wealth, and between colonies and trade, before the cool eye of Adam Smith in 1776 examined with some scientific detachment the causes of the wealth of nations. The many wars of the eighteenth century about marriage settlements and sickly children of royal marriage beds were fought in front of fortresses Tristram Shandy's Uncle Toby would delight to model, but they were also about commercial interests which only a statesman of genius could begin to understand. The early eighteenth century was greatly influenced by the failure of the Dutch to maintain their pre-eminent position; the late eighteenth century by the duel between France and England for commercial and colonial pre-eminence.

From the middle of the seventeenth century France had dominated Europe more completely than it had ever been dominated by a single power since the days of ancient Rome. This domination rested on the divisions among her neighbors and on her own wealth, population, and armed forces. With eighteen or nineteen million inhabitants she had more than three times the population of Spain, Italy, or England. Her army of a hundred thousand men in peace time, and more in war, was led by great generals and was the model for the rest of Europe. Her navy made her the third maritime power in the Atlantic and the first in the Mediterranean. She had the most skilled and highly organized bureaucracy in Europe. Louis XIV at her head was the observed of all observers. He himself held a fanatical view of the divine right of kings: "He who has given kings to men has desired that they be respected as His lieutenants, reserving to Himself alone the right to examine their conduct." All over Europe the same principle of absolute government had triumphed: in the Habsburg territories, in Bavaria, in Sweden, and, in its Byzantine and barbarous form, in Russia too. Only the Revolution of 1689 in England and the writings of John Locke were prophetic intimations that all this would pass away. It would not have passed away had there not been in the United Provinces of the Dutch the center of a continental opposition to Catholic absolutism which, linked with England's insular power and eccentric institutions, curbed Louis XIV at the zenith of his power. England and Holland under the House of Orange defeated the greatest military power in Europe. Only the Dutch could have served as a continental core of resistance to France. Spain was in decline, Austria was in conflict with the Turks (who had laid siege to Vienna in 1683), Prussia was only one of the many composite "territories" which with many smaller and some very small states made up the ramshackle Holy Roman Empire, and Sweden under Charles XII had eyes only for the Baltic.

The United Provinces was an aristocratic republic with a federal constitution. Only the predominance of the province Holland gave some coherence to its federal divisions. In time of war the House of Orange gave the leadership it needed. The Dutch had created for themselves a near monopoly of the sea-borne carrying trade of Europe. They were supreme in the Baltic trade, which provided the fleets of Europe with timber and naval stores. In the East they had conquered trade from the Portuguese. Their trade with Asia was in pepper, cloves, and nutmeg. They had ports of call on the way, in West Africa, at the Cape, and in India.[2]

If France was the model for Europe in the art of war the Dutch were the cynosure for commerce and shipbuilding. Their great trading companies, especially the Dutch East India Company, were imitated from Sweden to Portugal. Dutch strength lay in sound finance. The Bank of Amsterdam was the financial hub of Europe. Only in Holland and England were commerce and industry really free to develop in the war-torn Europe of the late seventeenth century. Only in Holland and England was there a powerful middle class. Only in them did the nobility and its standards not dominate the life of society. In science and technology, too, Holland and England were leading. So while 1648–88 had seen the greatness of France in war, in politics, and in the arts, in these years in finance and economics, in the influence of a middle class on social structure, in industry and overseas trade, in a diversity and tolerance in religion and all things of the spirit Holland and England had matured. Holland was to yield first place to England. Her resources were more limited and her population smaller. She had not the security of British insularity. Unlike the English the Dutch had no strong and growing domestic industry upon which to base their foreign trade. Mandeville put it with charm and clarity: "The Dutch perhaps have more shipping, and more ready money than we, but then those are only to be considered as the tools they work with. So a carrier may have more horses than a man of ten times his worth . . . He that keeps three or four stage-coaches to get his bread, is to a gentleman that keeps a coach for his pleasure, what the Dutch are in comparison to us; having nothing of their own but fish, they are carriers and freighters to the rest of the world, whilst the basis of our trade chiefly depends upon our own products." [3] The spread of English commercial enterprise into most parts of the known world was to bring it into conflict with the decaying Spanish empire in the West Indies, with the Dutch in the former Portuguese territories in the East Indies, and finally with the French in India and in America. With a small population, poor resources, and vulnerable communications Dutch statesmen were in no position to pursue similar adventurous policies.

In England the development of trade and the securing of a favorable balance of trade was part of government policy. The government had a fiscal interest in trade, and there were strong groups, such as the East and West Indian merchants, to influence government policy. Trade was vital to some industrial areas and in some cases vital to national security. Jamaican cotton was used more and more in the Lancashire cotton industry. West Indian dyes were used in the treatment of dark cloths of Yorkshire and the West Country. The swordmakers and gunsmiths of Birmingham had to have Swedish iron. The silk spinners of the English Midlands and the weavers of Spitalfield had to have raw silk from Smyrna and Leghorn. Merchant and naval shipbuilding was dependent on imported timber from the Baltic. Midland nails were sold in the American colonies, Yorkshire worsted in Germany and in Spain, and in Italy the nuns were "vail'd with fine Kersies and Long ells." Naval bases like Gibraltar and Minorca protected trade in the Mediterranean where it might be attacked by Spain, by the Empire from Sicily, by France from Toulon and Marseilles, and by the Barbary pirates from North Africa. In the Mediterranean rivalry was mainly between the French and English. The Levant trade gave a valuable market for European cloth exports, and the raw silks and cottons which were imported were of growing importance as materials for expanding home industries.

The Atlantic trade was of immense value to both French and English. The West Indies were the heart of this Atlantic system, which included also the mainland colonies from Spanish America in the south to Newfoundland in the north. The West African slave trade was a source of wealth to western European ports from Cadiz in the south to Glasgow in the north. Economic writers did not at first see the commercial potential of the North American colonies with their steadily growing populations. The value of West Indian products—sugar, tobacco, cotton, indigo, and dyewood—was obvious enough, and they had been among the first commodities to be "enumerated" under the Navigation Acts. West Indian colonists with their slave dependents were a firm market for British goods until the middle of the eighteenth century. Mercantilists thought that "every Englishman in Barbadoes or Jamaica creates employment for four men at home." The colonists of New England, it was thought, employed less shipping, consumed few English manufactures, and produced goods which did not fit so well into the system of a balanced trade. Colonies of settlement were supposed to be by nature competitive with England. A series of acts was passed to restrict North American industrial tendencies. These colonies also had the displeasing habit of trading with foreign West Indian colonies. They would sell their boards and planks and beams to the West Indies when, according to plan, they should have been making England independent of Baltic timber.

Apart from the conflict of interest between the New England colonies and the British idea of what colonies were for, there were chronic causes of friction between the four European powers which had interests in the Caribbean. Old Spain looked to New Spain for the bullion she needed for essential purchases in Europe. The Spanish empire which Spain could not develop attracted the attention of English and Dutch smugglers. Both England and France had vested and conflicting interests in the production of sugar. In the middle of the eighteenth century it was realized that the white population of the colonies of settlement was growing while the population of the West Indies was kept stationary by disease. The balance of interest shifted to this growing market, and after the Seven Years' War (1756–63) France was allowed to keep her sugar islands.

India and Southeast Asia were another area of trade and war. The disintegrating Portuguese empire was the prize. In the seventeenth century the Dutch had driven the English out of the Spice Islands. During the eighteenth century Dutch power declined in India. It was limited to the Southeast Archipelago. The struggle for economic supremacy in India became an Anglo-French duel. From it was to come the unique imperialism of the British in India. Founded by violence, treachery, and avarice, by incomparable daring, and by sustained revolution it was to create modern India. Its glories will never fade, and its failures and iniquities will be a lesson and a warning for all time. It started when the courage and iniquity of a few began the structure of a new world within the dissolving structure of the Mughal Empire.

The trading interests of the English East India Company were concentrated on the mainland round Surat, Bombay, Madras, and Calcutta. In 1685 James II had approved of the East India Company carrying out maritime reprisals for the harrying of its tiny posts. In 1715 it was not known that the dissolution of the Mughal Empire was at hand. The emperor still sat upon the peacock throne in the Red Fort at Delhi. In Bengal the East India Company had been troubled by the exactions of the Nawab of Bengal, Jaffer Khan. Two Englishmen made a march of three months from Calcutta to Delhi and by daring resolution and corruption secured "extraterritorial rights" from the panic-stricken and incompetent Indian headquarters. This grant produced dramatic developments forty years on, when the governor of the Company's establishment in Bengal became involved in a local Indian dispute. He backed one of the pretenders and used his extraterritorial rights to give that pretender sanctuary in the Company's area round Fort William at Calcutta. Suraja Dowlah attacked the Fort in June 1756. He took it and the death of some of his prisoners in the Black Hole of Calcutta was the germ of one of those atrocity stories which infect the record of the past. The real interest was not there. It was in Madras. The French were firmly established at Chandernagor a few miles up the river from Calcutta. In South India they had Pondicherry.

The few Englishmen who were in Madras decided to send off almost all of both their land and sea force to Bengal. In command was Robert Clive. He had to prevent Suraja Dowlah and the French from combining against him. Between June 1756 and June 1757 the British in Bengal were transformed from helpless fugitives into the effective rulers of the country. Indian society at the time was a sort of partnership between the Moslem conquerors and the old Hindu governing class. The Moslems ruled and the Hindus administered for them. Clive used the Hindu interest against the Moslems. Of the 3,000 troops at Plassey with which Clive pursued the 50,000 of Suraja Dowlah, 2,000 were Bengalis. The East India Company from a trading monopoly was being transmogrified into a political power. Great states may be to the moralist no more than robber bands, but they need more than robber bands, deathless courage, and, what is far less common, administrative skill of a high order. To the home government in Britain the economic success of the East India

Company brought its problems. Its cargoes of Indian textiles profoundly disturbed the English woolen interests at home. As India was not a good market for European exports she had to be paid in silver. The demand for silver kept alive the notion that the object of economic and strategic policy was the winning of precious metals. Tea from China and coffee from the Red Sea ports were more acceptable.[4]

In 1907 Sir Eyre Crowe wrote: "The general character of England's foreign policy is determined by the immutable condition of her geographical situation on the ocean flank of Europe as an island state with vast overseas colonies and dependencies, whose existence and survival as an independent community are inseparably bound up with the possession of preponderant sea power." [5] It was in the eighteenth century that the genuine meaning of sea power for Britain was revealed. As a maritime state Britain was in the literal sense of the word, the neighbor of every country accessible by sea. If she had sea power—that is if she could make her own sea routes secure and deny their use to an enemy in time of war—Britain could make her power felt in the Low Countries, southern Scandinavia, and Germany. Sea power enabled Marlborough to fight and win his battles in the very heart of Europe—Blenheim, Ramillies, Oudenarde, and Malplaquet. It was decisive in the struggle with the French for North America and India. But it is a weakness of sea power that only by indirection can it find direction out. Sea power made Britain the neighbor of every country with a shore. But she could not use their front door. She had to use the deep indentations which were so many back doors into the living room of Europe. The Baltic and the Mediterranean were the tradesmen's entrances. She used the western Mediterranean during the campaign of Marlborough. In 1713 she obtained Gibraltar and Port Mahon. Her defeat of the Spanish fleet at Cape Passero (1718) gave her control of the eastern Mediterranean. In the middle of the eighteenth century a French official wrote: "The English will rule the sea through their fleets and the land through their wealth, and America will furnish them with the means of dictating to Europe . . . France alone is in a position to prevent this catastrophe, and France must do so for her sake and that of all Europe."

It was not in fact at all likely that England would dominate Europe in the way this Frenchman feared. But it was very possible that a European power might dominate Britain. She was after all the odd man out— the enemy of kings by God appointed; a world of merchants who while they might sedulously ape had no fear or reverence for a lord; a world of common people who had little respect for the ordered hierarchy of the feudal age—they were a mob in which were stirring the seeds of rational thought; so many Bunyans who had begun an industrial pilgrim's progress. Sea power, too, can be intermittent. At least four times in the century the French organized potentially formidable attempts at invasion: in 1744, in 1756, in 1759, and 1779. They failed because of the luck of the weather and because sound and at times superb naval dispositions were arranged by the Admiralty. But with Ireland almost a fragment of Catholic Europe and with Scotland dreaming of a royal and feudal past the danger was real. There were seven wars with France between 1689 and 1815. "They were not wars for trade, although British trading interests were deeply involved. They were not wars for colonial empire, although they added very materially to our overseas possessions. They were not wars of religion . . . They were conflicts in which, for Great Britain, national security was the predominant issue. They were wars for the restoration and maintenance of the balance of power." [6] Admiral Mahan wrote of Queen Anne's War (War of the Spanish Succession): "Before that war England was one of the sea powers. After it, she was the sea power, without any second." After it England's security was not threatened for sixty years. There was no serious war for a generation. What was this sea power? and what this balance of power in which it played a part?

The fact that Great Britain and Ireland were islands meant that a navy was the best means of defense against invasion. A navy could be used to strangle at sea the trade of her continental foes while avoiding heavy commitments on land. But there were limits to the avoidance of land commitments. Allies might be defeated or might refuse to continue fighting on land for a partner who had no stomach for the dirty work. With her navy Britain could move troops where she desired and stop the enemy doing so by sea. She could transport small armies to strategic points to keep valuable bases out of enemy hands and to harass his large land armies. In the early eighteenth century the English view was that they should man their navy, conquer enemy colonies and, if necessary, pay others to do most of the soldiering.

All eighteenth-century armies were an amalgam of national and foreign elements (who comprised between one-quarter and two-thirds of all armies). Soldiers enlisted for long terms and fought not to die for a cause but to make a living.[7] In time of threats of foreign invasion the British would borrow troops from the Irish establishment, hire them from German principalities, or subsidize other nations to do the fighting. Only 9,000 of the 45,000 troops on the allied side at Blenheim were English. If the rank and file were scum and their officers gentlemen, often without professional skill, the practice of war was more civilized than ever before or since. It lacked the religious fanaticism of the seventeenth century and the national fanaticism of the American and French revolutionary wars. Success in battle "depended on skill of generalship rather than on force of arms, quality rather than quantity, and battles depended on manoeuvre rather than on destruction." [8] War was a dance of death in which the steps were few and stately.

The use of a navy in battle had the same formality as the use of an army on land. The English had a body of fighting instructions which was a tactical bible down to 1783. It was a set of standing orders as binding on the admirals themselves as it was on everyone else in the fleet. It was not possible to give any new instructions not in the approved list because they could not be linked to any signal given in the book. An expensive tool should not be lost or broken. No British fleet inflicted a whole-hearted defeat upon any enemy fleet in any stand up fight between Barfleur (1692) and The Saints (1782). Britain relied upon control of the seas as her main instrument of warfare. This was sound sense because of the increasing importance of commerce, the vulnerability of the British Isles to blockade, and their immunity from land attack. On occasions British forces had to fight on the continent, and the art of war which was practiced there had disastrous results when she had to fight in America, where the skirmishing of light infantry had replaced the formal maneuvers of disciplined lines.

What was the balance of power? In an essay on *The Balance of Power* in 1701 Davenant wrote: "All good Englishmen ought seriously to consider this reflexion which Machiavel makes, 'That when a Prince or Commonwealth arrives at that height of reputation, that no Neighbour Prince or People dares to Invade him (unless compell'd by indispensable necessity) he may do what he pleases: 'tis in his Election with whom he will make War, and with whom he will be at Peace; for his Neighbours being afraid of his Power, are all glad to be his Friends; and those Potentates who are furthest off, and have no Commerce with him, look on as unconcern'd, as if the Consequence could have no relation to them; and in this Error they many times continue till the Calamities are brought Home to their own Doors; and then 'tis too late, for they have nothing but their own private Force to oppose, which is too weak when the Enemy is grown so strong.' In all probability the French are now arriv'd to this formidable Pitch of Greatness." [9] Since 1648 when the devastating wars of religion had ended and more rational calculations could enter into the art of war and the skill of diplomats, a practice of territorial compensation in the settlement of disputes had become almost a theory of politics. The stability of Europe was a balance in which any substantial accretion of power by one political entity was to be met by the appropriate compensation to each of the others. Should one power try to establish its ascendancy each of the others had the liberty, the obligation even, to re-establish equilibrium by force.

In the late nineteenth century this technique of fine adjustments made in accordance with the rules of the diplomatic game was to give place to the confrontation of two accumulations of power by two opposing groups, a polarization which we know now as the balance of terror. That the stability of eighteenth-century Europe should have been but balance and that diplomatic wisdom should lie in skillful adjustments of the unforeseen—for example, the unexpected fertility of a supposedly impotent prince—may seem to suggest that reason has little power in human affairs. But as Hobbes once wrote there are two parts of our nature, the one mathematical and the other dogmatical. For the first, reason is final and no one in his senses will challenge the arithmetic of the figure in an account. But in the second, interest or passion will deny reason. We agree on the amount of the bill, but we will be damned if we will pay. When it was firmly believed that kings were by God appointed and that the accumulation of their possessions was determined by the mysterious sacrament of marriage and the secret processes of generation, when the differences in accumulation were pointed with the passionate antagonisms of irreconcilable religious beliefs, it was a miracle that any balance was achieved. We who have seen a Hitler seek a final solution of a social and religious difference by the technique of gas ovens ought not to despise the meticulous adjustment of the product of the marriage beds of kings by the professional if tricky skill of professional diplomacy or the ceremonial movements of eighteenth-century armies and fleets. Hereditary succession may seem a comic form of manifest destiny, but who will now say what the real form may be? At least the conception of the balance of power had a place for the recognition of an international community. No one state should be allowed to dominate the rest. It was the function of statesmen by vigilant inspection to discover and be prepared to counteract projects of encroachment which a powerful state might be tempted to form. But while the balance of power might adjust the frontiers of enlightened despots it could not control the forces which were shaping the empires of the East and of the West. The charm and the terror, the squalor and the glory of the eighteenth century lie in the interplay between the subtle movements on the European chessboard of power and the vast issues of empire and of commerce which were being settled in scuffles round the world from the St. Lawrence to the Himalayas and from Newfoundland to Patagonia.

In 1689 and 1701 coalitions were formed against Louis XIV; the Protestant and anti-absolutist powers of Holland and England curbed him at the zenith of his power. Louis might well think that he had a duty to move out from the natural frontiers of France, which he had reached, to eliminate the Protestant heresy of Europe which lurked in Holland and in England. But in the years from 1689 to 1713 England was to play a very decisive part in a great continental war. She contributed money (the Bank of England was founded in 1694), her sea power, some military contingents, and the genius of Marlborough. The first war (1689–97), King William's War, was to prevent the conquest of the Spanish Netherlands (modern Belgium); the second, Queen Anne's War, was to prevent the union of the crowns of France and Spain under a Bourbon king. The first was won largely by sea power. In 1692 a projected invasion of England was prevented by the victory over Tourville at Barfleur–La Hogue. In the second (the War of the Spanish Succession 1702–13) Louis had the Spanish empire at his disposal and Bavaria as an ally. There was only one fleet action—off Malaga, 1704—but the ubiquitous pressure of sea power sustained Marlborough's new war of movement in Bavaria and in Flanders. Never before had Britain been so involved in war. She had armies in Flanders and in Spain and fleets on many seas. Reforms in banking and taxation and brilliant inventions and improvisations in administration had seen her through. The Treaty of Utrecht (1713) saved France from ruin and apart from a little local fighting it gave Europe peace for nearly thirty years. Louis XIV had tried to secure the vast dominions of Spain for his family and the commerce of the Indies for his people. He had failed. No other country could then hope to dominate Europe. England obtained Hudson Bay, Newfoundland, Nova Scotia (captured by a force which included Massachusetts colonists), the island of St. Kitts in the West Indies—all from France—and Gibraltar and Minorca from Spain, with the then valuable trading concession (the Assiento) that she might supply African Negro slaves to the American colonies. The Spanish Netherlands were transferred from Spain to Austria. The phrases "a just balance of power" and "the balance of power of Europe" were used in the treaty itself.

Between the Treaty of Utrecht and the Seven Years' War the diplomatic maneuvers are so intricate that a summary would no more convey the reality than a *New Yorker* cartoon would give the inner life of a chess match between two masters. In Europe the powers were engaged in complex maneuvers seeking to keep a balance and push their own advantage. The diplomatic history was more complex in this period than it had been in the seventeenth century because there were now more pieces on the board: Russia, Poland, Sweden, Denmark, and Savoy. And the European stage was only part of a scene stretching from the New World to the ancient East in which the fate of the New World of the Americas and the gorgeous East of Asia was involved.

Some of the powers and interests were: (1) France wished to avoid war for at least a generation and to isolate the Austrian Empire by breaking up its traditional friendship with England and the Netherlands. When she had increased her fleet and filled her coffers she would break English power in America and in the East. In fact, she was to form an active coalition against the worldwide first British Empire of the last quarter of the eighteenth century. It was a coalition which included France, Spain, and Holland and the armed neutrality of Russia, Sweden, Denmark, Portugal, and Turkey. It was that coalition which secured the independence of the United States and placed Britain in a jeopardy from which she was only rescued by Rodney's victory in the battle of the Islands of The Saints (Les Saintes) in the West Indies (1782). (2) The Austrian Empire. This ramshackle accumulation of territories was the result of Habsburg marriage and of successful war against the Magyars and the Turks. It was a pageant of Europe's medieval past. Vienna was the seat of the most august dynasty in Europe and the meeting point where influences from Germany, Italy, Spain, and the Netherlands were mingled. The Austrian Habsburgs were the wearers of the crown of the Holy Roman Empire from 1556 to 1740. As the secular heads of the whole Christian society they felt they had the right and the duty to restore the religious and the territorial integrity of Christendom.[10] But the glory of Vienna had been developed both at the expense of the provincial centers and of the countryside. Its large army and its brilliant court life, where Charles VI personally composed an opera in which his daughters danced a ballet, were deceptive. The emperor had a devouring passion for the advancement of his religion, the slaughter of infidel Turk, and that his daughter Maria Theresa should inherit all his dominions intact and without dispute. While to many it seemed that a Habsburg domination of Europe might follow that of the defeated Bourbons, they were wrong. For (3) in the 1750's came the startling emergence of Prussia as a great military power in the European scene. In 1756 Prussia was "a new, half finished country, composed of scattered fragments joined under one Crown, as a result of various marriages, by the chance of various deaths, and by conquest—a State without real frontiers, without geographical unity, inhabited by subjects . . . who owned a common allegiance to one thing alone, the person and power of the sovereign." It had "an artificial and precarious unity; . . . it had to win or lose, advance or retreat, extend or

Europe in 1721

SWEDEN

Finland

Viborg

St. Petersburg

Stockholm

Esthonia

Gotland

Livonia

Courland

RUSSIA

Moscow

Lithuania

East Prussia

erania

Danzig

burg

gen

POLAND

Warsaw

Silesia

Galicia

Podolia

hemia

oravia

TRIA

ienna

Moldavia

Styria

Hungary

Transylvania

Croatia

Bosnia

Wallachia

mat

Servia

Bulgaria

OTTOMAN

Constantinople

Albania

EMPIRE

TWO SICILIES

Smyrna

Morea

Crete

Cyprus

disintegrate." [11] It was never satisfied since it was never secure. In the Seven Years' War the struggle of Prussia for existence was the main theme of the war in Europe and influenced the energy and resources of Britain and France in their struggle for empire in America and India. The rise of Prussia began a dualism in Germany—the struggle for supremacy between the Empire and Catholicism, supported by Austria, and the heretical king of Prussia. One effect was that in 1756 Austria broke off her entente with Britain and France her alliance with Prussia. (4) The United Netherlands had been in 1689 the key to English foreign policy. But there was a deep-seated disharmony between them. The English seemed to decide according to their own interests and to expect the Dutch to follow. George I was King of Hanover and the Dutch feared that he might make himself master of the Elbe estuary. The Dutch were Europe's warehouse, but they could not sustain the burdens of an imperial power. (5) The Spanish empire had been partly dismembered by the Treaty of Utrecht. The trading opportunities of its vast empire were exploited by other powers. In spite of its bullion from the mines of South America it had no money to buy the mercenaries which were the chips of the Euopean power game. The obstacles which Spain put in the way of trade in the West Indies infuriated British merchants. Spanish reprisals for the smuggling activities of British seamen were magnified into a tale of fiendish cruelties by Spanish Catholic devils against harmless Protestant merchants. Jenkins' ear was found to be worth a war (in spite of Walpole's vigorous dissent), and it has its place in the museum of famous propaganda tales.

For some time after the peace of Utrecht Britain pursued a policy of the balance of power in the sense of trying to control and if possible to weaken the strongest state in Europe. But which was the strongest state in Europe? From the beginning of modern European history almost, the antagonism of France and the House of Habsburg had been axiomatic. But there were new forces at work, and the many powers in Europe had other things to think about than to help England to keep the balance which she sought. England might desire no possessions on the continent, but she did thirst after trade, and, if trade were riches and riches power, as both economic theory and political experience seemed to agree they were, then England might be thought the strongest nation in the world. While England was trying to unite Europe against its strongest power that power might try to unite Europe against her. Pitt in 1755 criticized the doctrine of the balance of power saying "we have suffered ourselves to be deceived by names and sounds, the balance of power, the liberty of Europe, a common cause, and much more such expressions without any other meaning than to exhaust our wealth, consume the profits of our trade, and load our posterity with intolerable burdens." Looking back, he could see that for a time after 1716 the English Court had been eager to come to an agreement with France. George I of England was also ruler of Hanover and had his own small plum in the European pie. He wanted some Swedish territory on the southern coast of the Baltic. The French court had a traditional influence in Sweden. It was hoped that French influence with Germany and the northern powers might be some protection to Hanover threatened both by Sweden and Russia who were at war in the Baltic. In the Mediterranean England wanted peace so that her merchants could enjoy their trade with Spain, Italy, and the Levant. When the policy of Elizabeth Farnese, the wife of Philip V of Spain, seemed to threaten another European war, England, France, and the emperor of Austria concluded an alliance for pacifying southern Europe. It was followed by the defeat of the Spanish fleet off Cape Passero.

Renewed competition from French commerce discredited the view that she ought to be an ally against a powerful Austria. When the chronic state of friction between England and Spain developed into the war of 1739 England was dangerously isolated. It began to seem that a recovered France might unite Europe against England and that England could not unite Europe against her. Poland, Sweden, and Prussia were not concerned. There were local conflicts in Germany and Italy quite as important to those engaged in them as England's struggle with France was to her. England was interested in colonies and world trade. Austria was interested in her own balance of power problem in central and eastern Europe. The king of the new kingdom of Prussia feared that he might be attacked from the east by the Russians, from the south by the Austrians and Saxons, and from the west by the Hanoverians, while a combined British and Russian fleet blockaded and bombarded his Baltic coast line. The English on their side could fear that if France held undisputed control of Europe by land she might control the navies of the lesser powers—Holland, Denmark, Portugal, and Sweden. While even then invasion might not be possible, a small landing in Kent could have disastrous effects on the tenuous web of public credit.

The Seven Years' War in Europe was but one part of the worldwide struggle between Great Britain and France which had begun in the New World in 1754. It began with the invasion of Saxony by Frederick the Great in August 1756. He said that he was the quarry in a stag hunt organized by the kings and princes of Europe. Austria hoped to recover Silesia and to reduce Prussia to the position of a minor German state. Russia hoped to absorb East Prussia and Sweden Prussian Pomerania.

The French hoped that a conquest of Hanover would be a useful counter to be set against colonial losses when it came to treaty making. Austria in 1756 broke off her entente with Britain which had been getting less and less cordial through the 1740's and 1750's. France and Austria came together and the States General in Holland announced their intention of maintaining a strict neutrality so long as France had no hostile designs on the United Provinces.

Britain was in an acute dilemma between the interests and advantages in a maritime and in a continental war. She had her European interests. She needed European trade, for even in 1760 her exports to the colonies were only a quarter of her export trade as a whole. Portugal was the European terminus of the considerable trade which Britain had with Brazil. But in a continental war Britain could not make a decisive attack on France in Europe. An alliance with the Dutch might draw on them an invasion from France. Pitt once said that he would rather feed a war in Germany than have one carried on in Flanders. Hanover was the apple of George II's eye, and in a continental war Hanover would be difficult to defend. A continental war had to be carried on by the hired troops from small German states and by the British army, which its citizens distrusted and depised. In a colonial war Britain would be in her element the sea, and the French navy had been sacrificed for the sake of the French army. But a war in America could not be fought by sailors alone. Professional soldiers would have to be transported and adapted to the conditions of battle in the New World. Hired Hessians might prove poor tools for a forest job.[12]

These and other problems faced the elder Pitt in the Seven Years' War (1756–63). In the first half of the eighteenth century France and Britain had isolated their American disputes from the diplomacy of Europe. Now the colonial conflicts were merged in a struggle which stretched from Bombay to the Mississippi. It was dominated by (1) the military genius of Frederick the Great of Prussia who, with a kingdom of four millions, one-third that of Austria and one-fifth that of France, faced the armies of France, Austria, and Russia, and (2) the all-pervading influence of British sea power which was decisive from Madras to Florida, and (3) the vision of Pitt. For Pitt the major purpose of the war was to safeguard English North America by seizing Canada. But the war for the defense of North America was inextricably involved with heavy fighting in the West Indies, and war in the West Indies was dependent on the power of the British navy to keep French fleets bottled up in Mediterranean and Channel ports.

On the North American mainland there had been an expansion of the tiny coastal fringe. British settlements had increased from 400,000 in 1715 to nearly two million in 1760. The British settlements were comparatively thick, and they moved like a creeping tide controlled by the laws of private profit; in the 1750's they were emerging on the western slopes of the Alleghenies as the magnates of the seaboard invested in the unoccupied and fertile lands of the Ohio. The English unplanned tidal movement into the wilderness was met by the advance of the French, which was a planned advance through the capture and fortification of strategic points. The French system was based on the economics of the fur trade, the use of water communications, and the skilled diplomatic control of Indian tribes. Operating from the valley of the St. Lawrence it had between 1713 and 1754 extended from the Mississippi and the Great Lakes to the Appalachians. The weakness of the French was that in concentrating on the fur trade the settlers were dependent on France for their provisions and weapons, and the approaches to the St. Lawrence were threatened by British sea power and by the British occupation of Newfoundland and Acadia. The weakness of the British colonies was that they could rarely be induced to combine for military operations. The control of the mouth of the St. Lawrence and of the headwaters of the Ohio was vital to the security of both systems. In 1745 the capture of Louisbourg by a group of colonists who had combined for once and co-operated with British sea power was a great achievement. Unfortunately, at the Peace of Aix-La-Chapelle it had been handed back in return for Madras. In 1752 the French took the offensive to forestall English settlements west of the Alleghenies. A force of Indians led by the French destroyed La Demoiselle and wiped out an English trading post at Pickawillany. In 1754 the young George Washington, sent with a small body of Virginia militia to drive the French from Fort Duquesne, failed. The other colonies were not enthusiastic in support of Virginia, and the British government had to decide whether it would leave American frontier problems to the Americans and confine itself to protecting their Atlantic trade routes, or whether it would directly engage the French regular land and sea forces with its own. In 1756 the French captured Oswego, winning the allegiance of the western Indians, and were poised from an admirably designed chain of forts to press the British back from the mountains to their sea-board settlements. Pitt was clear that the growth of the North American mainland colonies had made them a central part of the old colonial system and that they must be protected.[13]

In the West Indies there had been war between the British and the French in the 1740's because of the rivalry between the French Caribbean sugar islands and the British. The French were more successful in the production of sugar and in trade with Europe and the North American mainland colonies; they were at a disadvantage in wartime because they had no permanent naval base from which to victual a large fleet (and food resources of tropical islands are slender for a hungry fleet), while the British had dockyards at Port Royal in Jamaica and English harbor in Antigua.

In 1757 the outlook in the West Indies and America was serious for the British. The loss of Minorca to the French had released units of the French Mediterranean fleet for the West Indies. The French using three naval squadrons from North Africa, the West Indies, and North America threatened Jamaica. The best English naval defense of the West Indies was to blockade the channel and Atlantic ports, but some French squadrons could always slip through.

In 1758 Pitt's plans matured. He had decided to make America the decisive theater of the war. A naval force under Edward Boscawen and troops under James Wolfe captured Louisbourg, the great fortress on Cape Breton Island. The French had lost the outer bastion to the St. Lawrence. The capture of Fort Frontenac threatened their communications between the St. Lawrence and the Great Lakes. The capture of the site of Fort Duquesne ended French ascendancy on the Ohio. An indirect attack was made against the French West Indies by the capture of Gorée in West Africa, which crippled their slave trade and hampered their sugar plantations. In September 1759 Wolfe's amphibious force captured Quebec and the counterattack which the French prepared was made useless because Edward Hawke had shattered French naval power at Quiberon Bay in November 1759, and the first ships to reach Quebec up the St. Lawrence in May 1760 were those of the British navy. Montreal surrendered in September. By command of the sea, the effective deployment in the American wilderness of first-class European troops, and the mobilization of colonial resources the French threat to drive the colonies to the seaboard had been overwhelmed.

While the battle for Canada was in progress the French had planned an attack on London. From Ostend 20,000 men were to land at Maldon, two marches from London; from Brittany 20,000 were to land in the Clyde estuary, cross Scotland, and seize Edinburgh. These were idle dreams unless they could have the support of a French fleet. Boscawen defeated one section at Lagos and Hawke the other at Quiberon Bay. The fleet action that saved London had also captured Montreal. At the other side of the world Clive's victory at Plassey in 1757 had made the British *de facto* rulers of Bengal, one of the wealthiest parts of India. Its resources could be used to destroy French power in the Carnatic. But sea power here too was decisive. The arrival of English seaborne reinforcements from Bombay forced the French to raise the siege of Madras. Sir Eyre Coote's arrival with a battalion of regular troops from England led to the defeat of Lally at Wandiwash in January 1760, and Pondicherry was forced to surrender to a combined land and sea attack in January 1761.

Spain entered the war in May 1762. Pitt intended to seize all French possessions in North America and the Caribbean. Rodney took Martinique in 1762. Havana fell in August 1762. An English fleet sailing from the East Indies captured Manila. Britain had acquired by her sea power so embarrassingly large an empire that many of her political leaders feared that there might be a combination of all the other colonial powers against her. Now that Canada was subdued the North American colonists were restive. They intended to trade with the West Indian islands whether they were French or British. In Europe Prussia at the close of 1761 was unconquered but desperate. She was saved by the death of the Tsaritza Elizabeth of Russia in January 1762, which broke up the coalition against Prussia. Frederick the Great was contemplating an agreement with Russia to partition Austrian and Danish dominions. The British were not prepared to pay subsidies for this purpose. They wanted Prussia to fight the French. To Prussia Austria was her real enemy. For these reasons and because Pitt had resigned in October 1761 the compromise Treaty of Paris was negotiated. By it France agreed to restore the territory of all Britain's German allies: Hanover, Hesse, and Brunswick were evacuated and restored. France ceded the whole continent of North America east of the Mississippi and the right of navigation on the Mississippi itself. Spain gave up her claim to the Newfoundland fishery. The right to cut logwood in Honduras was recognized. Britain agreed to restore Martinique and Guadeloupe (with St. Lucia as essential to its defense) and the French slave trading stations in West Africa. Britain restored Cuba to Spain and obtained Florida in exchange.

During the war Frederick the Great of Prussia had held his own against Austria, Russia, Sweden, the South German states, and France. One in nine of the Prussian population had perished in the war. Frederick himself wrote: "The nobility and the peasants had been pillaged and ransomed by so many armies that they had nothing left except the miserable rags which covered their nakedness." France had played a minor role on the continent. The peace settlement was a profound shock for her. It secured the maritime supremacy of Great Britain and the entry of Prussia into the ranks of the European power system. Britain restored her West Indian island conquests to France and by so doing assured to Prussia the recovery of her western possessions. Pitt considered that the peace was insecure. France had not been crushed. The restorations made in the West Indies weakened the British naval command in the Caribbean. In the American War of Independence Britain was to pay a great deal for the compromises of the Treaty of Paris.

CHAPTER IV

The Beginnings of Modern Industry, 1760-1815

> "The time has come," the Walrus said,
> "to talk of many things:
> Of shoes—and ships—and sealing wax—
> of cabbages—and kings—"

In the simple mind of a walrus, shoes and ships and sealing wax, cabbages
and kings, might represent British history in the second half of the eighteenth century. The kingly items may stand for the loss of the British
American colonies, the planting in many parts of the world of the seeds
of another British Empire, and the birth of those ideas and practices of
political liberalism, which shaped the Western World of the nineteenth
century. Sealing wax is an obvious symbol for the administrative skills
without whose existence the words of kings would be a breath moving
nothing. Shoes suggest the increased mobility of men and of materials
which in the eighteenth century was a prologue to an age of new technologies. Ships are a symbol of the network of trade which supported a
new scale of economic life. The homely cabbage may remind us that
the changes which took place were not only in minerals such as coal and
iron but also in the vegetable and animal world—that there was an
agrarian revolution before there was an industrial.

Mandeville wrote in the *Fable of the Bees:* "They are very seldom the
same Sort of People, those that invent Arts, and improvements of them,
and those that enquire into the Reason of Things: this latter is most commonly practised by such, as are idle and indolent, that are fond of Retirement, hate Business, and take delight in Speculation; where as none
succeed oftener in the first, than active, stirring, and labourious men such
as will put their Hand to the Plough, try Experiments, and give their Attention to what they are about." [1]

During the eighteenth century the two sorts of men—those that invent arts and those that enquire into the reason of things—were in the way of a useful co-operation between their diverse gifts and interests. The curiosity and scholarship of the sixteenth and seventeenth centuries was attracting the attention of active, stirring, and laborious men. Partnerships in many arts and new sciences were formed by practical men with capital to invest. Not only the secrets of nature but also the causes of the wealth of nations were being unveiled. The latent force of water, the expansive power of steam, the properties of coal, the possible but hitherto undreamed of scope of the wheel, the lever, friction, and the chemistry of acids and alkalis—from all these were derived new ways to meet the wants of men. And while the hidden processes of nature's working became better known, new understanding grew of the meaning of the economical use of natural resources. The adaptation of means to ends, hitherto traditional and often rule of thumb, became the subject of close enquiry and of statistical and sometimes even mathematical elaboration. The flirtation of mathematics and matter had begun; their later marriage was to give us automation and the bomb. Capital, interest, price, rent, and contract were to have their complex natures investigated as closely as were the properties of coal and iron. It was revealed by all this that the life of man need not be poor, nasty, and short.

What we know about the life and industry of the age which was the corridor to our own palaces of industry comes from the use of statistical methods and techniques of economic analysis which were begun in that age. They were not at the time advanced enough to be used on contemporary materials. There was, for example, no census of population until 1801, and we can only estimate that the population of England and Wales, which was then about nine millions, had increased by some three millions since 1750 and that most of that increase had been since 1780.[2] During the reign of George III the population of England and Wales had almost doubled. England within her little isle was growing almost as fast as the United States with her open frontiers to the West and her ports open to migrants from the old and wicked feudal world.

The causes of this increase in population are even now not completely understood. It was not the result of an increase in the birth rate. It was made possible by a decline in the death rate in the period from 1780 to 1810. Before 1780 there had been a certain balance between the movements of birth and death rates. In an agrarian society a slight rise in the death rate would set free more accommodation for other married couples and would be followed by a rise in the birth rate. Between

1760 and 1780 the ancient rhythm was broken. There was a slight rise in the death rate, the birth rate also rose, and after 1780 that rise was not checked. This change had many causes. There were improvements in medical services—in Edinburgh a great medical school had been in existence for thirty-five years. In London the great hospitals had been founded. The idea of having smallpox in a mild form as a protection against a more deadly one had begun to be accepted. More important than medical knowledge, which before the discovery of the microbe was working against unknown powers, was the general improvement in food and a new desire and opportunity to be free from dirt. It had been discovered that fruit was not the cause of fever, that artificial feeding of infants on animal milk was better than breast feeding by the most seemingly clean and healthy wet nurse. There was more and better food. The Irish had potatoes; the English had cabbages; and the cows, with turnips and swedes on which they could live through the winter, were a living store of fresh meat for town and country. Tea was replacing spirits as a common drink. Wool and cotton clothes were more easy to wash. The paving of streets reduced the diffusion of dung and dust.[3]

A growing population was moving about in new ways. It did not rush or march—the north of England did not invite a gold rush. But the population seeped into new areas, and it coagulated in new blobs and around old spots. There was almost a continuous flow of labor into England from Scotland, Wales, and Ireland. In the early part of the century a high proportion of the poorer people was engaged in domestic service. When labor was needed to develop the new industrial techniques—in iron works, cotton spinning, and canal construction, there were reserves which could be tapped. Such labor was attracted by the improved conditions which were offered. Dark and satanic the new mills and towns might seem to an aesthetic eye, but they were oases of light in the dim desert of the agricultural laborer's life.

In 1760 there were only two towns in England with a population of more than 50,000—London with 750,000 and Bristol with 60,000. Slight as it may now seem, the urban growth which took place in the later eighteenth century was in pattern and in scale something new in the history of man. The new towns were the tempting new frontiers of an old agrarian order. The young man who in the nineteenth century in the New World would go west, in eighteenth-century England went to the new towns. "A village," it was said, "is never the seat of the Arts." In the towns new crafts could be learned and more money could be earned and spent. It was not the old ecclesiastical or administrative centers which had the most rapid increase of population, but the new unincorporated towns. Not the cities of old England, but the free towns of a new and changing England advanced in wealth and numbers.[4]

There was not only a movement from the country to the towns, but also a movement of population from the south to the north. At the beginning of the eighteenth century the southern counties had one-third the population of England. In the south the old textile trades and the traditional agriculture predominated. During the century the south lost ground to the northwest and the west Midlands. The main changes were after 1780. The usefulness of waterpower for the new cotton industry, the proximity of coal and iron to the ports, and improved means of transport on canals and roads meant that the northwest came to rival the corn-bearing southeast. By 1800 Lancashire was more thickly populated than any other region outside London. By then there were almost two nations—an industrial and an agrarian. This fundamental change in the pattern of population was to shatter the mold in which the British constitution of 1689 was set. The Reform Act, 1832, was a political adjustment to a demographic change. The home market, which the new numbers provided, was to be a basis for an industrial order in the nineteenth century that had for its market the world.

In the nineteenth century Britain was to become the workshop of the world. It would be the first stage for the play of those liberal ideas which offered the promise of a world order in which political freedom and economic plenty were partners and not antagonists. The roots of her success may be traced in the eighteenth century. It is agreed by the experts that it was not until after 1780 that the various trickles of change in the techniques of agriculture, industry, and business organization had mingled into a stream which flowed toward that liberal utopia. Only after 1780 did the curves of production and export in cloth, in coal, and in metals show that a new age was born.[5]

In 1760 it was assumed in political circles that industry was a comparatively static and undramatic part of the national life. The coal and iron and glass produced, the great landowners took to be merely new if slightly unusual crops which would add to their normal rent roll. England was no doubt pregnant with a new age, but she had not yet been brought to bed. Industry was as yet only a foetus in the womb of an agrarian mother. In France the expansion in the output of coal and in the production of iron and steel and textiles was at that time faster than it was in Britain. It was the problems of trade which excited the analytical skill of pamphleteers and stirred the British councils of war. Industry in 1760 had not become a magnet to the rural population, nor was its dynamic power reshaping political institutions or transforming the attitudes of politicians and administrators. The industrial, like the rural, areas of the country were still supervised by the justices of the peace and the search for new administrative methods had barely begun.

Looking back, we can now see that there were present conditions which would favor industrial innovations. There was plenty of skill among the workers in the traditional industries and crafts. It had been observed in 1697 that English artisans "were allowed the best upon earth for improvements." The population was much smaller than that of France, but there were fewer internal checks on its movements. Few places, except in the west and north, were more than a long day's journey by cart from navigable water. Villages could be isolated for a whole winter. In Devonshire in winter the sledge competed with the pack horse. Coal for firing the potter's oven in Staffordshire was often carried by men, for no other beast of burden could get through the deep quagmires. But relatively speedy communications were on the way. The coach and van would replace the pack horse when better roads were developed. In 1760 the canal age had just barely begun.[6] Every improvement in transport meant a wider market, and a wider market stimulated a demand which could be met by bringing in the reserves of labor always to be found in a village economy. Where, as in the north, labor was really scarce, increased demand encouraged the use of labor-saving methods in productive processes. In a buoyant economy, sustained by age-old skills, stimulated by agricultural improvements and wider trade, a capitalist could invest in the new methods devised by ingenious men. The improvements in transport, the expansion of overseas trade, and the accumulation of capital in the service of many inventions had a snowballing effect. Every contrivance that made the wheels of industry turn more quickly and that cut down the time taken in the movement of men and materials was a saving of resources. The more quickly you could produce, the more could you transfer circulating capital to fixed capital, which would itself help to quicken production still more. Nor was England without the stimulus which comes from the gifts that immigrants may bring. Of the 810 merchants who kissed the hand of George III in 1760, at least 250 were of alien origin. Among the insular syllables of Hanway, Lloyd, Thornton, Walpole, Washington, Wilberforce, and Wordsworth, appear a Boehm, a Schoen, Montefiore, Modigliani, and Zimines.[7] But only after the Americans had won their independence did the pace really quicken.

Of the 26,000 inventions that belong to the century, far more than half were obtained after 1782. When the struggle with Napoleon came, it was necessary to do quickly what otherwise would have been done slowly. Napoleon closed the continental European shop and by so doing compelled the British, if they would survive, to sell to all the world.

In 1760 there were few signs of the far-reaching changes in industry which were to come. But agriculture was being slowly transformed. To meet the demands of a growing population the enclosure of scattered holdings into fenced units of production, under individual control, increased after the middle of the century. Enclosures were part of a movement which contemporaries spoke of as improvement. From the very nature of agricultural activities these improvements—enclosure, the opening up of waste land, improvements in farming practice, new crops and new types of machinery—would be made locally and would be slow to spread. They would happen piecemeal and had a local and not a national context. But their cumulative effect was a revolutionary change in the work of the farmer before the revolutions in the industries of textile and steel. The need for improvement was most obvious in the south and east Midlands. In the north too the general backwardness of the country discouraged scientific farming. But the improvements were made—in drilling in rows, in the use of marl and artificial grasses and crop rotation, and in stock breeding. The English aristocracy never lost touch with the land and after 1780 some of them attached prestige to schemes of agricultural improvement. Farmer George III himself followed the fashion.

After 1780 England ceased to be a corn-exporting country and became a net importer of wheat. The farm was now a factory producing the means of subsistence for the growing towns. When the Napoleonic war diminished the supply of foreign corn there was an expansion of farming, and between 1793 and 1803 there was a hectic period of enclosure at the end of which only half a dozen counties in England had more than 3 per cent of their land unenclosed.

Improvements in agriculture made it possible to feed a larger population and the agricultural population itself increased. It did not grow as fast as the industrial population, but it did increase, not only on the farms themselves but in the ancillary trades and crafts—the blacksmith's, wheelwright's, and mechanic's. Although the changes in industry were to alter the place of agriculture in the national life, as late as 1851 agriculture still employed one out of every four Englishmen over the age of twenty. Nor did enclosures destroy the small producers. The average agricultural unit in 1815 was an employer with two or three hands to assist him. The villages were not deserted.[8] Wealth might accumulate, but men in fact did not decay.

The cumulative and accelerating changes in the methods of production and distribution of goods and services which have been called an industrial revolution first appeared in the use of cotton, iron, and steam. They were an effect in things of common day of the penetration into the secrets of nature which was the inspiration of the scientific movement. In cotton, as Alfred Marshall noted, the replacement of manual dexterity by a mechanical process was to be expected, because a cotton thread is a thin cylinder easy to adapt to such operations. Iron, when its physical and chemical properties could be controlled, was a material which could replace the wood which would burn or splinter at the new speeds now given to ancient crafts. Steam was a new power, a mutation of that waterpower to which the worker had once had to go but which could now be brought to him. These three things—the use of machines which could perform at enormously greater speeds than the manipulative skill of men, the tapping of the powers latent in the fire and water used since the dawn of civilization, and the making of iron and steel which could be given the shapes that machinery needs and retain them when driven by the new power of steam—together made possible a new pace in the economic loom by which men must live.

The real innovation was that natural materials and forces could be put to do the work of men. The formulas of the chemist and the equations of mathematicians informed the raw materials found in nature so that they could take over the efforts of human fingers, hands, and feet. We can see more clearly now the significance of early machines when a new revolution in which the analytical and calculating activities of human brains are being taken over by machines is all about us. In the eighteenth century we see the use in man's struggle with nature of his new knowledge of its structure. The celestial mechanics of a Newton was given an earthly task.

But if machines were to take over much of the drudgery of men, it was only at the price of men taking on some of the characteristics of machines. A factory was a place in which men and women (and for a time children too) had to behave as though they were parts of a machine. It was this new service of the machine which was at the root of so much early horror at the factory conditions. If they were to live, men had always to adapt themselves to the movement of the sun and the course of the seasons. The new discoveries broke the organic rhythm and replaced it by an order which was mechanical, artificial, and within human control. When in the not very distant future the climates of the world are within the control of the appropriate government departments, we may face a similar shock to that given by the first stages of the age of machinery.

Aggregations of labor working to a strict timetable had, of course, existed before the cotton factories. Defoe had described the royal arsenal at Chatham in the 1720's. Guns and cannon could not be made in cottages nor could sail cloth for merchantmen and men-of-war nor could army boots and blankets in the numbers needed. The use of waterpower to turn the machinery used in the cotton industry or to swing the hammers and drive the blast of the new iron and steel processes led to the new factory organization. Waterpower meant that the productive processes in which it was used had to be where the water was. The spinning jenny of 1764 made it possible for one man or woman to work several spindles simultaneously. It did not interfere with the pattern of cotton spinning by families in separate cottages. But in 1779 the mule married the jenny to the water frame using the moving frame of the former and the rollers of the latter. For convenience many processes were now gathered into adjacent buildings near a bridge over a river from which power was taken. It was the application of steam which led to the centralization of production round the new source of power and which expanded the industry until it began to change the whole face of the country. The mule produced a strong fine thread of cotton from which the weavers could make muslins superior to those of India. But it meant that weaving became a bottleneck because mechanization was not applied to weaving successfully until 1801. Before spinning was mechanized it had taken five or six spinners to make the thread which a single weaver could use. When spinning had been mechanized the weavers for a time were the aristocrats of the artisan world, some of them sporting £5 notes in their hatbands to show how well off they were. When weaving itself was mechanized the hand-loom weavers suffered a long decline. Their sufferings were one of the first examples of the need for a planned mobility of labor which the penetration of life and labor by mechanical techniques would require.

The development of the steam engine came from a combination of a knowledge of the nature of latent heat with skill in the making of instruments. In 1782 the essential transformation of up and down movement into a rotary one had been achieved. It was known as a sun and planet motion. The first steam engine with rotary motion was used in a cotton mill in Nottingham in 1785, in Manchester in 1789, and in Glasgow in 1792. The expansion of the cotton industry which steam made possible transformed Lancashire into a frontier colony of a new age. The population of Manchester increased from 50,000 in 1790 to 100,-000 in 1815; that of Oldham from 400 in 1760, to 12,000 in 1801. The new industry was untrammeled by ancient prejudice or vested interest.

The industry was fortunate, too, in its sources of supply. In 1760 about three million pounds of raw cotton were imported, mostly from the West Indies and South America. In 1793 the invention of the cotton gin in the United States made the latter the main source, and in 1789 more than thirty-two million pounds were imported.

Cotton was the protagonist of the industrial drama now begun. But the woolen industry was still the leading industry in eighteenth-century England as it had been for centuries past. As late as 1800 its exports, valued at seven million pounds, were greater than those of cotton and iron combined. The industry was spread in scattered units of production from the southwest to the east and north. In the late eighteenth century it was to be concentrated round Leeds and Bradford. During the Napoleonic war its raw material was difficult to get from Spain. But toward the end of that war the first wool cargoes were received from New South Wales.

Before the eighteenth century, iron ore was smelted in the small charcoal-fired furnaces in Sussex, the Forest of Dean, South Staffordshire, and South Wales, where the ore was to be found near timber for charcoal. The forges and the mills used to make the finished iron products were not near the smelting furnaces or near to one another. The mills were as close as possible to waterpower, and the forges were near where coal was easy to get. The finishing sections of the trade became dependent on foreign supplies of iron imported from Norway and Sweden, Spain and Russia. The transformation of the industry came with the use of coal, in the form of coke, in place of the charcoal from the vanishing forests, for smelting the iron ore. The process was developed by three generations of the Darby family, ironmasters of Shropshire. In 1783–84 Henry Cort perfected a coal-fired reverberatory furnace known as a puddling furnace, in which the melted iron could be rid of its impurities. In 1790 Homfrey of Tredegar devised a method to remove surplus silicon from the ore before it was treated in the puddling furnace. These and other inventions made possible the malleable iron age in which from 1784 to 1875 Great Britain was the predominant producing country. By 1800 the blowing apparatus for the blast could be worked by Watt's steam engine in place of waterpower. The output of pig iron rose from 68,000 tons in 1788 to nearly 260,000 tons in 1806 and nearly 700,000 in 1830. With steam power, production could be concentrated—in South Wales and Staffordshire. At the same time new processes made possible the production of high-grade steel of known properties—tailored, as we say today of fibers and detergents, to particular needs—and by the end of the Napoleonic wars Sheffield had become the center of the steel trade. The iron industry vigorously cultivated the home market, mitigating the effect of fluctuations in demand. Iron was used for bridges; in 1787 the first boat built of metal plates was finished. In 1788 Wilkinson of the iron industry made forty miles of cast-iron pipes for the water supply of Paris. In 1812 the gas industry had iron pipes. Wilkinson himself had an iron coffin, and his resurrection was awaited by his devoted employees.[9]

Iron wheels and the use of mechanical iron hammers were to make possible the use of machines to make machines—the real prologue to our own speeding and kaleidoscopic scene. Coal and iron were the base of a new technology in place of wood and wind and water. Unlike the cotton revolution the development of coal and iron did not depend on large imports of raw material nor on the replacement of labor by machines. England had the largest coal reserves in western Europe outside the Ruhr.

The new methods of production, whether in organic material such as cotton or in inorganic such as iron and steel, involved a far more complex division of labor than had been known before, a redistribution of workers and their places of work, and the wider markets which require and support the changes in scale of operation and the more specialized forms it will take. Differentiation of activities involves co-ordination if a working unity is to survive. With machines and factories came improvements in communications of a most far-reaching kind. They were material and immaterial. Material in the form of canals, roads, and iron rails. Immaterial in the development of technical institutions for the advancement and dissemination of new technical skills; also in the weaving of a subtle network of credit on which the accumulation and distribution of capital depends. Moreover, the whole of the British Isles was the center of a network of trade which had been the main concern of those responsible for foreign policy in the eighteenth century and which many in the nineteenth century were to see as the first sketch of a world order, based on international division of labor that would bring peace and plenty.

The most obvious means of communication were the roads. Chesterton sang that

> The rolling English drunkard made the rolling
> English road.

Although English roads were the admiration of the continental visitor, many of them were fairly described as being as "God left them after the flood." Too often it was hoped that the broad wheels of wagons would flatten a track wide enough for a gentleman's horse. It was a revolution when it was decided that a road ought to meet the needs of the user and that the user was not to be expected to make the road. Considerations of strategy after the rebellion of 1745 led the central government to drive roads through the Highlands of Scotland. The Turnpike Trusts employed professional surveyors, and by 1815 there were about 20,000 miles of turnpike trust roads. Also for heavy goods short stretches of iron rail track could be used. In 1773 it was provided by Act of Parliament that milestones should be set up on the highways, that signposts be erected at road junctions, and that bridges be walled or fenced.

The roads were operated in conjunction with canals. London was at the center of the system. Raw materials from the London docks could be moved by canal to all points of the Midlands and the finished goods poured back into the metropolitan warehouses for distribution. Between 1789 and 1815 the East India, West India, and the Commercial and Surrey docks were built. As Adam Smith wrote: "Six or eight men by the help of water carriage, can carry and bring back in the same time the same quantity of goods between London and Edinburgh, as fifty broad wheeled waggons attended by a hundred men and drawn by 400 horses."

The canal era had begun in the early 1760's. The English rivers, improved under the stimulus of ideas derived from the Dutch, provided as early as 1724 some 1,160 miles of navigable water, and except in mountainous areas most of the country was within fifteen miles of navigable water. The canals greatly improved the internal arteries of trade. Landlords had better markets for the corn, timber, and minerals of their estates. Farmers could get marl, lime, and manure; builders and manufacturers bricks and stone, coal and cotton. Coal was the most important freight carried. Of the 165 acts passed between 1758 and 1802 to develop canals ninety were for the transport of coal. The improvement of rivers and the building of canals developed the skill of engineers and the techniques of labor management. It was necessary to control bodies of 400 to 600 men scattered over miles of country. These men—the navvies—were the pioneers of a new age. They brought new ideas to isolated villages, and they were the forerunners of those English navvies who in the middle decades of the nineteenth century were to build the railways of many lands.

Equally important was the invisible network of credit operating from London as a center. Businessmen might get their fixed capital by borrowing from relatives and merchants, or by ploughing back their own profits. But they needed also circulating capital for their raw materials, their wages, and general running expenses. By 1784 there were more than one hundred country banks in England alone. They were developed by traders and industrialists and by financial intermediaries such as attorneys and collectors of government revenue.[10] During the next ten years their numbers trebled. Their work was indispensable in the quickening of economic life.

When industry in the middle of the century was looked upon as a necessary, but subordinate, variation in the general agrarian pattern of economic life, the interest of analytical minds and the concern of statesmen and diplomacy was trade. It was in trade that the sources of national strength were sought. It was the merchant and not the poet who really surveyed mankind from China to Peru. It was trade that was at the heart of the theory and the practice of eighteenth-century politics. There was a theory that a planned and mutually co-operative economic community must be sustained. Trade and ships and security were all for one and one for all. There were the actual facts of trade—the variety, the competition, and the growth. The basic economic drives which, internally, were to create a new industrial order within an old and yet powerful agricultural way of life were, on the world stage, to disrupt the first British Empire and to create the liberal order of the nineteenth century. Trade implies the existence of an international division of labor of which the latent force was to shatter the political forms of the eighteenth-century world. Neither enlightened despots nor great landowners, however tolerant or worldly wise, could command the winds of trade to blow where they listed.

In 1760 Great Britain exported textiles, metal goods, tin, pottery, and cured fish. She re-exported tobacco, sugar, Indian calicoes, and leather. The export of woolen goods was more than a quarter of the whole. She imported wines, spirits, sugar, tea, coffee, furs, and silk, and raw materials such as wool, linen, hemp, and naval stores. Holland had the largest trade. Then came the West Indies, the American colonies, Germany, the East Indies, China, and Russia. But trade with the West and East Indies and China was growing more rapidly than with Holland. The idea of a guaranteed and controlled trade was general. The Navigation laws were intended to secure the ships and seamen needed for national defense. The enumeration of the commodities which a British colony might manufacture or might import only from England and the preferential rates of duty upon some colonial products were parts of a plan to control economic activity in the national interest. Foreign policy was directed to secure an increase of customers (not of colonies) overseas and with the minimum of interest in continental Europe. The merchant tonnage to sustain it was in 1760 about 500,000 tons. Soldiers (since the seventeenth-century civil war) were disliked as possible instruments of despotism. In England, Schumpeter has written, there was agreement "to prevent the rise of a professional army; and when that rise had become unavoidable, to keep the army as small as possible and prevent it from growing into a separate occupational estate with independent power and distinct interests." [11] So it was not the English *state* that conquered the colonial empire. The conquerors were adventurers who were unable to find a solid footing at home or men driven into exile. On the continent the first would have joined the armies of the prince. The exiles were carriers of that frontier spirit nourished by a free society.

The old colonial system was, therefore, mercantile rather than colonial. It tried to widen the opportunities for trade. It looked on Newfoundland not as territory to be painted red, but as a place where the fishermen of west country ports could dry their nets, pack their fish, and find safe harbor. The great voyages of Cook and others were a search for customers in the Pacific. Most of the revenue which served the public debt was drawn from customs and excises or charges upon trade. It was perfectly orthodox that an English politician—Grenville—should propose that customs duties should be levied to meet the cost of American government.

We who have lived through the period of the great depression and live even now in a period of creeping inflation and on the brink of the immeasurable destruction of atomic war, which could be triggered by a difference in economic dogmas, will not expect that the theory and the practice of eighteenth-century trade should coincide. It was in the eighteenth century that the foundations of modern economic science were laid. It was in the process of production that a succession of great thinkers—Locke in England, Hume and Adam Smith in Scotland, the physiocrats in France—saw the real power of creating wealth and the possibility of a surplus which, accumulated, would accelerate future production. Hume could write in 1752: "Not only as a man but as a British Subject, I pray for the flourishing commerce of Germany, Spain, Italy and even France itself." But the political and administrative factors involved in realizing the advantages latent in developing the diverse skills and natural advantages of the different regions of the world were the concern of political leaders.

To see that all good government must rest upon the consent of the governed does not of itself provide a blueprint of a workable constitution. To understand the causes of the wealth of nations does not of itself tell you how to unravel the tangle of interests and powers which time has woven. Industry and agriculture were a part of normal life. Until the fast-moving changes of the nineteenth century they were normal and undramatic. But trade had obvious peculiarities of urgent concern to the statesman. It involved shipping, and shipping, for an island, was closely linked with war. For internal purposes a government could secure the

peace and order which were its *raison d'être* by the control of communications by men and horsemen. It could administer justice through a system of magistrates who knew their neighbors and had for various reasons
their support. Even then there was a prolonged and acrimonious struggle
between local interests and central needs as we know from the care with
which His Majesty's ministers would supervise the shape of county things.
But ships are in direct contact with foreign powers. They are both elusive
and vulnerable. They can be controlled when they are in ports, but on
the open seas they have a freedom which no highwayman could enjoy
on land.

Trade is more easily controlled than industrial processes. What goes
into a ship can be examined. But the significance of the exchanges—the
effect on the country of the trade which took place through the medium
of shipping—was very difficult to understand. The merchants were the
experts which a government could consult about conditions in foreign
parts—their trade regulation and their currencies. On the other hand the
merchants were dependent on the government for their safety, their
standing with foreign powers, and for the provision of essential services
in the colonies with which they dealt. The theory of foreign trade has its
complexity as one aspect of the general problem of providing that network of law and order without which trade will degenerate first into
barter and then into loot. In internal affairs the authorities had early discovered the value and the need of providing the peace of the market.
To provide a network of law and order for the interchange of goods implicit in an international division of labor was far more intricate.

The general problem was complicated by three things: (1) the special
needs of the government for defense. Trade was a part of war potential.
In a war you would need ships and sailors; you would need the appropriate currency for the sinews of war. Common to both was the need
for certain essential supplies of timber and of hemp from the Baltic.
What could be got from America was not enough to maintain a navy.
(2) The concern of the government that vital industries should have
their essential supplies and that the markets for which they had specialized
should not be closed down. (3) The development of complex patterns
of trade, continuance of which at least seemed to depend on the skill
that government could use.

The British had a theory of a planned and mutually co-operative economic community. Imperial trade was to be conducted in British or colonial ships. This was a great advantage to the shipbuilders of New England. All European and East Indian goods had to be imported into
America by way of Great Britain. A long list of enumerated goods had

always to be exported by way of Great Britain. These included tobacco, cotton, indigo dyes, molasses, copper, fur, hides, skins, pitch, tar, turpentine, masts, coffee, whale fins, raw silk, and potash. The object was to get valuable raw materials and to deny them to European rivals. The nonenumerated exports of the colonies were free to move into southern Europe or other parts of the world, but if they were destined for northern Europe they had to be taken by way of Britain. It was a consistent extension of this policy when the Americans were forbidden to trade in manufactured woolen goods from one colony to another and when they were ordered not to develop an iron industry. Great Britain was in fact the natural market for most of the American products and the cheapest supplier of finished articles to her. Before the War of Independence the Americans loudly deplored the prohibition of an industry they were in no position to undertake. When the war was over trade increased. Efforts were made to develop Nova Scotia as a grain supplier to the West Indies in place of New England, but it was not possible. Illicit trade with alien America was a necessity to the West Indies.

One of the most important patterns of trade was that known as the Atlantic triangle. England exported manufactured articles to Africa. From Africa she took black slaves for the West Indies and the southern mainland states of America. From the West Indies she imported sugar. The West Indies paid for their provision from the American mainland in bills on London and in rum. The Americans had their accounts in these bills and for tobacco and timber settled by the export of manufactures to them.[12]

Another trade pattern was that for India and the Far East. The big ships of the East India Company brought Indian muslins and cotton and tea and spices. The cotton industry had not yet developed, and England imported cotton cloth. But as wool was not wanted in exchange because of the climate, bullion had to be exported.

After French sea power had been shattered at Trafalgar Napoleon tried to win his war by using his dominion over Europe to starve England into submission by depriving her of food stuffs and to ruin her by depriving her manufacturers of raw materials and by closing her markets for manufactured goods. The English declared the entire coast of the countries under France or in alliance with France to be in a state of blockade. "Napoleon defied England to dispense with the Continental market and the British Government in return defied the French Empire to dispense with all goods which were either of English manufacture or had passed through the English customs. The two nations . . . were in the position of two men who had both put their heads in a bucket, and were trying to see who could keep his head under the longer." [13] The English found new markets beyond the seas. The hemp and timber they could no longer get from Russia and Denmark they got from Bengal and from North America. Baltic corn was replaced by corn cultivated in Ireland. When the French invaded Spain the whole of South America, and also Oporto, Lisbon, and Cadiz, opened their markets to British goods. British goods found their way, too, even into the parts of Europe which were under Napoleon's control. "Undoubtedly," he informed his minister of commerce, "it is necessary to harm our foe, but above all we must live." By 1812 the British had abandoned their Orders in Council and Napoleon his continental system.

Napoleon, in fact, failed to develop French industry under the conditions of protection which the war provided. In England cotton and woolen textile industries continued to expand. Bonaparte's soldiers were wearing British great coats when they defeated the Russians in 1807. The iron trade was relatively prosperous. In agriculture the enclosure movement continued at a rapid pace; the Board of Agriculture set up by Pitt in 1793 publicized new methods and techniques. The output of tillage crops in 1815 was 50 per cent greater than it had been twenty years before. The protests of industry and commerce against the Orders in Council, the incidence of bad harvests and rising prices, and the burden of taxation led to an analysis of the nature of the economic order which was to lead, after the war, to the development of free trade and to a critical analysis of what the proper functions of government were in a free society.

CHAPTER V

A Balanced Constitution, 1760-1815

In the preceding chapter a sketch was given of the first consequences for ordinary men and women—in field and office and workshop—of the ability to control some of the forces of nature by a patient study of detail and a willingness to follow the argument wherever it might lead. Modern technology was not yet born, but the British Isles were quick with the seed of new knowledge about nature and nature's laws. Through every trade and industry might be traced the tiny rivulets of change, hurrying to form the mighty river of a world economic order which now carries the whole world toward an unknown sea.

In the world of politics, in the conceptions of social order, and in the administrative skills on which they depend, there were changes no less portentous. An economic order is no doubt bewildering in its complexity, but it is open to statistical analysis and its details can be averaged into sketches of plausible trends. Who made what, and who did this for how many, and for what price? And with what over-all effects on the bread by which men live? To such questions the economic historian can give an intelligible reply. It is far more difficult to lay bare the ideas, habits, passions, and delusions by which men are stirred, controlled, or comforted in their everyday life out of its economic shadow. To know how men get their daily bread may be difficult enough, but to understand how they settle their disputes and decide their common purposes is mysterious indeed.

The United States in the nineteenth century was to make a political and legal order which sustained an economic development of astonishing speed and range. The American people moved from the Atlantic to the Pacific weaving as they went a powerful industrial and agrarian order. No doubt the history of the frontier is a tangled tale, and no doubt the history of agrarian and industrial America in the nineteenth century will need the finest skill of the economist and the prolonged research of scholars before it can be told in full, but the grand design is reasonably clear. It took place in conditions which were in the light of common day. Even the adaptation of the American Constitution to the needs of her protean economic changes can be followed and explained.

But in the history of the British political system of the late eighteenth century we move in a very strange world indeed. The king of Brobdingnag gave, we know, his most courteous attention to the political lectures of Lemuel Gulliver, but we do not feel that he quite caught the spirit of what that Englishman was trying to convey; and if the late eighteenth century in English political life was not so very queer, as it had been when Swift was the Bernard Shaw of his generation, it had not yet moved into the light of common day. The theory of the constitution was subtle, confusing, and profound. The scope of government was narrow, and its practice often trivial, technical, and mean. But there are astonishing grandeurs which blaze against a background which is often dirty and dull. Between the accession of George III in 1760 and the final defeat of Napoleon in 1814, the United States was born in a War of Independence against the British system, the master of Europe was checked and finally destroyed by the stubborn resistance of the maritime power of a few small islands off his coast, and the principles of a parliamentary system of government were nourished by the experiences of those who had to work a constitution which was old and resilient, corrupt and competent. In philosophy and in literature in the eighteenth century, one may trace in Britain a movement from the rationalism of the Augustans to the romanticism of the Lake poets. We seem to move from Pope's theme:

The proper study of mankind is man

to Wordsworth's sense of:

Something far more deeply interfused.

But in the development of the constitution there is a movement from romanticism to utilitarianism. The mystery of kingship is lost yet it vanishes not into thin air, but lives on as a principle of unity in the system of representative government which came after. From an undergrowth of queer theory and stranger practice there springs the stem of a new system of government—the constitutional monarchy of the nineteenth century which made possible the liberal economic order of that era—a pattern of civilization which we now see to have been as unique within its scope and as transient in its glory as any of the imperial orders of the past. Its future we do not know:

History tells more often than not
of wickedness with will, wisdom but

> An interjection without a verb,
> and the godless growing like green cedars,
> On righteous ruins.   (*The Age of Anxiety*)

Its origins we must look at now.

One peculiarity about the eighteenth-century British system of government was its assumption of antiquity. Burke,

> . . . haughtier-headed Burke,
> that proved the State a tree,

spoke of "the powerful prepossession towards antiquity, with which the minds of all our lawyers and legislators, and of all the people whom they wish to influence, have been always filled . . . the stationary policy of this kingdom in considering their most sacred rights and franchises as an inheritance." And with antiquity went freedom. It was not that the British with insular conceit said that they never, never would be slaves; it was that intelligent visitors noted with astonishment that they were not. The constitution was thought to be a "pattern of perfection," but its perfection was not that of a new tool or of well-written articles of agreement; it was the perfection of garnered experience. "If ever God Almighty did concern himself about forming a government for mankind to live happily under, it was that which was established in England by our Saxon forefathers," wrote an essayist of 1771. No doubt his sense of history was not so good as that of a Gibbon or a Hume, but he was merely uttering what he sensed in the climate of his time. Jefferson himself was to justify the American position by direct appeal to Saxon precedent. In the attitude of eighteenth-century men to the constitution we find the same paradox as in their attitude to nature. The constitution was a part of nature. But to the eighteenth-century mind, nature was on the one hand an infinitely complex, but since Mr. Newton, a measurable and manageable mechanism—a celestial clock or watch, and on the other hand nature was the body of which God was the soul, and immanent in nature were the powers of good and evil known in our own hearts and in our enemies and friends. So it was possible to consider the clockwork of the British constitution as a domestic version of the clockwork of the universe and also to consider it as a microcosm of those powers of good and evil which move through the worlds of a Milton or a Blake.

During the eighteenth century the conception of the universe as a great chain of being was transformed into the conception of the universe as the coming to be of an increasing diversity, a more luminous reason and steadier virtues, as mankind moved from a savage past to a glorious future. The political implications of this change in metaphysical ideas were far-reaching. It is his sense of them that fires the genius of Burke. If there is no hierarchy from God to nothingness, if man is not an isthmus of a middle state then the whole influence of what Shakespeare called "degree" would be lost in the political order. The divinity that had hedged a king would shrivel like the fragment of a broken spider's web and some other base of political authority would have to be found. That king and statesman and poet were in the eighteenth century often mad— George III, Chatham, and Blake—had, no doubt, simple medical explanation, but their madness may be seen as a symbol of the tensions of their age.

After antiquity comes complexity. The contemporaries of George III were proud of the "mixed form of government" which combined by a skillful division of power the best of monarchy, aristocracy, and democracy. Jeremy Bentham was to make fine fun of this confusing "image" of a political three-in-one beloved of all working politicians. George III once called it "the most beautiful combination that ever was framed." This trinitarian theme was almost a commonplace and always confusing. To Locke the trinity was that of the executive, the legislative, and the federative; to Montesquieu it was the legislative, the executive, and the judiciary; but to George III and most of his subjects the important trinity was the old English trinity of King, Lords, and Commons. "This might or might not be identical with the trinity of monarchy, aristocracy, and democracy; and that might or might not be identical with the trinity of executive power, landed property, and money." [1]

The government was the king's government. The phrase His Majesty's Opposition would have been almost a contradiction in terms. By 1760 the dynasty had ceased to be an issue. With the passing of the deadly threat of a dynastic dispute and the incidental chance of disembowelment for treason against the King's Majesty, the divinity of kingship shrank to a powerful symbol of political unity. When real kingship died the conventions of cabinet government were born. But in 1760 the king was still a real king. A new reign was a new world. It was the king's business to see that the government of the nation was carried on. He had a right to demand advice, though no duty to do so. He had a right to choose his instruments. It was a constitutional axiom that he was free to choose and to dismiss his ministers. Politicians strove for office, or they would not have been politicians, but they would each and all declare their extreme reluctance to take or retain office unless assured of the king's favor willingly accorded. A man had a duty to support the government so long as in honesty he could. To try to impose oneself on the king by means of a systematic opposition, to "force" a change in the composition of the king's government was held to be factious and dishonest. You might by seduction win the favors which you craved, but a rape was breaking the rules of the game. To go into opposition required some excuse, however specious. A useful distinction was drawn between opposition to specific measures, for reasons of conscience, and "formed opposition," which was condemned by all as indecent and oppressive.

In the eighteenth century there was in fact no competing center of power in the country which could be set up against the king's right to choose a government. George III rightly believed that it was the duty of men of good will to accept office. It was absolutely necessary for the government to have the favor of the king. The members of his government were not collectively responsible for the policy which the king might pursue. The general opinion was that it would be unconstitutional for one minister to control the cabinet and engross the favor of the king. A prime minister had not emerged when George III came to the throne in 1760. Monarchy could not be depersonalized until the House of Commons had been so organized that it could do for government what in the existing conditions of political life only the king could do.

The king would select a group of ministers who, having the support of a majority in the House of Commons, could carry on the essential functions of government as they were then understood. No eighteenth-century politician had the power from his party following alone to lay down a policy or to dictate to the king his choice of ministers. The king could select the material for his administration from among the different party groups. Like little Jack Horner he sat in his corner; he put in his thumb and pulled out a plum and said: what a good boy am I. By relying on some he could free himself from the importunity of others. But he had to choose a workable combination. He could not with impunity flout the leaders of all the major groups.

The functions of government were the keeping of order, the protection of property, the conduct of commercial, financial, and foreign affairs, with the direction of whatever warlike operations these might unfortunately involve. When these vital matters were well in hand the control of the composition of the executive itself could be discussed. And such discussions—about the distribution of the sweets of office—were music to the politician's ear. "The due arrangement of men in the active part of a state . . . ought to be among its very first and dearest objects." But the cabinets themselves had to govern rather than to legislate. The king's service very seldom required legislation—except, of course, financial legislation. Very few of the proposed laws which seem, in retrospect, to have been most important were cabinet measures. Parliamentary reform was not; the abolition of the slave trade was not. Catholic Emancipation only became a matter of government when it might involve civil war and the destruction of property. "When a minister legislated, even on important matters, he often did so as an individual, not only technically, but politically. It did not often happen that a party program consisted of legislation, or that the merits of a legislative proposal were, in any sense, put before the electorate. Defeats on legislative proposals, even finance bills, did not usually involve the fall of the government." [2]

Governments did not initiate legislation to remold the social order nearer to the heart's desire. Such legislation—in poor law, enclosures, canal development, the making of roads—was secured by private legislation initiated by the co-operation of local agencies. For that reason the House of Commons could be described as being "a confused and scuffling bustle of local agencies." It was saved from the worst kind of logrolling by its own standing orders, which forbade a private member to propose the expenditure of public money. It was not "a congress of ambassadors from different and hostile interest, but a deliberate assembly of one nation." Its members were "as trustees, to act for the benefit and advantage of the whole kingdom." The stress on unity is understandable when one sees how precarious that unity still was, how recent were the memories of bloody divisions, and how turbulent were the forces beneath the surface of bewigged and ceremonial order. The men of genius in the eighteenth century, with no Freud to guide them, understood the terrors that lurked in the jungle of the unconscious and knew that the public order was as vulnerable as the order in their own lives.

Since 1689 government could only be carried on by the co-operation of king and Parliament. In the last resort the king could not oppose the deliberate resolution of the House of Commons. No ministry could pursue a policy to which the House of Commons was definitely opposed. "The people of a free commonwealth," wrote Burke, "who have taken care that the laws should be the result of general consent, cannot be so senseless as to suffer their executory system to be composed of persons on whom they have no dependence." In 1782 Lord North told George III, who, like Mr. Churchill in a later century, did not feel that it was his calling to preside over the dissolution of a British Empire, "in this country, the Prince on the Throne, cannot, with prudence, oppose the deliberate resolution of the House of Commons . . . Your Majesty having persevered, as long as possible, in what you thought right, can lose no honour if you yield at length, as some of the most renowned and most glorious of your predecessors have done, to the opinion and wishes of the House of Commons." In form a minister might seem to be crawling on his knees, but in fact he was able to shake a very real fist. The government was the king's government, but no individual minister could continue to hold office if the House of Commons was definitely opposed to him. Walpole had resigned as soon as he lost his majority in the House of Commons. In 1783 the Fox-North coalition compelled Shelburne to resign, even though he was supported by the King.

A government had to have the support of the House of Commons, but defeat of a particular measure or on a particular issue did not involve their resignation. "Ministers must not," George III once said, "mind being now and then in a minority." A minister ought to insist on anything which was really necessary to the king's service, but he could not insist on everything which he might think to be right in itself. The Commons were not in a position to nominate the ministers whom the king might use. They could criticize his choice and demand that they be removed, but the pattern of parties among their number, and in the country from which they came, would not yet support a prime minister, the formal and actual head of a group united on the principles and the details of a policy which the king must accept and Parliament implement. The king had plenty of room for maneuver, because one-third of the House of Commons did not belong to any party at all, and the other two-thirds was divided among three or more parties which had none of the characteristics of the parties the British were to create in the period after 1832. The House of Commons made its claim to supremacy an essential principle of the constitution. But it did so in the eighteenth century on the ground that its historical function was to be a check to the Crown. In theory and in fact it was looked upon by many people as a second-rate aristocracy.[3]

The theory of virtual representation—that the House of Commons did not mirror proportionally the interests of the country, but in some subtle but undefined way, interpreted their essential unity—is a good example of that desire for unity in a world clearly bursting with diversity which is the passion of the age. "So little was the principle of actual representation valued that early parliamentary reformers ignored or even denied it." All the emphasis, at first, was on making the House of Commons more virtuous, or more independent of the Crown, or more economical; only gradually did the inequalities of representation come to appear as the chief part of the grievance.[4] "Independence," rather than representation, was the basis of the Commons strength. It would protest as much against pressure from outside Parliament as it would against the influence of the king.

But even in the eighteenth century the king's government was carried on. If America was lost India was held, and the French Revolution was halted at Dover; moreover, the fantastic complexities of the administrative and electoral systems were transmuted into the powerful political system of the nineteenth-century liberal state. What were the secret processes of this transfiguration? How did the chrysalis of aristocracy survive to become the hard-working, far-flying, if rather dun-colored democratic butterfly we know?

The first answer is that the eighteenth-century English aristocracy had most complex and varied roots. The House of Lords and the House of Commons were fed from the same complex social order which in the world of industry was initiating the industrial revolution and in the world of thought was tracing the course of speculation from the comparative simplicities of Locke to the great utilitarian and idealist schools of the nineteenth century. Men of affairs had to be tough and technical and of great natural ability. Within the framework of inherited order there was a fierce competition for place and fortune. At every level the tension between the deference owed to birth and to inherited fortune and the challenge of natural ability was very great. We cannot trace in detail this life-giving competitive struggle, but we can sense it in all the great events. The simple-minded George III was driven to madness by the effort involved in accommodating himself to the problems presented by the genius of a Chatham and a Pitt and the pretensions of a Rockingham, a Bedford, and a North. In the House of Commons there was the tension between the men of genius, such as Burke, and the skilled manipulators of the details of political patronage. In the chaos of a changing world at large, there was the swagger of a Wilkes, the demonic energy of a Wesley, the scurrility of pamphleteers innumerable, and the prophetic vision of a Blake. The drive to master those natural forces which could give power and plenty was felt by men of energy and ability everywhere, now that new technical knowledge was giving them the tools for the job.

The contrast between the gyrations of the pygmy politicians of the court of George III and the vastness of the issues which were their concern in the New World of nascent American democracy and in the chaotic conditions of the dissolving Mughal empire of India, where greed and daring won a new British Empire, has been a theme of many historians. But we must not forget that it was those pygmy politicians who had in their care the seeds of time and that it was they who made possible the continuity of the political and administrative order in the British Isles, without which, in the nineteenth century, there might have been no Western democracy at all. They may not have had the greatness which we would like our ancestors to have had, but they made possible a slow but sure broadening of freedom from precedent to precedent. The success of the British constitution in the nineteenth century as a working system of political democracy in a changing world has led to the invention of a false pedigree for that constitution in eighteenth-century events. A Whig view of history has seen in the last half of the century the struggle of a rational party system to subdue an inept and corrupt record of patronage. With the wisdom of hindsight, it has been suggested that the American Revolution might have been avoided, that the rights of men might have been peacefully won in the British Empire, and that their proclamation in the French Revolution and their loss in the bloody sequels which it generated might have been avoided. One cannot, of course, ever prove that a utopia might not have been founded had our ancestors done what we now think that they could and should. But the historian can at least show that the conditions in which they worked were not as legend would sometimes suggest.

We now know that George III was not attempting to subvert the constitution. As Sir L. Namier has said: "He was not a politician, and certainly not a statesman. But in the things which he could judge without passion or preconceived ideas, there appears a basic honesty and will to do the right thing." [5] The constitution of which he became the king in 1760 was very complex indeed, and it was changing under the pressure of forces which a far greater man than he could not have fully understood or even partly controlled. A king cannot himself directly govern. He has to work through institutions and with the help of men and their supporters who are not the creations of his will. In a social order which is in dissolution or in which the hierarchy of traditional authority has fallen into disarray, it may be possible for a Lenin or a Napoleon to create new instruments of government. But in the late eighteenth century the British social order and its traditional political hierarchies were in fact in flourishing condition. That they did not understand or control the conditions which were to create the industrial democracies of the nineteenth century cannot be held against them. To no man and certainly to no institution is it given to know the future. To know the seeds of time would stop their germination.

Eighteenth-century governments, when George III became king, had a triple basis in the House of Commons. In a House of 558 members the absolute minimum for a majority was 279, and all the King's personal and official influence could not directly secure the support of such a number. Nor could any political leader, however great his possessions or however brilliant his gifts. In practice every government had to rely on the support of between 100 and 140 members who were permanently attached to the government of the day, either because they represented constituencies in which the government had a direct interest, or because they held administrative posts which made it to their interest to support the powers that be; on the support of about another hundred made up of party groups; and on the support—which was often vital—of a group of independents who were bound neither to the government nor to its opponents and were in fact in a position to judge ministers by results, and who expected to have the issues of the day expounded to them by able and eloquent speakers.

In 1783 there were some 178 members of the total of 558 that the most expert party managers could not place. And in 1803 of the 658, some 208 were doubtful. These men who belonged to no specific party were numerous and respectable and in some cases very powerful. It was they who brought about the fall of Lord North in the period 1780–84, when the American Revolution war was clearly lost. Both government and opposition had always to consider the views of over a hundred gentlemen unconnected with any parties or with the administration and whose conduct was unpredictable. They were often members for popular constituencies with what in those days were sizable electorates. They were not in competition for honors or for places of profit. In addition to the court, the administrative group, and the independents were the various party groups, the various heads of the "hydra faction" which George III so deeply hated. These groups or factions did contain a large proportion of candidates for office. Among them was the small class of potential ministers. They fell roughly into two groups: the men of great possessions and wide electoral influence: a Newcastle, a Bedford, and a Rockingham, and a small number of able and ambitious men of smaller fortune, such as Richard Rigby the manager for the Duke of Bedford, Edmund Burke the spokesman for the Rockingham Whigs, and Robinson the manager for Lord North. But it is vital to realize that in the then existing electoral conditions no one man could control in his own right more than twelve to fourteen parliamentary seats and, in fact, that very few did control more than five.[6] The grouping of the factions depended upon friendship —that friendship, the spirit of the little platoons which Burke so magnificently eulogized and which Charles Fox so warmly practiced—and upon leadership.

In the eighteenth century, as at all times, leadership was a subtle matter: in part that genius which lies in attention to necessary and dreary detail and in part that spirit which can inspire the dullest flesh. The professional politician who hoped to rise from minor office to the control of one of the great departments was often a man who was fascinated by the details of policy and administration—matters of trade and revenue and details of living administration. The younger Pitt once spent ten days in seclusion at Wimbledon mastering the details of the Bengal revenue system. Others were fascinated by the art of management—they nursed their following in constituencies and in Parliament as a great landowner would husband his estate. It was in the nature of the eighteenth-century system of government that the possession of office attracted a political following. And the following continued even when a man was out of high office, provided that he had a hope of return. A man who had either an alliance value because of his following or a nuisance value because of the same could keep such a following.

It has been noted that George Grenville, when he succeeded Lord Chatham in 1761, had neither a political following nor the necessary confidence to be a party leader. In a few years he had both. Beginning as a junior partner in the firm of Pitt and Temple he ended as a leader in his own right, with a larger following than Pitt's and a reputation greater than that of Lord Temple. He was conversant with finance and trade. The country gentlemen listened to him with respect. The younger Pitt at the end of seventeen years of supreme power commanded no more than fifty to sixty personal followers because he had taken no trouble to attach to himself such personal followers.[7] It was Chatham's weakness that although he was a House of Commons man in the sense that he would uphold the prestige of that House against the House of Lords, yet he did not appreciate the significance of the system of groups in the House and, when he left the Commons for the Lords, set himself to pulverize the groups and to select the pieces from the wreck for his own designs. It was his tragedy that although he won for Britain supremacy on the North American continent, yet he became the principal obstacle to the union of those most inclined to sympathize with the aspiration of the colonists for their freedom from the British tie.

An eighteenth-century government needed the support of the Crown, the ability to explain a policy persuasively to the Commons, and skill in managing a group of supporters. A general election was not an occasion for a people to choose a government. It was not a struggle in the country between two opposing parties. A general election was an occasion for an adjustment of the balance of power between the various groups. Before 1780 elections had little to do with politics and almost nothing to do with party. It was a time for the king and his ministers to conciliate or defeat the groups who were out of office and who wanted to get in. The political pattern of the House of Commons was not fixed to any great extent by the results of a particular general election. A dissolution

of Parliament and a general election were in the eighteenth century required by law after the lapse of seven years or on the demise of the
Crown.[8] In 1761 the number of contested seats was only forty-nine and
even in 1780 it was only eighty-six when the American war had for the
first time since 1714 produced a real political issue.

In normal circumstances an eighteenth-century government had little
to fear from the opposition. And eighteenth-century governments won
their general elections when they took place. But this was not because
the influence of the Crown could secure a majority for them. The Crown
had at most two or three dozen seats which it could directly control as
a patron of the boroughs concerned. And these it had to use to secure
the return of some of the necessary officials which government required.
Elections were won because arrangements were made for the electoral
patronage of private persons to be used in their interest. And the arrangements which were made did not involve the offer of hard cash by the
government of the day—for an eighteenth-century government had little
hard cash at its disposal—but by the promise of various advantages which
the government was in a position to confer.

On the proper use of patronage depended the healthy functioning of
the eighteenth-century system of government. Patrons were the hormones
of that Leviathan. Electoral influence was in the nature of a commodity
or service from which an income might be derived. Political power which
rested on a basis of electoral influence had to meet its costs of production.
In the absence of the great professions which in the nineteenth century
were the outcome of the development of new technical skills, and in the
absence of a secure income from investments, a gentleman had to look
to government office for the income which he could accept with honor.
A patron controlled the means of subsistence to which the younger sons
of an aristocracy based on primogeniture had to look. For centuries the
army, the navy, and many of the posts which are now in the professional
civil service and the legal profession and the Church of England were
more intimately connected with politics than they are today. The bishoprics, the deaneries, the prebends and the Crown livings, the higher posts
in the regular army, the navy and the revenue offices, and colonial gov-
ernorships were at the disposal of the government. One effect of this
was that all-embracing coalitions were not possible because, as Lord
Chesterfield once said, the leader of a coalition could not find pasture
enough for the beasts he would have to feed. There was a continuous
pressure of officeseekers on the means of subsistence which could be
found. It meant, too, that there were two main groups within the political
class—an active class who were seeking office and a passive class of more

or less independent men who were not seeking office. And, finally, it meant that in the life of political groups the technique of patronage was more important than political programs. Men were concerned less about a policy for the future than they were about the commitments they had already made.[9]

The constitution was not subverted by the king; it was to be transformed by time and the deep changes which it fostered. The effect of the American war, the rise of popular movements which had the same roots as the industrial and intellectual revolutions we describe elsewhere, and the influence of war with France led to the Reform Act, 1832, which is as important in the political development of Britain as the Revolution of 1689.

The American war not only swelled the numbers of the opposition, it gave them a policy and a cause. For a short time there was something resembling a two-party system. It occasioned Edmund Burke's superb analysis of the need for a union of principles and interests in a party system which would provide both the sails and the steering wheel of the ship of state. When the American war was clearly lost a change of ministry was to imply a reversal of policy and the policy to be reversed was the King's. Actually, Rockingham had not gone into opposition to resist the power of George III or to secure more liberal treatment of the American colonies. His policy statements and his patronage maneuvers do not survive with any glory the sceptical scrutiny of modern scholars. He shines with a reflected glory in history because he was the patron of Burke and the ally of Fox. His estates—in Yorkshire, Northamptonshire, and Ireland—were large and his historical knowledge was small. He looked back to an imaginary golden age when Whig principles had ruled, and he liked to attribute all evil in political life to the influence of the Crown. But his group was anticourt and antiwar, and circumstances made them the rallying point for all who felt the weight of contemporary discontents. In 1760 there had been no group openly committed to opposition. In 1780 the Rockingham party was a large and coherent group of seventy or eighty strong with Rockingham as a symbol of their unity and Fox their driving force. The loss of the American war enabled Rockingham to impose terms upon the King. His party intended to eliminate the King's personal will entirely from politics. In 1782 the influence of the king was at its lowest. George III himself believed that if Britain held on, France would crack, and he believed that a surrender to America would involve a surrender to Ireland and the dissolution of the British political and trading system. But public opinion was for peace.

In 1782 Rockingham died, and the combination of Fox and North was able to bring down the ministry of Shelburne who was the king's choice. This was a clear and brutal victory of party leaders over the King. The union of Fox and North was not so monstrous as legend might suggest. Like most political power groups of the century it was a union of convenience and necessity. When Fox and North were planning their coalition, they discussed whether the King should be allowed to be "his own Minister." Fox pressed the necessity of governing independently of the King. North replied: "I am clearly of opinion that the King should be treated with all sort of respect and attention—and, indeed, the appearance of power is all that a King of this country can have."

But George III's system of personal government did not come to an end with Fox and North. In 1784 he got rid of them and in the younger Pitt found a minister of his own choice who won the election of 1784 more decisively than any other eighteenth-century election. It was the result of a triple alliance of public opinion, the moneyed men, and the intelligent use of patronage. Over 160 of Fox's friends failed to return. There had been no more contested seats than usual. But many sitting members who were identified with Fox's plans decided that it was better to give up their seats than to incur the heavy cost of an uncertain electoral contest.

The defeat of the King over the American war did not mean that the existing party groups could now perform the function of providing an alternative administration. Nor did the success of Pitt mean that power was transferred entirely from the King to a prime minister. Pitt had been chosen by the King and remained the King's minister only so long as he retained the King's confidence. When George III became insane in 1788, Pitt's position was in danger, for it was accepted that the Prince of Wales as Regent might dismiss his father's ministers as his father had dismissed his in 1784. In 1807 George III was to dismiss Lord Grenville, the head of the "ministry of all the talents," and to recall Pitt's friends under Portland and dissolve Parliament to secure them a majority.

In the eighteenth century the choosing of the head of his government was by far the most important of the acts which the King had to perform. Nor did the prime minister so chosen necessarily form his own government. In 1807 George III entrusted that task not to Portland who became prime minister, but to a special triumvirate. A prime minister did not necessarily enjoy the largest share of the King's confidence.

The eighteenth-century politicians, "hunting in small packs," were averse to there being a prime minister who combined and unified the whole force and operation of government. The chief qualification for membership of an eighteenth-century cabinet was large landed property and aristocratic connections. Ability must rest on acres. Addington was the first prime minister to come from the professional classes. Part of the hatred and malignity with which Canning was assailed in 1827 was caused by his being born outside the traditional governing class.

But whatever the vagaries of royal displeasure and however purblind the party groups, a successful government needed a minister in the Commons who had the feel of the House. Someone had to present the mood of the Commons to the king and the other ministers. Before 1832 more than half of the ministers were in the House of Lords and often the proportion was two or three to one. For some time after 1783 Pitt was the only cabinet minister in the Commons.

In the beginning of his reign George III did nearly all business with his ministers in the room called the closet. He usually saw them one by one. A minister had no strict right to discuss anything in the closet but the business of his own department. If he were leader in the House of Commons or considered himself to be prime minister, he could range more freely. Obviously, on any question of real political importance the ministers would agree beforehand what they would say in the closet. What they would say in the closet, one by one, was often concerted in one or other of the great country houses of England. But some time in the reign of George III the cabinet formed the habit of concerting what they would do in the work of government without any suggestion from the king. With the increase of the work of government a cabinet tended to increase in size from about seven in the 1780's to fourteen during the French wars. Clearly, the business of government could not be personally controlled by the king. The cabinets would discuss any matter necessary to the well being of the country and they would put their collective decision to the king. But he retained the right to ask for their separate opinions. And it is important to remember that not until after 1832 had the cabinet responsibility for the initiation of an agreed program of legislation for which they were each individually and collectively responsible. Ministers were free to decide even on the merits of the legislation of the younger Pitt, who normally dominated his cabinet. They were free to speak and vote in Parliament as they thought fit on Catholic Emancipation, the repeal of the Test and Corporation acts, and the abolition of the slave trade.

When George III came to the throne there was no public opinion because there was no real public. Opinions there were, but it took a municipal form as when it "rained gold boxes"—the freedom of corporations upon Pitt in 1755–56. The corporations were oases of administrative activity and political experiment in the eighteenth-century world.

The city of London had a very definite public opinion of its own. There were conditions among the middling businessmen of London and Middlesex which favored the development of radicalism as a political force—meaning by radicalism the application to the art of government of the methods and ideas of those who had to make a living in the business world. London was the stronghold of Pitt and also of Wilkes. Wilkes has been compared to a city boss. He made his impression in the London world because he had there an audience of carpenters, engravers, coachmakers, and jewelers, who collectively possessed a great measure of power in London's peculiar system of government.

There was in London a city state of craftsmen and merchants who were free from the traditions and taboos of a landed aristocracy. To them a constitution was a machine which could be improved and not a mysterious growth to be worshipped. But in the 1780's the British public was not limited to London. The movement for parliamentary reform was nationwide; so too was the humanitarian campaign against the slave trade. The same forces which were transforming the economic life of the country would in time transform the life of Parliament as well. The mechanical improvements in the printing of newspapers gave them a large circulation and a revenue from advertising which made them independent of any direct government payments. The convention that the proceedings of Parliament were entirely confidential, to be divulged neither to the king nor to the people, could not survive in an age of mechanics and calculators. George Canning used the House of Commons as a sounding board even for foreign policy. He and William Huskisson went speechifying up and down the country to the great disgust of the Prince Regent. The time was coming when the House of Commons would have to consider the quality and the composition of public demand. The machinery of government would have to be geared to a new head of public steam.

In the late eighteenth century King, Lords, and Commons were the "supreme, irresistible, absolute and uncontrolled authority" in the British state. The king was no mere figurehead. He was a person to be considered in the inner councils of the nation. Even when the war policy against the American colonies had failed, his conception of government did not die. He was forced to accept Portland, Fox, and North, but, when they claimed the right of the cabinet to follow a policy determined by itself alone, the King could not agree. In December 1783 he wrote: "The times are of the most serious nature, the political struggle is not as formerly between two factions for power; but it is no less than whether a desperate faction shall not reduce the Sovereign to a mere tool in its hands."

Monarchy might be dying, but George III was not yet dead. When Fox's India bill, 1783, seemed to threaten a concentration of Indian patronage in the hands of the cabinet the King first organized its defeat in the House of Lords and then dismissed his ministers. He appointed the younger Pitt prime minister, and when the new government won the election of 1784 he had a minister in charge of his administration who was able to work through a Parliament in which that minister had a clear majority.

The king was old and the world was young and changing. The French Revolution in the short run—and the economic effects of new knowledge in the long run—would change the structure and texture of political life. There was an interlude before the war with Napoleon in which Pitt was able to reorganize the eighteenth-century administration. His reforms were a prologue to the sane and sober administrative arts of Peel and Gladstone in the nineteenth century. If they were limited by the influence of inadequate economic theories and the pressure of selfish interests, these were but conditions of our mortality, in which all theories are incomplete and few interests unselfish. Pitt had read Adam Smith, and his sense of the economic facts of life and their implications for the policies of government may have prevented a revolution in Britain and put her in a condition to survive the struggle with Napoleon.

Pitt "brought order to the nation's finances in a series of brilliant budgets." [10] Smuggling flourished in the eighteenth century because of the high rates of duty on tea, rum, wine, and spirits as bootleggers flourished in the United States under prohibition in the twentieth century. By reducing the duties to reasonable rates Pitt undercut the smuggler's price. By setting up a "Consolidated Fund" in 1787 he centralized and standardized the collection and distribution of revenue. He established a system of raising loans by tender and the impartial auditing of public accounts. He tackled the problem of the national debt. He even tried to reform the representative system of the House of Commons. He proposed to disfranchise thirty-six of the most corrupt boroughs, and to give the seventy-six seats thus vacated to the cities of London and Westminster, and to the large and underrepresented counties.[11] But he was defeated in the Commons, and faced with the hostility of the King and of many members of his cabinet he felt that it was futile to continue. He was able to secure the regulation but not the abolition of the slave trade.

Until late in 1792 Pitt thought that England could be kept out of the war against the French Revolution. In the early days Pitt hoped that the disturbances in France "must sooner or later culminate in a general harmony and regular order." King George III himself took a certain pleasure in the misfortunes of the Bourbon king. The French were doing what many thought the English had done in 1689. Old things were passing away and there was a hope of the regeneration of the human race. But the September massacres of 1792 hinted that the price of change might be high in blood; in January 1793 Louis XVI was executed, and in February France declared war. There was an idea in arms, an idea which was incompatible with the ideas, the habits, and the institutions of the British people.

The influence of the war was to consolidate the forces of order under Pitt and to drive the New Whigs—the political leaders under Fox who continued to support the Revolution—into the political wilderness. Pitt felt that it was not a time to make hazardous experiments and that one could not risk "the best constitution that was ever formed on the habitable globe." In his opposition to all large measures of reform he had the support of a majority of Englishmen. A contemporary said that there were twenty king's men for every one Jacobin. As the war continued with its hardships and alarms it was inevitable that there should develop a "stupid dread of innovation" and a "savage spirit" inimical to reform. A small minority among the higher classes might wish for a moderate reform and a large minority among the lower classes hunger for revolution but, as the administration was in fact far more competent than that of France and as the revolutionary ideas had their point blunted by the underlying facts of an increasing national prosperity, the eighteenth-century's fantastic, corrupt, and adept aristocracy survived to father the democratic institutions of the Victorian age. The country was not overrun. Industry and commercial activity steadily increased. Public expenditure rose from £27,500,000 in 1792 to £173,500,000 in 1815. The war did not become "the great industry, directing, distorting, and dominating the whole of the nation's economic life" [12] as war became in this century. But a population of some 17,000,000 survived in the British Isles the opposition of the continental 100,000,000 that Napoleon sometimes thought that he controlled. Sea power and some sound arithmetic and good administration took the winning tricks. The British maintained a navy of 140,000 men and land forces of 350,000; and if the forces of the East India Company, the local militia, the volunteers, and yeomanry are included the number was nearer a million. It has been estimated that in 1914 it took three war workers to maintain a single fighting man; in the Napoleonic wars it took one war worker to maintain two men in the fighting services. The technologies were simpler—sailing ships, canal barges, and horse-drawn vehicles or pack animals determined the size of campaigning armies.

There was one fundamental constitutional change occasioned by the war which was to have a sad and almost disastrous effect in later British political life—the Act of Union between Great Britain and Ireland, 1800. The worst crisis of the war with France was in 1797–98, when there were mutinies of the fleet at Portsmouth and the Nore in 1797 and a rebellion in Ireland in 1798. It was the rebellion which made Pitt determined to force a legislative union between Britain and Ireland. It was passed in defiance of the wishes of the majority of Irishmen by means of wholesale corruption.

The Irish problem sheds a grim light on politics in general and the limitations of the eighteenth-century British constitution in particular. It had not been possible to interpret or to adapt that constitution to keep the loyalty of the American colonies. They won their independence in war. The Irish could not do that. But the Irish question was to remain a frontier problem, where racial, religious, and economic factors created conditions which on the continent of Europe have been the seeds of war and the nursery of despotisms.

The Irish were poor. They had neither wood nor coal nor iron. Their resources were their land, their linen industry, and their cheap labor. These were not developed as they might have been, because politically Ireland was subordinate to the British Parliament, where the interests of British industry and trade interpreted in mercantilist terms were in control. In Ireland itself the land had been divided among a small number of conquerors of English origin and Protestant religion. Partition was difficult, and estates rarely came into the market because of the system of entails. The class of small landlords was small. The relationship between landlord and tenant was without any of the advantages of the English pattern. The landlord erected no building on his property and spent nothing to keep it in good condition. He was usually an absentee collecting his dues through a system of agents who were often in a position to defraud him and oppress his tenants. The landlords were too small a class to nourish a local society and tended to concentrate in Dublin. The middlemen had neither morals nor culture. The peasants considered that the land was theirs whatever the legal forms might be. Their farms were usually a disgusting sight. They were getting smaller and smaller wherever they were used for tillage. The grazing farms in the center of Ireland were large. The graziers—"the greatest graziers and cow raisers in the world," Arthur Young called them—were despised by the aristocracy and loathed by the peasants.

Politically, there were three main groups, all of them opposed to England: (1) the Roman Catholic majority who were without political rights in the country of their birth, (2) in the north in Ulster a Presbyterian population which like the Dissenters in England was excluded from political influence, (3) the Protestant Episcopalians who were anti-English because they regarded themselves as an English garrison in Ireland who were not paid enough for their garrison duties.[13]

In such conditions political life was a caricature of political life in England, which though fantastic and corrupt was vigorous and flexible. The Irish Parliament of 300 members was controlled by a majority representing rotten boroughs controlled by the great Irish families, who sold their support to the lord lieutenant. In 1691 an act passed in England for Ireland made it impossible for Roman Catholics to take any part in political life. They had, as Burke said, no *virtual* representation, that system "in which there is a community of interests and a sympathy of feeling and desires between those who act in the name of any description of people and the people in whose name they act," even though the trustees are not actually chosen by them. "The several descriptions of the people were kept apart as if they were not only separate nations but separate species."

The war with America had had some effect. It created in Grattan a leader of a new status. It led the British in 1782 to allow Roman Catholics to inherit property, to allow Irish ships to sail as British, and to give independence to the Irish Parliament (which had been limited since 1495 by Poyning's law).

During the war with the French Revolution and Napoleon it became urgent to keep the policies of the two countries in harmony. This could not be done so long as the Irish Parliament was independent. In England the king's government had the support of, although it was not the actual choice of, the legislature. In Ireland political leaders could not form such a government. Pitt had read Adam Smith's advocacy of political union. If it were accomplished, he thought that the parliament of a united kingdom could emancipate the Catholics and in time heal the breach between the Anglicans, the Presbyterians, and the papists (the official term in the eighteenth century for Roman Catholics). In 1798 a radical revolt in Ulster degenerated into massive agrarian disorders in the south. It was ended by General Lake at Vinegar Hill, June 1798, and the surrender of the few hundred French troops that had been landed in County Mayo in August. In October, Wolfe Tone was captured on board a French man-of-war in Lough Swilley and with his suicide in prison joined the ranks of Irish martyrs who held that the connection between Ireland and Great Britain was the curse of the Irish nation.

Pitt was afraid that unless the two countries could be united there could be no possibility of Catholic emancipation and that the French would always be tempted to invade. Union would offer security to the landlords and the possibility of Catholic emancipation and free trade for the Irish in the Empire. In 1800 the Irish Parliament by 158 to 115 voted its extinction. The 32 counties and 118 boroughs, represented by 300 members in the Irish House of Commons from 1692 to 1800, were reduced to 68 constituencies, which from 1801 to the Reform Act of 1832 were represented by 100, 64 from the counties and 36 from 33 out of the 118 cities and boroughs. A total of £1,250,000 was paid in compensation. Those who organized the bribery were often indignant that they had to court borough owners whom they would have liked to kick. The price of a borough went up to £15,000, and as much as 4000 guineas was paid for a single vote. In addition, there were forty-six promotions in the peerage and twenty ecclesiastical appointments. In the eighteenth century, when a vote or a seat was universally considered to be a piece of property, it would have seemed as immoral to expropriate boroughmongers as the bribery used now seems to us. In fact, E. Porritt, the historian of the *Unreformed House of Commons,* has given it as his considered opinion that he could feel no regret that an end was made to the Irish Parliament.[14]

The real tragedy was that Pitt, who had always considered that union and emancipation went together, found it impossible to secure the latter so long as George III held with insane tenacity to his view that it was incompatible with his coronation oath. Nor could Pitt carry the two other measures which he had originally designed to follow the Union—endowment of the Roman Catholic priesthood and tithe commutation. The first of these would have produced a priesthood that might have sided with the law, and the second would have removed one of the most fertile of all the sources of Irish anarchy and crime. It was not until 1838 that such a measure was passed. By then it was too late. The Irish union was to introduce into the House of Commons an Irish party which in the nineteenth century was to have a most damaging effect.

The first effect of the Union was the resignation of Pitt. His colleagues were divided and hesitant and the attitude of the Commons was doubtful; nor had he any inclination to force the King to consent to his suggestion that the admission of the Catholics and Dissenters to offices and of the Catholics to Parliament was advisable. When the King was adamant to the edge of insanity Pitt could but resign. He was succeeded by Henry Addington, whose father had been the family doctor of the Pitt family. With Pitt's help he negotiated the treaty of Amiens. In 1804 Pitt was again prime minister. In 1806 he died. The King sent for Fox and Grenville who formed what was known as the "ministry of all the talents," which spent some eight months in trying to negotiate with Napoleon. Its main achievement was the abolition of the slave trade. In 1807 it was dismissed because the King demanded a pledge that it would not advise concessions to the Catholics.

The "ministry of all the talents" was followed by a ministry under the nominal headship of the Duke of Portland, in which Spencer Perceval took the lead in the House of Commons and Canning and Castlereagh quarreled about the conduct of the war. When they fought a duel after the failure of the Walcheren expedition the government broke up. A new government was organized by Perceval and Lord Liverpool which by its steady support of the Peninsular campaign took a long step toward winning the war. In 1811 the King went permanently mad and a Regency Act was passed. But the Regent did not change his ministers. In 1812 Perceval was shot in the lobby of the House of Commons by a madman. Liverpool reconstructed the ministry and he and Castlereagh made peace with America in 1814 and with France in 1815.

CHAPTER VI

Britain's Wars with the Revolutions, 1760-1815

Today we face the search for political and administrative know-hows which will serve and control the new forms of social life engendered by the spirit of enquiry and experiment that has possessed us. We have

> ... planned to bring the world under a rule,
> Who are but weasels fighting in a hole.

As science makes the material and the living structures of nature subservient to the human will and

> Civilisation is hooped together, brought
> Under a rule ...

we have to find political forms and administrative techniques to contain and direct its protean and swelling progeny.

In the eighteenth century we have the prologue to the swelling scene. There we can see almost as in a slow-motion film the first stirrings of the powers and terrors that now encompass us. We can see how they were only in part controlled and in part only dimly understood by those who were involved. The structure of Europe was falling apart riven by the ideas of Locke and Newton. The political problem which the new thought implied was stated by Rousseau with the insight of genius: if kings are not by God appointed, if there is no natural authority among men, if force creates no right, then on what can legitimate government be based if not upon consent? Government by the consent of the governed would harness all thought in the service of peace and plenty. It could not then be foreseen that the units of the consenting governed would come to be those separate nations whose pedigrees would be more intricate and legendary than any royal race of kings and whose lust for territory would make Caesar's seem modest. The doctrine of nationality was to give at first a new balance to the European world, and, thereafter, to destroy it as a predominant world power, and from its inheritance all who come after may be hampered. We can see that the new knowledge working in the realms of social relations was to produce a theory that if the division of labor, which had been known since Adam delved and Eve spun, were fully understood, then men would see that peace and plenty, the ages' long-sought aims, would come from allowing an international division of labor freely to develop. A proper understanding of the economic facts of life would eliminate all serious political problems. Feudal and mercantile muddles would melt in the light of the new science of political economy, "as it were in the sun's rays." Society was the product of our necessities and government only of our wickedness.

The new economic and political ideas might serve to make over the feudal structure of Europe into something more rich and less strange—might, we may say, put all the Don Quixotes into useful and profitable stage-coach services—but they could not also provide for the extra-European world. Given the genius of Napoleon, the ideas of Rousseau might make a constitution and devise an administrative machine with which Frenchmen could freely live; in the special conditions of insular security England had inherited the traditions and the skill of an aristocracy, which had had the good fortune to produce the almost matchless genius in the political arts of a Walpole, a Chatham, and a Pitt. From this basis and helped by the speculative genius of a Hume, a Burke, and a Bentham it was possible for that complex set of institutions known as the British constitution to grow into a passable political habitation. But the architecture and the furnishings of this establishment have never fully been understood or approved either by the residents or by curious visitors. To change the metaphor, in the British Isles the political problem was temporarily solved by the development in its leaders of a political style which has never revealed its secrets to the investigation of experts from Bentham and the two Mills to the modern psephologists. And, finally, whatever the merits and shortcomings of the British insular system—the foster child of eloquence and slow time—it could not be extended to take in the political order which the new empire of commerce was weaving—as well expect Plato's philosopher kings to adapt their administration of a polis to the scale of imperial Rome.

British statesmen were not, even in the eighteenth century, philosopher kings. Burke said that great empires and little minds did not go together. Their minds were not little, but it would not have been possible even for a committee of statesmen, each as wise in action as Burke was deep in speculation, to have avoided the disruptions and the conflicts which occurred. There were three main factors which made this impossible: (1) Britain was only one among the varied competing principalities and powers of the European continent. The French saw no reason why it should not be their manifest destiny to save Europe from heresy in religion and the imperial thrust of English traders; (2) the development of trade and the spread of trading centers had meant that the political form which served a British island were stretched so far that the center could not have effective control of its periphery. A trading post on the shore of India or in the heart of Canada could not be handled as a lord lieutenant in an English county or a justice of the peace was handled from Whitehall. Even the most virtuous Senate of the high and palmy days of Rome could not have fathered those distant shores; (3) the complex imperial trading pattern had an imperfect unity, and the different segments of its circle had each its own complex history and frontier problems, diverse in their variety as the climate of the world. The British, who could not solve the Irish problem on their doorstep, could far less solve the distant problems in America and India.

Between 1763 and 1815 there is a succession of grandeurs and miseries flowing from the impossibility of shaping political forms to the movement of frontiers in the New World, and the interaction with that problem of the transformation of Europe. There are three main episodes which we must briefly consider: the American War of Independence, which has meant that the English political genius lost forever the chance of offering an empirical pattern of political tolerance to the world. There have been many empires: Roman, Chinese, and now a Russian, but while there was for a brief period a *Pax Britannica* for part of the Western world, there has never been a British Empire (with the unique exception of the control of India by a system of enlightened utilitarian despots). It is a reflection on our human condition that the break came because of the fine balance of power in a monarchical Court—it was a division between reason and the passions—the reason of many great writers and the passion of a King and the passion born of the political naivete and emotional self-interest of the American frontier. The thought of a capital can never fully inform a provincial periphery. There is little evidence that empires can be created or held together by the march of legions and an administrative *corps d'élite*. In any case by the very nature of her institutions Britain had neither. One may even venture the reflection that had any other European power had the relations that Britain had with the New World it would not have lost it. If the United States spoke French, German, or Russian can one doubt that it would be a portion of a European power?

In the case of America we may note briefly: (*a*) the political forms that were involved, (*b*) some of the political and strategic forces, (*c*) the economic pattern of the old colonial system. A colony was an extension in the beginning at least, of the homeland. How else could order be carried over into new found lands? A Robinson Crusoe who landed on a new shore had need of some of the divinity that hedges a king if the community around him was to be more than a robber band. A colony could not be entirely divorced from the legal order which had made it possible. It could no more invent an entirely new political system than it could an entirely new language. In practice the governor within his colony had power even more, extensive than the king at home. He had the authority of the master of a ship. He might call, prorogue, and dissolve the assemblies; he commanded the forces; he made peace or war; he exercised a supreme prerogative in ecclesiastical, financial, and judicial affairs. The problem of government in a colony was inherently more difficult than in the mother country. What custom willed at home in human relations, matrimonial and commercial, had in a colony to be guarded from decay, and technical necessities, such as currency and contract, had to be adapted to new conditions. But with the passage of time in colonies of settlement like America with a Lockean state of nature around them, the Hobbesian pretensions of a governor came to seem an irritating interference.

To the frontiersman government was only a rare occurrence. The merchant of the seaboard saw it as a mere bar to the smuggling which made men rich. The growth of a free market was hampered by the fumblings of a distant bureaucracy itself suspected of self-interest. Adam Smith had disentangled the causes of the wealth of nations from the obsolete web of the mercantile system. But what was theory in his pages was daily experience and daily bread to the colonists. They were a trading nation free from the traditions and the hierarchies of an agrarian aristocracy. The salt estranging sea was between them and the power-bred tangles of divided Europe. They had a good coastal, a thriving West Indian, and a growing European trade. But for English regulations they could develop the finest shipping in the world. They felt that they were being exploited in the interest of London plutocrats under a pretense of protection and tutelage. It seemed to them that British constitutional control and economic superiority were obstacles to a great expansion of their trade. They were not without their differences: in Canada a minority of British who wanted help to face the wilderness and the authority of France; in New England the Puritans had a state of nature which could be made an El Dorado if they were freed to do what common sense prescribed: take but "degree" away and self-interest guided by the inner light would build new Jerusalems of peace and plenty. In New Jersey and Pennsylvania the merchants of the coast and the settled farmers had their own struggles with the pioneers of the interior. The egalitarian spirit of the frontier was opposed to the nascent aristocracy of the few great families. In the South the great plantation owners producing rice and tobacco with black slave labor might ape the English country gentlemen, but they wore their aristocracy with a difference. Shakespeare's gentry do not thrive in plantations worked by innumerable black Calibans. A real forest of Arden is fatal to the courtly way of life. These men were producers and not administrators—they had not been trained by centuries of quarter sessions, and there were no judges of the king's bench on circuit to give a touch of majesty. Such stresses and divisions among two and a half million Americans made English control unthinkable. All could agree, whether farmer or merchant, that their lives could not be regulated by decisions taken 3000 miles away and only received months later from across a restless ocean.

On the English side there was perplexity and mingled exasperation and resignation. They, too, were traders. They were not imperialists in the high Roman fashion. Their trading minds could not rise to the conception of resident English communities abroad, self-sufficing microcosms of the homeland. They wanted the American continent and the islands taken as a whole to be a market for their manufactures and a source of products which could not be got at home. Tobacco, rice, and sugar from the West Indies and the colonies were indispensable. Naval stores from the northern colonies supplemented those from the Baltic. The fur trade from Canada down from the Lakes to the Ohio and Tennessee was valuable. It seemed to them that imperial trade was reasonably planned. In accordance with mercantilist principles it was conducted in British or colonial ships, a great advantage to the shipbuilders of New England. European and East Indian goods had to be imported into America by way of Great Britain. The exports of the colonists were divided into "enumerated" and "nonenumerated" goods. The "nonenumerated" were free to move into southern Europe (that is south of Cape Finisterre) or other parts of the world, but if they were destined for northern Europe they had to go by way of Great Britain. The "enumerated" goods had always to be exported by way of Great Britain. The object of this planning was to secure to England valuable raw materials and to deny them to European rivals. They could be paid for with English manufactured goods. A consistent development of this policy was to forbid Americans to trade in manufactured woolen goods from one colony to another and to stop their developing an iron industry. The attempt to bind the winds of trade by decree infuriated the American pamphleteers. In fact, the natural channels of a free trade would not have been very different from those which were decreed—as was found after America had won her independence.

The British politician and administrator did not discern America's future greatness. They were irritated by a disunity and lawlessness which they despised. The spirit of freedom could not be savored from so far away. They had to deal with immediate practical administrative and strategic problems. Europe was on their doorstep. They had not the freedom of the forest. In 1760, Plumb has said, the American problem was not as large as the problem of the Boers in the nineteenth century or of Ireland in the seventeenth century. It was a sort of remote Puritan Ireland useful for trade but no more useful than the West Indies, a convenient dumping ground for criminals, whores, and bankrupts.[1] And the eighteenth century establishments, which were a thin film of order spread by divine Providence over a mob of fallen men, had every need for such useful outlets. They had no open agrarian west to be a safety valve to the tensions of their turbulent towns or ordered farming settlements. The English appreciated that like the Corsicans or the Spartans the men of the New World were nearer to nature than those of the Old, but they were dependent on a financial umbilical cord, for without English credit the American economy—particularly the tobacco trade—could not have flourished. Their plenty in a state of nature was dependent on the support and protection of a complex pattern of power. At the Peace of Paris Britain had obtained Canada from France and the Great Western Plains of the Mississippi and Ohio valleys. But France still had New Orleans and Louisiana. She had control of the mouth of the Mississippi. The Americans had only the Indians, the elements, and their own divisions to deal with. The British had a frontier problem. Something had to be done about the future of the area of Detroit, Illinois, the Ohio, and Tennessee. There the interest of Canadian Indian tribes and American colonists intermingled. The British Board of Trade wanted to encourage the growth of trade and to keep the administrative costs as light as possible. Shelburne had a comprehensive policy for guiding settlement and allowing trade to develop in peace.

The Stamp Act was an attempt to raise a revenue of about £60,000 a year by a tax on legal transactions and on newspapers. A Sugar Act aimed at enforcing the system of trade while making it more reasonable. Alas for the use of administrative skills to control the winds of change or the passions of pamphleteers. The Stamp Act was a novelty. It was taxation for revenue and not for the sake of trade regulation. It raised

constitutional issues which were embedded deep in English history. Moreover, the people most hit by it were the classes most effective in the arts
of propaganda. And, of course, the policy of shutting up the west as an
Indian reserve was bound to be rejected. Canute could not stem an
incoming tide and Westminster could not stem the flooding of the west.

Professor Alden has written: "During the years 1763–65 the ministry
headed by George Grenville goaded the colonists into open revolt by a
series of ill advised measures. It undertook to restrict settlement on and
speculation in the lands beyond the Alleghenies recently won from
France; to maintain a standing army of redcoats of about six thousand
men in America; . . . to make permanent the offices of two royally chosen
superintendents of Indian affairs . . . ; to renovate the customs services
in America and to enforce the long laxly executed Acts of Trade; to
expand restrictions upon colonial paper currencies . . . ; to lessen the
trade between the colonies and the foreign islands of the West Indies . . . ;
to secure a revenue from America through a tax on molasses and, especially, the famous Stamp Act." This program, he continues, was "not
intended to establish British 'tyranny' in America." It was adopted "to
build more effective defense against France, Spain and hostile Indians; to
prevent war between the colonists and the Indians; to protect the interests
of British sugar growers in the West Indies; to assure to the mother country the benefit of her Acts of Trade; to buttress and rebuild British authority in the colonies; and to compel the colonies to assume a larger part of
the financial burdens of the empire." [2] It was hoped that a compromise
would be found if England were firm in essentials and generous in details.
But the legal fundamentals could not be adjusted to the political and
economic facts. As Richard Price put it in his *Observations on the Nature
of Civil Liberty:* "The case of a free country branching itself out in the
manner Britain has done, and sending to a distant world colonies which
have there from small beginnings, and under free legislatures of their
own, increased, and formed a body of powerful states, likely soon to
become superior to the parent state, this is a case which is new in the
history of mankind; and it is extremely improper to judge of it by the
rules of any narrow and partial policy; or to consider it on any other
ground than the general one of reason and justice." [3]

The Stamp Act could not be enforced. The stamps were burnt by the
rioters. The Stamp Act was repealed and replaced by a declaratory act
which stated England's right of sovereignty. John Dickinson and Samuel
Adams for America claimed that under the English constitution there
were certain laws of nature which kept even a sovereign power from
certain actions. Lord North then tried the ingenious idea of letting

the East India Company send tea to America paying a three-pence duty on entry while being excused the English custom duty of one shilling. The radical leaders in Boston organized the Boston Tea Party. In 1775 Burke in his great speech said: "Magnanimity in politics is not seldom the truest wisdom and a great Empire and little minds go ill together." But no great mind could then resolve the constitutional and administrative tangles.

It was not possible for the formal armies of eighteenth-century Europe to hold down a new world. The British with a small number of trained soldiers, mainly hired from Hesse, had to suppress a great number of partially trained men who had the whole eastern sea board in which to form, disperse, and reform. The British forces had to be maintained and supplied across 3000 miles of ocean over a period of years. There was always the unmastered hinterland and to master that meant using the Indians. Naturally, the Americans complained of the unnatural ferocity of a king who exposed his countrymen to atrocities of the savage as well as to the harshness of mercenaries.

If Britain were to win she had to do so quickly before her European rivals intervened. General Howe asked for 20,000 men for 1777, but he got only 2500. Lord North thought that Hessians were too expensive. His reputation depended on his economy. The world situation and British home politics made it urgent to end the war in 1777. New England was to be cut off from the rest of the colonists by a pincer movement of a force striking south from the St. Lawrence through the Hudson gap and one striking north from Howe's camp at New York. This failed when on October 17, 1777, Burgoyne hemmed in at Saratoga surrendered his army to the American force under General Gates. The French now came in on the American side.

It was now more important to defeat the French at sea than to subdue the American mainland. The Rockingham group advocated the prompt acknowledgment of American independence. Although Chatham on April 7, 1778, "sick and half mad" made his dying speech in the House of Lords protesting against the proposal to recognize the United States as a new country, he was for conciliation though not for capitulation. America was not interested in the terms offered.

Spain had laid siege to Gibraltar. The invasion of England was possible. The British navy had to supply the force in America, fight the French in the West Indies, guard the Channel, and try to keep the French fleet bottled up. George III took the bulldog view that he had not become King to preside over the dissolution of the British Empire. He thought that if America got her independence, the West Indies and Ireland would do likewise,

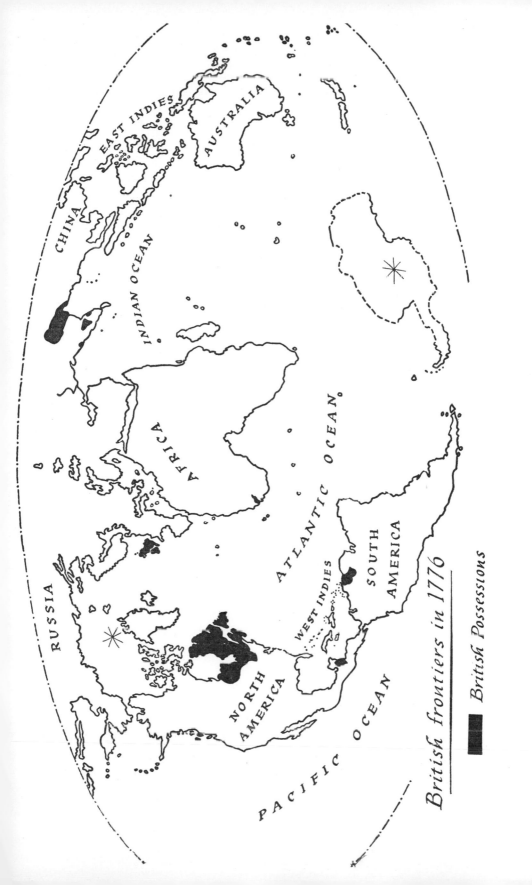

British frontiers in 1776 ███ *British Possessions*

to the economic ruin of Great Britain. In 1780 the northern powers of Europe had formed a league of armed neutrality to resist the British search of vessels on the high seas for contraband. In America isolated bodies of British troops were surrounded by a scattered host of American guerilla fighters. It was decided to establish a Virginian base at Yorktown on the peninsula near the mouth of the Chesapeake. In October 1781 the French fleet was outside, and inland there were two armies, one French and one American which ringed the British under the command of Cornwallis. He surrendered on October 19, 1781. A British fleet arrived too late on October 24. In April 1782 Rodney and Hood at the battle of The Saints ended the French threat to the West Indies and won back control of the Atlantic. But in February 1782, 193 members of the House of Commons voted for a speedy surrender. North's majority had sunk to a majority of one.

Shelburne hoped that it would be possible to secure a peace that would be the beginning of a new and more glorious period of British history. If the British traders had their trade routes secured, two self-governing units, Britain and America, could be partners in an Atlantic sphere of industry and trade. The Americans would penetrate the openlands of the Mississippi, while the British would, as a natural center of trade, link the expanding West with Europe and the East. Canada, Newfoundland, and Nova Scotia were to be retained by Britain. But to Franklin, Jay, and Adams, the American negotiators in Paris, he freely gave the interior of the continent. This was not pleasing to France. She disliked American penetration of the new west. But France had few cards to play. Her supremacy in the Caribbean had been ended by Rodney and her schemes in India countered by Warren Hastings. So between France and England the peace was a restoration of the prewar position in the West Indies, Africa, and India. France had fought to establish the new state of America and it left her in the lurch. Britain gave up East and West Florida to Spain but kept Gibraltar. The cession of Florida substituted friction between Spain and the United States for that which would have troubled Britain. Britain restored the status quo with her European enemies and renounced colonization on the mainland of America. But the strategic points necessary to her sea power had been safeguarded.

The great French historian Albert Sorel wrote that "the English only make up their minds to fight when their interests seem absolutely threatened . . . their history is full of alternations between indifference, which makes people think them decadent, and a rage which baffles their foes. They are seen, in turn, abandoning and dominating Europe, neglecting the greatest continental matters and claiming to control even the smallest, turning from peace at any price to war to the death." [4] In the war with France and with Napoleon the younger Pitt as a great peace minister had no wish to get involved. When it came, the war against revolutionary France was not an antirevolutionary crusade. The wars against France of the Revolution and against Napoleon when he arose were not wars for trade or empire but for security. As Napoleon controlled the land and Britain controlled the sea her empire was enlarged—a sea power that is shut out from the continent its enemy controls must inevitably become a picker-up of island trifles. Pitt had come to power after the humiliations and disasters of the American War of Independence. His aim was to restore British prestige in Europe and overseas. He negotiated a commercial treaty with France based on free trade principles. He thought, as his father Chatham had thought, that Britain's true interests were outside Europe in a wider world. There were, however, certain spots in Europe where British security could be threatened—the Netherlands, the Baltic, and the Mediterranean.

In 1790 he deterred France from backing a Spanish claim to the eastern shore of Nootka Sound in what is now Vancouver Island. It had become an important trading post for British ships in the China trade. When the Spaniards arrested some British trader there, Pitt threatened war and the Spaniards gave way. But while the British public could understand a maritime quarrel with Spain about a Nootka Sound, they were not interested in a quarrel with Russia about an obscure Black Sea fortress. In the Oczakov incident Pitt's opponents did not challenge the principle that there would be a duty to intervene if the balance of power was really threatened, but that in this case—an advance of Russia in the Black Sea, which might threaten the Turks—the threat did not justify the risk of war. Pitt's first defeat in diplomacy had been inflicted by the British public.

Fox declared that the fall of the Bastille was the greatest and best event in history. Burke sensed that far from being an extension to the European order of the British Revolution of 1689 it was a bid to remold the political structure of Europe in the light of a false theory of human nature, that the tool would be force, and that the price would be blood. The French Revolution went on to threaten all other powers in Europe. The Americans could safely follow Paine's common sense and the rights of man for they had a wilderness in which natural right could be given a local habitation and democratic institutions to protect them. To make a new order in a new land is one thing; to overturn all order in an old one quite another. Pitt was opposed to overturning the existing order and of releasing all peoples from their obedience to kings. He could not admit that France should reserve the "right of mixing herself in our internal affairs whenever she shall judge it proper, and on principles incompatible with the political institutions of all the countries of Europe." England would "never consent that France shall arrogate the power of annulling at her pleasure and under the pretence of a pretended natural right, of which she makes herself the only judge, the political system of Europe, established by solemn treaties, and guaranteed by the consent of all the powers." As late as February 1792 Pitt thought that we might reasonably expect at least fifteen years of peace. He held aloof from the kings of the Continent when they wanted to war with France in 1792. He viewed with relative unconcern the deposition of Louis XVI in August. But when the French invaded Belgium, threatened Holland, and defeated the Austrians at Jemappes (November 6, 1792) and when by a decree of November 19 they appealed to subjects to rise against their rulers in obedience to the law of nature and added that they intended to open the Scheldt contrary to existing treaties, Pitt was convinced that war was necessary. He demanded that France renounce her plan of "aggression and aggrandisement" and her attack on the whole system of Europe, its treaty rights, and its institutions. The French invasion of the Netherlands had touched a vital area of interest. Pitt wished to restore British security. But he did not commit himself to the general policy of the allied kings. He wanted to get France to abandon her conquests, withdraw within her borders, and abandon seditious propaganda in the internal affairs of other states. He was determined to recover Holland, Belgium, and the left bank of the Rhine from France. He varied between demands for "security" and a desire to make peace with the new military republic.

The war as it developed called for a continental rather than a maritime policy, for a Marlborough rather than a Chatham. But Pitt would not commit himself to the general policy of the allies. His eyes were on the wealthy sugar islands of the West Indies. But it was found that without a European policy Britain would have no allies at all. She was fighting, in fact, not for profit but for survival. Pitt had a British army of only 20,000 for the capture of French Haiti, raids on French Brittany, an offensive in the eastern Mediterranean, and a campaign in Flanders. The idea of conscription for service overseas was then unthinkable; even the French did not have it until 1798. By 1795 the French held all the coast of the Low Countries and were preparing to invade England. The weakness of sea power—that it encourages mere peripheral activities—was exposed. France could only be defeated by a blow at Paris and not by a blow at Haiti. If the British could not break into Europe, France under Napoleon might well break out. As an industrial, maritime, and commercial power Britain might be fitted to endure a long war. But Napoleon on his side was able to batten on Europe. The danger that France, by combining the fleets of Europe, might subdue even British sea power was defeated by four great naval victories: in February 1797 John Jervis beat the Spaniards at Cape St. Vincent, in October 1797 Adam Duncan destroyed the Dutch fleet off Camperdown, in August 1798 Lord Nelson destroyed Napoleon's fleet in Aboukir Bay, and in 1801 Nelson destroyed the Danish fleet at Copenhagen. Nelson's victory at the Nile stopped Napoleon's plan to seize Egypt and open the way to India. Britain captured the Cape of Good Hope (Holland being now on the French side), Pondicherry, Trichinopoly, Ceylon, Malacca, Amboina.

Britain had the East, but after 1795 she could find no foothold in Europe to resist France. In 1797 Austria was forced to make peace. In December 1797 a French invasion fleet sailed for Ireland. Bad seamanship and bad weather prevented them landing in Bantry Bay, which was fortunate for England for the army in Ireland was "in a state of licentiousness which must render it formidable to everyone but the enemy." In April 1797 the Channel fleet at Spithead mutinied. They would put to sea if the enemy appeared, otherwise not. Lord Howe rowed round from ship to ship with George III's pardon in his hand. In May 1797 the North Sea fleet mutinied at the Nore. The mutineers threatened to blockade the Thames. The same fleet under Admiral Duncan destroyed the Dutch invasion fleet at Camperdown. Pitt offered to allow France to retain her natural frontiers including the vital area of the Low Countries. When the French refused and made clear their determination to dominate Italy and Germany even Fox admitted that they were bellicose.

Pitt remodeled the whole fiscal system (including an income tax) and Britain mobilized her economic power to balance her military defeat. She entered the Mediterranean to aid Austria and Naples. Napoleon sailed from Toulon with a French army for Egypt. The battle of the Nile destroyed the French fleet and Britain had control of the Mediterranean. By 1799 the British fleet had a crushing superiority which could only be met by years of work by all the shipwrights of western Europe. By 1801 Lord Wellesley had ousted French influence from southern India. He destroyed the power of the Marathas at Assaye in 1803 and in 1805 the Grand Mughal accepted British protection. From Persia to India British power was felt. In the Middle East Sir Ralph Abercromby defeated the French army Napoleon had deserted at Alexandria. But Denmark, Sweden, and Russia laid an embargo on British ships in the Baltic. Prussia joined this northern league and invaded Hanover. The Danes occupied Hamburg to prevent the English trading with north Germany. On April 2, 1801, Lord Nelson destroyed all seventeen of the Danish first-line ships in their own harbor, Copenhagen.

A short-lived peace was negotiated at Amiens. Britain agreed to restore all her conquests to France, to Spain, and to Holland with the exception of Trinidad (taken from Spain) and Ceylon (taken from Holland). When it was clear that France was still expansionist and that the independence of Holland, Switzerland, and northern Italy was not secure Britain broke the letter of the treaty on the excuse that Napoleon had broken the spirit. The war was now between Britain controlling the seas and Napoleon the land. Industrial development gave Britain the ability both to arm herself and her allies and at the same time to sell cotton textiles to the world. In control of the seas she could supply coffee, sugar, raw cotton, spices, and dyes. Napoleon on his side could play off the ambitions and cupidities of the European powers. "It was the hunger for territorial aggrandisement which caused the powers who were joined in coalition against the French Revolution to come to terms with the revolutionary government—it was repartition, distribution, promises, even the simple hope of spoils from weaker states, which enabled France to divide her enemies, and to dissolve or forestall coalitions." [5] But Napoleon was a mercantilist. He understood battalions but not banking. He thought that exports were of extreme importance. He allowed European exports even to Britain. European wheat helped Britain in the famine years of 1809–12. Europe needed the imports from the East which Britain controlled. Napoleon's new order in Europe, which reached its apogee in 1807, was self-destructive. The internal communications of Europe were not good enough to absorb Europe's output. French farmers had to export. Exports imply imports. While Napoleon's armies tried to man the customshouses of a continent the Rothschilds were negotiating British bills within his fortress.

Napoleon was crowned Emperor in 1805. He mismanaged his invasion plans. England had no force or foothold on the continent except in Sicily. Then from Russia and from Spain the fatal cracks began. Russia wished to reach Constantinople. As Napoleon extended his influence into Germany he was bound to collide with Russia. The British hesitated between trying to attack in the north across the rivers of the Netherlands and using Malta and Sicily as bases to strike at the underbelly of Napoleon's empire in north Italy. In 1805 Austria entered the war against Napoleon. He left his invasion base at Boulogne to meet and destroy the Austrian army on the Danube. The invasion of England was off. Nelson made it impossible in the future. Following Villeneuve's fleet to the West Indies he returned and arrived off Cadiz in the "Victory" on September 28 and on October 21 off Cape Trafalgar the British line split the line of the French fleet and in the pell-mell battle Nelson had prepared for, the French fleet was destroyed as an effective force in the unfinished war.

An invincible naval power faced an undefeated land empire. At Austerlitz December 2, 1805, the French army smashed the Austrian army and the Austrians lost all their influence and possessions in South Germany and Italy. Pitt died on January 2, 1806. In October 1806 the French destroyed the Prussian army at Jena. By October 25 the French were in Berlin. The British captured the Cape of Good Hope; they captured Buenos Aires, but the inhabitants rose and captured them! Sea power is not infallible. A naval expedition to the Dardanelles failed. There was mutiny at Malta and of Indian troops at Vellore in Madras. Viscount Castlereagh had less than 12,000 troops of the regular army to reverse the calamities of the globe.

On June 14, 1807 Napoleon destroyed a Russian army at Friedland. On July 9 the Emperor Napoleon and the Emperor Alexander met on a raft on the Niemen at Tilsit and made an aggressive pact against Britain. To complete his master plan for a Europe which could destroy the British Empire of the sea, Napoleon attacked the Spanish peninsula. The British now had allies and the use of ports on the European coast line. The terrain of Spain and Portugal was too broken for the French army to use its formal battle line. Sir Arthur Wellesley arrived at Lisbon in April 1809. In his own words: "I went abroad and took command of the Army, and never returned, or even quitted the field, till the nations of the Peninsula . . . were delivered from the French armies; till I had invaded France . . . till the general peace was signed at Paris." Wellesley's success in Spain was the result of an intelligent strategic eye and attention to administrative detail. He saw that the French armies paid for their marching prowess by an inability to stand still. They must starve unless they moved in search of food and forage. Wellesley had command of the sea and his army could be supplied from a line of ports parallel with his march. He could pay for his goods. The British Treasury played its part in his army's supply. He had Portugal mapped at four miles to the inch. In the winter there were fox hunts for his officers and sound snug buildings for the troops. The French in the winter could not stay in the open to attack a foe which was as snug as a bug in a bed.

The struggle between Napoleon's armies and British ships continued. By the Berlin decrees, November 1806, Napoleon declared the British Isles in a state of siege. No vessels coming directly from Britain or her colonies would be received in any port under his control. Britain replied by Orders in Council that neutral vessels going to or coming from enemy ports must proceed by way of Britain. Napoleon by the Milan decree of November 23 replied that all ships touching in British ports were to be confiscated. The unfortunate neutrals were between confiscation in Napoleon's ports and detention by the British navy. But Napoleon's subjects were more goaded by his controls than the merchants of the world were by British search parties. The British developed their trade in South America and in the Levant. Europe could not live without sugar, coffee, and cotton. Napoleon's armies had not only to march into Russia, but against smugglers in the northern ports. Britain was indeed driven into war with the United States over the use of her sea power. The radicalism of the French and the frontiers of the New World were a promising basis of agreement. But the depredations of French privateers and the extension of the common rights of men to black men disturbed an initial harmony. It was significant that world trade problems should have drawn France into Spain and toward Moscow and Britain into naval conflict with the United States.

It was easy for Napoleon to exploit the differences between the British and the United States. He needed neutral shipping in French ports and he had never been in a position to control it on the high seas. At the very time that he was planning his attack on Russia to force her to apply his continental system against British trade he was willing to give full freedom to American ships. The British government claimed the right to recapture, without any form of trial, English sailors, or those presumed to be such, found on board American vessels. The British government held that a belligerent had a right to seize contraband of war going to an enemy port and that no neutral could carry on trade in time of war which had been closed to it in peace. The United States was feeling her way to the doctrine that the freedom of the seas meant that a neutral flag must be respected cover what it might. The critics of the British government at home argued that as North America was the sole power in the world beyond the reach of Napoleon and its navy could never be incorporated in the enemy fleet it was in the political interest of Britain to conciliate the United States. President Madison summoned England to relax her orders in February 1811. In June 1812 the British government agreed that it would cancel restrictions on American trade. It was too late. There were interests in Congress which wanted war. Western nationalists wanted to eject all European powers from North America. The purchase of Louisiana from Napoleon tempted land speculators to look across into Spanish Florida with covetous eyes. Spain and Britain were allies in 1811. It might be possible, too, to conquer Canada. The chief sufferers from the war were to be the New England merchants who had opposed it from the first. In the last months of 1814 peace was painfully negotiated. It was Britain's interest to trade with and not to fight with the United States.

CHAPTER VII

The Age of Reason
in British Thought

From the English Revolution in 1689 to the French Revolution in 1789 we have a prologue to the swelling scene of our own age. We are moving to our destiny impelled by ideas which were first stated and forces which were first analyzed in that period. It was the last period of an economic order which had the rhythm of the seasons, the last in which the world of Caesar and Vergil was in tone with the life and thought of living Englishmen. In the eighteenth century the mathematical structure of the material and social worlds was unveiled; mind entered into matter, and the attempt of men to control the cosmos, to make it as malleable as their own minds, had begun. The age of reason found nature intelligible and believed that it was controllable in the service of human felicities:

> . . . still advancing bolder, led him on,
> To Pomp, to Pleasure, Elegance and Grace;
> And, breathing high Ambition thro' his Soul,
> Set Science, Wisdom, Glory in his View,
> And bade him to be the *Lord* of all below.

The peace of the Augustans was a pause before the march of reason into a secular millennium.

Reason was the surface show. But the higher reason tried to reach, the deeper were its roots found to be. The philosophers who began by thinking that the world was very like a watch were led to the realization that it was more like a thought. Was there not, as Hume said, "a certain degree of analogy among all the operations of nature, in every situation and in every age"? Are not "the rotting of a turnip, the generation of an animal, and the structure of human thought" energies that bear some remote analogy to each other? The same observation that suggested utility might be the basis of morals could also suggest to a different genius that "the roaring of lions, the howling of wolves, the raging of the stormy sea, and the destructive sword, are portions of eternity, too great for the eye of man." The age of utility was also the age of romanticism, the age of scepticism, the age of Methodism. When Hume was finishing his *Treatise of Human Nature* in 1738, John Wesley at Aldgate wrote: "[I] felt my heart strangely warmed; I felt I did trust in Christ and Christ alone for salvation." The adventures which wrecked the prosaic mind of Swift's Lemuel Gulliver were symbols of the changes in scale, of the mysteries of time and space, and of the trembling balance between reason and the passions which ordinary men must face when they have begun to uncover the secrets of nature.

In the eighteenth century it was possible to think of Western Europe as one great republic embracing several states wherein the life of reason made the different political forms almost irrelevant. If there were despots they could not but be enlightened when Reason was abroad and Voltaire was its prophet. The reason of common men under the guidance of philosophers would come to see nature as it really was. The seemingly mysterious and dangerous cosmos would be reduced to manageable order. *Les philosophes* were, as Whitehead said, "men of genius, clear-headed and acute, who applied the seventeenth century group of scientific abstractions to the analysis of the unbounded universe." Reason was the key to nature and in nature would be found the means to all that reason could wish. In some unbalanced minds absurd fictions about reason and nature would lead to fantasies about earthly millenniums. But the creative writers, seriously concerned to ease the tension between the nascent power of a new scientific method and the customs and traditions which were the work of ages, produced masterpieces of order and clarity, and the men of action, in the social and political world, outlined the institutions in which the Western world still lives.

The age lies between the religious wars of the seventeenth century and the economic liberalism, religious toleration, and democratic aspirations of the nineteenth. The communism of the twentieth century is a heresy of the age of reason. After 1689 we have the prologue to the American, the French, and the industrial revolutions. In literature the novel, in politics the party, and, in philosophy, empiricism was born.

England was, of course, a mere province of this European republic of nascent reason. She had no enlightened despots—only some dull German kings. She was committed to an empirical method in politics. She had made her adjustment to the claims of the Papacy in the sixteenth century. In that struggle, which, to Voltaire, was the center of the battle, England had merely to conduct some mopping up operations as the aftermath of her Civil War. It was, however, a factor in her foreign policy, because it involved the dynasty which was a catalyst in her changing constitution. She had a form of government which proved to be as useful in practice as it was absurd in theory. The most serious struggle was with Enthusiasm —that sense of a false feeling of divine presence which could lead simple men and foolish mobs to destroy the social order. The greatest English work on the philosophy of politics—Hobbes's *Leviathan*—had been written in the middle of the seventeenth century to counter the anarchy implicit in the claim of any boy or wench who could read the Scriptures to have the authority of God for defiance of the magistrate.

In England the ambiguity of the appeal to reason and to nature was sensed almost from the beginning. John Locke himself adopted what he called "a plain historical method" to be brought into "well bred company and polite conversation." We might have a love of truth which the mind "embraces in its native and naked beauty," but we were "in the state of mediocrity; finite creatures furnished with powers and faculties very well fitted to some purposes, but very disproportionate to the vast unlimited extent of things."

In England the continuity of her institutions was matched by the continuity of her ideas. In medieval Europe the extent of natural knowledge had been thought to be determined not by the object but by its origin. All knowledge was natural which came from human reason. But reason was the servant of revelation. At the Renaissance the idea was developed that divine power pervades nature herself, and the dualism between the Creator and creation was abolished. We could know not merely *natura naturata* but the creative process (*natura naturans*). Shakespeare put it clearly and neatly: "Nature is made better by no means but nature makes that means." In the seventeenth century Galileo had said that we should find truth not in God's word but in his work and that his work would be understood by those who knew nature's handwriting, which is mathematics. Observation and exact measurement would tell us all we need to know. The eighteenth century held that Galileo's dream had become in Newton the reality of common day. James Thomson in *The Seasons* expressed the natural satisfaction of Englishmen:

> Let Newton, *pure Intelligence,* whom God
> To Mortals lent, to trace his boundless Works
> From Laws sublimely simple, speak thy Fame
> In all Philosophy.

The use of Newtonian concepts in social questions had far-reaching effects on the eighteenth-century climate of thought. But here it should be noted how the English with their habit of compromise managed to combine medieval, Renaissance, and Newtonian ideas. It was a weakness of the eighteenth-century scientific scheme, Whitehead has pointed out, that it provided none of the elements which compose the immediate psychological experience of mankind.[1] Hume himself knew that from a dance of particles whether in the sun or in the brain of the observer it was not possible to derive a spark of thought or a quiver of feeling. The inadequacy of Newtonian mechanism as an intelligible record of the full glory of the natural world meant that poets and men of letters filled in the Newtonian outlines with colors from the Platonic and the medieval palettes. The harmony which Pope celebrates in his *Essay on Man* is an organic and not a mechanical one. God works in nature by a *plastic* power which produces new forms by a process of growth:

> Look round our world; behold the chain of love
> Combining all below and all above
> See plastic nature working to this end,
> The single atoms each to other tend,
> Attract, attracted to, the next in place
> Form's and impelled its neighbours to embrace

The eighteenth century believed in a great chain of being.[2] Locke had written: "That there should be more species of intelligent creatures above us than there are of sensible and material below us is probable to me from hence, that in all the visible corporal world we see no chasms or gaps. All quite down from us the descent is by easy steps, and a continued series of things that in each remove differ very little one from another" (*Essay Concerning Human Understanding,* Bk. III, c. 6). Addison in the *Spectator* (No. 519) wrote: "The whole chasm in Nature, from Plant to a Man is filled up with diverse kind of creatures, rising one over another by such gentle and easie ascent, that the little transitions and deviations from one species to another are almost insensible." In Thomson's *Seasons* this becomes

> the mighty chain of being, lessening down
>   from infinite perfection to the brink
> of dreary nothing, desolate abyss
>   from which astonished thought, recoiling turns

and is combined with a vague pantheism which anticipates Wordsworth:

> Inspiring God! who boundless Spirit all,
> And unremitting energy, pervades,
> Adjusts, sustains, and agitates the Whole.
> He ceaseless works *alone,* and yet *alone*
> Seems not to work; with such perfection fram'd
> Is this complex stupendous Scheme of Things.

> But, tho' concealed, to every purer Eye
> Th' informing Author in his Works appears.

If the poets were inclined to be satisfied with the general reflection that

> All are but parts of one stupendous whole
> Whose body Nature is and God the Soul

and if social philosophers liked to play with Newtonian models for the analysis of human history a host of new sciences was developed by social oddities: eccentrics like Cavendish, by Unitarians and Quakers, by untaught mechanics like James Brindley. In the study of dyes, the development of guns, diving bells, the study of bills of mortality, and in the collection of animals and fossils there was in operation an empirical method which was blazing the trail from Newton to Darwin.

You could not go directly from Newton to chemistry, botany, geology. Nor could you go directly from Locke's *Human Understanding* or Hume's *Treatise of Human Nature* to the life of *Robinson Crusoe* or the life of *Tristram Shandy*. But from Newton and Locke came two things which dominated the century: (1) that the social order had a rational basis—and this was to be the inspiration of the new science of economics, and (2) that there was reason in nature.

This nature could be used as a norm by which human actions could be judged in the satire of Swift or the exhortations of Addison. New forms of literature were addressed to a wide public. There was a circulation of a common currency of critical prose. As W. H. Auden has said, the past had given us the Saint, the Knight, the Courtier, the Gentleman; now we had the philosopher—not as the brain of a small hierarchical community but as an essential hormone quickening a national life. Philosopher came to be a common term applied to any gentleman who did not believe in witchcraft. And it was high time that gentlemen—particularly if they sat on a judicial bench in quarter sessions—should cease to believe in witchcraft. Now that the stars were known to have an ordered path gentlemen might with advantage follow their example. Given the recent passions of the Civil War, given the need, if kings were not by God appointed, to control the social scene without divine assistance, given the uneasy feeling that the Christian tradition could not survive the elimination from the history of mankind of the legendary elements which had accumulated, it was well that gentlemen should feel that nature, as reason could know her, prescribed balance, elegance, and even honesty in their behavior. A Stoic touch in every magistrate, in every merchant, and in every landowner had its advantages. There was a natural dialectic, too, for the more the appeal to the mathematical order in nature was developed the more the development of the imagination and all those feelings and passions which were not covered in the current theories were fostered. English insularity has always encouraged the fantastical. In the age of reason the passions were nourished as never before. The age of reason suffered a sea change into the age of romantics.

The eighteenth century is one of the great periods of British philosophical thought. The influence of John Locke (1632–1704) pervades the age. Santayana has called him the father of psychology, of theoretical liberalism, and the godfather of the American political system. Had his mind been more profound his influence would have been less: "His philosophy held in solution many different and incompatible elements which have since been separated by the labours of his successors. No one of them, when taken by itself and carried to its logical conclusion, is as plausible as the confused mixture of them all." [3] Voltaire placed him above Plato. He considered that he had set forth human reason as clearly as a good anatomist shows the pattern of the human body. In his *Essay Concerning Human Understanding* (1690) Locke had enquired into the possible range of human knowledge. As we would test a razor before shaving or examine the lenses of a telescope before stargazing, so we should examine the mind to see what it could do.[4] This was an odd procedure, because we ascertain the utility of any tool by using our mind, but the competence of the mind we can only ascertain by using it. He had therefore to assume the existence of the very competence which he set out to establish. And when he wanted to explain how the mind works he had to assume that it knew the parts of the physical world which were needed in the explanation. "The fact is that Locke constantly speaks as though we had some way of knowing what the world is *without knowing it,* and can thus settle whether certain processes through which we have gone or can go have given or will give us knowledge of it." [5] He assumed that we can study the working of the mind by the "historical plain method" of looking into it and writing an account of what we see. As we only know what we can see by looking into our minds and as we have no direct knowledge of what is outside them, it is not possible for us to know anything for certain about the physical world. We know the picture in our minds, but we can hardly go out of our minds to see whether that picture resembles the world outside.

George Berkeley (1685–1753) accepted Locke's principles and let the argument lead him as far as it would go undeterred that it might be awkward to admit that we did not know anything that was not in our minds. He admitted that there was no reason for believing in the existence of a physical world resembling what we had before us in our minds. Locke had said that secondary qualities—the whiteness and the sweetness of sugar, the warmth of life, the color of sunsets, and the smell of blood— were dependent on perception: the blind do not see the sun or the sick taste the wine the bon viveur savors; Berkeley said that it was the same with the primary qualities of extension, shape, movement, and the solidity of a body. "The table I write on I say exists, that is, I see and feel it. . . . There was an odour, that is, it was smelt; there was a sound, that is, it was heard: a colour or figure, and it was perceived by sight or touch. That is all that I can understand by these and the like expressions" (*Principles of Human Knowledge,* para. 3). The sensations we have are orderly and could only be caused in us by an intelligent spirit. This we call God. "So-called laws of nature are simply the rules according to which God excites ideas in us; these rules are not necessary, so that what are usually called miracles are possible." [6]

It is not possible here to consider the contradictions which lurk in Berkeley's own position. He was concerned to deny the existence of that physical world which Locke had taken for granted. But he is led to say what he does by considering the physical conditions of perception and, therefore, he tacitly takes for granted the existence of the very physical world he wants to show does not exist. He had, however, says Whitehead, made all the right criticisms, at least in principle, of the mechanistic theories of the eighteenth-century philosophers. Locke had made the mind a mirror which knows that it mirrors what it does not see. It is the photographic plate which says "how fine is my grain and what a pity I had not focused myself more accurately." But if one starts from the immediate facts of our psychological experience, as an empiricist ought to do, one is led to an organic conception of nature, for we have memory of the past, immediacy of realization, and a sense of the shape of things to come. Berkeley pointed out that the small round blob which the viewer sees is, not the four-square castle tower which is really there. I see a point of light and not a giant star from which it comes. Neither the blob nor the twinkling star *which you see here,* are the real ones which you suppose exist at a distance.

David Hume (1711–76) extended and systematized the introspective psychology of Locke. His *Treatise of Human Nature* almost lovingly develops the sceptical implications of eighteenth-century empiricism. He has confused, exasperated, and inspired a variety of critics. Some say that the human mind was only rescued from the impasse into which Hume drove it by the critical philosophy of Kant. Some honor him as the supreme spirit of British empiricism which, temporarily obscured by the cloud of idealism from Samuel Taylor Coleridge to F. H. Bradley in the nineteenth century, today shines once more in its full glory. He had a profound influence not only on the theory of knowledge but also on the development of the economic and political theories of the utilitarians. In his *Dialogues Concerning Natural Religion* he destroyed the argument from design on which theology was resting. "A fleet, whose purposes were salutary to society, might always meet with a fair wind: Good princes enjoy sound health and long life: Persons born to power and authority, be framed with good tempers and virtuous dispositions. A few such ventures as these, regularly and wisely conducted, would change the face of the world; and yet would no more seem to disturb the course of nature or confound human conduct than the present economy of things, where the causes are secret variable and compounded. Some small touches given to Caligula's brain in his infancy, might have converted him into a Trajan; one wave, a little higher than the rest by burying Caesar and his fortune in the bottom of the ocean, might have restored liberty to a considerable part of mankind. There may, for ought we know be good reasons, why providence interposes not in this matter; but they are unknown to us; and though the mere supposition that such reason exist, may be sufficient to *save* the conclusion concerning the divine attribute, yet surely it can never be sufficient to establish that conclusion." [7] His attack on religion was so deadly that he dare not publish it in his lifetime, and to this day theologians find it difficult to believe that he meant what he said. Here we can only touch the surface of his profound and confusing work.

In the *Treatise of Human Nature* he tried to show that what we know is "limited to a series of sensations, passions, and emotions, together with mental images of them, and that it is groundless to believe in the existence of anything else whatever, even of ourselves." [8] He spoke of his speculations as appearing ridiculous, and H. A. Pritchard has said that in fact they are ridiculous. Ridiculous because Hume tried "to describe the whole of the process by which we come to know and endeavour to increase our knowledge, as if it were conducted by a mind in which all rationality had been left out." [9] The merit of Hume's scepticism is that it forced all serious philosophers to admit the reality of mind. Hume is the real father of Hegel. The scepticism of Hume is the starting point of the English idealist philosophers T. H. Green and F. H. Bradley.

Hume's scepticism was that "reason is nothing but a wonderful and unintelligible instinct of our souls," but reason could give us a "sceptical understanding of the limits within which reason is able to operate." He divided knowledge into two provinces—the analytical, and all apprehensions of matters of fact. In the first, knowledge in the sense of intellectual insight is possible—we know that 2 plus 3 are 5 and we can demonstrate the properties of a triangle. In the second, outside mathematics and logic we have no real knowledge but only belief. That fire burns and water drowns, that the sun will rise, we most verily believe and would be fools if we did not. But such truths by which we live cannot be demonstrated. All probable reasoning, which includes all the natural sciences, and all history and morals are nothing but a species of sensation.

It is not solely in poetry and music that we must follow our taste and sentiment, but likewise in philosophy. In the field of matters of fact, knowledge is a name only for certain fundamental beliefs to which we are instinctively and irrevocably committed. We are such stuff as beliefs are made on.

The doctrine of natural belief is the heart of Hume. Reason—the demonstrative reasoning of the mathematician—will not explain any of the ultimate characteristics of our experience: awareness of external reality, the casual pattern which informs it, the appreciation of beauty, and our judgment of actions good or bad. In the world of experience natural belief must take the place of rational insight.

Hume's scepticism and his clear insight into the social order were vital to the eighteenth-century's conception of the science of economics and the history of mankind. With Adam Smith and many others he shaped a tentative science of society which would explain the past and control the future. It surveyed mankind from China to Peru in the sure and certain hope, and with the benevolent intention, of releasing reason from its servitude to superstition and the passions. The secrets of nature were being uncovered, and society, a part of nature, would be revealed in its simple and naked beauty. Out of this analysis came some techniques which are still with us, such as the system of representative government in its British form and modern economics. Some of the most penetrating statements of the realities of political and social life were inspired by the weaknesses of its theories. Dr. Johnson and Edmund Burke added the insight of genius to the speculations of the early social scientists.

Hume's starting point was that man, like other animals, is more an active than a reflective being. He would have agreed with Hobbes who wrote: "From the principal parts of our Nature, Reason and Passion, have proceeded two kinds of learning, *Mathematical* and *Dogmatical:* the former is free from Controversie and Dispute, because it consisteth in comparing Figure and Motion only; in which things, *Truth,* and the *Interest of Men,* oppose not each other: but in the other there is nothing undisputable, because it compareth Men, and medleth with their Right and Profit; in which, as often as Reason is against a Man, so oft will a Man be against Reason" ("Epistle Dedicatory to William Earl of Newcastle," in Hobbes's *Human Nature*). Hume thinks that it is possible to have a scepticism which will limit the influence of passion and leave men free to appreciate the social order which they have always had. The philosopher can show that while there is not a war of all against all but a subtle system of mutual interdependence, this natural order by which men live may be distorted and even disrupted by passionate beliefs which have no ground at all. No one could seriously believe in the divine right of kings or in the origin of society in a social contract. But if one considers the social order with the common sense we use in everyday life, then it is clear that we are alive and that we should not be so had our ancestors not survived. The conditions of survival of the human race in the past must have been satisfied. We know from our experience now what some of these conditions must have been. Our ancestors must have contrived to defend themselves against wild beasts so much stronger than they were. Had there ever been a Hobbesian state of nature we should not now be here. Because we are here there must have always been the rudiments of division of labor, property, contract, and law.

In his analysis of justice Hume had two opponents: those who said that justice should be done though the skies fall—that there were certain standards intuitively grasped which were independent of utility and interest—and the social contract writers who said that the authority of the magistrate was grounded on a conveyance of right and power. Both, Hume said, were mistaken. The principles of justice are artificial. They are not natural in the sense that paternal affection, mother love, and the attraction between the sexes are natural. But though they are artificial they are not based on contract, because the keeping of contracts is itself one of the principles of justice. Contract is a social concept and cannot be the ground of the conditions which must be antecedent to it. The principles of justice, Hume concludes, are the outcome of customary behavior which commands our approbation because of its utility.

The analysis of the social order was a great achievement of the eighteenth century, and in its British form is immortal in Adam Smith's *Wealth of Nations*. It led to the development of the classical liberal theory. It was the root from which modern economic science has flowered. The questions which it raised have been the concern of all the political philosophy of the West. The English having beheaded one king and chased away another had to improvise a political theory which would explain a system in which neither divine right, nor enlightened despots, nor the absurdities of the concept of the sovereignty of the people had a place. They developed an empirical system of ordered liberty indefensible in theory but impressive in practice.

Before we examine the serious and seminal work of Adam Smith we must glance at the delightful Mandeville (1670–1733). He was one of the most successful authors and widely famed men of his day. The *Fable of the Bees: or, Private Vices, Public Benefits,* was published anonymously in 1714. Mandeville had a style which was a medium for popular philosophy, lacking only the quality of poetry. Sometimes one feels that there is more wisdom and fun in Mandeville than in any other eighteenth-century writer. His prose is light, swift, and serious. It is a stream which sparkles though it runs deep.[10]

That private vices were public virtues followed from Mandeville's definition of virtue. When he wrote, some theologians held that virtue was a mastery of self given by divine grace; others held that it was conduct in accordance with the dictates of pure reason. Swift had parodied the latter in the Houyhnhnms, the wise horses who so discountenanced poor Gulliver: "As these noble Houyhnhnms are endowed by Nature with a general disposition to all Virtues, and have no Conception or Ideas of what is evil in a rational Creature; so their grand Maxim is, to cultivate Reason, and to be wholly governed by it."

Mandeville adopted both the theological and the rational conception of virtue and amalgamating them declared those acts alone to be virtuous "by which Man, contrary to the impulse of Nature, should endeavour the Benefit of others, or the Conquest of his own Passions out of a Rational ambition of being good." As one would expect, when he examined the world in the light of this formula, he could find no virtue there at all. The affairs of the world were not managed in obedience to any such rigorous view of morality. If all actions were to cease except those dictated by the pure idea of the good, trade would end, the arts would be unnecessary, and the crafts be almost abandoned. Mandeville showed that the ascetic idea of morality was incompatible with the facts of economic life and the rationalist idea of conduct with psychological fact. He faced the belief that the laws of right and wrong must be "eternal and immutable" with the observation that, in point of fact, they were temporary and variable.

There is in Mandeville the germ of utilitarianism: ". . . it is manifest, that when we pronounce Actions good or evil, we only regard the Hurt or Benefit the Society receives from them, and not the person who commits them." It was his belief that philosophers tend to rationalize certain dominant desires: ". . . we are ever pushing our Reason which way soever we feel Passion to draw it, and self-love pleads to all human creatures for their different views, still furnishing every individual with arguments to justify their inclinations." He had a feeling for the gulf of time and effort which divides us from the primitive: "It is the work of ages to find out the true use of the passions." He saw the social order as an adjustment made in the course of ages between men's passions and desires and the scarce means in nature for their satisfaction. In Paradise man was "wholly rapt up in sublime Meditations on the Infinity of his Creator, who daily did vouchsafe intelligibly to speak to him and visit without Mischief." The golden age could not be civilized: "No societies could have sprung from the Amiable Virtues and Loving Qualities of Man, but on the contrary all of them must have had their origin from his Wants, his Imperfections and the variety of his Appetites."

Berkeley beautifully parodied Mandeville in 1732: "Leave nature full freedom to work her own way and all will be well. . . . There cannot . . . be a stronger instance of prejudice than that a man should at this time of day preserve a reverence for that idol Virtue, a thing so effectually exposed and exploded by the most knowing men of the age, who have shewn that a man is a mere engine played upon and driven about by sensible objects; and that moral virtue is only a name, a notion, a chimera, an enthusiasm, or at best a fashion, uncertain and changeable, like all other fashions." We "shew people how to serve their country by divesting themselves and causing the streams of public spirit and self love to unite and run in the same channel." Berkeley also criticized him by an incisive summary: ". . . that there is no God or providence: that man is as the beasts that perish: that his happiness as theirs consists in obeying animal instincts, appetites and passions: that all stings of conscience and sense of guilt are prejudices and errors of education: that religion is a state trick: that vice is beneficial to the public: that the soul of man is corporal, and dissolveth like a flame or vapour: that man is a machine actuated according to the laws of motion." He continues his implied criticism, saying that this philosopher who is, according to his own principles, "an organ played on by sensible objects, a ball bandied about by appetites and passions . . . this curious piece of clock work having no principle of action within itself, and denying that it hath or can have any one free thought or motion, sets up for the patron of liberty, and earnestly contends for *free-thinking*."

Hume and Adam Smith took Mandeville's analysis with more calm. If vice, indeed, produces all the good in the world then, said Hume, there is something wrong with our terminology. In the course of ages law has given security, security had made possible plenty, plenty has encouraged curiosity, and curiosity has given civilization. It would be prudent to understand this order by which we live. Here was the root of modern economics. It was to make possible a quantitative and analytical development of the history of civilization which Voltaire and Gibbon in their different ways were providing. In the eighteenth century the moving frontiers in the New World of America and in the ancient East of India, the growth of towns, and the varying fortunes of agriculture gave an edge to the interest in the causes of social change. If the universe were "a mighty maze but not without a plan," in the microcosm of the human scene the economist could give some account of its working order.

Adam Smith wanted to give the world a complete social philosophy. "Philosophy by representing the invisible chains which bind together 'the disjointed objects in nature' endeavors to introduce order in this chaos of jarring and discordant appearance." His originality lay in his attempt to analyze the whole range of the economic process with the purpose of discovering the nature of the order which underlay its seeming chaos. In 1749 he had the notion that there was a latent order in human affairs which could be released by the removal of foolish restrictions. "It requires no more than to leave her [nature] alone and give her fair play in the pursuit of her ends that she may establish her designs. . . . Little else is required to carry a state to the highest degree of affluence from the lowest barbarism but peace, easy taxes and a tolerable administration of justice: all the rest being brought about by the natural course of things." The composition of the *Wealth of Nations* was spread over the next twenty-seven years to 1776. In 1759 in *The Theory of the Moral Sentiments* Adam Smith developed a doctrine of a beneficent order in nature shown in the providential adjustment which Providence had made of the forces of external nature to the innate propensities of human nature. He developed almost a cosmic division of labor between God, who looked after things in general, and man, who minds his own business.[11] "The care of the universal happiness of all rational and sensible beings, is the business of God and not of man. To man is allotted a humbler department, but one much more suitable to the weakness of his powers, and to the narrowness of his comprehension: the care of his own happiness, of that of his family, his friends, his country."

In the *Wealth of Nations* the benevolent deity is dropped. Economic order is not a deduction from the general harmony of the universe. It is established by an appeal to some self-evident principles of human psychology, by the citation of historical object lessons, or by inference from contemporary experience. It is an average or statistical harmony and not a pervading spiritual one. Being so, Adam Smith can note its defects without decrying the workmanship of its author. The Mandevillian vice of self-love has a central place: "The natural effort of every individual to better his own condition when suffered to exert itself with freedom and security, is so powerful a principle that it is alone and without any assistance, not only capable of carrying on the society to wealth and prosperity, but of surmounting a hundred impertinent obstructions with which the folly of human laws too often encumbers its operations." This natural liberty could be restored in 1776 if the legislation which restricted free choice of occupations, free trade in land, internal free trade, and international free trade was abolished. Adam Smith radiated a sunny optimism. He has little sense of social disharmonies. While he attacks the mercantilists for their intervention, he at the same time shows how ineffective their interventions were: "One gets the impression that smuggling is God's way of removing the obstructions of foolish politicians who want to upset His wise and liberal reign with tariffs and prohibitions." [12]

In Adam Smith is foreshadowed the liberal theory that the duties of a government are limited to protecting society from internal violence and invasion by other independent societies, the establishment of an exact administration of justice, and the duty of erecting certain public institutions and certain public works. Given that the proper functions of government were so slight it was possible to devise a system of representative government in which those who did these things formed a microcosm of the macrocosm they served. This theory of self-government in which citizens were obeying laws which they themselves had made was hailed as a solution of the problem of good government which had troubled Western Europe since the Greeks. The strength of this theory was to help Victorian England to her political and imperial greatness. The weakness of it was to hasten her decline and to generate the mythologies which now plague the world.

John Locke in his *First Treatise of Government* had demolished the theory of Filmer: God had set some men above other men, fathers above sons, men above women, and kings above all others. "The Lord and Master of them all," Locke said, had not "by any manifest Declaration of his Will set one above another." But if kings are not by God appointed some other ground for law and order must be found. His "Strange Doctrine," as he called it, was that "everyone has the Executive power of the Law of nature." "We are born free as we are born rational." But government is necessary because of the imperfections of human nature and the scarcity of natural resources. "In the beginning of the World—was *America*. But in the modern world government is needed to protect *Property* not only in the extended sense of lives Liberties and Estates but also in the narrower sense of the *Labour* of his *Body*, and the work of his hands." Political authority has its source in the governed and may be revoked and reallocated at their good pleasure. The holders of authority must frame their policies in accordance with the law of nature. They must make the life of individual citizens their supreme consideration.

The difficulties of the Lockean political mode are obvious. If Locke had hoped that the law of nature might be made as clear as mathematics the hope was not fulfilled. David Hume gave an incisive demonstration that whatever the necessity for government, its origin and its existing forms could not be contractual. Government must depend upon the opinion of the governed if only in the sense that men must fear it too much to chance resistance. Given the limited techniques of eighteenth-century administrations Hume was not troubled by our modern problems of the scope of torture and propaganda.

Eighteenth-century administrations could rely on the inertia of custom and had every reason to know that sleeping dogs do not bite. Hume's criticism—that governments had their origin not in any contract but in the acceptance by the many of the useful functions carried out by a ruling few—led to a close analysis of the history of governments. It was found that the origin of governments was far more complicated than had at first been supposed. And the tension generated by the growing economic order and the venerable complexities of existing institutions led to an analysis of the process of political change. The analyses of Locke and Hume were widened, deepened, and corrected by the genius of Swift and Burke.

Swift (1667–1745) was born in Dublin, the grandson of a fiercely royalist clergyman of Herefordshire. In Ireland he got the best education which the English governing class there could offer. He was in residence at Dublin College when the Revolution of 1689 put an end to normal life in Dublin. He crossed to England, and off and on until 1699 he was secretary to Sir William Temple at Moor Park. In that world he absorbed the social attitude of the post-Restoration Whigs. It had the tough energy which we see in the social satire of Restoration comedies. After the animosities of the Civil War they were on guard against the fantastic and the hypocritical. Swift was the spokesman of the Protestant aristocracy in Ireland. As an Anglican he held to a middle way between the sheer faith of the Roman Catholic and the sheer inspiration of the Puritan. The Puritan regime he saw as a political tyranny, the seizure of power by a minority. He opposed the enthusiasm of the Puritan, the claim to have a particular knowledge of the Divine mind. Swift appealed to common sense, by which he meant a particular sort of reason—not the reason of the moralist nor the reason of the rational divines but the funded experience of mankind. "Reason itself," he once wrote, "is true and just, but the reason of every particular man is weak and wavering, perpetually swayed and turned by his interest his passions and his vices." He measured the stupidity of individual political and public figures against the good sense and decency inherent in the social body. Cunning individuals for their own discreditable interests pervert the common sense of average men. It is the function of the critic to expose such unscrupulous agitators who might otherwise destroy political and social stability. A free man will assert the tradition of reason against stupidity and bestiality.

Swift had an ironic invective, breathtaking and mysterious in its subtlety. In his prose there are depths and vistas as deep and distant as those in Shakespeare's poetry. The structure of a paragraph can be as subtle as a play. He can use a deadly literalness to achieve the terrors of an Inferno. He is the supreme master of English prose. He was a satirist of critics without taste, pedants without imagination, and scientific experimenters without common sense. *Gulliver's Travels* is not only an excellent parody of the contemporary accounts of travels into remote parts of the world, it is also a dazzling presentation of theories about man and society. The contrast between the Lilliputians and the Brobdingnagians hints at man's middle state, neither angel nor worm. His theme is the Fall of Man and the limitations of reason.[13] The original institutions of the Lilliputians were admirable, but later the people fell into "the most scandalous corruption" by the "degenerated nature of man." In the voyage to the Houyhnhnms Swift is hinting that anyone who believes in the adequacy of reason without Christianity must see himself as a Houyhnhnm and the rest of mankind as Yahoos. The inexhaustible benevolence of the Houyhnhnms who believe that "reason alone is sufficient to govern a rational creature" is probably a parody of Shaftesbury's *Characteristics*. The Yahoos were believed to have been descended from original refugees who "degenerating by degrees became in process of time, much more savage than their own species in the country from which the two originals came." *Gulliver's Travels* is not contrasting the evils of civilization with the virtues of primitive peoples. What is wrong with Europe is not that it has been civilized but that its civilization is falling into decay. In a voyage to Laputa Gulliver discovers "the Springs and Motives of great enterprises and revolutions in the world, and of the contemptible Accidents to which they owed their success. How a Whore can govern the Back-stairs, the Back-stairs a Council and the Council a Senate." As Bolingbroke was to echo him: "A chambermaid may slip a banknote into a gripping paw as well as the most subtle demon of hell."

Lord Acton said that Burke at his best was England at its best, Hazlitt that it had always been with him a "test of the sense and candour of anyone belonging to the opposite party, whether he allowed Burke to be a great man . . . in arriving at one error he discovered a hundred truths."

Edmund Burke (1728–97) was born in Ireland, the son of an attorney, a profession then held in little repute. Dr. Johnson said of Burke that in the House of Commons he "gained more reputation than perhaps any man at his first appearance ever gained before." Horace Walpole said of the same occasion: "His name was Edmund Burke . . . an Irishman, of a Roman Catholic family, and actually married to one of that persuasion. He had been known to the public for a few years by his essay *On the Sublime and Beautiful* and other ingenious works; but the narrowness of his fortune had kept him down, and his best revenue had arisen from writing for the booksellers." Horace gives us here the feel of the weight of aristocratic insolence which pressed on Burke and other men of genius. He was an Irishman; he was related to Roman Catholics; he was poor; he was rumored to be writing for the booksellers. The pen might be mightier than the sword, but a courtesan might be more influential than a lord. For a man to sell his pen was as tricky as for a woman to sell her virtue. Burke had had a literary and journalistic career of about ten years before at the age of thirty-seven he entered the House of Commons. In the early part of his career he had the support of the Marquis of Rockingham, by hereditary wealth one of the most powerful men in England, who was twice prime minister. Rockingham leaned heavily on Burke. Burke was the brain of the Rockingham Whigs.

Burke was consistent in all he wrote and said. *The Vindication of Natural Society,* 1756, stated the same principles as those which were the nerve of his speculations about English, American, Indian, and French politics. Burke sensed the explosive implications of the popular doctrines of the age. He did not say that God was dead, but he did indicate the consequences of thinking Him to be so. In the *Vindication* he shows that the arguments used to destroy religion could be used to destroy government. What would become of the world if the practice of all moral duties and the foundations of society rested upon having their reasons made clear and demonstrable to every individual. "Is not the same reason available in theology and in politics? . . . We are indebted for all our miseries to our distrust of that guide which Providence thought sufficient for our condition, our own natural reason, which rejecting both in human and divine things, we have given our necks to the yoke of political and theological slavery . . . We first throw away the tales along with the rattles of our nurses. Those of the priest keep their hold a little longer; those of our governors the longest of all."

The implication of this parody of Bolingbroke is that to substitute abstract speculation for an understanding of inherited institutions will lead to chaos or tyranny. He knew (as J. M. Keynes was to discover in this century) "that civilisation was a thin and precarious crust erected by the personality and the will of the very few, and only maintained by rules and conventions skilfully put across and guilefully preserved." [14] "The order in which we find ourselves is not going to last or to be improved by our choosing a new set of rules of any special voluntary pact. Those we have arise from the relations of man to man, and the relations of man to God, which relations are not matters of pact. On the contrary the force of all the pacts which we enter into with any particular person or number of persons amongst mankind, depends upon these prior obligations."

When Burke uses the metaphor of growth and life in social institutions he is making the point that institutions transcend the lives of individuals. Institutions do not grow—the British Constitution is not a vegetable, nor is the greatest Duke a venerable oak—but they are not made in the way that machines are made. Institutions are the result of human actions, but they were not contrived for the purposes which they now fulfill. A sound political constitution is the product of generations of adjustment and contrivance. A "disposition to preserve and an ability to improve taken together" was Burke's conception of statesmanship. But "when the reason of old establishments is gone it is absurd to preserve nothing but the burden of them." "The laws reach but a little way. Constitute government how you please, infinitely the greater part of it must depend upon the exercise of the powers which are left to the prudence and uprightness of ministers of state." "It is the business of the speculative philosopher to mark the proper ends of government. It is the business of the politician, who is the philosopher in action, to find out proper means towards those ends and to employ them with effect." "We are born only to be men. We shall do enough if we form ourselves to be good ones. It is therefore our business carefully to cultivate our minds . . . to bring the dispositions that are lovely in private life into the service and conduct of the commonwealth; so be to be patriots is not to forget that we are gentlemen." One is tempted to say of Burke that he distilled the wisdom of political speculation in Western Europe. It had begun with Plato's Republic and was relevant to the life of men before that life was transformed by the scientific revolutions through which we are now living. He is the political sage of the prescientific West.

"Burke," Augustine Birrell wrote, "as he regarded humanity swarming like bees into and out of their hives of industry, is ever asking himself, How are these men to be saved from anarchy?" It was the wonder of order in society that impressed him as it is the wonder of order in nature that impresses the naturalist. What in Plato's Republic was secured by the authority of a small group of philosophers, trained in administration and inspired by a knowledge of eternal things, had in some parts of the world come in part into existence from a conjunction of causes it was almost impossible to analyze. Tradition in public affairs and prejudices in personal were safeguards of these gifts of time. "Prejudice is of ready application in an emergency; it previously engages the mind in a steady course of wisdom and virtue and does not leave the man hesitating in the moment of decision, skeptical, puzzled and unresolved. Prejudice renders a man's virtue his habit; and not a series of unconnected acts."

Burke was not unaware of the technical and practical problems of the social order he defended. Adam Smith said that he was the only man, who, without communication, thought on economic topics exactly as he did. He appreciated that living as we do, under conditions which are temporal and terrestrial, there must be a limitation on human purposes because there is a scarcity of means. The economic order which Adam Smith had analyzed was direct evidence both of the deep roots of civilized society and of the delicate and complex conditions upon which it depended. Burke is here in line with Hume, who had seen that the institutions, economic and political, which had come down to us out of the past had been the outcome not of abstract speculation but of adjustments in human nature to its situation.

In the case of the dispute with America it seemed to Burke that it was a clear case of the development of a separate community with traditions of freedom similar to those of the British and that it would be absurd to discuss the dispute in terms of formal legal rights. From six capital sources, he said in 1775, "of descent; of form of government; of religion in the northern provinces; of manners in the southern; of education; of the remoteness of situation from the first moves of government (seas roll and months pass, between the order and the execution; and the want of a speedy explanation of a single point is enough to defeat a whole system); from all these causes a fierce spirit of liberty has grown." The question was "not whether their spirit deserves praise or blame, but—what in the name of God, shall we do with it?" And he went on to state the theme which is the heart of English liberalism—that it is will, not force, that is the basis of the state: "Do not dream that your letters of office, and your instructions and your suspending clauses, are the things that hold together the great contexture of this mysterious whole. These things do not make your government. . . . Do you imagine . . . that it is the land tax which raises your revenue? that it is the annual vote in committee of supply which raises you your army? or that it is the mutiny bill, which inspires it with bravery and discipline? No, surely not. It is the love of the people; it is their attachment to their government, from the sense of the deep stake they have in such a glorious institution which gives you your army and your navy, and infuses into both that liberal obedience, without which your army would be a base rabble, and your navy nothing but rotten timber."

When the French Revolution began, Burke had been in politics for thirty years. He had fought George III and Warren Hastings. He had struggled to reform British India. He had fought against the misgovernment of Ireland, against the African slave trade, the oppression of Catholics and Dissenters, the imprisonment of debtors. He had some knowledge of the technique of reform. As early as 1769 he had seen the possibility of a violent upheaval in France. But how was it possible to recast a whole constitution? "To make a government requires no great prudence. Settle the seat of power; teach obedience and the work is done. To give freedom is still more easy. It is not necessary to guide: it only requires to let go the rein. But to form a *free government;* that is, to temper together these opposite elements of liberty and restraint in one consistent work, requires much thought, deep reflection, a sagacious, powerful, and combining mind." In 1689 "it was the case of a legal monarch attempting arbitrary power." In France in 1789 it was "the case of an arbitrary monarch, beginning, from whatever cause, to legalise his authority." Britain in 1689 "got rid of the man, and preserved the constituent parts of the state." The French in 1789 "got rid of the constituent parts and kept the man."

What Burke feared was "the degenerate fondness for tricking short cuts, and little fallacious facilities, that has in so many parts of the world created governments with arbitrary powers." Defects in wisdom are then supplied by the plenitude of force. Abstract innovators can cause a dissolution of a nation into a mere aggregation of individuals, make a reapportionment of property by political machinery, and produce an era of merciless war and tyranny forged out of anarchy.

CHAPTER VIII

The Workshop of the World, 1815-70

The growth of British economic power in the fifty years after 1815 may never be explained to the satisfaction of scholars. The emergence of a great power has the mystery of the appearance of a great man. Its origin and nature are never fully explained. But at least something of what was not understood at the time may become clear to the hindsight of scholars. And if they cannot see into the seeds of growth they can often find the seeds of decay. All men must love history, for in it they can study how those before them came to have their day and, in the end, were the victims and not the masters of their fate. The rise and fall of British industrial supremacy is a well-documented case study for those that have come after.

When so many vital things must remain in the dark it is useful to state what on the surface is clear. A sunspot or a new star can be recorded though the forces that were the cause are not fully understood. Between 1815 and about 1875 there were many profound changes in the British way of life which will always be of interest to the world in general because: (1) they led to a brief period of British supremacy in world affairs, the nature of which it is important to understand; (2) the changes were part of the numerous changes in the life of Western Europe then beginning and which continue now, with a terrifying acceleration, throughout the world. Britain was in fact the cradle of a new industrial power which may serve to make glorious our material life, but only if it is partnered by continuous political skill and wisdom. We do not yet know whether political man has it in him to be an equal partner with his economic brother. The full implications of the penetration into the daily toil by which men have won their daily bread of the most subtle powers of thought have yet to be revealed. Not since, in the Mosaic legend, dust became flesh has there been a more profound revolution than the transformation of the work of hand and muscle by the life of mind. Every tool and every machine is becoming the body of a mathematical equation. The most abstract thought can become the most potent material power. Plato's great myth of the Guardians trained in pure mathematics that they might be philosopher kings has had a new and awe-inspiring twist and realization. Plato's Guardians were to avoid the crippling and distracting labors of the craftsmen. In our new republic it is the work of the craftsmen that the mathematics of the Guardians is transforming. What once was ignoble to the philosopher is now the object of his most subtle care. Platonic forms shape every detail of our lives. We have found an Aladdin's lamp, and we have to master the language of the genii it commands.

The rhetorical and speculative opening may be excused because the period of British history with which we are now concerned was, to contemporaries, so deeply stirring and so little understood. With Macaulay they were impressed with the physical, the moral, and the intellectual improvement since the Revolution of 1689 of which they were the heirs. They were right to feel that something unique had occurred and that there was in the air the promise of intoxicating achievement. It was fitting that the spirit of the age should have inspired political leaders to seek how they might secure the greatest happiness of the greatest number. The naive Utopian writers of the eighteenth century had had an intoxicating vision of peace and plenty secured by the use of reason in the control of the passions. But now these airy nothings were given material form and substance by the use of reason in mine and mill and forge, in the work of the plough, and in the breeding of cattle and of sheep.

Some of the more obvious surface facts may be given first. Afterward, we can consider how they have been interpreted and how they have been misunderstood. Between 1816 and 1875 Britain was to become the world's workshop, the world's banker, and the world's trader. She was also the world's stud farm. By 1860 she was supplying half the world's output of coal and manufactured goods. In 1830 world production of coal was about 30,000,000 tons, of which Britain produced four-fifths; in 1870 it was about 220,000,000 tons, of which Britain produced half, the United States a fifth, and Germany, France, and Belgium a quarter. Exports of coal rose from 500,000 tons in 1830 to nearly 14,000,000 tons in 1870. In 1870 the external trade of the United Kingdom was greater than that of France, Germany, and Italy combined and three times that of the United States. The output of pig iron had risen from 700,000 tons a year in 1830 to about 3,800,000 in 1859–61, and to over 6,500,000 in 1871–73. While many industries were dependent on the coal fields, the main growth had been in cotton. Cotton was the one industry into which mechanization had cut deep by 1820. Textile operatives were more than 10 per cent of the working population in 1841.

The meaning of these and other figures (which have their place in the tables of economic textbooks) is that between 1815 and 1851 occurred the most rapid economic development of domestic resources in the whole of British economic history. Between 1700 and 1780 the rate of growth in the output of British industries had been about 0.9 to 1 per cent per annum; between 1780 and 1870 it was more than 3 per cent. From 1740 to 1800 the average real income per head had risen by a half; between 1800 and 1860 it had doubled; and by 1900 it would have doubled again. This was something new in the world's history. It was a good example of what modern economists call the self-generated take-off. There was a transition from an agrarian and commercial economy to one which was geared to machine production for an international market. It was the first transition of its kind. It involved the exchange of a surplus of manufactured goods for food and raw materials. Britain, in making the transition, was a pioneer in the nineteenth-century pattern of foreign trade, when the world was divided into new countries producing raw materials and old countries manufacturing them. It involved the ploughing back of at least 10 per cent of the national income into investment in place of the customary 4 or 5 per cent. This accumulation of capital made it possible for a population growing at the rate of 200,000 a year to be maintained at an increasingly higher standard of living. It was brought about by the action of individual entrepreneurs working in relation to market forces and in the individualistic and competitive spirit of the age. It was facilitated by government policies, but it was not the result of direct planning by the state. It was, in fact, the considered opinion of most economic experts before 1860 that while a government ought to remove all impediments which interfere with the people providing for themselves, it could do very little more than that and, indeed, ought not to try.

The primary causes of this mutation in British economic life may never be known. But as Gibbon said about the rise of Christianity, there are secondary causes we can study. As the name "industrial revolution" has been given to what happened, it is necessary to give some idea of the variety and intricacy of the changes that were involved. The industrial revolution does not mean that agricultural laborers went or were hustled through some revolving door into a factory. The people of Britain did not become a nation of factory workers. They were not driven into dark satanic mills to have the key turned in the doors while a boss-class squeezed them for surplus value. Machinery played its part, but the innovations were wider and more subtle and complex than the simple substitution of mechanical for manipulative processes. It seems inevitable, looking back, that the spirit of scientific enquiry growing ever stronger since the beginning of the seventeenth century would touch, and with its touch transform, the traditional crafts and techniques of the world, and in that transformation scene Britain had certain clear advantages. She had long been supreme in many of the traditional skills and crafts.

In 1815, 34 per cent of the employed population of England and Wales was still engaged in agriculture and fishing activities, and in agriculture she had some of the best agricultural land in the world and one of the best agricultural climates. Her system of land tenure, though it was anathema to radical reformers because it involved an unparalleled monopoly of ownership, was in fact a system of quasi-co-operative enterprise between landlord and tenant in which the former was responsible for the provision of capital and the latter had a share in improvement, so that the land got the intelligent management and the stimulus of a technical ingenuity to which it could respond. There was great variety. As late as 1840 wooden ploughs drawn by oxen could be seen a few miles from Brighton. But Small had discovered empirically the optimum curve of the mold board, and the precision given by new engineering tools had made it possible to produce the new model on a large scale. The art of deep drainage for heavy soils, the development of four-course rotation, and the management of periodical leys provided the winter keep which made possible the establishment of the British pedigreed stock industry. With the development of scientific stock farming on permanent pastures Britain became the stud farm of the world. Men who knew nothing of genetic science, nutritional science, or veterinary science were yet able to produce breeds which have stamped an English seal on the face of the sheep of three continents and peopled the pastures of the world with British pedigreed cattle. Jonas Webb's Southdown sheep in 1861 were sold to New York, Buenos Aires, Melbourne, New Zealand, France, Germany, and Russia. Robert Bakewell's Leicester sheep and the Shorthorn cattle of the brothers Collings earned Britain her title of stud farm. At least one of the secondary causes of Britain's industrial supremacy is to be found in the vigorous empiricism of her agricultural diversity.

She had another natural advantage in the proximity of her coalfields to her ports. There were five coastal coalfields which could deliver their products almost straight into vessels for shipment to a great domestic market like London or for export as ballast and makeweight. When the railway had been invented, the proximity of coal and iron made Britain the maker of rails for the whole world. There was a shortage of skilled engineers, industrial chemistry was in its infancy, but the railway iron of the English and Welsh furnaces was the best in the world. An American agent wrote in 1835 that "all countries in the world must get their railway iron in England where it is manufactured so rapidly and so perfectly that it is useless to pretend to compete with this branch of industry." Until the late 1840's Britain had no competitor in this, not even in the United States. The 1820's were an age of iron, when rails, pipes, bridges, boats, churches, and even pavements of iron were contemplated. The general adoption of iron in steamship construction began in the 1840's.

In the use of the raw materials coal and iron Britain had every advantage. She has been described as a museum of geological specimens encompassed by the surrounding sea, itself a highway to the markets of the world. The British government itself was a pioneer in the development of geological surveys—a survey was begun in 1835 and completed for England and Wales in 1884.

It has been well said that the industrial revolution was an historical as well as a geographical happening. The British economic grandeurs and miseries are not intelligible if we forget how very immature, unstable, and highly specialized were the industries she possessed when the great transformation had begun. Very few of the workers of the world were in factories. The typical Englishman in the 1840's was still a countryman. Although by 1851, the year of the Great Exhibition, there were more people living in urban than in rural areas and the Englishman was becoming a townsman, he had not become a factory hand. It was not until the last decade of the nineteenth century that the factory became the dominant form of organization in the majority of industries. In 1834 there were in the cotton mills about 210,000 to 230,000 people, or one in eighty of the population, less than one-third of those employed in domestic service or one-eighth of those engaged in agriculture. When Britain was the undisputed workshop of the world, only 1,700,000 out of a total population of 21,000,000 were employed in great industry. It absorbed less than one-quarter of the principal occupation groups. The most numerous group after agriculture was that of domestic servants. Domestic servants and agricultural workers were more than double those engaged in manufactures and mining. In 1851 those employed in the principal nonmechanized groups of industry were about 5,500,000 and outnumbered those in the mechanized (including coal) by three to one.

We shall get a more balanced picture and be better able to understand the power and the problems of the British people if we glance at the conditions in agriculture, textiles, coal, and iron and, closely linked with them, the revolutions in transport. In England and Wales in 1851, 20.9 per cent of the working population was engaged in agriculture, 11.1 per cent in textile manufactures, 10.3 per cent in the clothing industries, 5.5 per cent in the building trades, and 4.0 per cent in mining. Manufacturing industries other than textiles and clothing employed 11.3 per cent of the total—less than in domestic service. Of these industries the largest was the metallurgical, 3.5 per cent. Transport employed 4.1 per cent. In Scotland the position was similar, though there was an even larger proportion in agriculture, 22.7 per cent; 18.8 per cent in textiles, 8.4 per cent in clothing, and only 9.3 per cent in other manufactures.

Agriculture is not a single industry but a group of industries. In 1830 it employed nearly a million families, more than 4,500,000 persons or 28 per cent of the nation. It contributed more than a third of the national income. Before the repeal of the Corn Laws in 1846 the farmers were still the people who really determined the nature of British government. During the French wars and with the swift growth of population the margin of cultivation crept visibly up the hills (as it was to do again in the world wars of the twentieth century). In the postwar depression some of the land which had been enclosed for corn went back to grass. But there were 200,000 new mouths to be fed every year, and British agriculture was well-equipped to adjust methods of production to the most productive use of many different kinds of soil. Light soils which had lain in semi-idleness or waste land were brought into production. On heavy soils deep drainage and scientific stock farming on permanent pastures made steady progress.

By the middle of the century scientific farming was in full operation, and the railroads were bringing the farmers into touch with the great new urban centers. There were three main branches of production: grain farming, which provided the raw material for milling, brewing, and baking; sheep farming which gave wool and mutton; dairy and fat stock farming to give meat and dairy produce and the raw materials for soap, oil, glue, and leather. The cultivated acreage (some 27,000,000 acres in 1851) was almost equally divided between arable and permanent pasture. The Midlands and the western counties were two-thirds grass; the eastern counties two-thirds arable. The case for agricultural protection rested on the difficulties of producers of grain, for they had to face not only foreign competition but also the inelasticity of the demand for bread. Fat stock and dairy farmers had not the same problems. Many landlords were as much interested in the return from the coal mines, railways, and urban developments on their land as they were in the price of bread. There was a diversity of interests to shape the political ends of the landlord class and the agrarian world. In the north of England, in the Midlands, and South Wales the gentry could enlarge their incomes by the lease of mineral rights. Some mined their own coal directly. Some passed from coal to railroads, and a few from railroads to sea transport. Only in the south and west, where large-scale industry offered no alternative employment, was it necessary to use the poor law to provide allowances in aid of wages.

The landlords had great power and privileges because they were the virtual monopolist owners of the soil. In 1874 half the country was owned by less than 8000 persons, a concentration of ownership fiercely denounced by Chartists and free traders and of deep concern to J. S. Mill and the classical economists. But in spite of the large area of land held under family settlements there was a very active land market. There was perhaps more invested in agriculture in the 1850's and 1860's than in any other period of English history. The role of the landlord was to exercise a stewardship of the national patrimony in the fertility of the soil. They had to encourage good husbandry through their oversight of their tenants. Their rents were no more than a return upon investment in a concern in which the landlord took a share in the risks as well as of the profits. That was the theory, and in many cases it was the practice. Retired manufacturers often gave to their land the same kind of care that had given them success in industry and commerce. But in many cases the interests of agriculture were sacrificed to sport. It was unfortunate that although the cost of drainage schemes was high and the cost of introducing new scientific techniques expensive, no British institutions emerged which were specialized to supply rural credit.

In 1846 Sir Robert Peel applied the logic of free trade to agriculture itself. For a quarter of a century after that application British farmers were to enjoy great prosperity. Between 1850 and 1870 the improvements of the best farmers became the practice of the average. British farming carried more livestock in proportion to its area than many parts of Europe. The wars in Europe and in the United States gave British farmers a respite from some of the implications of free trade. In 1868 some 80 per cent of the food consumed within the United Kingdom was produced within the country, and the proportion of livestock was as high as 90 per cent. There were about 250,000 compact farms, nine-tenths of them occupied by tenants and more than half large enough to employ between them a million laborers, an average of about seven. The use of fertilizers had become an exercise in applied science. But the farmer was still helpless against hoof rot, foot and mouth disease, and swine fever. Inventive ingenuity had overflowed from industry into agriculture. But the invisible world of the microbe had not yet been explored.

It was in the cotton industry that replacement of skilled fingers by a mechanical rotation of inanimate matter had first taken hold, for spinning involves essentially the manipulation of a cylinder. The new industrialism was made manifest first in the textile mills. Yarnmaking had been revolutionized in the half-century before 1830. The transition to mechanization was independent of the skill of the engineer and even of the power steam engines. In 1771 Jedediah Strutt and Richard Arkwright built a series of cotton mills along the Derwent and began the development of factory production and the revolution in the ancient industry of spinning. The power used was water. By 1800 cotton spinning had become to a large extent a factory industry. The Strutts had some 1500 to 1600 workers at Belper and Milford, Robert Owen some 1600 to 1700 at his mill at New Lanark, and there were large country colonies in Scotland and one in Wales. But the number of "cotton lords" was small compared with the host of petty employers with their score of workers. In 1816 the large firms accounted for about 14,000 out of the 60,000 cotton factory operatives. It was not until after 1815 that steam power replaced water and brought the industry into the towns. In weaving, effective mechanization came later than in spinning. In 1830 the power loom as distinct from the hand loom was efficient and economical only for coarse cottons. The power loom did not get near its modern form until 1841. The hand loom weaver was not finally superseded before 1860.

The development of the cotton industry was the result of a complex conjunction of many varied and subtle causes. The introduction of East Indian cottons into Europe during the seventeenth century had created a demand for clean, light-weight, and colored clothing. The cost of transport of the raw material was low compared with the finished product, so that there was no need for the manufacturing process to take place where cotton was grown: a spinning mill does not have to be in a cotton field. An industrial spider could now spin his commercial web. The countries that produced the raw cotton were not ready for industrial development, and the British who were, had the water power, the humid climate, and later the coal supplies and the engineering skills, for the development of a large factory industry.

It is not surprising that the cotton industry provided economists with a classical example of territorial specialization. Lancashire had a suitable climate, a convenient port, and coal supplies. In a fiercely competitive industry only the strongest could survive, and apart from a strong group in Clydesdale, the counties of Lancashire, Cheshire, and Derbyshire obtained a virtual monopoly of cotton spinning and weaving. The invention of the cotton gin by Eli Whitney in 1793 had solved the problem of supply. In 1800–1804 the annual average of retained imports of raw cotton was 56,000,000 pounds weight, in 1830–34 it was 152,000,000, and in 1850–54 it was 707,000,000. Between 1840 and 1880 the output of yarn per operative doubled, and in weaving output per man rose nearly two and a half times. The only serious check was the cotton famine during the American Civil War; when it was over the wave of new investment made possible by the Limited Liability Act of 1855 and the opening of new markets in China, Asia, and Africa renewed the prosperity of the industry. By 1886 it could be said that there was scarcely a nook or corner in the habitable globe where the products of the spindles and looms of Lancashire did not find a market. But there was a shadow on the brightness of the competitive individualism of the British textile industries. The best English artisans were lacking in the knowledge of machine drawing and designing and in the chemistry needed for the dyeing and finishing trades.

If one is tempted to think of the industrial revolution as a transformation—at the touch of the fairy wand of science—of the toil and sweat of human limbs into the purr and throb of glistening machines, the coal industry will bring one back to earth. The national economy of Britain rested on the extraction of coal. From an approximate 10,000,000 tons in 1800, the output of British mines rose to 44,000,000 tons in 1850 and to 154,000,000 in 1880. Coal was an essential factor in the nation's trade and, through the work of the British mercantile marine, in world trade, too. From less than half a million tons in 1831 the export trade rose to 1,500,000 tons in 1841 and to 8,000,000 tons in 1861. The economist Jevons in 1867 feared that there might be a fatal pressure of population on the supply of coal. The wave of population, he picturesquely put it, will break upon the furthest shore of our Black Indies and roll back upon itself.[1]

The extraction of coal was a blind struggle for undifferentiated quantity production. The advance of machinery was slow. Machinery was used only on the surface—for pumping, winding, and ventilation. The work of getting the coal was done with pick and shovel and gunpowder. Human muscle, male, and until 1842, female in some pits, was the prime mover except where an endless rope haulage operated by stationary engines could be used along the main roads. In 1816 Humphry Davy had provided the gauze-protected light, and in 1845 Faraday had hinted at the part played by dry coal dust in colliery explosions, but it was not until 1850 that the scientific basis of mine ventilation began to be understood. There were, of course, great qualitative differences in the kinds of coal used—steam coal and other varieties—but these were the work of nature and not of man. In the nineteenth century coal was a magnet to the industrial population. In some areas the economy was based upon the production of coal and the sale of coal outside, for example, South

Wales and the northeast. In others coal was the foundation of manufacturing industries—in west Yorkshire wool textiles, in south Yorkshire a steel industry. In the east Midlands coal was the basis of a large group of miscellaneous metal industries. In most of the coalfields iron ore was found close to the coal so that coal-producing areas became iron- and later steel-producing areas.

The principal characteristic of the industry was its diversity. It was an agriculture of the underworld. It has been likened to "a series of farms in a country of valleys and mountains, varying in their productivity from the flat lands by the rivers, through the medium farms on the lower slopes, up, through farms of gradually decreasing fertility, to the fields that are half rock at the limits of cultivation on the higher slopes." [2] There were geological differences: the depth of the coal seams from the surface and the thickness of the seams, the chemical composition of the coal, the presence of faults in the seams and their inclination. There were geographical differences: the proximity of a market or a port and the availability of water for the condensation plant. Every mine had a history, often as living for its workers as the history of a village or a town. Except in the northern coalfields extraction depended on small subcontractors who engaged to mine coal at an agreed price and employed their own labor.

From the seventeenth century onward Britain had been a pioneer in the smelting of iron ore. By what the French called le systeme anglais— the use of coke in place of charcoal for smelting ore and the puddling of liquid cast iron to change it into tough wrought iron—the British iron industry had quadrupled its output between 1800 and 1830 and its product was the cheapest in Europe. In Scotland between 1828 and 1831 J. B. Neilson found that raw coal could be used to smelt the local ores provided that the furnace blast was heated. A great Scottish iron industry rose after 1830 to rival that of South Wales and Staffordshire. In 1820 a ton of pig iron needed eight tons of coal to make it, by 1850 it could be produced, using the hot blast, by two tons. Neilson's invention made possible the use of anthracite and led to development of the United States iron industry. By these and other inventions the output of pig iron rose from 700,000 tons a year in 1830 to some 3,800,000 in 1859 and to over 6,500,000 in 1871. The invention of the steam hammer in 1842 improved the quality of wrought iron and freed foundries from using unsuitable waterside locations. The use of the hot blast reduced the fuel bill by a third. Production rose ninefold between 1830 and 1870 and prices fell from over £10 a ton in 1825 to £3 in 1866.

In 1850 steel was almost a semiprecious metal. It was used for cutlery, tools, jewelry, and small articles. The world's output was about 80,000 tons, of which Britain produced a half. Then, in 1856 the Bessemer method of blowing air through the liquid iron made possible cheap mass production of steel. By 1870 the output was eight times that of 1850 and the steel age had dawned. Steel in bulk was a material for an immense range of industrial purposes. It made possible the use of the most precise measurements in machine tools and the most subtle tailoring of the properties of the material used. The mind of man was coming to control the structure of the matter he used. In 1850 there was a wide range of machine tools, but they were small, slow, and inadequate in precision. The steam engine needed the skill to bore a fine cylinder, turn a true piston, and plane a valve face. In 1855 Whitworth produced a machine which could measure to one-millionth of an inch. In 1862 self-hardening tool steel permitted a 50 per cent increase in the speed of cutting tools. By 1870 engineering workshops could do many things in quantity which in 1850 could be done only slowly and with difficulty. The mind was making for itself hands of hitherto unbelievable power and precision. The low price of British coal was an important factor in the transition from the age of iron to the age of steel.

The iron masters at first gave a cool welcome to cheap steel. They were suspicious of science, and they thought, too, that the process of making basic steel was better adapted to the ores of the continent than to those of Britain. But by 1886 they had taken to the new sorcery. They spoke of fractional percentage of phosphorous and sulphur with respect. In 1879 the Bolckow Vaughan works at Middlesborough had placed themselves at the disposal of Gilchrist Thomas, who had solved the problem of phosphoric ores, and a new era in the metallurgical industries of Britain and the world had begun.

The new world of industry would not have been possible without a web of communications to sustain its diversities. In Britain, where water communication was easy and warlike frontiers almost unknown, Roman roads, in the sense of a straight and firm way between two places, were not wanted after the Romans left. Roads were to be made by the feet of freemen and the beasts they owned. The result was that British roads got steadily worse from the time of the Romans to 1700. Then, in the eighteenth century energetic persons secured from Parliament the creation of Turnpike Trusts which had the power to construct and maintain a specific piece of road and to levy tolls on certain kinds of traffic for its upkeep. By their work, in the words of a contemporary, "journeys of business are performed with much more than double expedition . . . Everything wears the face of dispatch." By 1815 the Trusts had made the best system of local communications in Europe. Their further development and that of Macadam, whose idea was that a road "ought to be considered an artificial flooring forming a strong, smooth surface at once capable of carrying great weights and over which carriages may pass without meeting any impediment," was postponed to the twentieth century by the coming of the railroad. On the main British turnpike roads, passengers, mail, and parcels moved at almost ten miles an hour.

The opening of the Liverpool-Manchester Railway in September 1830 wedded the locomotive to the railroad and made possible twenty miles an hour. Speed was born of the marriage of steam and iron. By 1850 the best trains were running at thirty-five to forty miles an hour, stopping at stations which were often "ornamental structures of costly character" and with refreshment rooms which, compared to the old coaching inns, were havens of warmth and light. Europe had sixty miles of operating railroad mileage in 1830 and 65,000 miles in 1870. By 1870 the world had built one-sixth, 130,000 miles, of the rails it was to possess. The development of railroads was self-stimulating. Cheap and speedy traffic created more traffic. Latent demands were uncovered. Farmers could meet the challenge of free trade. The iron, coal, and engineering industries were stimulated. The railroads killed the coaching industry, but they stimulated urban transport and the passenger and goods-carrying trade. They employed 65,000 male workers in 1851 and 174,000 in 1881. But this was only a fraction of the 750,000 who were engaged in all forms of conveyance, which was almost as many as those occupied in the building trades. It was British iron that made possible the world railway mileage of 200,000 in 1880. It had well-nigh girdled the earth in forty years.

British leadership in metallurgy and marine engineering was to secure her in the same period one-third of the world's shipping tonnage. The new era began with the launching of a new line of fast sailing clippers in 1837 on the Indian and Australian hauls. By 1850 nearly 60 per cent of the world's ocean-going tonnage was British. In 1851 composite ships consisting of planks on iron frames were laid down. In the 1840's the steamship had a poor record for safety. In 1856 less than 4 per cent of the passengers arriving in New York came there by steamship. But during the 1850's and the 1860's the steamship became safer, more efficient, and more economical. By 1870 the sailing ship had lost the cream of the North Atlantic traffic and was losing on all other routes except the Australian. The Suez Canal in 1869 opened the nearer Orient to steam but not to sail. Between 1865 and 1885 British steamship tonnage rose from 1,000,000 to 4,000,000; sailing tonnage fell from 5,000,000 to 3,500,000.

Because Britain had been the first to specialize in the development of new industrial processes—particularly in textiles and in iron—and because she had an abundant supply of coal, which an industrial age would need, it was in her interest to remove political barriers to the development of markets for her goods and to the supply of the raw materials which she needed. The new economic order of the machine would not cause a reduction of the population in England, as it did in Ireland. Agriculture would have to submit only to a relative and not to an absolute reduction in importance. In 1815 special interests were in possession of vested rights to which they clung. But it was found possible to dissolve them in a general affluence: the Corn Law of 1815, the differential duties in favor of West Indian proprietors, the monopoly of the East India Company, and the navigation laws protecting shipping—all were ended. There were also heavy duties on raw materials of industry and on foreign manufactures. But the principles of free trade were supported by the promise of peace and plenty which international specialization in the production of raw materials and the development of manufacturing industries would bring. In 1820 the London and Edinburgh merchants petitioned against "every restrictive regulation of trade not essential to revenue." Commerce it was held would be "a source of reciprocal amity between nations and an interchange of production to promote industry, the wealth and the happiness of mankind." By 1852 the work of Huskisson, Peel, and Gladstone had secured the triumph of the principles of free trade. The world did not follow.

In 1816 the British government undertook the suppression of the Barbary pirates and made the high seas safe for international trade. In 1821 it restored the prewar gold basis of international exchange believing that free gold and trade expansion went hand in hand. In 1822 the new republics in Central and South America were allowed to export to Britain in their own ships, and countries in Europe were allowed a share in British colonial trade in return for reciprocal concessions. In the 1830's it had become obvious that the existing system of customs and excise was archaic and irrational, incapable of meeting either the needs of the revenue or of trade. In 1841 Sir Robert Peel reduced or swept away the duties payable on 750 articles. He lowered the cost of living without exposing home industries to undue competition. An income tax of 7d in the £ on incomes over £150 replaced the indirect taxes which had been abolished. In 1845 he was convinced that the same principles should be applied to wheat as to other articles of trade. There was to be "total and absolute repeal for ever of all duties on all articles of subsistence." In 1849 the repeal of the Navigation Laws opened the carrying trade as well as the import of grain to all nations. Gladstone completed the work of Peel. His principle was to tax for revenue only with no attempt at incidental protection; to make no difference between colonial and other imports; to avoid taxation on food and to concentrate on a few articles such as tea, tobacco, and alcohol, once luxuries but now conventional necessities. He saw the income tax as a temporary expedient to bridge the gap between a fall of revenue from tax remission and the increase of revenue from rising consumption. He would "let the nation's wealth fructify in the pockets of the people." Bliss was it in that dawn to be alive and to be rich was very heaven. By 1870 there were only seventeen dutiable imports. Five of them (sugar, tea, wine, spirits, and tobacco) contributed nine-tenths of the customs revenue. The income tax was a source of revenue to replace the duties.

William Huskisson, Peel, and Gladstone had set the people free. But the economic loom of the world does not operate in a legal or a political vacuum. In the high and palmy days of the *Pax Britannica,* and the international free trade of the Cobden era, there were many problems in the economic life of Britain both internal and external which were portents of the difficulties of the present age. The physical basis of British foreign trade was slender. It was very much a cotton problem. Of the £36,000,-000 of exports in 1820, cotton goods were £16,500,000 or 47 per cent, woolens and linens 20 per cent, metals and glass 10 per cent. When in 1830 total exports had crept up to £38,300,000 the proportion of cotton goods had risen to over half. The cotton industry had the double advantage of the revolutionary innovations in the manufacturing process at home and in the production of the raw material abroad. The large markets abroad made possible economies of scale which the home market alone could not have supported. The U.S.A. and Latin America were the areas most involved. After 1830 a third area, Australia, was brought in because the demands of the woolen industry were beyond the capacity of Spain and Germany to supply. Merchants complained of the partial closure of European markets to British goods. Germany was the best British market in Europe, but the formation of the Zollverein threatened to replace the inefficient fiscal system of the old and numerous German states with a solid wall of tariffs. The Board of Trade was of the opinion that the only way of securing German tariff concessions was to repeal the Corn Laws and to admit German grain. The relatively unprotected markets of the East were more open to British textiles. British exports to the East—mainly of cheap calicoes—rose from less than a million yards in 1814 to over 57,000,000 yards in 1832. In 1833 the China trade which had been a monopoly of the East India Company was thrown open. In the years from 1816–20 to 1838–42 the increase of British exports was in south Europe, Africa, Asia, and Central and South America. These were new regions for marketing. The established markets of north Europe, U.S.A., and British North America were taking slightly less at the end of the period than at the beginning.

After the repeal of the Corn Laws, 1846, British overseas trade was stimulated by the boom in railway and iron steamship building and by constantly improving means of transport and communications. In 1830 a message from London to Calcutta took from five to eight months; by 1850 using the overland route via Alexandria and Suez, a month; by 1870, using the direct cable to Bombay, a few minutes. In 1867 the Atlantic cable made possible a market in futures. The discovery of gold in California, 1849, and Australia, 1851, meant that the era of free trade was unimpeded by the exchange difficulties which had often hampered the British economy in earlier decades. There was a world demand for the railway iron and the engineering and metal goods, made by British skill, to equip the new industrial economies of Europe and North America. There was an increased export, too, of fully manufactured goods. But the proportion of cotton and wool to the total fell—from 58 per cent (in value) in 1842 to 42 per cent in 1873—while the proportion of iron, coal, and machinery rose from 11 to 24 per cent. There was also a favorable turn in the terms of trade. Exports bought a relatively larger quantity of imports, and a growing proportion consisted of food, especially bacon, eggs, butter, and cheese.

This rise in the value of exports was one cause of the boastful optimism of the 1850's and the 1860's. Of the international position at the end of 1851 the *Times* said: "Insulated in position, with a mixed political constitution, the asylum for refugees from all nations, showing her flag on every sea, and thrusting her manufactures into every market, unable to sympathise entirely with either monarchs against people or peoples against monarchs, she commands the respect, the fear, and even the admiration of mankind, but not their love or free co-operation" [3]—not knowing, one may say with the Eastern sage, in anywise the mind of Allah, not knowing her own heart or what it would some day suffer. For command what she might, she could not command the roots of her own prosperity to grow and forever nourish her. These roots were subtle and complex, and they have not even now been untangled by scholars. British imports always exceeded her exports. The invisible earnings of her merchant marine, her commercial and banking houses, and the return on her overseas investments redressed the balance and gave her a surplus. In the mid-nineteenth century there was an average annual deficit of £27,500,000 in merchandise trade. But they were more than offset by "invisible" exports, of which one estimate puts the shipping earnings (1851–55) at £18,700,000, foreign investments at £11,700,000, and trading and other services abroad at £11,900,000. Over half the retained imports (by value) consisted of raw materials and 39 per cent of food stuffs. More than half of the imported raw materials were for the textile industries, and, of the imported food, over a third was grain and flour and nearly a quarter sugar and other tropical products.

Investments abroad rose from £10,000,000 in 1815 to nearly £100,-000,000 in 1825 and £700,000,000 in 1870. By 1875 foreign investment had reached a total of not less than £1,000,000,000, and British shipping was earning £50,000,000 by services all over the world. Until the early 1850's most of these investments had been in Europe, for example, railway finance had been a strong link between London and Louis Napoleon. After 1857 the main flow was to India (the building of her railroads 1856–69), Australia, and Canada. Britain was investing in the underdeveloped countries of the world. The investments went into railroads and harbor installations. A very large proportion was spent on materials of British manufacture, the cost of freight in British ships, and the salaries of British engineers and managers. Vast new territories for white settlement were opened up and the Indian continent was unified. Returns on British capital rose from £12,000,000 per annum in the early 1850's to over £50,000,000 in the early 1870's. This was a useful reinforcement of the British balance of payments. It should be remembered that until the financial crises in Turkey and Egypt in the 1880's the British government did not think it right or expedient to intervene officially with other governments on behalf of their bondholders. Lord Palmerston might threaten to use the big stick of the British fleet to protect the person or the property of a British citizen, but it was not to be used to collect the interest on investments.

It has been estimated that of the £2,400,000,000 added to the capital of the United Kingdom between 1865 and 1875 nearly a quarter was placed abroad, a sixth in houses and other buildings, and a tenth in railways at home. That generation did not secure its expanding income through lack of thought for those who should come after. It saved abundantly and invested prudently. It developed foreign markets and was ready to supply them with the kind of goods they could most plentifully absorb. It concentrated on providing the development of those business services which the whole trading world required. The question now is whether what was done in the spirit of the times and with the skills to hand could and should have been done differently. The outlines of a world economic order were drawn by the finger of profit-seeking capital. Could an early welfare state have eliminated the poverty of the poor at home? The question may never get a satisfactory answer. Indeed, it is possible that it is no proper question at all. It involves intellectual and institutional anachronisms of the wildest kind. But it does prompt us to consider what were some of the problems, recognized at the time, of the relation between political power and economic life.

In the early nineteenth century the obvious vitality and the seeming harmony of the economic order were to many a comforting demonstration of the power of reason in society. The swift development of industry was providing a society which seemed to flourish without the aid of government. The market which the economists had analyzed was creating indirectly the peace and plenty which philosophers had failed to plan. Of course, no economic thinker of repute really believed in a laissez faire which denied the need for the use of political skills. But industrial progress seemed to be producing a form of society in which governments would have less to do. On the vital question what should be the functions of government the economists were tantalizingly obscure. An economic order implies a social order. Some form of private property, the enforcement of contracts, and the suppression of violence were necessary if the subtle adjustments of human interests that the mechanism of price provides were to be enjoyed. If the legal forms which the market of the economists requires could be provided, then the competition of several million wits sharpened by self-interest might give a daring and insight to the planning of the economic order that no bureaucracy can achieve. But as we have seen the new industrial order had to make its way through a tangle of controls inherited from a feudal and mercantile past. The old legal order had to be pruned so that the new economic shoots might grow. The free trade movement cut back the old fiscal system and the privileges of the agrarian world. But at the same time political leaders were forced to consider what new legal forms were needed to channel the new powers latent in the application of the new science to age-old methods of production.

The new loom of industry had to be matched by a fresh and subtle web of law. One of the most important and subtle of the latter's strands was connected with the currency. Whatever the merits of the theoretical discussion, force of circumstances decided that there must be a central bank, with a clear responsibility to safeguard the public interest in a pure and stable currency. "Free trade in banking is synonymous with free trade in swindling . . . it was a matter for regulation by the State and came within the province of police." The Bank Act, 1844, gave to the Bank of England the ultimate monopoly of the note issue. It became the controlling element in the country's credit structure. It had an obligation to the public interest in its policies, and it was not at liberty to act merely for the benefit of its shareholders. The government supported it in times of stress such as the crises of 1847, 1857, and 1866.

In 1844 William E. Gladstone was the chairman of a committee on companies. Its problems went to the very heart of economic liberalism. What were the legal instruments which would make possible the co-operation of every man in his own interest for the good of all? How were the savings of the people to be converted into instruments of production? In 1844 the law was so obscure that it was said that a man had either to be a knave or a fool to venture his money in partnership with a stranger. As H. J. Habakkuk has said: "The story is a classic case of the conflict between legal logic and economic needs." [4] In the United States, from an early period, it was easy for a company to get the legal status of a corporation. It was a legal entity, separate from the individuals who composed it, with powers to sue and be sued and with limited liability for its shareholders. In England, before the nineteenth century, to become a corporation a company had to obtain a royal charter or an act of Parliament. Without these, in the eyes of the common law, companies were simply partnerships; mere collections of individuals, every one of whom had an unlimited liability for the debts of the company in which he was joined. Up to 1854 the balance of British legal and official opinion was against the general introduction of limited liability. Organized commerce was mainly against it. But Lord Palmerston and George Bramwell (who suggested that the word Limited should be obligatory after the company's name) secured the acts of 1855 and 1856, the crucial step for Britain in the evolution of the modern joint stock company.

While company law had to lay down how men could co-operate in the use of their capital, trade union law was concerned with the marketing of labor. In 1800 the Combination Acts had been passed because it was feared that unions of workmen under cover of trade activities might engage in revolutionary propaganda. When the fear of revolutionary activity had died down, it was seen that to allow combinations of workers for the purpose of bargaining about wages would facilitate the organization of industry and trade. In 1824 and 1825 the Combination Acts were repealed. But while this removed a statutory prohibition against combinations, it left the unions liable to prosecution under common law if they were in restraint of trade. The courts developed a doctrine that it was an obstruction of an employer to persuade a worker to leave his service unless he were paid a certain scale of wages. In 1871 the Trade Union Act laid down that the purposes of any trade union should not, by reason merely that they are in restraint of trade, render any member of such trade union liable to criminal prosecution for conspiracy. This was not the end of the story of the work of the state in the regulation of the market for labor. Vital as the problems of the trade unions were, and were to be, they touched only the fringe of the nineteenth-century problem of population and poverty.

There is a vital flaw in any attempt to find a natural harmony in the economic order. The more subtle and complex the development of industry, the less is it probable that the value of any particular worker in a free market will be equal to the cost to him of buying the goods and services which to be a citizen he needs. There would, indeed, be a divinity that shapes our ends if the price at which it was profitable to employ the lowest-paid worker would keep him and his family in a condition in which he and they would be no burden to others. Factors other than labor which enter into the pricing process of a freely working economy can be scrapped, sold at a loss, or transformed into something that will pay should they in their existing form and quantity not be worth using. But there can be no profitable junk heap for old hands as there is for old automobiles. If the example seems a violent one it may serve to bring out the great difficulty and almost terror of the problem of population and poverty in the period of mid-nineteenth-century affluence.

Between 1801 and 1881 the population of Britain rose from 10,500,-000 to 29,710,000. Though many families led lives, poor, nasty, brutish, and short, and without the blessing of solitude, conditions were such that their numbers could increase. The economic system was able to provide food and shelter for a population which doubled between 1801 and 1851 and at the same time to find employment for a stream of Irish immigration and to equip the majority of them with a fund of £15 per head beside their passage money to the New World. Our sources of information about the changes in population are not very good before 1837, when a public registry of births was established. Recent research has suggested that a fall in the death rate became really important from about 1820 and not from 1780 as had previously been thought. It was in the industrial districts that the increase of population was especially rapid. Cotton clothes, cheap soap, pottery, iron ware, houses of brick and tiles, piped water, and paving all helped to prevent the scourge of epidemics which might have been expected. But the death rate may have risen in some large towns between 1820 and 1840, although for the country as a whole it fell. Not until 1829 was the pumping of water by steam engine from rivers to reservoirs, where it could be filtered before delivery to pipes in streets and courts, begun by a young engineer, Thomas Hawkesley, in Nottingham. The rapid increase of population and its greater mobility meant that labor was always plentiful. There is overwhelming evidence of economic waste and of personal misery in the conditions of the lower rank of laborers. For one thing, a large part of the child population was in a state of dirt, ignorance, and savagery with no order or discipline save what was imposed by the need to come to terms with brute violence among family and neighbors. Waves of utter destitution would overwhelm the poor as a result of periodical unemployment. Factory production benefited more and more people. The fall in the price of textiles reduced the price of clothing. Boots took the place of clogs, hats of shawls. Tea, coffee, and sugar became common necessities. But there were always masses of unskilled or poorly skilled workers whose incomes were wholly absorbed in paying for the necessities of life. There was always the basic problem of reconciling the cost of building and maintaining housing accommodation with the wage level of those who were in need of it.

CHAPTER IX

Wellington to Gladstone

The British could not have survived in the struggle with Napoleon had they not been sustained by the changes in economic power, which contemporaries could only imperfectly understand, and by a competence in administration, the relation of which to the complex structure of the constitution was even more dimly grasped. The age of reason was becoming an age of improvements, but the transition involved contrasts bewildering in their fantasy. The mad King of 1811 was succeeded by the Regent, who was a false and selfish debauchee, gross and palpable in his absurdity, without, said Leigh Hunt, "a single claim on the gratitude of his country or the respect of posterity" and yet "he made the greatest contribution ever made by an English monarch to the enduring beauty of his country"—in London Regent's Park, the Nash terraces, Regent Street, and the splendid sweep of Carlton House Terrace, and, in addition, the Pavilion at Brighton, the Royal Lodge at Windsor, and the restoration on a grand scale of Windsor Castle.[1] His government was the sober administration of Lord Liverpool from 1812–27, which attracted to itself most of the conflicting groups which had struggled against each other in the previous decade. George Canning joined in 1816 as president of the India Board and became foreign secretary after the suicide of Castlereagh in 1822; Wellington joined in 1818. It attracted bright young men with a future, like Palmerston, Peel, and Huskisson.[2] Liverpool "was representative of his age in a way that few statesmen have been, for he reflected both its prejudices and its enlightenment in exact proportions ... He seems, at one moment, to be looking back to the eighteenth century, at another to have set his face towards the prosperous commercial world of the high nineteenth century." [3]

The governments from 1807 till 1830 were Tory. Fear of the French Revolution had made them hostile to all large changes and produced a scepticism as to the good to be derived from any change.[4] "Either they would defend anomalies as the fruit of the unconscious wisdom of the past, or they would take it for granted that the wit of man was incapable of patching and repairing the old constitution without destroying it altogether." [5] They were against parliamentary reform because it would disturb the balance of the constitution; for the same reason they were against Catholic emancipation. They considered that the government was the king's government. As late as 1832 Wellington was saying that he could not refuse office if he were pressed by the king to undertake it even though the policy to be pursued was repugnant to his own convictions.

With the passing of George III into final madness in 1811 and death in 1820, the governments were ceasing to be the king's governments for reasons wider and deeper even than the vulgar absurdities of the Regent (after 1820 George IV) and his royal brothers. A system of government associated with the memory of Pitt was developing an administrative competence and a familiarity with new economic ideas which enabled it to take the strain of the postwar economic dislocations, with their accompanying riots by hungry and angry men, and the inflammatory appeal of radical orators and journalists, who were familiarizing the people with Tom Paine's democratic and religious views. The government came to believe in the period 1817–20 that there was a widespread conspiracy with a central committee of revolutionaries in London. They were perhaps misled by the evidence available to them from justices of the peace, from other local officials, and from spies. In a social order under strain from new and little understood forces of economic change and without any serious police force (the Metropolitan Police date from 1829), the fear of the mob was very real. But the leaders of the Radical party were persons of such varying aims and ideas that it is impossible to suppose that they could ever enter into such a conspiracy. William Cobbett, who distrusted radical clubs and hated commerce and commercial men, had little in common with radicals of the type of Bentham, Mill, and Ricardo. None of these radicals had much in common with the physical force party represented by Arthur Thistlewood, who engineered the Cato Street conspiracy in 1820 to murder the whole cabinet.[6] The fear that "seditious leaders" might rouse a deluded people to take arms against a sea of troubles was bound up with traditional conceptions of political authority. Local family power as well as the power of central government was challenged by the new demagogic politicians.[7]

The basic error of the Tory government of Liverpool at the end of the war was the belief that it was the true end and object of all statesmanship to secure the stability of the state and not to provide for its growth. It was Peel who was to discover that in a changing world the true con-

Europe after the Congress of Vienna

NORWAY

Trondhjem

Bergen

Christiania

AND

Scotland

NORTH

Edinburgh

DENMARK

Copenhagen

SEA

Jutland

Schleswig

Holstein

MECK LENBU

Ireland

Dublin

GREAT BRITAIN

Hamburg

Bremen

HA

NOVER

Berli

Wales

England

Amsterdam

The Hague

N. ETHERLAND

U

London

P. Cologne

R

GER

Brussels

Aix la Chapelle

LUX EMBURG

HESSE

S O

Paris

Rhine

BADEN

WÜRTEM BERG

CONFED

BAVARIA

FRANCE

Basen

Zurich

SWISS

Munic

Bern

CONFEDERATION

Tyrol

Ca

Bordeaux

Lyons

Turin

Milan

Lombardo-Vene

SARD

Genoa

Toulouse

Marseilles

Nice

Parma

STATES

Ve

MONACO

TUSCANY

Oporto

PORTUGAL

Corsica

Florence

Elba

Lisbon

SPAIN

Barcelona

Rome

Madrid

Olivença

Balearic Is.

Sardinia

INIA

Seville

Tangier

Gibraltar

MEDITER

R

Melilla

Algiers

TUNIS

MOROCCO

ALGERIA

SWEDEN

Finland

Nizhni Novgorod

St. Petersburg

Stockholm

BALTIC SEA

Riga

R U S S I A

Moscow

Königsberg

S I A

Posen

Warsaw

POLAND

Don

Breslau

NIC

gue

Bohemia

ATION

Moravia

stria

Galicia

Ukraine

Dnieper

DON COSSACKS

Vienna

BudaPest

Bessarabia

Moldavia

hia

AUSTRIA

HUNGARY

Crimea

Transylvania

Danube

Slavonia

Croatia

Wallachia

BLACK SEA

Belgrade

Bucharest

Servia

Dalmatia

OTTOMAN

Sofia

Adrianople

Roumelia

Constantinople

RIATIC SEA

Albania

THE

Naples

TWO SICILIES

EMPIRE

Salonica

Ionian Is.

Athens

Morea

NEAN

Crete

SEA

Cyprus

Malta

servative must change the institutions of the state as the only sure and certain hope of their preservation. Even before 1830 the infra-structure was changing. The legislature had as a result of war conditions become used to giving increased power to the executive. Pitt by his abolition of sinecures and by impartial distribution of government contracts had severely limited the whole flow of Crown influence. In 1822 it was even a question if the influence which the Crown could exercise were further reduced, whether it would be possible for a cabinet to conduct the government of the country. Liverpool had in fact neither an efficient patronage system nor a disciplined party machine. A government could not be sure to get its way in the Commons even on a major matter of policy —in 1816 the Commons threw out the income tax which both the prime minister and the chancellor of the Exchequer thought essential to fiscal stability. The pressure of individual members of the House of Commons for the appointment of committees to investigate questions in which they were interested and the vigorous agitation of orators and journalists did not provide a competent opposition well rooted in the constituencies and able to provide an alternative government when the one in power blundered. The Whigs were rich in talent, but their influence as a party was small because they were divided and because their record during the war with Napoleon had been poor.

There is a change in the political climate after the death of Viscount Castlereagh in 1822. "He had been an able war minister and an able foreign minister. He had brought to a victorious conclusion the war against Napoleon, he had made a just peace, and he had refused to commit England to the policy of the Holy Alliance." [8] But he was identified with all the stern measures which had been taken to repress the disturbances of 1817–20. He had introduced few measures of domestic reform, and he allowed no one else to do so.[9] The government which was reformed after his death passed under the control of men like Canning, Peel, and Huskisson. They were well aware of the need for large reforms in the law and administration of the country. They were in touch both with the new economic ideas and the new industries and commerce which were to shape the century. With the co-operation of Prime Minister Lord Liverpool they were to carry out moderate measures of reform—Peel humanized the criminal law by abolishing the death penalty in nearly three hundred cases and established the Metropolitan Police; in the sphere of commerce and industry Huskisson revised and modified the Navigation Acts, modified the customs tariff in the direction of freer trade, and repealed the combination laws. Huskisson and Canning were preparing to modify the Corn Laws, when in 1827 the ministry was dissolved by the stroke which incapacitated Lord Liverpool.[10]

George IV as Elector of Hanover had the right to conduct personally his electoral foreign policy. He disapproved of Canning's liberal policy. But he was forced to recognize the new South American republics and came to admire Canning's wit and brilliance. When Liverpool collapsed Wellington hoped that he would be selected as his successor. When George IV selected Canning, Wellington, Eldon, Peel, and three others resigned. Many of the Tories regarded Canning as a mere adventurer. Wellington disliked both his foreign and his domestic policy. Peel would not serve under him because he was in favor of Catholic emancipation. The result was that Canning made a coalition with the Whigs. Had he not died almost at once a permanent alliance between Whigs and left-wing Tories might have been effected. As it was Lord Goderich, a "transient and embarrassed phantom," formed a government which fell to pieces before it met Parliament, and Wellington formed a ministry in 1828. The Duke was not a good prime minister. He could never understand that policy was a matter of opinion as well as authority. It was said, too, that he had a "social contempt for his intellectual equals, and an intellectual contempt for his social equals." [11] The Canningites soon resigned, and Wellington was left at the head of a solidly Tory cabinet. He decided that Catholic emancipation was necessary to preserve law and order in Ireland. O'Connell had organized a Catholic party which was prepared to take the offensive against the Protestant landlords in Ireland. Civil war was the only alternative to concession. George IV, like his father, was adamant against emancipation of the Catholics. Unlike his father he could not go off his head. But he put up a fine performance. "Threats to retire to Hanover, tears, and even kisses, were all tried to shake the ministers' attachment to the Bill, but all in vain, and the King boldly dismissed them from office." [12] But he found that he would be left without an administration and decided to yield his opinion to "that which is considered by the Cabinet to be for the immediate interest of the country." "After much whimpering, many protestations, and constant invocations of the Almighty's name, he gave his consent to the Bill." [13] In this way an alien element was introduced into the Parliament of the United Kingdom. The Irish party was to bedevil the work of government for a century.

The death of George IV in 1830 and the accession of William IV opened the way to the Reform Act of 1832. The death of a king at that time necessitated a general election, and in the new Parliament radicals pointed to the bloodless July Revolution in France which led to the over-throw of the Bourbons. Lord Grey proposed a reform of Parliament, a gradual reform without danger to the institutions of the country. Welling-ton replied that he "was fully convinced that the country possessed at the present moment a Legislature which answered all the good purposes of legislation, and this to a greater degree than any Legislature ever had an-swered in any country whatever." What he really meant was that it was a link of influence which enabled the executive and the legislature to work together. Where he was wrong was in supposing that the country could continue to tolerate a system which not only had so many absurd anoma-lies but was unable to respond with enough elasticity to the new inter-ests and the new ideas of a changing society.

The Reform Act of 1832 is an excellent example of the British skill of muddling through. An aristocracy muddled through to a democracy, taking many of the aristocratic virtues with them; and they muddled through from an age of privilege to an age of numbers. The democratic implications of the act were not in fact revealed for more than a genera-tion, and when in 1867 the Niagara of democratic rapids was shot there were institutions and conventions which would prevent the ship of state from being swamped.

During the eighteenth century the dynasty had ceased to be an issue. The Hanoverians had been accepted, dull though they might be, and if they had helped to lose America they had preserved the liberties of Eng-lishmen. The British had not become a province of any enlightened Eu-ropean despotism. But the insoluble contradiction between a political sys-tem which associated a royal executive with a parliamentary struggle for office was becoming clear. In theory King, Lords, and Commons shared political power, and freedom was in danger if one of them achieved su-premacy in the state. The government was the king's government. Pitt had repeatedly declared that he would not be forced upon the king by Parliament nor come into his service without his constant. George III in 1784 and 1807 had been able to get powerful public opinion on his side by claiming that the dominant parliamentary gangs were aggressors against the balanced constitution of which he was the upholder. The writ-ers of the *Federalist* had seen the king as the absolute master of his own conduct in the exercise of his office. The American president had been conceived as an elected king with the essentials of executive power re-strained by the right and proper elected legislative organ. But the British people could not plunge into a new order of a written constitution with-out abandoning the aristocratic niceties by which they lived. Nor by 1832 could they continue to rely on the system of representation which they had inherited.

It had been essential in the eighteenth century that there should be co-operation between Crown and Parliament, a co-operation secured through the following which the Crown had in the Commons. The Crown had never been in the position to pack the House of Commons with its supporters. It had been able to secure two or three dozen seats so that the necessary men of business could be elected. To get a majority it had had to make arrangements for private persons to use their patronage in the interest of the Crown. Nobody, whether king or political leader, could win an election in the open constituencies because there were not enough of them. A government which had the support of the king needed also the support of other members, and that could only be secured by the offer of advantages only a government controls. Of the 245 English constituencies in 1780, the greater number was beyond government intervention. Of the 485 borough seats about 240 were controlled by patronage. It has been estimated that 52 peers had a decisive control of influence in the election of 113 seats and 67 commoners a similar power over 108. In all, 119 patrons disposed of 221 seats. The 40 English county constituencies were a political seismograph. They registered the underlying political convulsions. No county was under the absolute dominance of a single patron though in about ten of them one or two leading families had an admitted primacy. Next in importance came the large boroughs which had over 1000 voters. In 1780 there were about 20 boroughs with over 1000 voters, ranging from Westminster with an electorate of 10,000 to Lincoln, Hull, and Leicester with about 1100. The heads of many families sat in the House of Lords and their younger brothers and dependents in the Commons, which was sometimes called "a parcel of younger brothers." The link of influence was the principal method of securing harmony between the executive, the Commons, and the Lords.

By 1832—and even earlier—changes in the distribution of population, in the value of money, and in the economic interests of the governing families had thrown this subtle machinery out of gear. It was obvious that continuity with the past would, in a nascent industrial society, merely provoke a revolution. At the very least it would be necessary to correct defects in the representative system occasioned by time and to restore the confidence of the people, which it no longer enjoyed. It could no longer register in a general election the vital changes in popular opinion or the pressure of particular interests. The Act of 1832 was not a democratic measure. In the crucial debates of 1830–32, it was agreed by both Whigs and Tories that democracy was an unpalatable and dangerous form of government, that a "stake in the country" was an essential qualification in those who claimed political power, and that landed property had a special part to play in guaranteeing the stability of the political order. But it was essential to satisfy all reasonable demands and to remove all rational ground for complaint from the minds of the intelligent and independent portion of the community. In particular, it was desirable to secure that the respectable elements of the new centers of population should be given political weight. The national electorate was to be enlarged by the new elements which were connected with property, had a valuable stake in the country, and a deep interest in its institutions. It was to be a question of balance and proportion. The influence of land and of numbers was to be so balanced in the election of the House of Commons that collision with the Crown and the House of Lords would be avoided. The privileged wealthy of the past admitted the new unprivileged wealth, created by the economic changes of a hundred years, to the closed circle of the ruling class. Property of certain kinds was to be accepted as a certificate of probity and good behavior. The purpose of the act was to win over the prosperous middle classes to the side of the governing order and so inoculate the constitution against the dangerous disease of government by the people.

The Reform Act of 1832 was a complicated compromise framed to meet a pressing need. It was opposed by Peel without hope, and its passage was assisted by Melbourne without desire. Any summary must be imperfect—as well map a landscape in a fog. Included in its highly legalistic provisions was a mass of vastly different franchises, including the perpetuation of many old franchises. The edges of the pattern created were different in different parts of the country. But it can be said that it managed to attach to the working constitution the bulk of the property, education, and intelligence of the nation—the manifest education and intelligence, but not, of course, the latent.

The Whig supporters of the bill said that it represented, with rough accuracy, the most that could be pushed through Parliament and the least that would satisfy the country. It was a practical remedy for four specific grievances: the nomination of members of Parliament by private individuals, the election of members by closed corporations, the expense of elections, the inadequate representation of the large towns. The first grievance was met by the abolition of all boroughs with an electorate too small to preserve their independence and too isolated to be easily enlarged, the second by the £10 household franchise, the third by providing for the registration of voters and a reduction in the duration of elections, the fourth by giving seats to the industrial towns of the north and the Midlands: Manchester, Birmingham, Leeds, and Sheffield. The opponents of the bill argued that by suppressing the small borough it was confiscating private property and corporate and customary rights, that the new experimental system of representation was as full of anomalies as the old and could not be permanent, that influence would pass from the landed to the industrial areas of the country, from the sound slow thought of the countryman to "active pushing and intelligent people," that the king's government could not be carried on because the executive would not have the patronage it needed, and that it was a thin end of the wedge—the noble hierarchy of Kings, Lords, and Commons would soon be level with the plane of petty shopkeepers and small farmers.[14] Peel said in debate: "I was unwilling to open a door which I saw no prospect of being able to shut." And Mr. Brooke of George Eliot's *Middlemarch* said of the Reform Act that it was "a sort of A. B. C. you know, that must come first before the rest can follow."

The dusty details we need only roughly sketch. They were to be the source of ample incomes to the legal profession for more than a generation. For as Frederic Maitland has said, the right to vote in Victorian England was inextricably bound up with the ownership of property. The unreformed House of Commons had 658 seats: 188 county seats, 465 for the boroughs, representing 114 county and 262 borough constituencies, and 5 university seats for Oxford, Cambridge, and Dublin. The reformed Parliament had the same number of seats, but in England fifty-six of the smaller boroughs were totally disfranchised and some others had their representation reduced. Twenty-two new boroughs were created with two members each and twenty with one member. The representation of some counties was increased. Altogether in England 126 new seats were created. In Wales one new district, Swansea, was created, and separate representation was given to Merthyr Tydfill. In Scotland eight new seats were given to the burghs, and in Ireland four large towns and Dublin University received an additional member. Broadly, one can say that the boroughs gained at the expense of the counties. The latter had 253 seats with 464,000 electors, while the former had 405 seats with only 349,000 electors. But in practice many of the small boroughs were essentially agricultural and were to return representatives of the landowning class. But the number of county seats had been increased from 188 to 253 and the number of borough seats reduced from 465 to 405. This meant that direct territorial interest had been fortified at the expense of the pre-reform system of the influence of patrons or the control by close corporations. It was of some importance for the future that Wales, Scotland, and Ireland had increased their representation at the expense of England. Before 1832 Wales had 24 members, Scotland 45, Ireland 100, and England 489. After 1832 Wales had 29, Scotland 53, Ireland 105, and England 471. It was possible for these peripheries with the assistance of an English minority group to dominate Parliament. In spite of the redistribution of seats the domination of the south of England over the north continued. A quarter of the population of England in the south had a third of the representation, while a quarter in the north had only an eighth.

The unreformed franchise had been less than 500,000. The electorate immediately after 1832 was 813,000. This was about one-thirtieth of the population. It was 1 in 7 of adult males—in England 1 in 7, Scotland 1 in 8, and Ireland 1 in 20. The new qualification which was most important —that of the £ 10 householder—was a most ambiguous category. It was an index neither of a class nor of a standard of living. In a few boroughs where rents were high it brought in the majority of householders. In some it excluded entirely the manual worker; in many it took in the skilled, while rejecting the unskilled laborer. In the long run the important thing was that the right to vote was not now based on mere prescription, but on the rent of a house. The rise in wages and in rents which followed in the 1840's was to enfranchise many new voters. The Act of 1832 added some 200,000 to an existing 500,000 and in the next generation changes in the value of money were to add some 600,000 more.

The indirect consequences of the Reform Act of 1832 surpassed, as J. S. Mill was to write, every calculation. It brought home to the existing generation "a practical consciousness of living in a world of change." It gave the first great shock to old habits. "It meant that the constitution would not be treated as something fixed for ever, but as a set of institutions which could be changed as public opinion changed."

The Reform Act had created a new political climate to which political institutions would have to be adapted. For more than thirty years it was to condition the prerogatives of the Crown, the conventions of Cabinet government, the development of parties, and the relation between the opinions and interests, which are the mind and body of social life, and the political institutions which must serve and guide them. Only the bare surface of the teeming and often burning issues can be touched on here.

The effect of the extended franchise was to make it impossible for the King or Queen to secure a House of Commons amenable to the ministers of his or her choice. This was not immediately understood. Both William IV and the young Queen Victoria were inclined to think that the electorate would support a government which the Crown had chosen. The danger was that had the Crown become associated with a particular party it might have been crushed between an increasing electorate and an intensified party struggle.[15] The solution was for the Crown to recognize that the choice of ministers must be determined by the result of a general election. This also implied that organized opposition to the government in power was not only constitutional, but politically respectable, because such an opposition was a latent alternative government, ready to take over when the government in office should resign, either with or without a general election, as circumstances might make convenient. So long as a group of ministers could be found acceptable to the existing House of Commons a general election was not necessary until the legal term of the House had expired. It was not until the present century that it became crystal clear that it was for the government in office to determine whether an appeal to the electorate was necessary to clarify the distribution of political parties in the House.

The relation between the House of Commons and the electorate was uncertain before 1867 because the development of parties after 1832 was for over thirty years tentative and confused. When parties became vitally important after 1867 they tended to provide themselves with mythical pedigrees. The Whigs liked to find their ancestry in the Roundheads and the Exclusionists of Charles II times. The Tory party looked back to Clarendon. The Labour party showed a romantic affection for the Diggers and the Levellers of Cromwell's day. The reality is much more complex. The constantly changing class structure of English society has been reflected in the development of the parties. As new problems have come to the front in politics new parties have sprung up to grapple with them and new principles and new men have sheltered behind old names.[16]

After 1832 the complex of interests and divisions in the traditional governing class was modified by the problems created by the early stages of the industrial revolution and the need to come to terms with the enlarged electorate. But the electorate after 1832 was not large enough to provide the basis for an effective Radical party. It seemed to the young J. S. Mill in 1832 that there was "nothing definite and determinate in politics except Radicalism." There had always been a radical tradition in English politics. In the eighteenth century radicalism had been nourished by the rationalism which believed that the time had come for man's reason to be master of his passions. The tree of liberty was to be replaced by a machinery of justice. The economic order which had been uncovered by the work of Adam Smith was to be given a rational political dress. In the war against France, before Napoleon's imperial thrust had given

Britain a unity in self-defense, there had been a division between those members of the ruling classes who feared his working model of a more egalitarian order and those who thought that at least some of the rights of man might be secured for British agricultural laborers and mechanics. Eighteenth-century governments had every reason to fear the savagery of urban mobs, whipped to frenzy by reckless pamphleteers and mob orators, before competent police forces were devised. Law and order were not then in the power of effortlessly superior and rational Houyhnhnms, because the Yahoos had reason, emotion, and plenty of physical strength. There was also opposition from an upper and middle class which ramified through the whole vigorous eighteenth-century society. There was the opposition of men of business to the extravagance and insolence of aristocracy. There was the long suspicion of government, nominally Anglican, felt by the Nonconformists. And, finally, there had been the critical analysis by the Benthamites of the limitations of a traditional and privileged order which to an unprivileged eye was only a gilded muddle.

That the institutions which had been the slow birth of time should be tested by the measure of their utility for a new industrial society was the demand of the philosophical Radicals. The airy nothings of the rights of man could, they thought, be given a local habitation, and a clear and measurable content, in the lives of ordinary men and women. Through their influence slavery was abolished throughout the British Empire in 1833, the Poor Law was reformed in 1834, and the first grants given to public education. But with the limited franchise of 1832 they were unable to establish a third political party in the House of Commons. Independent landowners were still after 1832 the largest single group in the House of Commons, followed at a long interval by lawyers, merchants, manufacturers, and holders of naval and military commissions. There was a general agreement that no man could pursue a political career with integrity unless he had a competence of his own. Macaulay solved the problem by earning a fortune in India. Peel was the son of a cotton millionaire. Gladstone was the son of a Liverpool merchant, Disraeli married a wealthy widow, and Cobden would have had to retire had he not received £75,000 by public subscription when he had nearly ruined his own calico printing business. The House of Commons was no place for a workingman.

The Radicals in the House of Commons may have represented the opinion of those who did not yet have the vote. But they had the weakness of men who were defending the interests of a class to which they did not belong. Many of them were afraid of the extension of the franchise for which the working class were asking. Others believed too strongly in the principle of free competition in economic life to win the support of those who wanted some state regulation of the industrial "free for all." In the constituencies their indifference in religion and their supposed freedom in morals lost them the support of pious and prosperous Dissenters. Melbourne was weighing his words carefully when he told Queen Victoria in 1839 that the Radicals in the House had "neither ability, honesty, nor numbers."

But if a third party of radical reformers was not established in the House of Commons, the character and organization of the traditional party groups were profoundly changed. The extension of the suffrage, limited though it was, meant that the men who wished to govern had to establish their contacts with the new electorate. The Reform Act of 1832 had provided for a registry of those qualified to vote. It was left to those who had the right to vote to see that their names were on the register. It was because an efficient register would determine the electoral success that the political parties which had been in the eighteenth century a parliamentary phenomenon made their way into the constituencies and gradually covered the country with a network of their organizations. Between 1832 and 1841 Peel, who saw the vital importance of registration, linked up a central party organization with a network of local associations. The Carlton Club of the Tories was a point of union and the center of organization for the whole party. It was the center of electoral information, the meeting place of the party election committees, and the main collecting point for party subscriptions. There, it was said, a delegation from a local constituency could find "a very rich man, who would do exactly as they liked, with extremely low opinions and very high connections." There they would find the young man who "looked like the rosebud which dangled in the button of his frockcoat." [17] The Whigs on their side had a convenient party center in Brookes. The Radicals established the Reform in 1836. The period from 1832 to 1867 was the golden age of the political club. It was a link between the leaders and the constituencies. But it was not until after the Second Reform Act of 1867 that the local party organizations in the constituencies were to try through their central association meetings to make a direct contribution to the formation of party policy at the center.

In 1832 the Whig party believed in nothing in excess. Privilege was the safeguard of freedom. It was the duty and privilege of property to extend the empire of reason. The prerogative of the Crown and the privileges of the two Houses of Parliament were necessary safeguards to the rights and privileges of the people. Universal suffrage would destroy an ordered liberty and create a lawless tyranny. Grey's government in 1830 had only three commoners in a Cabinet of thirteen. Lord Grey had set out to show that in the days of Jacobitism and democracy it was possible to find real capacity in the high aristocracy. There was an intricate network of aristocratic connections among the old constitutional Whigs of England. The Whig centers were the town and country houses of the great magnates —estates such as Woburn, the home of the Duke of Bedford, or Holland House. There were interests which had been attached to them for generations—a large part of the money interest in the city of London and some of the manufacturing interests in the industrial north. Many of the utilitarians saw the need for joint action with the Whigs. Lord John Russell was the last great Whig, and he became the first Liberal. The ideas of 1689 were still living ideas to him. But he became a link between the aristocracy and the new economic ideas of the classical economists. He was a friend of Nassau Senior, and he introduced the Poor Law Act of 1834. He was in favor of religious freedom and wanted to keep the Church in its proper place—a small one. He was to live to congratulate Bismarck on his campaign against Roman Catholics in Germany. The Whigs were to be in office from 1832 to 1841, with a diminishing degree of parliamentary and outside support. Between 1834 and 1840 they were to be defeated some fifty-eight times in the House of Commons.

If the Whigs represented a blend of eighteenth-century rationalism with the constitutional traditions of 1689, the Conservative party represented the economic interests most severely threatened by the new industrial and commercial order. There was a grain interest, cattle interest, and sugar interest. The Whigs would protect liberty by keeping government weak. The Conservatives wanted a strong government which would reform traditional institutions so that they would be preserved in a changing society. Like the Red Queen, they saw that to stay where you are you may have to move fast.

Sir Robert Peel was the architect of the new party. His first apprenticeship in government had been during the war with Napoleon. As Home secretary from 1821, with a short break, to 1830 he had got rid of the old system of spies and agent provocateurs, had reformed some parts of the criminal law, and had established the Metropolitan Police for London. He considered that ministers were not in office to implement a party program, but to act as the king's confidential advisers. He was to play an important part in modernizing British institutions and administrations to meet the social and economic needs of the nineteenth century. He started the modern police, the modern civil service, and modern financial administration. Gladstone was his apprentice and tried to finish what he had begun. Peel did not himself create the new party organization which the new registration of voters had made necessary. But he saw its necessity, and it was F. R. Bonham, the Tory election manager caricatured as Mr. Tadpole in Benjamin Disraeli's *Coningsby,* who reorganized the party from his desk in the Carlton Club.

Peel in his leadership of his party in the new House of Commons avoided what he considered factious opposition and was prepared to support a Whig government whenever its members espoused conservative principles. He was not prepared to ally himself with Radicals to secure a Whig defeat. His difficulty was that many of the country gentlemen who supported him from 1832 to 1846 did not share his views either on the nature of society or the importance of political economy. His great ministry of 1841–46 was the model which Gladstone admired and sought to emulate in 1868–74, and his solid virtues were to be the opportunity for the vicious attack of Disraeli and the rise to power of that masterly charlatan.

Before 1832 the functions of a government had been mainly executive. Changes in the law were proposed by independent members and carried, if wanted, by the combined action of both sides. After 1832 it is significant that the business of the House of Commons was continually on the increase and the proportion of time which the government took increased too. It was recognized by all parties that the government must have time for its essential business. One of the essentials of Cabinet government is that ministers, who must be members of the legislature, shall be able, by the rules of procedure, to state and defend a policy and secure the legislation and the money which its implementation will require. The dependence of the Cabinet upon a House of Commons which neither the Crown nor the House of Lords could control in the eighteenth-century manner, involved the development of a principle of collective responsibility. The possession of power might be the sole object of political warfare, but honor required that you agree in principle with those you joined, and solidarity was needed for efficiency in the government in power. It came to be clearly recognized that openly avowed and tolerated differences of opinion upon matters standing for immediate action would be fatal to a Cabinet.

The most significant political event after the Reform Act of 1832 was the Repeal of the Corn Laws, 1846. It was an act of intelligence and integrity on the part of the government of the day, completing a policy of economic liberalism whose pedigree went back to Adam Smith, and it created a condition of party confusion which was only resolved by the extension of the suffrage by the Reform Act of 1867, the second step of the British constitutional tortoise along the democratic path. Two earlier episodes must be briefly mentioned if the constitutional niceties involved are to be understood. In 1834 Melbourne offered his resignation to William IV when the latter objected to the reconstruction which Melbourne wished to make of the Cabinet. The resignation had been accepted, the King clearly believing that he had the right to make his own choice of ministers in eighteenth-century style. Peel took office in a minority and failed to get a majority when he appealed to the new electorate. Peel said in his Tamworth manifesto that "he had a firm belief that the people of this country will so far maintain the prerogative of the King, as to give to the Ministers of his choice not implicit confidence but a fair trial." Although he did not get a majority at the general election Peel continued in office and only resigned when after several months it was obvious that the House of Commons would not support him. He saw, he said, "the greatest prejudice to the cause of good government and to the prerogative of the Crown" in "exhibiting the executive government without control over the House of Commons." The king's government must have the support of the House of Commons and that support could now only be won in the constituencies. The second episode was in 1841. The Melbourne government had suffered a series of defeats in the Commons, but made no offer of resignation. Peel argued that it was "at variance with the principles and the spirit of the constitution for a Ministry to continue in office without the confidence of the House." Russell and Macaulay in reply argued for the Whigs that while inability to perform the administrative duties of government was ground for resignation, a government did not have to secure general support for its legislative program. Peel retorted that legislation and administration were so interwoven that it was utterly impossible to draw a line between them and that the claim of a government upon public confidence "was infinitely stronger on account of their legislative measures than on account of their administrative acts." Already legislation was a tool of policy and a government must be able to get from the House the tools for the job.

The Repeal of the Corn Laws in 1846 raised fundamental issues about the relation between government and parties in the cabinet system which was developing in Britain. By 1845 many of the big landowners, particularly those with urban and industrial properties had little interest in the protection which the Corn Laws gave them. The Board of Trade officials had come to take the merits of free trade for granted. Peel himself had come to the view that the Corn Laws ought to be modified before the crisis caused by the failure of the potato crop in Ireland forced his hand. Russell, the Whig leader, had also been converted to repeal, announcing that he would agree to repeal, as he had agreed to parliamentary reform, because he wanted to avoid a struggle which would be deeply injurious to the aristocracy.

When Peel found that he could not carry his cabinet with him he resigned and, when Russell was unable to form a government, he returned to office and carried the repeal of the Corn Laws because it was the course which the public interest really demanded. His critics led by Disraeli said that he had no right to assume responsibility for a policy which was not that of the party to which he belonged. He was not entitled as the leader of a party to act on his view of the national interest unless he could carry his party with him. When, after he had carried the repeal, he was defeated by a combination of the protectionists in his own party, the Whigs, and the Irish, he resigned, refusing to dissolve and go to the country. Cobden invited him to go to the country on the cry of "Peel and Free Trade." The country should be ruled by its middle class—the reform bill had decreed it and the passing of the repeal had realized it. Peel was not prepared for what he considered to be an unnatural combination with those who agreed with him in nothing but the principles of free trade. When Peel was driven from office, his party lay in ruin. Disraeli argued that free politics was more dangerous than free trade. Only by maintaining the independence of parties, could one maintain the integrity of public men and the power and influence of Parliament itself.

The effect of the disruption of Peel's party was that from 1846 to 1852, from 1858 to 1859, and from 1866 to 1868 no ministry had a stable majority. For a time the very names of the parties were unstable. The terms "Conservative-Liberal" and "Liberal-Conservative" came into use. Some of the Peelites, including Gladstone, drifted over to the Whigs. Gladstone who distrusted Palmerston almost as much as he distrusted Disraeli, joined Palmerston's administration in 1859. In the confused condition of parties, the process of forming a new administration became tedious and even ridiculous. The Aberdeen Coalition 1852–55 included six Whigs, six Peelites, and one Radical. Contemporaries called it a "tesselated pavement" and "a clique of doctrinaires existing by Court favour." In 1855 it collapsed from inability to conduct a war—the Crimean—which it had been unable to prevent. The period showed the dangers which threaten constitutional government when there are no clear party lines with broad-based popular support. The Queen, advised and assisted by the Prince Consort, had more to do with the formation of governments than it is wise for a constitutional monarch to have. In this period Disraeli learned how to use her influence, a skill which he was to abuse after 1874, and Gladstone came to see the need for an extension of the suffrage given in 1832. By 1858 the real issue was, as Disraeli said, "whether parliamentary government is compatible with our existing institutions. The House of Commons is broken into sections which, although they have no unity of purpose or policy, can always combine to overthrow the Queen's Government however formed."

The confusion of parties in the Commons inherent in the limited franchise of 1832 had helped the House of Lords to survive as an important part of the machinery of government. Immediately after 1832 the Lords had acquiesced in the reforms which the Whigs and their Radical supporters had introduced. But when the Whigs and the Radicals could not co-operate and the latter were allying themselves with the Irish members, the courage of the House of Lords revived. The Whigs were not prepared to ally themselves with Radicals in an attack on the House of Lords. By 1842 the Lords were in a strategic position. They would pass measures which it would have been dangerous to refuse because of the state of public opinion. But they could prevent any systematic development of a liberal policy by the Whigs and their Radical allies. It was with the support of Wellington in the Lords that Peel was able to carry the repeal of the Corn Laws. After 1846 the Lords were prepared to pass Factory bills, which controlled the activities of the industrial interests that had favored free trade in corn, but they were opposed to any amelioration of the conditions of the Irish peasant or to any reduction of the privileges of the Established Church.

In 1856 the Lords "rejected," in the words of Bagehot, "the inestimable and unprecedented opportunity of being tacitly reformed." It had been proposed that the Queen should create life peers. The Lords could not prevent her exercising her undoubted prerogative to do so, but they could decide that a life peer might not take his seat in the House of Lords. The fact that the Prince Consort was believed to favor the inoculation of the Lords with some scientific and literary talents may have stimulated the Lords to defend their privilege of dullness. But though they won the battle of privileges in 1856, they lost in their contest with Gladstone in 1861. They rejected a measure which repealed the excise duty on paper—the last lingering survivor of the taxes on knowledge. They had a good tactical case, for in rejecting one bill which repealed a tax they could not be said to be denying funds to the executive government. The annual budget then consisted of a number of separate bills and in rejecting one bill which repealed a tax, the Lords had destroyed no vital financial plan. Gladstone, as chancellor of the Exchequer, retaliated by persuading Prime Minister Palmerston that the Commons should be asked to assert that it had the power "in its own hands so to impose and remit taxes and to frame bills of supply that the right of the Commons as to manner, measure and time may be maintained inviolate." Also, Gladstone in 1861 combined in one bill the entire financial scheme of the year, so that the Lords could neither amend nor reject a budget without a direct challenge to the Commons. This they were not to do until 1910, and it was to be their political euthanasia.

Before 1870 the power of government moved only over the surface of social life. But in 1859, it was becoming clear that the compromise of the Reform Act of 1832 could not endure. The problems of an industrial society and the problems of an international society in which the industrial revolution born in England was now at large would need a more potent and complex machinery of government than the aged Whigs or the sleepy Tories could provide. William E. Gladstone in 1859 was fifty years old. He said of himself in 1850 that he was "outside the regular party organisation of parliament." He had been a Peelite, and after 1846 the Peelite rump was doomed. He had sat in Parliament since 1833 and had held office of Cabinet rank as early as 1845. His first speech of importance in the House had been a defense of the treatment of slaves on his father's Demerara plantations. In 1838 he had published his book *The State in Its Relations with the Church,* in which he upheld the view that the English state recognized as among its duties the support of religious truth, as embodied in a particular church, against religious error. In 1839 he had opposed an increase in the parliamentary grant for education because the grant was distributed to all religious denominations.

In the confusions of Gladstone's powerful mind, one can see in little some of the tensions of that age. A Christian order was ceasing to be one, and the system of government, which had served an agrarian island with a trading empire, was becoming every year less relevant to the problems of a new kind of industrial society. Looking back, we see that there were really two interlocking problems—the machinery of government and the scope of government. In the case of the machinery of government the vital issue was that the Reform Act of 1832 had destroyed the prescriptive ground on which the old constitution had rested. The British were not committed to the unsolvable problem of finding a legislature which should embody the will of a sovereign people, but they were committed to the task of finding some means by which citizens should be associated in the selection and the dismissal, when necessary, of their political leaders. The compromise of 1832 could not be adapted to the changes in the distribution of population and the changes in the composition, interests, and ideas of its component parts. The Reform Act had created constituencies and political habits which could survive in a stage-coach age. It could not be adapted to the age of railways, increasing literacy, and the development of the organized interests of employers and workingmen.

We may glance at three different aspects, perhaps one may say, three different levels of the problem: (1) the anomalies of the electoral system and the political habits associated with it, (2) the economic changes which influenced the pattern of political events, and (3) the movements of thought which strove to penetrate beneath the veil of common political practice and the surface changes in economic life to the realities which they covered.

(1) After 1832 for many years the average voter still wanted to be represented by the social leaders of his own local community. But the average voter was not a fair sample of the politically conscious citizens of the local communities which were to be represented. The eighteenth-century boroughs with only a handful of voters had been abolished, but in the new constituencies the number of voters was often small enough to make it possible by direct and indirect means to purchase the margin of votes needed for success. After 1832, although it was usual for less than half the constituencies to be contested because of the cost of elections, the balance of local interests and the possibility of dividing the spoils in double-member constituencies made compromise possible, yet the contests were more than double those of the eighteenth century. The Reform Act itself did not transform the intricate pattern of influence and tradition. The provincial interests were not dependent on the party machinery such as it was in London; the party was dependent on them. The social system depended locally on long established "interests," and the political system continued to register that influence in all the forms it took—landlords over tenants, masters over servants, employers over workmen, clergy over their congregation, and the customers over the shopkeepers. Even the poorer unenfranchised classes could use their influence by withdrawing their custom from a public house of the wrong party affiliation. The respectable classes exercised the influence which was theirs by custom.

The Reform Act of 1832 had not been intended to destroy legitimate but only the illegitimate influence of property. In a county election it was a matter of conventional courtesy to seek the permission of the landlord before canvassing his tenants. The landlords were not only owners of lands, they were also magistrates, patrons, customers, chairmen of committees, local sportsmen, and officers in the militia. The decencies had to be observed.

In addition to customary control and influence there was an element of violence and fraud. The business of an election was usually in the hands of the candidate's agent, who took care that his principal was not aware of the precise technical details involved. As a character in Disraeli's *Coningsby* put it: "I do not see how we can win . . . we have polled all our dead men and Millbanks is seven ahead." A borough election might well cost £5000 a side. At times the professional pugilist and the underworld of the tavern, the race course, and the slum were mobilized for an appropriate fee. Often it was essential to have the public house on one's side and that was best secured by lavishly treating the electorate to the landlord's beer at the candidate's expense. It was not until after the second Reform Act of 1867 that the secret ballot and a moderately efficient Corrupt Practices Act took the Dickensian sound and color out of the electoral arts.

One consequence of the narrowness and complexity of the franchise was the attempt to influence the government by organized pressure from outside. Two attempts were outstanding—the Chartist movement and the Anti-Corn Law League. The first was a complete failure and the second was not the success it has sometimes been believed. The root of the first was in the disappointment of the working class with the Reform Act of 1832. They had thought that it would provide a machinery of improved legislation by which their grievances would be removed. It seemed to them that it had merely effected a transfer of power from one domineering faction to another. An exclusively working-class movement was brought into being. Lovett, Hetherington, and John Black formed, in 1836, the London Working Men's Association "to draw into one bond of unity the intelligent and influential portion of the working classes in town and country and to seek by every legal means to place all classes of society in possession of equal political and social rights." They attacked what they called the rotten House of Commons, saying that a majority of the House was elected by only 151,493 votes and that one-fortieth of the male adult population had power to make laws binding upon millions. In 1838 William Lovett produced the People's Charter. It had six points; manhood suffrage, vote by ballot, equal electoral districts rearranged each census, annual parliaments, no property qualification for candidates, M.P.'s to receive salaries. That all of the points except annual parliaments are now in operation does not mean that the charter was wise in its generation. The development of transport and the liquidation of the hierarchies of a semifeudal society had to be carried much further by the industrial revolution before the British constitution could be geared to the seeming simplicities of one man one vote, one vote one value.

The Anti-Corn Law League was a more sophisticated affair and showed some of the tough and technical problems which faced political propaganda in the 1840's. From 1815 onward there had been present in the country a strong body of opinion opposed to the protection of agriculture. Until 1830 the opposition was local and sporadic. In 1836 an Anti-Corn Law association was founded in London following a steep rise in wheat prices. In 1838 another was formed at Manchester from which the Anti-Corn Law League was to be developed. The League had wealth, able leaders, single purpose, and solid middle-class support.[18] Richard Cobden appreciated from the first that the Corn Laws must be repealed in Parliament and that Parliament could only be moved by political action.

The League had a most favorable climate of opinion in which to work. The intellectual elite was, in accordance with the principles of political economy, against vested interests. The intoxication of industrial innovation led to lyrical extolling of industry and commerce. Aristocratic misrule was to give place to business competence. The owner of ten thousand spindles faced the owner of ten thousand acres. Much of the financial support for the League came from the owners of large mills. Dissenters saw in an attack on agricultural protection a meritorious attack on the parson's tithes and on the Established Church which taxed the poor man's bread. Charitable men and women could support the League as a scientific attack on the real causes of poverty, the dislocation caused by government interference with the natural course of trade.

The technique of the League was to distribute a torrent of tracts and handbills which presented the question of the Corn Laws as a religious, moral, and social problem quite separate from party politics, and to lobby extensively, which at the time was held to be an intrusive and an intolerable infringement on the independence of M.P.'s. The League divided the country into twelve areas, each with its own permanent lecturer. The organization for distributing tracts was used to get comprehensive reports on the electoral position in the constituencies. The electoral law was very complicated. There were 576 types of freehold qualification, 400 of copyhold, and 50 of occupying tenancy. As one leaguer wrote: "In the warfare of registration the solicitors rise to the rank of Generals." In that warfare the League concentrated on getting as many free traders as possible placed on the register and as many protectionists as possible struck off. They anticipated in many ways techniques of party politics which are now common. They had to secure the support of newspapers which had an independent circulation of their own. This was not cheap for, as one leaguer wrote, the press was not *"a self-acting machine and wants as the yankees would say an Almighty power of grease to set it going."* The energies of the League when the crisis of 1845–46 came were directed to a decisive struggle at the expected general election of 1848. Their influence was at most indirect. But they provided a sketch of the political shape of things to come.[19]

By the middle of the century it was agreed by most reasonable people that certain changes in the 1832 settlement were necessary. Since 1832 a new industrial kingdom had been created in the north of England, centered round Manchester, of which the constitution took no account. Few workingmen had the votes, and that meant that working-class opinion could only influence parliamentary action by direct pressure. The working class distrusted the middle-class free traders. They did not like the idea of free trade in labor. The pressure on the government was thus divided. The Reform Act of 1867, when it came, arose out of exigencies in the House of Commons itself. But some change in the franchise and a considerable redistribution of seats was necessary if the life of the House of Commons was to be vitalized by a touch of popular power. A situation could not continue in which five out of six males were voteless and in which one-half of the borough population of England had thirty-four seats and the other half 300.

(2) To the hindsight of the economist there are two sections of the period we are considering. From 1820 to 1849 prices were falling and from 1849 to 1874 they were rising. In the first period in spite of an increase in production, stimulated by tariff reforms of William Huskisson in the 1820's and of Peel in the 1840's, and the improvement in communications begun by the railroads, the telegraph, and the penny post, the working classes of the country were worse off than in almost any other period of English history. This was the result of the disorganization of the labor market, which meant that workers were not in a position to make a successful fight for a higher standard of living. Between 1810 and 1830 money wages were falling and from 1830 to 1850 were practically stationary. Also, though prices as a whole fell between 1820 and 1849, the commodities which fell most were not those consumed by the working classes. The price of raw materials, particularly iron, fell with improvements in transport, but agricultural food products fell less rapidly than the average, or actually rose in price. This was primarily due to the Corn Law of 1815.

In the second period the discovery of gold in Australia and California led to the growth of pioneer communities with a demand for the goods which Europe was well equipped to supply. Their effective demand for manufactured goods gave a fillip to trade at home. The Companies Act of 1861 encouraged the development of limited liability, and large numbers of new enterprises were started under the stimulus of abundant, loanable capital and an optimistic spirit of expanding trade. Transport facilities made enormous strides. There was a rapid increase in production of coal and iron. The Bessemer process of steel smelting had been introduced in 1858. Money wages between 1852 and 1870 were rising fast. Food product prices, except for meat and butter, were stationary or rising only a little. The rise in prices was in commodities such as coal, iron, cotton, indigo, and tin, which have a comparatively indirect effect upon the purchasing power of the working classes. The relative price changes of the period were in favor of the consuming classes. The population of England and Wales rose from 18,000,000 in 1851 to 20,000,000 in 1861 and 22,750,000 in 1871. The wage bill rose 30 per cent between 1861 and 1871.[20] With the price of food almost unchanged the rapid increase in the wage bill of the nation left a considerable margin for other expenditure. Savings bank deposits increased. The consumption per head of tea, sugar, and other once luxury commodities rose. The working classes had an opportunity of raising their standard of life, and they were in a much more favorable bargaining position than they had been in the 1840's.

This economic skeleton of the social body which the X ray of the economist reveals explains in part why in the 1840's there was so much talk of class divisions while in the 1850's and 1860's it was more a discussion of interests. The railroad interest was a dominating factor. Bagehot claimed that railroads had some 200 members of Parliament supporting them. There was the city interest, the licensed victualers, the attorneys, and even the ecclesiastical lawyers, all in a strategic position to check legislation which might be injurious to them. Government was relatively feeble. At the core of the House of Commons was a cousinhood of landed families which included nearly half the members. It was this pattern which was to be changed by the reform acts of 1867 and 1884.

(3) We may glance at some of the movement of ideas which both reflected and influenced the changes which had taken and would be taking place. When population was increasing and when trade and industry were expanding faster than they had ever done before, it was the concern of contemporaries to understand the scope and nature of the changes taking place and to adjust the machinery of government to meet the political problems they were bringing. On the nature of the changes the economists were the most penetrating commentators. On the machinery of government needed the Benthamites offered the most persuasive advice. The fundamental concern of the economists was to show the conditions needed if the wealth of nations was to be increased. Adam Smith had been concerned to attack the specific abuses of existing govern-

ments hindering the co-operation for which men were in their own interests prepared. Free trade in land and a free choice of occupations within and between countries would add immeasurably to the wealth of nations. If the state would prevent violence and administer justice and cease to be the servant of vested interests it would release powerful forces toward profitable co-operation. The utilitarians from Jeremy Bentham to J. S. Mill were the most influential writers on the problem of the proper scope for government now that the springs of economic well-being were beginning to be understood. "The guides of English legislation during the period and individualism . . . accepted the fundamental ideas of Benthamism . . . the immediate and practical object was the extension of individual liberty as the proper means of ensuring the greatest happiness of the greatest number." Common to both the economists and the utilitarians was the assumption dear to the rationalist movement of the eighteenth century that matters of opinion could be settled by discussion. The obvious vitality and seeming harmony of the economic order were a comforting demonstration of the power of reason in society. The industrial progress which was taking place seemed to show that the essentials of human order were rooted more firmly in men's stomachs than in their minds. The market which the economists had analyzed was providing indirectly the ideal republic which no philosopher king could plan. The tableau of human progress was being woven by the economic loom.

In all this there was one dangerous obscurity. What did governments need to do in order that the economic loom continue to hum? Some form of private property, the enforcement of contract, and the suppression of violence were required before the subtle adjustments of human interests that the mechanism of price provides could be enjoyed. But to admit the need for the enforcement of contracts was to abandon the philosophy of individualism which some economic thought seemed to imply. And in addition to the problem of contract was the problem of the pattern of property. Property is an historical category, and it was idle to assume that the forms of property inherited from the past would be appropriate to the economic order of the future, for it was against certain forms of property that the early economists had most convincingly inveighed. "That great man," wrote Thomas Hodgkin in Labour Defended (1825), of Adam Smith, "carefully distinguished the natural distribution of wealth from the distribution which is derived from our artificial right of property." And J. S. Mill was to argue that the system of landed property in England did not satisfy the conditions that the freedom of an economic market required. And his criticism of the peculiar English land laws could be extended to all the monopolistic elements secreted in an ancient and landed aristocracy. There was a living past with which contemporary statesmen must deal.

The implications of the analysis of the economists had to be carried out by politicians and administrators with the constitutional tools and the political practices which had come down to them. The actual policies which they carried out fall into four groups: (1) the attack on those privileges which were indefensible in theory and lacked the political power to resist reform. Of these the most famous was the free trade movement which swept away the old fiscal system and the privileges of the landed aristocracy; (2) the provision of a legal framework for the free co-operation of men assumed to know their own interests. Here the most obvious need was the development of company law which would provide a sensible system for the conversions of private savings into instruments of production. Equally important was the legislation which regulated the freedom of workmen to combine. At the beginning of the century the Combination Acts had been passed because it was feared that unions of workmen under the guise of trade activities might engage in revolutionary propaganda. As the fear of revolutionary activity died down the Combination Acts were repealed in 1824 and 1825 on the grounds that combination of workers for the purpose of bargaining about wages would help the organization of industry and trade. But it was not until the Trade Union Act of 1871 that the trade unions were given a clearly defined legal scope for their various activities. And 1871 was not to be the end of the story.

(3) There were the problems connected with those social and individual needs for which forces of the market do not, in fact, provide. Effective demand in the economic sense is always lacking for the services of the parson and the schoolmaster. Before Darwin, all save the atheistic poor and the philosophical Radicals felt that some form of organized religion was necessary to the existence of society. The Evangelical party in the Church of England made possible much humanitarian legislation which the philosophical Radicals could never have carried alone. The experience of the Methodists had far-reaching effects on party and trade union organization. The High Church party was stung by the attacks of its critics into the Oxford movement. Coleridge said that the Church of England transplanted to every parish of the United Kingdom a germ of civilization, "that in the remotest village there is a nucleus round which the capabilities of the place may crystallise and brighten."

Whatever the spiritual case for the Church of England might be the political leaders of the country after 1832 had to face the problem that the organization of the Church would have to be reformed. Ecclesiastical sinecures had to share the fate to which in an industrial society all sinecures are doomed. The growth and movement of the population made it necessary to reorganize the financial and administrative system of the Church of England. Its accounts, if not its creed, would have to bear inspection. In 1836 Parliament created a Permanent Ecclesiastical Commission to equalize the incomes of the various bishoprics and to reorganize their territorial extent.

The problem of the Church of England was intricate and technical. But it was comparatively simple compared with the problem of education. Religion in the nineteenth century was a receding tide, but education was the little cloud no bigger than a hand which was to cover all our skies. The peculiarity of the English educational story is that it was not possible until after 1867 to get Parliament to agree to a scheme of national education. There was no doubt about the shameful facts. There was a frightful state of brutal ignorance and heathenish irreligion. But the Dissenters would not stand the parson in a state school. The Established Church would not stand anyone else. So the government had to limit its educational policy to the giving of meager grants to two great voluntary organizations, the National Society of the Established Church and the British and Foreign Society of the Dissenters. The price paid for this sectarian passion was that England entered the fierce economic competition after 1870 with artisans who were the least trained, and a middle class which was the worst educated in Europe.

Finally, (4) the condition of Ireland, where the aristocracy was absentee, the Church an alien power, and the population near to starvation. English rule was little more than a provisional government in a half-conquered country. A population of 8,000,000 in 1841 depended upon a primitive system of tillage. In 1841 more than 80 per cent of all farms were under sixteen acres and only 7 per cent over thirty acres. Free trade and the great famine of the "forties" led to a change from small to large holdings, and from tillage to pasture. By 1851, 26 per cent of all farms were over thirty acres and only 51 per cent under sixteen acres. The population had sunk to 6,500,000. In Ireland the law regarded the landowner as the sole owner of the farm, whereas in fact and in equity the tenant was the co-owner. The tenant in Ireland, unlike the tenant in England, provided the stock and the improvements and if dispossessed had either to starve or to emigrate. In 1870 Gladstone tried to give legal recognition to the co-ownership which in fact and in equity existed. The failure of the British Parliament to solve the problem of the relation between economic, political, and religious forces in Ireland was to create in the United States the political force of Irish-Americans, one of the

most dangerous enemies England has ever had, to create an Irish proletariat in some English cities, the Irish Nationalist party in the House of
Commons, and to destroy the English Liberal party of Gladstone for a
generation. This Achilles' heel of the British political system is a grim
warning of the dangers which lurk in the limitations on human skill and
sympathy which the past may impose on even a well-meaning present.

Sea Power and the Balance of Power

The influence of Great Britain in the world was at its height in the period from 1815 to 1850, before the breath of technological change had given life to vast new political powers in whose presence Britain would be an elderly and infirm David surrounded by youthful and boasting Goliaths. For at least a generation after Waterloo Britain had so much influence in international affairs that there was almost a *Pax Britannica*. The character of that now almost legendary world can easily be misunderstood. Britain was a "leading rather than a dominating power." [1] Her influence was based on an effective naval strength—on a fleet which, being made of wood, could not suddenly be outbuilt—latent military resources, and a swelling financial and industrial supremacy. She had no territorial ambitions in Europe and she had no imperial ambitions. She dismantled her control of trade and abandoned the restrictions of the Navigation Acts. She was willing to negotiate on something like a basis of equality with the new United States. Her Achilles' heel lay in her empire in India which was a byproduct of her struggle with revolutionary and Napoleonic France. Her frontiers there involved her in a latent contest with the Asiatic front of the moving mass of Russia and in the strategic problems of securing her sea routes to them.

Sea power as we have seen has its limitations. At the Congress of Vienna, 1815, which secured the peace of Europe for forty years, Britain had acquired islands and harbors essential to the sea power of wooden ships: Heligoland, Malta, Mauritius, Trinidad, St. Lucia, Tobago, the Cape of Good Hope, and a protectorate in the Ionian Islands. In 1824 by a treaty with the Netherlands her possession of Singapore was recognized. It outflanked the straits of Malacca and made the British Empire in India for a time secure. A Cabinet memorandum of December 26, 1813, laid it down that her representatives at the coming peace talks were "to evince a desire to conform as far as possible to the general interests of the continent . . . to avoid everything that might countenance a suspicion that Great Britain was inclined to push them (her allies) forward in the war for her own purposes." The Mauritius was to be retained "as being, when in the hands of an enemy, a most injurious naval station to our Indian commerce, whilst it is of little comparative value to France." Malta was to remain British; the Cape of Good Hope retained "as a position connected with the security of our Empire in the East." [2] While she would allow no questioning of her maritime supremacy by which she had survived and through which Europe had been helped to free itself from the empire of Napoleon, Britain held to the principle that all seas were freely open to all and that the British navy would keep the seas open for the common benefit, suppress piracy and the slave trade, and prepare and publish charts of every ocean. It has been said by a distinguished American jurist, Professor Quincy Wright, that "the inconsistency of neutrality with an effective international law was obscured during the nineteenth century because Great Britain had so firm a devotion to law and liberty that British control of the world, facilitated by the doctrine of neutrality, did not wholly destroy the rule of law. Neutrality lasted because it facilitated the *Pax Britannica*. Its influence in weakening the law of nations was not observed because the law of England was substituted." [3] As Santayana was to ask: when will the world have again such sweet boyish masters?

Britain was never the master of the world. In the nineteenth century she had secure bases from which to exercise her influence in the world. She could ward off threats to key points in her communications—the Baltic, the English Channel, Gibraltar, and the Straits. The Cape of Good Hope served the route to India before the Suez Canal was cut, and the coming of the steamship made it a vital artery of trade and war. A policy of free trade opened her empire to the foreign traders of the world. She believed that her revolutions in agricultural and industrial processes could serve mankind. Before 1850 the conditions of warfare in Europe were such that if war broke out there would be time for the British to mobilize their strength. Palmerston could even threaten war: against France in 1831, unless France withdrew from Belgium; against France in 1840 over the Near East; even against the United States, if a British subject, Alexander, were executed for killing a man in 1837 in a raid into the United States territory arising out of a Canadian rebellion. But her sea power could not keep Russia from her subjection of Poland, nor prevent France from invading Spain, nor protect the Turks from a Russian attack in 1828–29.

The successes and the failures of British influence need to be seen in

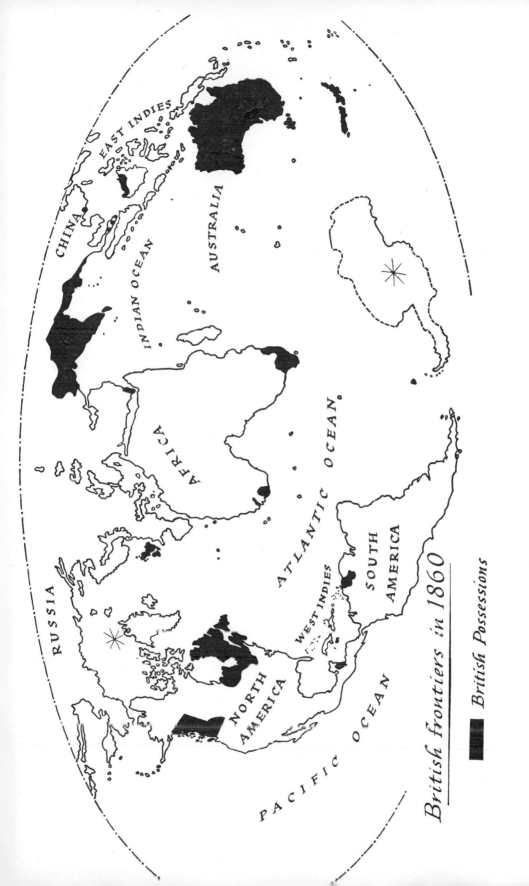

British Frontiers in 1860

■ *British Possessions*

the context of (1) the ideas and the interests which were stirring in the British Isles themselves; (2) the state of the European continent, where forces utterly beyond the power of the British to control or even to influence were stirring beneath the pattern of order made at the Congress of Vienna; (3) the influence of the accelerating changes in industry and commerce which was to create the finally United States of 1865, the self-governing dominions of a new British Empire of which Canada in 1867 was the first, and to open China and Japan to the ideas and the techniques of the nascent industrial West; and (4) the interaction between the British conception of the balance of power on the continent of Europe, the strategic necessities of her frontiers in India, and the protection of her settlements and possessions scattered round the world.

The British Isles after 1815 were not only the center of the new revolutions in industrial methods, they were also the stage of a political transformation by which a museum of aristocratic political pieces was made over into an effective legislative and administrative machine. The prerogatives of an ancient monarchy became the privileges of a new industrial people. Some useful cuttings from the tree of eighteenth-century rationalism were grafted on a long-established aristocracy. A working system of representative democracy was developed, and the social problems caused by the unfamiliar effects of rapid economic change were brought under some competent political and administrative control. What in the United States was done in the conditions favorable to political experiment, which the open spaces of the West provided, had in the British Isles to be done in the confines of small islands where new and strange frontiers between agriculture and industry, between masters and men, and between rich and poor had to be controlled by a single political system. Britain was too small to enjoy the safety valve of federal diversities.

We cannot, of course, say that it would not have been better had Napoleon occupied Britain and given her a new Norman administrative system in which the ideas of Tom Paine and Jeremy Bentham might have helped to create an early welfare state. No one can say what benefit the British would derive from a new Domesday book published with the help of modern techniques. The point is that this did not take place, and the Britain of the *Pax Britannica* was politically an aristocracy only slowly changing into a partial democracy. The constitution may not have been a Venetian oligarchy, as Disraeli was pleased to call it. The king's government was carried on with excellent practical wisdom, but it was not a system of government of the people, by the people, for the people. Castlereagh and Canning, Wellington and Melbourne, Palmerston and

Peel had none of the characteristics of political leaders who serve in systems of universal suffrage.

The men who were responsible for foreign policy may have been of eighteenth-century vintage, thinking in terms of the old regime, of which since the French Revolution the brains were out, and calculating the balance of power which was to become incommensurable, but they were braced by the criticism of an entirely new world of economic and rational analysis. The social order might be old, but new ideas and new economic forces were felt along its blood and thrilled along its nerves and in its brain. The new ideas which were transforming industrial and social life had their influence on the calculations of the ancient art of diplomacy. Even a Machiavelli would have had to take note of a spinning jenny and a steam engine. It has been said that wisdom lies in masterful administration of the unforeseen. In a period of nascent mechanization the unforeseen was never more fecund in problems for statesmen to solve. For the leaders of a constitutional monarchy like Britain, as distinct from the great despotic powers of Europe, in internal affairs it was difficult to judge how far the freedoms their peoples had were dependent on the support by the state of the Protestant form of Christianity. They had only the most confused ideas about the role which the state could play in the shaping of a new industrial society. In external affairs they could not know how quickly or in what ways the new order of international trade and commerce about the world would alter the balance of power which was their professional concern. Both those responsible for internal order and those responsible for the external defense were told by the leaders in the new science of political economy that the economic order which division of labor, speeded by new industrial techniques, was creating would make otiose their careful and anxious calculations. Internally, the old order of privilege and hierarchy would, by the magic forces of a free market, be transformed into a crystal palace of humming plenty. Externally, the balance of power was a feudal delusion which would vanish when nations were allowed to find their real interests in the economic interests of their industrial and commercial leaders seeking to serve the markets of the world. In trade and industry was perfect peace. The balance of power was a cloud that was dragonish, which would vanish and leave not a wrack behind if the sun of reasoned international self-interest were allowed to shine. The advice of the experts to their political leaders, whether they thought of them as being too like Machiavelli or too like Polonius, was to be good and let who will be clever. In particular, the British government was not to think because some remnants of empire were left that it was an eagle flying over a land of freedom. It was a hen sitting on eggs of freedom which would quickly hatch.

The statesmen who had in fact to play politics knew that there were short-term problems which no long-term abstract theory could decide. There was the difference between the despotic and the constitutional powers of the European system. They could not ignore British strategic interests in the Levant, the Cape, or the movement of the Asiatic front of Russia in the direction of the Indian frontier. The European order was of a complexity which no sea power could control. Europe could not as a whole adopt the principles of Adam Smith or John Locke. The United States was new, free, and good. The European continent from the Arctic Circle to the Mediterranean was old, a patchwork quilt of despotisms, constitutional systems, and simple corruptions, and, of course, politically speaking, as wicked as could be.

The international problem for Britain was that the facts of political life in Europe were very different from the dream of universal order cherished by English Radical thought. In the British Isles religious tolerance (with many exceptions), constitutional liberties (often dependent on an archaic legal system), and national sentiment had found a working harmony. The constitution could in fact be changed, and the administrative techniques—primitive as they now seem—were not, except in the case of Ireland, made impotent or monstrously distorted by racial or ideological tensions. The issues which the British had to face in Ireland and in India were the cause of peripheral disasters, but in Europe such matters were the very stuff of politics. Britain had comparatively simple internal problems; those of Europe were incredibly complex. Britain solved neither the Irish nor the Indian problems. Europe had racial and ideological problems in which the influence of Britain could only be slight—problems which are still unsolved and may be forever unsolvable.

Before the French Revolution the many political systems of Europe had been the result of the long history of an interaction between the principle of kingship and the force of local custom. The map of Europe had been traced by the genealogy of kings and the vitality of small republics. There was nothing wrong or outrageous in an agglomeration of subjects who had nothing in common but their allegiance to a king or a republic—Venice ruled Italians and Slovenes, the king of Denmark ruled Germans and Swedes.[4] Speech, race, and religion did not have to fit into the same political mold. The struggle for power was carried on with traditional and formal institutions. The courts of the great powers shared a common humanist culture. With the French Revolution the old hierarchy had had a great fall and not all the king's horses nor all the king's men could put it together again. The dynastic basis of political order was replaced by a search for a pattern of sovereign peoples. The eighteenth-century dynasties had been quasi proprietary in character and had emphasized territory. The new order would be concerned with human communities.[5] Opposition to autocracy based on an hereditary dynasty, if it took the form of a claim for a self-government, could lead to constitutional development if there were no claim to territorial change. This was the condition in England (except for the case of Ireland, where the only solution was a twentieth-century civil war). The claims to self-government and to self-determination were congruent. In France the development of self-government was not easy because the French did not, in fact, find a constitutional form which would implement their theory of the sovereignty of the people.

Outside France and England and a fringe of states along the North Sea the problems were much more serious. The principle of self-determination —the right of communities supposed to have a claim to a political unity other than what they had historically come by—involved a struggle for changes in political frontiers which could be fatal to constitutional development. Irredentists make poor constitutionalists. All over Europe acute disputes about the territorial framework of the political order retarded constitutional development.[6] A most serious problem was that often the leaders of a movement for self-government were in fact led by a land-owning class in the countryside allied with an upper middle class and intelligentsia of the towns, both descended from former conquerors of an alien peasantry. When Swift wrote the Drapier letters against the English government he was not thinking of the Catholic Irish peasants; even Jefferson was not thinking of the slaves of old Virginia. Europe was littered with Irelands and her politics torn by Swifts. A European Burke is unthinkable. All over Europe "national and religious conflicts interlocked with agrarian movements, envenoming each other." [7] Europe had in fact to deal with all the problems of the United States without the aid of a moving frontier, a common language, or the hope of the final surgery of civil war.

The doctrine that the consent of the governed was the legitimate ground of political power was easy to accept in Britain, where the salt surrounding sea had imposed a working sense of common traditions; in the United States, where racial and religious differences could be diluted by space and virgin resources; in France, where her frontiers were almost as neat as a Descartian proof. For a time, indeed, the idea of nations rightly struggling to be free seemed to promise the creation of a political framework for a new economic order based on an international division of labor. Mazzini had a vision that nations had been constituted inside humanity to divide the intellectual life of the world as labor was divided between individuals inside a nation. Inspired by Cobden the members of a French society adopted the federation of Europe as their aim. Given the unification of Germany and of Italy, Europe might have a political order which would support her economic loom. But there were at least two difficulties: at the Congress of Vienna Germany and Italy could not be made single political systems. Germany in particular came to resent that she had not been among those present when Spain, Portugal, France, Holland, and England were apportioning the world. The age of discovery had been dominated by the coastal periphery of Europe and its heart-lands were to claim their place in the sun. It was discovered that there were more nations than early theorists had supposed.

In 1815 Germany and Italy were disunited through dynastic fragmenta-tion. In 1848 Englishmen knew of four nationality problems—the unifica-tion of Germany and Italy, the independence of Hungary, and the resur-rection of Poland. In 1849 Palmerston was saying: "Austria stands in the centre of Europe, a barrier against encroachment on the one side and against invasion on the other." Should the Hungarians be entirely sepa-rated from her it would be "such a dismemberment of the Austrian Em-pire as will prevent Austria from continuing to occupy the great position she has hitherto held among European powers." [8] But there was more than Austria to be fragmented by an appeal to a principle of national self-determination. More than a dozen smaller nations were engulfed in the Habsburg and Ottoman empires, in the eastern fringes of Prussia, and in the western fringe of Russia.

British statesmen in 1815 had to deal with a Europe in which there were three main groups: (1) France and Austria, European great powers whose political ambit still covered almost the entire continent; (2) Prus-sia, the newest and the least among the great powers, but in her latent challenge to Austria threatening the keystone of the whole European arch; (3) flanking Europe, but never altogether of it, Russia and Great Britain herself. At the Congress of Vienna Russia had secured a frontier which made no concessions to liberal or nationalist sentiments. She pressed on the Ottoman Empire, which in the eastern Mediterranean held a key position between three continents, and she hung a sword of Damocles over British routes to India. By controlling Turkey she could bar the British road by land through the Levant or by sea through the Mediterranean to India. Advancing in central Asia she could threaten the northwest frontier. The Treaty of Unkiar Skelessi (July 1833) made Turkey almost a protectorate of Russia and led Palmerston to say that "the Russian ambassador becomes the chief Cabinet minister of the Sultan."

The strategic problems were complicated by ideological differences. As Castlereagh wrote in a famous state paper of 1820, Europe was "divided into two great masses, the Western, consisting of France and Spain, the Eastern, of all the other continental states still subsisting . . . under the form of their ancient institutions." The Congress of Vienna, by binding up the various states of Germany into a single and undivided power, had given "a great degree of additional simplicity as well as strength" to the Eastern portion. Russia, Austria, and Prussia had a common belief in autocratic government and a common fear of a resurgence of 1789 and 1793. The Western powers stood for liberal and constitutional government. Because the West and the East thought differently they might act differently. They could also ignore ideological differences where the balance of power was concerned. Between 1830 and 1854 there was enough free play in the European diplomatic alignments to make it possible to keep the peace. But in a longer view we can see that just as the economic expansion of Western economic power has loosened the ancient structure of the whole world and is breathing life into that dead dust, so in Europe of the nineteenth century the principle of nationality was to disintegrate the feudal and dynastic structure of Europe beyond its western constitutional fringe. Austria was to be destroyed. The conflict between Austria and Russia in the Balkans was to precipitate the war of 1914. The dissolution of empires as the result of World War I (1914–18) was to be a prologue to the swelling scene of totalitarian states.

The influence of Britain after 1815 on the almost fissionable material of post-Napoleonic Europe could only be peripheral. Some frontier problems concerned her vitally, but she could only influence them indirectly. Palmerston held that Britain should watch attentively and guard with care the maintenance of the balance of power. He was not prepared to interfere by force of arms with changes in the internal government of foreign countries. He was on the side of constitutional monarchy as against despotism. Gladstone held that interference in foreign countries should be "rare, deliberate, decisive in character and effectual for its end."

Britain was only peripherally involved in the jungle of European frontiers. She was directly involved in her own frontier problems scattered as by the winds around the oceans of the world. The loss of the American colonies had left her with fragments of settlements, trading posts, and naval stations. The dry bones were to live. But Britain had little desire to care for, and no desire at all to extend, this second empire after 1815. But the parts were bound to her by ties which she could not cut, though her radicals and economists hoped that they would dissolve or wither away. After 1783 she still held Upper and Lower Canada with small populations, half French and half English—two nations warring in the bosom of a single state and with frontiers almost defenseless against the United States—New Brunswick, Nova Scotia, Newfoundland, the Hudson Bay trading stations, Bermuda, the Bahamas, Jamaica, Barbados, the Windward and Leeward Islands, Honduras, and the Falkland Islands. There were trading posts in West Africa. In Asia there were the provinces of Bengal and the presidencies of Bombay and Madras under the East India Company, as well as Penang. In 1788 and 1803 penal settlements were established in Australia, which are now New South Wales and Tasmania. There was no plan to build another empire. In 1815 Britain took only islands and stations which were needed for strategic reasons. She could have had the pick of the Spanish and Dutch island empires and of what was left of the French. Britain paid the Dutch for what she took. She returned Martinique, Guadeloupe, Cayenne, Réunion, and Pondicherry to France; Surinam, the Moluccas, Java, and in 1824 her settlement in Sumatra to Holland.

Where settlements were retained the frontier problems between an industrial power and the savages or the wilderness, were, in spite of the hope of theorists and the anxieties of statesmen, almost as inevitable as those of the United States itself. Between 1837 and 1867 over three-quarters of a million people left Britain and Ireland for British North America and nearly another million for Australia and New Zealand. Outside Canada, Australia, and New Zealand, Britain had incurred commitments which it would have been shameful to abandon. From the Cape of Good Hope she was drawn into a continent where no frontiers could be fixed and into contact with the Boers, whose native policy made either withdrawal or peaceful settlement impossible. In the West Indies the abolition of the slave trade made the British Colonial Office responsible for the re-creation of a society in the West Indies. Small forts occupied in West Africa to suppress the slave trade were centers from which commercial and political expansion would spread when the value of the tropics was realized and the tools by which white men could enter them had been made. The navy could only police a coast line. When steamers could use lakes and rivers and railroads pass the rapids and the falls, governments had to become roadmakers, railway builders, and constructors of ports. After 1850 British investment began to move from Europe to the underdeveloped areas of the world. Of the £800,000,000 to £1,000,000,000 of British foreign investment between 1850 and 1875, about two-fifths went to British possessions. It was only by the development of a trade in tropical products, such as palm oil, cotton, and gum that the trade in men—slavery—could be suppressed. The Congo was to show the dangers of shirking imperial responsibilities when trade has already brought together two unequal civilizations.

In India the East India Company had tried in vain to set limits to the expansion of its territories. During the revolutionary and Napoleonic wars with France, fear of her had stimulated attacks on her protégés in the south of India. In 1839–42 fear of Russia was to draw Britain into a disastrous campaign in Afghanistan. When the British went to India many Indians were as much strangers and foreigners to each other as the white man was to them. Had the Indian tribes of the American West been Hindu and Mohammedan civilizations of great antiquity and dissolute administration, what would have happened? The transformation of the economic relations between India and Britain is some evidence of the complexity of the British problem in India. The East India Company had been tenaciously conservative in its policy. The pattern of trade had been a reciprocal exchange of manufactured woolens and hardware for cottons and silks. When in 1813 the trade monopoly of the Company was abolished, there was a rush of English cotton goods to India and a cessation of India's cotton textile exports to England. But this did not mean that agriculture was substituted for industry in India as a result of her connection with Britain. India was not an industrial country when the British went there. Indian weaving was not wholly destroyed. The finest and best manufactures, such as those of Dacca, were ruined, but the coarser kinds of weaving survived and a division of labor was achieved by which India imported her finer goods from Lancashire and made her coarser goods at home.[9]

Modern independent Malaya is the most prosperous and best-governed state in Southeast Asia. This is, in part, the result of local officials and a reluctant British government undertaking responsibilities against the wishes of either Gladstone's Liberal or Disraeli's Conservative government after 1867. The assumption of responsibility was reluctant, but was forced upon the British government because attempts to control disorders in the Malay states led to the acceptance of a direct responsibility for government within a constitutional framework of indirect rule.

In the Pacific, too, British statesmen and officials devised remedies for particular evils, and policies were the outcome of decisions which had to be taken in particular emergencies. There was something to be said for the view that the authority of the British Crown was often a power under Providence for peace and order in extensive regions of the earth.

In 1839 the number of British subjects living overseas was only 1,200,000. In 1853 most of the colonial preferences had been abolished. In 1854 less than one-quarter of overseas trade was done with the colonies. Where there was any possibility of local self-government it was hoped that they would depart in friendship and in peace. Cobden in 1836 looked on colonies as accessories to the unjust privileges of aristocracy, the navy, the army, the church, and the corn laws. Sir George C. Lewis in 1841 argued that neither for tribute, military assistance, trade facilities, as outlets for immigration, or as penal settlements were the colonies of any possible value as possessions. Sir James Stephen wrote in 1849: "It remains for the Canadian to cut the last cable which anchors us to them . . . the same process is in progress in the Australian colonies." Of the smaller colonies, including New Zealand, he wrote that "these detached little islands with their indigenous populations were wretched burdens which in an evil hour we had assumed." And Earl Grey, secretary of state for the colonies, in 1846 felt that the acquisition of African land would be "not merely worthless, but pernicious—the source not of increasing strength, but weakness." And in 1860 the economist, Cairnes, wrote that "in commercial policy, in territorial policy, in military defence, the colonies, in the teeth of example, advice and remonstrance, have pursued their own way. We have abandoned all the objects for the sake of which our colonial empire was founded. We are unable to impress our will upon our colonies in any particular, however in itself reasonable or just or apparently necessary for their safety or ours. We retain the privilege of spending yearly £4.5 millions on their protection and receive in requital prohibitive tariffs and ironical allegiance." An assistant under-secretary for war considered that the presence of the British flag all over the world added very much to English weakness. All Englishmen were "little Englanders" in the middle of the nineteenth century, and it was asked whether as the "thirteen colonies had once revolted from us because we proposed to tax them for our benefit, might not we, who were taxed for the benefit of our colonies, now revolt from them." The British government and people had neither the ideas nor the institutions which could in any way further the development of a British imperial order.

In Canada the existence of a politically conscious and alien French Catholic community and the proximity of the republican institutions of the United States encouraged the development of responsible government. This constitutional revolution by which the governor, as the head of the executive appointed by the Crown came to accept policies which were presented to him by a cabinet responsible to an elected colonial legislature, took place between 1839 and 1854. It was carried out by instructions from the Crown in despatches to the governor. In 1839 the colonial secretary, Lord John Russell, considered that such responsible government was entirely incompatible with the relations between the mother country and the colony. By 1854 it was recognized that it could not be too distinctly acknowledged that it is neither possible nor desirable to carry on the government of any of the British possessions in America in opposition to the opinion of the inhabitants. The powers of the Crown were never formally abolished. Constitutional conventions were accepted by which the sphere of colonial self-government in Canada grew from a limited autonomy into a complete self-determination—the dominion status of the British Commonwealth of 1926. The British had, in fact, let pass any hope or fear of empire they may ever have had. In 1859 the government of Canada asserted its right to "adjust the taxation of the people in the way they deem best, even if it should unfortunately happen to meet with the disapproval of the Imperial ministry." The British theory of complete international free trade was dead beyond its shores. The principle of self-government had overridden the principle of free trade, the root of Britain's power and the economic theory of her finest minds. One free people could not govern another free people, and free men could not compel free men to be free in industry and trade. Dominion tariffs were to grow unpruned by any imperial knife. In 1867 the British North America Act set out a federal constitution which the self-governing colonies of British North America—French and English—had devised for their own particular needs. Responsible government, once it had been established in British North America, would not be denied to Australia and New Zealand.

The development of trade and commerce was to involve Britain in frontiers more distant than the northwest frontier of India, the middle west of Canada, or the deserts of Australia. In 1825 China, Korea, and Japan with a quarter of the world's population were inaccessible to the trade and commerce of the Western world. The Mughal Empire in India had been taken over by the East India Company; the Ottoman Empire which bordered eastern Europe was thought to be in slow dissolution. But the Chinese Empire had lost no territory since 1700 and had in fact been extended by the acquisition of Tibet. The emperor of China loosely governed an area stretching from the Pacific to the Pamirs. Europe had had its theory of a Holy Roman Empire, the Dantesque image in the terrestrial globe of the unity of Heaven; confined and pestered in this pinfold here, it was yet the temporal shadow of the Christian heaven. But in China the emperor was the sole legitimate representative of heaven in mundane affairs. He rejoiced in the political theory that there could be

nothing in the nature of international relations in the Western sense between equal sovereign states, because there could only be one legitimate
government in the world. The relation of all other monarchs to him
could only be one of vassalage. No guilt of conquest could trouble his
soul, for all states which he might conquer were merely revolted vassal
states retrieved after a temporary and regrettable secession. No problem
of the balance of power could worry him, for the Chinese Jehovah had
not bothered to permit a Chinese Satan to fall. The court of Peking permitted merchants from Europe and North America to trade at Canton
under rules laid down unilaterally by the local Chinese authorities.

The British had by far the largest share of the volume of western
trade which went to Canton. The business was conducted by the East
India Company and by merchants from India operating under licence.
When in 1834 the British terminated the East India Company's monopoly
by act of Parliament and the China trade was thrown open to free competition on the British side, the Chinese bureaucracy would not enter
into any official relations. In 1839 the first Anglo-China War began. It
was not a war to force opium upon China but to remedy the harsh conditions imposed upon foreigners. The British demanded official intercourse on equal terms with the provincial administration for the settlement of disputes arising out of the trade at Canton, the payment of an
indemnity, and the cession of the island of Hong Kong. The Treaty of
Nanking, August 1842, provided for the cession of Hong Kong and for
the opening to foreign trade of other ports in addition to Canton. The
British disclaimed any intention of seeking for themselves in China rights
and privileges which were not available to other nations. They promoted
the development of the efficient and incorruptible Chinese maritime customs service. Great inroads had been made into China's seclusion, but
she had not opened regular diplomatic relations with foreign governments'
representatives and except for recreation allowed no right of travel for
foreigners outside the five treaty ports.

If Britain kept out of other wars between 1815 and 1854 it was not
because of any doctrine or practice of isolation. The British government,
unlike the government of China, did not consider that it was the only
representative of Heaven. It could not, like the government of the United
States, announce a Monroe doctrine for a new world where men could
enjoy life, liberty, and the pursuit of happiness while their virtues shone.
British statesmen were too near a divided continent, itself a mere peninsular of Asia, to feel perfectly secure whatever their strength and influence might seem to be. They could not follow Cobden and have no foreign policy, leaving it to the loom of trade and commerce to weave the

web of peace. They had been deeply involved in the settlement made at the Congress of Vienna. Castlereagh had put into practice there the idea of a European concert or league, which he had inherited from the Younger Pitt. The preface to the Vienna settlement had been the Grand Alliance, the defeat of Napoleon, and the need for a European settlement which would contain within her old frontiers the power of France.

The Treaty of Vienna (1815) was made by statesmen who were attached to the principles and practice of the balance of power. For Castlereagh the balance needed was a France back within her frontiers of 1790 and held by a barrier of states to north and south. France was to be kept out of the Low Countries and the Rhine. Belgium was united to Holland to make a strong Dutch state. France retained Alsace-Lorraine, but Prussia got the districts south of the Rhine. Piedmont was strengthened with Genoa, Austria with Lombardy and Venetia. In the center was an independent and neutral Switzerland. Spain and Portugal were given their old boundaries. Sweden was given Norway from Denmark. Russia took a large part of Poland, including Warsaw, and the Emperor Alexander kept an army of one million men, more than good judges thought necessary. The smaller states had been sacrificed to the larger so that the pieces on the board might not complicate too much the game of public safety. British maritime supremacy was consolidated. The property claims of individuals who had suffered were fairly met. A doctrine of international rivers was laid down. The slave trade was declared inhuman. There was originality in the arrangements for guaranteeing the settlement. Castlereagh hoped to hold the existing order together using traditional methods under the mediating hand of Great Britain. He looked for what he called a "European Commonwealth." Britain was, however, to be an impartial umpire and not a member of the team. Sea power is better for umpires than for players.

There were forces below the surface of the Vienna settlement of Europe which were to transform the old order into something sinister and strange. The pattern of three Eastern despotic powers and the Western powers stirred by the principles of representative government could not endure. In 1820, when there was a revolution in Spain and the three military monarchs of central and eastern Europe—Russia, Prussia, and Austria—wished to intervene actively, Castlereagh would not have England join a league of despots. His state paper of 1820 is one of the most famous in British history.[10] It states the principle of nonintervention—that England would not interfere by force in the internal affairs of other states. The system of European co-operation which Castlereagh had done so much to promote died with it. If our Allies, he wrote, "will be theorists,

we must act in separation." "The union for the reconquest and liberation of a great proportion of the continent of Europe from the military
dominion of France was never," Castlereagh wrote, "intended as an union
for the government of the world, or for the superintendence of the internal
affairs of other states." [11] The stability of all existing governments was
menaced more or less by the fact that so many states of Europe were
"employed in the difficult task of casting anew their governments upon
the Representative principle." But "the notion of revising, limiting or
regulating the course of such experiments, either by foreign council or by
foreign force, would be as dangerous to avow as it would be impossible
to execute." There was the Eastern bloc of despotic continental states,
Russia, Austria, and Prussia, and "for purposes of internal tranquility"
Austria and Prussia might be regarded as component parts of a united
Germany. In the West were France and Spain. There were in addition,
since the Congress of Vienna, "but few pieces on the board to complicate
the game of public safety." He continued: "The principle of one State
interfering by force in the internal affairs of another in order to enforce
obedience to the governing authority, is always a question of the greatest
possible moral as well as political delicacy" and "to generalise such a
principle and to think of reducing it to a system, or to impose it as an
obligation, is a scheme utterly impracticable and objectionable." Only
mischief could be expected from a system of constant European interference upon the volcanic masses in which the principle of representation
was abroad. And no country having a representative system of government could act upon a system of intervention. Britain could interfere
with effect, but she was the last government in Europe which could be
expected or could venture to commit herself on any question of abstract
character. In 1824 Canning stated that Britain would be "no party to
a general interference in the concerns of other states." She would be
prepared "to interfere" only "on *special* occasions" which in her opinion
justified such interference.[12] Canning deprecated the laying down of "fixed
resolutions for eventual probabilities," and declared that "cases must
arise upon facts which it is utterly beyond the power of human foresight
to combine and calculate beforehand." [13]

Palmerston in 1830 had to deal with one such unforeseen contingency.
In 1830 the Belgians revolted against the Dutch and issued a declaration
of national independence. The French had a good case for intervention
to restore order. They had, too, a French royal prince as candidate for
the Belgian throne whom the Belgians were willing to accept. A settlement
by which Belgium was to be neutral and independent was devised by
Great Britain and accepted by Belgium. The Dutch objected and in 1831

invaded Belgium and were only kept from Brussels by the advance of a French army into Belgium. With the French in Belgium and the British fleet in the Downs ready for any emergency, the danger was extreme. In 1793 Pitt and Grenville had gone to war with France to keep Belgium and Holland independent of her. No British statesman would allow French influence to dominate in Belgium. Palmerston told the French they must leave Belgium, and when they agreed to do so the crisis was over.

Palmerston had no systematic policy about foreign relations. He would do what seemed best in the interests of Britain on each occasion as it arose. But he did not wish to be a mere umpire between the conflicting principles of despotism and democracy. He considered constitutional states the natural allies of Britain; it was the duty of an English ministry to be attentive to the interests of such states. He hoped that he would be able to keep parliamentary France apart from despotic Russia. From his twenty years at the War Office he knew the extent of Russia's military power. The British navy was supreme on the sea, but a combination between France and Russia would mean that the most formidable military power in the world could advance to India overland while the French navy, powerful in the Mediterranean, could obstruct Britain on the sea. In 1834 he took a chance which offered to form an alliance of the constitutional powers, Spain, Portugal, France, and England. He saw in the Quadruple Alliance of 1834 "a powerful counterpoise to the Holy Alliance of the East." [14]

Unfortunately, there was no real community of economic interest between France and Britain at that time. British and French trading interests were fighting bitterly in Greece, Spain, Africa, and the Pacific. But Palmerston continued to believe in the political advantages of union with France. In the Eastern crisis 1839–40, Palmerston had to prevent a division of Turkey into two separate states, one a dependency of France and the other a satellite of Russia. Successful experiments in steam navigation on the Red Sea and the Euphrates had greatly enhanced the importance of the overland routes to India in British eyes. Palmerston won a victory over Mehemet Ali, over France, over Turkey, and over the majority of his colleagues in the British Cabinet. As Disraeli wrote in *Tancred,* it was "a great monument alike of diplomatic skill and administrative energy." In 1839 Mehemet Ali and his son Ibrahim Pasha had annihilated the Turkish forces of Sultan Mahmud II sent to subdue them. The Turkish fleet surrendered at Alexandria. Palmerston tried to set up a European combination to restrain Mehemet Ali from profiting by his conquests. France had still Napoleonic dreams of Egypt, and Mehemet Ali would have preferred to be the vassal of France rather than of Turkey.

When France would not agree to a compromise Palmerston concluded a convention between Austria, Prussia, Russia, and Britain in 1840. A British fleet appeared at Alexandria. Mehemet Ali was induced to withdraw his army back into Egypt. In 1841, in the Straits' Convention, all the Great Powers, including France, pledged support to Turkey and pledged the sultan to close both Bosporous and Dardanelles to ships of war. Russia thought she had gained an advantage by stopping British and French warships at the Dardanelles; England and France by stopping Russian ships at the Bosporous.[15]

Tsar Nicholas I was delighted at the separation of England from France over the Egyptian crisis of 1839 and to make it permanent asked England to enter into a secret alliance against France in 1840. Palmerston in his refusal explained to Nicholas the doctrine of obligations by which a British Cabinet and Parliament can be bound. "Changes which foreign nations may choose to make in their internal Constitution and form of Government . . . are considered in England to be matters of domestic concern, which every nation ought to be allowed to settle as it likes . . . But an attempt of one Nation to seize and to appropriate to itself territory which belongs to another Nation, is a different matter. It may derange the existing Balance of Power." The British government held itself at full liberty to resist such attempts upon the principle of self-defense. But Nicholas must trust to the general tendency of the policy of Great Britain "which leads her to watch attentively, and to guard with care the maintenance of the Balance of Power." [16] It was not possible for the British government to enter into binding engagements without the approval of Parliament, and Parliament might not approve of an engagement which should bind England prospectively. Had the tsar really understood this advice the Crimean War might have been avoided. He would not have played with proposals for the partition of the Turkish Empire. He did not invite England to rob Turkey of Egypt in the south, while he robbed her in the north. But he did not heed the warning that Palmerston had given in 1841. The Crimean War occurred because Britain held that Russia was "seeking to obtain a virtual protectorate over the Christian subjects of the Porte" and that the claims put forward by Russia were irreconcilable with the assurance that no extended power or influence was sought in Turkey. In 1840–41 the problem of the Straits had been recognized as an European concern. In 1853–54 the very future of the Ottoman Empire was endangered by Russia's action, and it, too, was a common concern of the powers. The Crimean War began "because a nationalist and defiant Turkey would not yield to Russian demands which she held to be humiliating and threatening to the maintenance of her empire. France and Britain joined her, and Austria openly swung towards the allies because they were not prepared to allow Russia to settle her scores with Turkey by herself and to gain thereby complete ascendancy in the Balkans and Asia Minor." [17]

The Crimean War ended forty years of peace. In the next fifteen years the great powers of Europe fought four wars which completely transformed the map of continental Europe. After the Crimean War the powers of Europe had an entirely new attitude towards the distribution of forces there. Napoleon III was intent upon securing a general rearrangement of the map of Europe upon national lines. Austria tried to consolidate its position and influence in Germany and abandoned the practice of collaboration with Prussia on which the settlement of 1815 depended. Prussia began to think that she would have to fight for her existence against Austria. Russia, which since 1815 had by her close association with Austria and Prussia prevented German dualism from degenerating into open antagonism, had herself become a revisionist power and wanted to free herself from the conditions imposed upon her by the Peace of Paris in 1856.[18] Great Britain tried to withdraw from continental troubles. Radicals felt that the time had come to apply the philosophy of laissez faire to foreign policy. Tories argued that Britain's national interest lay overseas. The principle of nonintervention became the shibboleth of all ministries between 1865 and 1870. They would use "firm but moderate language to deter the strong." [19] Her credit and her power, Gladstone wrote in 1869, "form a fund, which in order that they may be made the most of, should be thriftily used." [20] This was not the nonintervention of Canning and Palmerston, but an almost complete abstention from continental affairs. In continental Europe the Gorchakovs, Cavours, and Bismarcks made diplomacy an instrument not for the preservation of peace, but for the promotion of war. In the new conditions of war on the continent created by the railway and new techniques of mobilization and firepower Britain was powerless to intervene even had she wished to. Within a month of the opening of the Franco-Prussian War ten battles were decided and 300,000 were killed, wounded, or made prisoner. A British expeditionary force could have numbered at most 10,000 men. The idea of nationality had sown dragon's teeth and Britain had no means to pull them up.

CHAPTER XI

Economic Vicissitudes, 1870-1914

In the middle of the nineteenth century Britain was the world's workshop, the world's carrier, and the world's entrepôt. She had been the frontier of a new civilization born of a marriage of new scientific method and ancient skills. It is the fate of all successful pioneers to be replaced by those that follow after. The pioneers of new mechanical methods could not long remain unchallenged. The new industrial Mephistopheles could not serve indefinitely only a British Faust. Like the Sorcerer's Apprentice, Britain was soon almost overwhelmed by the new powers she had unleashed.

The new methods were conditioned by a unique economic climate. A free internal market and the possibility of worldwide trade had made possible a division of labor which stimulated the use of machinery in textile production, the use of iron, and the consumption of coal. The factory, the bank, and the merchant were all for one and one for all. A growing industrial population in Europe and above all in nineteenth-century Britain wanted increasing supplies of food and of raw materials from the world at large. Britain, Europe, and the United States were to become the world's workshop and the whole world their granary and source of raw materials.

There had been, as we have seen, a dream of peace and plenty nourished by an international division of labor. A system of laissez faire within each nation state would co-operate in international anarchy to the relief of man's estate. The dream was to become the nightmare through which we have lived. Why, we do not really know. But we do know that the political implications of complete freedom of trade between the producers of different nations were not accepted by the old empires or by the new states of Europe or by the nascent industrial power of the United States, eager to develop its own economic empire beyond the Mississippi. The causes of our present welfare and our dreadful woes lay not merely in a rejection of a Cobdenite millennium. The process of change in production and distribution had in the middle of the nineteenth century only just begun. The consummation of the marriage between new science and old crafts would produce a progeny which, like the Titans, would dethrone all the ancient gods. In textiles, in coal, and iron Britain had been the first to be served by the new powers. But the natural resources of other countries were far greater than hers, and the technique of putting nature to the question, so that she might give up her secrets for the use of men, could not be confined to a few small islands off the coast of Europe. Christians believe that the implications of the Incarnation are universal. The Cross has been the symbol of the brotherhood of man. The first machine age and all that it implied for the use of natural resources for human needs was also worldwide in its implications. It was a mutation in the pattern of human activities, and its end no one can foresee. Once clearly established in the British Isles it was certain to range the world. It was a process of change which could not fail to accelerate. What had been at first empirical, fumbling, and local would become experimental, planned, and universal.

Between 1870 and 1914 the world came into possession of a larger increment to its economic wealth than it had ever known before. The railroad, the steamship, the prospector, the builder, and settler opened to production and trade the areas that had previously been of little commercial importance. Science was "comforting man's animal poverty and leisuring his toil . . ."

In the United States alone there was an area larger than the Roman Empire open for development by its industrial and commercial leaders. Between 1870 and 1910 over 80,000 miles of new railway were opened in continental Europe (excluding Russia and Turkey), 38,000 miles in Russia, 158,000 miles in the U.S.A., 24,000 miles in Canada, 27,000 miles in India, and over 50,000 miles in Latin America. In the same period the world's supply of shipping grew from 16,800,000 metric tons in 1870 to 34,600,000 metric tons. From 1880 to 1914 the international trade of the world as a whole nearly trebled.

At the center of this vast web of world trade was the British capital market. British industry had more than doubled its output between 1870 and 1913, but in the world as a whole there had been a fourfold increase. In 1870 Britain produced nearly a third of the world's output of manufactures, in the closing years of the nineteenth century about a fifth, and in 1913 only about a seventh. In 1880 Britain produced nearly as much steel as the whole of Europe, but in 1913 only about a fifth. In 1880 she produced three times as much coal as Germany and more than twice as much as the United States, but in 1913 her output was only about one and a half times that of Germany and rather more than half that of the United States. In 1890 the American steel output exceeded the British and in 1913 it was four times as great. In 1893 Germany overtook Britain as a steel producer, and in 1913 her output was more than twice that of Britain. The rate of British industrial growth after 1880 fell to less than 2 per cent per annum, while that of Germany had risen to 3.9 per cent and of the United States to 4.8 per cent.

On the surface the shape of things to come had cast warning shadows. The British economy seemed to be overspecialized. In 1914 she was dependent on her manufactured exports to finance three-quarters of her raw materials (apart from coal) and one-half of her food. The first comprehensive census of production in 1907 showed that the staple trades of coal mining, iron and steel, and textiles accounted for 46 per cent of the total "value" added by manufacture of British industries, employed nearly a quarter of the working population, and supplied 70 per cent of all British exports.

In 1907, too, 60 per cent of the insured population in manufacturing industry was concentrated in four main areas: South Wales, the northeast coast of England, Lancashire, and mid-Scotland. Since 1870 agriculture as a source of employment and means of livelihood had greatly declined. The late nineteenth century was a period of large-scale agricultural decline in England. It was in that period that the countryman ceased to be a representative figure of English life and that the long-standing traditions of village society began to crumble. Henry Strakers were in the wings to do their turn after Hardy's yokels. The Great Depression of 1874 had stimulated economic nationalism in the world outside Britain, and agriculture also had to adapt itself to the challenge from the products of world granaries brought nearer by improved transport. Although England still had one of the more productive farming industries of the world, she had carried industrial specialization to an extreme limit. On the eve of war in 1914 the number of persons engaged in agriculture was only 8 per cent of Britain's employed population, compared with 33 per cent in Germany and 43 per cent in France.

The British system had in some things shown great adaptability and it was tough, skillful, and experienced. In others there were signs of serious maladjustments and inelasticity. In 1914 British shipyards still supplied 61 per cent of the world's total tonnage of shipping. In cotton the number of spindles and looms in use had increased 45 per cent between 1885 and 1914. The yardage of piece goods exported in 1909–13 was nearly half as much again as it had been in 1880–84. In 1860 the output of coal was 80,000,000 tons, an amount equal to one-half the world supply. In 1913 it was 287,000,000 tons, of which 34 per cent was exported, and the industry employed 1,100,000 men. But the products in which she excelled were being supplied by her former customers. Her technological ability in the new and expanding industries was in general inferior to that of Germany and the United States. Although many of the major innovations of the nineteenth century had originated in Britain, they had been commercially developed elsewhere. Britain had invented basic steel; she had been the first to produce solid-drawn weldless steel tubes, but the development of these had been in Germany. In 1879 she had experimented in electrical metallurgy, but in 1900 the United States led in it. In 1913 Britain imported no less than nine-tenths of her synthetic dyes and dyestuffs from the Continent. In 1907 the newer industries of motor vehicles, electrical goods, chemicals, artificial silks, and certain types of machinery employed only 5.2 per cent of her labor force and were responsible for less than 2 per cent of her manufacturing exports. In 1912 the automobile industry in the United Kingdom produced some 25,000 vehicles when the United States produced 485,000. Britain's share of the world's manufacture of all kinds of electrical products was 13 per cent, whereas that of Germany was 31.9 per cent and that of the United States 28.9 per cent.

To see the British problem in perspective one must look at the general character of the industrial changes in which she and all other nations were involved. The revolution in textile manufacture had been an application of mechanical principles to the naturally cylindrical fibers of the cotton plant or the cylindrical embellishments of the sheep. What the wheel had once done on the macro level of transport the new textile machines could do on the almost micro level of the thread. But the first mechanization had affected only a few industries. After 1870 cylinders and rods moving at great speed became common to industry in general. After 1850 the number and accuracy of machine tools steadily increased. After 1860 increased supplies of cheap steel and the mass production of standardized universally used components, such as screws, made the new machines as universal as old tools. What printing had been to learning, machine tools were to production. As the machines became more accurate and more prolific (for there were now machines to make machines), the implications for production of applied science were partly revealed.

The developments in industry at the end of the nineteenth century were the practical outcome of the previous hundred years' achievement in pure science, thermodynamics, electro-magnetism, chemistry, and geology. In 1884 the steam turbine was invented by Parsons, and its power transformed the speed and carrying power of ships, and, linked with the new electromagnets in the dynamos of Siemens, made possible central power stations. In chemistry the periodic table of the elements stimulated the search for the ones which were missing and opened up the world of modern alloys. New forms of matter and new forms of energy could be linked in ever more productive combinations. In the last quarter of the nineteenth century a great deal came to be known about the association of particular minerals with particular geological ages and types of formation. The laws which govern geological phenomena were not only of concern to those who, like Mr. Gladstone, were concerned to defend Mosaic cosmology, but they could serve to guide the miner and to uncover the world's supplies of petroleum.

The probing of the makeup of raw materials and the release of new forms of energy meant that the supremacy enjoyed by a particular industry might be undermined in a very short space of time. That sails should give place to iron and steam or that horses should be replaced by motor cars everybody knows, but they are only particular examples of continuous and accelerating processes of production and distribution. The discovery that iron could be worked with coal gave Britain her predominance in the iron industry. The invention of the hot blast created a great Scottish iron trade. The inventions of Bessemer and Siemens caused the industry to move to the coast where the imported ores needed would be cheapest. The Thomas process made Germany the chief European producer.[1] Before 1850 the United States had been a leading builder of wooden ships; her supremacy was undermined when ships came to be made of iron.

Before 1914 the economist could find a deep satisfaction in contemplating the fine and intricate web of industry and trade which had come into existence as a result of the striving of individuals without any central control. It was an economist who smiled with deep satisfaction when he heard that a Gestapo leader had in 1941 asked to be told the headquarters of the black-market. A market is for the economist like the medieval God—its center is everywhere and its circumference nowhere. The economic order of liberal theory, like the honeycomb of Darwin, had come from adaptation and selection through many generations and had had no shaping spirit from on high. An "invisible hand" had indirectly secured that from the conflict and co-operation of a billion wills of individuals pursuing what seemed best to each, a self-regulating order of great common interest had emerged. This theory was very gratifying to those who were producing cotton goods for every clime, whose ships were on every sea, and whose golden sovereigns or their paper equivalent were in every till. But there were critics. One wrote of "three thousand unco-ordinated small units . . . all without cohesion, without nucleus, loose higgledy-piggledy, running hither and thither, jostling, chasing, fighting, the whole curious phenomenon involving an enormous waste of money, energy, time and power." In fact, of course, an element of central control was always present, in that the state was responsible for the legal order without which the co-operation of individuals in economic activities would have been impossible, and also for a variety of services which experience, reinforced by theory, suggested some central organization must perform.

The increase in the population of England and Wales between 1871 and 1911 was 13,300,000, greater than in any other forty years. The increase was achieved with less pain and less loss than ever before. Fewer men died when they were in their full powers; fewer women—though the family might still be, as Bernard Shaw called it, the mother's workhouse and the daughter's prison—were worn out by excessive child bearing. More children lived to maturity. The percentage of the total population of Britain aged fifteen to sixty-four inclusive rose from about 60 per cent in 1891 to nearly 64 per cent in 1911.[2] Because there were more people at the peak of their mental and physical power and skill, training experience could yield fruit for a longer period. The national income after 1870 was growing faster than before. Behind the squalor—the lot of the very poor was probably more miserable at the opening of the twentieth century than it has ever been—and behind the glamor—the fashionable Edwardians displayed a vulgarity in marble halls and open spaces which, even now, infects the subtlety of Henry James and the charm of Max Beerbohm—there is almost statistical certainty that real incomes were growing at a rate that had never before been sustained for so long.

It is estimated that the national income of England and Wales was in 1867 £32 per head of the population and for the United Kingdom £27 per head. It is known that half the total went to rather less than one-tenth of income receivers and therefore the great majority had incomes well below these general averages. But it could be said that there was an amount which, evenly spread, would have provided a modest comfort, but no more, for all. It was this sense that the horribly poor like the horribly good need not always be with us that was the inspiration of the Fabian socialism of the turn of the century. However scandalous the inequality of income in the early twentieth century,

> "see how cross-eyed the pride of our world-wide crusade
> Against Nigerian slavery, while the London poor

> In their Victorian slums lodged closer and filthier
> Than the outraged alien . . . ,"

it was just a little less extreme than it had been forty years before. After 1870 the masses of wage earners were improving their position even more than were the middle class; the increase of moderate incomes seemed to contemporary statisticians to be outstanding; and it is possible that the aristocracy experienced some diminution of income—though the prophecy of Lord Salisbury that the poor would make all the laws and the rich would pay all the taxes had not yet been fulfilled.

It was this vigorous, competitive, hideous, and yet dazzling community which was the great exporter of the capital which made it possible to open up the vast but hitherto untapped resources lying in the hinterlands of new continents. All the undeveloped parts of the world were calling for investments. Nearly a quarter of the £2,400,000,000 which was added to the capital of the United Kingdom between 1865 and 1875 was placed abroad, while a sixth went into houses and a tenth into railways at home. By 1875 the heavy investment needed for the equipment of an industrial society—the railways, docks, towns, and their equipment and services—had taken place. The spread of mechanical transport and communications and the speeding up of manufacturing processes made investment at home more immediately productive than it had been before, and investments in railways and other enterprises in the American West brought a large flow of cheap imports much more quickly than comparable investment in the 1850's and 1860's. It has been argued that the effort and the expense which went into the development of the colonial empire were at the cost of improvements which might have been made at home. This is to ignore the indirect gain which came from bringing new areas with new products into a worldwide system of multilateral trade. The small volume of direct trade with many new colonies often contained an element which played a vital part in some more complex interchange of other types.[3]

The dominating theme of British economic life between 1870 and 1914 was her increased involvement in international trade. More and more of the goods produced or consumed in Britain had to be sold or bought overseas. Foreign investments brought large new productive areas into relation with the British economy. This caused a relative increase in the distributive, financial, and other services in the British way of life.[4] By 1914 there had developed a unique and subtle system of multilateral trade. The United Kingdom sold her manufactured goods to primary producers who got the money to pay for them from their own sales to continental industrial countries and the United States. The industrial countries of Europe paid the primary producers and the United States by their sales to the United Kingdom. In this system it was possible for Germany to be not only the United Kingdom's chief competitor in manufactures but also her best customer. The United Kingdom exported pig iron and acid steel to Germany and took in return semimanufactured steel products. The increased demand by the continental and other industrial countries for the products of the primary producers enabled the latter to buy more British exports and the British to buy greater quantities of continental manufactures.

In this way a vast external trade had become a vital part of British economic life. In 1907 about one-quarter of the goods produced in the United Kingdom was exported while one-fifth of the goods consumed came directly from imports. If we allow for the home-produced goods which incorporated other imports, the total of retained imports was about one-third of the total national consumption. In addition to its own trade Britain, as financier, carrier, insurer, and commercial agent, had a direct stake in the trade of half the world beside. No country has ever had so great an interest in the worldwide growth of commerce and in the free movement and security of capital everywhere. Before 1870 a great part of Britain's trade had been bilateral, and only a small surplus or deficit had to be settled through multilateral exchange. As British import requirements became vast and varied and the area of profitable investment widened with the greater speed of communications and the international mobility of labor, there was a fall in the proportion of wants which she could meet by goods purchased from those areas which were her best customers or where she had most investment. Before 1870 most of British capital exports had gone to continental Europe and to the older centers of the United States. But in the 1860's they were going to India (for railways); in the 1880's to the American West; in the 1890's to Australia, the Argentine, and South Africa; in the early 1900's to Canada, the Argentine, and Brazil. By 1914 about half of British investment overseas was in the Empire—Canada, India, and Australia being the most important borrowers. About 20 per cent of all British foreign investment was in the United States and another 20 per cent in Latin America, nearly half of which was in the Argentine. As the range of British export goods was limited—coal and iron and textiles—in those few countries where she had a clear surplus in her balance of trade that surplus had to be large and, to make that possible, those countries had to have a large surplus with the rest of the world.

In this intricate pattern India was a vital part. For India and other Asiatic countries could sell large amounts of food and raw materials to other industrial countries as well as to Britain. In 1910 probably one-half of Britain's deficits was covered by receipts from India, for India had a large import surplus with Britain and also paid regular dividends on large past investments.[5]

Today any part of the world may be hit by a bomb fired from any other part, but in that lost nineteenth-century heaven of British financial supremacy it was possible for a payment received in any part of the world to settle a debt incurred in any other part. The pivot of the delicate system was the London capital and money market. A large part of the world's trade was financed by sterling bills of exchange and the international gold standard. The United Kingdom was far in the lead of other international lenders. She annually invested abroad a sum equivalent to her total current receipts in interest and dividends earned on her overseas capital holdings.

This British position was inherently transient. Her power to supply financial services and capital to the outside world was dependent on her own international earning power. The village moneylender had to be a vigorous and prosperous blacksmith as well. After 1900 the area from which she earned her surplus had shrunk. The goods by which she earned that surplus were in large part the cotton textiles, which were most vulnerable to the competition of newly industrialized countries. British coal exports, too, had an importance out of all proportion to their size—which indeed was large. Had there been no coal exports, a large proportion of British shipping would have had to leave her ports in ballast (for her export goods were not bulky and her imports were) and freight rates would have been higher. The coal export trade helped Britain to carry her industrialization further than she otherwise could. In the body of her economic life her coal exports were hormones which nourished every tissue however peripheral. But coal was a wasting asset because with increased demand less and less fertile mines and seams were being worked. The structure of the industry made it very resistant to improvements in organization and technique. Mine owners were, in their resistance to change, almost the peasant proprietors of the underworld.

The great foreign trade in coal had developed since 1870. In 1800 the annual output had been a bare 10,000,000 tons. The number of workers in the industry had risen from about 200,000 in 1850 to 1,127,000 in 1913. The number of coal miners was increasing faster than was the employed population as a whole. In 1913 about one-tenth of the employed males were in coal mining. The increased demand from abroad had been a main cause of this growth. In 1860 the export trade had been a bare 10,000,000 tons; in 1900 it was five times as great and in 1913 it was 98,000,000 tons, about one-third the total output. In 1913 the world output of coal was about 1,200,000,000 metric tons of which the United States produced 517,000,000 and Europe 605,000,000, and Britain produced nearly half of that. The United States, Britain, and Germany were responsible in 1913 for nearly all the export trade, and the British share of the total was about two-thirds.[6]

While it was inevitable that Britain should lose her industrial leadership to countries which had larger internal markets and more abundant natural resources, her own industrial development after 1870 was still very rapid. The technical basis of British industry changed radically between 1870 and 1914. In 1871 the textile and clothing industries employed more people than all other manufacturing industries together: 14.3 per cent of the employed population of England and Wales was engaged in agriculture, 9.3 per cent in textile manufacturing, 8.5 per cent in making articles of clothing, 6.3 per cent in the building trades, and 4.5 per cent in mining; in Scotland: 17.3 per cent in agriculture, 14.2 per cent in textiles, 6.6 per cent in clothing, and 13.9 per cent in other manufacturing industries.[7] While in 1914 as in 1870 the same industries dominated economic life, they had come to concern themselves with the production of an almost entirely new range of commodities. Coal mining, the major textile industries, cotton and wool, and the building industry did not greatly change their products. But in the iron, steel, and engineering industries there were sweeping changes in the character of the things produced. In the iron and steel industry the most important change was the substitution of steel for puddled iron, and in engineering there came into existence a whole series of virtually new industries.[8]

It was the abundance of coal which had made possible a great British iron industry, and the fact that the coalfields were near the coast helped the growth of shipbuilding and the shipping trade, while the concentration of population nourished the railways. The demand for rails had caused a boom in the iron industry in the 1870's, but by 1876 the market for iron rails was dead. The use of puddled iron reached its peak of 2,800,-000 tons in 1882 and then declined. In 1870 Britain had produced less than 250,000 tons of steel, but in 1913 she produced 7,600,000 tons. In 1879 Percy Gilchrist and Sidney Thomas showed how to line a blast furnace to take up the phosphorous in iron and initiated the use of basic steel in place of the acid steel of earlier processes. The consequent rise of the Bessemer industry in Germany and the United States forced the British to concentrate on high-quality steels produced by the open-hearth process. This revolution marked the end of British predominance in the iron and steel trade. In 1870 Britain had provided half the pig iron of the world.

In 1913 the United States produced three times as much and Germany half as much again as Britain. In 1890 the United States and in 1893 Germany passed her in the production of steel. In 1913 the German production was twice and that of the United States four times that of Britain.

The new steel industry had to be organized in a very different way from that of wrought iron. The latter was largely a manual process dependent on the skill of experienced workers. The new steel industries were based on large-scale production and the use of skilled metallurgists. As one writer put it in 1907: "The rule of thumb is dead in the workshop, the day is with the engineer and the chemist with their methods of precision." [9]

The loss of her supremacy in iron and steel, the rising cost of her natural asset, coal, as deeper seams had to be worked, and a decline in Britain's percentage of world trade from 22 per cent in 1871–75 to 15 per cent in 1913 were no doubt unavoidable. Gulliver in Brobdingnag could not cut the figure he had in Lilliput. The industrial revolution had left its British cradle and was crawling round the world. But there were failures by the British to do what perhaps they might have done. The nature and extent of those failures are not easy to define. It is of the very nature of a period of economic progress that some industries must decline, and if they are centered in a particular area that area may decline with them. Tin mining, for example, reached its peak about 1870 and fell away after 1890. Copper mining was in continuous decline after 1850 and had almost disappeared by 1900. The linen industry contracted in England after 1860, but maintained itself in Ireland and Scotland. The new industry of jute developed in Scotland in the second half of the nineteenth century. After 1874 the falling prices of the Great Depression slowed up the growth of both agriculture and industry. But if they did not advance as quickly as before, other activities essential to a complex economy—the distributive and financial services—were very much alive. In shipbuilding, too, Britain retained her predominance. The replacement of wood and sail by iron and steam was a generation later than the railway revolution in land transport. In 1870 British sail tonnage was still four times as great as steam. But in 1869 the Suez Canal was opened. By 1890 steel had replaced iron in hulls, reducing their weight and increasing their carrying power, and the use of steel in boilers made greater pressure possible and reduced fuel consumption.

British industry, like industry in any part of the world, had to be adapted to conditions of place and time. In the early nineteenth century she had had exceptional opportunities to develop the steam engine in the way she had. In the late nineteenth century the United States had special advantages for the development of the motor car—the demand and the tradition of mass production and interchangeable parts. Of course, the automobile was made possible by a conjunction of a variety of discoveries and improvements in several trades—an internal gas combustion engine of 1860, the high-speed Daimler engine of 1883, the pneumatic principle discovered in 1845 and applied to cycles in 1888, light-weight alloys, and electricity for ignition. The United States had plentiful oil. In Europe the motor car was long a luxury, and in Britain the Red Flag Regulation, which required that such a vehicle be preceded by a man with a red flag, was not repealed before 1896.

Britain had developed industries in which she had no enduring advantages. But it is the essence of a technological era that there are no enduring advantages. Who can say now whether the equator or the poles will have the greater advantages in the productive and distributive techniques of an atomic age? As competition inevitably developed Britain had to discover and maintain those branches of work for which she had an aptitude and to withdraw from the rest. By 1900 she had gone far to adapt herself to international competition. There was a great expansion in the staple trades and in exports. The new industries of the motor cycle and electricity were doing well.

English agriculture in 1870 compared favorably with that of other countries. But it had latent weaknesses. The leadership was narrow. It made a wasteful use of labor because the labor was not properly trained. There was only small provision for the collection and diffusion of technical knowledge. The ownership of land was closely concentrated. In 1873 nearly half the total area of England and Wales was owned by 4217 persons, each of whom possessed 1000 acres or more. In the whole United Kingdom in 1879 there were 901 landlords with estates of over 10,000 acres each, of whom forty-four owned more than 100,000 acres each.[10] The landowners, in fact, were a powerful pressure group with a firm grip on the machinery of government. In the interests of their industry and way of life they secured and defended rules of apprenticeship, rates of pay, speed of work, and opportunities for leisure and amusement. In the development of land, economic advantages are easy to subordinate to questions of political and social prestige. English land law had two notorious defects. It prevented the proper utilization of land, and it made the parliamentary franchise almost incomprehensible to the layman. For the latter criticism we have the authority of the great legal historian, Frederic Maitland, who wrote: "It may have been supposed that one part at least of our law would be plain, the law relating to the

Parliamentary franchise. But it never will be plain so long as it depends on a real property law essentially nonsensical." Investment in agriculture was hampered for the same reason. It was not possible to establish a registry of titles because it was not possible to register what could not be determined. Land titles drag at each remove a lengthening chain.

During the period of agricultural prosperity from 1860 to 1874 tenant farmers had been discouraged from investing in improvements because of the fear of eviction without proper compensation. In 1875 they were given safeguards against such eviction by the Agricultural Holdings Act. Then the depression of the 1880's, when the age-old farming world felt the first tremors of the changes that science in the fields and crops would mean, and the beginning of a scientific study of agricultural techniques led the landowners to give up the privileges which as a powerful interest group they had held at the expense of the community. In the 1880's there was a popular outcry against entailments, and the Settled Land Act, 1882 was passed. In 1880 the Ground Game Act entitled farmers to kill hares and rabbits. In 1906 the Agricultural Holdings Act gave compensation for damage done by game and freedom to determine the choice of crops and the disposal of produce. But with all these changes the Land Requisition Committee during World War I was surprised at the expense and delay involved in any transfer of land in Britain as compared with such transfers on the Continent.

In Ireland the land issue was the heart of the matter, for there "all the circumstances, all the associations, and all the accretions which had grown around the naked idea of contract were different from England." Half the land was owned by about 700 persons. But these were absentees who differed in religion from their tenants. They did not have the idea of social obligation that in England was imposed by the political and administrative responsibilities of a landlord—from quarter sessions to the House of Lords. In 1870 an effort was made to create by law in Ireland the partnership between landlord and tenant which in England was a matter of custom. The act gave compensation for disturbance and for improvements. It failed because with rising prices the farmer preferred to pay the increased rent his landlord asked rather than be evicted and claim his compensation. When, after 1878, prices fell, evictions increased, and the agrarian issue in Ireland grew to a national and class war. In 1881 Mr. Gladstone was convinced that the land laws of Ireland did not allow her to enjoy the benefits of a system of free contract. Not in Ireland could private vices be public benefits. In 1885 a real attempt was made to settle the Irish land question by creating a peasant proprietorship, the purchase money being advanced by the state. But by then it was too late.

The Irish had a war chest in the United States and could buy arms and men, dynamite, and assassins. In 1903 and in 1904 fresh legislation prepared the way for the complete abolition of landlordism in Ireland, but it could not prevent the final tragedy of civil war.

The Irish tragedy is evidence of the degree to which it was luck, rather than good management, that by 1870 had given the British people so many of the conditions which in 1776 Adam Smith had seen to be necessary to a nation's wealth. However imperfect they might be, there was a market in land, there was mobility of labor, and in each of the diverse areas of production a keen competition between the various manufacturers with only an occasional monopoly to meet special conditions. Within Great Britain there were no separate nationalities which preferred to be poor and self-governing, rather than rich in the political and social order of an alien culture. Had all the Welsh been Roman Catholics or had all the Nonconformists lived in Scotland the problem of minorities might have made democracy and the liberal economic order, which should go with it, as precarious in Britain as it has been in Europe. Only in Ireland did the coincidence of economic, religious, and racial differences produce the passion which in the United States the great open spaces helped to cool and a complex federal system of government to control.

The influx of Irish labor sometimes undermined the local government of an English city. From the 1880's onward there was an influx of Polish and some other Jews afflicted by the revival of anti-Semitism in Europe. This had some effect on the labor market and social life of a few districts in London, Manchester, and Leeds.[11] But immigration was only a minor item to set against the emigration of nearly 2,000,000 persons from Great Britain between 1871 and 1911. For England alone the importance of this emigration was less than for Britain as a whole, since it is highly probable that a smaller proportion of the English moved overseas than of the Welsh and Scots, and certain that England had a net inflow of population from Wales and Scotland.[12] In any case, the natural increase of population between 1871 and 1911 was about nine times the loss from emigration.

The British problem before 1914 was not one of many nations within a single state. It had the more manageable but difficult problem of the rich and the poor. Economic science had derived its prestige from the discovery that there was an order in society which was not the creation of the planning skill of any group with legal authority over all, but the outcome of spontaneous co-operation of individual wills through the market. The economist had shown how under conditions of scarcity—which, since Eden, has been the human condition—an orderly production of goods and services might come from individual freedom of choice. Each for himself would produce more than enough for all, and the hindmost would at least be well nourished when the devil got him. But this analysis of the economist assumed that there would be an impartial administration of the laws which are necessary if the market is to work at all. Scarcity cannot be mitigated without a system of property and contract, as David Hume had clearly seen and stated. J. S. Mill had traced the root of the Irish troubles to the absence of those two essentials. But property and contract as every lawyer knows, and needs no Marx to tell him, are almost as subtle and complex as life itself. After 1870 the government of Britain became more and more concerned with two main tasks: (1) where there was reason to believe that the free play of individual choice and judgment would be beneficial, the government had to secure that there should be neither force nor fraud nor the obstruction of legal forms to hamper the creative power of individual self-help; (2) where the play of individual choice and judgment did not in fact produce the goods and services which common sense suggested—and experience confirmed—were desirable and possible, the government had to try to provide them. If the mechanism of the market was to produce what it could, that mechanism had to be properly serviced. Things necessary to civilized life that a market could not provide the government should provide if possible.

With the wisdom of hindsight we see that neither for ownership nor use of land, nor for the accumulation and application of capital, nor for the hire and fire of labor was the market reasonably organized. Nor to contemporaries did it seem likely that either education or health or safety or the provision of the statistics and fundamental research upon which the life of industry depends would be forthcoming without the intervention of government. The end of politics, the great eighteenth-century statesmen had believed, was to provide and maintain a system of law which would make it possible for men to enjoy as equals life, liberty, and the pursuit of happiness. It was realized, as the intricate patterns created in industrial and commercial activities by mechanization and many inventions began to appear, that the functions of the state would become almost as intricate as industry itself.

The criticism has been made that before 1914 the export of capital set up foreign industries which produced goods to compete with British exports. And, clearly, if you sell a man a sewing machine he may not only cease to buy your shirts but he may also sell his own make of shirt to your former customers. It was inevitable and desirable that the new methods of production should become worldwide and that the international division of labor should not be a pattern of dig, sweat, and muck there and the power, shine, and purr of machines here. As the leading industrial countries specialized in more advanced industrial processes, they were only too eager to exchange their different special products profitably. Germany, as we have seen, was both Britain's best customer and greatest rival. But foreign investment must necessarily be at the expense of home investment. In the United Kingdom, as elsewhere after 1900, real income per head was no longer growing as quickly as before. "The British economy at the beginning of the twentieth century passed from its remarkable late Victorian growth to a condition by no means stagnant or declining, but showing slower progress. And the main reasons for the change were a failure to exploit favorable economic conditions at home and even greater concentration than before on dealing with the outside world in circumstances in which the advantages from so doing could not go on increasing so easily as they had done a little earlier." [13]

The world demand for primary products had begun to run ahead of their supply and to increase them resources were developed that were slightly less accessible or slightly less easily worked than those which had been developed earlier. Before 1914 there was sufficient coincidence of private profit and social gain to say that uncontrolled investment paid. But the price mechanism and the profit motive may have faltered in their task of determining the right order for the public interest of developing a distant ranch or re-equipping a local factory or mine. In an economic system dominated by small firms there is great elasticity, because a manufacturer has little inducement to continue in production once his margin of profit has diminished. It is when industry is in the hands of firms with large resources that the elimination of the unfit is slow, if only because they may mobilize political support for their failing economic prowess.

In the United Kingdom the whole political tradition in the nineteenth century was against any tariff protection and against any movement for the creation of centralized administrative units and concentrated production. The economic theorist was critical of monopoly as being inefficient, while the socialist saw in economic concentrations the threat of an arbitrary power over the worker's life. The export trades depended upon their ability to adapt themselves to a variety of markets. In the United Kingdom before 1914 coal and iron, steel, shipbuilding, and textiles were for the most part small family businesses. We know from the stock exchange lists before 1914 that the small firms were able to raise the money they needed from wealthy private individuals who could assess their prospects from personal knowledge and that they were able to finance expansion by plowing back their profits.

Before 1914 industry proper—distinct from the banking, insurance, and transport undertakings—did not get a large part of its capital from the issue of public quoted shares on the stock exchange, which tapped the savings of the general investing public. Another criticism is that after 1900 the development of the trade union movement and the social legislation which was the first faint outline of the later welfare state tended to weaken the pressure of economic forces on the worker and that among employers, too, the demand for greater stability and security grew. After 1900 there was a rapid increase in the proportion of the national income which was spent by local and central government. Expenditure on the social services quadrupled between 1900 and 1910. The organization of the market for labor was improved by the Labour Exchange Act, 1909. Compulsory insurance against unemployment was introduced in 1911. But these and other state activities were all of them implicit in the great economic liberal tradition properly understood as it had developed from Adam Smith to Alfred Marshall.

CHAPTER XII

The Preface to Democracy, 1867-1914

Benjamin Disraeli in a letter to Queen Victoria likened the debate on the Reform Bill of 1867 to "an affair of Inkermann." The passing of the bill was indeed the prologue to profound political and constitutional changes. The way in which it came to be passed was in character with the period it was to supersede. Lord Russell was in his seventy-fourth year and wanted to give his name to a second reform bill. There was general agreement that the franchise must be adapted to the changes in wealth and population which had taken place since 1832. But there was no agreement about the details. Lord Morley wrote that "the great reform was carried by a parliament elected to support Lord Palmerston and Lord Palmerston detested reform. It was carried by a government in a decided minority. It was carried by a minister and by a leader of the opposition neither of whom was at the time in the full confidence of his party." The opposition to reform was, John Bright said, an objection to any transfer of power from those who possessed it to the working class. They regarded the workmen in Britain as the southern planter regarded the Negroes who were so lately his slaves. They might work and pay taxes, but not vote. In the 1850's and 1860's there had been many tentative reform bills, but they had not been vindications of any principle but useful maneuvers to attract small marginal groups of members.

When Lord John Russell's Cabinet could not agree on the details of reform and was not prepared to dissolve Parliament because a general election would only have brought to light the divisions in their ranks, they resigned and Lord Derby took office. Disraeli after some playful maneuvers secured the passage of a bill which virtually doubled the electorate. Disraeli's maneuvers included a host of fancy franchises—for graduates, those with £50 in government funds, membership of the learned professions, and the general principle that it would be contrary to the constitution to allow any class a predominance in the electorate. One-quarter of the voting power would belong to the aristocracy, one-quarter to the working class, and the remainder to the middle class. These proposals were transformed because of the confused political condition in the House of Commons and the general feeling that the House would be regarded as utterly incompetent unless something were done. The act as passed added 938,000 voters to an electorate of 1,056,000, Disraeli having decided that if it were done it were well that it were done quickly.

The implications of the new franchise were far-reaching. Amid the dusty and technical details we may note that: (1) something like a lodger franchise was given to the boroughs with the result that the voters in the boroughs were doubled, in Birmingham trebled, and in towns like Leeds, Blackburn, and Bolton quadrupled; (2) that after the Act there were politically two Englands—a democratic England of the towns and an aristocratic England of the counties. For while in the boroughs the artisan had the vote, in the counties (and they included towns which were more flourishing and populous than many boroughs) neither the small tradesman nor the miner nor the agricultural laborer had the vote. Although there had been some redistribution of seats (one member being taken from boroughs of less than 10,000 inhabitants and forty-five seats redistributed so that Liverpool, Manchester, Birmingham, and Leeds had three members), 4,000,000 people in the large towns returned only thirty-four out of 334 boroughs members, and the small rural boroughs with a population of half a million between them were of greater weight electorally than the 10,000,000 of the metropolitan, the Midland, and the northern boroughs. Only in the large industrial towns was there a sweeping change in political forces. They became, after 1867, fields for experiments in party organization. The counties remained the strong-holds of the old order. Until the 1880's economic prosperity helped to sustain and invigorate the old hierarchical system. The British constitu-tion, as Lord Derby sapiently said, was still "a monarchy limited, an aristocracy tempered and a House of Commons not altogether demo-cratic."

The pessimists feared that the changes of 1867 would give to mere numbers a power that they ought not to have. Disraeli hoped that it would never be the fate of the country to live under a democracy. Salis-bury thought that there was nothing in the nature of things to make us suppose that the freedom of those who are not on the side of the govern-ment will be better observed where the government is the creature of a multitude than where it is the possession of one. The optimists, such as Gladstone, thought that the great social forces which move onward in their might and majesty were marshaled on his side. He had "a rational confidence in the intelligence and character of the people." He ventured to say "that every man who is not presumably incapacitated by some constitutional consideration of personal unfitness or of political danger, is morally entitled to come within the pale of the constitution." This was too much for his then chief, Lord Palmerston, who wrote to him, "I entirely deny that every sane and not disqualified man has a moral right to a vote. . . . What every man and woman too has a right to, is to be well governed and under just laws, and they who propose a change ought to show that the present organization does not accomplish those objects." Gladstone had the Biblical touch so familiar in the later Labour party: "Did Scribes and Pharisees" he asked, "or did shepherds and fishermen yield the first, most and readiest consent to the Saviour and the company of His Apostles? . . . in studying the great questions of policy which appeal to the primal truths and laws of our nature, those classes may excel who, if they lack the opportunities, yet escape the subtle perils of the wealthy state."

It may be interesting to turn from these high and cloudy thoughts to glance at the mire, the tangles, and the fun of the actual electoral and political scene.

A county was more than a geographical unit. It was a self-contained society. The agricultural estates in the counties were social institutions, and the recognition of this induced a political concord between landlord and tenant. Owners of large estates had an influence over the tradesmen living in neighboring villages. Estates tended to vote as a unit, and electioneering was limited to organizing the transport needed to get the voters to the poll. There was no general canvass because it would have been an impertinence to canvass a man's tenants without his permission. In 1868 only thirteen of the county members were strangers to the counties they represented. The political character of the county was decided almost entirely by its landlords, who were the recognized leaders of social administration and judicial work. Only men with local family connections were approved as candidates, or men of extensive property, who might be merchants or manufacturers, whose behavior warranted their being accepted as country gentlemen.[1]

About 54 per cent of England and Wales and rather more of Scotland were in the hands of owners of over 1000 acres, and almost 80 per cent was in estates of over 100 acres. In the English counties the Conservatives before 1885 won more than twice as many seats as their opponents. The root of their strength lay in a kinship of outlook and interest between landlord, farmer, and village. The amount of land occupied by smallholders was not very great. There were about 250,000 smallholders as well as independent merchants and tradesmen in the small towns and villages. But the political effectiveness of these independent interests was weakened by its scattered nature and a lack of leaders. The liberalism of the villages was only latent until 1885. The Radicals had the support of the dissenters and potentially of the agricultural laborers, but they had no chance of winning a seat until the Reform Act of 1884 gave the latter the vote.[2]

In Scotland, Wales, and Ireland the counties were strongly anti-landlord. In Scotland the few Conservative strongholds were either the creation of a few local landowners who were known personally to the farmers or the result of a Conservative tradition going back to the eighteenth century. But the small laird, the big farmer, the banker, and the newspaper editor were the leaders of society in a small Scottish county. By 1868 the Liberals, as the party of national patriotism, could count on carrying all but six or seven of the sixty Scottish seats, although their hold on the counties was not very secure. Scotland had retained at the Union (1707) its own educational and legal systems and had its own vigorous church, so there was no open challenge to national feeling such as the Anglican Church gave in Wales and Ireland and the English administration in Dublin. The party managers of the Conservative and Liberal parties were able to treat Scotland as if it were an extension of England. As the ablest Scots did not go into politics, the quality of Scottish M.P.'s was low. Scottish liberalism had a family atmosphere, and when a labor movement developed at the turn of the century it was unable to keep its allegiance.[3]

In Wales the Reform Act of 1867 put the dissenters in a majority in almost all constituencies. The industrial revolution had created a new urban Wales alongside the old Wales. The evangelical revival had cut off the people from the old ruling class. The religion of the chapel created the social climate of the new Wales. Before 1867 the gentry, who were churchmen, had controlled Welsh representation. But the clergy, the gentry, the large farmers, and a narrow circle of Anglican workingmen who looked to England were only a quarter of the population. Dissent was a popular Welsh movement.[4]

Before the Ballot Act of 1872, which abolished open voting, the condition of politics in Ireland was very odd indeed. The great majority of seats were not contested. When they were, in the countryside the landlords or their agents brought their tenants in droves to the polls. The troops of the British administration were parceled into small groups to see that there was no fighting or at least no serious injuries. Between 1868 and 1874 the Home Rule movement introduced a purely Irish party in Irish politics, and when in 1874 the ballot destroyed the power of the landlords the Irish Home Rule party did its best to paralyze the working of the British House of Commons as the center of power of the hated Union.

In England the boroughs were of three kinds: (1) Small medieval towns like Calne, Rye, and Bridgnorth which continued until 1885 to return more than half the borough members and more than one-fifth of the House of Commons. As no borough with a population of less than 10,000 had a second seat after 1867, the compacts to share the seats between the contestants, which had been common before 1867, were no longer possible. The small boroughs looked either to a tug of war between rival candidates with money to spend in the town or for a member who would stay for a long time as their representative, foster local industries and contribute to local charities. Some of the smaller boroughs became adept at fleecing the rich aspirant to a political career. Perhaps the happiest small boroughs were those which were near great estates to which they could look for representatives to flatter their vanity and cherish their needs. (2) There was a middle group of about seventy-five medium-sized towns (between 16,000 and 50,000) where, if they were provincial centers like Cambridge or Lincoln, old family connections would linger on or the owner of a large industry could be given the same deference as would be given to a large landowner in the countryside. But (3) in the big towns the whole pattern of life inclined them to liberalism or radicalism. The Conservative party, to the sceptical workingman and his vigorous and competitive employers, was associated with aristocratic exclusiveness, the privileges of the Church of England, and hostility to industry and trade. It was sometimes said that the Conservatives could leave the counties to take care of themselves while they did what they could in the large towns with bribery and improved organization.[5]

Before 1867 the task of getting electors on the register, which since 1832 entitled them to vote, was undertaken by local party notables with the help of a local solicitor. In 1861 the Liberals had set up in London the Liberal Registration Association with the task of co-ordinating the constituency registration associations. Control was kept in the hands of the parliamentary whips. It was something like a party headquarters in the modern sense of the term. The registration associations were not representative bodies. They were self-electing and self-perpetuating. After 1867 great changes were necessary. The electorate was larger and, after the Ballot Act of 1872, free from direct influence of landlord, employer, or customer; after the Corrupt Practices Act, 1883, the cost of a contest for almost any seat was within the means of men with moderate means, or no means at all, if they represented a cause for which subscriptions could be raised. A group of party members of all classes developed in every constituency, united in the pursuit of common aims in place of the individual candidate with his party committee. There was a development of political clubs, a growing influence of a provincial press, and a new interest in municipal elections. Both liberals and conservatives opened social and political centers for workingmen. Constituency associations were grouped into national unions and national party conferences were held.

In 1867 the Conservatives decided to form a National Union of Conservative and Constitutional Associations "to afford a centre of communication and action between local associations supporting constitutional views." The new Union was put on the map in 1872, when its conference was accompanied by a banquet in the Crystal Palace at which Disraeli laid down the general principles of Conservative policy. In 1870 Disraeli established a Conservative Central Office. He started the first great party machine, and it may have been through this that he won the general election of 1874. In 1877 Joseph Chamberlain started the National Liberal Federation. This gave the Liberals a new method and almost a new set of ideas. It led to a discussion about the merits and demerits of political organization. The Conservative Union had made no claim to determine the policy of the Conservative party. It was intended to be a mere handmaid to the party. It was for the Conservatives in the Commons and the Lords to decide the great issues of policy. The object of the National Liberal Federation was to determine the attitude of the Liberal party outside Parliament to the questions of the day.

It was a revolutionary doctrine in 1877 to suggest that the party outside Parliament should dictate a policy to the party inside. The Whig wing of the Liberal party disliked the idea of a policy-making machine in Radical hands. Disraeli thought that the new Liberal organization was one of the causes of the Liberal victory of 1880. For a time there was friction between the National Liberal Federation with its headquarters in Birmingham and the leaders of the party in London. When, in 1886 Joseph Chamberlain left the Liberals over the Irish Home Rule issue, the National Liberal Federation came under the control of Gladstone and the parliamentary leaders. By then the foundations of a modern party system had been laid. There were constituency associations of a representative character grouped into a national federation and assisted by a national headquarters. There was the party annual conference and the party election manifesto. These had been made necessary by the extension of the suffrage and the drastic tightening of the electoral laws. The technique of the mass organization of voluntary supporters with a national headquarters to co-ordinate their activities was being developed. But effective control was in the hands of the leaders of the parties in Parliament.

Before 1868 general elections were not really general. Only about half the seats were contested. Often the Liberals could not find candidates in the counties nor could the Conservatives find them in the boroughs. In 1859, 374 seats were uncontested. After 1867 the number uncontested fell rapidly until 1880, when it reached about 110, which was to be normal until after World War I. In Ireland it dropped from fifty-six uncontested in 1868 to seventeen in 1880.[6]

The compromise of 1867 could not long continue. The violence and corruption in the smaller boroughs and the almost ridiculous contrivances of the Irish herding of the county voters led in 1872 to the Ballot Act, in spite of the hostility of the House of Lords and the latent disapproval of the House of Commons. Disraeli affected to see in it a divorce of political life from publicity. It was the blow given to the landlords in Ireland by the ballot which led to the development of the Nationalist party in Ireland. Nor could the distinction between the urban and rural franchise continue. The distinction between the towns in counties, where the artisan did not have the vote, and towns which were boroughs, where they did, could not last. By 1884 there was no one to oppose the principle that the householder and the lodger in the counties should have the vote on the same terms as the householder and the lodger in the boroughs. The extension of the household franchise to the counties tripled the county electorate, from 900,000 to 2,500,000. It was to lead to the creation of elected county councils in 1888 and the transfer to them of the administrative power which had for centuries been in the hands of the justices of the peace. One could not deny the vote for local government to those who had been given it for central. County councils were to be vital organs in the development of a future welfare state, and they were to mobilize and train much political talent.

The act of 1884 on the franchise was followed in 1885 by one on redistribution. This was made essential by the growth of new urban areas which were grossly underrepresented. One example must suffice—the small boroughs of Cornwall, Devon, and Wiltshire with a gross population of 100,000 had more seats than the 2,000,000 in the industrial Midlands. The act of 1884 had gone far to abolish the influence of the landlord; the act of 1885 abolished the preponderance of small agricultural boroughs. All boroughs of less than 15,000 inhabitants were merged in the county. Boroughs hitherto not separately represented with 50,000 inhabitants or more received one member and larger boroughs more in proportion. Seventy-two boroughs disappeared altogether and thirty-six lost one member. The long predominance of the southern over the northern constituencies and of the agricultural interest over others was ended. It could be said that the Conservative principle of representing communities was replaced by the Radical principle of the representation of majorities.

The changes in the electorate and in the grass roots of political life led to profound changes at the center of political life in the Cabinet in the Commons and in the Lords. The position of the prime minister whose party was clearly supported by a majority won in a general election was strengthened; so, too, was the position of his chief opponent, the leader of the Opposition, which was the alternative government available to Her Majesty. For a time it appeared that Britain might enjoy the benefits of a splendid alternation between Tweedledum and Tweedledee—that the good and the bad, the ins and the outs, might magnificently alternate; the ship of state be carried before a breeze of progress now to port and now to starboard. In 1868 Gladstone's Liberal party had a majority of about 100, and Disraeli, saluting the new electoral power, resigned as soon as the result of the election was known. In 1874 it was the turn of Disraeli to win by nearly a hundred. But in the second Gladstone administration of 1880–85 the pressures of a changing world were obvious, and when in 1886 Gladstone attempted to solve the Irish question by a measure of Home Rule his party was shattered, and the Liberals were not to return to effective power until 1906, by which time the nascent Labour party was an intimation of the domestic problems of the twentieth century.

In the period after the Reform Act of 1867 party election manifestos were still the personal appeals from the party leader and not a statement of future policy prepared and endorsed by the leading men in the party. The party leaders were not committed to any particular reform. An election was fought around an issue which the party leader had chosen: in 1868 with Gladstone it was the disestablishment of the Irish Church, in 1874 the abolition of the income tax, in 1880 Turkish atrocities, and in 1886 Home Rule for Ireland. But Gladstone was the first major statesman to stump the country, and Derby in 1868 referred to the "balderdash and braggadocio in which Gladstone has been indulging on his stumping tour." Great informality marked the choice of a party leader. Disraeli, who followed Derby in 1868, said that "Lord Derby never appointed me to the leadership, but the party chose to follow me." It was recognized that the Queen could have sent for the Duke of Richmond or for Edward Stanley instead of sending, as she did, for Disraeli. When Disraeli lost the election of 1868 the Queen sent for Gladstone as the recognized leader of the Liberals, and when in 1880 the Conservatives were defeated a delicate situation arose which revealed the changes in the balance of power in the constitution. Gladstone had formally resigned the leadership of the Liberal party in 1875, but he was the de facto leader of the attack on Disraeli's 1874–80 administration, and it had to be explained to the Queen that it would be wise to send for him because neither Granville in the Lords nor Hartington in the Commons could offer effective leadership either in Parliament or in the country.

Gladstone considered that his Cabinet of 1868–74 was "one of the finest instruments of government that ever were constructed." It was, he thought, the closest to the perfection which his mentor, Peel, had achieved in 1841–46. It was really a unity and not a mere assemblage of departmental ministers. Gladstone was to be for sixty-five years a member of the House of Commons. He retired from politics in 1875, when he was sixty-six, after forty-three years in Parliament and six as prime minister. He was to return to the premiership in 1880 when he was seventy-one, and twelve years later he was once more prime minister. The great work of his Cabinet of 1868–74 was to continue the work of Peel. He initiated the modern civil service, reorganized the army, and reformed the judiciary. The eighteenth century had been without a modern police, a modern civil service, and a modern system of state revenue. Peel gave Britain the first. But Gladstone in 1870, for practically all departments except the Foreign Office, made entrance by competitive examination obligatory. He introduced a famous series of budgets. But, underneath, his party was an uneasy combination of Whigs and Radicals, and when he temporarily retired in 1875 the Whigs were to follow one leader, the Radicals another, and the Irish a third. His weakness was that he was only interested in the Treasury and the Board of Trade, and in the army and navy in so far as they affected the estimates. Until 1886 he never lost his hold on the House of Commons. But he developed a liking for addressing great popular audiences in provincial halls. What he took from them in vapor he poured back upon them in a flood. He came to believe that he could best divine God's purpose by consulting the uncorrupted minds and hearts of men in masses everywhere. This latent demagogy made him most unpopular with the Queen. But toward her he behaved with absolute constitutional propriety. He denied her any right to know the individual opinions of members of the Cabinet. The Cabinet he held should show a unity before the Crown and a unity before the Commons.

Disraeli's Cabinet of 1874–80 was a masterpiece of a very different kind. It was a small Cabinet—six from the Commons and six from the House of Lords. He intended, he said, to change the old oligarchy into a generous aristocracy round a real throne. He manipulated the limited intelligence and the strong emotions of the Queen for party purposes. He tried to make her feel that she was a partner in the determination of the highest policy. He kept her acquainted with the views and feelings of the various members of the Cabinet. When he left office in 1880 the Queen continued to correspond with him and to exchange confidential information, a course contrary to the spirit of the constitution, which required that the Queen should take the advice only of her ministers, so long as they have not resigned. Gladstone came to feel real hatred for Disraeli. He sometimes thought that he was the Beast in Revelation. He disapproved of Disraeli because he considered that he had corrupted the public life of England and seriously warped the mind of the Queen. Disraeli for his part considered that Gladstone was an "unprincipled maniac . . . an extraordinary mixture of envy, vindictiveness, hypocrisy, and superstition." As Lord Granville said, the two men "disliked each other more than is common among public men." Disraeli is a mysterious figure. He was an artist in the art of power. He was a successful Bolingbroke. After 1846 he had become the leader of the defeated and inarticulate landlords. He was to create the new Tory party, and seeing that a Tory party of mere landowners was an anachronism he aimed to secure the support of all those groups that Gladstone alienated. Peel and Gladstone both broke their parties. Disraeli did not.

In the second Gladstone Cabinet 1880–85 it was clear that there would be no simple movement from the careful aristocracy of the 1870's to a democracy of responsible and respectable workingmen who would secure that freedom would broaden slowly down from precedent to precedent. The Queen had resented Gladstone's attacks on Disraeli's (now Lord Beaconsfield) Eastern policy. She only asked him to be prime minister because the Whigs Hartington and Granville told her that it would be safer to have him in the Cabinet than as a popular leader outside. Hartington said, "The spirit of the Constitution is that the ablest and most powerful member of the Opposition should be called on to take the position of the retiring Government." Gladstone found himself beset by forces which were divided on nearly every issue of politics. On the one side the Whig leaders, Granville and Hartington, were considering when it would be safe to turn him out. On the other the Radical twins, Charles Dilke and Chamberlain, the latter in the Cabinet and the former outside, were pressing the policies of a new radicalism born of the extension of the suffrage in 1867 and the economic pressures from the vitality of a finally United States and recently united Germany. Gladstone's Cabinet was three-fourths Whig and one-fourth Radical, which was the reverse of the political forces in the country. The decline in world prices since 1874 was having a depressing influence on the landed interest. The Irish question was coming to a head since the Ballot Act of 1872 had destroyed the political monopoly of the landed aristocracy there. The African continent was producing the problems presented by political frontiers which were also frontiers between races and between different ages of economic development.

In 1885 the government resigned after a defeat on its own budget. There could be no general election until the new constituencies required by the reforms of 1884–85 had been organized. Lord Salisbury had to take office until there could be an election in 1886. The result of the general election was the return of 249 Conservatives, 335 Liberals, and 86 Parnellites, the Irish party dedicated to securing Home Rule. Salisbury decided to meet the new House of Commons and compel the Liberals and Irish to combine to defeat him. Gladstone had been converted to Home Rule and would have been willing to support the Conservatives to carry it had they wished to do so. When at the age of seventy-six Gladstone was called upon to form his third ministry he was engaged in a violent controversy defending the literal truth of the account of creation in Genesis against T. H. Huxley. Queen Victoria said to one of her friends: "She does not in the least care but rather wishes it to be known that she has the greatest possible disinclination to take this half crazy and really in many ways ridiculous old man for the sake of the country."

Gladstone's Home Rule scheme for Ireland was shattered by the opposition of Chamberlain. It is just possible that a more wily Gladstone might have played Chamberlain for the sake of Ireland. But Gladstone considered Chamberlain to be an insincere careerist. When his Home Rule Bill was defeated and he asked for a dissolution, Gladstone felt that he was appealing from the corruption of the upper ten thousand to the upright sense of the masses. On the other hand, one of his opponents, Lord Randolph Churchill, in his election address gave a hint of the style a popular appeal to a mass electorate might require: "This design for the separation of Ireland from Britain—this monstrous mixture of imbecility, extravagance and political hysterics— . . . the united and concentrated genius of Bedlam and Colney Hatch would strive in vain to produce a more striking tissue of absurdities. . . . The British constitution is to be torn up to gratify the ambition of an old man in a hurry." Gladstone's conversion to Home Rule lost him the support of the great Whig families and of the Radical Chamberlain. Party lines had been disrupted by the unresolved Irish problem.[7]

Lord Salisbury emerged as the leader of the Conservatives in the government of 1886–92. Foreign policy was his dominating interest. He was the last prime minister to sit in the House of Lords. He had the double burden of the premiership and the Foreign Office, and his government was handicapped by having a prime minister in the House of Lords absorbed in foreign affairs while in the House of Commons its leader, Smith, was unable to exercise effective control. Randolph Churchill, the leader of the Tory democrats, was as much an inconvenience to the Tories as Chamberlain had been to Gladstone, and his resignation opened a way for George Goschen, the accredited representative of the Liberal Unionists. Salisbury himself did not believe any good could be effected by inspired ventures in legislation. But he thought that legal provision should be made to accommodate existing institutions to changing social conditions. Under the influence of Chamberlain his government was to carry out much of the Radical legislation which Gladstone had regarded with distrust. One of the most important was the Local Government Act, 1888, which created the present structure of English local government because it applied to the counties the principle of an elected council which in 1835 had been applied to the English boroughs. His government also made education free and made some provision for the agricultural worker.

The political confusion of the time is shown by the result of the general election of 1892, which returned 269 Conservatives, 46 Liberal Unionists, 81 Irish, and 273 Liberals. The Irish held the balance of power and once more Mr. Gladstone at the age of eighty-two was to form a government—his last. Queen Victoria said that she would in no way "interfere in the formation of this iniquitous government." Through the mediation of the Prince of Wales she persuaded Lord Rosebery to take the Foreign Office. In the House of Commons Gladstone had with the support of the Irish only a bare majority of forty. In the House of Lords the majority against Liberals and Home Rulers was overwhelming. So much so that Gladstone sent Queen Victoria a memorandum pointing out that although Liberal views were supported by a majority of the English-speaking people "they were hardly at all represented, and were imperfectly known in the powerful circle within which the Queen had personal intercourse. It seemed to him that there was a widening gap between the upper and the more numerous classes." When the Home Rule Bill came to the Lords from the Commons it was defeated by 419 to 41. Gladstone, if the doors of his senses had not been gradually closing, would have dissolved then and there on the issue of the place of the House of Lords in the constitution.

When he resigned on the grounds of age and sickness, the Queen on her own initiative sent for Lord Rosebery. He was in an impossible position. He was, he said, shut up in the House of Lords which was so unanimously opposed to his government that he might as well have been in the Tower of London. In the Commons his government had only a narrow majority and its leader there was Sir William Harcourt, who was bitterly opposed to him. Harcourt rightly complained that his task was impossible because the ministers on whom all the vital issues depended —the prime minister, the foreign secretary, the first lord of the Admiralty, and the secretary of state for the Colonies were all in the Lords. His position as leader in the House of Commons was impossible. The government resigned in 1895, and Salisbury, forming a government, dissolved and won a clear victory—340 Conservatives, 71 Liberal Unionists, and against him 177 Liberals and 82 Irish. In his Cabinet the Conservatives, the old Whigs, and the Radical Imperialists formally coalesced. Salisbury, Goschen, and Chamberlain were in the same Cabinet. Chamberlain took the Colonial Office with far-reaching results for the British in South Africa. Had he gone to the Home Office it is possible that much of the social legislation for which the Liberal government of 1906 was to be famous might have been anticipated. The Salisbury Cabinet contained eight peers, but its inner life was controlled by Salisbury, his nephew Arthur Balfour, and Chamberlain.

The course of the South African War made Chamberlain one of the strongest members of the government. He persuaded Salisbury to dissolve in 1900 and to win what was known as the "khaki election" because of the propaganda theme "every seat lost to the government is a seat gained by the Boers." Chamberlain thought that imperialism and social reform should go together. He had a dream of economic unity for the empire. We must not, he thought, by adherence to economic pedantry lose opportunities of closer union with our colonies. He was to develop in 1902 a tariff reform program. For some time Lord Salisbury had been failing, and in 1902 he resigned. King Edward VII sent for Balfour to succeed him. This was perfectly correct, because since 1891 Balfour had been the leader of the Conservatives in the Commons. It was said at the time by the journalist James Garvin that Balfour had been made prime minister because the ruling families desired that the minimum of change should be made. It is one of the ironies of history that if Balfour was intended to bar the way to Chamberlain the result was to open the way for the far more radical David Lloyd George of the Liberal government, under Asquith in 1906.[8]

Balfour as prime minister was soon in difficulties with a Cabinet which was divided on the policy of tariff reform, which Chamberlain was pressing. Balfour claimed that, as once Catholic Emancipation had been an open question, and free trade itself, so now he was not required to profess a settled conviction when he had not got one. "Whatever be the merits of the question," he wrote, "why should the fact that some of us differ and many of us hesitate about it, break up or tend to break up the present Cabinet." A dissolution of Parliament was not desirable because it was "not a felicitous moment for putting the party fortunes to the hazard." Balfour sensed that the old order was passing and that a new pattern of political life would be drawn by the democratic forces moving beneath the surface of the gilded Edwardian era. He determined to make things as shipshape as he could before these new powers were in control. In domestic policy he carried through the Education Act of 1902, by which responsibility for elementary and secondary education was given to the new system of local government which had been created in 1888. He established an Irish Land Purchase Scheme in an effort to lower the temperature of that feverish island. He passed a Licensing Act of 1904 which settled for a time the English sectarian passions about the frequency of alcoholic consumption. In foreign policy he was determined that the Anglo-French Convention of 1904 and the alliance with Japan should be concluded before he went. And—of vital importance for British survival in the war which came in 1914—he initiated the Committee of Imperial Defence, a subtle device by which the political autonomy of the British dominions was flatteringly confirmed, while, at the same time, their potential value as allies in a dangerous war was harnessed to the Cabinet as the directing organ of British policy and administration. While Chamberlain reacted to the centrifugal nationalism of the colonies by a rushing mighty wind of ill-conceived tariff proposals, Balfour concentrated on developing the still small voice of consultation on matters of life and death which awaited immediate action.

In December 1905 Balfour had to decide whether he would resign, or himself ask the King for a dissolution. It is one of the subtleties of the British constitution—which has a parallel in the British game of cricket which allows the batting side to declare and put the other side in if such a course seems to be in its interests—that the government in power may either ask for a dissolution of Parliament and thus go to the country on its record and promises, or it may resign, thus compelling the Opposition to take office and itself go to the country because it needs fresh support in the Commons, which only the electorate can give, or because the legal term of the existing House of Commons is near its end. Balfour in 1905 may have hoped that the dissensions which existed in the Liberal party might be revealed to the damage of their reputation. Most of the constitutional experts were agreed that it was dangerous to take office in the last months of an expiring Parliament. There would be little time for the new government to show its quality. But the Liberal leader Sir Henry Campbell-Bannerman took office. To refuse would he said "be ascribed to division or to cowardice." In forming his Cabinet he had a diversity of interests to harmonize. The chief difficulty came from the Liberal Imperialists, Sir Edward Grey, Richard Haldane, and Herbert Asquith. When the Cabinet was finally formed Asquith was at the Treasury, Haldane at the War Office, and Grey at the Foreign Office. Lloyd George was at the Board of Trade, and outside the Cabinet but in an important junior post was Winston Churchill.

At the general election of 1906 the Liberals recovered the power which they had lost when Gladstone's party was shattered by the Irish Home Rule issues in 1886. The election itself is a fitting prologue to the age of high argument mixed with propaganda to which we are now inured. The Liberal party relentlessly exposed the confused economic thinking of the Tariff Reform case. It was also able to play on the fears and prejudices which some aspects of Conservative policy had aroused. The Education Act of 1902 had "stirred into life one of the fears of Protestant England"—that Rome would be on the rates, that is, good Nonconformists would be paying local taxes to support jesuitical education. The Licensing Act of 1904 was invoked as a beery "Mr. Bung the Brewer," leering from Liberal posters. Imperial preference was said to threaten a return to the "hungry forties" and a "dear loaf."

More important than the sweeping Liberal victory of 377 Liberals to the Conservative 167, in addition to the 83 Irish almost solid for Home Rule, was the appearance in the House of Commons of a Labour party of 29. The election, as Balfour sensed, inaugurated a new era. The new Labour sputnik would become one of the great constellations of the parliamentary skies. It was a party different from the older Conservative and Liberal parties, whose leaders had been in Parliament and had created their organizations in the constituencies to bring in the new electorates created by the Reform Acts of 1832, 1867, and 1884. The Labour party had not been called into being by party leaders inside Parliament. It had begun outside Parliament. In 1899 the Trades Union Congress had instructed its parliamentary committee to call a conference on the question of labor representation in Parliament. It met on February 27, 1900, in London and was attended by delegates from the trade unions and also by representatives of the Independent Labour party (I.L.P.), which had been formed in Bradford in 1893, the Social Democratic Federation, and the Fabian Society. A Labour Representation Committee was appointed, and in 1903 it made the vital decision that members elected to Parliament through the efforts of the committee should "abstain strictly from identifying themselves with, or promoting the interests of, any section of the Liberal or Conservative parties." In this complex way the pressure of British socialist thought was to be harnessed to the machinery of Parliament. The House of Commons is so supreme a political organ in British life, that, once a labor movement had members in it, such members would become a Parliamentary Labour party whose relations to the mass organization outside would be very similar to those of the Conservative party in Parliament to its mass organization outside.[9]

The new Liberal government went into action with a fleet of contentious measures. The most important were about education, trade unions, plural voting, licencing, and land valuation. There was, in fact, a whole world of sensible state activity which had the support of an English rational and empirical tradition stretching back through the Fabian analysis of social tissue (as Sidney and Beatrice Webb called it) through the philosophical collectivism of T. H. Green, the utilitarian collectivism of J. S. Mill, to the vigorous common sense of Tom Paine. Little of it had any need of ideological props from continental socialism. There were children to be fed, a system of education that went beyond the three R's to be begun, the relation between the organization of workers to determine their wages and their organization to exert political pressure to be settled, and innumerable anomalies in the franchise and a fantastic system of property in land to be adjusted. There was work for a generation of rationalists and empiricists in finding the new legal, fiscal, and political forms for a changing industrial world. There were also the peripheral racial and religious fanaticism in Ireland, and in England some awkward, almost ancestral, memories of the pope before Henry VIII and Cromwell before 1689 to infect the discussions. But there was no serious fear that reason aided by growing plenty would not provide at least an outline of the Good Society.

The British were to get their welfare state, but the manner of its coming was to be by a way which the fantasies of the most imaginative Utopians could never have conceived—not even the H. G. Wells of *When the Sleeper Wakes*. Looking back to the years 1906–14 from a 1962 in which it is no longer merely theological to speculate whether there will be a 1963, one has the feeling that "a battle, a strife, an agony, was travelling through all its stages—was evolving itself, like the catastrophe of some mighty drama." The strife and agony were trivial before 1914, but in the British scene there was a touch of violence and a note of hysteria which were intimations of new and deep disharmonies. It is idle to speculate whether the trivial British problems about the place of women in political life (they were slashing pictures, burning public buildings, setting fire to pillar boxes, and generally playing with the "dangerous drug of violence" which it is the supreme function of the political art to control), the wisdom of giving Ireland political autonomy, and the redistribution of income and capital in accordance with economic principles (with the authority of that fifth most respected profession—the economic—which now joined the church, the law, the armed forces, and the medical) would have been solved had not the disaster of 1914 transmogrified them every one.

For the first time since Napoleon a British Cabinet had seriously to consider the possibility of a direct challenge to British insular security. The question of *dreadnoughts* was at least of equal importance with the question of the political power of trade unions. A British foreign secretary had to consider the possible combinations and permutations of real imperial powers which were also nations in arms. With the passing of the political power of the landed aristocracy the relation between a new democracy and the protean forms of an industrial world in accelerating change had to be worked out. And these wide general issues were bedeviled by the unresolved Irish question. The Irish question and the social problems were both entangled in the constitutional question of the place of the House of Lords in the British Constitution.

After 1867 the procedure of the House of Commons had been streamlined to handle the legislation needed to implement the policy of governments which had to deal with an industrial society. The main changes had been precipitated by the attempt of the Irish members after 1875 to paralyze the House of Commons as the central political organ of the hated union. Their systematic obstruction led to the introduction of a closure procedure by which a government supported by a majority in the House of Commons could stop debate and proceed to a vote. A unitary state with a cabinet system of government cannot afford the luxury of a filibuster. By 1902 a reasonable scheme had been developed by which the government controlled sufficient time of the House of Commons to get its legislation and financial provision accepted so long as it retained its majority. This had been done without sacrificing the rights of the Opposition and of private members to the time they might need for the performance of their duties. This is one of the technical, tedious, but vital changes in the political life of Britain since 1832. The procedure of the House of Commons from the seventeenth century until the middle of the nineteenth century had been designed to protect the members against the possible overriding influence of an executive representing the Crown and wielding its influence. With the coming of nearly universal suffrage and the problems of an industrial society it had been necessary to protect the government of the day against the obstruction of private interests or sectarian passions. The procedural reforms had made the House a tool with which the executive got the legislation and the financial resources that it had to have after reasonable opportunities for criticism and the statement by the Opposition of its considered alternatives.

The streamlining of the House of Commons was bound to involve a collision with the House of Lords once the Commons felt the impetus of the forces of reform. Mr. Balfour made the collision certain when, as soon as the Liberal government of 1906 was in office, he decided that the House of Lords must play the important, delicate, and difficult game of passing measures from the Commons which it considered to be moderate and rejecting those which it held to be outrageous. The Lords would pick and choose from the measures of a Liberal government and so play on the divisions which they not unreasonably assumed would exist within the Liberal Cabinet itself. This meant, as the Liberals said, that "the second chamber was being utilised as a mere annexe of the Unionist Party." It was, in the words of Lloyd George, being used not as a watchdog of the Constitution but as Mr. Balfour's poodle. The Lords passed a Workmen's Compensation Bill, the Eight-Hour Day, Trade Boards, Labour Exchanges, and the Trades Dispute Bill of 1906. The Conservative or Unionist party had a clear eye for the industrial workers in the new democracy. But they destroyed the Liberal government's Education Bill, a Plural Voting Bill, and a Valuation Bill. By the end of 1908 Asquith, who had succeeded Campbell-Bannerman, said that the Lords had blocked the government's policy in education, temperance, and land reform, the disestablishment of the Church of England in Wales, and Irish Home Rule. Even then, so resilient can be the obstinate stiffness of ancient British institutions, the House of Lords was by no means done for. But in 1909 Lloyd George as chancellor of the Exchequer introduced a budget which proposed increased taxation to meet the cost of the navy, which the German Empire had decided to challenge. The Lords, against the advice of their ablest members, decided to reject the budget. They were claiming the power to compel a government to go to the country on its financial policy. This struck at the very heart of the Constitution by removing the center of control, above the electorate itself, from the House of Commons.

The rejection of the budget was followed by a complex of subtle maneuvers and a din of invective, personal and public. It was established that the King must dissolve Parliament when in the opinion of his Cabinet it is desirable that he should and that he must exercise his prerogative to create peers if such an exercise should be necessary to secure the passage of government legislation. There were two dissolutions in 1910, the first on the issue of the budget and the second on the place of the House of Lords in the Constitution. It was understood that if the government won the second general election of 1910 that the King would be prepared to create enough peers to pass the bill abolishing the Lords' veto were they to be so foolish as to reject it. In a sputnik age this may seem a war of kites and crows, but at the time it was political drama in Hercules' vein. Two things must be noted here: The British Constitution had shown that it was capable of fundamental self-amendment, and the inner crisis was the problem of Ireland. After the first election of 1910, though the Liberals still had a majority, it was dependent on the support of the Irish vote, and the Irish were determined that the Lords' veto must go because it was, as it always had been, the bar to Irish Home Rule.

It could be said that since 1867 the British had been trying to find political forms to serve an industrial society. Their glories had been born of sheep and sails and international finance. For a short time they had been the workshop of the world, but in this period their long-established agricultural industry had felt the destructive force of changes in world transport and their industrial supremacy based on empirical techniques was challenged by new methods and by resources far beyond anything a small island could command. They enjoyed certain obvious advantages. Only in Ireland did their politics suffer from the disrupting passions of a national minority and religious rancor. There had been a striking homogeneity in British economic life. When after 1875 British agriculture suffered severely from the opening of the wheat states of America and improved transport of cereals, there was no serious development of an agrarian party because the owners of land were also shareholders and company directors. There had been no farmers' party because in the main the interests of landowners and farmers were found to be the same. There had been no irreconcilable minorities.

In the religious world the sectarian controversies between the established Church of England and the multitudinous Protestant sects were never very serious because the life blood of all of them was drained away by the slow decline of Christianity. Only some parts of the Christian ethic remained as a serious political force. His theology was a personal idiosyncrasy of Mr. Gladstone and had little political force. The position of the statesman has always been more analogous to the doctor than it has been to the priest. The politician is responsible for the health of the social order as the doctor is for the body's health. The Radical Dissenters who were the English admirers of the French Revolution were convinced that the teaching of Jesus Christ and the teaching of science were practically the same for all personal and social problems. For those who did not accept the divinity of Christ, the Utilitarian school, from Bentham in the eighteenth century to J. S. Mill and Sidgwick in the nineteenth, had provided the basis for social and political decency and order. However pagan the personal life of the English proletariat, socially they had always adhered to an empirical version of Christian ethics. That every man has a duty to do what he could to reduce the misery of others had been held to be self-evident by the bulk of the middle and the working class. Some envy had been felt for those members of all classes who might genuinely claim by reason of their temperament or their exceptional insight into the nature of this terrifying universe that they did not find this duty self-evident. This empirical temperament, which might be described as seventeenth-century puritanism without its Biblical ideology, was strengthened in the period we have been discussing by the economic facts of life.

The frontiers of British life were not in the open spaces of a New World but along the mean streets and in the smoke-laden atmosphere generated by an early machine age. The grass roots of political life were in the urban problems of the Midlands and the north. Unity was preserved because it is fairly clear that any attempt to deal seriously with the problems of a raw industrial area, or a complex agrarian community feeling the winds of change, or a financial house that has its filaments around the world will find a common empirical and numerical set of problems to be solved. The unity of England was the unity of the machine and the calculator—long prepared from the Reformation and through the Age of Reason. This empiricism was in the case of the Liberals given a theoretical stiffening by the analytical studies of the economists. Their initial analysis confirmed the case of the Puritan for honesty and of the master and the workman for freedom. Even the great conservative case which we hear in Burke—that the state is a partnership of the living with the dead and those yet to be born and that what you would do must be done from the place where you now stand and with the habits and customs which you now have—that truism had reinforced the sceptical and empirical tradition. The veneration of the conservative for the actual, for all that is a late birth of time, gave him some insight into the tough and technical process of securing lasting reforms. He would know that the health of the body politic depends upon the proper use of the dangerous drug of violence. He would agree with J. M. Keynes that civilization is "a thin and precarious crust created by the personality and the will of a very few, and only maintained by rules and conventions skilfully put across and guilefully preserved."

However thin and precarious the crust of civilization might be in the nineteenth century, it had to be stretched and thickened if it were not to be broken and submerged by the new movements which the use of new and ever-changing methods of production was causing in the life of men and women everywhere. In trying to understand their world men had almost accidentally begun to change it, and they must now either control or adapt themselves to the changes which had begun. Hitherto, the life of men had been poor, brutish, and short, save for a gleam of peace and glory here and there. It was the promise of the new scientific method in the business of earning a living that henceforth men would be delivered from the barbarism which scarcity imposes, to the civilized life which plenty makes possible. Hume in the eighteenth century had noted that security gives plenty, plenty leisure, leisure curiosity, and curiosity civilization. Curiosity had stumbled on the new tool of mechanized industry, and if only security could be guaranteed an unimagined plenty was within the reach of all.

It was the sober hypothesis of the philosophical liberal and the almost pathological obsession of the philosophical anarchist that the new industrial processes would simplify the problem of security. The purr of the new machines would be accompanied by a softening of the harsh voice of the law. Economic science had shown that there was an order in society which had not been made by either king or priest, for division of labor and the mechanism of exchange had in fact brought the human race out of the darkness before recorded history into the contemporary dawn of a civilized life. Whatever political empires had come and gone the economic order had always been intact, for had it ever been broken the human race would not have survived. This had been the argument by which Hume in the eighteenth century had dismissed the fancies of the social contract thinkers. It had been simplified for the American revolutionaries by Tom Paine into the aphorism that society is the product of our necessities and government of our wickedness. In the middle of the nineteenth century the English Liberals developed it into a theory of the limited state—that the state should do only what was necessary to be done for the latent harmony of human needs and human abilities, human desires and wills to be released into a social order of peace and plenty.

This classical liberal theory is one of the great achievements of the Western mind. It implied that there should be a government of law and not a government of men—that in a civilized community there should be a body of rules which were general and impartial, and knowing those rules and that they would be firmly administered (because the political authority would have a monopoly of coercive power) the citizens would, in peaceful competition and co-operation, subdue the forces of nature to their rational wills. This classical theory is still the basis of the democratic state in the free world; a denial of its premises is the basis of all totalitarian systems. It is not possible here to consider the intellectual and moral problems which are involved.

British experience since 1870 has a relevance for the great issues we have just barely touched. Britain was on the frontier of the movement from an agrarian order to the new and protean industrial patterns. In Britain the rule of law had, it was agreed by the French philosophers of the eighteenth century and by the Americans in the New World, been developed with great subtlety and power. By an appeal to it the British had with a good conscience beheaded a king, and by an appeal to it their revolted colonies had paralyzed the will to deny them independence. But the rule of law in England had in the course of centuries acquired an incredible technical complexity. "We have," wrote Sir Henry Maine, "turned our laws over to experts, to attorneys and solicitors, to barristers above them and to judges in the last resort." Not until 1878 was a revised edition of the statutes begun in place of the previous unsystematic mass. English law had been concerned, too, with the structure and working of an agrarian and commercial society. It had in the nineteenth century to be adapted to the problems of an industrial society whose nature was not easy to understand (for as Whitehead remarked nothing in nature— not even a flash of lightning—reveals itself at once). Society was being continuously transformed by new advances in pure and applied science and by its efforts to adjust itself to its internal problems of changes in the length of life and in the fertility of its members, by adjustment of the rates of development of consumer and of capital goods, and, in the details of economic life, by the search for the customs which would do for the new world of mechanized production what had been done by the old customs for the farm and the craft.

Of course, there had always been areas of industrial and commercial activity in which the problems of change and of numerical calculation had been understood. But these special areas of calculation were dotted about a wide agrarian plain. In the past, too, they had each their own rhythm, which was as well established as the rhythm of the seasons in agriculture, the way of life of the sailor, the merchant, and the disciplines of the ancient crafts. The law had no doubt been adapted over generations to the diversities of these different worlds. It had now to be adapted to the sudden quickening of the process of change in all productive activities. A hierarchical landed order had to be transmuted into the more flexible order needed by an industrial state. The challenge of the new industrial to the old agrarian order was not so serious as it might have been—as it was in the American Civil War—because in England the ownership of land was concentrated in comparatively few families, who were united by blood with the rising manufacturing interests, so that there was a kind of osmosis of power and influence between them. Because there was no peasantry and because the manual worker in the towns did not have the vote before 1867, the transition was comparatively peaceful.

There were, however, a host of problems to be solved, and the tensions of the political scene today are evidence that they were not completely solved. The most obvious problem was the organization of the labor market. An industrial society involved a greater mobility of labor and a greater specialization of occupations (and a greater increase in rate of change of mobility and specialization) than agrarian societies had ever known. The new mobility and specialization would have profound effects on the traditional structure of the family. The more intricate the web of industry became the more difficult it might be for the members of a particular family to determine how best to prepare themselves for their livelihood. After 1870 the problem of the organization of the labor market became a problem which the government could not ignore. The study of *Unemployment* by William (later Lord) Beveridge in 1908 showed that while the visible and legal obstacles to the mobility of labor, such as laws of settlement and of apprenticeship (attacked by Adam Smith), had been abolished the impalpable but no less real barriers of ignorance, poverty, and custom remained. The system of odd jobs was one of the causes of pauperism.[10] While the markets for other commodities were increasingly organized the market for labor was still left to ill-informed individual action. Because the prevailing method of getting work was personal application at a place of work, one could say that labor was hawked from door to door. Fresh men would enter a trade under the influence of local development in one place though men of the same trade were standing idle elsewhere. If the market were better organized and changes in demand for different forms of labor made known to those concerned, the stagnant pools of unemployed labor would be drained into a circulating stream. With an organized market it would be possible for children to be given guidance in the choice of a career and for the educational authorities to plan the technical training which would be required. The start of an organized market for labor was made with the Labour Exchange Act, 1909. In 1911 a scheme for compulsory insurance against unemployment was begun, because it was held that a flexible industrial structure might involve unemployment of which the incidence on individuals should be met by a general provision. The cost of the relief of unemployment caused by the flexibility of efficient industry could be made a charge on the industry itself.

The provision of labor exchanges by the state was only part of the organization of the market for labor. Trade unions among the better-paid workers had spread a knowledge of the market for labor and helped to break down the pools of labor which might have been bargaining in isolated ignorance. They might be regarded as creating a stock exchange in muscular skills. But the development of unions of workers for the purpose of negotiating their conditions of labor raised problems for economic theory and the legal concepts of mid-nineteenth century law. The dominant opinion before 1870 was that the freedom of action which should belong to individuals in a free society implied their freedom to combine to secure the things which apart they never could. A workman had the right to guard his own health, convenience, comfort, and safety and to bargain collectively for them if it appeared to him that collective bargaining were necessary. But collective bargaining for the raising of wages was condemned as being either futile or immoral—futile because in the long run the forces of the market would be sure to prevail, immoral because if it were effective it would be so only as an exercise of monopoly power. The mathematical economist Francis Edgeworth pointed out that nobody would be able to make any contract with a clear conscience if it were his duty to consider whether his gain was another's loss. If the trade unionist were told that his actions tended to diminish the total national product he could answer that as an "economic man" he was not concerned with the total product. The total product might be diminished but his share might be increased. A tariff system may diminish the total of the world wealth but it might well increase the share of the country with a good tariff.

The economic analysis was complicated by the legal confusions. The state had for centuries made some effort to regulate conditions of labor by statute. The state had an aversion to any combination within it (worms in the entrails of Leviathan) which might challenge its power. In 1799 all combinations of workmen to regulate the conditions of their work had been declared illegal. In 1800 a new general consolidating act "to prevent unlawful combinations of workmen" was passed. It declared illegal *every* combination for obtaining advance in wages, altering the hours of work, or preventing any person's employing whomsoever he might think to employ. Fresh legislation in 1824 and 1825 removed all criminal liability of combinations to determine wages or hours of work. But some of the judges developed a doctrine that conspiracies in restraint of trade were criminal offenses at common law.

On the *civil* side the courts held that a union whose member had defrauded it could not sue him and it was necessary to pass the Trade Union Act of 1871 to give the unions power to enforce a contract. In 1901 the House of Lords in the Taff Vale case held that a trade union was responsible for the damage caused to a railway company by procuring breaches of contract by its employees. The economical and social consequences of this decision were such that the Trades Disputes Act, 1906, was passed which exempted trade unions of all types from *all* actions in tort. This was necessary to protect the funds of the union, which, of course, included funds for sickness and unemployment and funeral benefits. The 1906 act went further and provided that no action done by a person in furtherance of a trade dispute to procure a breach of contract was actionable. In popular language it had placed trade unions "above the law." In 1908 Osborne, a member of a trade union, invoked the law to prevent a union from spending its money upon political objects. But a trade union although registered under the Trade Union Act, 1871, had no corporate *persona* beyond its power to sue or be sued in its registered name. If a union were not a corporation how was it to be limited in its powers? The Lords held that bodies constituted by statute, even though not corporations, could not act beyond the powers directly or indirectly conferred upon them. In 1913 legislation was passed to remove the restriction on political activities and other objects outside the ambit of the definition given in the act of 1871, although a trade unionist could contract out of the political obligations.[11]

The state after 1870 was more and more involved in considering what ought to be done to provide those services which were necessary to civilized life but which had not been developed by the existing forces of supply and demand. Of these the most important were educational and health services.

In France and Germany education had always been regarded as public service as essential as defense and justice. In England it was regarded as incidental to the missionary's duty to save the souls of the poor. If they could come to God by the Bible, the Bible they should be able to read. After 1832 some state assistance was provided through the medium of meager grants to two religious organizations, one of Anglicans and the other of Nonconformists. By 1870 it was clear that private enterprise with or without grants from the state had failed to provide the elements of education for even half the children of the country. The Liberal party had been torn to pieces on the issue of the Established Church and Nonconformity, and the Tories had been opposed to general elementary education from an instinct of self-preservation. When in 1867 the vote was given to the ordinary artisan it was essential that the failure of private education should be made good by state action. The Education Act of 1870 provided that elected local school boards should make good the gaps in the voluntary system. In 1880 attendance was made compulsory up to ten years old. In 1891 school fees were abolished in most schools. But it was not until 1918 that all fees were abolished in elementary schools and full time attendance required to the age of fourteen. The act of 1870 was, as H. G. Wells once wrote, "not an Act for common universal education" but "an Act to educate the lower classes for employment on lower class lines and with specially trained, inferior teachers who had no university quality."

After 1870 the English had not only to "educate their masters," the enfranchised artisans, they also needed to train the workers for the thronging new industrial techniques and to educate their industrial leaders. Forster, who introduced the bill of 1870, said that despite their powerful sinews and determined energy the uneducated laborers of England were in danger of being overmatched by the well-taught workers of other countries. To meet this need for technicians in industry and competent clerks in business and in the new and growing civil service, education other than elementary was encouraged. The Local Government Act of 1888 set up county councils and county borough councils, and they developed technical education. A central department for education, the Board of Education, was created in 1899, and in 1902 Balfour abolished the school boards and transferred their powers to the counties and county boroughs, which became responsible, under the supervision of the Board of Education, for the development of both elementary and secondary education.

The development of public health services took a peculiar form in England because of her pioneering efforts in the development of the new industrial methods. In 1834 the problem of the poor had been tackled by the setting up of a very new machinery of elected local Guardians of the Poor under the supervision of a special central department, the Poor Law Commissioners. Between them these bodies had investigated the relation between disease and poverty. Were people sick because they were paupers or paupers because they were sick? Progress was hampered not only by imperfections in the current economic analysis of the causes of destitution but also by the fact that the whole invisible world of microbes which does so much to cause disease was not known to exist until after the work of Pasteur in 1858. But if people could not see microbes they could smell bad drains. One byproduct of the revolution in the iron industry was that it became possible to make drains which would not burst, as well as railway lines which would not buckle. By 1869 both Gladstone and Disraeli were deeply interested in the provision of clean water, the removal of refuse, and the provision of reasonably safe and healthy houses. After 1871 the whole technique of preventive medicine began—the exploration of the unseen world of bacilli which determines our health, as the upper air determines our weather. The political and administrative problem was to develop a medical service which would prevent disease without undermining the independence of the ordinary worker. The problem was complicated by the fact that the Poor Law authorities had since 1834 provided some medical services for paupers in an effort to prevent the destitution sickness can cause. By the time of the Royal Commission on the Poor Law of 1905–9 it was clear that if health was good for the pauper it was good for the poor who were not paupers. The root difficulty was that while a generous establishment of sanitary provision for the prevention of disease and destitution was a common service which did not conflict with any principle of individualism, medical relief was grudgingly given in order to avoid pauperization and thus deprived itself of effectiveness. The development of medical treatment as a preventive measure against potential destitution was tentatively begun with the National Insurance Act of 1911.

In the opportunities offered by the development of the biological sciences and in the experience derived from the work of government departments and local authorities which had to deal with urgent problems of destitution, housing, sanitation, education, and preventive medicine lie some of the causes of the rise of the Labour party. The Industrial Revolution had created problems which were unknown in the agrarian societies of the past. If kings were not by God appointed, neither were the existing patterns of ownership of land and buildings and other capital resources. There was obviously some sickness in what was, in 1900, only partly an affluent and very much an acquisitive society. Could not this sickness be cured by publicity and measurement? And if the measurement led to suggestions for public control of what hitherto had been a field of private enterprise, was there any objection in principle to the extension of public control if it could deliver the goods?

CHAPTER XIII

Sea Power and Imperial Powers

Should the world survive the destruction threatened by the nuclear might of a prophetic power, the history of the *Pax Britannica* in the years between 1870 and 1914 will always have an interest as the prologue to the era of terror in which we live. The dissolution of its gentle and pervasive influence was a symptom of the limitations of the political ideas and institutions which had been worked out in Europe since the end of the Middle Ages. The armed prophets, whom Machiavelli had understood so well, were to tear its fragile web and the life of millions was to be made "poor, nasty, brutish, and short." As Santayana was to write: "Things come round in this world; the ruffians may be upon us some day when we least expect it and philosophy may have to retire again to the sanctuary." He was optimistic, for there is now no sanctuary to which philosophy can retire. Totalitarian states will not favor even a speculative and secular monasticism.

In this chapter there are three themes which we must briefly consider: (1) the nature of the power which was the basis of the *Pax Britannica,* (2) the ideas which were the roots of its life and in part the cause of its death, and (3) the relations between the British political system and other world powers in Europe and in a wider world.

The basis of British power in the world of separate states was sea power. But sea power had, even before the age of air and space, obvious limitations. It could not be a weapon of empire. A navy cannot do the work of Roman legions—it cannot march and it cannot man a Roman wall—except at the neck of a sea-girt promontory. It could be used to safeguard the peace of the seas. It made intervention possible when the scene of action was within the range of the navy, and it could be an effective weapon against states which, like France, were vulnerable to naval action. But it could not be used to help the Poles against the Russians, or the Armenians against the Turks, or the Danes against the Russians and Austrians.[1] It had sometimes to be used in a way which disturbed the men responsible. "A bombardment is a horrible thing," wrote Lord Granville in July 1882 of the British bombardment of Alexandria, ordered by the Gladstone Cabinet, "but it will clear the air and accelerate a solution of some sort or other. It is well for a country whose strength is maritime, that naval demonstrations should not be thought to be absolutely without a sting." [2] By 1897 the balance of opinion among naval experts was sceptical of the ability of the fleet to force the Dardanelles unless accompanied by land-based military measures against the forts.

So long as Britain was sheltered by a powerful fleet she could not be destroyed, but she could not control Germany, Russia, or Austria, and, in the United States, as the New York *Herald* said during the American Civil War: "Four hundred thousand thoroughly disciplined troops will ask no better occupation than to destroy the last vestiges of British rule on the American continent and annex Canada to the United States." [3] In 1909 the British public had become aware of the real danger from Germany when their homeland was threatened by the strongest military power in Europe backed by a navy which had been specially built to open the way to invasion. While the British fleet was an all-purpose fleet for the protection of the sea lanes of the world, the navy designed by Tirpitz was built to command the sea between Europe and the British Isles. To Sir Edward Grey and all responsible British statesmen there was no half-way house in naval affairs between complete security and utter ruin. But this is to anticipate.

With the fact of sea power went a complex system of ideas about the economic and political facts of life—what one may call the liberal philosophy of life, at once the glory and the ruin of the British peace. It had two main elements, the doctrine of free trade and the aim of self-government for all people on earth. In Gladstone's speech at West Calder, Midlothian, November 27, 1879, we hear prophetic intimations of the Wilsonian conception of self-determination, which was to complete the disintegration of what, after the 1914–18 war, remained of the nineteenth-century hope of a world order. Mr. Gladstone offered six principles of foreign policy: good government at home, the preservation to the nations of the world of the blessings of peace, the cultivation and maintenance of the concert of Europe ("common action is fatal to selfish aims"), the avoidance of needless and entangling engagements ("if you increase engagements without increasing strength, you diminish strength"), acknowledgment of the equal rights of all nations ("in point of right all are equal"), and, finally, "the foreign policy of England should always be inspired by the love of freedom." And of all these six the greatest was the principle of the equality of nations—"the principle of the equality among nations lies . . . at the very basis and root of a Christian civilisation." [4]

These principles depended on the assumption that if nations were free—neither in bondage to a tyrant power nor themselves enslaved by the evils generated in those who are tyrants over others—then their governments would not undertake more functions than would be necessary to the development of the energy and foresight of their individual citizens. Internal laissez faire, properly understood, would make possible a harmonious philosophical anarchy among free and sovereign states. Such was the vision. What were the facts?

It was true that Britain did not look for her livelihood to any system of imperial exploitation. She looked for her livelihood to her trade based on her industrial skills and to the investments which they had made possible. If peace, liberal ideas, and free trade were to prevail in the world, her position would stand. That they would so prevail was a belief which rested on the modest assumption that there was no special merit in the British success. There was nothing in the nature of man, or in the history of the different portions of mankind, to suggest that the experience of the British Isles could not be shared by all. Indeed, as Britain had been a pioneer others might well learn from her example to avoid her mistakes. This was, of course, an astonishing illusion. It ignored the peculiar good fortune which had favored the British Isles, it ignored with a false modesty their peculiar if not unique virtues, and above all it ignored the significance of the pressing problems with which her own statesmen were struggling. How all occasions did inform against Mr. Gladstone and examples gross as earth deny his premises we can see most clearly now.

A textbook on the colonies in 1883 made it clear that the policy of England discouraged any increase of territory in tropical countries already occupied by native races. It was unwise to extend imperial rule to aid British trading and philanthropic enterprise beyond existing frontiers. The world's unappropriated regions would remain open to British commerce without the assumption of the unpopular liability of ruling them. It was particularly foolish to push forward land frontiers in Asia and in Africa beyond the protective reach of British sea power. Gladstone stigmatized the acquisition of Cyprus and Fiji, the invasion of Zululand, the occupation of the Transvaal and Kandahar, and the purchase by Disraeli of shares in the Suez Canal as "gratuitous, dangerous, ambiguous, impracticable and impossible engagements." But however inconvenient to existing theory, the frontiers of empire (and not only those of Britain's) did move. They might not move as swiftly as those of the American nation, flowing swiftly to the Pacific and rising as a new sea of civilization where once the Indian had scalped and the buffalo roamed, but move they did.

Ominously, in those parts of the Queen's dominions which had no serious problems of racial difference, or of contacts between new commerce and ageless savagery, the basic principle of liberal free trade had not been accepted. The United States was already snug behind its tariff walls, and when responsible government was conceded to the Canadians and the Australians they adopted tariff policies of their own. It was no doubt true that some colonial statesmen were "in such ignorance of the principles of political economy that of the writings of Adam Smith and Mr. Ricardo they seem never to have even heard." But it was held by all responsible British political leaders that the principle of self-government was even more important than the principles of political economy.

Even in the case of the settlement of British people overseas where there were no problems of contact with old civilizations, as in Asia, or ageless savagery, as in Africa, there was no theory available to cover the facts of political growth. Even in the internal affairs of the established kingdom of Great Britain there was great uncertainty both in theory and in practice about the proper functions of government. For the technique of extending a political order to cover economic expansion and the movements of peoples that may accompany it, there was almost no theory at all. Classical political thought had not dealt with this. The United States having an open frontier, and a written constitution into which it could be tucked, had comparatively little trouble until the present century. The British had to accept the principle of self-determination as an internal disorder of the regions under their flag. This made impossible either the realization of the liberal theory of free trade or the development of a political order to do for the areas opened by sea power and the railroad in four of the world's continents what in the United States was done for the area opened by the covered wagon and the railway.

Two other consequences of the principle of self-government must be briefly mentioned before we consider more closely the real world of powers and conflicts in which for a time the web of British peace remained unbroken. (1) While it was a principle laid down by Mr. Gladstone in 1872 that Britain would not annex any territory great or small, without the expressed wish of the people to be annexed, freely expressed and authenticated by the best means the case would afford, it was also a belief that any national war by which the political unification of a nation was brought about was a just war. While liberal theory at home emasculated the political power of England, on the Continent liberal theory was often allied with aggressive nationalism. What might be life on the frontier of the American West could be destructive of peace and order in the thickly populated and diverse cultures of the Old World. (2) The nature of the British constitution precluded any Machiavellian skills. Kings and aristocracies, it was held, might govern other peoples, but one people could not govern another. Democratic government was thought to be inherently incompatible with imperial rule. One people might assimilate another; they could never govern another. A free empire was a contradiction in terms; it must be a federal system or disintegrate. Not merely could the British not be an empire, neither their theorists nor their men of action had in them the stuff of Caesars or their sycophants. Their democratic institutions seemed often to make it impossible that they could do what was vital to the survival of their own homeland. The British government could not undertake to declare war for any purpose unless it was a purpose of which the electors approved. "If the Government promised to declare war for any object which did not commend itself to public opinion, the promise would be repudiated, and the Government would be turned out." 5

That British policy must have the approval of the representatives of her people did not alter the political facts of life in Europe or the problems of the world beyond, though it might be a handicap in dealing with them. The question of the balance of power in Europe was still there. Because Britain as an insular world—an industrial and trading power —was concerned only for her security and had no continental ambitions, she was prepared to support the stronger European power, provided that it were friendly. She would interfere in force in Europe only when Europe had become acutely dangerous to her security. Mere "isolation" was no danger in itself. As Salisbury put it in a memorandum of May 29, 1901: "If we had succumbed in the revolutionary war (with France and Napoleon) our fall would not have been due to our isolation. We had many allies, but they would not have saved us if the French Emperor had been able to command the Channel." In the period after 1900, the British could not reach Berlin, but the German army supported by a superior fleet could conquer England. When the British homeland was threatened by the strongest military power in Europe, backed by a navy which might open the way to invasion, the course was set for the war of 1914. British statesmen in the period after 1906, however limited their vision and however improvised their policies might be, saw the realities of the European situation in clearer perspective than did their radical doctrinaire critics. But how had this position arisen?

In the pattern of world power after 1870 there were three vital conditions: (1) the continuing decay of the Turkish Empire; (2) as that empire decayed there was in the southeast of Europe no political principle to offer an effective basis for a political order which could be a barrier to the extension of Russian imperialism to Constantinople and the northwest frontier of India. The principle of self-determination, which was life to France and England, would be death to the Austro-Hungarian Empire and was incompatible with the survival of both the Russian and the Turkish empires; (3) in addition to the problems of the frontiers between Mohammedanism and Christianity and between Greek Orthodoxy and Catholicism, the German people, from the Middle Ages, had never found a political form appropriate to their intellectual and cultural attainments. They felt—to put it crudely—that the people of Beethoven and Goethe ought in no way to be inferior in the world to the people of Shakespeare, Newton, and Locke, particularly, as they appreciated their great men while the British did not. The English Philistines had need of cultural guidance. In this wicked world cultural leadership had need of the support of political power. The German sword—and navy—should uphold the honor of the German pedagogue. Linked with the drive of the German people for political greatness was at least a partial failure of the French to find for themselves a constitution which would carry out the great principles of the French Revolution. The working of a European Concert for purposes of justice, peace, and liberty with efficiency and success was the ideal of Gladstone's life in foreign policy, but the powers involved were out of tune.

These European differences recall the failure of classical Greece to achieve a viable political unity for those

> Aegean isles
> and promontories of the blue Ionian shore
> —where in her Mediterranean mirror gazing
> old Asia's dreamy face wrinkleth to a westward smile

which had been

> with their virtue, dispersed
> and molten in the great stiffening alloy of Rome.

Could not the Europeans of the nineteenth century have learned from the wisdom of the *Federalist* and achieved a federal constitution? Had they to repeat in a wider world the failure of the ancient Greeks? Could not the peoples who gave us Montaigne and Pascal, Newton and Locke, Goethe and Beethoven, Tolstoi and Chekhov, aided by all the unifying technologies that the nineteenth century was producing, have found a unifying basis of political order?

Of course, in a stable world, had Europe been merely a larger and more populated archipelago of Grecian vice and eccentricity, the sober virtues of American federalism might have prevailed. But the European world was losing all its ancient forms and loyalties as they melted under the influence of the rays, at once quickening and disintegrating, of the rising sun of science; and European order was flowing out into the world in a very different way from which it had moved in the eighteenth century. In the United States new knowledge and new methods could people and develop west of the Mississippi an almost empty area as large as the Roman Empire. But the impact of Europe was on the savagery of Africa, the medievalism of the Arabs, and the diverse civilizations of the ancient East. Where the British had the equivalent of the American West—in Canada, in Australia, in New Zealand—their record was modest and respectable. English Radical and Liberal ideas found their gardens in those wildernesses and assiduously cultivated them. Self-government, peace, equality, and economy—most of the Gladstonian virtues—were there developed. Systems of responsible government were encouraged and the pattern of a future Commonwealth outlined. The tensions which were to end in the disasters of World War I were generated in the interaction between the problems of the European balance of power and the frontier problems of a divided Europe in Asia, Africa, and the Middle East.

The British problem was revealed in four periods, the policy of four statesmen, and in the frontier problems of four areas: (1) Russia, Turkey, and the Dardanelles with Disraeli's handling of the Congress of Berlin, 1878, (2) Gladstone's handling of the African problems in their seemingly simple form in Egypt and in South Africa, (3) Salisbury's handling of the partition of Africa, and (4) in the last phase before the war of 1914 the Anglo-Japanese Treaty and the naval understanding with France by which the British under Balfour and Lord Lansdowne tried to meet the threat to their security latent in the development of Germany's naval ambitions. Such an outline sketch as can be given here has a delusive simplicity. It cannot cover the complexity of the changes in the European balance of power or the minutiae of diplomatic maneuvers which took place, as a great diplomatist has said, in a fog as impenetrable as that of war itself. The outcome—war and the ending of the *Pax Britannica* with its vision of democratic institutions slowly broadening down from precedent to precedent—we know, but the why and the how in the minds of the chancelleries of the world we cannot attempt to follow here.

There were deep and accelerating forces which are clear now but were difficult to judge at the time and impossible to control. The power to concentrate military and naval forces was increasing under the influence of scientific developments. The strength of the British navy depended on the secure control of a chain of coaling stations round the world. While in the 1860's and the early 1870's British naval superiority over other countries had remained unchallenged, by the 1880's the position was rapidly changing. Though greatly superior to that of France, the British navy had not a "strategic sufficiency" to deal with the possible combination of France and Russia if a third power such as Italy were neutral but unfriendly. The navy had not fought a real fleet action against a first-class naval power since the Basque Roads of 1809. The Naval Defence Act of 1889 was intended to make the navy superior, at least on paper, to the combined navies of any two European powers. The precise meaning of this so-called "two-power standard" was much disputed because Britain had long and vulnerable lines of sea trade and communication, widely dispersed territories, and many tempting prizes to offer in the shape of ports, bases, and coaling stations, and there were uncertainties about the attitude that neutrals might take in the event of war. Developments in guns and torpedoes and ship designs and armor had completely upset the old static relationship between attack and defense. By 1904 the submarine and the mine had made close blockade impossible. After the Franco-Russian alliance of 1894 it seemed possible that France might threaten invasion, keeping the British army tied to Britain and preventing reinforcements being sent to India in case of Russian attack. Dock facilities had to be extended at the Cape, Mauritius, Hong Kong, and Gibraltar. The increasing importance of the Suez Canal for trade and for the strategic route to India meant that the Mediterranean was vital to imperial strategy. After 1900 it was a problem how to give the Dominions and self-governing colonies an active interest in naval defense without destroying the British Admiralty's system of centralized control. Up to 1897 British naval expansion was based on the possibility of war with France and Russia and the strategic importance of the Mediterranean, the Suez Canal, and northwest India. But in 1897 two new facts appeared: the rise of the German navy and the extension of international rivalry to the Far East. These radical changes in the realities of power must not be forgotten when the details of diplomatic memoranda are scrutinized.[6]

If the shape and power of fighting ships were changing, so too were the means of communication about the empire and the world. A network of communications—railway, telegraph, shipping—was being woven. In 1870 a direct and independent cable from England to Bombay was completed; in 1872 London and Adelaide were brought into telegraphic communication; in 1876 the cable between Sydney and Wellington was laid.

The Suez Canal shortened the voyage to India by 5600 miles. It became the great highway of British traffic to India, Burma, Australia, and the Far East. Egypt became the half-way station between Southampton and Bombay. The words of statesmen were no longer slow, like drifting clouds, but swift as light itself.

Even more important than the new web of communications was the fact that the legal and political forms—the political nest in which the eggs of industrial and commercial revolutions had been hatched—were no longer suited to those vigorous chicks. Competitive industry and finance had taken wings and were abroad in the world, and few had any idea how they might be controlled. We know today the challenge of the problem of underdeveloped areas. Can the free world in the conditions of the cold war find legal and administrative forms through which to channel the technical resources and skills which will bring the conditions of political freedom to peoples who for long ages have had a life "poor, nasty, brutish, and short," before they are freed by the political slavery the Russians command? Can the freedom which was first developed in the poleis of classical Greece be sent, even with the aid of modern technologists, into the many hearts of darkness which still exist before they have been lit up by the red star of Russia?

In the period before 1914 the issues seemed simpler than they do now. It was simpler because there was no demand for representative government as a right which could not be refused. Except in the case of white colonies of settlement in Australia and Canada the demand for representative institutions as the right of every so-called nation had not been thought of. In principle all dependencies were being prepared for self-government. But in the case of India, which Sir Thomas Munro had believed would one day govern itself, most members of the Indian Civil Service did not think it could. There were many colonies under Crown government—the Crown Colonies—where a governor ruled as the representative of the Crown with no check save the advice of a council and the free expression of public opinion—in West Africa, the Caribbean, Mauritius, and Ceylon, the commercial stations around the Straits of Malacca, Hong Kong, and the Falkland Islands. Stations which had been merely occupied for war or depots of trade with nonwhite populations did not seem in 1870 to be candidates for self-government. As the Duke of Wellington had once said: "A constitution for Malta! I should as soon think of elections in an army or a parliament on board a ship." That political institutions might with the right help and guidance be developed as swiftly as a factory or an assembly line had not been grasped. Electoral arts were thought to be traditions which might grow, not tools which could be borrowed. We now export our institutions as we export our cloth or our valves. The problem then did not seem so complex as it does now, because the scope of political action, the varied uses to which political institutions might be put, was thought to be slight. The problem might be how to give to the Congo the blessings of Gladstonian liberalism. It was not how to find a substitute for a Chinese or Russian five-year plan in such areas. It is difficult to remember how very slight were the powers which, before 1914, *could* be used beyond the frontiers of the white man's industrial world when we are discussing whether they were *rightly* used.

Returning to the four periods mentioned, we have first the Eastern crisis from 1876 to 1880. In this Disraeli had a commanding position. The Congress of Berlin, 1878, was the last peace congress, actually so called, to be held in Europe. There was no great war in Europe for thirty-six years after it. Russia had gone to war with Turkey in 1877. The policy of London was at the time one of conditional neutrality—neutrality provided Russia respected British interests in Constantinople, the Straits, Egypt, and the Suez Canal. In March 1878 Turkey was forced to sign the disadvantageous Peace of San Stefano. Salisbury at the British Foreign Office and Disraeli (Lord Beaconsfield) were determined to upset two of its main provisions. They were determined not to allow Russia to create a big Bulgaria, a state with a seaboard on the Black Sea and the Aegean. So large a state would, as a vassal of Russia, upset the balance of power. Second, the Russians had taken Batum, Kars, and Ardahan and seemed to threaten an overland way to Suez and the Persian Gulf. Great Britain insisted on the submission to a congress of the whole terms of San Stefano. Salisbury had been profoundly influenced by his term of office as secretary of state for India and wanted effective securities for the free passage of the Straits "at all times, as if they were open sea." At the Congress of Berlin, Turkey in Asia, the Straits, and the maintenance of her Mediterranean interests were the keynotes of British policy. Turkey, Salisbury thought, could no longer stand alone. He hoped that in Constantinople and in the eastern Mediterranean, British influence could be made predominant. He feared that the Arabs and the Asiatics would look to the Russians as the coming man, now that Turkey was in seeming dissolution. Russian influence over Syria and Mesopotamia would, through the connection of Bagdad with Bombay, make the British hold on India more difficult. The British needed a place of arms in the Levant where their ships could be ready for action. In return for a guarantee of Turkey in Asia against Russia the British secured the right to occupy and administer Cyprus. Cyprus, Disraeli told the Queen, was "the key to Western Asia." Four years later Gladstone was to occupy Egypt and the need for Cyprus passed.

This brings us to our second theme—the occupation and ultimate annexation of Egypt by Gladstone, contrary to his intention as well as contradictory to his principles. Egypt and Tunisia had become fields of European investment. Joint Anglo-French intervention in financial affairs had been established in 1876–79. During the years 1880–82 an Egyptian national movement was endangering the continuance of the khedive's rule. This involved a threat to the peaceful development of Anglo-French financial policy. Canning and Palmerston had always held that the contraction of a loan by a British government with an undeveloped power was undesirable because it ultimately involved interference with internal affairs. Now British financial interests in Egypt were so great and the financial situation of Egypt so unsatisfactory that interference even by Gladstone, who normally desired to encourage and not to repress national movements everywhere, was unavoidable. His view was that "the root and pith and substance of the material greatness of our nation lies within the compass of these islands, and is, except in trifling particulars, independent of all and every sort of political dominion beyond them." When Disraeli had acquired about 44 per cent of the shares of the Suez Canal in 1875 he was not thinking of any possible occupation of Egypt. He thought that Constantinople, and not Egypt and the Suez Canal, was the key to India. An empire based on naval supremacy and free trade did not need to extend its territory. The Suez Canal made Egypt of an importance for trade and strategy almost as great as Cape Town. But neither Disraeli nor Gladstone wanted to occupy the country.

The British would not have entered on the Egyptian adventure had it been possible to continue Anglo-French co-operation. But the French Chamber was convinced that Bismarck was plotting to draw the country into foreign complications, and the fall of Gambetta in 1882 ended Anglo-French co-operation. The military *coup d'état* under Arabi Pasha was anti-European and anti-Turk in character. When Sir Garnet Wolseley had destroyed Arabi's army at Tell el-Kebir it was impossible to quit. There was no effective government left. The Mahdi revolted in the Sudan and defeated Egyptian troops. The British government wanted to pull out after the rescue of outlying garrisons in the Sudan, and to defend only the ports in the Red Sea, where the navy could give support. But the work of evacuation involved sending General Charles Gordon, and when he was besieged and killed in Khartum the Egyptian policy of Gladstone's government ended amid storms of criticism.

The upshot was that the British were left responsible for the government of Egypt, not directly, but indirectly through a British agent and consul general in the person of Sir Evelyn Baring. He had to secure the consent of an international commission which he could not carry without the vote of Germany, and Germany used her veto to bring pressure to bear on Britain in the interest of Germany's European ambitions and fears. In 1887 Salisbury complained: "I heartily wish we had never gone into Egypt. Had we not done so, we could snap our fingers at all the world." Because France and Russia habitually opposed her Britain could only govern Egypt by keeping Germany on her side. "Berlin and not Cairo," wrote Baring in 1886, "is the real centre of gravity in Egyptian affairs." [7]

At the other end of the continent of Africa a different problem was developing. In New Zealand it had been easy to place financial and military responsibility for the control of the Maoris in the local administration. But in South Africa neither Cape Colony nor Natal had responsible government. The Bantu people, then known as Kaffirs, were far more dangerous than the Maoris of New Zealand. A group of people in Great Britain was concerned to check injustice and inhumanity to the natives on the part of the Boers of the Orange Free State and the Transvaal. So long as South Africa remained an agglomeration of disunited provinces there was a danger that a war of any one of them with the Zulus would involve serious consequences for all the rest and involve the British government as well. In 1871 responsible government was given to the Cape. In 1875 it was proposed that delegates from all the states and provinces should meet in Cape Colony in the hope of securing a possible union of South Africa in some form of confederation. But the attempt to bring under a single government two independent republics, two Crown Colonies, and an ancient dependency newly given responsible government was a failure. In 1876 the Boers were at war with the Zulus. The Boer's system of government was, in British eyes, at once oppressive, meddlesome, and factious, incompetent in peace and war, and financially ruinous. The Transvaal was annexed.

It seemed to the British that early confederation was the only way to avoid direct responsibility for the "turbulent, advancing colonial frontiers of the subcontinent." [8] Confederation, Gladstone thought, was the only hope the British had of bringing about healthy relations between the colonies and republics, Boers and Britons, colonists and natives. The Cape naval base was the only major imperial interest Britain had. When confederation proved impossible, the Gladstone cabinet was divided over the issue of withdrawing from the Transvaal. Those who were for withdrawal did not want to "create another Ireland in South Africa"; those who were against did not want to abandon the native population to Boer oppression. By the Pretoria Convention (August 1881) a compromise was made: on the one hand imperial suzerainty and the appearance of control of Transvaal native and frontier policy; on the other self-government was restored to the Boers. But almost immediately the Boers were intervening in Bechuana tribal wars. By 1884 there were fears of a German-Transvaal conspiracy to seize hegemony in South Africa as German annexations in Southwest Africa advanced inland toward Bechuanaland and the Transvaal western frontiers. Boer control of Bechuanaland might shut out the Cape from the interior. The Colony and Protectorate of Bechuanaland were proclaimed in September 1885.

The problem of South Africa was to end in the Boer Wars, the generous peace of Vereeniging (1902), the creation of the Union of South Africa, and the final defeat there, after World War II, of the liberal tradition.

We must look now at our third theme: Salisbury's handling of the partition of Africa. "Are we to attempt the creation of another India in Africa," Harcourt asked in 1889. Throughout the 1880's British ministers tried to keep the African hinterland open to British trade by international agreements and the reservation of exclusive spheres of influence. But the autarkic aims of continental imperialism made it impossible to secure adequate diplomatic guarantees of free trade. Before 1870 the protection of our communications with India had been the vital consideration in determining the retention of imperial dependencies, but after 1870 the future of tropical Africa arose in a new form.

To assume control of immense areas of tropical Africa and of groups of islands in the Pacific was repugnant to the policy of British governments. With the utmost reluctance they were driven to acquire a new empire to protect the old. The prospect of the reform of Turkey had become remote. After the Suez Canal was built Cairo was important to protect the route to the East. They failed to stabilize Egypt as they had failed to stabilize Turkey. The missionary societies did not favor such expansion either. In West Africa small forts had been retained to suppress the slave trade. In the 1880's and 1890's the Colonial and Foreign Offices objected to any extension of administrative responsibilities. A proposal for a protectorate in the Niger was refused in 1882 because "the coast is pestilential; the native numerous and unmanageable. The result . . . would be almost certainly war with the natives, heavy demands on the British taxpayer." Neither the government nor the public wanted "to get mixed up in" the turbulent affairs of Ashanti. The Colonial Office refused to subsidize or guarantee loans to private enterprise.

Officials in West Africa were warned continually against accepting formal responsibilities beyond existing frontiers. British policy toward East Africa and Zambesi was entirely defensive in purpose until 1888. The sultan of Zanzibar's offer to place his territories under British protection was refused in 1880. In return for Bismarck's support of British policy in Egypt, a large sphere of influence in East Africa was conceded to Germany in 1885.

From 1884 on the Foreign Office had to give priority to imperial interests in East Africa over those on the West Coast. British vulnerability in Egypt made it dangerous to compete seriously with the continental powers in West Africa. The political future of the East Coast was of real importance to Indian and imperial interests. The suppression of the East Coast slave trade was a concern of humanitarian societies in Britain. The highlands were suitable for European colonization. A settlement colony was possible. Unoccupied African territories were valued according to their proximity to the Suez India life line, their mineral wealth, and their suitability for colonization.[9] With the developing technologies of the West and the projection of the strategic struggles of European powers around the world, the central heart of darkness of Africa could in the late nineteenth century no more remain inviolate than the far side of the moon in the twentieth. British policy in West and in East Africa was a response to British needs in Egypt and the South.[10] In 1870 the map of Africa was full of vacant spaces (they fascinated the youthful Conrad). Nothing was known of the basin of the Congo, geographically the heart of it all. But the infiltration of light from economic interests had begun. During the American Civil War Europe had turned for cotton to West Africa. In eastern tropical Africa the commercial center of Zanzibar imported British cottons and exported ivory and cloves. In 1873 the great Zanzibar slave market was shut down. In 1876 slave trade by land, and slavery itself in 1897, were abolished in the British Protectorate.

From 1870 African journeys of exploration took on an increasingly political character. The British had been interested in the exploration of the Niger for half a century; but now French, German, Italian, Portuguese, and American interest was shown. In the 1870's in West Africa leave of four or five months a year was needed by all who worked there. (Saki's *Unbearable Bassington* was quickly disposed of there.) After 1897 the great advances by Manson and Ross in tropical medicine made continuous and economical administration by Europeans possible. Only on the Niger and the Congo could river steamers be used. Horses and oxen were of little use because of the tsetse fly. Railroads were essential, and they would need government support if, as in India, they were to be built. After 1880 British relations with Africa could not rest on the influence direct and indirect of sea power alone. Up to 1880 we had been, as Lord Salisbury explained to the House of Lords, "masters of Africa, practically, or the greater part of it, without being put to the inconvenience of protectorate or anything of that sort, by the simple fact that we were masters of the sea and that we have had considerable experience in dealing with native races . . . We left enormous stretches of coast to the native rulers in the full confidence that they would go on under native rulers, and in the hope that they would gradually acquire their own proper civilisation without any interference on our part. Then suddenly we found that that position, however convenient, had no foundation whatever in international law. We had no right over all those vast stretches of coast—we had no power of preventing any other nation from coming in and seizing any portion of them." [11]

The advance of foreign enterprise forced British ministries from their noninterventionist resolutions. Changes in international law made spheres of influence depend upon effective occupation. To allow a struggle for supremacy between white traders of different nationalities would mean the degradation of the natives and the possibility that national sentiment might provoke war. There would have to be, Salisbury decided, a selective regulation of the British advance; the black man had the right to be rescued from the curse of the slave trade, the right to share in the religion and civilization of which the white races were the trustees, and the right to be well governed. Between 1888 and 1892 Salisbury began to forestall foreign advances toward the Nile Valley and the East and Central African highlands. Cairo, not Constantinople, was now the pivot of security in the Mediterranean. He determined upon a prolonged occupation of Egypt. The security of Egypt, he thought, depended upon keeping Uganda and the entire Nile Valley under imperial control. The Foreign Office carried out a deliberate expansion to meet a long-term conception of the empire's strategic needs. But he did not want to place fresh burdens of cost and responsibility upon the British taxpayer. The extension of British rule was to be economical and tentative. Chartered companies were used—the Niger Company in 1886, the East African Company in 1888, and the Rhodes South African Company in 1889. The British government reserved the right to supervise their native policy, kept exclusive control over their foreign policy, and the right to withdraw their charters. But the government avoided going to the Treasury for grants-in-aid or to the Commons for legislative authorization.

The pattern of moving frontiers in Africa was shaped at least in part by the tensions which were unresolved in Europe—and not only in Africa but on the northwest frontier of India too. Russia did not seriously contemplate the invasion of India, but she knew the value of a threat to India as an asset in her European political strategy. Bismarck thought that even if colonies were valueless in themselves, they were sensitive spots where Britain could be pressed. Looking to British difficulties in Egypt, in South Africa, in New Guinea, Bismarck's successors in Germany could try to blackmail her into acquiescence in their European policies. There was a possibility that France would encircle and infiltrate British West African possessions. This was stopped by Lugard's West African frontier force and a convention in 1898. There was a possibility, too, that the French would establish an east-west sea to sea axis a few degrees north of the equator, cutting across the Upper Nile Valley. This was stopped at Fashoda in 1898. But in the same decade there had been tension between France and Britain in Indo-China. In 1893 France invaded Siam, 90 per cent of whose trade was in British hands. But more important was the need to keep a buffer state between the French frontier in Indo-China and that of India. The British government did not want a great military power on her southeast flank. The Russians got the impression that France had braved the risk of war with Great Britain in Siam and sent a Russian squadron to visit Toulon in 1894. In 1894–95 China had been defeated in the Sino-Japanese war and France in the south and Russia in the north were moving in to secure concessions. It was feared that there might be plans for connecting the Russian advance from the north with the Indo-Pacific empire that France was building from the south, and ousting Great Britain's commercial interests in the Yangtse Valley.

The importance of the Malacca Straits to the China trade helped to focus attention on the whole Malayan area. The Foreign Office and the Admiralty were little interested in the Malay States for their own sake, but they were concerned with the China trade and the strategic importance of the Straits of Malacca. They had to give men on the spot—such officers as Sir Andrew Clarke and Sir William Jervois—sufficient authority over local rulers to deny a pretext of intervention to any other power.

Germany was mainly a continental power. To protect her frontiers she wished to divert the other European powers from the continent. She hoped that Britain might be persuaded into an alliance with her. But Great Britain was concerned with her world position and had no interest in Germany's hegemony in Europe. As Salisbury put it in a memorandum of May 29, 1901, "the liability of having to defend German and Austrian frontiers against Russia is heavier than that of having to defend the

British Isles against France." [12] In any case the British government could not undertake to declare war, for any purpose, unless it was a purpose of which the electors would approve.

By 1900 the *Pax Britannica* was doomed. The conditions which had made it possible, a balance of power in Europe and an acceptance of British supremacy at sea, were not to continue. The vision of spreading peace and growing plenty as the industrial techniques of Western civilization were diffused around the world was to become the nightmare in which we have lived, as it was realized that political skills could not meet the problems generated by economic change in a world so culturally diverse that the peace of Europe depended on a balance of power in which three tottering and almost medieval empires were involved—the Russian, the Austrian, and the Ottoman—and the *Pax Britannica* on a pattern of naval power which was wide open to attack by any political system that was prepared to use force to attain its ends. In 1890 Britain had found that she could not prevent a combination of three European powers which threatened a partition of China. The building of the Trans-Siberian Railroad by Russia turned the flank of the front which British sea power had opposed to her Far Eastern policy. Britain decided to ally herself with Japan so that she could concentrate her naval forces in the Mediterranean. As the German naval challenge was revealed, an Anglo-French entente made it possible for the French fleet to guard the Mediterranean while the British fleet held the North Sea, the Channel, and the Atlantic beyond.

These changes were necessary because of the strategic basis of British existence as an independent power. There were seven strategic areas of the world before the air age. Three were oceanic: the Atlantic, the Indian, and the western Pacific. Four were continental: Europe with North Africa and the Levant, Africa, Russia, and Central Asia. In the nineteenth century the *Pax Britannica* rested on British control of two of the oceanic areas—the Indian and the Atlantic Oceans—and of one of the continental —Africa. For a century after Napoleon, Africa was a buttress to the British control of the Atlantic and Indian oceans and their shores. New Zealand was a bastion to the East. West Africa was a control point on the Atlantic route. In World War I the British naval position in the Atlantic and the Indian oceans was not secure until German East and German Southwest Africa had been cleared. Command of the Atlantic could be turned by a power which had control of the western coast of Africa or the eastern coast of South America. The Mediterranean had become a secondary concern in British strategy even before air power was to reduce it to a mere river flowing through the European area. It was a useful short cut to the Indian Ocean, but there was another route.[13]

The great land wars of the British had been fought in the area between the Atlantic and the heart of Europe—in France, Spain, and the Low Countries, from where a deadly thrust could come to the Channel, the very moat of British freedoms; or in the area between Europe and the Indian Ocean—Egypt, Iraq, Palestine, and the Black Sea, for a hostile power on the Nile, the Niger, the Tigris, or the Euphrates could threaten either the command of the Indian or the Atlantic oceans.

CHAPTER XIV

British Thought
from Blake to Darwin

The life of science and the life of industry and politics do not, even today, move in step. But their interrelations are the urgent concern of governments. Even the other side of the moon can be on a Cabinet agenda, or influence a party program. Before the last quarter of the nineteenth century the spirit of science was moving over the social life of men, but the currents which it stirred were not deep or swift. Men sensed a change in the air. They did not know that their own transformation had begun. They saw they had a new tool; they did not know that a new cosmos was coming into their ken.

In Britain the reactions to the changing spirit of the times had some special features. She was a pioneer in a new form of industrial organization; she was only a province of the mind of Europe and a province with some very odd highways and by-ways; and she had developed a liberal state which could never be imperial. The universal implications of the new industrial methods would not in her case come under a national political control. In almost any other political system the new powers would have been used to further imperial designs. It might have been well for the world if they had. But interaction between the new knowledge and social change was at the time local and superficial.

From 1770 to 1830 the effect of mechanization was far-reaching in certain basic British industries. The great advances were in textiles, in iron and steel, and in the use of steam. The innovations were in improvements in automation and in the use of power. Neither large factories nor simple machines were new. By 1830 no country was so mechanized, no country so statistically-minded, as England. But the basic changes had been inventions and not scientific discoveries. The industrial developments had little systematic connection with the real life of science. The science used was simple and the crafts were old. The formative period of modern science in which its character, its methods, and its problems were established ended about 1830. The pattern of the atomic structure within the molecule and the reasons why certain arrangements are possible or stable had been glimpsed with the discovery of valency by the English chemist Sir Edward Frankland in 1852, which led to Friedrich Kekule's classification in 1865 of the elements according to their combining power. Electrolysis was discovered by Sir Humphry Davy in 1807; catalysis which speeds up reactions in 1836. But the applications of these discoveries were not to come until the last quarter of the nineteenth century. About the year 1870 the modern age with the technical ascendancy of science begins. The influence of inventors of a completely new type—a Bessemer, Siemen, or Armstrong—begins to impinge on basic industries. Before 1870 the precise control of operations by accurate timing and sampling was novel. The technology was empirical. In the Great Exhibition of 1851 the displacement of coal and iron by oil and steel was not even hinted at. What science really implied with its shaping power moving into the heart of nature was only dimly grasped. The *Pax Britannica* from the fall of Napoleon to the unification of Germany was based upon a comparatively simple technology.

It is useful to recall these scientific and industrial truisms because it sets some of the intellectual troubles of the time in a cooling perspective. Men need not have bothered so much about the things that did bother them. What was to come was much worse than they ever dreamed. And yet it could be argued that had they solved in their day the problems they could have solved the world would not now be the fearful place it is.

The two great debates of the period were over mechanism and freedom, over the discontinuity and creationism which dominated popular religion, and the principle of continuity which dominated intellectual life. Intellectual clarity was dimmed by religious emotion. The problems are difficult enough. When mixed up with questions about the authenticity of the Scriptures discussed by scholars who had not, and could not then have had, the linguistic and archeological tools they needed, they became hopeless. A few philosophers kept their heads—F. H. Bradley and J. McTaggart among them—but they had no mathematical language with which to speak to the scientists.

With these two debates were associated the disputes between empiricists and idealists. As J. S. Mill wrote in 1838: "... between the partisans of these two opposite doctrines there reigns a *bellum internecinum*. Neither side is sparing in the imputation of intellectual and moral obliquity to the perceptions, and of pernicious consequences to the creed, of its antagonists. Sensualism is the common term of abuse for the one philosophy, mysticism for the other. The one doctrine is accused of making men beasts, the other lunatics. It is the unaffected belief of numbers on one side of the controversy, that their adversaries are actuated by a desire to break loose from moral and religious obligation; and of numbers on the other that their opponents are either men fit for Bedlam, or who cunningly pander to the interests of hierarchies and aristocracies, by manufacturing superfine new arguments in favour of old prejudices." [1]

With the empiricist/idealist dispute was linked the political issue between the utilitarians with their many forms of hedonism and the philosophical idealists—S. T. Coleridge, T. H. Green, Bradley, and others— who were concerned to analyze what is really involved in a social order. They tried to restate the insight of Burke to an age which—temporarily as we now know—had no need for political philosophy. They were not successful. One result of their failure is that the world is now menaced by the unifying power of a fighting creed and by a fissiparous doctrine of national self-determination.

In the eighteenth century, as A. N. Whitehead has said, the radical inconsistency between the conception of nature as a vast machine and man himself, a part of nature, yet a self-determining organism, enfeebled thought.[2] The position of Kant in European philosophy stems from his efforts to resolve the dilemma that man as part of nature is to the last particle of his brain and body bound in a determined pattern, while in his everyday life he knows that he is free, responsible, and guilty, too. Poets and men of letters have not normally the philosophic genius of Kant. But they were aware of the dilemma which taxed his powers. The problem for the poet was that the scientific vision of the external world was spiritually barren. He was driven to seek nourishment for his poetic impulse in a cosmos of his own.

William Blake (1757–1827) was the English poet who reacted most violently against the Newtonian conception of the universe:

> The Atoms of Democritus
> And Newton's Particles of light
> Are sands upon the Red sea shore
> Where Israel's tents do shine so bright.

He made Christ a seer and a naturalistic rebel, the enemy of restraint. Blake's devil is Reason whose high priests are Newton and Locke. There may be, as J. S. Mill said, "in the English mind, both in speculation and in practice, a highly salutary shrinking from all extremes." "It is rather," he added, "an instinct of caution than a result of insight." In Blake there is a full rejection of the generalities of the eighteenth century. "Great thoughts are always general," Dr. Johnson had remarked, "and consist in positions not limited by exceptions, and in descriptions not descending to minuteness." Sir Joshua Reynolds had remarked that our bodies are roughly alike; so too are our minds. But for the "general uniformity and agreement in the minds of men" it would not have been possible to establish the rules of art. Blake had retorted in a marginal comment: "to generalise is to be an idiot." He wrote:

> He who would do good to another must do it in Minute Particulars.
> General Good is the plea of the scoundrel, hypocrite and flatterer;
> For Art and Science cannot exist but in minutely organised Particulars.

And:

> I must create a System, or be enslav'd by another Man's.
> I will not Reason and Compare: my business is to create.

It would have seemed ridiculous to Blake to make any separation of art from moral problems and beliefs. He wrestled with such salient problems of human life as the proper place of intellectual control in the total economy of the personality, the place of impulse, the relations between authority and those it controls, the relations of the sexes, and the folly of moral generalities.[3] It is not fanciful to see in Blake's "I will not Reason and Compare: my business is to create" a parallel to Goethe's statement: "A man born and bred in the so-called exact sciences will, on the height of his analytical reason, not easily comprehend that there is also something like an exact concrete imagination." "Beauty," he continued, "is the manifestation of secret laws of Nature which, were it not for their being revealed through beauty, would have remained unknown for ever."[4] Which is Keats' "Beauty is Truth, Truth Beauty."

The only way to escape the effects of the Newtonian doctrine of mechanism was to discover that it was not mechanism at all. This the scientists were to do in the course of the nineteenth century until of the Newtonian universe not a wrack remained. But the poet and the plain man of 1800 could not know this. They only knew science as the prisoners in Plato's cave saw the shadows on the wall. They had to make what sense they could of life by using all the powers of what "concrete imagination" they had. The danger was that they might be led into private worlds of experience and private worlds of morals. Romanticism was the appeal to the concrete against the abstract, to the passions, which Hume himself had noted are the springs which drive the hands of the clock of reason, to childhood as the mystery from which the rational self emerges, and to the dark gods of classical Greece from the easy rationalism of Cicero's Rome. On the continent of Europe such romanticism was driven into nihilism. Between 1830 and 1850 "the romantic faith in love and in the future," wrote Nietzsche, "turned into the craving for nothingness." The implication of the Newtonian system which Hume had only playfully noted—that God is dead—was taken by the Europeans very much to heart. In England romanticism, except in the case of Blake, remained, with theology, mild, muddled, and constitutional. Under J. S. Mill's guidance the British came to recognize "the importance, in the present imperfect state of mental and social science, of antagonistic modes of thought: which . . . are as necessary to one another in speculation, as mutually checking powers are in a political constitution." [5] We owe the Romantics one great debt through Coleridge, Keats, and Hazlitt: Shakespeare's genius was revealed beneath the inept criticisms with which Augustan wits had covered him. (How silly the spirit of an age may make a great man outside his own craft is shown in Hume's estimate of Shakespeare in his *History of England*.)

The early eighteenth-century writers in England had been interested in truths which they thought were universal and demonstrable. They had viewed with suspicion thought which was merely personal or, worse still, peculiar.[6] This distrust of originality and love of orthodoxy was in part the result of the popular view of science as the mastery of nature's simple laws, in part the result of the patronage of a small aristocratic class whose members had achieved a balance in their own social life, but knew from painful experience how cracked many of their number were as individuals and how tenuous was their hold on political power. They could not know that a few scraps of the sciences used with moderate administrative competence would make the mob that broke their windows, and even burnt their town houses, almost as balanced, sceptical, and bored as themselves. A very little applied science could make a Gulliver out of any Yahoo.

In the meantime, before the new science reached into the workshops, along the canals, and into the railways the world of politics and art was very small indeed. In 1753 the poet John Armstrong did not put the fashionable class in London at much more than 12,000. In 1812 Francis Jeffrey (1773–1850) of the *Edinburgh Review* guessed that there were about 300,000 persons who read for amusement or instruction among the "middling classes of society," and in the higher about 30,000. It was for this limited public that Jeffrey could comment in the *Edinburgh Review* of November 1814:

"An habitual and general knowledge of the few settled and permanent maxims which form the canon of general taste in all large and polished societies—a certain tact, which informs us at once that many things, which we still love and are moved by in secret, must necessarily be despised as childish, or derided as absurd, in all such societies— though it will not stand in the place of genius, seems necessary to the success of its exertions" (*Contemporary Reviews of Romantic Poetry,* ed. by John Wain. London, 1953).

The power and the weakness of the Romantic poets was that they had all to aim at being true to their own peculiar genius without the support of "commonly accepted symbols to represent and house . . . the deepest feelings" of their readers.[7] In the middle eighteenth century it had been thought that after a long process of trial and error poetry had at last reached a satisfactory form of expression."[8] For Pope it had. But then Pope was a unique genius and not just an outstanding example of a "general rule." And Pope too could use some commonly accepted symbols to represent and house the deepest feelings of his readers. But those symbols did not survive into the later eighteenth century.

The romantic poets had to think that they were unique and gifted beings whose duty it was to find perfect expression for the visions revealed to them. A. E. Housman said that there were only four good poets in the eighteenth century and they were mad: Collins, Smart, Cowper, and Blake. It was Poor Kit Smart who, as Browning said:

> . . . pierced the screen
> Twixt thing and word, lit language
> straight from soul.

But Smart, like the Wesleys, took the Bible as seriously as did Bunyan. The Romantics did not. To Wordsworth the dichotomy between the mental and material worlds was antipathetic. He sought in his own pantheism an adjustment between Newton's mechanical order and Blake's "innumerable company of the heavenly host." In his *Prelude, or, Growth of a Poet's Mind,* the central theme is the development of Wordsworth's sense of the intimacy of natural objects. They provide a stable background to his emotional life.[9] He is sometimes "able to create for the reader the feeling he has derived from 'natural objects,' thereby making those feelings part of the common stock of human experience and hence capable of being brought to bear on other modes of experience."[10] Today we can appreciate Wordsworth because for us "at the heart of all science is the impersonal mode of experience . . . it gives a . . . subtle penetration of even the most intimately personal experience by a new mode of feeling, e.g., in the experience of pain—something in my pain is uniquely, ungeneralisably mine, but something is common to all men . . . Known in this mode the individual is not unique and mysterious; he is an animal entity in a material cosmos, an organisation of appetites and aptitudes identical with others of his species. And these facts are as vivid and exciting, as real and true, as *important*, about *oneself, to* oneself, as the personal facts." [11]

In Wordsworth the relation between the personal and the general is stated almost wistfully:

> How exquisitely the individual mind
> (and the progressive power perhaps no less
> of the whole species) to the external world
> Is fitted: and how exquisitely, too—
> Theme this but little heard of among men—
> The external world is fitted to the Mind:
> And the creation (by no lower name
> Can it be called) which they with blended might
> Accomplish.

The opposition between the mechanical and the vital was a central theme of Coleridge's later writing.[12] Coleridge wrote to Wordsworth that the aim of the *Prelude* should have been to refute the school of Locke, to show how man's senses are evolved from his mind or spirit, and to show how the doctrine of redemption rescues mankind "from his enmity with nature." In the *Statesman's Manual* Coleridge wrote in 1816 that the Bible reveals that "the elements of necessity and free-will are reconciled in the higher power of an omnipresent Providence, that predestinates the whole in the moral freedom of the integral parts."

Samuel Coleridge (1772–1834) lived in an "age of anxiety." He transformed the mechanistic psychology of the eighteenth century, revived the older tradition of Platonism, and introduced to England the new idealism of Germany.[13] It was with his help that the Rhine flowed for a while into the Thames. He had known the Lockean tradition from the inside. In 1794 he wrote to Southey: "I am a complete necessitarian. I go further than Hartley, and believe the corporality of *thought*, namely, that it is motion." The leading idea of his harmless and extravagant scheme of Pantisocracy was to try the experiment of human perfectibility on the banks of the Susquehanna. In the second generation the little society was to combine "the innocence of the patriarchal age with the knowledge and genuine refinement of European culture." After a year in Germany (1798–99) he read philosophy seriously and in 1801 was rejoicing that the mind was not a machine registering sense impressions but a creative force in the shaping of truth. He was confident that he could prove the reputation of Locke, Hume, and Hobbes to have been wholly unmerited. He was convinced that Descartes and Locke had "untenanted Creation of its god," and substituted

> a universe of death
> for that which moves with light and life informed
> Actual, divine, and true.

In 1797 and 1798 he had composed his greatest poem, "The Ancient Mariner." In 1802 he composed the ode "Dejection," lamenting the decay of his poetic powers.

Wordsworth had claimed in the Preface to *Lyrical Ballads* that poetry was "the breath and fine spirit of all knowledge." Coleridge underpinned Wordsworth's intuition with a philosophical structure borrowed from Kant. Kant had said that "imagination" was a power active and creative in our knowledge, however commonplace, of the world. Kant in his criticism of the empiricism of the eighteenth century put imaginative power at the very center of human experience. Coleridge felt that this gave a philosophical ground for Wordsworth's claim.[14]

Keats (1795–1821) distinguished from the poet who was "Wordsworthian or egotistically sublime" the poet whose essential quality was "Negative Capability," that is, the capacity to be in "uncertainties, mysteries, doubts, without any irritable reaching after fact and reason." Had he not died so young Keats might have found a Shakespearean balance even in the age of anxiety. He once wrote: "I have good reason to be content, for thank God I can read and perhaps understand Shakespeare to his depths." For John Keats the world was a place in which we alter nature. We construct from our experience a personal identity. Human life was a "vale of soul-making." [15]

Tennyson had neither the intellectual passion of Keats nor the personal vision of Wordsworth. While Wordsworth was the poet of nature Alfred Tennyson claimed to be a poet of science. He was an early convert to evolutionism. Carlyle said that he was "a man solitary and sad, as certain men are, dwelling in an element of gloom, carrying a bit of Chaos about him, in short, which he is manufacturing into a Cosmos." [16] With many Victorians he was on a darkling plain:

> Swept with confused alarms of struggle and flight
> Where ignorant armies clash by night.

Frederick Temple in *Essays and Reviews* (1860) stated their trouble. Was this a "world of mere phenomena, where all events are bound to one another by a rigid law of cause and effect; was the universe 'a dead machine' and the order of all things . . . not merely an iron rule from which nothing can ever swerve, but an iron rule which guides to nothing and ends in nothing." [17] Such a supposition might be possible to a logical understanding; it was not possible to the spirit.

In Memoriam (published in 1850, but composed, most of it, after the death of Arthur Hallam in 1833, which it commemorated) had stated the dilemma somewhat obscurely. "Its faith is a poor thing," Eliot has said, "but its doubt is a very intense experience." [18]

> Are God and Nature then at strife
> That Nature lends such evil dreams?
> So careful of the type she seems,
> So careless of the single life;
>
> . . . . . .
>
> 'So careful of the type?' but no.
> From scarped cliff and quarried stone
> She cries, 'A thousand types are gone:
> I care for nothing, all shall go.'

Henry Sidgwick, the wisest of the Victorians, tells us that there were some stanzas of *In Memoriam* which he could never read without tears. He felt in them "the indestructible and inalienable minimum of faith which humanity cannot give up because it is necessary for life." [19] John Morley said that it "lent the voice of pathetic music and exquisite human feeling to the widening doubts, misgivings, and flat incredulities of the time" (Morley, *Recollections,* I, 14–15). Huxley declared Tennyson to be "the first poet since Lucretius who has understood the drift of science." [20] The drift of science in Tennyson is that nature is cruel and wasteful and also gives meaning and direction to life:

> . . . I see in part
> That all, as in some piece of art,
> Is toil cooperant to an end

which may not be Lucretian in power but is not so very far from the Kantian theme that history is the process in which men have become rational; that the existence of the irrational and immoral elements in man —pride, ambition, and greed—has led to the development of society. The Victorians, as F. H. Bradley was to point out, could not think seriously about first principles in metaphysics, and it is not surprising that Tennyson as their poet of philosophy, science, politics, and morality should have been forced to concentrate on the composition of melodious scores; to drop the kernel of meaning and to retain only the husk of melody. [21]

> The woods decay, the woods decay and fall,
> The vapours weep their burthen to the ground,

> Man comes and tills the field and lies beneath
> And after many a summer dies the swan.

In what have been called the Victorian sages—Carlyle, Ruskin, Arnold —the same tension is felt. They were driven by their gifts to be as articulate as they could about the mystery they felt and the particular evils they claimed to know. J. S. Mill said of Carlyle: "I felt that he was a poet, and that I was not; that he was a man of intuition, which I was not; and that as such, he not only saw many things long before me, which I could only, when they were pointed out to me, hobble after and prove, but it was highly probable he could see many things which were not visible to me even after they were pointed out." As Byron might have said, Mill's brightness and Carlyle's darkness exchanged gestures of extreme politeness.

The relation between Carlyle and Goethe is not fortuitous. Goethe was concerned with everything that Newton had left out, and Carlyle more particularly with everything that Bentham and other would-be social Newtons had left out. Even J. S. Mill after communion with the spirit of German philosophy was mainly concerned with "the inductive laws of the existence and growth of human society." Carlyle was admired for his feeling for humanity. Engels translated him. Dickens dedicated *Hard Times* to him. Emerson chose him as a correspondent. Huxley wrote that *Sartor Resartus* had convinced him that "a deep sense of religion was compatible with an entire absence of theology." *Sartor Resartus* has been said to stand with *Tristram Shandy* and *Ulysses* as the most original prose work of its century.[22] When Carlyle said that history was "the essence of innumerable biographies," he was stating the obvious with passion. It is so true that the need to say it is a measure of the fictions it was meant to destroy. It has been said that he was a historicist, that his Heroes were those who knew the way the world was going. This is misleading. Carlyle simply felt how much was left out that matters to the souls of men in the contemporary political techniques. He did for his age what Rousseau did for his and D. H. Lawrence for his.

It would not be too sweeping to say that the troubles of the Victorian sages—Carlyle, Ruskin, Matthew Arnold, and others—were that they did not understand the significance of the penetration of mathematical analysis into every detail of men's lives. The enemy was mechanization, and mechanization was thought of as something that destroyed the balance of man and nature which had been built up through the ages. Only a genius of the order of Picasso could have helped them by showing that the most ordinary things can be metamorphosed into works of fine art, that art need not be an imitation of nature, that the distinction between the Beautiful and the Ugly is aesthetically untenable.[23] Something of the possibilities of the new mastery of matter was shown in the Crystal Palace built by Paxton for the Great Exhibition of 1851. But over the greater part of life in the nineteenth century mechanization meant a multiplication of debased copies of things which had once been informed by the human spirit. This was unavoidable because mechanization did in fact involve urbanization and urbanization meant that old patterns of social relations which had had some beauty were disrupted, and that dung and death, to say nothing of copulation and birth, took on a new terror when divorced from their age-old vegetable setting. The problem was made even more fearful by the fact that a crucial factor of the life of towns was not known—the part of the microbe in the dissemination of disease. Cleanliness may be next to godliness but not the cleanliness which used water to flush the privies into the rivers, rejoicing that the bad smell had gone, but unaware that the real cause of infection was being spread more widely. The trouble was diagnosed by D. H. Lawrence in this century. In *Nottingham and the Mining Countryside* he wrote: "The English are town-birds through and through, today, as the inevitable result of their complete industrialisation. Yet they don't know how to build a city, how to think of one, or how to live in one. They are all suburban, pseudo-cottagy, and not one of them knows how to be truly urban." [24] We do not, of course, know that men can ever learn how to be truly urban. But in the first three-quarters of the nineteenth century the problems of urbanization—aesthetic, administrative, sanitary, and social—were only beginning to be experienced.

It is this problem of squalor, in the sense that men's material setting is not adjusted to their biological needs and rhythms, which may explain the peculiar Victorian emphasis on delicacy. In a passage in William Cobbett's *Advice to Young Men* (1830) he explains to the young husband why his wife has need of privacy. One has only to consider the lack of privacy which women and children of the poorer classes endured in the back-to-back houses of the new industrial towns to understand how the intimacies of daily life could become almost pathologically obsessive. Prudery was a protective coloring of the poor and not so poor against conditions which pressed on them with the terror of the unknown, for birth had not modern care, nor had procreation a technique of birth control, nor syphilis and gonorrhoea any help but from the quack.

These urban tensions may explain the irritating near-phobia of Thackeray about sexual irregularity with his use of the words "pure" and "purity" with frequent irrelevance. His good women have a "pure fragrance," his portraits of saints and martyrs "pure eyes" and one lady "pure feet." [25] In Trollope's novels physical desire is treated as "a male peculiarity" which even men can "transcend" when they are in love.

The novels of Charles Dickens are a record of the fear, the mystery, and the complacency of the new urban world. "When the mood was on him his understanding of the sensual and social effects of the whole railway revolution was deeper and wider than that of his contemporaries.[26] The railways meant that the "various ranks and classes of mankind" were brought "into more familiar intercourse and better humour with each other," and in railroad travelers a "general tone of mutual frankness and civility . . . *so new in the English character.*" But the mixing of the classes hardly extended to the poor.[27] Dickens does not describe a third-class railway journey. *Blackwood's* in June 1855 said that Dickens was "perhaps more distinctly than any other author of the time, a *class* writer, the historian and representative of one circle in the many ranks of our social scale. Despite their descents into the lowest class, and their occasional flights into the less familiar ground of fashion, it is the air and breath of middle-class respectability which fills the books of Mr. Dickens." [28] But Dickens never exalted the political power of the middle class. He did not think that it was so wide that its interests would coincide with those of the people as a whole. He had in the 1840's a fear of mob violence—and who has not—but his fear came "from a psychological pacifism based on an introspective knowledge of the hidden depths of bestiality in every man." [29] There is one outstanding thing about all his reporting of the Victorian world. In *Oliver Twist* he said that he had aimed to describe the dregs of life *"so long as their speech did not offend the ear."* [30] The whole atmosphere in which Oliver lived in London would, as Mr. Humphrey House has said, have been drenched in sex. But Dickens does not even obscurely hint at such a thing.[31] The dung, the drunks, and the general feel of sick and dirty bodies all around was so oppressive in fact that for very relief they were omitted from print. It is a common experience. If "dainty delicacy living in the next street" was not to be offended by an accurate account of the squalor of the slums by a Dickens, equally when the nastiness of the trenches of the 1914–18 war was first experienced it was not described in the drawing rooms of the home front.

Whatever the problem of poets and men of letters and the personal problems of ordinary men and women who were moving into the first really urban civilization, there was the more general problem of the political order on which they had to depend. "Obedience to a government of some sort has not been so easy a thing to establish in the world," J. S. Mill wrote. What were the possibilities of government for the new industrial society? Wherever a "habitual submission to law and government" has been "firmly and durably established" and yet "the vigour and manliness of character" preserved, three conditions have been fulfilled, Mill thought: (1) a system of education, beginning with infancy and continued through life which gave the individual "the habit, and thence the power, of subordinating his personal impulse and aims, to . . . the ends of society"; (2) "the existence in some form or other of the feeling of allegiance, or loyalty." There must be something which is settled, something permanent, and not to be called in question; (3) a strong and active principle of cohesion among the members of the community.

In the century after 1776 there were many reasons why in Britain the analysis of the nature of government should have been of such urgent concern. Whatever the merits of British institutions they would have to be greatly changed if they were to cope with the basic problems brought by the first machine age—a greatly increased population and its tendency to concentrate in towns. For nearly a hundred years the analysis of Malthus was to hang like a cloud over the spirit of the times. Again, the contemporary theories about the social life of men were Janus-faced—on the one side they seemed to promise that all would be well if the last king were strangled with the entrails of the last priest and the natural harmony latent in the desire of rational men allowed to become manifest; on the other side they implied that it was part of the natural order of things that men should use their new-found knowledge to introduce improvements always hitherto desired but only now clearly possible.

J. S. Mill felt in his blood and along his nerves the transition from eighteenth-century optimism to nineteenth-century confusion and perplexed responsibilities. In two essays—one on *Bentham* and the other on *Coleridge*—he brought together the doubts which troubled him. He saw them as "the two great seminal minds of England in their age." He said that "whoever could master the premises and combine the methods of both would possess the entire English philosophy of their age." Bentham, after David Hume had established the empirical method of study in things of the mind, had carried the warfare against absurdity "into things practical." In Bentham, a rare union of self-reliance and moral sensibility had made him challenge the British constitution and the legal profession. He had made the public familiar with the idea that their laws and institutions were "in great part not the product of intellect and virtue, but of modern corruption grafted upon ancient barbarism." Because of his work innovation was no longer scouted *because* it was an innovation; establishments were no longer considered sacred because they were establishments.

Bentham had given England what she most needed at the end of the eighteenth century—a challenge to its complacency and a criticism of its compromises. On the continent of Europe the philosophy of the enlightenment had done its work completely and "scarcely one educated person was left who retained any allegiance to the opinion or the institutions of ancient times." In England there had been concessions on both sides, between the philosophy of the time and the traditional institutions. While the continent of Europe suffered from "the extravagance of new opinions," England suffered from "the corruption of old ones." The result was that in England government was regarded as a necessary evil. It was expected to confine itself to the bare minimum of functions—questions of *meum* and *tuum,* the protection of society from open violence, some of the most dangerous modes of fraud. Bentham demanded that the corrupt institution should be liquidated and that the functions competent government ought to perform be scientifically determined.

The weakness of Bentham was that his was the empiricism of one who had had little experience. "He was," said J. S. Mill, "a boy to the last." His idea of the world was that it was "a collection of persons pursuing each his separate interests or pleasure, and the preventing of whom from jostling one another more than is unavoidable" might be attempted by hope and fears derived from three sources: the law, religion, and public opinion. To J. S. Mill, the weakness of the Bentham approach was that it ignored all the forces which in the course of history may have made it possible to use the prescriptions of a Bentham. Given that society had attained a certain level of spiritual development then it could use the Benthanite formulas. But how had that level been reached and on what did it depend?

Bentham said that since the general interest is the object of government, a complete control over the government ought to be given to those whose interest is identical with the general interest. J. S. Mill sees this for the nonsense it is: "It would be difficult to find among theories proceeding from philosophers one less like a philosophical theory, or in the work of analytical minds, anything more entirely unanalytical." Doubtless Mill had in mind the biting comment that Disraeli had made in his *Vindications of the English Constitution* (1835): "The blended Utilitarian system of morals and politics then runs thus: 'Man is only influenced by self-interest; it is the interest of man to be a tyrant and a robber; a man does not change his nature because he is a king, therefore a king is a tyrant and a robber. If it be in the interest of one man to be a tyrant and a robber, it is the interest of fifty or of five thousand to be tyrants and robbers; therefore we cannot trust an aristocracy more than a monarch.

But the external principle of human nature must always hold good. A privileged class is always an aristocracy whether it consists of five thousand or fifty thousand, a band of robbers or a favoured sect; therefore the power of government should be entrusted to all; therefore the only true and useful government is a representative policy, founded on universal suffrage . . .' Let the Utilitarian prove that the self-interest of man always leads him to be a tyrant and a robber, and I will grant that universal suffrage is a necessary and useful institution. A nation that conquers the world acts from self-interest; a nation that submits to a conqueror acts from self-interest. A spendthrift and a miser act from self-interest. To say that a man acts from self-interest is only to announce that when a man does act, he acts."

Mill found in Coleridge a hint of a serious philosophy of government which would provide what Bentham had omitted. Coleridge saw that it was not enough to denounce the corruption of the past; the past had to be understood. What was it in the nature of men and in the problems of social order that had made the institutions of the past possible and, indeed, necessary in their time? J. S. Mill said: "No one can calculate what struggles, which the cause of improvement has yet to undergo, might have been spared if the philosophers of the eighteenth century had done anything like justice to the past." Coleridge saw the value of the past. What Bentham would reform Coleridge would first understand.

J. S. Mill was particularly interested in Coleridge's statement: "It is the chief of many blessings derived from the insular character and circumstances of our country, that our social institutions have formed themselves out of proper needs and interests: that long and fierce as the birth, struggles and growing pains have been, the antagonistic powers have been of our own system and have been allowed to work out their final balance with less disturbance from external forces than was possible in the Continental States." [32]

The theme of the special condition in Britain, the result of insularity, was to become of growing importance in the nineteenth century. What Coleridge sensed in the 1830's was to be given one of the wisest, most provocative, and impish statements by Walter Bagehot in 1867: "We have made, or rather stumbled on, a constitution which, though full of every species of incidental defect, though of the worst *workmanship* in all out-of-the-way matters of any constitution in the world—yet has two capital merits: it contains an efficient part which, on occasion, and when wanted, *can* work more simply and easily, and better, than any instrument of government that has yet been tried; and it contains likewise historical, complex, august, theatrical parts, which it has inherited from a long past—which *take* the multitude—which guide by an insensible but an omnipotent influence the association of its subjects. Its essence is strong with the strength of modern simplicity; its exterior is august with the Gothic grandeur of a more imposing age." [33]

That the constitution survived the French Revolution and the year of revolution, 1848, and was adapted, but not scrapped, to meet the challenge of both universal suffrage and modern technology is an odd and impressive fact which the most acute scholarship has not yet explained. One of the causes was that the extension of the scope of state action rarely took place until it had been discussed from every possible angle and often had been tried out in a modest form before being applied in a general way. The moral case had been discussed and the practical difficulties explored before the state assumed the responsibility of a new province. To many of its critics this meant that government action in the provision of goods and service vital to a civilized life was often too little and too late; on the other hand it was never too soon or inept.

There were two problems involved in the discussion of the scope of state action which dominated this period. The first was the relation between the economic order, which since Adam Smith had come to be more and more subtly analyzed, and the social order of which it was a part. On social order the development of historical studies was to throw more and more light and reveal more and more complexities. The second problem was the nature of the state itself. A philosophy of representative government was never clearly developed. So long as the British complex of institutions worked without open violence or obvious decay, the problem of the relation of the one and the many, of the individual and the community, was not pressed. But there is in the writing of Coleridge, Disraeli, T. H. Green, F. H. Bradley, and others an awareness of the issues involved.

On the first problem, the relation of the economic order to the whole social order, there was the valuable work of the English socialists of the period 1820–30: John Grey, *Lecture on Human Happiness* (1825); William Thompson, *Inquiry into the Principles of Distribution of Wealth* (1824); Thomas Hodgkin, *Labour Defended* (1825); and J. F. Bray, *Labour's Wrongs and Labour's Remedies.* Their theme was that the natural harmony among men which the eighteenth century had believed to be possible was prevented by the existing rights of property. Tom Paine had said: "The great part of that order which reigns among mankind is not the effect of government . . . society performs for itself almost everything which is ascribed to government . . . government is no further necessary than to supply the few cases to which society and civilisation are not conveniently competent . . . how often is the natural propensity to society disturbed or destroyed by the operations of government." [34] The socialists held that it was not government but the existing rights of property, the outcome of violence in the past, which were the cause of the rich getting richer and the poor getting poorer. In fact neither the economists nor the socialists their opponents seriously considered what system of property and law would secure the practical working of the market which was the model economists used in their analysis of the causes of the wealth of nations and its distribution. But J. S. Mill did note two urgent problems: (1) that the system of landed property in England did not satisfy the conditions that a free market required. This criticism of the land laws in Britain—and still more in Ireland—could be extended to all the monopolistic elements secreted in societies where custom rules or violence preys; (2) there is no necessary connection between the market value of a man's labor and the cost of what he will need to be a full citizen. However complex the industrial order may become it will not necessarily follow that the value of any particular worker in the market will equal the cost of the standard of living which in the interest of the community he ought to have. It may be bad for production to pay a man more than he is worth, but what he is worth in his job will not always cover the cost of the health services and the education his children ought to have.

The second problem, the theory of representative government, was bedeviled by the confusions in utilitarian theory. Were they assuming that men pursue pleasure and avoid pain, and that, from that psychological assumption, it would be possible to work out a code of rewards and punishment which might be administered by a competent despot? As J. M. Keynes was to write in this century: "Communism is the *reductio ad absurdum* of Benthamism." Or were they saying that it is an intuitive judgment, which anyone can on introspection confirm, that the good is pleasure? On this issue Mill, too, was to attempt a clarification. But there remained the problem of the relation between the individual and the community.

In his *Constitution of Church and State* Coleridge had stated simply and lucidly the problem involved: "The difference between an inorganic and an organic body lies in this: in the first—a sheaf of corn—the whole is nothing more than a collection of the individual parts or phenomena. In the second—a man—the whole is everything and the parts are nothing. A state is an idea intermediate between the two—the whole being a result from, and not a mere total of, the parts, and yet not so merging the constituent parts in the result, but that the individual exists integrally

within it." If the community is only a collection then the majority however large has no authority over the minority however small.

The history of social and political institutions had a valuable part to
play in the critical analysis of the schemes of reformers from the utilitarians at the end of the eighteenth century to the Fabians at the end of
the nineteenth. But the study of history had most disturbing effects in
the life of the mind. The German schools of history at the end of the
eighteenth century were bound to stir profoundly the English climate
of opinion which, in spite of the Scottish genius of Hume, had not come
to consider seriously the implications of historical scholarship for Christianity, particularly in its British Bible Protestant form.

In England in the eighteenth century it was "a time of formalism in the
Church . . . when the most valuable part of the meaning of the traditional
doctrines had faded from the minds even of those who retained from
habit a mechanical belief in them." [35] Mark Pattison pointed out that
rationalism in England had not been an anti-Christian sect outside the
Church making war against religion. It had been a habit of thought by
which men tried to make good the peculiar opinion they might happen
to cherish. In the eighteenth century "the great majority of writers were
employed in constructing a *via media* between Atheism and Athanasian-
ism, while the most orthodox were diligently hewing and chiselling Christianity into an intelligible human system, which they then represented,
as thus mutilated, as affording remarkable evidence of the truth of the
Bible." From 1689 to 1750 every endeavor had been made to show
that there was nothing in the contents of revelation which was not agree-
able to reason. After 1750 concern shifted to the proof of the authenticity
of the Christian record. "The Apostles were tried once a week for the
capital crime of forgery." In the first period religious experience was
eliminated. In the second the power of using speculative reason in theology declined. The weakness of eighteenth-century theology was not in
having too much good sense but in having nothing else beside.[36] It was
into this anemic Christianity that in the 1830's and 1840's the leaders of
the Oxford Movement tried to instill a revived Anglicanism.

To John Henry Newman the Anglican claim to represent a middle way
between Calvinism and papalism came to seem untenable. His secession
to Rome was a great shock to English opinion, a shock from which
Anglicanism has never recovered.[37] The new historical scholarship in
Germany involved the reconstructing of the world of thought of the
Apostles as an archeologist might reconstruct a vanished civilization. It
meant that Jesus would emerge as a great moral teacher who died like

Socrates a martyr to the truth. It meant to Matthew Arnold that there might be an "Eternal not our selves that makes for righteousness" and "that the prevailing form for the Christianity of the future will be the form of Catholicism; but a Catholicism purged, opening itself to the light and air, having the consciousness of its own poetry, freed from its sacerdotal despotism and freed from its pseudo-scientific apparatus of supernatural dogma. Its forms will be retained, as symbolizing with the force and charm of poetry, a few cardinal facts and ideas, simple indeed, but indispensable and inexhaustible, and on which our race could lay hold only by materialising them." [38]

J. H. Newman squarely faced the issue which was involved. His mind, as James Anthony Froude wrote, "was world wide. He was interested in everything which was going on in science, in politics, and literature. Nothing was too large for him, nothing too trivial, if it threw light upon the central question, what man really was, and what was his destiny." Newman had, in fact, a lively appreciation of the work of the great sceptic David Hume, who had drawn a distinction between what could be demonstrated, for example, the properties of a triangle, and what cannot be demonstrated but which we cannot but believe—that fire burns and water drowns. Newman tried to establish that conscience was something that presents itself to us with all the denseness and weight of an ineluctable fact, like the property of fire or water. By a critical study of the limitations of language and of logic he tried to restore the Christian faith. Moral truth could not be adequately explained and defended in words at all. Language is an artificial system adapted for particular purposes which have been determined by our wants. Half the controversies of the world were verbal ones and could they be brought to a plain issue they would be brought to a prompt determination. The parties involved would perceive either that in substance they agreed together or that their difference was one of first principles. Newman has in his very different way something of the sweep of Hume and the penetrating rigor of F. H. Bradley. But not even Newman could cast out Newton. And in the generation from 1845 to 1870 Newtonian mechanics was to impinge on the Victorian mind in a most sinister way.

In 1835 the young Charles Darwin, then twenty-six, had visited the Galapagos islands during the voyage of the "Beagle." The Galapagos species and the fossils and living forms of South America were the start of his views on the origin of species. He looked for a theory in which all past and present organic forms could be shown to have been produced by laws on the model of Newton's law of gravitation. In 1835 he read

Malthus on the pressure of population against the means of subsistence. It struck him that, given such pressure, different variations in living things would survive at different rates. He had a theory with which to work. In 1844 he wrote a long essay on the subject. He saw that the hypothesis that a process of natural selection should have produced the wrath of the tiger, the wisdom of the serpent, and the voice of the turtle required two sets of laws: the laws which would produce variations from one generation to another, and the laws of survival. He contributed the second. His natural selection was a statistical law of the redistribution of matter and energy among competing consumers. It showed how increasing order would be automatically generated—eye of toad and hive of bee—from unordered variations by the operation of a purely mechanistic principle. Wallace who had the same idea compared its action to that of the governor of a steam engine. The built-in response of a Newtonian mechanism would lead living things to multiply, evolve, and inhabit the earth.

When the *Origin of Species* (its full title: *On the Origin of Species by Means of Natural Selection, or the Preservation of Favoured Races in the Struggle for Life*) was published in 1859 it occasioned an upsurge of religious and nihilist passion. The explosion produced shock waves which help the scholar to chart the many strata of Victorian hopes and fears. The 1850's were a period of intense spiritual anxiety and intellectual restlessness. For one thing the devil had come into their world by the back door of geology. At the end of the eighteenth century William Smith, an English surveyor constructing canals, had shown that the distribution of fossils through the various geological layers was not compatible with the doctrine that they were relics of the Mosaic Deluge. In the 1850's Philip Gosse, a specialist in marine biology, offered, in *Omphalos: An Attempt to Untie the Geological Knot,* the thesis that there had been no gradual change of the earth's surface or gradual development of living forms but that all had been created slapdash as it was—the fossils put there by God to test the faith of men. Good Victorians, to whom geology had become a country week-end hobby shared without embarrassment with ladies, did not take kindly to this suggestion of unsporting and ungentlemanly celestial behavior. Carlyle said that it was breaking the rules of the game and that lying was not permitted in this universe.[39]

By 1850 most people were prepared to accept that the varieties of living things they knew had not been created separately but had come gradually to be, that God had moved not only in a mysterious way but had allowed a considerable time for His operations. Herbert Spencer, who had appointed himself general philosopher of the age, had produced a definition of evolution which had the merit of many syllables and no meaning. Evolution he said was "an integration of matter, and a concomitant dissipation of motion; during which the matter passes from an indefinite, incoherent homogeneity to a definite coherent heterogeneity; and during which the retained motion undergoes a parallel transformation." But he had coined the phrase "survival of the fittest," though to his chagrin he had not seen how it would help the Darwinian hypothesis. Where Darwin's *Origin of Species* hurt the ordinary churchman from Mr. Gladstone downward was that its hypothesis of natural selection implied that there was no immanent progress in the history of life. Before him the common theory of evolution was that living things had changed, becoming more and more fitted to the conditions in which they lived. Stags had grown antlers in the mating season because their ancestors had been angry at that season. The ancestors of giraffes had stretched for food. Our brains had grown so large because our ancestors had thought so hard. For Herbert Spencer there was convergence on a desirable end when every individual would have achieved a perfect adaptation to his environment. The Darwinian hypothesis of natural selection offered only a divergence from an unknown beginning. It was a material determinism in whose operation blind accident had played a small but necessary part.[40] Darwin did nothing to establish a transition from non-living to living aggregations of matter. But he did convince the world that there had been a continuous historical process linking the growth of animals and plants now alive with ancestors immeasurably remote; that the wonder and variety which we now had, including man himself, had been secured without design.

Only one example of the problems which this raised, but it is a fundamental one, can be noted here. The young T. H. Huxley in 1860 could write that "the absolute justice of the system of things is clear to me as any scientific fact. The gravitation of sin to sorrow is as certain as that of the earth to the sun . . ." In 1889 he announced: "I know no study which is unutterably saddening as that of the evolution of humanity." The slow rising of mankind had been attended by "infinite wickedness, bloodshed and misery." And in 1893 in the Romanes Lecture, "Evolution and Ethics," he noted the distinction between knowing *how* good and evil have come about and knowing *what* is good and evil. "Social progress means a checking of the cosmic process at every step and the

substitution for it of another, which may be called the ethical process . . .
The ethical progress of society depends, not on imitating the cosmic
process, still less in running away from it, but in combating it." Matthew
Arnold had made the point earlier:

> Nature is cruel, man is sick of blood;
> Nature is fickle, man hath need of rest.
> Man must begin, know this, where Nature ends;
> Nature and man can never be fast friends.

CHAPTER XV

World War I and After, 1914-39

The war of 1914–18 was only in name a world war. But it was a war which affected every continent. With a few exceptions every country in Europe was in it. Every country in Asia, except Tibet and Afghanistan, was affected by it. The whole of Africa and almost the whole of the nations of America were involved. A history of Britain cannot include a history of the war, for it was a wider story than hers. The Dominions fought alongside the United Kingdom. Some 700,000 men from the British Isles were killed or died of wounds in the armies; nearly 57,000 Canadians, 60,000 Australians and 17,000 New Zealanders lost their lives. The Indian army lost 62,000 men in action. The total strength of the British armies in the field on November 1, 1918, was 5,300,000, of whom 3,200,000 were in the theatres of war, 1,600,000 in the United Kingdom, and 480,000 in India. But to understand the history of modern Britain some of the more obvious facts about the war need to be kept in mind. Here we shall briefly consider how it was that Britain was involved at all, the general character of the war, an outline of its course, and its effects on Britain's position in the world.

There were three main causes of the crisis of July 1914 which led to Britain's ultimatum to Germany. There was a serious flaw in the European pattern of international order among sovereign states—the weakness in the Balkans, where the Austro-Hungarian and Russian empires had racial, religious, and strategic interests which were tangled and easily inflamed. This Balkan appendix was part of the European body. The Dual Alliance, ratified in treaty form in 1894, provided that if Russia were attacked by Germany or by Austria supported by Germany France would support Russia. Since 1908 it had become obvious that if Austria were to attack a Balkan Slav state, Russia would intervene against Austria and Germany intervene against Russia. On June 28, 1914, the Archduke Ferdinand was assassinated at Sarajevo by a Bosnian Serb of Austro-

Hungarian nationality. The murder was planned from Belgrade by a Serbian secret society because Ferdinand stood for Habsburg federalism and that threatened the establishment of a greater Yugoslavia. The problem for diplomacy was not new. In previous years the Austro-Hungarian government had not gone to war against the South Slavs because of the risk of Russian intervention and the uncertainty of German counter-support. The war of 1914–18 was not planned. Some countries were more ready for war than others, but that does not mean that the former contrived the coming of the war. The commitment to Austria by Germany was treated as more rigid than it need have been, and Germany made a virtue of preventive war against Russia and France out of the case which could be made for securing an Austrian political victory over Serbia.

The subtle and often confused diplomatic maneuvers in the fog of diplomacy were complicated by the concern of military experts (particularly in Russia and Germany) with the problem of timing. The development of railways and roads had made it possible to deploy and supply large bodies of men. "The mobilization fuse" could explode "millions of men into the enemy country." [1] But like modern rockets, the armies, once launched by rail and road, could not be recalled. Germany felt that her ally Austria, if she was to achieve political rehabilitation, needed to chastise Serbia, if the stabilization of Russian hegemony in the Balkans was to be prevented. It seemed to many in Germany a good moment for a showdown, before Russia could have built her Baltic fleet and her strategic railroads. Apologists for the Central Powers (Germany and Austria) have blamed the provocative attitude in Belgrade, the consolidating of their front by France and Russia, and the misleading posture of neutrality by Britain. It is with the latter that we are concerned here.

Britain could not have prevented the war because the Cabinet (a Liberal government was in office) could not have agreed to give a specific guarantee to Russia through France against Germany. A private warning would have been taken by Germany to be bluff. An encouragement to Russia and France would have been misleading. Britain could not go to war unless there were a united government and public opinion for it. With the Liberal pacifist tradition strong, with the naive intellectual tradition that a great war was financially impossible, with the peculiar Liberal belief that Germany as a great commercial power must be as such disposed to peace, with the knowledge that Germany had a powerful and internationally minded socialist movement and a trade union movement opposed to militarism, with Russia as the classical enemy for the Conservatives of the British Empire in Asia and for the Liberals as the despotic enemy, in the person of the tsar, of democracy, with France under suspicions by many liberals as seeking a war of revenge—a British preventive intervention to stop the drift to war was not within the realities of British politics.

In any case Germany had discounted British intervention. One strategic school in Germany would have liked to seek rapprochement with Russia against Britain—would have liked "to set the Whale against the Bear." The General Staff in Germany believed that the issue would be settled in battle in the plains of Flanders and Poland. Their timetable for the successive defeats of France and Russia left no occasion for the intervention of a British army, which could not be more than trivial in its thousands beside their millions, and took no heed of the long-term effect of sea power. It was not foreseen in France and Germany, it was hardly realized in Britain, that the issue of Belgian neutrality would become the crucial issue. When Germany decided that an advance through Belgium was essential to her military strategy she gave Britain a unity which would have been otherwise impossible.

The main features of the war, from the British point of view, were: the dislocation of the German timetable by the intervention in Flanders —made possible by sea power—of a small British professional army, and the consequent stalemate on the western front from the channel to Switzerland leading to (a) an "unimagined war of flankless armies scratching each other's faces across an endless thorn hedge," [2] a war which involved a percentage of casualties among the attacking forces on either side never known in history and believed to be incompatible with the maintenance of morale. It was the first hint to the twentieth century that groups can go to their death as easily as a Hotspur to his single doom. (b) The mobilization of industrial manpower to the support of battles—a partnership of Vulcan and of Mars—undermined the economic life of Britain and of Europe and was an intimation of what political power could do with industry if the will were there. (The present Russian technological space probe can be seen in germ in the fumblings of desperate political leaders for new weapons of war.) (c) The entry of the United States into the war resulted in a peace treaty which only she could have enforced.

That the Treaty of Versailles was not enforced when the United States withdrew into what, in the 1920's, must have seemed splendid and moral isolation led to a pattern of power in Europe in which it became impossible to stop the resurgence of Germany into the most repulsive political form the West has so far known and to the rise of a new secular religion and imperial power in Russia, the third Rome of Dostoevskian prophecy, and a third Rome armed with the powers of a succession of technological revolutions. The end is not yet. Britain in the period before 1914 had shown that industry and commerce are no substitute for political power. She produced a constitution for the cradle of the early industrial revolution. She could not give political form to that industrial revolution as it moved into the hitherto unchanging masses of the world. Germany was to show after 1918 that there is no guarantee that all the virtues may not be wedded with political evil; Russia that it is possible to use technologies in peace as, among democratic systems, they have hitherto only been used in war. The *Pax Britannica* died in 1914; it could not have survived without a will to power which was the antithesis of its very essence. There is now no balance of power possible or, if there is, it is by means which we cannot now foresee. Past politics are outmoded by modern technologies. Intimations of the terrors amid which we now live were given in the 1914–18 war.

In 1914 Britain, because of her sea power, had a voluntary, long-service army. Half her 250,000 men were overseas. She had to have garrisons in India and elsewhere. Some trained units had to be retained at home so that for the first encounter barely 100,000 men were available. These—the First Hundred Thousand as they were nostalgically to be remembered—were the best-trained, best-organized, and best-equipped force with which Great Britain ever started a war. But they were a flea bite to the 5,000,000 trained men (1,500,000 immediately available in the West) of Germany and the 4,000,000 of France. Even Belgium, caught with her army undergoing reorganization, could mobilize more men in August 1914 than could Great Britain.[3] On the Continent the nature of armies had been transformed by industrial developments. By skillful administration in peacetime the details of mobilization could be polished and the railway timetables adjusted so that a day or so might be gained against the enemy in the initial concentration and deployment. But once the forces had been launched from their railheads maneuver was still clumsy. The internal combustion engine had not yet transformed the pace of armies. The men moved on their feet and were supplied by horse-drawn transport. In 1918 the British forces were served by 500,000 horses and 200,000 mules. Air reconnaisance was in its infancy. A Royal Flying Corps observer did report the wheeling movement of von Kluck's army to the southeast in August 1914. When the German sweep through Belgium failed and the French unskilled thrust at the German center was parried there followed the trench warfare, with millions of men dug in from the Channel to Switzerland in parallel lines and with a no man's land between them.

This trench warfare had much in common with the siege warfare we know in Shakespeare's *Henry V*. But it differed from siege warfare of the past in that medical services were better and machine guns, poison gas, and flame throwers were more deadly than arrows, mortars, and "Greek fire." H. G. Wells had foreshadowed the coming of ironclads. The penetration of the trench system needed bulletproof armor. An armored vehicle with caterpillar tracks to span the trenches and to cross open country was developed by Colonel E. Swinton backed by Winston Churchill (then first lord of the Admiralty). It was called the tank—one of the first secret weapons. It appeared first on the battlefield in September 1916, but its influence was not decisive till 1918. The war till the end was very slow. It had the pace of marching soldiers. The motor truck —on hard tires—could take materials to the trenches. But in fighting the pace was that of the infantry. Cavalry on the Western front was useless before a machine gun: "Two squadrons of horse were sent to charge, in column, up a straight, treeless rising road for half a mile and take a little wood at the top. There were many machine guns in the wood. No horse or men either got to the wood or came back. They were all in a few seconds lying in the white dust, almost in the order they rode in, the officer in command a little ahead of the rest." [4] But the campaigns for the capture of Jerusalem and the final advance to Damascus and Aleppo were great exploits of cavalry, and they showed—not that cavalry had any future—but that mobility would be decisive in future wars.

In previous wars the main British fleet had been placed in a strategic position so that it could destroy the enemy fleet should the latter venture out. Against the French the British Grand Fleet had lain in the mouth of the English Channel, supported by naval bases along the south coast. The defeat of the enemy was only a means to the protection of sea communications. In previous wars the enemy had been to the south and west of Great Britain. Germany was to the east of the English Channel. The British main fleet was put at Scapa Flow in the Orkneys where it could prevent a break-out of the German fleet to the north into the Atlantic. The Straits of Dover were mined and watched. The Russo-Japanese War of 1904 had shown the possibility of the mine and the torpedo. Between 1906 and 1914 British naval policy had been to concentrate her capital ships in home waters. The ships were of the dreadnought type, which after 1904 had outmoded all existing battleships and remained the type of capital ships until after 1945. Two vital changes had been made: the turbine gave greater speed and less vibration, which assisted the accuracy of gunfire; the decision was taken in 1914 to burn oil fuel only.

On August 4, 1914, the Royal Navy had twenty battleships and four battle cruisers in home waters and three battle cruisers in the Mediterranean; the German High Seas Fleet had thirteen battleships and three battle cruisers. The German Admiralty could afford to concentrate in the North Sea and thus reduce their inferiority in numbers compared with the British Grand Fleet. They did not have to keep command of the sea. For two generations the British Empire strategically had been a system of coaling stations and cable stations. These had to be preserved. The German naval power depended upon coal from neutral ports and upon communications by wireless telegraphy from a few powerful transmitting stations recently erected in the German colonies.[5] In the Mediterranean the German squadron took refuge in the Dardanelles and by August 10 did not threaten the sea route through the Suez Canal. The British failure to destroy the "Goeben" and "Breslau" in the Mediterranean was a factor in bringing Turkey into the war on Germany's side. There were as yet no ocean-going submarines to menace British shipping. Instead, the Germans had five fast merchant ships armed as commerce raiders and eight cruisers. In the first five months of war German surface raiders sank 203,000 tons of British merchant shipping. The five armed merchant ships were easily hunted down. But six expeditions to seize German colonies in every part of the world which they might use as base or refuge had to be dispatched: Togoland, the Cameroons, German East Africa, German Southwest Africa, German New Guinea, and German Samoa. The communications of German commerce raiders had to be silenced not only because of trade but because of the convoys of troops from India and the Dominions.

Germany thought that the British Grand Fleet would try to destroy their High Seas Fleet. But the British Admiralty stuck to the principle that so long as an enemy fleet was not at large it could do no damage. The Battle of Jutland, May 31, 1916, when, it was said, Admiral Jellicoe could have lost the war in an afternoon but did not, was indecisive as a contest in hits made and ships sunk but decisive in strategy because the German High Seas Fleet never challenged again. It was kept as a threat and a bargaining factor. To destroy British shipping Germany concentrated on submarines. In 1917 merchant ships were being sunk by submarines at a greater rate than new ships could be built to replace them. In one month, April 1917, 870,000 tons were lost, and Britain had food for no more than six weeks. The submarine menace was met by hydroplanes, depth charges, spotter aircraft, armed convoys, and Asdic—the detection of submerged submarines by sound, developed from a suggestion made in 1912 after the sinking of the "Titanic" by collision with an iceberg. With the mastery of the submarine the more distant blockade was established by the use of navy "certificates" for neutral traders.

As early as 1878 the first army balloon school was formed at Woolwich. But it was France that had first recognized the potential value of the airplane for military purposes—the aerial equivalent of cavalry scouts. In December 1911 the British Committee of Imperial Defence, impressed by the German Zeppelin, had begun to form a flying service. In 1912 a Flying Corps was formed; in 1914 the Royal Naval Air Service. The normal performance of airplanes in 1914 was 70 to 75 mph and two to three hours flying time. In the summer of 1915 the Germans produced the Fokker with a machine gun firing through the propeller. The first real fight for the command of the air was during the battle for Verdun in 1916. Over the Somme battlefield in the autumn of 1916 the British Royal Flying Corps had a local superiority. German Zeppelins began an intermittent night bombing of London and other cities in 1915. Casualties and material damage were slight, only 1,413 civilians lost their lives in air raids. The raids had a slight effect on the output of work, and in one case caused a riot in which troops had to restore order. In World War II civilians were to be as steady as the troops in the trenches of the first war. In 1917 a formation of twin-engined bombing planes—the Gothas —raided London in daylight. The Smuts Committee reported in August 1917 that aerial operations with the devastation of land and the destruction of industrial and populous centers on a vast scale might become the principal operation of war. In April 1918 the Royal Air Force had a total of 22,000 planes (of which 3,300 were first-line strength) and nearly 300,000 officers and men—the most powerful air arm in the world.

It was possible for the democracies to learn the trade of war as they went along. Once the German blow at the heart of France was parried, the latent administrative skills and the deep resources of scientific methods could be developed to make a civilian and peaceful people terrible in war. There were many difficulties to overcome. World War I of 1914–18 differed, for the British people at least, profoundly from the second of 1939–45.

The first volunteers lived in the spirit of Shakespeare's *King Henry V:*

> Now all the youth of England are on fire,
> And silken dalliance in the wardrobe lies;
> Now thrive the armorers, and honour's thought
> Reigns solely in the breast of every man.

C. E. Montague in *Disenchantment,* the best record of the gray disillusionment which the long agony of mud and blood was to bring, noted of the first volunteers: "Each of them quite seriously thought of himself as a molecule in the body of a nation that was really, and not just figuratively, 'straining every nerve' to discharge an obligation of honour." [6] But it was not realized that in this war it would be necessary to harness the factory to the battlefront. It was a war for freedom. But tensions would develop between the home front (Blighty) and the trenches. "When a man enlisted during the war he found himself living the life of the common man in a Communist State. Once inside he had no more choices to make than a Russian under the Soviet. His work, his pay, his food, his place and mode of living were fixed from on high. He might not even decide whether he should remain a soldier or be turned, say, into a miner." [7] On the home front the mechanisms of a free industrial society had painfully to be adjusted to the conditions imposed by the need to feed and clothe and arm the fighting front. It was only slowly realized that the war would be a supreme contest in applied economics. In the first rush of voluntary enlistment skilled men went out and either were killed or were got back with difficulty to the mine or factory where the need for them was dire. Trade union officials who would have gladly fought in the trenches would not allow changes in the working rules which might have saved those already there. That industry would have to be deliberately organized for war production was only realized under the pressure of the most dangerous losses. In 1916 Churchill was to say in the House of Commons: "I believe that before the end of this war . . . all shipping will certainly be taken over by the Government and regulated in one form or another . . . I believe that all important employment will be regulated by the State for the purposes of war. I believe that prices will have to be fixed so as to secure to the poorest people . . . the power of buying a certain modicum of food . . . I am sure that we shall come to a national organisation of agriculture." But in 1914 there was not and could not have been any state machinery to organize the nation for the emergency which had arisen. It was done at last. But it could not have been done had not the fortunes of war on the Western front given the British a vital pause in which to find their salvation.

The Germans invaded Belgium on August 4 and by August 18 had forced the Belgian army back to Antwerp and were preparing to envelop the uncovered left of the French army on the Sambre. Unknown to them —because of the British use of sea power to choose where they would land—the British Expeditionary Force of one cavalry and four infantry divisions had begun crossing on August 9, landing at Havre and Boulogne (not as the Germans expected through Ostend or Calais), and on August 19 were concentrated behind Maubeuge. Advancing to join the French, it met the Germans near Mons. The battle of the twenty-third checked the German advance, and this, with the previous Belgian resistance, upset the German timetable. The British and the French were pushed back. When in early September the French moved northeast from Paris against von Kluck's advance, the British were able to penetrate the gap between two German armies, von Kluck to their right and von Bülow to their left. The French had stretched the German lines, and the British pierced a joint. This battle of the Marne was a strategic success for the Allies, checking the German advance just in time. In the meantime fresh British forces had been drawn from garrisons overseas. They were too late to save Antwerp, but by October 18, reinforced by two Indian divisions, the British were in a position to stop the German drive to the Channel ports and to roll up the Allied line from the left. By the end of November 1914 the German drive to Paris had failed, and they had not reached the Channel ports. By December 1914 major operations were suspended on the Western front and the pattern of trench warfare was being drawn. This pause was vital to Britain.

During the course of the war some 22 per cent of the adult male population of the British Isles were recruited. Not only had the armies to be supplied and civilians fed and clothed but some export trade had to be maintained. The controls which made this possible were developed to meet the pressures of emergencies. At the outbreak of the war the government found that it must guarantee the solvency of the banks. When the military necessity was obvious the government took over the railways. When the refineries were paralyzed by the failure of sugar imports from Central Europe it took over the purchase and importation of sugar. It found that when it had to fix prices, control and centralized purchase had to be pushed back from finished articles to the raw material. For infants to have diapers at controlled prices, the government had to buy cotton crops in bulk. It was driven to experiment with the control of the production of essential food stuffs. The control of commodities drove it to the control of shipping. In shipping it was found that private trading and state trading could not exist side by side during the risks of war. The shipping industry opposed control at the beginning of the war, as imperiling the flow of essential supplies. But as the submarine attack developed the available tonnage had to be concentrated on the shortest routes and supplies purchased on the credit of the state in the nearest markets. The essential supplies were secured, but the cost in adverse exchanges, indebtedness, and commercial dislocation was very great.

A British army of millions was created. Until well into 1916 the lack of arms, especially of heavy guns, and munitions of every sort put the

Western front in peril. By March 1915 the demand for munitions and the rush of skilled workmen to the colors had created a situation in which firms lived by taking on one another's employees. The government had to limit the movement of workmen, and dilute the labor which was to be had. The shortage of skilled labor could not be met by persuading skilled men to let the unskilled do their job, for the unskilled could not. Dilution involved dividing the job into its component parts and devising foolproof machines for the different parts. The foundations of labor regulation were laid down by the Munitions of War Act, July 1915. The basic principle of the act was that the worker remained a civilian, and with all the rights and privileges of civil law, but his industrial rights were severely limited. In the controlled establishments, where the worker had to surrender some of his industrial rights, the profits of the employer were also limited. Lockouts were made crimes and arbitration was made compulsory.

Since the opening of the West in America and the cheapening of transport Britain had relied more and more upon imported foods. In 1914 Germany could feed her whole population for six out of seven days in the week without imports, Britain could only feed herself from Friday night to Monday morning, or feed 15,000,000 of 47,000,000 people, or all her population for 125 out of 365 days. This meant that during the course of the war calories had to be counted as carefully as rifles and shells. Calories meant shipping space and toward the end shipping space meant American troops. The various problems of labor, munitions, food, and shipping involved the creation of ten new ministries and over 160 boards and commissions before the war was done. By 1918 the British army was the best supplied of all the combatants.

It has been said that an Allied strategy did not exist. There were at least six separate and distinct wars, with a separate distinct and independent strategy in each, until November 1917 when an Allied Supreme War Council was set up. War involves the direction of the whole power of the nation as a means to the end of victory. The supreme command has to be in the supreme authority of the state—in the case of Britain the Cabinet, which is H.M. Government. "It is for the statesmen," wrote David Lloyd George, "with such advice as they can command, to survey the battle area as a whole on land and sea, to examine the needs and possibilities, to make their plans and to dispose of their resources to the best advantage." The snag lies in the phrase "such advice as they command," for you cannot use good advice that you do not understand and you cannot be given good advice by those who do not understand you. Statesmen have to make the vital decisions about policy, but they may lack the knowledge of war and its problems in spheres which vitally concern policy. The terms of a partnership between the statesmen who have to decide, the experts who have to advise (a General Staff), and the leaders in the field had not been worked out. Winston Churchill held that it was part of the business of a civilian minister to prepare plans of campaign, Lloyd George complained that Sir William Robertson, the chief of the Imperial General Staff from December 1915, withheld from the Cabinet essential facts about policies which he supported but believed that the Cabinet would oppose. He claimed that had the government not overruled the Admiralty the submarine menace would not have been overcome and the war would have been lost by the Allies. There is evidence that the Germans were even more inept than the British in solving the problem of the relation between policy, technical knowledge, and battle experience.

In 1915 the Germans had the interior position on the Western front and they had superior railway communications. The Russians had suffered disaster at Tannenberg. Their losses were large and they had inadequate reserves of munitions. On October 20, 1914, Turkey joined the Central Powers and the Black Sea route was barred to Russia's allies. Troops had had to be sent from India to safeguard the Suez Canal and the Persian oil fields, on which the British navy now largely depended for its fuel. It was necessary, if possible, to reopen the Black Sea route. The attempt was the Gallipoli expedition, which was to become the Homeric legend of the Anzacs (the Australian and New Zealand troops). It began with a decision by the Cabinet "to prepare for a naval expedition to bombard and take the Gallipoli Peninsula, with Constantinople as its objective." How ships were to take a piece of land was not explained. The naval bombardment of the Turkish forts guarding the Narrows began on February 19, 1915. The Greeks were impressed and offered to mobilize the Greek army for a march on Constantinople. The proposal was vetoed by the Russians for political reasons. The British had now to withdraw or to supply an army of their own. A second bombardment of the forts in the first week of March was followed by a third on March 18, when three old battleships were sunk and one new battle cruiser severely damaged by floating mines which had been overlooked. The naval action was stopped until combined operations could begin on April 25, 1915, when landings were made near Cape Hellas. By May 8 a deadlock had been achieved at a cost of 20,000 casualties. Before the final withdrawal in December 1915 and January 1916, 400,000 troops were involved and 18,000 British, 8000 Australians, and 2600 New Zealanders were killed.

Three days before the landings at Gallipoli the Germans had attacked

on the western front at Ypres, using poison gas. The German Supreme
Command had, fortunately for the British and the French, little faith
in the new weapon. They lost much of its advantage by disclosing it
prematurely. As a discharge of gas from cylinders is dependent on a
favorable wind and as a west to southwest wind was the most frequent
in Flanders, the Allies were to have the advantage in retaliation until
gas shells had been produced to replace gas cylinders. There was a deadlock in the West, but it was not safe for the Allies to take any chances
there and use their control of the sea to attack in the Middle East. In
April 1915 the British were holding only thirty miles of the front,
while the French held 400 miles. In 1916 the British held 60 miles. A
campaign in Mesopotamia had miscarried. An overoptimistic advance to
Bagdad following an initial success had been checked at Ctesiphon
(November 22) and British troops were besieged in Kut-al-Imara. At sea
the submarine had had menacing successes but that battle was not fully
joined because the Germans could not ignore the protest caused by the
loss of American lives in the sinking of the "Lusitania" and British concern about American opinion was limiting the Allied blockade.

In February 1916 the Germans attacked once more in the West at
Verdun. The British helped to relieve the pressure on the French by
taking over twenty miles of front between Arras and Lens and launched
the Somme offensive on July 1. It was "a day of an intensive blue summer
beauty" and in its beauty the British army lost 50,000 men. The new
armies trained since August 1914 bore a percentage of losses no professional army of the past had been deemed capable of suffering and retain
its morale. It was a superb and terrifying vindication of the power of
men to endure. In the whole Somme campaign the British were to lose
400,000 men, France 200,000, and Germany 500,000. In between the
firing and the killing, trench life continued. It was a life "squalid beyond
precedent." It was "a life of mud and stench and underground gloom."
It was also "the jealously close, exclusive, contriving life of a family
house in an urban cellar." [8] It involved a divorce between the men in
the line and the higher command which only the existence of an intense
will to win could survive. The mind and the limbs of war were almost
fatally divorced. The technique of briefing, of the control of men in battle
was primitive. Armies clawed at one another like dinosaurs whose brains
had imperfect communication with their bloody claws and limbs. The
fog of war and the confusion of battle which in previous wars had been
for days were here for months. Until the development of aerial recon-
naissance, and of the tank to penetrate the wire and give protection against

machine guns, the armies were so many moles trying to do what only eagles and hounds could properly do.

Life for most men at the front was poor, nasty, brutish, and short, and not solitary enough. But the will for victory in fact was never destroyed. And the Somme was the turning point of the war. (The destruction of the finest youth of a whole generation of Western Europe may have made it a turning point in Western civilization.) By the end of 1916 the German position on the vital western front had changed for the worse. In May 1916 Jutland had confirmed the British command of the sea. By the end of 1916 the Turks had been repulsed in Egypt. British troops were across the Sinai Desert and menacing Palestine. In Mesopotamia the British were advancing to Bagdad.

In 1917 the initiative in the west was never with the Germans. But the British and French armies were badly worn. A great offensive by General Nivelle, April 16–May 7, had failed, and for a brief period the French army was on the verge of collapse. The Germans, however, did not reach the Belgian coast. The United States had declared war on April 2, but it was clear in October that Russia would be out of the war before the former could give effective assistance on land. In October, too, the Germans broke through the Italian front at Caporetto and a dozen French and British divisions had to be sent to Venetia to stem the Italian rout. In March 1918 Russia had a peace dictated to her at Brest Litovsk.

The Russian collapse, the exhaustion of the French armies by the bloodshed of 1916 and 1917, and the natural unwillingness of the Americans to allow the 100,000 of their troops who had reached France to be incorporated temporarily into Allied formations nearly caused complete disaster in 1918. Germany switched her troops from the Russian fronts and in an attack on March 21 on the St. Quentin-Arras front—when a real fog neutralized the British machine gun defense—drove back the British Third and Fifth Armies which bent but did not break, and Pétain, contemplating a retirement upon Paris, was prepared to lose contact with the British. When disaster seemed imminent unity of supreme command was at last achieved when (March 26) Ferdinand Foch was appointed to co-ordinate the Allied operations. By July 1 the worst was over. On August 8 the reorganized British and French armies struck. In September and October the whole front was on the move and by November 11 the Central Powers had to accept the Allies' terms.

Early in 1917 President Wilson had challenged the Allies to state their war aims. In August 1914 the British First Hundred Thousand had felt that they were to reclaim "a sour, soiled, crooked old world" from bullies and crooks "for straitness, decency, good-nature, the ways of common men dealing with common men." [9] International politics is never a matter for common men dealing with common men. The problems which had faced the Congress of Vienna in 1815 were, as Lloyd George said in the House of Commons in April 1919, insignificant compared with those which had to be settled at the Paris Conference.

As Clemenceau once remarked, President Wilson had a way of talking like our Lord and behaving like Lloyd George. Knowing the superb isolation of the United States in the nineteenth century from a wicked Europe and knowing something of the problems that the collapse of three empires, the Ottoman, the Austrian, and the Russian, involved for the peacemakers of 1918, we can understand his dilemma. But it was most unfortunate that the armistice concluded with the Central Powers was based on the ambiguous terms of Wilson's Fourteen Points as amplified subsequent to their first formulation in an address to Congress in January 1918. The Fourteen Points included (1) general propositions about open covenants of peace openly arrived at, absolute freedom of navigation upon the seas, equality of trade conditions among nations, the impartial adjustment of all Colonial claims, (2) specific territorial settlements based on the restoration of conquests, and self-determination. The last phrase was not used in the Fourteen Points. The phrases used were "autonomous development" and "clearly recognizable lines of nationality." Wilson's commentary also made it clear that open covenants openly arrived at would not exclude "confidential diplomatic negotiations involving delicate matters." The British could not accept a doctrine of complete freedom of the seas which would destroy the power of blockade. And no one of the Allies wished to see the restoration of German colonies. In the exhaustingly complex discussions at the Peace Conference Britain was in a strong position. She secured the suppression of the German fleet and colonies, the doctrine of blockade was not destroyed, her strategic position in the Middle East and on the route to India was not lost, and the constitutional evolution of her Empire was recognized—the Dominions were to sign as separate sovereign powers.

The Germans as all the world knows were to develop a propaganda campaign against the treaty based on its inconsistencies, real and alleged, with the Fourteen Points. This diverted attention from the greedy and vindictive war aims which they themselves had got ready in the expectation of victory. By 1922 it was probable that no one in Germany considered a successful war of revenge morally reprehensible. General Hans von Seekt, a brilliant Prussian staff officer, was emulating Scharnhorst's subterfuge after Jena when he had secretly reconstituted the Prussian army in defiance of Napoleon. By all round evasion and violation of the Treaty of Versailles, a great army in miniature was created; and even more important, manufacturing potential was co-ordinated for military requirements.

The main defect of the Treaty of Versailles was that it was not enforced. From the moment on March 19, 1920 when the Treaty failed to secure ratification by the United States Senate, it was not enforceable. No power was in a position to do in Europe after 1918 what Britain had done after 1815. Conditions in Europe after 1918 were far less favorable to the enemies of despotism than they had been after 1815.

J. M. Keynes thought that Europe might have looked forward to a very different future if either Lloyd George or Woodrow Wilson "had apprehended that the most serious of the problems which claimed their attention were not political or territorial but financial and economic." He added that "the events of the coming year will not be shaped by the deliberate acts of statesmen but by the hidden currents, flowing continually beneath the surface of political history, of which no one can predict the outcome." It is the great illusion of liberal thought that if you take care of the economic pence the political pounds will take care of themselves. It is another illusion that because during a war which you did not start you have fought like lions, in the peace that follows your enemies will attend like doves to any serpentine wisdom you may show.

The European situation was one about which Britain alone could do very little. The tensions within Europe were already moving out into the wide world. The British control of the sea routes of the world could not be maintained. The progeny of national sentiment and ever more procreant technology would place the democracies in the position of a sorcerer's apprentice who has no master able to restore order by a tranquillizing spell. The European problem was that, as a result of the war, the Austrian Empire had been parceled out among half a dozen succession states. The Germant remnant of Austria became a top-heavy and economically precarious state of under 7,000,000 population, of which nearly a third was in Vienna. This Balkanization was not created by the Treaty of Versailles. It was already latent in the disruptive process of national liberal uprisings within the Austrian Empire. But the principle of self-determination, while it fragmented Austria, could not be allowed to Germany, which it would have enlarged. Lloyd George saw the danger of having Germany surrounded by a number of small states, many of them consisting of people who had never previously had a stable government and each of them containing masses of Germans. A customs union from Danzig to Sicily was tentatively discussed, but American attitudes at the time were not interested in the development of European unity. The intellectual view, of Smuts, was that "Europe is being liquidated" and that the League of Nations must be the heir to its great estate.

The period between 1919 and 1939 is bisected by 1929. In the first half Russia had fallen away to the East to suckle and rear the terrifying monster with which she had been quickened by the scientific word of the West. America left Europe to make the best of the peace made upon the basis of an American program. When America could not ratify the treaty France lost her military guarantee, Britain, also, was released from her obligation, and France lost one of the main guarantees of security which she had been given in return for renunciation of her demands in the Rhineland. Britain could not make this good, for any guarantee she might offer in the West would not cover France against German "indirect aggression" in eastern Europe. In the French view a Polish Sadowa would be for Germany the best preparation for a new Sedan. Britain as a world trading power wished to see the earliest possible revival of international commerce and the economic revival of Germany herself. There was much ill-judged talk of a French domination of Europe, when in fact the power of France was very fragile.

In Britain, too, the old controversy between limited and unlimited intervention was always present. The Labour party supported the idea of a general settlement based on an unlimited guarantee to support collective action against an aggressor who refused to submit to arbitration. The Conservative party preferred specific commitments in a limited area. Keynes had written in 1922 that there were two opinions in the life of a nation, not as in former ages "the true and the false" but "the outside and the inside." There was "the opinion of the public voiced by politicians and newspapers; and the opinion of the politicians, journalists, and civil servants expressed in limited circles." The distinction between popular and technical opinion was further complicated by the distinction within popular opinion between the dogmatism and definiteness of the press and the living indefinite belief of ordinary men. He believed that "inside opinion gradually percolates to wider and wider circles; they are susceptible to time, to argument, common sense or self-interest." And on the truth of this belief the hope of democracy depends.

In the case of international relations a healthy relation between inside and outside opinion was never developed. "The people hoped and believed that the League would be effective. The governments who knew better, did not dare to try to disillusion them. The whole international structure rested upon an equivocation." [10] With the United States absent from it the League was a very different one than had been envisaged in the peace negotiations. In particular any sanctions which its working might involve would fall particularly heavily on a naval power, and its exercise by Britain alone could easily involve her in Anglo-American friction. At the Washington Conference of naval power in 1921–22 Britain ended the Anglo-Japanese alliance in deference to American and Dominion wishes.

Britain abdicated her position of naval supremacy and, in common with the United States, opened the way for future Japanese predominance in the Far East. In 1816 Britain from a sentiment of solidarity and a recognition of common interest with her Allies had wiped the slate of subsidies clean. In 1922 the United States Congress decided that the Europeans were not allies in a common cause but debtors. Britain pointed out to her debtors that she was owed by her allies more than twice as much as she owed the United States; she would have to ask from them not all they owed but what she would have to pay her creditors. It was not until 1925 that Europe's primary production passed the level of 1913, and before the great depression Europe was dependent on lavish American loans. When that flow ceased Europe collapsed and all debtor states except Finland defaulted in their war debt payments. Up to 1931 Britain repaid nearly $2,000,000,000 or about three-quarters of all the payments made to the United States.

In 1924 the Geneva Protocol was proposed. It was a supplement to the Covenant of the League of Nations. It was supposed to be a system of pooled security whereby the power of nations would become the servant of international justice. There was to be a system of arbitration which no international dispute, whether juridicial or political, could escape. All disputes were to be settled by pacific methods. All disputes would be settled in the last resort by arbitrators whose decision would be final. Sanctions, which are, of course, involved in the principle of the finality of arbitration, would be applicable to every resort to war and not merely, as hitherto, to war in breach of the covenant. The Labour Prime Minister, Ramsay Macdonald, was in power during the debates, and it fell to his successor, the Conservative Prime Minister, Stanley Baldwin, to make the decision to reject the protocol. It is unlikely that any British government could have accepted it. The Dominions were opposed, and it was not true that it provided for the settlement of all disputes, because it could not deal with those which involved a wish to change the system of existing legal rights. Beyond its juridicial defects lay the lack of power to implement its sanctions. In its place in 1925, in the Pact of Locarno, Britain agreed to a limited liability. At the time there was a British foreign secretary (Sir Austen Chamberlain) favorable to France, a French minister (Aristide Briand) with a liberal policy, a German minister (Gustav Stresemann) adhering ostensibly to a policy of fulfilment of Versailles. Great Britain, France, and Italy agreed to protect Germany's western frontier against attack from either side. There was no undertaking in regard to Germany's eastern frontier with Poland. Europe emerged into "the pale sunlight of Locarno." Germany entered the League of Nations on September 10, 1926.

Locarno was called by Chamberlain "the real dividing line between the years of war and the years of peace." But the period of optimism was not to last long. The great economic depression of 1929 was a shattering blow to the political self-confidence of the democratic world. The experts relied upon could not see even into the economic seeds of time. In 1930 the National Socialist party won more than a hundred seats in the German elections. A new force had appeared in European politics— the use of words to prepare the way for guns. This was not to be the competitive dissemination of half-truths with which competitive industry was familiar in the world of advertising and against which it was assumed that good democrats had developed an immunity in their life of freedom. This was a new technique of the big lie complicated by the technique of saying what you intended to do and of relying on creating a disbelief favorable to yourself by the very enormity of your proposals. This was an Iago who saw and said that all the democratic Hamlets were sicklied o'er with the pale cast of thought. A more healthy if equally dangerous challenge came in September 1931, when Japanese troops attacked and disarmed the Chinese garrisons in Mukden. By the end of the year they had overrun the whole of Manchuria. In 1933 both Germany and Japan gave notice of their withdrawal from the League. In the case of Japan the weakness of the system of collective security was mercilessly exposed. The question of sanctions against her could not be seriously raised. The Washington treaties had put Japan in an almost impregnable position in the Far East. In Europe in 1936 Ethiopian resistance against Italy collapsed, and after an effective defiance of the League Italy resigned from it in 1937.

The British could not believe that the rantings of Hitler's *Mein Kampf* were a practical manual of daily conduct from which he would never deviate. Hitler was a demonic Machiavelli to whom the conditions in Europe created by the Treaty of Versailles were an almost perfect field for the exercise of the strategy and tactics of state building by blackmail and terror. Germany had after 1918 her industrial potential and her central geographical position. The principle of self-determination had surrounded her eastern and southeastern frontiers by a number of small states whose stability was uncertain. "As Hitler consolidated his hold on Germany, most of the small countries on Germany's borders and beyond based their policies on the hope that they would be spared, that the blow would fall on someone else." [11]

This Balkanization of eastern Europe had thrown the burden of upholding the provisions of the Versailles peace settlement against a resurgent Germany squarely on the Western powers. Once Hitler had reoccupied the west bank of the Rhine he could only be stopped in the east by the use of force. Hitler could have been stopped in the east by an agreement between Britain, France, and Russia. This was not possible because neither Romania nor Poland was prepared to accept Russian help against Germany. To protect the independence of the small countries of Europe against Hitler, Britain and France would have had to make an agreement with Russia which seemed to expose the same small countries to a threat which was equally serious. In particular, Russia wanted the military details which would allow the transit of Russian troops through Poland written into any treaty. Britain could not build up a diplomatic and military combination of the pre-1914 kind. An effective combination to contain Hitler would have involved either an agreement with Russia which sacrificed the independence of small countries lying between Russia and Germany, or complete rearmament in peacetime with the supply of arms to any country willing to join her. She would have had to do for Europe against Germany what the U.S.A. is now doing for the free world against the U.S.S.R.

CHAPTER XVI

Aspects of Democracy, 1914-39

Machiavelli liked to distinguish between the influence of fortune and necessity. In the history of Britain after 1914 one has to distinguish between the influence of men's growing insight into and control over the sources of power in the world of nature, which had so long been hidden, and the contingencies of war, with its specific trials and tribulations for a complex but insular community. It may be that a growing insight into the processes of the mechanical and the living world—into the structure of matter and the life of the cell—paralleled an increase in self-knowledge and that the great novelists from Stendhal and Tolstoi to Chekhov and Joyce had made a break through, in their study of the individual, comparable to the penetration of the secrets of nature which physicists, chemists, and biologists had made. The pace of the seven league boots of science may have been matched by the removal of some of the seven veils of the mind, but in social and political studies most was still hidden. Only in the case of economics had there been the development of a technique which could give an X-ray picture of the body politic to supplement the speculative interpretations of the political philosophers from Plato to Hegel and Marx.

One vital effect of World War I was to break the traditional patterns of political thought and behavior, established since the Renaissance, and cause an examination of their working in order to reassemble them to meet the exigencies of war. On the European Continent this was to lead to the development of the totalitarian systems in the East and in the West. In the case of Britain her island security and her links with an extra-European world enabled her to carry forward her traditions of order and liberty into a strange new postwar world. They were to survive the economic and political alarms and changes of the interwar years and to ride out the storm of the war of 1939–45. It will be of some interest to see their fortunes in an atomic age. It might be argued that Britain was strengthened after the war when the Irish irreconcilable minority was purged from her already complex system. The principle of universal suffrage was accepted as a necessary condition of political life. The promise, or perils, of imperial adventure were avoided. Britain might still save the world by her example; she would never order it by her power.

At the outbreak of war in 1914 the political wisdom—conscious or unconscious—of the prewar leaders was vindicated. Asquith brought an almost united people into the war. The Expeditionary Force was an efficient tool for the job which had immediately to be done. The navy denied the enemy the use of the seven seas. The enemy lost the war he had envisaged, and Britain and her Allies had time to adjust themselves to the war that he might devise. In Britain a free state had to create a nation in arms and contrive that its fields and factories should be an assembly line to the battle fronts. Partly by good luck and partly by good management the armies were raised, the ships were built, the people were fed and—except in the Dublin Rebellion—there was almost no disorder. The political and administrative machinery were so improved and the administrative arts so developed that the system survived the postwar years of economic dislocation and the threats of new pagan despotisms.

There was nothing to be surprised at in the British record. Santayana has reminded us that courage is the commonest of the virtues. The human race could hardly have survived if it were not. When it is understood to be the right and proper thing to do, there is almost nothing easier to face than death. There were, of course, nastinesses in the war which were not known in World War II. The social structure was very aristocratic, and it was an aristocracy vulgarized by new industrial and financial leaders who had not yet found their manners. It was also rather confusing to adjust the equality of the trenches to the great inequalities of the home front. It was almost embarrassing that an almost feudal cavalry class had to get off their horses and lie in the mud while industrious mechanics protected them with machine gun fire. The war was in fact a vast experiment in the use of new industrial methods and new arts of management. Ajax and Hercules were level with Thersites, and the squire and his relations with the industrious mechanic. Had not so many been killed it would have done them all a world of good.

The British people were fortunate in their political institutions. If the system was aristocratic, in the sense that political leaders had been drawn from a relatively small class and that the permanent officials had been selected by a system of competitive examinations which favored the Universities of Oxford and Cambridge, yet on all frontiers of political, economic, administrative, and social life there were conditions favorable to osmosis. The British social structure had not the glorious fluidity of the Texan frontier, but it was not rigid, and since 1900 at least a healthy mobility had begun. A Labour party had already established itself in the central organ of political power—the House of Commons. The industrial revolution which had been nourished by a widespread tradition of skilled crafts had inoculated the population with the scientific spirit. In the seventeenth century a copy of the Bible could inspire ordinary men and women with the strength in unity of a chosen people. In the twentieth century the precision and co-ordination which are implicit in machinery were absorbed into the flexible discipline of troops and the orderly service of civilians. One of the seeming weaknesses of a free state is its greatest strength: so little has been done by government that there is an almost unlimited reserve of abilities and know-hows on which to draw. The less the scope of government in peace the easier it is to create new organs to meet the exigencies of war. There was tremendous waste and inefficiency, mercilessly exposed by innumerable writers at the time and since. One remembers G. B. Shaw pointing out that as a war correspondent in his compulsory khaki he was more conspicuous to the enemy than a bug would be on a bed, while a foreign colleague in the full glory of a rainbow uniform was almost invisible.[1] On the other hand, one is impressed by the way in which rational techniques did creep in. The life history of the louse was assiduously studied by scientists at war, who carried them snugly in belts against their flesh. Siegfried Sassoon, one of the most bitter critics of the blood and mud of Flanders, was himself helped by W. H. Rivers, who used the new techniques of Freud, to solve the problems presented by shell shock and other war neuroses.

The normal Cabinet system before 1914, though it had been based on deep mutual confidence and absolute secrecy in its internal working, could not run the war. There were three problems: to adapt the conventions of peacetime responsible Cabinet government to the needs and pace of war, to discover the best working relations between civilian ("frocks") and military leaders ("brass hats"), and to improvise administrative techniques which would help a democracy realize its will to victory. Broadly, the first and the third of these three aims were brilliantly achieved in 1914–18. The second was not, though it was in the war of 1939–45.

By November 1914 a committee of the Cabinet—a War Council for the conduct of the war—had been established. But the Cabinet as a whole did not abdicate its authority. It was impossible that a Cabinet, drawn from one party only, should be responsible for the conduct of the war. The Opposition would have been in an impossible position. If they criticized the government they might be thought unpatriotic; if they did not criticize, it would be assumed that they approved what was done. The first Coalition was formed on May 26, 1915. It was an unwieldy body of twelve Liberals, eight Conservatives, one Labour member, and Lord Kitchener. There was duplication between the War Council and the Cabinet as a whole. In December 1915 the War Office was responsible for the campaigns in France and the Dardanelles, India was conducting a campaign in Mesopotamia, the Foreign Office was responsible for operations against the Senussi in western Egypt, and the Colonial Office for a campaign in West Africa. Sir William Robertson, who became chief of the Imperial General Staff in December 1915, urged the setting up of a small war council charged with the co-ordination of policy and strategy in every theatre of war in which Britain was concerned.

In December 1916 Lloyd George displaced Asquith as prime minister by a campaign of intrigue and propaganda which was a classic of its kind. In wartime there could be no appeal to the electors. Had Asquith taken the issue to the floor of the House of Commons he might have won, but he was not willing to damage the unity of the nation. Lloyd George was clear in his own mind that it was his duty to change the conduct of the war. He detached the Unionists from Asquith and forced them to work with him. The war could hardly have been won without his driving power and his courage as head of a wartime government. But the price paid in the future was to be heavy. The Liberal party was to be destroyed and that was to mean that the brains were out of the British left. Lloyd George came nearer to being a dictator than any other leader in British history. The means by which he displaced Asquith were unparalleled for chicanery either before or since. The mildest statement that has been made about him is that he was protean beyond the average. The most savage comment—made with the insight of genius —was by J. M. Keynes: "Lloyd George is rooted in nothing; he is void and without content" and referred to him as "this goat-footed bard, this half human visitor to our age from the hag-ridden magic and enchanted woods of Celtic antiquity." [2] Both before and after the war he was known for his ability to deceive with truthful words so delicately phrased that his interlocutors caught only those he wished them to hear. He could charm a bird from a bough. He could scatter official inertia to the winds. He liked individualism in office and unorthodoxy in administration. He was a supreme civilian war leader. With victory he was to become an unscrupulous politician, distrusted by nearly every political leader.

In December 1916 Lloyd George was clear that a Cabinet of twenty or more could not run a war. He was clear, too, that a prime minister could not run the House of Commons and run the war. He formed a War Cabinet of five, which became the central organ for the direction of the war. Representatives of the Dominions and of India could be included when necessary, and the War Cabinet was then an Imperial War Cabinet. The British constitution had produced its Public Safety Committee. It was the directing organ of an elaborate machinery which assembled and co-ordinated the resources of the nation to win the war. It developed a complex system of committees which tapped the technical and intellectual resources of the country. It was the embodiment in political and administrative forms of the spirit which held that

> There is but one task for all—
> One life for each to give.
> What stands if Freedom fall?
> Who dies if England live?

The complex machinery could not be run with the informality of the prewar Cabinets. In 1917 Lloyd George appointed a small secretariat responsible for an agenda and a timetable. Its functions were to see that the persons and papers that the War Cabinet had to see should be seen and that the Cabinet should be briefed with all the materials available for the decisions which it had to make. The secretariat was able to co-ordinate the working of the Cabinet with the activities of particular departments and with the committees, in which members of the government and high officials explored the problems to be solved, and the Cabinet was not overworked. The secretariat enabled the Cabinet to keep the essentials in its own hands, while the preliminary work was done by whatever committees it might appoint. The permanent secretariat was continued after the war. Its origin can be traced to the Committee of Imperial Defence before the war. For the Cabinet to have a secretariat charged with putting into shape its agenda, providing information for its deliberations, and recording and communicating the decisions made to the departments concerned may seem trivial. But it is on such trivia that the lives of states may depend. The War Cabinet solved the problem of adjusting a parliamentary executive rooted in party politics to the unity required by war.

The problem of the relation between the politician and the service chiefs was never really solved. Asquith would not play the part of an amateur strategist or foist his opinions on men who had made soldiering the study of their lives. Lloyd George knew that a man who had made a subject his life study might hug his own opinion in the face of new and bitter truth. It was for the statesman, he held, "with such advice as they can command, to survey the battle area as a whole on land and sea, to examine the needs and possibilities, to make their plans and to dispose of their resources to the best advantage." War involves the direction for a special purpose of the whole power of the nation. The supreme command of the British people in arms could only be the Cabinet, the supreme executive power in the state. The handling of the armies, navies, and air forces must be left to professional experts. But they were very different from the experts which politicians use in time of peace. The civil servant can be trusted to carry out in peacetime a plan with which he may not agree. But the soldier or sailor in war will find this difficult to do. The terms of a working partnership had not been worked out before the war. Lloyd George has made the specific charge that the chief of the Imperial General Staff withheld from the Cabinet essential facts about policies which he supported but believed that the Cabinet would oppose. On land the high command had its way. The general strategy of the land fighting was their policy. At sea the government compelled the admirals to take the measures necessary to meet the submarine menace.

On the home front after an initial delay the machinery of government was geared to the job. Ten new ministries and over 160 boards and commissions were created. Because the whole idea of conscription was alien to the British political tradition there was from the first a serious misdirection of manpower. In the initial rush of volunteers men had joined the armed forces and left industries with a desperate shortage of manpower. In 1914 there was no central state department able to determine the order in which men should be withdrawn from industry. It was not realized that manpower would have to be husbanded and directed. In spite of all "the astonishments of war" the distribution of manpower between the forces, the factories, and the fields was worked out. Ministries of Labour, Munitions, National Service, and Food were developed. On the home front the worker's freedom of movement was checked, his wages controlled, strikes forbidden, and work defined. His recreations were limited, his consumption of liquor and the building of his homes curtailed. Britain was able to feed her entire population only from Friday night until Monday morning—she had to import the rest. A Ministry of Food which showed respect for scientific advice, combined the traditions of the peacetime civil servant with the experience of the business expert, decentralized its machinery, and was scrupulously fair in its distribution was able to secure that the people were fed.

The government would have been powerless had it not had the co-operation of the industrial, commercial, and labor organizations. The government's legal powers were of less importance than the force of public opinion and the knowledge of the groups concerned that their co-operation was a duty. There were, of course, flagrant abuses in profiteering and conscription dodging. An army of mercenaries may "save the sum of things for pay," but it will leave a trail of looting and rape. The passage of a free people through the wartime valleys of death, shortage, and uncertainty left its trail of fraud and cowardice. No doubt there were "hard-faced men" who did well out of the war, but Leviathan in mortal conflict cannot purge all the worms from its entrails. On the whole, when it was possible to tell people what to do to help in the war effort, the response was clear and strong. But the four years of war were not a rehearsal for any five-year plans. The system of co-operation rested on the fear of defeat. The priorities of materials and skills involved were dictated by the enemy. The home front in 1914–18 was not, as in 1939–45, in the direct line of fire, but there were few families which had not given hostages at the front to the proud death which feasted there.

Peace has its difficulties no less alarming than those of war. It was many years after 1918 before the menacing shape of things to come was even faintly discerned. It was a part of the hysteria caused by the strain of war that it had come to be regarded as a war to end war. Since 1945 the West has learned that the ending of a war may be more deadly than the opening. We have to beware the terms of a peace even more than we fear the opening battle moves. The breakthrough of a foe who has long secretly prepared his thrust may be less deadly than the settlement which may be made in the confusions and delusions of a long-desired peace. In Britain after 1918 one should allow for the peculiar exaltation of spirit, combined with the slow degradation of morale, which a long war imposes. Lloyd George in 1918 was of smaller stature than he had been when he took supreme power in 1916. Perhaps no human being could have stood up to his ordeal of responsibility and have kept a sense of proportion. To many he seemed to have become an unscrupulous politician determined to maintain power.

The political life of Britain between 1918 and 1939 falls into two periods: from 1918 to 1929, during which the difficulties experienced could still be attributed to the effects of the war; and from 1929 to 1939, when it was clear that all the basic principles of the world before 1914 had really passed away. For a brief period, until the elimination of Lloyd George from effective political life in October 1922, Britain was threatened with all "the improvisations of an intermittent and incalculable dictatorship." Three days after the Armistice Parliament was dissolved. A general election was needed, but it was designed by Lloyd George to secure another five years of power for himself and his Conservative allies. The Conservatives went to the poll as a party united behind Bonar Law. He was a tough Canadian, of Ulster Nonconformist stock, a Scottish businessman who had become leader of the Conservative party when Balfour retired in 1911. He had been an invaluable partner to Lloyd George since 1916 and was to be so until 1921, "hanging onto the coat tails of the Little Man and holding him back." The collaboration of the faun from Wales and the Glasgow businessman was close and mysterious. The Labour party withdrew from the Coalition and fought on the platform of "No More War." Lloyd George was to fight on the platform that the man who had won the war would provide a land fit for heroes to live in. There could be no clear issues between the parties because serious political controversies had been suppressed since 1914. The election was a fight of the Conservatives and all personal supporters of Lloyd George, against the Asquithian Liberals and Labour. The Asquithian Liberals could be accused of having hampered Lloyd George's efforts to win the war because they had asked in May 1918 that the charges made by General Frederick Maurice against Lloyd George be investigated. All who had voted against the government in the Maurice debate were in the general election of 1918 treated as members of the opposition. At the election the government supporters secured 533 seats, the Liberals 29, and Labour 59. With the Irish and some independents the total opposition parties were only 174. Although his majority was so large, Lloyd George had to keep the Coalition together if he were to remain in power, for the Liberal party was hopelessly split. It was one of the tragedies of the war and of the complete distrust which Lloyd George was to inspire that the Liberal party was never again either to form a government or to function as an effective opposition.

The Conservative leaders in Lloyd George's postwar coalition government came to suspect that he might try to form a center party with the Conservatives on his right and the Asquithian Liberals on his left. Many Conservative members came to believe that a continuation of the Coalition would break the Conservative party beyond recovery. The dynamism of the "Glendower in a bowler hat" had smashed the Liberal party to pieces, and Baldwin feared that it would do the same to the Conservatives. In 1922 a meeting of Conservative members at the Carlton Club decided to end the Coalition, Lloyd George resigned, and Bonar

Law became Prime Minister. Lloyd George would never again exercise effective political power, and the party struggle between the wars would be between the Conservatives and Labour.

In Britain the common dangers of the trenches and the common fatigues of the industrial and agricultural fronts had removed any opposition to universal suffrage. The Representation of the Peoples Act, 1918, extended the franchise to all adult males and to women at least thirty years old. The procedure of registration was simplified so that fraud or the expenditure of party funds for the manipulation of the register was useless. All elections now took place on the same day. But this simplified electoral law made it even more important that the parties have an organization to provide competent leaders and communicate to the electors ideas and programs relevant to their problems. The Labour party, nourished by the hopes of a world without war and a New Jerusalem based on a minimum standard of material welfare guaranteed to all and heartened by the seeming inability of Conservative power or Liberal thought to control the economic forces which had stricken so large a part of British economic life, was to form a government for the first time in 1923 and again in 1929, and when not in power was to be His Majesty's Opposition.

Between the wars both the Conservative party and the Labour party in Britain had some common advantages: an absence of virulent internal problems of religion or of race which might cause fear to cast out thought (religious sectarianism was still alive, and in educational policy required careful handling, but it was not a killing disease); and both parties had a deep if inarticulate understanding of the nature of industrial society. The worker in the factory was as wise in his industrial environment as the peasant in the past was thought to be in his. And as nine people worked in industry for every one in agriculture, and in 1939 half the British people lived in towns with a population of more than 250,000, and as agriculture itself was quickening to the magic touch of science, there was no fear of a deep cleavage between town and country. If there were only two major parties—the one in power and the one in hope of power —the community could adapt itself by trial and error to a changing world. As Mr. Bassett, the author of the *Essentials of Parliamentary Democracy* has pointed out, democracy "does not mean majority rule, but government by voluntary agreement; that agreement, necessarily never complete or final is roughly attained in practice by the interaction of parties following each other at relatively short intervals in the exercise of governmental power. Under the operation of such a system, the doctrines and policies of the contending parties, however divergent they may be at any point of time, tend to approximate." ³ Such a party system is an expression of the real unity of the state and of the differing views about specific policies which have to be decided. An opposition can see that power does not corrupt the government. Should those in office falter on matters which concern the welfare of the state, the opposition is an alternative government on hand to introduce changes which may be necessary.

The techniques involved in governing became more complex every year. After 1918 the British people had to feel their way to adapting their institutions to universal suffrage and to the provision of the services needed by all the citizens of a modern state. The quality of those services depends on the level of the national income, but cannot be left to be determined by the level of each individual's earnings. The line between such services as health, education, and unemployment insurance, which are a common interest, and the goods and services which individuals may buy for themselves and their families is one of the vital moving frontiers of the welfare state. What in the United States had been given by abundant natural resources and what in Germany and Scandinavia had been matters of state policy even before the twentieth century, the British had now to provide by their political and administrative skills— in education, health, and housing. Because Britain had been the frontier of an industrial civilization, there were large areas which had to be replanned. The political forms and the administrative machinery would depend upon the vitality of the economic and social order.

Between the wars there were very serious economic adjustments to be made by a country whose basic industries had been developed in the conditions of international trade—and comparatively primitive technologies—before 1914. The interplay between the political and social life of a modern industrial state is intricate and of vital importance. Should their relations go seriously wrong the results may be disastrous. The subtle life which we know in a Turgenev or a Chekhov may body forth a Stalinist state; the Germany which was the heart of European scholarship, philosophy, and music may be distorted into the frenzy of the Hitler regime. In the United States the relations between social and political forces were determined by the traditions of her Constitution, the skill of the Supreme Court, and the abundance and, until recently, the isolation of the American way of life. In Britain, so small and so suddenly shaken by the changes in the economic structure of the world, their solution was a problem for the political parties. Parties have to be the brokers between new knowledge and the ways of living of ordinary men and women. A party, as the genius of Burke sensed, must provide the link between the power which a government must have if it is to exist and the persuasion it must use if it is to be free. The tree of liberty need not be nourished by the blood of tyrants, provided that its roots are dug and its branches pruned with proper party skills.

After the fall of Lloyd George, the new Conservative leader Andrew Bonar Law won the election of 1922. The Conservatives had 344 seats, the Labour party 183, the Independent Liberals 60, and the National Liberals 57. The Conservative party was supported by only two-fifths of the votes cast and just over one-quarter of the whole electorate. Lloyd George could still play with the idea of a new alignment of parties which would have the support of one third of the electorate. It was rumored that he was working like a little dynamo to break up the Conservative party. Sir Ivor Jennings has written: "Brutus might have said that Lloyd George was ambitious—to split one party which had just won an election against most of its leaders; to split a second party which had just doubled its representation; and to fuse with liberals who felt that they had been turned out of office by a trick in 1916 and deprived of seats by lies in 1918." [4] It was not to be. In May 1923 Bonar Law's health collapsed and King George rightly invited Mr. Baldwin to become prime minister.

Stanley Baldwin, Rudyard Kipling's cousin, was known to be fond of pigs, of country life, and of the classics; he was also an industrialist nurtured in an atmosphere of piety, frugality, and wealth. In 1919, when financial secretary to the Treasury, he had anonymously given one-fifth of his wealth to the nation. He had negotiated the American debt settlement when chancellor of the Exchequer in Bonar Law's government. He was convinced that Lloyd George was a corrupter of public life. Until 1940 the mystical, impetuous, and intuitive Baldwin in collaboration with the brisk, efficient, and unimaginative Neville Chamberlain led the Conservative party. In 1923, when the new Parliament was only a year old, Baldwin asked for a dissolution, although he had a majority of eighty-eight over all other parties combined. He had decided that he could not introduce protection, which he thought was a remedy for unemployment, without a specific mandate from the electorate. It is possible that he feared Lloyd George might shelve the Conservatives by dropping free trade and going all out for a policy of tariffs.

The results of the scarcely comprehensible decision to dissolve was that the Conservatives lost nearly ninety seats and a Labour government took office for the first time in British history. At the election the Conservatives had 258, the Liberals 159, Labour 191, and others 7. In the circumstances Baldwin did not resign at once, but met the new House of Commons. The Liberal leader Mr. Asquith had then to decide whether he would support the Conservative government or, by supporting the Labour party, put it in office as the next largest party to the Conservatives. When he decided on the latter course Baldwin resigned and Ramsay Macdonald became the first Labour prime minister of a government which was in office but, being dependent on Liberal support, not in power.

There is no mystery about the rise of the Labour party. It was not inevitable, because, had Gladstone and Chamberlain managed to cooperate in the 1880's, the Liberal party might have developed a working-class policy which would have attracted the industrial worker and the agrarian laborer enfranchised in 1867 and 1884. The theology of Gladstone, the truculence of Chamberlain, and the protean quality of Lloyd George are all elements which may have determined the political failure of the Liberal party. There were more general conditions favourable to the Labour party. It was clear to all students of social life after 1880 that the scope of government action would have to be widened. In the British constitution the power of the Queen in Parliament, in practice of the House of Commons, was so pre-eminent that it was the only effective tool for the work of social amelioration.

The Labour party had developed before 1914, mainly as a pressure group, to secure legislation in the interests of the long-established trade union organizations. In 1918 a vital change had been made by Arthur Henderson. This Labour leader was born in Glasgow, the son of a Scottish cotton spinner. He had moved to Newcastle-upon-Tyne, where he was apprenticed at the age of twelve at the Robert Stephenson locomotive and foundry works. He had been included by Lloyd George in his War Cabinet of five because of his skill as an adviser on labor problems. In 1918 he broadened the basis and strengthened the organization of the Labour party. A new constitution in 1918 opened the party to "workers by hand and brain." The structure remained as it had been since 1900, federal, an association of trade unions and socialist societies, but individuals could now join local Labour parties. Henderson, at the same time, strengthened the central machine and brought in a wide range of experts to serve on advisory committees. After 1918, the Labour member of Parliament, like his Conservative or Liberal colleagues, had his own constituency organization to which he was responsible. The object of the prewar party had been "to organise and maintain in parliament and in the country, a political labour party." Under the new scheme, drafted in collaboration with Sidney Webb, the formula was changed. It was now: "To secure for the producers by hand and by brain the full fruits of their industry, and the most equitable distribution thereof that may be possible, upon the basis of the common ownership of the means of production, and the best obtainable system of popular administration and control of each industry and service."

In 1923 Prime Minister Ramsay Macdonald of the first Labour government had an impossible task. Because he was dependent on Liberal support he did not have control of the timetable of the House of Commons and of the details of bills which a Cabinet needs to implement a new policy. The end came in October 1924, when the Liberals supported a vote of censure and the Labour government asked for a dissolution. At the election which followed, the Conservatives won 419 seats, the Liberals 40, and Labour 141. The Liberals had clearly dropped to third place, and the possibility of a Labour government alternating with a Conservative government was now one of the facts of political life. Those who did not want a Conservative government would have to vote Labour, and vice versa.

The position of the Labour party as a possible alternative to Conservative governments was strengthened by the failure of the General Strike in 1926. This failure destroyed a myth which had been spreading in peripheral Labour circles. The strike itself arose from the lamentable condition of the coal industry and the obstinacy of the coal owners and the miners. The majority who joined the strike viewed their action simply as support of the miners in an industrial dispute. But it was clear that a general strike to be successful would have to be a revolution. There was in Britain no point in having a revolution when in the sovereignty of the King in Parliament, unlimited by any written constitution, there was a machine competent to make any changes in the industrial and social life of the country that can be made by government. The defeat of the General Strike opened the way for the Labour party to consider what precisely were the changes in the economic and social life of Britain that it wished to see. With universal suffrage and a single sovereign legislature, and a single civil service bound to serve those who had a majority in that legislature, there was no impediment, except the nature of things and the limitations of human skill in economics and administrative arts, to the building of the New Jerusalem. Unless it were blinded by the motes in its own eyes a Labour government was free to remove the evils a Conservative could not see.

The root of the Labour party's faith was the Christian and Protestant idea that, as R. H. Tawney put it, "the love of God, whom one has not seen, is not compatible with advantages snatched from the brother whom one has." It owed something to the radicalism of the late eighteenth century, when Joseph Priestley had held that a proper knowledge of the teaching of the Christ, whom "the universal parent of mankind" had "commissioned to invite men to the practice of virtue," and an under-standing of the mechanisms of nature would make possible a terrestrial millennium. Since 1800 our knowledge of the mechanisms of nature had greatly increased, and economic analysis had given a penetrating insight into the structure of industrial society. It might appear that the abolition of "all advantages and disabilities which have their source, not in dif-ferences of personal quality, but in disparities of wealth, opportunity, social position, and economic power"—and what could be fairer than that?—was a very simple thing to do. One had only "to create organs through which the nation can control in co-operation with other na-tions, its economic destinies, plan its business as it deems it most con-ducive to the general well-being; over-ride, for the sake of economic efficiency, the obstruction of vested interests; and distribute the product of its labour in accordance with some generally recognised principles of justice."

The problem was not so simple as the Labour party supposed. On one of the most momentous issues before 1939—the causes of unemploy-ment and of the trade cycle—the experts were divided. The economists had always known that the working of self-interest was generally bene-ficial "not because of some natural coincidence between the self-interest of each and the good of all, but because human institutions are arranged so as to compel self-interest to work in directions in which it will be beneficial." After 1918 it was clear that some changes in human institu-tions would be necessary if self-interest were to work for the common good with the new powers and in the conditions which new knowledge was creating. The *Liberal Industrial Report,* 1928, sought to show the "unreal character of the supposed antithesis between Socialism and Individualism. While there was a place for public concerns to under-take work of great importance which for various reasons did not attract private enterprise on an adequate scale, and where unavoidable condi-tions of monopoly made private enterprise dangerous, it was the function of the state to establish an environment in which normal competitive conditions could flourish with the greatest efficiency and the least possible waste." [5] At the time the Liberal thinkers had neither the political power nor the technical knowledge to offer an effective alternative either to the Conservative party's experiments in protection or the Labour party's dream of nationalization.

In what ways political action can improve economic life and adjust the search for plenty to the love of freedom and the duty to be fair was, after 1939, most thoroughly to be explored. But in Britain, before 1939, the problems were how to aid the industries which had been most hardly hit by the war and the worldwide diffusion of the industrial revolution, and how the obvious gaps in basic social services, such as education, health, and the organization of a market for labor, could be made good. After 1918 the discussion was dominated by the experience of state control during the war years. This gave some countenance to naive theories of nationalization and industrial democracy. There were almost intoxicated visions of the application of the democratic process to industry itself. These visions were fed by a passionate desire to secure the elements of social justice in a country which had been united in war and by the grim facts about the poor deal in education, health, and other basic social services which the condition of the 1914–18 conscripts showed them to have received.

At first nationalization seemed merely to be a question of constitution-making for the industries concerned. The concentration of many of Britain's great industries made it seem feasible to have them nationalized. But it was soon brought home to serious students that Britain had to avoid the fatal rigidities of an old industrial structure in a changing world and that nationalization was not the best way to get flexibility. Before 1927 it could be argued that Britain was only temporarily aground on economic difficulties caused by the dislocations of war. After 1927 her difficulties could no longer be attributed to the effects of war, but were seen to be the result of the conditions of a new industrial and commercial age. The problem of flexibility in an industrial civilization, where Britain was now only one workshop among many, dominated the economic discussions of the decade from 1929 to 1939.

The basic elements of the problem were enumerated by J. M. Keynes. He agreed with the most simpleminded members of the Labour party that the obvious faults of the economic order were its failure to give full employment to those able and willing to work, and its arbitrary and inequitable distribution of wealth and income. But Keynes saw more clearly than most how complex were the tools which would be needed to make any amelioration. The state would have to exercise a guiding influence on the propensity to consume, partly through its scheme of taxation and partly by its control of the rate of interest. He thought that some socialization of investment would help to reduce unemployment. Given these technical tools the actual ownership of the means of production would be comparatively unimportant.

The most serious problem of the interwar years, and one which still lives vividly in the folk memory of the British Labour movement, was that of unemployment. Before 1914 the mean figure round which unemployment moved was of the order of 4.5 per cent, but after 1918 in only one year, 1927, was it less than 10 per cent, and at times it was more than 21 per cent. Unemployment arising out of personal qualities and defects cannot be foreseen, but unemployment arising out of industrial fluctuations can. A risk which might be overwhelming and impossible to estimate by a single worker or a particular industry may be measurable when considered collectively. In 1911 a scheme of compulsory unemployment insurance had been developed by a brilliant team of civil servants and applied to a particular group of industries—building, construction work, shipbuilding, engineering—which although liable to fluctuations were not thought likely to decay. The scheme was compulsory to avoid the predominance of bad risks; it required a definite relation between contributions paid and benefits received in order to exclude bad risks; it made the state a contributor so that it could give stability and exercise control.

The extension of the scheme in 1920 to a great part of the field of industrial employment meant, in the postwar conditions of industrial instability, the abandonment of nearly every principle of a sound insurance scheme. It became a system of public assistance for those who were thought to be fit for work. It was fair neither to the unemployed themselves nor to the community as a whole. The difficulties of its administration were a major problem of the 1930's. In addition to unemployment insurance one of the most important prewar reforms had been the establishment of labor exchanges which would improve the marketing of labor. In the interwar years it became obvious that it was necessary to improve the market for capital so that the investor would not be as much at sea as the worker himself in his search for useful openings. In fact, between the wars the economists were seeking the analytical tools and the administrators the procedures which, after the war of 1939–45, were to make possible a workable and efficient frontier between what are now called the public and the private sectors of the nation's economic life.

In the first postwar years Mr. J. M. Keynes had urged that Britain should "hold to free trade in its widest interpretation as an inflexible dogma to which no exception is admitted." Britain should hold to it even when she received no reciprocity of treatment. In 1927 only 2 to 3 per cent of British imports were liable to protective duties. But in 1932 the Imports Duties Act saw the beginning of a new protectionism. It gave protection to some home industries, a basis for preference within the empire, and a basis for reciprocal agreements with, or retaliation against, foreign countries. The Ottawa agreement widely extended this principle of imperial preference. The government had assumed the difficult task of co-ordinating a three-fold policy of protection to British agriculture, trade agreements with countries in the sterling area, and imperial preference. The government also made itself responsible for some control of the allocation of British capital resources. Whereas before 1914, 20 per cent of new capital went into home and 80 per cent into foreign investment, after 1932, 89 per cent was for home, 9 per cent for the empire, and less than 2 per cent for foreign countries. Between 1929 and 1936 the whole structure of British finance was transformed. Free trade, no taxation except for revenue, the lowering of the cost of living by every means, the gold standard, and the punctual discharge of international obligations—all basic principles of the world before 1914—had passed away. The political influence of nationalism and the technological impact of scientific research on industrial life were creating entirely new economic uncertainties for the businessman which involved the government in administrative problems never before tackled.

It is in this context of uncertainties and innovations that the crisis of 1931, which was to have such serious effects on the nascent Labour party, should be viewed. At the election of 1929, Labour had been returned to power with 288 seats, the Conservatives 260, and the Liberals 59. It was Labour's bad luck to take office at the beginning of the Great Depression. The crisis of 1931 was the outcome of the impact of a world economic crisis on the vulnerable British economic order. The Labour government did not know, because no one then knew, how to handle the problem of unemployment. The increase in public expenditure and the decrease in revenue brought about by the deepening depression resulted in a run on sterling as call money was removed from London. In a debate on February 11, 1931, Snowden had told the House of Commons about the extreme gravity of the country's situation. A three-party committee —the May committee—was set up to review expenditure and explore possible economies. Its report published on August 1 advised a cut of over £80,000,000 in the social services. This would have involved a reduction in the current unemployment allowance. The issue divided the Labour Cabinet of Ramsay Macdonald. A majority would have accepted a reduction in unemployment allowances, but a minority would have resigned. In the circumstances Macdonald could only tender the resignation of the Cabinet, and it became the duty of the King to see that a government was formed which could carry on in a crisis, until a general election should be feasible. Macdonald was persuaded that it was his duty to head a new three-party "national" ministry, including three other members of the old Cabinet—Snowden, J. H. Thomas, and Lord Sankey. There is plenty of evidence that Macdonald regarded himself as only temporarily sundered from his old associates and as the head of a government with strictly limited objectives. The national government "was regarded as a purely temporary expedient. Its life was expected to be short. When its task was completed, Parliament would be dissolved, and the three parties would contest the general election independently." The Labour party has created a legend of betrayal by a leader who, corrupted by the insidious appeal of the traditional governing classes, had lost his understanding of the righteous Labour world. But it is clear that Macdonald as the retiring prime minister could not throw aside all responsibility for seeing that the King's government was being carried on and the immediate crisis dealt with.[6]

When the general election did come, before the end of 1931, the heart of the matter was the conflict between the Labour ministers in the national government and their former colleagues. The national executive of the Labour party had decided that "automatically and immediately all members and supporters of the National Government cease to be members of the Labour party." The Labour party's manifesto for the election said that the capitalist system had broken down and that the National government was seeking from the electorate a mandate for the impossible task of rebuilding capitalism. The General Council of the Trades Union Congress spoke darkly of "a secret alliance with those forces of reaction against which the trade union movement has fought throughout its existence." Mr. Lloyd George said that he declined "to assist a mere Tory ramp to exploit a national emergency for Tory ends." Snowden, for the National government, said that the one issue was "whether we should have a strong and stable government in this time of national crisis, or whether we shall hand over the destinies of the nation to men whose conduct in a grave emergency has shown them to be unfitted to be trusted with responsibility."

The result of the election was that the Labour representation fell from 288 to 52. The National government had 556 seats. In terms of votes the defeat was not catastrophic for the Labour party. It retained the support of seven out of eight of its supporters. But the analysis of the results in the constituencies showed that there was no such thing as a solid working-class vote and that in an emergency men and women would vote as citizens.

It was unfortunate that in the next four years Prime Minister Macdonald had no real party following and that the second in command, Baldwin, led the largest party in the House. The fact that a large Labour party in the country was so poorly represented in the House of Commons weakened the proper functioning of the British constitution, which has need both of strong government and strong opposition. But the small

Labour party in the House did not sulk or secede. In 1935 it was back to a reasonable strength of 154. It was in this period of party weakness and anomaly that the government failed to meet the complicated, obscure, and dangerous menace which was developing on the continent of Europe. It was in this period that Oswald Mosley, who had in the 1920's been regarded as a possible future Labour prime minister, but had later been expelled, developed his comic and ugly Fascist party. It declared itself the politics of youth and vigor, "the steel creed of an iron age which would cut through the verbiage of illusion to the achievement of a new reality." Mosley had energy, intelligence, courage, oratorical power, money, and social position, but the uniform, the theatrical floodlit meetings, and the paramilitary organizations were entirely foreign to British political habits. The ideas of Conservative, Labour, and Liberal party thinkers were in sad disarray, but they were not so confused as to fall for hate and hot air.

The real weakness of British governments after 1931 was that they could not develop a policy which would be effective against Hitler or Mussolini. The Labour party was prepared to support rearmament provided that it was in support of a collective security which did not exist and could not be created.

After 1918 the Cabinet system of government in Britain was being adapted to the problems of the twentieth century. Before 1914 the theory of cabinet government was generally understood, but the growing complexity of government made some changes in procedure necessary. In Britain the Cabinet, as the central organ of government, has to determine policy and get from Parliament whatever legislation may be needed to implement that policy, and it has to co-ordinate the complex pattern of departments which are the mind and muscles of the modern state. In this Cabinet system—probably unique in its concentration of political power—the executive is in the legislature as the yolk is in the egg. Its members must be members of either the House of Commons or the House of Lords. It would be difficult now for a prime minister to be a member of the House of Lords. The chancellor of the Exchequer has always been a member of the House of Commons. It is in the Commons that the Cabinet must present and defend its policy. It is in the Commons that it has the support of a majority for the legislation it will need. It is in the Commons, too, that it will defend the actions of any minister or official that are criticized.

The political history of Britain has produced a constitution in which whoever has the support of a majority of the elected House of Commons can do whatever in this modern world can be done by government. Sovereignty—in the sense of the final source of law—belongs to the Queen in Parliament. The King or Queen in Parliament has, since 1688, determined to whom the Crown shall descend, excluding from the throne all Roman Catholics and all who may marry Roman Catholics. When in 1936 Edward VIII had been advised by the prime minister of the United Kingdom, after consultation with the Dominion governments, that his marriage to a divorced commoner would impair if it did not destroy the symbolic character of his office, he signed a declaration of abdication to which effect was given by His Majesty's Declaration of Abdication Act, 1936. This act provided for the exclusion of Edward VIII and his issue from the succession to the throne.

The King in Parliament has united England, Scotland, and Ireland into a United Kingdom and has given Northern Ireland a special form of local autonomy and Southern Ireland her independence. It has introduced universal suffrage by stages and varied the qualifications of a member of the House of Commons, altered the composition of the House of Lords, determined the relation between Lords and Commons, and created and continuously adjusted an intricate administrative and judicial machinery.

The working of the system depends upon the observation, by the Queen and the prime minister and his cabinet, by the most fleeting member of Parliament or the humblest official in the administration, of certain rules of the game, which English writers on law and politics have called the *conventions* of the constitution. These rules of the game might be called the spirit of the constitution. The inner core of these conventions is the principle that the prerogative powers of a monarch will be exercised only on the advice of politicians who have the support of the elected House of Commons. The residuary powers for the preservation of the state which legally are with the sovereign are actually at the disposal of the government of the day. The government is composed of servants of the Crown, but by convention those servants will be members of the legislature and supported by a majority in it. They will be chosen by the Queen's prime minister, and they will be individually and collectively responsible for the policies they follow. It is a vital convention that the prime minister may advise the Queen to dissolve the existing Parliament, which being done, a general election will give the country the opportunity to change the membership of the House of Commons and incidentally the party in office. The British can have a general election whenever it is necessary that they should, and the election may be in effect a choice between two political parties or a decision about a particular policy—to introduce protection or to join the Common Market. And, of course, if the emergency should warrant such a step, the Queen in Parliament can by ordinary legislation prolong indefinitely the life of an existing Parliament.

We know so little about the psychological forces involved in ceremonial, and we have so many reasons to respect and even to fear the power of symbols—the hammer and sickle, the swastika, and the fasces have been the death of millions—that the British have some reason to think that they have been lucky in their political history which has brought it about that the ceremonial presence and the actual operations of the state are in separate institutions. The prime minister is not a head of state. Her Majesty the Queen has now only two clear personal responsibilities in the political life of Britain: the selection of a prime minister— a matter of form because the leader of the party which can form a government is usually not in doubt—and the refusal of a dissolution of Parliament should it ever wrongfully be asked for.

To understand the position of the prime minister is to understand the British constitution. He selects not only the members of the Cabinet but all the other political posts which must be filled. There are some sixteen important offices outside the Cabinet itself and altogether about one hundred which change with a change of government. Before 1939 there was a steady accumulation of power in the office of the prime minister. With the King's consent he appointed and could dismiss a minister, and the number of ministers was increasing. He was consulted about key appointments in the civil service: The official world is a permanent one, but which official shall be the official head of a great department under its political chief may be a matter for the prime minister. He had to settle disputes between the different departments of the government, and their number was increasing. He was the chairman of the most important committees through which the government prepared its policies. In the office of the Cabinet secretariat he had the beginnings of a highly organized machine for co-ordinating the preparation of policies.

Before 1939 three driving forces of the modern state were highly developed: (1) the House of Commons, in which the government would present its policies, in which the official Opposition would function as the most formidable critic of the government—and as the alternative government should the one in office fail; (2) the Cabinet, the political head of the national executive; (3) the permanent civil service. The civil servants are in law servants of the Crown, and it is a *convention* and not law which makes the vital distinction between those servants of the Crown who are the political leaders and the permanent nonpolitical officials.

The civil service, in its modern form, is not a hundred years old. It had been realized as early as 1854 that it would be impossible for politicians to carry the burden of staffing government departments by the distribution of public jobs to private friends. When so many activities were being professionalized, the service of the state had to be made a profession too. Gladstone decided that the civil service must be recruited by competitive examination to permanent posts. The selecting body then established—the Civil Service Commission—was able to draw on the output of the national educational system developed after 1870 and on all the bright young men who had not the desire or the finance which might promise success in business or the older professions. The service grew in size as the scope of government widened. But the most remarkable thing about it was the smallness of the administrative, or policy-making, grade—in 1939 only 2000 members. The essential of their art was an ability to transact business by word of mouth with their opposite numbers in the world of business, science, and politics, by tough and technical discussion in committee and by a mastery of the art of drafting. The great British civil servants always had the ability to take a line, expound it, persuade, and convince. Their tough and canny practice was shaped before 1939 by a century of experience. They were the hidden glands which gave Leviathan its sanity and its power.

The British civil service, like the Monarchy, Parliament, or the Cabinet, is unique. One cannot say politicians deal with opinion and civil servants with truth, that civil servants deal with what is permanent in policy and the politicians with innovations. One can only say that the civil servant does that part of the work of government which is not done by Parliament or the Cabinet. The civil servant is the kind of expert which the party system and the British system of responsible government require. The power and competence of the Cabinet, the strength and resilience of the administrative machinery, the subtle partnership between the politician in office and the permanent official in his department is the nearest thing that the modern world has had to the Platonic idea of a philosopher king. It is not the dream of a philosopher now; it is the tough and canny practice shaped by a century of experiments. Before 1939 it had done much to anticipate the dangers of 1939. Between 1939 and 1945 the staff of permanent officials was supplemented by larger numbers of academic persons and businessmen. This partnership of civil servant, don, and businessman was a dazzling success. After 1945 the technique of co-operation between political leaders and professional administrators made the welfare state possible. On its skill in adjusting the people's will, as it is elicited by the party process and political debate, to the realities of economic and social forces the survival of democratic government has depended.

CHAPTER XVII

The End of Laissez Faire, 1914-39

The British Isles in the twentieth century could not keep the industrial, commercial, and financial lead which had been theirs during the nineteenth. They were not born great; in part they had achieved and in part they had had economic greatness thrust upon them. They had no permanent advantages in the age of new technologies comparable to those given by the juxtaposition of coal, iron, and ports, the basis of British supremacy in the first machine age. By 1900 Germany was leading the world in chemical and electrical industries and the United States in the techniques of mass production. The cumulative annual increase of manufacturing production from 1873 to 1913 had only been 1.8 per cent for the United Kingdom; for the United States it had been 4.8 per cent, and for Germany 3.9 per cent. In the new shape of things to come—the world of electricity, oil, synthetic rubber, dyes, rayons, and plastics, a world in which in one generation the motor, the plane, the tractor, the power station, and the laboratory would change in every detail the life of common men— the British would have to face formidable problems of adjustment: not least because they had been more highly specialized in the old pattern of industry and trade than any other country in the world. In 1910, 48 per cent of the population of England and Wales was occupied in manufacturing and mining as against 40 per cent in Germany, 33 per cent in France, and 30 per cent in the United States. On the eve of the 1914 war, Britain was importing four-fifths of her wheat.

By its very nature industrialization—the penetration of the methods of production by the power of organized thought and the informing of men's tools by the mathematical equations of their finest minds—was certain to accelerate, and the economic well-being of any country would come to depend on the skill with which it could adapt itself to these protean forms. The spread of industrialization was bound to cause changes in the basic pattern of the world's economic division of labor. The simpler types of manufacture were developed in what had been mainly agrarian areas, and the British textile industry inevitably declined before the multitudinous manipulative dexterity of the Indians and the Japanese, once the know-how of textile machinery had been exported. Countries of moderate size, such as Germany and Britain, had to concentrate on the manufacture of high-quality goods in which their skill and advanced technologies could have full play. Very large countries, such as the United States, would be able to develop the full range of manufactures that new technologies made possible because they could use their political power to protect the economic advantages given by their internal mass markets.

There was a change, too, in the terms of trade between the producers of primary goods in the agrarian areas of the world and the industrial centers. "Up to about 1900, a unit of labour applied to industry yielded year by year a purchasing power over an increasing quantity of food," wrote J. M. Keynes in 1919. "It is possible," he added, "that about the year 1900 this process began to be reversed.... But the tendency of cereals to rise in real cost was balanced by other improvements; and —one of the novelties—the resources of tropical Africa then for the first time came into large employ, and a great traffic in oil seeds began to bring to the table of Europe in a new and cheaper form one of the essential foodstuffs of mankind." [1] The improvements were to continue. After 1918 the agrarian areas of the world were transformed by the work of the biologist and the chemist. The output of primary products was so stimulated by new knowledge while the demand for them in the industrial countries did not grow as fast as formerly (because of a falling birth rate) that the fall in the price of these products may have been one of the causes of the depression of the 1930's.

For Britain there was the double problem: the newcomers to the industrial revolution could produce textile goods more cheaply than could Britain, and at the same time the loss of income which the primary producers suffered when the terms of trade had moved against them led to a reduction in their purchase of Britain's more sophisticated industrial output. The quantum of world trade fell by a quarter between 1929 and 1932, and Britain as a great world trader was heavily hit. The peculiar pattern of world trade in the nineteenth century which had helped to nourish the *Pax Britannica* had gone. Then, primary producers had borrowed to buy railways, ports, installations, and machinery and had paid for their loans with the money from the agricultural products they sold. Britain was hit not only by the general decline in trade but also by the impact of the competition in textiles from the nascent industries of the once "unchanging" East.

Before 1914 Britain had tried to make good her loss of industrial supremacy by cultivating her financial subtlety. In 1918 she had many of the financial institutions and the banking skills which might have helped to stabilize a world economic order rocking in the wake of war. But she had been too weakened by the war to have the necessary power. She was an industrial dwarf in the clothes of a financial giant. But if she stumbled, other countries had not even learned to walk. The United States did not do the job which she alone had the power to do. In fact, the essential knowledge was not available to any government. "Few realised," Keynes wrote, "the intensely unusual, unstable, complicated, unreliable, temporary nature of the economic organisations by which Western Europe had lived for the previous half century." [2] To see into the oddity of the past is not itself a map and torch for the unknown future. Before 1914 the economic frontiers of industrial Europe had been moving frontiers. The central network of European trade depended on a regular supply of raw materials and food stuffs from areas far away. Between 1890 and 1914 Germany had become more and more dependent on imports of primary products from other continents and Britain had obtained less than one-third of her imports from Europe.

The export of capital from Europe had made possible spectacular developments outside Europe. Inside this credit empire Britain had had the leading part. In the seven years before 1914, for the construction of railways in countries which produced food and raw materials, she had provided £600,000,000. Sterling was a common currency of international trade. The success of the gold standard mechanism depended less on the perfection of the mechanism than on the way in which it was used. Although the United Kingdom before 1914 was the world's largest creditor country, at no time did she use this position to accumulate large stocks of gold. She imposed no political obstacles to the free export of capital. The subtle mechanisms of stable exchange rates and the gold standard could be used by international traders as an ordinary man uses his bank they did not have to understand its inner life. The free and open market of the British Isles absorbed a large proportion of the world's total export of stable products. Continental countries and the United States could finance their purchases of primary products from overseas by their exports to the United Kingdom. The United Kingdom was the conductor of an orchestra which gave forth promising harmonies of peace and plenty. After 1914 that world passed away. The disintegration of the multilateral system and the conception of planned economies begin in 1914. In the last three years of peace the national income of the United Kingdom had averaged about £2,300,000,000 annually, of which some £1,950,000,000 had been devoted to consumption, and not quite £350,000,000 saved; well over half the savings had been invested abroad.

Britain had to share her prewar financial supremacy with a new and powerful partner. After the 1914–18 war, the long-term, capital position of the United States changed from a net debit of from £400,000,000 to £600,000,000 in 1914 to a net credit of close to £1,200,000,000 by 1922. There was no longer one center of decision in moments of crisis. All the world had need of a stable system of international finance. But Britain had not the means herself to reintegrate the different national centers of trade and finance. New York had the means, but New York had neither the machinery nor the incentive to use her means in the way that London had used her surplus in the past. After 1929 the single world economy, disrupted by the war, was replaced by a multiplicity of national economies each concerned with its own well-being. The war had broken up powerful economic units and multiplied the number of nation states. Before 1914 the population of Germany and Austria together was more than that of the United States. After 1919, of the twenty-nine European states only five had more than 40,000,000 and ten had less than 5,000,000 population. During the war the United Kingdom had sold £1,000,000,000 of foreign investment, and though by 1929 her total investment was higher than in 1913 the frontiers of the British empire of investment had contracted.

The cessation of American lending during the Great Depression further contributed to the international collapse. The wiring of the world economy was short-circuited. In 1929 the United States owned 38 per cent of the world's monetary gold; in 1939 her stock had risen to 59 per cent. Humanity was now really crucified on a cross of gold. The United States had followed a policy of claiming the repayment of her war debts and also a policy of protection. As the president of the Chase National Bank put it: "The debts of the outside world to us are ropes about their necks, by means of which we pull them towards us. Our trade restrictions are pitchforks pressed against their bodies by means of which we hold them off." [3] In September 1931 the Bank of England was forced to suspend gold payments. The postwar efforts to restore the multilateral economic liberalism of the nineteenth century had finally collapsed. It was inevitable after 1931 that international trade should be drastically reduced and that states should try to defend their currencies and protect their industries. No unitary or even federal constitution had been devised to give a legal and political framework to an international economic order. The *Pax Britannica* had gone, and the life of many states was to be more isolated, less prosperous, and shorter than they had hoped.

Had there been no war in 1914, the United States would still have become the world's greatest creditor. The marriage of technology with her virgin resources could not but produce a race of industrial and financial giants. The genie of the lamp of mechanism would not indefinitely serve a British Aladdin. Her cotton industry was certain to contract. Britain's exports of cotton goods fell by 38 per cent between 1913 and 1925. The United Kingdom's share in world cotton exports fell from 68 per cent to 44 per cent, and the total production of cotton piece goods fell from 8,000,000 square yards in 1912 to 3,300,000 square yards in 1930. Coal was almost as vulnerable as cotton. Without the war substitutes for coal would have grown in importance. While the world consumption of coal had remained almost constant between 1913 and 1924, the consumption of petroleum trebled, the output of lignite nearly doubled, and new sources of hydroelectric power were developed in the United States and in Europe. In 1914, 96.6 per cent of the world's mercantile tonnage was coal fired; by 1939 the proportion had fallen to 54 per cent. Moreover, productivity in coal mining was increasing much more rapidly in other parts of the world than in the United Kingdom, where many mines were deep and old. Coal exports slumped from 87,000,000 tons in 1913 to 48,000,000 tons in 1929. These weaknesses were natural in a country relatively small and with industries adapted to times which technologically were past.

The world has waded so deep in blood that the dead of one country in World War I may be remembered only as a slight drop in a statistician's curve. What the dead, had they lived, might have done, it is idle to speculate. But their loss had economic effects. In the United Kingdom some 745,000 men (about 9 per cent of the men aged 20–45) were killed during the war and about 1,700,000 wounded, of whom 1,200,000 received disablement pensions. As Kai Lung said of a different episode: "It was for a long time after unusual to meet anyone whose outline had not been permanently altered by that occasion." The decimation of the age groups normally most economically productive surely had some deleterious effects on the economic and political "know-how" and energy of the interwar years. The largest physical loss was the sinking of over 40 per cent of the British merchant fleet (8,000,000 gross tons). Shortage of manpower and steel meant that in spite of all efforts the tonnage of the merchant fleet in 1919 was 14 per cent lower than before the war.

While the capacity of British merchant shipbuilding yards had increased during the war by about 25 per cent, the capacity of the world's had doubled. Some industries such as textiles, for which raw materials and shipping space could not be spared in war, had had to contract their output. Engineering had had to expand its capacity. In the coal mines it had been necessary to use the seams most easily worked. Imports in 1918 are estimated to have been 27 per cent in volume and exports (including re-exports) 63 per cent in volume below the 1913 level. Distant markets in the Far East, India, Canada, and Latin America had had to be neglected, and the United States and Japan had supplied what the British could not. While ploughshares are being made into swords the anvils are not at hand to make other things. The British mart had become a temporary fort. To the end of 1919 loans to the Dominions and to European allies totaled £1,828,000,000. There was a net sale of rather more than 10 per cent of Britain's long-term foreign assets. Many assets in enemy countries and in Russia were lost by confiscation (perhaps 5 per cent of her total foreign investments).[4]

What is most remembered about the interwar years is the high unemployment, the depressed areas, and the great depression of 1929. But as Lord William Beveridge has put it: "Across this waste period of destruction and dislocation, the permanent forces making for material progress, technical advance, and the capacity of human society to adjust itself to new conditions continued to operate." Between the wars there was, in fact, a substantial and fairly steady advance in the average standard of living—an advance which was retarded but hardly reversed in the slump after 1929. By 1939, the total net national income is estimated to have increased 40 per cent since 1920. The average real income per head in the decade 1930–39 was 17.7 per cent higher than it had been in the past decade. This rate of increase was not so fast as in the previous decade, nor so fast as it had been in late Victorian days, but it was better than it had been in the Edwardian.[5] The interwar years received the benefit of technological changes started before 1914. An improvement in the terms of trade was accelerated at the onset of the Great Depression and reversed only when employment was improving again in the middle 1930's.[6]

The volume of industrial production was nearly 80 per cent higher in 1937 than in 1907, and the real income per head of the population about 30 per cent higher. The decline of the old staple industries—textiles and coal—was inevitable. The stresses and strains and the consequent distortions that war imposed had made the change more rapid and more difficult than it otherwise might have been. British exports suffered more than those of other Western nations because so much of them had gone to the great pre-1914 producers of food and textile fibers. Technological innovations were certain to damage most severely the industries which before 1914 had enjoyed a natural advantage. In the United States similar changes took place, but there it was only a matter of redistributing industrial processes within a common political framework. Britain was a New England entirely surrounded by water, whose Chicago was in another political system. Britain might sometimes have the name of empire, but unlike the United States she had no Middle West and West into which she could expand.

Surveys of income and of living conditions in several large towns suggest that between 1919 and 1939 the condition of the people was a good deal better than it had been a generation back. A substantial minority of families could still not buy the minimum of food, clothes, and shelter necessary to a healthy life, but it seemed that a very slight further redistribution of income would bring everyone well above the subsistence level. The continued rise in the proportion of the population engaged in the professions, entertainment, transport, distribution, and public services was evidence of improved conditions. In spite of the severe unemployment in the old staple industries and in certain areas, the actual waste of manpower may have been lower than it had been in the casual labor and unemployment of Victorian days. The structure of society and the organization of the labor market were being informed by the quantitative precision which is the very life of modern industry. Another symptom of improved conditions was that the consumption of alcohol from the early 1930's always remained below one-half the level of the early years of the century. In spite of a ninefold increase in price the consumption of tobacco more than doubled in the fifty years after 1900. An estimate of the national income per head of population in 1938, computed by the Department of Economic Affairs of the United Nations, gave the United Kingdom $481.2, the Netherlands $321.8, and France $243.9.[7]

After 1913, if Britain were to have kept her relatively high level of prosperity, she would have had to make drastic shifts in the use of her productive resources and have shown great ingenuity in the development of new products. In 1913 she produced 11 per cent of the world's output of chemicals, but that was less than half the production of Germany and less than one-third that of the United States. Nearly two-thirds of the exports of manufactures before 1914 belonged to commodity groups which were to have a declining share of world trade in the interwar years. In 1924 only 49.7 per cent of the total power consumed by all branches of British industry was electrically generated, as compared with 73 per cent in the United States and 67 per cent in Germany. In 1925 Germany had an export market twice the size of the British, and the United States five times as large. In engineering exports Britain's share in world trade dropped from 30.4 per cent in 1913 to 25.6 per cent in 1930, mainly because there was a static or only slowly rising market for the prime movers and textile machinery, the boiler and the boiler house plant in which she had specialized in the past, and a rising market for agricultural machinery and machine tools in which the United States was leading the world.

Four periods can be distinguished in the economic history of the inter-war years: 1919–25, a period of inflation in which a spinning dance of European currencies might have been specially devised to illustrate an economic lecture on the meaning of money; the later 1920's, a period of expansion and large-scale lending; 1929–33, the world economic crisis; 1933–39, a period of partial recovery in which the bandits of the totalitarian world prepared their bid for world power.

In the first period, from the spring of 1919 to the early summer of 1920, there was a boom accompanied by a steep rise in wages and in prices followed by a slump from which the country did not recover until the end of 1922. The confusion of the currencies and the vagaries of economic nationalism made trading, as Lloyd George once put it, like "playing billiards on an Atlantic liner." The co-operation of the Bank of England and the Federal Reserve Bank of New York and the efforts of the economic and financial organs of the League of Nations managed to secure some financial order. In the second period of expansion and large-scale American lending, the volume of British industrial production increased by 12 per cent. But this was less than one-half the rate of growth in Germany, France, or the United States. Britain, too, was selling less, compared with before the war, than any other European country save Russia.[8] Unemployment was 1,500,000 or 12.2 per cent of the working population by 1929. Of this unemployment, two-fifths was concentrated within the staple trades of coal mining, iron and steel, ship-building, and textiles. In the United States the economic activity was so great that the unfortunate idea was born that the secret of perpetual progress had been discovered. Slumps, it was held, were things of the past and unemployment a disease of the effete, dole-giving countries of the Old World.

In the third period hopes were dashed and illusions dispelled by the depression which began in 1929. The mechanism of the international gold standard laboriously reconstructed after 1919 collapsed. Britain was driven off the gold standard, and the world in general was taught some of the economic facts of life. The quantum of world trade fell by one quarter between 1929 and 1932. The self-adjusting international system was no more. The nineteenth-century dream of international harmony based on a self-regulating international division of labor dissolved. After 1931 it was inevitable that trade should be drastically reduced and that states should adopt what measures they could to defend their currencies and protect their industries. In the fourth period, while there was partial recovery, the Axis powers were able, amid the ruins of economic liberalism, to prepare for war. They used for their own purposes the tools which the states in the liberal tradition were reluctant to use for theirs. It was mainly from resources controlled by countries with which they intended or expected to be at war that both Germany and Italy obtained their war reserves. Germany by her control of imports made foreign exchange available for the materials she wanted for war. From a position of clear inferiority in 1933 she achieved one of overmastering ascendancy by 1938.

It is within this general world pattern that British interwar experience may be considered. The first shock, after World War I, came over the dispute about reparations. "We have been moved already beyond endurance, and need rest," wrote J. M. Keynes. But rest was not to be known again so far in this century. The war expenditure of the United Kingdom had been about three times that of the United States (excluding loans to allies in each case), and in proportion to capacity it had been between seven and eight times. Whatever Germany might be made to pay in reparations would have to be earned from activities which would be highly competitive with those of Britain herself. Textiles, chemicals, machinery, and vehicles accounted for over one-half of the export trade of Germany and for nearly two-thirds that of Britain. The British in the end received from war debt repayment and reparations a sum roughly equal to the payments which she was to make to the United States. The economist Hubert Henderson put the position in 1932 as one which might be "likened to that of a self-contained village community, in which there are two cobblers in keen competition with one another. If a heavy annual fine were imposed on one of the cobblers which he could only pay by cutting his prices and working overtime, the result would be bad for the other cobbler, and would not be any less bad if he had to pass on his share of the receipts from the fine to the lord of the manor." [9]

Before the war, Britain's share of world export of manufactures had fallen from 38 per cent in 1876-80 to 27 per cent in 1911-13. She had temporarily made good the adverse balance of payments which this caused by winning an increased share of the world's shipping, insurance, and other commercial services. With these "invisible" exports she earned a surplus which financed a growing export of capital. An income of over £200,000,000 from overseas investments and £130,000,000 from shipping and commissions paid for the import of some 60 per cent of British food and supplies and left £180,000,000 for investment abroad. In the 1920's her external earnings were still large enough to finance her imports and leave some surplus for foreign investments. But after the slump of 1929 the income from invisible exports was so greatly reduced that she was driven to start living on her overseas' capital. There was a catastrophic fall in the volume of British exports between 1918 and 1939. In 1913 exports had been over a third of the total industrial output of the United Kingdom. In 1939 they were about 15 per cent. The industries which suffered the most lasting contraction in their export trade—coal, shipbuilding, and cotton—were concentrated in particular areas—South Wales, the Clyde, Tyneside, and Lancashire. There was between 1918 and 1939 some redistribution of British industrial resources, with rapid developments in the Midlands, in London, and in the Southeast. The main losses took place in the cheaper goods. Britain developed more highly finished and specialized products among consumer goods and in industrial equipment. The increases in the new did not offset all the losses in the old. The volume of world trade as a whole fell away after 1929 from the level of 1913. Of that declining volume Britain had a declining share.

It has been said that the position need not have become so serious if the British economy had been more flexible. Her exports tended to be largest in those commodities which were expanding least in world trade. But flexibility was not easy to achieve. In the 1920's efforts were made to restore Britain's position as a great financial center. This led to the restoration of the gold standard in 1925 at prewar parity. Unemployment was concentrated in the export trade, and efforts were made to facilitate the transfer of labor from export trade areas into others. But these had only a limited success. With the wisdom of hindsight it is now said that it should have been possible to modernize the methods and equipment of the basic industries, such as coal, cotton, steel, and engineering. Britain should have adapted her economy to a smaller production for export and a larger domestic trade.[10]

It was obvious in the mid-1920's that the old industrial north was yielding place to the Midlands, and the unemployment in the former was almost double what it was in the latter. The industrial center of gravity in the nineteenth century had been in the north, where coal was cheap, and in the 1920's about two-thirds of the 5,250,000 employed in the great staple industries were north of the Trent. There were three outstanding groups: metals, chemicals, and engineering; textiles; mining and quarrying. They accounted for nearly two-thirds of the 9,000,000 employed in all British manufacturing and mining industries. Another 9,000,000 were employed in transport and communications, commerce and finance, public administration, public utilities, professional and personal services, and defense. Under 1,400,000 were in agriculture, horticulture, and fishing.

The staple industries were handicapped not only by long-term forces of technological change, which were making their methods out of date, and by the development of competition in other countries, which the industrial revolution had reached, but also by the distorted development imposed upon them by war. In the case of coal the war had starved the mines of equipment. Mining activities had had to be concentrated on the seams which were most easy to work. Exports had had to be restricted so that the domestic needs of a beleaguered island could be met. After the war was over the disorganized industry was not able to meet the large demands of the reopened markets of the world. The government controlled domestic prices at a low level, and the urgent needs of continental Europe made the price of the limited amount of coal licensed for export rocket. The strike in the United States coal fields, followed by the French occupation of the Ruhr in 1923, was an artificial stimulus to the industry, masking its real weakness until 1924. Even then a government subsidy to the mineowners hid the truth from most people until May 1926, when a national coal stoppage touched off the abortive General Strike, in which the economic and political delusions of the postwar world combined to stage a tragicomedy which showed that the British people, while they might lack economic genius, retained their constitutional wits. In 1927 the coal industry was free from the feverish influence of fortuitous and temporary demands and the soporific effect of subsidies. It had to face the realities of a world learning to economize in the use of coal and to develop alternative sources of power—the internal combustion engine and the swelling flow of oil into ships and trucks. In 1914 the proportion of the world's mercantile tonnage dependent on oil was only 3.4 per cent, in 1932 it was 40 per cent, and in 1939 it would be 46 per cent. The British coal industry was one of the chief sufferers in the depression of 1929; its output declined by one-fifth, and, in 1932, 41 per cent of the workers in the coal industry were unemployed. The export of coal, including bunker coal, fell from 98,000,000 tons in 1913 to 46,000,000 tons in 1937. The great expansion in manufacturing industries of the 1930's did not bring an increase in the consumption of coal. The Coal Mines Act of 1930 tried to find a permanent cure for the weakness of the industry. There were then some 1400 collieries with 2500 mines with an average output far below those of the Continent. A Coal Reorganisation Commission was established to promote reorganization by amalgamations.

The position of the textile industry was even more serious. Depression among the world's primary producers to whom Britain sent much of her export was then compelling them to seek cheaper sources of supply, to reduce their total purchases, or to manufacture for themselves. India increased her own output of cotton goods and also bought large quantities from Japan. In the 1930's less than 60 per cent of the British output of cotton piece goods was exported, as against nearly 90 per cent of a far larger output in 1907. Africa was able to buy some of the simpler products, and in 1939 the exports to Africa and Asia were about equal. Lancashire was most severely hit by this change in the textile markets of the world. Her exports in 1913 had been far greater than the sum of the cotton exports of the rest of the world. During the war the shortage of shipping had made it impossible for cotton producers to get their normal supplies of raw materials. From 1917 to 1919 the trade was regulated by the Cotton Control Board which concentrated production on the higher grade goods. This had compelled customers in Asia to look elsewhere for low-quality fabrics. The magnitude of the contraction in the cotton industry, in the absence of any great revolution in techniques, was unique in the economic history of the world. Before 1914, cotton goods had been nearly a quarter of the total exports of the country. Her share of the world consumption of raw cotton had been about one-fifth. In 1939 it was less than one-tenth. Cotton goods are what the country beginning in industrial methods can most easily produce. By 1939 over four-fifths of the world consumption of cotton textiles were supplied by local industries. Where home production had not replaced cotton goods imported from Britain, Japan's exports had cut in. It is estimated that two-thirds of the British export losses in the cotton industry could be attributed to the development by former customers of their own industries and one-third to the successful competition of the Japanese.

The woolen industry suffered far less than the cotton. During the war it was clothing armies and could not extend its plant to meet foreign demands. Raw material was in short supply because shipping space was tight and the chief sources of supply were remote—Australia, New Zealand, and South America. War, too, and the general spirit of change decreased the home demand for wool. The weight of wool that women wore was aesthetically reduced. The adoption by Asian countries of Western habits of dress offset in part the decline in European consumption of wool. Britain did not keep her new markets in the Far East in the face of local industries after 1924. But in 1937 the output of her main finished woolen products was only 16 per cent less in volume than before 1914.

During World War I the iron and steel industry had been adapted to the needs of war. The new works were first class, but they were sited for the exigencies of war and were in the wrong place for ordinary commercial business in peacetime. Productive capacity was far greater in 1920 than in 1914. Blast furnaces capacity had increased from 11,000,000 to 12,000,000 tons and steel capacity from 8,000,000 to 12,000,000 tons. During the period of European recovery, 1924-29, Britain's pig-iron trade did not revive and the expansion of her steel output was only moderate. It worked at half capacity, unemployment was heavy, and profits were low. World demand for the class of material Britain was best fitted to produce had fallen and British prices had risen. The heavy steel industry needed to be rebuilt with plants larger than any it had ever had. There was worldwide change from the use of wrought iron to basic steel. The changes Britain needed in her iron and steel industry were structurally greater than those in any other country. The depression of 1929-32 fell with crushing force on the British iron and steel industry. The home production of pig iron dropped by over 50 per cent between 1929 and 1932 and the production of steel by 45 per cent. In 1932 the Import Duties Advisory Committee recommended the imposition of a temporary duty of $33\frac{1}{3}$ per cent on many classes of iron and steel. It was hoped that this would encourage reorganization. But the high tariff by increasing the industry's competitive power in the home market weakened some of the previous spurs to reorganization. There was, however, a revival after 1933. By 1937 steel output was more than a third greater than in 1929. This was caused by the recovery of ship-building and constructional engineering in general, the expansion of the motor industry, the substitution of steel for timber in coal mining, and rearmament.

The iron and steel industry has some obvious characteristics. In it a very large volume of homogeneous fluid material has to be handled in very big individual masses. It clearly aches for skilled planning. The product of the higher stages of production are the rails and machinery and these are needed at the lowest stages for the coal and iron mines by which the industry is fed. This favors vertical integration, and by 1930, 70 per cent of the British output of iron and steel was turned out by twenty firms. In 1932 ten vertical groups had 47 per cent of the pig-iron capacity and 60 per cent of the steel capacity. But these British giants were pygmies to the American eye. The twenty had an output of steel less than one-third of that of the United States Steel Corporation. The large British firms were not specialized enough, and their economic policy was influenced after 1932 by the British Iron and Steel Federation's power of political negotiation. During World War II, the industry passed under control, and once again its operation was governed by strategic needs.

World War I had a most shattering effect on the shipping industry. In 1918 the world's fleet was slightly greater than in 1913, and British tonnage was less. The capacity of the world's merchant shipbuilding yards had doubled, and the British capacity had increased by about 25 per cent. Britain had to extend her building capacity to make good the wartime sinkings; the world had had to build its own ships when the belligerents could not build them. But if the world's fleet was greater, the world trade was less. By 1925 about one-ninth of the world's shipping was laid up in port. Britain's share of world production fell from 60 per cent in 1913 to 49 per cent in 1922–25. In 1927–30 there was a revival. International trade revived; there were new types of ships—oil burners, oil tankers, the electro-turbine, and the motor ship. British industry responded and the proportion of world tonnage launched in the United Kingdom rose from 49 per cent in 1922–25 to 53 per cent in 1927–30. But she could not do so well in the new type of shipbuilding as she had done in the types before 1914. Her great resources of steam coal made a change to ships using the new fuels less urgent for British shipowners than for those in other countries. If you have a good old car there may be no economic necessity for a new one. In 1927–30 Britain built 65 per cent of the world's tonnage of steamships but only 41 per cent of its tonnage of motor ships.

The position of agriculture has in Britain always been peculiar and complex. That today only about a million—a bare one in twenty—of the working population are engaged in agriculture is a feature of the British economic order found nowhere else in the world. In the United States the proportion is about one in five. Agriculture, because of the early British industrial revolution, has a position less politically powerful than in any other great state. Britain had taken as much land into cultivation by 1870 as was profitable under a free trade regime. After 1870 there was a trend away from cereals, especially from wheat, to livestock. The opening of the West in America and the cheapening of ocean transport encouraged a change from wheat to meat production. After 1890 refrigeration made possible larger quantities of meat imports. To meet this overseas competition Britain concentrated on high-quality production. Technical improvements after 1920 in refrigeration brought chilled meat from the Argentine, butter and lamb from New Zealand. British production then shifted toward milk, eggs, and vegetables, which suit a sheltered home market and for which a rising standard of living and a better understanding of dietetics created an expanding demand. During the 1930's, British agriculture was concentrating on livestock and livestock products, in place of crops, for direct human consumption. The meat, the dairy, and the poultry industries were also becoming more dependent on imported feeding stuffs. The result was that except for the later years of the war of 1914–18 the arable area declined continuously from 1872 to 1939. From 1891–1913 about 45,000 acres a year went out of cultivation in Britain, half was lost to rough grazing and half to nonagricultural uses. After 1913, over 100,000 acres a year were lost, about three-quarters to rough grazing and one-quarter to other uses. Within the shrinking agricultural acreage there was a decline in the corn area in favor of grass. In 1870 Britain was a carpet of arable with a pattern of grass; in the 1930's it was a carpet of grass with a pattern of arable.

Before 1914 the British agricultural industry had lost its traditional leaders. Before the depression of the 1890's farm relief had been supplied by the land-owning class. The depression wiped them out as an economic and political power, and the control of British agricultural production was in the hands of the farmers themselves. The system was one midway between the peasant system of the Continent and large-scale capitalist undertakings for plantation crops. About 28,000,000 acres would under any circumstances be under grass and about 12,000,000 under crops. There was a margin of 6,000,000 which by subsidy or protection could be turned from grass to crops. In normal peace conditions one-third of the population could be fed on home production. By raising the area given to crops this could be raised to one-half. But the other half would depend upon the ability of the British to pay for food from abroad and to protect the routes by which it had to come. Or so it seemed in 1918. But while in 1938 Britain produced less than two fifths of her food requirements, during World War II she produced four-fifths. Before 1939–45 only two-fifths of farm land was arable and the rest permanent grass. During the war the proportions were reversed.

In 1918 the achievements of 1939–45 could not be foreseen. The agricultural policy of the government was uncertain. There were moves to increase efficiency. Plant and animal diseases were controlled, education and research encouraged, the special credit facilities which the

British banks, preoccupied with foreign trade, had not provided were set up. But there was also a confused and conflicting policy of subsidy and protection. In 1924 a sugar beet industry was begun. In 1932 the Wheat Act provided a guaranteed price for a specific quantity of wheat grown in the United Kingdom. In 1933 a Marketing Act combined internal marketing arrangements with the regulation of imports by quotas. A policy of imperial preference increased the percentage of food imported from empire countries from 38 per cent to 50 per cent. The bare possibility of empire self-sufficiency in food stuffs was fortunately not pursued.

Between the wars the British economy was shielded from the force of the development of industry around the world by the exceptional terms of trade which industry enjoyed in the purchase of primary products and by the assets which she had in her overseas' investments. Even in 1938 the net income from overseas' investments was enough to pay for one-fifth of all British imports. With the addition of her net earnings on invisible account—from shipping and other services—it paid for over a quarter of her imports in that year. But the long-term trends were serious. The development of new countries, such as the early United States, and some parts of the colonies of settlement—Australia and other British Dominions—will, in the early stages, create a demand for imported manufactured goods—railways and similar equipment are examples. But this is a passing phase. In the long run the new societies will develop their own industries. In densely populated and ancient communities such as India and China there is a drive to develop new industries to mop up the hidden unemployment which lurks in densely populated agrarian communities—village Newtons and mute inglorious Miltons lurk in their thousands at the bottom of the deep hierarchies of the ancient East and even in areas nearer Europe, as we can guess from the pages of Chekhov or Tolstoi. When the unchanging East welcomes change, its nations become competitors for food and raw materials in the markets of the world and also competitors in the sale of the export of mass-produced industrial products. The industrial revolution which was born with much pain in early nineteenth-century England can disseminate its own progeny with astonishing ease. In these conditions Britain needed great flexibility in her industrial structure if she were to maintain an export trade which would support her economic life. She could no longer be the workshop of the world. What other activities would be sufficiently remunerative?

New industries were, in fact, developed. The fall in the employment in the basic trades of coal mining, iron and steel, shipbuilding, and textiles was almost exactly counterbalanced by the great increase of employment in new industries—motor vehicles, electrical engineering, heating, and welding appliances. By 1939 the British industrial structure was on the way to being adapted to the new conditions of her economic life. A symptom of the changes taking place was that over the interwar period as a whole while more than half a million people migrated *to* the London area 400,000 moved *away* from the northeast coast and South Wales. Such a redistribution, while it means that the nation will not die, does mean that there will be some hardships for those who because of their training, location, and age are unable to move. The average rate of unemployment in the depressed areas in 1932—where the staple industries were contracting—was 38 per cent of the insured population compared with 22.5 per cent for the country as a whole. In South Wales it was 41 per cent and in West Cumberland 46 per cent. In the long run, for the psyche of British political life, the slow misery which these figures imply was even more damaging than the bloodshed of the Somme.

In the development of new industries there were some handicaps dating from the 1914–18 war. In the case of the motor industry the plants during the war had been devoted to the production of airplane engines and shells, while the government imported the vehicles it needed from America. The American output of cars increased from about 500,000 in 1913 to over 2,000,000 in 1920, while the British output was kept stationary by the necessities of war. For the same reason the small export trade was lost. But during the 1930's when the cheap car displaced the motorcycle, American output of the latter declined and the British became not merely the largest producer but the main source of world export of motorcycles. The development of the motor car meant, of course, a reduced demand for railway equipment. The world output of motor vehicles grew from about 500,000 in 1913 to over 6,000,000 in 1929. The United States had four-fifths of the world output of motor vehicles and most of the export trade. The British production was only one-tenth that of the United States. Because of their large internal market, the United States has concentrated on goods which lend themselves to mass production, of which motor cars are a famous example. The British have used their experience and traditions of skilled workmanship in the shipbuilding and marine engineering industries. In the late 1920's Britain was the principal exporter of steam engines, railway equipment, textile machinery, and heavy electrical machinery. In the engineering industries she could meet the more varied demand for the capital goods which the world might need. Not only could she provide the costly and elaborate durable goods but she might also develop the cheap and simple time-saving ones. But here there was another lion in her path. During the interwar years machinery was applied to nearly all the few industrial processes which had hitherto defeated it. The British machine tool industry was making few of the special equipments needed for the rapidly growing motor and light engineering industries. In 1935 she was more dependent on foreign types of machine tools than she had been in 1913. It should not be forgotten, however, that during the 1920's and 1930's Cambridge was the metropolis of physics for the entire world. 1932 was "the most spectacular year in the history of science," when Sir John Cockcroft went skimming down King's Parade, saying to anyone whose face he recognized, "We've split the atom. We've split the atom." It is not given to men to see into the seeds of time.

CHAPTER XVIII

World War II and the Atomic Age

The German attack on Poland on September 1, 1939, brought Britain into the war in fulfillment of a pledge made on March 31 of that year and reaffirmed in the Anglo-Polish agreement of August 25, 1939. Britain had committed herself to aid Poland in the event of a clear threat to Polish independence which the Polish government was prepared to resist forcibly. The German attack was sudden and overwhelming. The crossing of the eastern frontier by strong Russian forces on September 17 made the end inevitable. On September 27 Ribbentrop left for Moscow to discuss the future of the occupied territories with Stalin. The economic agreements which were signed on October 24 gave Germany oil, timber, iron ore, grain, and chemicals—more than enough to offset the effect of the British blockade. It also meant that for the rest of 1939 and the first half of 1940 only seven German divisions were needed on the eastern front.

It was the intention of Hitler to conquer France and dominate Russia west of the Urals. He was not thinking of a hegemony but of a domination of Europe. He was prepared to kill, enslave, or transport as many millions of peoples as might be necessary to create living room for a third Reich which would last a thousand years. He was not too concerned to conquer Britain, thinking that the breakup of her empire would benefit the maritime powers of the United States and Japan. He made a peace offer on October 6, but without waiting for the reactions to it he ordered his armies to prepare for an attack against Holland, Belgium, and France. When the British and French decided to cut off the Norwegian iron ores by mining Norwegian territorial waters south of Narvik, the Germans were ready and occupied the south of Norway and the vital ports of Trondheim and Narvik. On March 18, 1940, Hitler met Mussolini on the Brenner Pass, where Mussolini gave an assurance that Italy would enter the war.

The German attack on Holland and Belgium by air and land began on May 10. On May 14 the Germans broke through the French front between Sedan and Namur, crossed the Meuse, and fanned their tanks out into the open country. This was the new Blitzkrieg technique. Not only had the Germans, as in 1914, wheeled through Belgium (and in 1940 also through Holland), but, smashing a hole at Sedan, they broke the axle on which any allied counter wheel into Belgium might have turned. The Polish campaign had shown that armored forces backed by air superiority could penetrate a defense which had no proper antitank and antiaircraft weapons and penetrate to a great depth. Nothing could now save France. The small British expeditionary force was saved because it avoided being trapped by retreating to the Channel coast. Also, on May 23 Rundstedt halted his armored forces for regrouping, and in the three vital days the British made good their retreat to the beaches of Dunkirk, where a bridgehead could be held long enough for 330,000 British and allied troops to be taken off in some 900 vessels—from 200 naval crafts to small craft of every kind which the navy had brilliantly assembled (May 26–June 2). On June 14 German troops were in Paris. On June 16 Petain sued for an armistice. On June 21 the armistice provided for a German occupation of northern and Atlantic France leaving the French government in control of the remainder of France and the French fleet and colonies untouched. On June 10 Mussolini had declared war on France and Britain, rushing to the help of the victors, as it was known that he would.

Britain was now alone. Oddly, her spirit was high but her defenses within her coasts were almost nonexistent. Tanks, however, could not smash through the Channel. The might of German armor would need to be ferried. Barges needed air cover or they would be sunk by ships moving freely on the seas which the British still commanded, provided their ships had air cover against Hitler's bombers. The stage was set for one of the small decisive battles of the world—the Battle of Britain—which, had it been lost, would have made Britain a German colony and faced the United States with an incalculable menace from all the ship-yards of Europe and the ports and airfields of Africa.

Hitler waited for Britain to sue for peace. He also ordered plans for invasion to be issued on July 2 and signed the preliminary directives on July 16. He thought that an air assault backed by a threat of invasion might lead to the overthrow of the Churchill government by a peace party. His propaganda machine, which had had some success by saturating the French troops behind the Maginot line in the winter of 1939–40, was turned on Britain and the world, particularly the United States. Odysseus had his crew's ears stopped against the Sirens' song. The British ignored the example. While they and all the world waited for Hitler's battle move anyone in Britain could listen to the threat and cajolery, "mantled in light's velocity," which Goebbels offered. The techniques then used have since been developed as part of the cold war. The Nazi pattern had a thoroughness and crudity and silliness which, re-read, almost bring to life that evil menacing world. There was the attempt to sow fear and alarm; for example, on June 30, 1940, any housewife could hear on her radio: "During this ominous lull before the mighty storm there is an opportunity for the thoughtful to reflect . . . It happened in Poland. It happened in Norway. It happened in Holland. It happened in Belgium and it happened in France. Why should it not happen in Britain?" On August 10 at the beginning of the Battle of Britain she could hear: "The German High Command calmly execute, hour by hour, . . . their carefully considered plans leading without delay or undue haste to the sensational conclusion." More simple on August 13 was the invitation to: "Hang Churchill and his Jewish bosses; let us make peace and cut our losses." With some sophistication, Fritzsche, one of the Nazi star performers on the air, said on August 20: "Yesterday an imposing world empire, fascinating in its splendor and tradition—today a country brought to the edge of the abyss by the obstinacy of its leaders." The theme of German propaganda to the United States was that the British were pursuing a deliberate policy of appealing to American moral sentiments in the interests of British imperialism. On September 13, 1940, the United States listeners were told that the British "make up stories about the anti-Christian attitude of Nationalism Socialism . . . These writers probably never read the story of the poor man whose name was Jesus and who preached exactly that which the Fuehrer is so resolutely turning into practice."

On June 18 Mr. Churchill had said in the House of Commons: "Hitler knows that he will have to break us or lose the war. If we stand up to him all Europe may be free, and the life of the world may move forward into broad sunlit uplands; but if we fail, then the whole world, including the United States, and all that we have known and cared for will sink into the abyss of a new dark age, made more sinister and perhaps more prolonged by the lights of a perverted science. Let us therefore address ourselves to our duty and so bear ourselves that if the British Commonwealth of Nations and Empire last for a thousand years men will still say: 'This was their finest hour.' "

There was in fact more than fine words in the British David's ears as he faced Goering's Goliath. He had a stone in his sling—the Spitfire. The

Battle of Britain which began on August 10 had been lost by Goering even before it was begun. For a great strategic battle the forces assigned had too little superiority. In August 1940 the Germans had more than 3000 first-line aircraft concentrated at bases in France, Belgium, Holland, and Norway. But only 1000 Messerschmit fighters were allocated against the British strength of some 700 Spitfires and Hurricanes. It was not enough. The eight-gun Spitfire had been developed from the design of the British monoplane which in 1933 had raised the world speed record to 400 mph. When in 1935 Hitler proclaimed that Germany had air parity with Britain a program to expand the R.A.F. had begun. By 1939 a system of ground observation and radar had improved the chances of interception. The German fighters had to protect their bombers attacking British towns and airfields; the British fighters had only to attack the enemy. British fighters which were shot down fell on home ground and could live to fight another day—in some cases even on the same day.

The object of the German attack was to destroy the British fighters. When, at the end of October, the British fighter command was not broken, but still operational, the Battle of Britain was over. The airfields of southern England had not been put out of action; the system of communications and interception had not been disrupted. On October 12 the invasion of Britain was postponed until the spring of 1941. Hitler, suspicious that Britain was relying on the hope of Russian and American aid, made his preparations to attack Russia in May 1941. The attack in fact began along the whole length of Russia's European frontier on June 22, 1941.

The Battle of Britain was "a battle the like of which was never waged before and, as surely as Crecy and Agincourt, will never be waged again." For the first time in British history "a housewife carrying her shopping basket could pause, look up into the sky and watch armed men engage in the bloody business of exterminating each other; a farm labourer at harvest could for the first time also look and see the victims of battle dropping into his barley." [1] The civilian population had the exhilaration of being in the front line. Bombs fell indifferently on the aged and infirm and on the young and strong. The older generation who remembered trying to guess the trajectory of large shells as they lay in the trenches of the Western front could renew the experience, with bombs in place of shells, and with the difference that they were in their own cellars or under their own tables and with wife and cat to share the boredom and the fear. There was a network of wardens' posts over the area, and it was the function of the wardens to record the fall of every bomb and to supervise the rescue work which any "incident" might require. The word "incident" became part of the technical vocabulary of the battle. It was a word "wonderfully colourless, dry and remote." [2] It covered events ranging from destruction by enemy bombs of two foxes to a major disaster in March 1943 at Bethnal Green Underground station when 178 people were killed and 62 injured.

The civilians could, in fact, "take it." The Germans were to take even more later in the war. Looking back, the terrifying thing is that there is almost no limit to what human beings can take. On September 7 the Germans flew in 350 bombers and fighters in two great waves. They suffered losses which made it clear that day raids would cease. But they got through, fired the docks, and, guided by the flames, night bombers attacked London till dawn. 305 people were killed and 1337 seriously injured. On the night of September 18–19, 350 tons of bombs fell on London—more than the total weight of bombs dropped on the whole of Britain during World War I. From September 7 to December 31, 22,000 people were killed in Britain, 13,000 in London itself. For the whole war the total killed by air raids and rockets was 60,000—about 30,000 in London.

Before the German attack on Russia Hitler entered the Balkans. On April 17, 1941, the Yugoslav army capitulated. On April 27 German forces entered Athens. Rommel opened his offensive in the western desert of North Africa, where the British had been rounding up the Italians. On December 7 the Japanese attacked the United States at Pearl Harbor. Hitler grossly underestimated the American military potential and industrial strength. But for a time the German declaration of war on the United States provided a new area of operations for her U-boats off the American Atlantic coast and in the Caribbean. The shipping losses in 1942 and in the spring of 1943 were to tax the allies to the limit. The Japanese could not be held by the British in the Far East, and they threatened Australia and India, with the possibility of a move across the Indian Ocean into Madagascar. There were, however, fatal flaws in the German position. When the German armies were trapped by the Russian winter and the shadow of Napoleon's Moscow fate was in their minds, Hitler in December 1941 announced his personal assumption of command on the Russian front. He saved their morale that winter but he destroyed their future. Never afterward could his subordinates get a hearing for a policy which was against his intuition.

On March 11, 1941, an "Act to promote the Defense of the United States" became law. It became known as the "Lend Lease" Act. It permitted President Roosevelt to equip with arms—and any materials necessary—any country whose defense he deemed vital to the defense of the

United States. On April 11, 1941, the President issued a proclamation opening the Gulf of Aden and the Red Sea to American shipping. War material could be sent directly to the British forces in the Middle East. On April 25 the President announced that measures would be taken to protect American shipping carrying goods across the Atlantic on British account by extending patrols deep into the Atlantic. In August Roosevelt and Churchill met at sea and drew up a joint declaration, the Atlantic Charter. In it they jointly expressed the hope that after the destruction of Nazi tyranny there would be a peace in which men might live out their lives in freedom from fear and freedom from want. The Charter was, if nothing else, a counter to the program of the Nazi New Order. In that order the world was to be divided into six "continental blocs"—Europe and Africa under the leadership of Germany and Italy, the Far East under Japan, Russia, North America, South America, and what would be left of the British Empire after the defeat of England.

In 1943 the course of the war turned against Germany. In October 1942 the Eighth Army had attacked at El Alamein—Montgomery won a great victory over Rommel. In November American and British forces which had sailed in separate convoys from the United States and Britain landed on both the Atlantic and Mediterranean coasts of French North Africa. Allied forces in July 1943 landed in Sicily. The Germans were by December 1943 clearly in final retreat in Russia. The battle of the Atlantic had been won. In June 1944 Anglo-American forces landed in Normandy and by September had liberated Paris and Brussels and reached the German frontier.

The final victory was made possible by a combination of all the different forms of attack which could be brought to bear against the enemy by sea, land, and air. Every aspect of the war was changed by the influence of science—an influence which has changed our world and may change the solar system itself. On the sea the development of radar in great secrecy in Britain turned the tide against the submarine, because it became possible to detect a submarine on the surface at night and in poor visibility by day. The day of large battleships passed, and the aircraft carrier became decisive. On land the technique of the German Blitzkrieg, in part the suggestion of British writers like Liddell Hart and J. F. C. Fuller, made the war of 1939–45 as remarkable for swift strokes as the first had been for sluggishness. Motor transport made desert warfare of a new kind possible. For two and one-half years, from the Nile delta to Tunis near the site of ancient Carthage, a new kind of warfare which was speedy and fluid was developed. It has been compared to sea warfare in its independence of fixed defenses, its rapid maneuvers, and its decisions by superiority in gun powder and armor. The stretches of desert impassable to armored vehicles were the shoals and rocks of sea navigation. Long-range desert patrols were like the raids of submarines at sea. The technical balance changed more than once. At El Alamein the appearance of American Sherman tanks in large numbers turned the scale. The American jeep replaced the army mule. In the air, in less than forty-five years, air power developed from nothing to a stage more destructive in its effect than any other weapon designed by man. Armies are confined to the land and have only certain channels of advance. Navies are confined to the sea and are intrinsically limited to certain objectives. The air forces are confined neither to the land nor to the sea and a change in their objective can be brought about almost as swift as thought.

The new techniques do not mean that the art of war is adequately developed. There were basic misunderstandings and illusions in the British and American attitudes to the very heart and meaning of the conflict. At the beginning the British did not realize the basic facts of the German economy. German preparation for war and her initial victories made the blockade ineffective. To the end of 1942 it was believed that the German economy was strained to the utmost, that bombing would compel her to divert production from war production to civilian economy. In fact, it was the latter which was at last being reduced in order to increase war production. The great bombing attacks from March 1943 to March 1944 "did not produce direct results commensurate with the hopes once entertained . . . Huge areas in many towns all over Germany were severely stricken and some were devastated, but the will of the German people was not broken nor even significantly impaired, and the effect on war production was remarkably small." [3] The final bombing strategy was a combined effort of the British and United States air forces. The cooperation was close and continuous and a common strategy was worked out at the highest level.

There were more subtle and more serious differences. When in 1943 the German U-boats had been defeated, the German land advances against both the East and the West checked, and the reconquest of Europe made possible, the British wanted by an Italian campaign to pin the German strategic reserve south of the Alps and then to attack across the Channel. The Americans distrusted the Mediterranean. It was to them "a kind of dark hole, into which one entered at one's peril. If large forces were committed . . . the door would suddenly and firmly be shut behind one." When the invasion of Normandy did take place there was a difference between the British desire for a thrust on a narrow front to the Ruhr and the American conception of a general advance along the whole Western front. And even more disturbing was the preoccupation of the Americans with a nonexistent British imperialism and a blindness to the aims of Russian Communist imperialism. American dislike of Britain's past made them blind to Russia's future. "Their illusion on the subject of Russia lasted, as I know myself," wrote Lord Attlee, "right through the Potsdam conference and after. It was only the Berlin blockade which opened their eyes—too late." [4]

Reason and passion have never kept in step. It is clear to all that the application of scientific method to ever-widening spheres of human behavior is shrinking our world, but there is evidence that we are more deeply divided than ever before. Diversities cut more deeply than in the past, and there is a real danger that the more we are together the more divided we shall be. And if that is too pessimistic a view, it cannot be denied that the creation of political institutions to soothe our passions and harmonize our interests does not necessarily keep pace with the development of technologies which can serve as tools to our fears, our greeds, and our prejudices. In this context there is a particular interest in the fate of the British political system. In the two centuries before 1914 it had provided a hopeful lesson in the techniques by which change could be reconciled with stability and an increased control over nature by human skill be won without generating uncontrollable tensions in the social order. Even in the rushing muddy torrents of the early industrial revolutions, freedom did, in fact, broaden down from precedent to precedent. Economic change did not generate the increased social tension which makes revolutionary violence inevitable. British experience was a decisive refutation of Marxist theory. There was some hope, too, that the British insular experience might be significant for the world at large. The British classical liberal theory was implicitly universal. A parliament of man and a federation of the world might, it seemed, be made possible by the spread of an international division of labor which, by removing the fear of want, would widen the empire of reason. Life, being no longer poor, nasty, and short, could cease to be brutish and begin to be wise. And if it were too much to hope that the small British example could school the world, there was every hope that in the United States—that other Eden—the peace and plenty which make possible our loves would be so dazzlingly displayed that no political leaders could anywhere refuse allegiance to the political principles that had made such human happiness possible. The scientific method which had removed the fear of want was linked with a political method which would fulfill the hope of peace.

The course of World War II was to shatter all these illusions about the relation between the political, the economic, and the intellectual life of men. Indeed, one now fears that the insular security of the British and the wide open and abundant spaces of the New World—temporary factors both—had generated such illusions by temporarily removing the need for serious political thought. We have dreamed of peace and plenty, and we are now awake once more in a Machiavellian world.

A terrible dilemma must be stated at the very beginning if the part now taken by one of the smaller characters in the political drama—the British Isles—is to be understood. The dilemma is this: suppose that freedom is not implicit in the conditions by which men live; suppose, that is, that the order and the freedom of a Britain or of the United States are not latent everywhere in human society waiting merely for the lifting of some easily removable obstacle; suppose that they are the result of a unique conjunction of circumstances, that the merit was not in ourselves, and therefore in all men, but in our stars; suppose our virtues were due to fortune and not to necessity—then it has grimly to be considered what we must do when fortune turns. The British had assumed that where they had gone all would follow. The Americans could note with satisfaction that they had gone even further and that the way was now clear to all. But if the British are not followed, nor the American stream-lined model either, the British experience has the special value that it shows the problems which face a free people who have not the power to secure freedom for other people. What is the place of such a free people in an unfree world? What could Machiavelli have taught Athens? Since the defeat of Hitler and the rise of Russian imperialism, the problems of the British people have been: (1) the relative weakness of their economic and political power; (2) the very special impact of the post-1945 world on their affairs arising from the fact that in the past, British power was so very much a product of an international order of peace and trade (because the old British Empire was so much a matter of opinion and so little a matter of power, it has been more hardly hit than it would have been had it been dissolved by defeat in war and not by changes in ideas); (3) the far-reaching changes in her institutions and her way of life that the new conditions have imposed; (4) to understand what has been taking place and still more to try to make what has happened to her understood by others who may be involved.

Britain's relative weakness at the end of World War II and at the beginning of the atomic and stellar age is clear enough. In the nineteenth century the great powers had populations of the order of 30,000,000 to 40,000,000; today they have populations of the order of 100,000,000. Today, the United States has 6 per cent, the U.S.S.R. 7½ per cent, India

14 per cent, and China 22½ per cent of the population of the world. Their economic power and their political unity make it possible for the United States and the U.S.S.R. to keep the peace beneath the shadow of the bomb. Mr. Khrushchev put it with bearlike simplicity to Mr. Nixon in Moscow on July 24, 1959: "We are the two most powerful countries, and if we live in friendship, then other countries will have to live in friendship. But if there is a country which is too warlike, we could pull its ears a little and say: 'Don't you dare; fighting is not allowed now.' " [5]

It would be tedious to set out all the factors which prevent Britain from having the kind of power had by peoples who can match a population of 100,000,000 or more with political and administrative unity. In these matters, quality is a function of quantity. Only after a certain size is it possible to secure the efficiency of staff structure, the quality of equipment, and the economies in administration that modern fighting forces need. No doubt, were the 250,000,000 Europeans blessed with a single political and administrative structure, they could match the apparatus of modern war which the United States and the U.S.S.R. now have. But Europe is not politically united, and the most fearful present and the most dreadful future cannot undo all the past. European political unity would be as surprising as the resurrection of the Holy Roman Empire. There is, therefore, no European power able to afford the full apparatus of modern war.

The British people themselves cannot feed more than half their number from their own resources. Britain has practically no major industrial raw material except coal. She is indefensible against nuclear attack— a mere aircraft carrier grounded off the coast of Europe. Such facts are clear as day. Less obvious, but as vital for her way of life, is that the goods and services she enjoys have been got from an exceptional development of international trade. If she is to make any significant contribution to the keeping of the peace of the world, her economic life must be strong and sound. She cannot be even a little platoon in freedom's war unless she is a humming factory as well. And here again the factor of size is decisive. Her international trade is large. But her domestic trade is three times as large. The internal market of the United States is more than three times the size of the British. And the economic advantages of size are so great that in a single year (1950–51) the mere increase in output of the U.S.A. exceeded the *total* output of Britain. The economic advantages of size are more than equal to the arithmetic ratio of the larger to the smaller population.

Britain is unavoidably a small power. What, then, is her position in the world? Before giving a bare outline of her fortunes since 1945, two misconceptions must be removed. Britain is not an imperial power, and she is only geographically a part of Europe.

In November 1942 Mr. Churchill said that he had not taken office in order to preside over the liquidation of the British Empire. But then Mr. Churchill—as Walter Lippmann said in 1957—was so big that he made the British power look bigger than it was. But no number of Churchills could have kept Britain an imperial power. It is one of the tragicomedies of history that President Roosevelt regarded Russia as relatively free and the Chinese as wholly free from the British taint of imperialism. But if Roosevelt and the American people did not understand the position, neither did the British people themselves. The American people did not understand imperialism. They thought it was a bad thing. But, having almost an empty continent to themselves, they did not have to face the problems arising when traders and settlers overseas have to be supervised or protected because there is no effective political power where they are, and the home government cannot move their frontiers to a plan that providence or fortune inspires. The British people had acquired an empire as a by-product of trade and commerce, but, given their constitution, it was impossible for them to organize the administrative and the warlike tools which imperialism—the deliberate and planned extension of a way of life and method of government to or, where necessary, over an alien people—requires. English democrats were always unwilling to finance the equivalent of Roman legions or Roman roads. Imperial power could not be representative, and a government which was not representative overseas would, they feared, soon cease to be so at home. And in any case, one cannot build Roman roads on sea lanes.

If the British people were not willing to become an imperial power, something had to take the place of the missing imperial power. The Empire has become a Commonwealth. That constellation in the political sky became visible to the whole world when the sun of British power had sunk. It set with tropical suddenness. The irony is that the preservation of the freedom of that Commonwealth is now an American responsibility, which self-interest or self-preservation may encourage her to meet.

The bare facts are not common knowledge. They amount to one of the most sudden transformations in the history of the world. In 1945 some 550,000,000 people were ruled from Britain. In addition, another 50,000,000 in Egypt and other Arab states were dependent in various ways. By 1959 over 500,000,000 of the 600,000,000 had become completely self-governing, either as voluntary members of the Commonwealth or as independent states. Of the remainder, over half were well on the way to self-government. All that will be left will be a difficult heritage of some East and Central African territories, a scatter of islands, and perhaps some oil sheikdoms of the Persian Gulf. If the passing of imperialism is not to mean the coming of anarchy, one has to assume that political talent and administrative skills are in latent supply awaiting only the call of necessity. In all parts of the world we must assume that the practices of barbarism and the customs of tyranny are mere dross which can be removed from the pure metal of communities taking the stamp of freedom. If the Saxons of early England could, as Maitland said, jump from primitive runes to the doctrine of the Trinity, natives everywhere can leave witch doctors for Jefferson or Mill or Marx. Perhaps the specter of colonialism loomed so large in the American mind because in World War I many great empires had been swept away but the British had remained; and in World War II the empire of Germany over Europe and the empire of Japan over two-thirds of China and much of Southeast Asia had flourished for two or three years and then their rack dissolved leaving not a wisp behind—while again only the British remained. But this time the British, too, was dissolved soon after. In place of the Empire there is the Commonwealth and a variety of dependent territories moving rapidly to Commonwealth status. The independence of former colonies has greatly enlarged the Commonwealth. It has been neatly said that "the members of the expanding Commonwealth, like the heavenly bodies, in growing seem to have grown apart." [6] However starry their future may be, there is no question of the existence of a new political system entering the international order as a unit in the way in which the United States, Soviet Russia, or Communist China are units.

The members of the Commonwealth have no common constitution. They have now no common adjective—for the term "British" has been dropped. There is, in fact, no political bond at all. In 1914 the King declared war on behalf of the whole British Empire; in 1939, on behalf of the United Kingdom, the Indian Empire, and the Colonies, but Canada, Australia, New Zealand, and South Africa declared war separately, while the Republic of Ireland was neutral throughout, greatly to the danger of the western approaches and the survival of the free world. In any future war the Queen would declare war only on behalf of the United Kingdom and the remaining colonies, if there were any. Some of the new countries in the Commonwealth would certainly declare their neutrality. The Queen is now head of the Commonwealth. But the Commonwealth of which she is the head includes three republics—India, Pakistan, and Ghana. Some others have declared their intention to become republics. Britain is one of the twelve members of which the Commonwealth is composed. Whatever the nature of the unity the twelve may be thought to have, it is not and can now never be that of single political power. It is neither British nor imperial. It has not even common aspirations. The members—other than Britain—have a relation with Britain which is conducted through the Commonwealth Relations office in London instead of through the British Foreign Office. That relation is closer between each of them and Britain than it is between each other.

Britain will find in her membership of the Commonwealth no conditions which could make her a great power in the American or Russian way. Nor will she find greatness by merging herself in a European unity. There has never been any sentiment in favor of Britain being a part of a politically united Europe. A European bloc, including Britain, with common political institutions which would make it a great power in the American and Russian sense is a Wellsian dream. Labour would not compromise the Socialist experiment made in Britain. Both Labour and Conservatives have seen, in the priority of obligations existing among members of the Commonwealth, basic obstacles to a European federation including Britain. The economic necessities of Britain may lead her to enter a European Common Market. The conflict between a European tariff and imperial preference may be resolved by an acceptable compromise. But no economic unity with Europe will be allowed to impair the political autonomy by which the British and their Dominions must live or die. In World War II, Britain's chief support came from extra-European sources. It was to Canada and to the United States and to other members of the Commonwealth that she looked for ultimate succor. It was with those powers that she built up the most intimate alliance the world has ever seen. "In the struggles which may lie ahead, I do not think that many of us would object to our forces and our fortunes being controlled by a joint staff headed by an American. But I think we should refuse absolutely to lose our identity and power of decision in a purely European combination." [7] In this matter of life and death, the telephone, the circulation of papers, and the know-how of administrative co-operation are the heart of the matter. The more terrifying the massing of potential power the more we know that the outcome will depend upon the nerve and know-how of the political leaders who control subtle administrative machines—the blend of "extreme personal integrity with a wearily expert knowledge of the way things get done." If Britain were to enter a European association on a permanent and deeply committed basis, more problems would remain than would be solved. A European military power would not be able to guard Britain's worldwide commercial interest. The large domestic market would have enormous advantages, as we know from American experience, but Western Europe has not all the raw materials which British manufacturing industries need. Politically, the role of belonging simultaneously to a federation of Western Europe and a commonwealth in the world would be baffling.

After 1945 Britain had to work out a new pattern of relations with other states in a world dominated by powers of a new order of magnitude. British freedom of action was reduced when the Germans and the Japanese began to lose the military initiative and the prospects of an allied victory grew more certain. The British Foreign Office was then at a disadvantage in many of the larger political issues because there was no Anglo-American political liaison corresponding to the organization on the military side. It is the fate of democracies to fight so singlemindedly when they are at war that they sacrifice even the future they fight for, and throw away what even an incompetent tyrant might preserve. It is a tragedy of history that democracies can win their wars, using, when necessary, every Machiavellian move that victory may require, yet they are incapable of using—to save themselves—the forces mobilized to win the war. As Germany moved to her military ruin, the conferences at Teheran, Yalta, and Potsdam merely registered the balance of power as in fact it then was. The Russians knew that the Western powers would give way to almost any extent rather than use force. They had their plans and they put them into effect. British or American acquiescence was irrelevant. The Russians were more hostile to Western parliamentary democracy than they were to National Socialism as a form of government. Roosevelt had more concern for the mote of colonialism in the British political outlook than he had for the beam of tyranny in the Russian world view. When the atom bomb was used on August 6, 1945, the British and American governments could have compelled the Russians to accept their terms. The bare statement of the possibility is enough to make us realize how unthinkable it was to use such power to save Central Europe. Even deeper than the incapacity of the democracies to use force, except in self-defense in open war, was the conviction on the part of the British and the United States governments that there was no hope for the world without the collaboration of Russia. Mr. Churchill put this view to Stalin on April 29, 1945: "There is not much comfort in looking into a future where you and the countries you dominate, plus the Communist Parties in many other States, are all drawn up on one side, and those who rally to the English-speaking nations and their associates or Dominions are on the other. It is quite obvious that their quarrel would tear the world to pieces and that all of us leading men on either side who had anything to do with that would be ashamed before history." [8] I doubt whether a naked Stalin would blush before Clio!

But if the British Foreign Office was anxious to secure collaboration with Russia so that the world should not "cleave and slain men solder up the rift," to the Russians the need and even the desirability of collaboration with the Western democracies lessened as the collapse of Germany became more obvious and more complete. The shameful treatment of Poland at, and after, Yalta (February 1945) foreshadowed the future cold war pattern of relationships between the Western powers and the Soviet Union. While the West maintained in principle the demand for Polish freedom and independence they knew what the Russians intended their puppet government to do.

The facts of political life could not be faced at once in their naked truth either in Britain or in the United States. In December 1946 Bevin was arguing that Britain's position in world affairs was an intermediary one between the United States and the U.S.S.R. When Churchill at Fulton, Missouri, on March 5, 1946, foreshadowed a "fraternal alliance" of the United States and Britain for the cold war in a dangerous world, his speech was sceptically received. But the economic facts and the perils of the free world could not long be ignored. In February 1947 the British government told the American government that it could no longer afford the cost of its commitments in Greece and on March 12 President Truman announced that the United States would take over this commitment as part of a policy of maintaining the security of the "free peoples of the world" against the threat of totalitarianism. George Marshall announced in June 1947 the European Recovery Program, which was to Western Europe a supreme example of American generosity and vision and to the Soviet Union a move in the cold war. The Soviet reacted by the creation in October of the Cominform (the Information Bureau of the Communist Workers' Parties), master of all dullness in propaganda techniques. But it was not yet realized in the United States that the containment of the Russian threat, begun as soon as Germany had dissolved in ruins, would involve a watch and guard of the whole periphery of the Soviet bloc from Norway round to Japan. Before the Czech coup of February 1948 Herbert Morrison had accused the Soviet government of aiming at "triumph through chaos," and Bevin had accused it of aiming to dominate Western as well as Eastern Europe. The statement of the aims of the vanguard of the proletarian world revolutionaries is of an appalling dullness, but it is easier to believe Russia's rulers mean what they say than it was to believe Hitler meant what he said.

However grim and clear the facts might be they could not remove immediately the differences between British and American opinion which had their roots in their very different histories. One of the terrors of

British leaders in the first year of World War II was that they might say anything which might be taken to imply that the United States had any special interest in the British stand against Hitler. At the end of the war it was dangerous to say anything that might imply that the "special relation" created by Churchill in his dealings with Roosevelt had not gone forever with the coming of peace. The United States does not appear among the allies or the commitments specially mentioned in formal statement of British policy on defense until 1950. If the Free World were not to be taken over bit by bit by the U.S.S.R. the British had to show that they could get on their feet after the exhaustion of war, and that, whatever appearances might suggest, they were not, in fact, an imperial power. They had to be good and let who would be clever. A poor relation living on immoral earnings and unable to put her house in order would get little help from the United States. Among the British themselves the radical and socialist traditions were opposed to any Churchillian capitalist power of the West. Nor, in fact, was the ordinary British citizen enamored of the tendency in the United States to see the Germans as their favorite Europeans or of the assumption that British pride and prejudice were the only barriers to a federation of Western Europe.

Between the end of the war in 1945 and the establishment of N.A.T.O. in 1949 a great change took place. Britain made a respectable economic recovery. It was accompanied by an almost strip-tease discarding of any shred of her once imperial power. The U.S.S.R. made it clear that, as they had once been encircled by capitalist powers, it would be their business to see that the United States be encircled by Communist powers in the future.

In August 1945 President Truman terminated Lend Lease. To Britain this sudden termination was, in the words of Lord Keynes, "a financial Dunkirk." Some replacement was essential. It was found in December 1945 in a negotiated loan of $3,750,000,000 from the United States and $1,250,000,000 from Canada. The terms were hard, but in the circumstances they could not be refused. 1946 and 1948 were years of impending economic disaster for Britain, disaster which was only avoided by great administrative skill. Peace had to have her victories no less renowned than those of war. In 1945 there were 5,000,000 men under arms in all parts of the world and 4,000,000 civilians were at work on production and other tasks to support them. By the end of 1946 the armed forces were a little below 1,500,000 and in 1948 below 1,000,000. The supporting civilian numbers had been reduced to 500,000. Economic reconstruction had to be carried out while meeting unavoidable responsibilities overseas. Many of the latter were the result of the war itself.

The British had been responsible for the liberation of Libya and Greece. British troops had received the Japanese surrender in Indo-China and Indonesia. In 1946 many Frenchmen believed that the British only wanted to take their place as the dominant power in the Levant. In Southeast Asia and in North Africa the British could not give the French the unconditional support they wanted because to do so would have alienated opinion in many new countries, including members of the Commonwealth. In Palestine the American support for Jewish immigration and the British obligations to the Arabs were in clear conflict.

Within this tangled web one simplification could be made. The British Empire in India could and must be dissolved. In the closing years of the wars there had been a conference at Simla to plan the future course of British relations in India. Jinnah, the leader of the Moslem League, insisted that there should be two separate independent states when the British went. When a deadlock had been reached at the end of 1946, the Labour government announced in February 1947 its intention to transfer power to the Indians by June 1948. The new viceroy, Lord Mountbatten, was certain that would be too late and that there was no practical alternative to a rapid withdrawal. The British government agreed and on August 15, 1947, India and Pakistan became two independent states. Many problems were left unsolved—Moslem-Hindu fanaticism in areas where they were intermingled, the fate of the princely states of Hyderabad and Kashmir, the division of the waters of the Indus. But the decision was unavoidable and the result, in spite of bloodshed and terror for many, a hope for the future. It confirmed without any shadow of doubt the sincerity of the British claim—made far back in her imperial history—that her colonial rule could only be justified by its success in preparing the way for political self-government. When India, Pakistan, and Ceylon had become independent states a new Commonwealth was born. Complete independence would be the right of all British colonies the moment that, in terms of size, economic viability, and other relevant factors, such as the possibility of a workable administrative machinery, it was practicable. On all the frontiers of British influence, self-government was the goal. The independence of India and Pakistan made it easier for Ghana and Nigeria to follow. And so since 1947 has been seen "one of the most sudden and momentous transformations in the history of the world": [9] India and Pakistan, 1947; Ceylon, 1948; the Central African federation, 1953; Ghana and Malaya, 1957; Nigeria, 1960; Sierra Leone, 1961; and the West Indies as soon as that pattern of islands has worked out a constitution.

The policy of the British Isles in the new postwar world was outlined in a statement on defense in 1948: "The fulfillment of the main object of the United Nations—the maintenance of world peace—depends on the ability and readiness of the Great Powers to keep the peace. The United Kingdom, as a member of the British Commonwealth and a Great Power, must be prepared at all times to fulfill her responsibilities not only to the United Nations but also to herself. For this purpose, the first essential is a strong and sound economy, with a flourishing industry from which to draw the strength to defend our rights and to fulfill our obligations." It was recognized in 1949 that the "establishment of collective security on a world-wide basis under the United Nations had not been achieved," and it was noted that research and development, which "for the most part must remain secret," were being devoted "to the production of unconventional weapons." This was a clear hint that Britain would have the atomic bomb. In April 1949 the Western powers signed the North Atlantic Treaty. It had been in existence before it appeared on paper. The Soviet blockade of Berlin, begun in June 1948, had been broken in May 1949 by a massive airborne operation. N.A.T.O. was to consist of the fifteen powers, mutually acceptable to each other, which were able and willing to come together for common defense against a potential aggressor. It was the first alliance in history from which it was impossible for any power to contract out of its obligations should the test of war come. The physical intermingling of its integrated headquarters (S.H.A.P.E.) was carried so far that an attack on any one power would, in fact, be an attack on all.[10]

The immediate effect of N.A.T.O. was to restore the confidence of the Western European peoples. The potential aggressor had been clearly recognized. But the cold war had not yet revealed its global scale. The Far East, the Middle East, Africa, and Latin America were not yet fully engaged. That Russia would make mischief by all means short of war had not been fully realized. Where free peoples had their own democratic constitutions and the necessary administrative tools they were immune from the Communist attack, but only a part of the free world had such constitutions and into all other parts the Communist powers would try to penetrate.

In September 1949 the Soviet Union stated it had the atomic bomb. In August 1948 the "Partisans of Peace" had been set up as a Communist propaganda instrument to frustrate the growing unity of the West and in April 1949 they held a world Congress in Paris and in March 1950 they launched a "Peace Appeal" from Stockholm. So, with the atom bomb to scare the West and a "Peace Appeal" to lure or lull Asia and Africa, the Russians had developed the propaganda technique of Nazi

Germany. All through the bombing of London in the winter of 1940–41 one could listen to Goebbels' special peace program, which had the signature tune "Rock of Ages" and a woman announcer who cooed: "Do we women of Germany and of England really want war?" The essence of such propaganda technique is to make a careful study of the divisions open or latent in your opponents' ranks and then to try to pry them apart by a ceaseless repetition of emotionally loaded phrases or facts. The big lie must be spread by the use of small truths. There are plenty of small truths about the different nations of the free world which it may be a pleasure for some of them to hear about the others, but which serve, in fact, only the evil which their common enemy intends them.

In this climate of lies and threats the Western allies kept their heads. For the technique is dangerous only when it is not understood. But there were many lines of fracture the Soviet could hope to exploit. The fear of Soviet aggression was now greater than fear of German aggression had ever been—for, after all, Hitler had neither the ideas nor the tools for the job of world power—but it was not always palatable to the British people that the German past should so soon pass into oblivion. In February 1950 General MacArthur was authorized to allow Japan to take part in international conferences. Having lost their historic China, the United States had adopted Japan. But Japan and Germany were Britain's most formidable economic competitors. When in June 1950 the Korean War broke out and in December 1950 it was feared that the United States might attack the Chinese mainland with atomic weapons, Clement Attlee flew to Washington to dissuade Truman from such a move.

Early in 1951 the British government stated that there was "an urgent need to strengthen the defenses of the free world." It began a program which was the biggest the British could undertake without going to a war economy. Substantial aid was given by the United States and Canada. In 1953 the Communists were named for the first time in official British statements on defense as the potential enemy. In the British view her defense problem had two parts: her obligations and commitments in resisting "the Communist campaign known as the cold war"; the preparations which Britain must take together with her Commonwealth partners and allies against "the risk the Communist policy—whether by accident or design—might force her . . . to defend herself against a direct attack."

By 1953 Stalin was dead, the Korean War ended, and both the United States and the Soviet in the spring of 1954 exploded hydrogen bombs. The British government formally stated that it was convinced that "the long-term aims of world Communism" appeared to be unaltered. It was clear that one of the principal Soviet aims was to weaken the strength and cohesion of the Atlantic alliance. The British government noted the advantages which world Communism had in a cold war. It gave an explicit account of the theory of deterrence—"the primary deterrent remains the atomic bomb. . . . We intend as soon as possible to build up in the Royal Air Force a force of modern bombers capable of using the atomic weapon to the fullest effect." In 1955 it said that it would produce the hydrogen bomb and noted that the dangers of infiltration and subversion had increased. In 1956 it said that the relaxation of political tension was illusory and that the Communists still believe in their ultimate triumph. Although in 1957 it was clearly stated by the British government that there was no means of providing adequate protection for the people of the United Kingdom against the consequences of an attack by nuclear weapons, yet it decided that only by the possession of her own nuclear deterrent could peace be preserved. In 1958 it was stated that if the U.S.S.R. were to launch an attack, even with conventional weapons only, the Western allies "would have to hit back with strategic nuclear weapons."

The case for Britain retaining her own was: the experience of the Bomber command in World War II gave promise that the British could make good use of any bombs they might have; the United States might not be willing to use atomic weapons unless she were directly subject to nuclear attack; there might be interests vital to Britain for which she would be prepared to strike though her allies were not. More generally, if Britain were to renounce atomic weapons and the U.S.A. and the U.S.S.R. did not, Britain would have weakened her standing. If the U.S.A. and the U.S.S.R. did renounce them, British security would be reduced, for with 200 Soviet divisions facing the West and with about 30,000 Soviet aircraft and a Soviet fleet including 500 submarines, only so long as there was a nuclear deterrent would peace be preserved. Safety, as Churchill had said as early as 1955, was "the sturdy child of terror." But, although the balance of terror between the two great super powers of the United States and the U.S.S.R. with their hydrogen bombs might prevent a direct conflict, the cold war may continue indefinitely, and in the cold war the intricacies of power and influence are too bewildering and dangerous for Britain to forgo her own strategic nuclear deterrent. In 1961 that deterrent is the V-bomber force equipped with British free-falling nuclear bombs. "The force," says the last British report on defense, laconically enough, "has the capacity and efficiency to penetrate to its assigned targets." David has retained his sling.

There is, of course, a very "delicate balance of terror." It may be possible in the near future that any city in the world could be instantly destroyed from any other place in the world—on or under water or on or above ground. But peace would not be more secure if there were a standing army of a hundred divisions to face whatever hundreds the Russians or the Chinese could mobilize. A war of all against all has, in fact, been prevented by the setting-up of the Leviathan of immediate annihilation—the nuclear bomb.

By 1954 the problems of the cold war were becoming worldwide. The United States wanted German troops for the defense of Europe. But while the United States had a vision of the unity of Europe, the British were not thinking of a Europe with supernational institutions. The British contribution to the Council of Europe, by a series of conferences in 1947–48, was lukewarm. The creation of the six-power European Coal and Steel community in 1951, and of the European Economic Community (the Common Market), while they had contributed a great deal to the recovery of Europe, had contributed little to its defense. In 1954 S.E.A.T.O. and in 1955 the Bagdad Pact involved the Middle East and the entire periphery of the Soviet bloc (except the Indian subcontinent) in the cold war. S.E.A.T.O. seemed to be the only way to stem the tide of Communism in Southeast Asia after the collapse of the French position in Indo-China in 1954. Early in 1955 the Americans signed a Mutual Defence Treaty with the Chinese government on Formosa. In October 1955 the Soviet Union made a general offer of economic aid to the Middle East and early in 1956 a specific offer to Egypt of Soviet aid for an atomic power station.

Most of the peoples of the Middle East, particularly the Arabs, were unconscious of any threat from the Soviet. They were more concerned about the latent power of Palestine and the imperial interests of the West. The Soviet government seemed to assume that President Nasser could be made into a dependable satellite by the supply of arms, economic aims, and technicians. It hoped to use its standard technique of getting the maximum propaganda advantage from a minimum of actual contribution. As the British had agreed to withdraw their force from the Canal Zone in 1954, the way was open for Nasser to organize, with Russian help, the forces of Egypt, Jordan, and Syria for an attack on Israel. The latter struck first. In this situation Great Britain and France decided to intervene. The Suez crisis of 1956–57 precipitated a bitter and hysterical debate. It was made clear to the British and the French that they had not the material strength to carry through a policy of armed intervention to which the United States was opposed. British opinion was dangerously divided and below the surface an agonizing reappraisal of British power in the world was made. If there was any comfort to be drawn from the tragedy it was that a war between small powers could fairly easily be stopped. The Hungarian crisis had shown that the United States was not prepared to go to war with the Soviet Union to liberate Hungary. That wars between great powers were not likely and that wars between small ones could be stopped was the verdict of some experts.

But the problems of the cold war remained. Both Britain and the United States had an interest in the stability, prosperity, peace, and independence of the states of the Middle East. But their commitments were different. In the Palestine War of 1948–49 the Jews and Arabs had used American and British weapons against each other. To the United States the Middle East was a vital link in a global chain of defense round the Soviet periphery. It was also a land mass to cut off the Soviet Union from Africa which, in enemy hands, could outflank the defenses of the United States. For Britain, the Middle East had once been vital for the control of their route to India. But with India independent, the British had no need of a major base in the Middle East to support an Indian army. The Suez zone could be given up and Cyprus could provide all that she would need to meet any disturbance within the area of her responsibilities. The British were interested in the defense of trade. The United States was interested in the worldwide defense against the threat of Communist aggression.[11] But both Britain and the United States had a common problem: they were in the invidious position of wishing to defend countries which did not wish to be defended from dangers the existence of which their governments denied in public. Similar differences may arise in Africa. Strategically, the loss of that continent to the Soviet Union could be a disaster to the United States; economically it is an important and largely untapped source of minerals in which the American continent is becoming progressively less self-sufficient.[12] But politically both the sources of order and also of disorder are in that colonialism which in American political folklore is almost the original sin.

The Commonwealth, we have seen, is not the British Empire under another name. Its members cannot form a united political unity. But its members may derive from their memberships a sense of some security of status in a disordered and dangerous world. Their sense of security may help to mitigate that passion of nationalism which is shattering so much of the world order we have. The principle of self-determination unchecked could be as destructive as nuclear fission. It is a paradox of our time that the economically most backward countries are most determined to secure that national sovereignty which the largest are considering how they can best resign. At least all members of the Commonwealth find that it offers an alternative both to standing completely alone in a harsh and dangerous world or to being absorbed into some larger unit of sovereignty. But although most members of the Commonwealth began their independence with systems of government closely related to the British parliamentary form, most of them have departed from the British form, nor is there any reason to suppose that they will renew its spirit. It is possible that as the political links weaken the economic links will grow stronger—that the life of international trade will flourish when colonial frustrations have vanished. There are more businessmen in India than there were before independence. Britain is still the best customer of most members of the Commonwealth, and the system of imperial preferences and the practice of the sterling area have something of the flexibility of these political understandings which are the life of a single state. Even imperial preference has been whittled away, and the sterling area is not exclusive to the Commonwealth: some nonmembers belong, Canada does not, South Africa is half in and half out. Some of the newest members of the Commonwealth are those most likely to question its advantages.[13] It has not been the object of British policy since 1945 to make either the sterling area or the Commonwealth a closed and exclusive economic association. Economically, "the Commonwealth is an intricate system of reciprocal relations and mutual benefits within a larger worldwide system. It functions as such and for just so long as its members find advantage in it." [14] As an English philosopher, T. H. Green, said of the nature of human society: "It is made possible by a reciprocal recognition of identity and difference."

The Commonwealth has certainly no common system of defense. Gibraltar, Malta, and Cyprus belong to a defense system for purely British responsibilities. No future war would be fought by the Commonwealth as a single defense unit. No member of the Commonwealth is likely to go to war with another, and that is more than can be said of members of the United Nations.[15] In the world as it is and as it will be for some time to come, the United States is in a position to protect New Zealand, Australia, and Pakistan far better than Britain could. There are two kinds of Commonwealth members: those of British and European descent—Canada, Australia, and South Africa—and others such as India, Pakistan, Malaya, Ceylon, and Ghana, where the British have never been more than a small educated class. There is no question, therefore, of the diffusion of a common English culture. The English language is, of course, an international medium of communication, but it is neither

exclusive to the Commonwealth nor universal within it. There is, however, the vital political fact that the members of the Commonwealth do
two things in common: they meet in periodic conferences of either prime
ministers or ministers of finance, and in them no interpreters are necessary; they exchange state papers—that is to say, the Commonwealth
statesmen are part of the inner administrative club on which the future
of the free world depends.

CHAPTER XIX

The Price of Victory
and the Cost of Welfare

The British war effort against Hitler in 1939–45 was out of all proportion to her economic strength. Before the war it would not have been thought possible. In six years of fighting the British used the equivalent of three years of their total production. The expenditure by public authorities on goods and services rose from one-fifth of the national income to about three-fifths. For more than five years nearly every man and woman under fifty without young children was subject to direction to work, often far from home. The call up of women would have impressed ancient Sparta, and Hitler's failure to do the same was one of his gross miscalculations. The severest taxation in the world was linked with a continuous pressure to save. Food and clothing were rigorously but fairly rationed. There had developed "an implied contract between government and people; the people refused none of the sacrifices that government demanded from them for the winning of the war; in return they expected that the government would show imagination and seriousness in preparing for the restoration and improvement of the nation's well being when the war had been won." In that implied contract was one of the roots of the future welfare state.

There were dangers for the future in that implied contract. The victories of peace may need efforts which, though not so bloody, require more brain and effort than those of war. The war effort involved a "financial imprudence without parallel in history." To avoid the complete destruction Hitler had planned for them, the British jeopardized their economic survival as a nation. Bread which is cast into the torrents of war is seldom returned on the waters of peace. The British sacrificed the export trade which in time of peace they would need to provide their food and work. For 50,000,000 people living in an area one-third the size of Texas and specialized in their industries to serve the markets of a world which the war had transformed, the recovery of their export trade was a matter of life and death.

It was necessary to adapt the British economy and British way of life to rapid technological changes, to alarming manifestations of political power, and to the play of ideological passions never before known in the history of the world. A British Machiavelli—had there been one —could not have guessed at half the problems fortune would bring to his island home.

The change from war to peace was managed with commendable skill. The mistakes made at the end of World War I were avoided. During the struggle the problems of the coming peace had been coolly examined. As early as the end of 1940, when Hitler was planning Europe's next thousand years, a minister had been appointed to "plan in advance," as Churchill put it, "a number of practical steps which it is indispensable to take if our society is to move forward." In 1943 Lord Woolton as minister of Reconstruction made a tentative survey of things to come when the peace should be won. The problem of demobilization was neatly solved. In 1918 demobilization plans based on the need for a man's skill and not on the time he had served in the forces had collapsed in the face of mutinous resistance. In 1945 demobilization was based on age and length of service. By the end of 1946 over 4,250,000 men and women had been released from the forces, and the number engaged in making munitions was proportionately reduced. The nation's manpower in the forces, or supplying them, fell from 42 per cent to less than 10 per cent. Plans were also made for an orderly disposal of surplus stocks.

The dispersal of victorious armies, navies, and air forces is one thing; to find the rhythm, the pace, and the thoughts for a new and ever-changing world is quite another. With her capital depleted and her productive powers impaired Britain had to meet, in the first years of peace, needs which were in fact greater than she had met before the war. The material damage to be made good was not slight. Nearly half a million houses had been completely destroyed or made uninhabitable by bombs. The damage done to homes, factories, railways, and docks, and to the British prewar merchant fleet, three-fifths of which had been sunk, was about £2,600,000,000 at 1950 prices. The British merchant marine had fallen from 17,400,000 gross tons in 1939 to 13,400,000 gross tons in 1945. Her industrial plant had been run down because for six years of war proper maintenance could be given only to industries of immediate military importance. The loss there was of the order of £1,200,-

000,000. Exports had had to be cut to less than a third of the prewar volume, and essential supplies during the war had had to be paid for by the sale of property owned abroad by British citizens and British business firms. A billion pounds had been raised in this way. But this had not been enough, and goods had been got on credit, with the result that the sterling balances held by foreign countries in London had increased by about £3,000,000,000. All this was in addition to the help given by American Lend Lease. The over-all position was a deterioration in Britain's external capital position of about £4,800,000,000. The day to day needs of the British people, too, were pressing. In six years of war they had received less than three years' supply of household goods. The food supplied in war had been only enough to keep them fit to fight.[1]

An expansion of British output was essential. But expansion takes time. Some additional resources for current use beyond what the British could themselves produce were wanted at once. By August 1945 it was clear that unless substantial new aid were secured from the United States to fill the gap left by the ending of Lend Lease the country would be "virtually bankrupt and the economic basis for the hopes of the public nonexistent."

The British, as mentioned earlier, got immediate help by borrowing $3,750,000,000 from the United States and $1,250,000,000 from Canada. From 1948 to 1950 there were further grants and loans from the United States under Marshall aid. The effect of the generous and timely assistance of the United States to Britain under the European Recovery program brought an immediate improvement in a hard if not dangerous condition. In the first two postwar years food shortages had led to the rationing, for the first time, of bread and potatoes. In the severe winter of 1946–47 coal stocks dropped so low that electric power stations had to close or reduce their generating hours, and factories producing goods for export had to stop work or work part-time. In February 1947 there were 1,800,000 temporarily unemployed in Britain. By 1948 there was a small favorable balance of trade. The wartime rationing of clothing and textiles was ended in March 1949. The American economic transfusion was bringing the patient round. British industrial production was rising. In the first half of 1950 it was the highest ever before recorded. Britain was at last living within her means and able to set aside part of her income to replace some of the capital losses she had suffered during the war. She undertook a capital investment program of more than one-fifth of her national production. In the first half of 1950 the volume of her exports was nearly half as much again as before the war. By 1951 the immediate task of postwar recovery had been accomplished. The British government agreed to the suspension of Marshall aid from January 1, 1951.

With the wisdom of hindsight we can now see that in the immediate postwar years the representatives of the United States and Great Britain failed to build the world economic system for which they hoped. The United States believed that the economic problems of the time could be met by drafting detailed codes of basic principles. It was hoped that a postwar economic order could be created which would be universal in principle and with no clutter of alliances or special arrangements between the individual members of a world community. This assumed that economic policy could be made in a political vacuum and that world peace could be woven by co-operation in the economic field. These American principles have been called legalism, universalism, and economism.[2] They were the shadows cast by English liberal thought of the *Pax Britannica* across the vast and fertile spaces of the New World. The British, for their part, were troubled by the American desire to draw a misleading distinction between the economic nationalism which they would tolerate (it was the father of their own prosperity) and economic imperialism which was the unclean spirit they must exorcise. The United States was exasperated by the British tendency to be obsessed with the troubles of the past. Keynes himself was inclined to think more about the risks of unemployment than about the dangers of inflation. The British, too, failed to show a real awareness of the precise and strictly defined conditions concerning the ending of Lend Lease as they were to apply (and in fact were applied) at the end of the war. While the Loan Agreement of 1946 gave Britain the essential assistance she needed, the convertibility of sterling which it prescribed was doomed to failure. The shock of this failure brought about the collapse of all the economic plans of Britain and the United States for a worldwide order. It saw, too, the end of the special relationship between Britain and the United States. The generous and successful offer of Marshall aid was made to Europe as a whole and not to Britain alone. In face of the threat of economic collapse in Western Europe and of Soviet political infiltration, the United States moved away from an excessive reliance either on universalism or on Britain alone toward regional arrangements.

When Britain had been helped to her feet she had to decide where she must go. This was not easy precisely because her economic life had been so closely interwoven with the pattern of the prewar economic order of the world. The universalism of economic co-operation was sound economic theory to the United States, but to the British it was a way of

life. Ever since 1846 Britain's commercial policy had been one of un-
qualified free trade. Her economic structure had grown in that climate
and was adapted to it. Even in 1960 more than one British worker in
three in manufacturing industry was producing against orders abroad, and
four shillings out of every pound was spent by consumers on imported
goods and services. In the growth of her economic life Britain's assets
had been her coal deposits, her skilled workers, managerial experience,
financial institution experience and resources, ocean transport, and worldwide markets. But for more than half a century her manpower and resources had been moving into the types of industry made possible and
necessary by the new sources of energy—electricity, the gasoline engine,
and atomic power—and the penetration into every fiber of industrial
production of the magic touch of scientific thought.

There is an almost Miltonic quality about the transformations in industrial activity that the scientific spirit has brought about. Our "spirits
reprobate" can "in an hour what in an age" the past

> With incessant toil
> and hands innumerable scarce perform.

More than a quarter of the goods produced in Europe today and an
even higher proportion in the United States either did not exist fifty
years ago or were only in an experimental stage. The structure and the
processes of industry are becoming as subtle, unstable, and protean as
the mind of man itself. In the use of new materials, the use of new
sources of power, and in devising new processes Britain has played an
important part. She was the first to discover how to make artificial silk
and synthetic fibers, the first to have a whole chain of radar stations, and
the first to have a fully electronic television service at work. The jet engine was developed by an officer in the Royal Air Force. In the international triumphs of nuclear physics the work of Rutherford, Chadwick,
and Cockcroft was of the first importance. British scientists were throughout the war by and large more effective than those of any other country.
During the period of stringency after 1945 the Labour government took
the courageous decision to develop atomic energy independently of the
United States (the McMahon law, 1946, had forced their hand). It
decided also to build a major oil refinery in England in order to be less
dependent on the Persian Gulf or on dollar imports.

The British manufacturing industry had grown during the war and
continued to grow after the war. The volume of production in manufactured goods was 43 per cent greater in 1957 than in 1948. Since 1945
world markets have grown very fast. The increased demand has been

for goods which Britain was well able to supply. The trade in manufactured goods has expanded with great rapidity. In 1938 the value of
world trade in manufactures was little more than it had been in 1913. By
1950 it was already some 50 per cent higher, and it continued to rise by
nearly 7 per cent per annum till 1957. But while technical progress has
continued to be rapid and industrial capacity has greatly expanded, Britain has found trading conditions difficult. Her exports increased between 1858 and 1960 only half as much as Germany's or Sweden's and
less than a third as much as Italy's, France's, or Japan's. Since 1953 her
production has risen less than half as much as has that of continental
Europe. Her export prices have risen more than theirs. It has been said
that Britain's economic life has been falling behind in vigor, ingenuity,
industry, and imagination. Only the future will show what is really alive
and what has really died in the British industrial tradition. But some of
the general causes of her precarious position can be explained. There are
at least four subjects to be considered: the adjustment of her staple industries—the bases of her nineteenth-century power—to the changing
world, the promise of her new industrial inventions and activities, her
financial standing in that world, and the economic policies of her governments.

Although since 1945 the whole balance of industrial power has shifted
and the interrelationships between individual trades have been revolutionized, the basic industries of Britain have prospered. 207,000,000
tons of coal were mined in 1959 compared with 227,000,000 in 1938,
when the alternative energies of oil had not matured. The industry employed 699,000 men in 1958 compared with 782,000 in 1938. The industry had all of the considerable problems of policy which have to be faced
in a period of rapid technological change. Before the 1914 war Britain
sold about a third of her output of coal abroad. In 1955 she imported as
much as she exported. During the 1939–45 war coal exports virtually
ceased. By 1942 the coal problem was one of deficiency. Efforts to overcome the shortage by redirecting former miners into the pits, by fuel economy campaigns, and by the development of open-cast mining were only
partly successful. A committee of mining engineers (the Reid Committee),
appointed in 1944, reported on the failure of the coal industry to undertake any major technical improvements or to concentrate its operations.
In 1928 one worker was employed for every five tons of saleable coal
mined in Britain; in the United States one for every fifty tons. The mines
were undermechanized. The National Coal Board, formed in 1947 when
the mines were nationalized, has secured great improvements. Output per
man shift became the highest in Europe. Production of deep-mined

Industrial Employment

NATURAL RESOURCES

COAL

IRON ORE

WORKERS IN INDUSTRY

- 400,000
- 200,000
- 100,000
- 50,000
- 25,000
- 10,000

Clydeside

NORTHERN IRELAND

Tyneside

Tees-side

West Riding

Merseyside

Potteries

West Midlands

South Wales

East Anglia

Home Counties

N

Miles
0   20   40   60

From BRITAIN: THE OFFICIAL HANDBOOK (1962 edition), by permission of the Controller of H. M. Stationery Office.

coal rose from 175,000,000 tons in 1945 to 202,000,000 tons in 1958 when, in addition, 14,000,000 tons of open-cast coal were mined.

Britain may cease to be a coal-exporting country, but for a generation to come coal must be the source of the greater part of the power and heat which she requires. The breakdown of fuel supplies during the severe winter of 1947 was a dramatic proof of the dependence of the British economy on coal. Nationalization was the inevitable outcome of the history of the industry before 1939. But nationalization does not remove the basic problems. Coal is only one source of energy, and it must compete with oil, water power, natural gas, and, in the future, with nuclear energy. Before 1914 Britain was completely self-sufficient in her fuel supplies, and she was a net exporter up to 1939. From 1939 to 1957 there was an almost continuous shortage of all kinds of fuel. The rationing of coal to domestic consumers only ended in 1958. But the British coal industry is today still the largest industrial employer in the country and supplies some 85 per cent of the country's energy requirements. It is not easy to estimate the supply and demand for energy. A plan of 1950 looked forward to a production in 1961 of 240,000,000 tons a year of deep-mined coal, of which 25,000,000 to 35,000,000 would be for export; another plan in 1955 put the output in 1965 at only 230,000,000 tons and calculated that all of it would be needed at home. From 1956 to 1959 there was a small decline in the total consumption of energy in all forms, and a decline in the consumption of coal of the order of 27,000,000 tons. This meant that at the end of 1959 there was a surplus of 30,000,000 tons in stock over the 20,000,000 tons needed for normal needs. Underlying these planning vagaries is the basic problem of the demand for and the supply of energy. In 1913 the consumption of primary energy was coal, 189,000,000 tons; oil, 2,000,000; in 1959 coal, 197,000,000; oil, 56,000,000; and nuclear energy, 2,000,000. Where energy is concerned it is not easy to see into the seeds of time.

The output of steel rose 55 per cent from 1938 to 20,000,000 tons in 1959. During the 1930's the competitive position of the iron and steel industry was weak, and certain branches were threatened with extinction. But in 1945 a period of great activity began, and the industry has been able to produce steel at prices lower than those of any other country. In engineering a continued scarcity of labor encouraged technical innovation and labor-saving methods and the output of engineering goods by 1957 was in volume nearly twice that of 1938. In 1955–56 engineering goods accounted for about 40 per cent of the total exports of the United Kingdom as against 22 per cent of the total in 1937–38. In 1953–54 the motor industry was the main contributor to the expansion;

in 1954–55 it was the machinery trade. Before 1939 the United States supplied the bulk of motor vehicles in international trade, while the United Kingdom led in motor cycles. During World War II the manufacture of private cars in Britain almost ceased because the industry was making munitions. After the war the home market for cars was limited by administrative action, and the motor industry became one of the main factors in the export drive. One of the outstanding British developments was the production of tractors, especially those for agricultural use. By 1956, 109,000 tractors a year were being produced (of which 92,000 were exported) as compared with a bare 12,000 a year in 1935–38.

The tonnage of shipping launched in 1954–58 was one-third more than in the corresponding period before 1939. Between 1952 and 1959 one-half the gross tonnage launched in Britain took the form of oil tankers. During 1939–45 British shipyards had had to concentrate on flexibility to meet the demand for various types of ships, while the United States provided the immense quantity of standard ships needed (a job which Britain had done in 1914–18 to meet the submarine menace of that war period). By 1949 the United Kingdom was building over 45 per cent of the world tonnage under construction. For several years Germany and Japan were out of production. If the British proportion of total tonnage launched fell from over 40 per cent in 1949 to 27 per cent in 1954 and 15 per cent in 1959, it was the result of the inability of British shipbuilding yards to expand because of the chronic shortage of labor and materials, which was a consequence of persistent inflation.

Textiles was the one great staple industry to show a continuous decline. Cotton exports were one-quarter of all British exports in 1913 and less than 3 per cent in the first half of 1959. Before the war Lancashire had 35 per cent of the world trade in cloth; in 1961 about 7 per cent. There were obvious reasons for this decline. Cotton textiles are the first arrivals in an industrial revolution because the mechanization of the manipulation of a cylinder—which cotton thread is—can be quickly developed. Cotton is easy to grow in many countries, and the training of workers in textile manufacture is comparatively easy. During World War II the British cotton industry had been severely restricted both in its productive capacity and in its raw materials, for which shipping space was limited. The nature of its products was controlled in the interest of exports and government demands. At the end of the war a shrunken industry was not able to meet the immense demand at home and abroad. In Britain clothes rationing had to be retained until 1949. The structure of the world's cotton industry had been transformed since 1938. Japanese capacity had been mainly destroyed during the war, but there had been great expansion elsewhere, particularly in those countries which before 1938 had been Britain's chief customers. By 1955 Lancashire could no longer insist that its export trade was essential to itself and to the nation. It was concentrating on a last-ditch defense of its home market. In 1958 Britain became a net importer of cotton cloth. The British government, like the American, had to assume some direct responsibility for its ailing textile industries. Lancashire could not face unbridled foreign competition in its home market. Producers such as Hong Kong had costs of production so low and quality of output so respectable that Western textile industries could not compete.[3] Only in the case of wool did Britain retain her pre-1939 textile predominance. In 1955 her exports were larger in quantity than they had been before the war.

British industry has shown initiative in the development of new sources of energy in the creation and use of new materials. New sources of energy have come from a great development of mineral oil refining. The United Kingdom is now the fourth largest oil refiner in the world. In terms of coal equivalent (1 ton of refined petroleum = 1.7 ton of coal) its output in 1959 was 62,000,000 tons. There is an important export trade. Because the United States is now a very large net importer of petroleum products, the United Kingdom has had to find 87 per cent of her supplies in the Middle East.

The development of atomic energy began in Britain when, in 1945, the government decided to produce an atomic weapon. The United Kingdom Atomic Energy Authority is organized in two groups—a research group at Harwell and an industrial at Risley. The contribution of nuclear reactors to the energy pool will be small for some time to come, but within a decade or so one-quarter of the electricity generated in the United Kingdom may come from this source. It is thought that atomic energy might contribute the equivalent of some 9,000,000 tons of coal by 1965.

The production of man-made fibers goes back to 1880, but not until 1930 was it on a large scale. Between the world wars, technical advances and changes in fashion with demands for lighter fabrics favored the growth of the rayon industry. Since World War II the production of artificial fibers has become a vital factor in the British way of life and in her industrial techniques. In 1900 world production of artificial fibers was 2,000,000 pounds; today it is 6,000,000,000 pounds, or 15 per cent of the total world production of fibers of all kinds. Nylon alone has one hundred separate industrial functions. The United States is the leading producer (25 per cent), and the United Kingdom is fourth (7.8 per cent). As man-made fibers rely on the skill of labor more than on the quantity of material resources (as with cotton), it is an industry well suited to British abilities and needs. In 1932 the annual production of plastics was 20,000 tons; by 1958 it had expanded twentyfold. J. W. Crawford of Imperial Chemical Industries in 1932 discovered the tough, light transparent plastic called "perspex," a substitute for glass. The polyesters (commonly used in conjunction with glass fiber) are a byproduct of the discovery of terylene, first patented in Britain in 1941. The United Kingdom is now the third largest producer of plastics (after the United States and West Germany). Readers of H. G. Wells's *War of the Worlds* will remember that the Martian invaders made great use of aluminum after they had landed on a Surrey common. Wells knew that aluminum in a combined state is abundant in nature, coming next to oxygen and silicon. Production from bauxite started in Scotland in 1896, the electricity needed coming from a hydro-electric plant. Britain now uses a larger tonnage of aluminum than any other metal. In 1958 her manufacture of some 33,000 tons of fabricated or semifabricated aluminum products was five-fold that of 1938. Used in the construction of ships it has made possible a larger carrying capacity and greater safety by lowering the center of gravity. Used for low-tension distribution lines it has lowered the capital costs of electricity distribution by 30 per cent.

It is impossible to foresee what will be the effect on the British way of life of the growing mastery of the inner structure of matter this century has seen. It is transforming the structure and the distribution of industry, the standard of living, and the relation between the public and the private sectors of the life of the community. In the structure of industry over £1,000,000,000 was invested in the petroleum refining and nuclear energy industries between 1945 and 1959. Between 1950 and 1956 investment in Britain by firms controlled by the United States accounted for 7 to 10 per cent of all net capital expansion in the British manufacturing industry. The infinite variety of the products which may stem from a new process or technique has altered the whole balance of industrial power and revolutionized the relationship between individual trades. Some 65 per cent of all firms employing more than 500 people have diversified their interests; Unilever Ltd., for example, is a holding company controlling 500 subsidiaries at home and abroad. Distillers Co. Ltd. has 105 affiliated companies; Imperial Chemicals operates 70 factories. The largest 200 United Kingdom corporations own one-third of the total net assets in the private sector of industry. The de facto financial control of the country's manufacturing assets may be in the hands of 3 per cent or less of the total shareholders. The separation between ownership and control in industry was never wider. On the other hand the public sector of industry now employs over 2,250,000 people, more than double the number in 1938.

The report of the Central Statistical Office on national income and expenditure gave an X-ray picture of the growth and changes in the British economy for the eleven years from 1949–59. It showed that domestic production had increased every year except two—1952, when it declined, and 1958, when it was stationary. The 1949 level of domestic output, in real terms, was increased by 30 per cent, while imports rose by 45 per cent. The additional supplies were used to increase personal expenditure on consumption by a quarter and public authorities current expenditure by a fifth. Capital formation was increased by 55 per cent and exports by 40 per cent. The national income per head of the working population of the United Kingdom rose at an average rate of 2.8 per cent per annum. If this continued for twenty-five years the British standard of living—allowing for changes in age composition and size of population—would be doubled. Twice as many new motor cars were bought in 1958 as in 1938, over seven times the number of refrigerators, and over five times the number of washing machines. There has been a movement of population away from the traditional areas of manufacture in the textile, coal mining, and heavy engineering industries of the north and west toward the areas of the new trades of electrical engineering, light chemicals, aircraft, and motor vehicles in southern England and the Midlands.

One of the most important factors governing the quality of British economic life and responsible for her precarious position, in spite of her technical know-how and continuous resilience, has been her failure to get back her prewar position as a great international creditor. Before 1939 she had been able to build up her investments overseas because the total of her receipts in international trade was greater than her payment for imports. She had a margin to invest. In 1939 she had a surplus of foreign assets over foreign liabilities of about £4,000,000,000. The war changed that surplus into a deficit of perhaps £1,000,000,000 or more.

One of the most important causes of Britain's weakness in the world has been her inability since 1945 to keep a margin of saving to supply out of her own resources more than a fraction of the needs of the countries, in the Commonwealth and elsewhere, which before 1939 had looked to her for finance. In the period 1945–55 Britain did not get out of her unaccustomed position as a net international debtor. Still less did she rebuild the great net surplus of foreign assets which she had had before

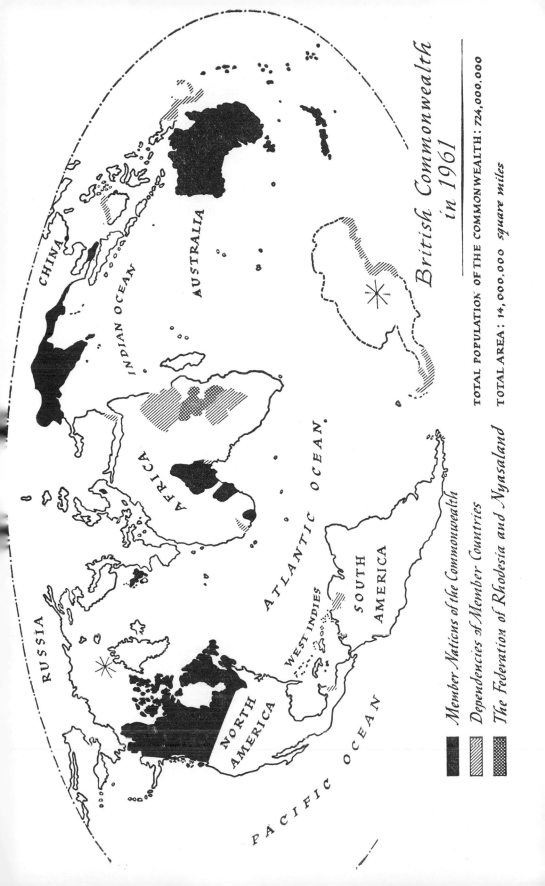

British Commonwealth
in 1961

TOTAL POPULATION OF THE COMMONWEALTH: 724,000,000

TOTAL AREA: 14,000,000 square miles

CHINA

AUSTRALIA

INDIAN OCEAN

AFRICA

RUSSIA

NORTH AMERICA

ATLANTIC OCEAN.

WEST INDIES

SOUTH AMERICA

PACIFIC OCEAN

Member Nations of the Commonwealth

Dependencies of Member Countries

The Federation of Rhodesia and Nyasaland

1914. In two years out of three after 1945 she could count on the *invisible income*—from foreigners using British ships, the spending of tourists in Britain, earnings on her overseas investments, payments from foreign governments, and the earnings of the financial work of the City of London—to turn the deficit on her visible trade into a payment surplus. But of these sources only those from travel receipts and the financial services of the City of London are really holding their ground. Military spending overseas and colonial welfare grants are a growing cost. Britain no longer earns a net income from shipping. British ships carry a smaller share of world trade and also of British imports and exports. The unsympathetic observer will say that Britain should forget that she had ever been a great lending nation. She could reply that her skill in directing the export of capital has some use in the world. She has the specialized institutions, the financial connection, and the long experience. The grants and loans made by the United States to the British were not intended to be invested abroad. But the economic recovery of the world was helped by the fact that of the £1,663,000,000 imported from the dollar area by way of gifts and loans between 1946 and 1949 over £1,000,000,000 was provided as capital for the nondollar world.

Britain's currency—sterling—is still the basis of half the world's trade and the protection of that currency must be the concern of her government. The Sterling Area—like the British constitution—is neither so cunningly devised nor so confused as an outside observer might suppose. During the nineteenth century the economic development of the non-European world was tied up with a British set of financial institutions, business connections, and trade centering on London. London performed a banking function for many countries, particularly those parts of the Commonwealth which were then in course of colonization and settlement. The growth of trade pivoted largely on the British market, was financed by British capital, and made use of British banking facilities. The pound sterling was the natural means of the settlement of trading accounts. It was also the most economical and accessible reserve to hold when foreign exchange transactions were centered so thickly in London.

This extensive use of sterling and the British arts of banking were in existence long before the establishment of central banks or the emergence of any defined group of countries to form a separate bloc. A Sterling Area began to emerge when the suspension of the gold standard in September 1931 forced the countries which made an extensive use of sterling to decide whether to link their currencies with gold or sterling—by choosing which they became members of what was called "the Sterling

Area." There were in fact no rules, formal or informal, of membership. But at the outbreak of war in 1939 the right to buy gold with sterling was suspended, and the members of the group agreed to limit their purchases of foreign exchange to what they needed for the settlement of essential external payments. The term "Sterling Area" was first used officially on July 17, 1940, for a group of commonwealth countries formed for a particular purpose at the beginning of the war. By 1950 it contained about a quarter of the world's population, and its members carried on about a quarter of the world's international trade. It had members in most climatic and geological regions of the world. Almost any commodity in which men trade could be found within its area, but it was not self-sufficient. Its members had to trade with nonmembers quite as much as among themselves. But the collapse of the Anglo-American postwar universal plans did mean that the sterling area became something of a club whose members discriminated against outsiders in trade and freedom of capital movement. The members accepted duties in return for the benefits of membership. The characteristics of a club overlaid the earlier banker-customer relationship between Britain and the other members which had been its prewar feature. But since the Commonwealth economic conference of 1952 there has been a move away from the club idea to a multilateral system. By 1957 there was almost no trade discrimination in the Sterling Area (apart from the colonies) which favored Britain against Europe and very little which favored Britain against the United States. The banker-customer relation prevailed once more. The Sterling Area group of countries banked in London. But it was far more dangerous for Britain to be such a banker in 1957 than it was in the 1930's. A customer is free to withdraw his deposit from his bank. The British in addition to their liabilities to the Sterling Area had short-term liabilities in 1957 about two and a half times their reserves. To avoid a fatal run on these reserves the British economy needed to be very stable.

In the early 1940's the British government had stated that one of its primary postwar aims would be to maintain a high and stable level of employment. The heavy unemployment which so many feared did not in fact occur. In the 1930's unemployment had rarely fallen below 10 per cent of the insured workers. It was heavily concentrated in the older industrial areas of the country and in the export trades. At times more than half the workers in some industries were unemployed, and many were without work for years on end. Since 1945 the level of unemployment has remained well below 3 per cent. It has rarely been more than half a million. The systematic short-time working of the 1930's had been replaced by systematic overtime. The pressure of demand implicit in this high level of employment has made it impossible for the government to prevent inflation. Prices rose on the average 4 to 5 per cent a year, and between 1946 and 1957 the aggregate increase amounted to 65 per cent. In part this was caused by the attempt to do too many things at once: to repair the damage and deterioration caused by the war, to improve the social services, to keep up a heavy rearmament program, and to keep up a high level of investment both private and public. Whatever its causes, inflation has meant recurring balance of payment crises and, in the industrial world, a serious waste and misdirection of resources. Persistent inflation has caused a chronic shortage of skilled labor and materials. During the 1930's Britain lost many of the benefits of technical advance by underemploying her resources. During the 1950's she lost almost as much by the inflationary diversion of resources from their most efficient uses. This internal inflation, in the opinion of some experts, was the root cause of British weakness and of her failure to accumulate a sufficient reserve and to achieve a position in international trade strong enough to be immune to the impact of international rumor.[4]

Those who pointed to the dangers of inflation were often denounced for recommending deflation and mass unemployment. The fear that mass unemployment might suddenly reappear dominated the thinking of most British trade unionists. They continued to believe that it is possible to have both stable prices and a level of demand that means there are more jobs available than men to fill them.[5] The demand for labor was so strong that wage rates were bound to rise whether or not the trade unions had bargained for them. A cooler appraisal of the situation would suggest that it was not the duty of the government to make the maintenance of employment the be-all and end-all of policy, whatever might happen to the value of money. The duty of government is to maintain the conditions which would make a high level of employment compatible with a stable value of money.[6]

The deleterious effects of inflation are subtle, profound, and far reaching; for example, the reduction in tax rates since the end of the war brought little alleviation of the real tax burden because the inflation of money values pushed large numbers of people into higher income brackets subject to higher rates of tax. When there is a progressive taxation system, during rising prices the man with a constant real income has to pay tax on a constantly increasing proportion of it. In the working of industry the difference between wage rates paid to unskilled and skilled workers has been halved in many industries. Real wages per head in manufacturing industries have risen between 1948 and 1955 by some

22 per cent, while real salaries per head rose only about 7 per cent. All this is part of the wider problem that technical changes tend to blur the individual contribution to production while social policy has blunted the sanction of unemployment. Large bodies of workers are so well organized that they cannot be discharged. Many firms are so large that they cannot be allowed to fail. The nationalized industries employ about a tenth of the total working population. By 1951, railways, London passenger transport, long-distance transport of goods by road, electricity, gas, coal mining, cable and wireless, air services, iron and steel, raw cotton marketing, and the Bank of England had been nationalized. After 1951, iron and steel, raw cotton marketing, and most of the road transport had been returned to private enterprise. These state-operated concerns have to compete for labor, materials, and capital in the open market, and in the last resort their output and price policies are determined by the pressure of organized labor and by the reactions of consumers to changes in market conditions. The economic realities are masked by the political commitment that the failure of a nationalized industry must be legally impossible.

Because of the difficulties of the post-1939–45 war years the British economy until 1950 was still to a large measure under central direction. Clothes were rationed until 1948; petrol until 1950, and food until 1952. Until 1948 the state had a most powerful control over the character and location of new building through a system of building licenses. But between 1951 and 1958 this elaborate structure was dismantled. The quantitative control of imports disappeared, state importing ceased, the organized commodity markets were re-established, price control, rationing, and building licenses were abolished and rent control relaxed. By 1958 the government had come to rely mainly on monetary and fiscal measures.

A budget is the skeleton of a state. Budget changes reveal the great change in the power which government can bring to bear on economic life. In 1890 the central government expenditure in Britain was £13,-000,000 or about 9 per cent of the national income. It included an item of £500 for a clock presented to the Emperor of China. In 1950 the government expenditure purely in money terms was thirty-eight times greater than in 1890 and was 40 per cent of the net national income. It included subsidies for the provision of wigs and for the support of grand opera. As the size of the budget has grown in relation to the national income the government can bring more direct pressure to bear on the life of the nation. Nearly half the total volume of investment is now financed by public authorities, including local authorities and the nationalized industries. The government has said that it "is pledged to foster conditions in which the nation can, if it wills, realise its full potentialities for growth in terms of production and living standards." [7]

Since 1945 Britain's national income has steadily increased. The real national income was in 1956 almost 25 per cent above the pre-1939 level and probably 70 per cent higher than in 1913. This means that the problem of basic poverty can be solved. The poor may be always with us, but they do not have to starve, and their abilities need not run to waste. The care of the sick and the aged, the education of the young, the training of the adolescent, and a reasonable income even when unemployed are within the power of government to provide. There has been no serious challenge to the principle that the government has such responsibilities. The Welfare State in this sense has too many roots in the bitter experience of the British industrial frontier of the nineteenth century and too deep a support from the moral standards of the sceptical majority as well as those of the religious minorities to be evaded by any political party. It is part of the responsibility which knowledge brings. The World War II, which caused such accelerations in the development of technology, caused also a more scientific study of social structure. If we know more about the structure of matter and about the working of our minds, we know, too, far more about the inner forms and movements of the social order. Nor has the dependence of the welfare state upon the economic order—the means by which scarcity in nature is best adapted to our insatiable desires—been forgotten. There has been a continuous and close analysis of the causes of the hardening of Britain's industrial arteries, and prescriptions for her rejuvenation are systematically sought. She has given much thought and effort to scientific research and the development of new industrial methods.

Britain earns over £4,000,000,000 per annum from the export of goods and services (nearly 25 per cent of the gross national product). The expansion of her economy and the increase in her standard of living must depend largely on the development of new processes and new products. British manufacturers have to buy 75 to 80 per cent of her imports of food and raw materials. The dividing lines between research, development, and production are indistinct. Some of the leading new industries have arisen from a foundation of scientific knowledge in a way that older industries did not, but advances have sometimes been empirical, and practical achievement has outstripped theory or contradicted it. The Marconi Franklin short-wave transmissions were made in 1922, in the face of scientific scepticism, before the theory of the ionosphere which explained them had been developed. Research cannot be socially directed to serve social objective. Clerk Maxwell was not aiming at radio. Professor Kipping did not anticipate the use to which silicones would be put. Lord Rutherford could see no practical use for his work on the atom.[8] The relation between research and economic progress is as subtle as the relation between knowledge and happiness. In our knowledge of nature there is no frontier which we can accept as final.

Organized research in industry, as it is known today, did not exist until the late nineteenth century. In 1876 Thomas Edison set up in the United States the first well-equipped laboratory. In the United Kingdom the National Physics Laboratory was established in 1900. Before World War I the British government's annual expenditure on scientific research was little more than £600,000, and private industry did not spend more than £1,000,000. But expenditure on research and development in real terms doubled between 1930 and 1938 and again between 1948 and 1950. In 1955–56 about £300,000,000 were spent on research and development in Great Britain—£185,000,000 by private industry. This would be about 1.6 per cent of the gross national product (at market prices) for the year 1955. Industry's own expenditure on research and development was about 0.8 per cent of industrial output. The corresponding American figures would appear to be that research and development expenditure corresponded to 1.5 per cent of the United States' gross national product (at market prices) and industry's own expenditure on research and development was about 1.9 per cent of net output. The large internal market in the United States makes it possible to set up five or six pilot plants where only one would be economic in Britain, and so the over-all burden of research in industry may be much lower than in Britain. It is not often possible to trace a direct link between pure research and its industrial application. There is an international cross fertilization which it is not possible to trace. The feasibility of printing electrical circuits was first demonstrated in Britain, but it was developed commercially in America. The use of resins to desalt water was discovered in Britain, but it was applied to the softening of water in the United States. The electronic computer, the "Pyrene" type of fire extinguisher, and penicillin were pioneered in Britain.

Agriculture is the occupation of two-thirds of mankind. The transformation of its techniques by the spirit of science, which has already transformed manufacturing processes, will change the social and political pattern of the world. In Britain the position of agriculture has always been unique and complex. Because Britain was the pioneer of the industrial revolution and because she became dependent on world trade, agriculture since 1870 has had a position less politically powerful than in any other first-class power. That only about a million people, barely one in twenty of the working population, are engaged in agriculture is a distinctive feature of the British economy found nowhere else in the world. In the United States the proportion is about one in five. But even in Britain the experience of two world wars and the disruption of the nineteenth-century pattern of international trade caused a revolution in agrarian political thought. The government has become the final arbiter on prices. The course of production is shaped by differential prices, fixed in advance. Either by guaranteed produce prices or by direct money grants farmers are helped to create the capital needed to raise output. Public money has been made available for long-term improvements in the land. Before World War II Britain produced less than two-fifths of her food requirements. During the war she produced four-fifths without any increase in her labor force and, indeed, with the substitution of 80,000 woman for as many men. Wheat increase was nearly doubled, potatoes were more than doubled. Before the war only two-fifths of farmland was arable, the rest being permanent grass. During the war these proportions were reversed. In terms of calories for human consumption Britain produced about 31 per cent of its food supply in 1938. By 1958 this had risen to nearly 40 per cent. An increase in agricultural production of over 60 per cent since 1938 had been achieved in spite of a slow decline in the number employed on the land.

Government policy in economic affairs has to consider some basic facts: (1) the most important factor in the growth of national real income is the rate of growth of total output of goods and services per head of the labor force. During the 1950's there was an average increase of about 2 per cent in output per head. (2) The growth of the economy must be interlocked with the growth of exports. The growth of the economy is dependent on the country's competitive power. With the export of manufactures Britain buys the imports of four-fifths of all raw materials used by industry, and half her food and feeding stuffs. Her overseas' investment and invisible exports now buy only one twenty-fifth of her imports, whereas before 1939 they bought one-fifth. (3) Her exports have been promising in some lines: cars, commercial vehicles, aircraft, office machines and equipment, new chemicals, electronic and other precision instruments or apparatus, heavy civil engineering and contracting work, heavy and light electrical equipment, etc. In others, mainly the established lines of British exports, such as coal, shipbuilding, the older textiles, leatherware, clothing, and footware, exports have greatly declined. (4) Britain is the *only* one of the leading industrial economies to show since 1951 four things together: (a) a decline in its share of the world's trade in manufactures, (b) the biggest rise in *export prices,* (c) the lowest rate of investment in private enterprise, which makes all its exports, and (d) the slowest rise in productivity.[9]

The government stated in April 1961 that the maintenance of full employment was an important contribution to the encouragement of growth because periods of industrial recession and heavy unemployment discourage capital investment in industry.[10] But if the balance of payments were to deteriorate continuously because of excessive internal demand, the result would be far more damaging to the country and at the same time to business confidence and to industrial development than if the government took moderate action to check excessive pressure of demand,[11] adding that the motive power for economic growth could not be created by the government alone. Industry must adapt itself to changes in demand, use facilities for education and training at all levels, and boldly plan investment for increased production and reduced costs. "It will not be possible to expand production, increase exports, and maintain full employment, without the fullest co-operation of employers and workers individually and collectively in the introduction of new plant and methods, and in ensuring that increases in incomes are not such as to raise the general level of costs." Among experts there is a widening agreement on the need to halt the inflation in the home market, to increase competition by foreign supplies in the home market, to eliminate the restrictive and other uneconomic practices of trade unionists as well as those of employers, to make a more "affluent society" pay more for its health and other welfare services and reduce its farming, food, and other subsidies.[12] The vital need is to ensure that resources *will* be switched from the home trade to exports, because the home market is less protected, less subsidized, and less profitable. It would mean that the welfare state benefits, the farming and industrial grants and subsidies, and the protective tariffs would cease to be *generalized* and applied only in *specific* cases of need or strategic requirement. The problems of elasticity imposed may involve a drastic—and agonizing—reappraisal of some party dogmas.

CHAPTER XX

Politics and Government, 1939-61

The most fundamental influence in the political life of the democracies of the West in the present century has been the responsibility which comes from the increased power knowledge brings. We have now such power, direct from our knowledge of the structure of matter, indirect from a growing insight into biological and social change, that Faust is a mere sorcerer's apprentice beside us. With every day that passes more of the world is our neighbor and a government may be responsible, not merely for the poor, sick, and aged of its own people, but for the survival of men, women, and children anywhere. It is becoming as true of the social order as it is of the physical that, as Whitehead said, any local happening shakes the whole universe.[1]

In the nineteenth century there could only be a rough and ready understanding of the forces of social change—the understanding a family doctor has of individual sickness unaided by an x ray or the pathological laboratory. The analysis of political institutions was comparatively simple because the scope of governments was limited. They were responsible for internal order and external defense and for the provision of a few services which experience had shown to be necessary not only for a civilized but for any life at all. Governments moved only over the face of the social waters. The ship of state sailed a sea whose currents it might chart but whose denizens it did not disturb.

Britain's experience of this changing world has had some elements peculiar to herself. In her case the scope of government has steadily increased, but the theory and the practice of that increase were influenced by the pattern of her economic life which had resulted from adherence to the doctrine of free trade, by her particular fortunes in the two great wars of 1914–18 and 1939–45, and by the power and subtlety of her political institutions. Of the latter it may be said without effrontery that they are probably the best the world has so far seen, but it must be added at once that there is no certainty that they will be adequate to the tasks which they will have to meet.

It is part of the British destiny that the very conditions which enabled her to develop political institutions of such outstanding quality were also the conditions which have generated problems so formidable that she may fail to solve them. The industrial revolution was cradled in Britain, before it spread its terror and its plenty round the world. The idea and the practical know-how of democratic self-government were also cradled in the British Isles, but it is not yet certain that they too will circle the globe, nor can we be sure that we know all the conditions necessary to their survival anywhere at all. Whatever happens cannot destroy the value of their experience so far.

Even before 1914 there had been a great development in the scope of government action. The British might stand firmly by the principles of free trade, but the policies of other states were such by 1900 that 45 per cent of her exports went to protectionist countries. The twentieth century brought a far more complex interplay between political action and economic life than had been expected. In foreign investment, central banking, and the development of railways the states of the world were playing an increasing part. If states were finding it necessary to reach down to the lives of industry and commerce, business was reaching up. F. W. Taussig wrote in 1911 that the future of democracy would depend upon its success in dealing with the problems of public ownership and regulation. There was a growing interest, too, in the use of taxation as a means of social adjustment. Before 1871 a direct income tax had been a device almost peculiar to Britain. Democracy meant an electorate of consumers with whom indirect taxation was unpopular. Progressive taxation, scientifically based and collected in proportion to income or wealth, came into favor. As Gunnar Myrdal has shown, the highly developed areas of the world were successful in defeating the Marxist prophecy of growing inequality and misery by their domestic social policies. The social services and full employment policies of the welfare state defeated revolutionary communism.[2] That these same measures were to cause an economic and social disintegration of the world economy produced, as we have seen, some of Britain's most serious political problems in the middle of this century.

It is in this wider context that we must place the British planning after World War II and her present welfare state. They were developments of ideas which had been maturing for over half a century. In 1909 Lloyd George had included in his budget the whole gamut of fiscal devices: heavy duties on tobacco and liquor, death duties on personal estates, a graded income tax supplemented by an additional "super-tax" on incomes above a certain level, a duty of 20 per cent on the unearned increment of land values, and a charge on the capital value of undeveloped land. In the fifteen years before 1914 government expenditure doubled a budget which had previously taken fifty years to double. In 1920 Paul Cambon could say to Churchill: "In the twenty years I have been here I have witnessed an English revolution more profound and more searching than the French revolution itself. The governing classes have been almost entirely deprived of political power and to a very large extent of their property and estates; and this has been accomplished almost imperceptibly and without the loss of a single life." [3] This was a courteous exaggeration, but it was also a prescient anticipation. By 1937 some 5 or 6 per cent of the national income was being redistributed from the rich to the poor. In 1939 people in Britain whose net incomes after paying tax, were £6000 or more a year, numbered about 7000. In 1949 they numbered only seventy. The private sector of the British economy in 1950 still included four-fifths of industry, but private enterprise had to operate within a complex framework of state regulation and subsidies and government control of trade and credit.

In all this there have been no leaps in the dark. Governments have done their work under a cloud of economic witnesses. This has had its dangers. As one of them has said: "The most extravagant propagandists of go-easy illusions, the most pushing salesmen of enervating Fools' Paradises, have been found among economists of diverse schools of thought." Practical men, as Keynes delighted to point out, are too often the slaves of some defunct economist. By and large, the British have had the good fortune that their practical men were guided by economists who knew their job. But the social order cannot live by economists alone. There is a practical point as to whether history has given a particular community the political institutions strong and subtle enough to use the analyses of the economists when they are correct; and there is the climate of opinion favoring some particular interpretation of the brotherhood of man. The British have been fortunate in their political inheritance; their machinery of government has made good use of the economic fuel to be had. Their ideas of social justice have had some embarrassing crudities, but they have retained the balance of a middle way. In Britain there has always been a close relation between the Protestant inclination to use the Bible as a textbook on the experiment of living and the empiricism of the scientist who sees in nature's laws the word of God. Radical Dissenters in the early nineteenth century thought that the teaching of Jesus Christ and the lessons of science were the same. The utilitarians from Hume to

J. S. Mill and Sidgwick were good Samaritans who did not believe in God, but held that it was self-evident that every man has a duty to do what he can to reduce the misery of others. On two points there was a tendency for economists, statesmen, and philosophers to agree: the poverty of the poor was the chief cause of that weakness and inefficiency which is the cause of their poverty; and privilege can be enervating to those who have it. When Attlee wrote in 1937 that "the existence of wide disparities of wealth, with a consequent segregation of the community into separate classes, is inimical to a true social life," he was only saying as a Labour leader what P. H. Wicksteed, the subtle Unitarian economist, had written nearly half a century before: "The plea of the privileged classes is in reality a plea to be left in a hothouse instead of being brought out into the open air, a plea to be allowed to belong to a clique instead of to a nation." [4] A severe handicap for the British in this century has been that utilitarian ethics, so long the ground of their democracy, has been riddled with criticism and that the Protestant ethic which was its partner has been weakened by the decay of Christianity. The decencies continue to be observed, but one is hard put to find reasons why they should. "Balance," wrote Demetrios Capetanakis, "is the secret of the English genius." On what it balances contemporary philosophers do not say.

In the development of the scope of government action, Britain has only done what many industrial states have done. But in the timing and in the technique of that development the experience of the two world wars played a great part. In those wars her power to lead the world was lost and the weakness they caused in her is still a peril to the world. In World War II she was not even a great power in the final arbitrament. But in her organization for war she was in the second war as in the first most thorough and systematic. War experience had profound effects on her welfare state.

The war years made clear that there are conditions when national planning is essential, and they provided a knowledge of the techniques to be used. It had always been known that the conditions of a siege economy would justify rationing. The web of private enterprise is woven in conditions of public confidence which war may destroy. In the 1914-18 war, hundreds of improvisations—originating in shortages of sandbags or shells or food and the more fundamental scarcities of shipping and manpower—in time fell together into a pattern. Few saw the logic that informed it. But in 1917 the War Cabinet realized that the social and administrative structure of the state had been transformed and that much of what had been done would be permanent. By 1918 at least two-thirds of all gainfully employed workers were in activities directly subject to some form of government control. But most of the control organizations operated by the Board of Trade and the War Office were abolished in 1919. A few lingered till 1921. But the general effect of the war had been to lessen the inequality of incomes. In 1924 the real income of the very rich was only half what it had been in 1914, and the poorest of the working class had gained most.

In social services (education, health insurance, and pensions) there was a steady expansion in the interwar years and about £10 per head was being spent by 1939. In 1925 the Conservative party under Stanley Baldwin had taken up the social reform work of the Liberal government of 1906. The 1908 and subsequent Pension acts had made the payment of pensions dependent on a means test, as well as tests of nationality and residence. The Widows', Orphans', and Old Age Pensions Act (1925) was compulsory and contributory. With National Health Insurance, Workmen's Compensation, and Unemployment Insurance it gave a fairly complete scheme of protection against the major risks that might affect the working classes. In 1937 Neville Chamberlain was telling a National government demonstration: "In the model State that all of us are striving for we would like to see conditions so framed as to enable its subjects to create happiness for themselves. If we are to achieve those conditions the people must be strong and healthy. If they should fall victims to accident or disease, they should have available the best of medical science. They should be able to command an income sufficient to keep themselves and their families at any rate in a minimum standard of comfort. They should have leisure for refreshment and recreation. They should be able to cultivate a taste for beautiful things, whether in nature or in art, and to open their minds to the wisdom that is to be found in books. They should be free from fear or violence or injustice. They should be able to express their thought and to satisfy their spiritual and moral needs without hindrance and without persecution." This was a commitment to "full employment" in a year when there were 1,500,000 still out of work. It looked to a "minimum standard" welfare state five years before the Beveridge Report. It acknowledged the challenge of leisure two decades before positive proposals were made in any party manifesto. It reaffirmed the tradition of even-handed justice and religious tolerance when Fascists marched in London and persecution held sway in Europe.

Before 1939 the state's role in industrial affairs had also widened and deepened. From being a policeman it had become a Father Christmas. But its intervention was selective and hesitant. The Safeguarding of Industries Act (1921) had levied an ad valorem 33 per cent import duty on certain products of key industries. The Finance Act of 1925 stimulated the United Kingdom rayon industry by levying customs' duties on the importation of natural and artificial silks, and in 1927 a Cinematograph Act provided for a statutory quota of British films. In 1931 the United Kingdom abandoned the gold standard for a managed currency. But the over-all control and planning of industrial activity remained in private hands. Keynes could fairly claim in 1926 that "the outstanding faults of the economic society in which we live are its failure to provide for full employment and its arbitrary and inequitable distribution of wealth and income."

During World War II more than half of the country's productive resources were devoted to war purposes. With the remaining half Britain had maintained a tolerable standard of living and for the poorest class one that was higher than they had known during the peace. This had been achieved by drastically curtailing production for export and fixed goods, such as housing and generating stations. In war the problems of peace had not been ignored. It was vital to win, but it would have been foolish to die from the shock. In 1941 and 1942 War Cabinet committees were examining the main problems of postwar planning. In November 1943 Lord Woolton was appointed minister of Reconstruction. By 1944 the Treasury was warning that the Brave New World after the war would be dependent on the existence of some basic economic necessities, for example, essential imports and the control of inflation. What had been endured would be a part of history. Adventures recollected in tranquillity might be a joy to individuals but they would not feed a community. The world owes no people a living.

By the end of the war a belief in the value of planning had taken root. It was accompanied by a too optimistic assumption that the technique of planning was comparatively simple. It is one thing to plan for efficiency in war and quite another to plan for prosperity in peace. In war there had been two simple tests: the needs of the fighting forces and the minimum needs of the civilian population. In war the government was the final purchaser and the effective consumer of the war essentials produced. The government had its shopping list and that list implied a system of rationing for the consumer. The rationing was accepted because the pantry was the civilian's trench or tank. The monotony of his food and the drabness of his clothes were his share of the blood, tears, and sweat of the fighting men and their dependents.

When the war was over it took some time for the realities of peace to be understood. As early as January 1943 Mr. Churchill had written: "A dangerous optimism is growing up about the conditions it will be possible to establish here after the war. Unemployment and low wages are to be abolished, education greatly improved and prolonged; great developments in housing and health will be undertaken; agriculture is to be maintained at least at its new high level. At the same time, the cost of living is not to be raised. The question steals across the mind whether we are not commiting our forty-five million people to tasks beyond their capacity to bear." It was not everywhere realized how far during the war Britain had deliberately unbalanced her economic system—that she was in the position of a workman who saves a child from drowning and ruins his only working suit. The techniques which had stiffened the sinews of war would not give the plumpness of peace. Nor would the sunshine of a free market dissolve all the miseries individuals may suffer, or the advantages of the few which the many may envy. The vital question was how Britain was to be organized so that her citizens should be made equal and yet remain free. The problem suggests a theme of Whitehead: "It may be impossible to conceive a reorganization of society adequate for the removal of some admitted evil without destroying the social organization and civilization which depends on it." [5] The evil is inequality; and yet civilization clearly depends upon it. If some were no better than others, we should all be much worse.

It has been said that "a passion for equality is the one thing that links all socialists; on all others they are divided." [6] Clearly, before 1914 there were inequalities about which it was reasonable to feel passion. In the 1890's over 30 per cent of the inhabitants of London were living in poverty. In the years 1911–13, 1 per cent of the population received 20 per cent of the total national income. It could be held that the English class system was "a blend of a crude plutocratic reality with the sentimental aroma of an aristocratic legend." But in the last fifty years governments have been combating the inequality of ownership by means of both death duties and of progressive income taxes, which make it difficult to accumulate a fortune. The redistribution of income has gone so far that the number of incomes above £6000 a year, after payment of taxes, has fallen to a negligible figure. The ridiculous position has been reached when *any* increase in inequality, however modest—for example, a slight reduction in standard rate of income tax—is held to be immoral because although the lower incomes will not be *reduced* they may not be *increased* as much as the higher ones.

The postwar legislation which created what we call the welfare state was more comprehensive than any previous legislation. It had its origin in the Beveridge Report of 1942, and its aim was not merely to relieve the poor and rescue the unlucky or improvident, but to guarantee to every citizen certain standards of income, health, and opportunity for self-improvement. The state accepted the responsibility for the economic well-being of every individual and family. The effect of the various acts —Ministry of National Insurance Act, 1944, the National Insurance (Industrial Injuries) Act, 1946, the National Health Service Act, 1946, and the National Assistance Act, 1948—was that there were no longer substantial numbers of people outside the income limits for national insurance, or beyond the scope of the system of national health services (by doctors or hospitals), or wholly dependent on the benefits given after a means test by the poor law authorities. The details would be tedious and misleading unless they were given in many chapters. It is important to notice that expenditure on social services as compared with the total of private income (personal incomes plus undistributed business profits) is not more than about 12 per cent. The total grants as compared with the total of personal income (the extent to which individuals are dependent on the welfare state for money incomes) is about 7 per cent.[7]

Political democracy, as Santayana noted, was a late and artificial product, a means for the better and smoother government of certain states at certain times. It had arisen by a gradual extension of aristocratic privileges and through rebellion against abuses. It was compatible with a very complex government, a great empire, and an aristocratic society. All this was true of British democracy at the turn of the present century. In the period after 1939 aristocracy, as it was known in the nineteenth century, has been rubbed out by the inland revenue office, and an empire has vanished, but the complexity of government has steadily increased.

In a revolutionary and warlike age the essentials of Cabinet government and of the parliamentary system through which it functions have been retained. In 1940 the existing complex machinery of government had to be shaped into a system of thought and action which could evade the defeat which nearly the whole world thought was coming, and prepared for a part in the victory which the British believed would come though then they knew not how. The essentials were three: the powers of a prime minister used by a leader of genius, Winston Churchill; a Chiefs of Staff Committee, his finely tempered tool for the job; a network of committees which could use every skill in thought and action which might serve the cause. In May 1940 the long period of waiting without any real setback to German prestige and the bitter disappointment caused when British troops had to be withdrawn from Namsos and Andalsnes in Norway led to a debate in which the government's majority, normally 200-odd, fell to 81. Leo Amery had called for "a real National government" in the debate and said to the existing Chamberlain government what Cromwell had said to the Long Parliament: "You have sat too

long here for any good you have been doing. Depart, I say, and let us have
done with you. In the name of God, go." Chamberlain hoped that his
government might be reconstructed on the basis of a national coalition in
which the Labour party would join. When that was not possible he
thought that Lord Halifax might head a new government. But it was
Winston Churchill who was asked by the King to form a national government. Lord Halifax held that a peer could not discharge the duties of
prime minister in war because he would have had no power to guide the
assembly upon whose confidence the life of the government would depend.

Churchill assumed the general direction of the war subject to the War
Cabinet and the House of Commons. As minister of Defense he supervised and directed the Chiefs of Staff Committee. In the perils of the
time Churchill could summon whom he pleased. "Once the main arrangements had been settled with the leaders of the other parties, the attitude
of those he sent for" was, he said, "like soldiers in action, who go to
places assigned to them without question." He quickly set up an organization which was subtle, swift, and full of power. His War Cabinet had at
first only five members. The number of those who attended steadily grew.
The chancellor of the Exchequer had often to be present. But the five
were the only ones who had "the right to have their heads cut off on
Tower Hill if we did not win." They alone were responsible for the policy
pursued. Churchill as prime minister could do whatever he thought should
be done for the winning of the war as minister of Defense. The union in
the same person of the civilian powers of a prime minister and the military
powers of a minister of Defense was a good example of the flexibility of
the British constitution. Churchill set up a Defense Committee (Operations) and a Defense Committee (Supply), and both of them were bodies
of the greatest flexibility. The new machinery enabled him to give a
unifying direction to almost every aspect of the war. The decisions coming
from the top were strictly, faithfully, and punctually obeyed. As prime
minister and minister of Defense Churchill could send out a daily flow
of minutes and directives to the departments and the Chiefs of Staff Committee. The latter was thus in daily contact with the executive head of
the government and in accord with him had full control over the conduct
of the war and the armed forces. The control of operations by three chiefs
of staff under a minister of Defense, who was also the prime minister,
with all the powers actual and latent of that office, made possible a
standard of team work, mutual understanding, and ready compromise
which had not been seen before. Supreme control of the forces was exercised by a professional committee working under the real head of the
government. The service ministers—for the Army, Navy, and Air Force

—were virtually confined to administrative tasks. The problem of the relation betwen civilians and service chiefs, which had so bedevilled World War I, was largely solved.

Strategy cannot be realized if the sinews of war are weak; and the sinews are economic. There had to be a system to do for the economics of war what the chiefs of staff and many committees which served them were doing for the fighting. Scarce goods and manpower had to be allocated as advantageously as knowledge would allow. In 1939 there was no machinery to collect the economic information required. But an Economic Section of the War Cabinet and a Central Statistical Office were developed. The lord president of the Council became the head of an administrative machine responsible for economic policies. It was significant that the chancellor of the Exchequer, who was responsible for the financial shadow which was cast by the grim substance of war economy, was neither the chairman of the Economic Policy Committee nor a member of the War Cabinet.

The experience of 1939–45 had given the British government some central machinery for investigation, thought, and action. The Cabinet had developed an intricate and well-planned committee system. This was organized in two layers—ministerial and official—and was served by the Office of the Cabinet, a mature form of the Cabinet secretariat of World War I. The actual pattern of committees is a matter for the prime minister, "who can alone justly measure both the problems and the personalities involved." The pattern is never actually described. The Cabinet is the supreme political organ, and it is a fundamental principle of the British constitution that the members of the Cabinet are collectively responsible for what they do. The Opposition in the British system is a hungry lion seeking what it may devour. The government will not help to feed it by giving detailed information about its committee structure. "The Cabinet as a whole," Herbert Morrison has said, "must be responsible for everything that happens. How the Cabinet does its business, and to what extent it delegates certain things to Cabinet committees is the Cabinet's business because it accepts responsibility." The purpose of the committee system is to make certain that nothing will come before the Cabinet which has not been made as ready for decision as the resources of the machinery of government will allow. During the Labour government of 1945–51 there was the Defense Committee, Economic Policy Committee, Production Committee, Future Legislation Committee, Committee on the Socialization of Industry, and many others. The Lord President's Committee was at one time a sort of general purpose committee for domestic matters.[8] The committees do not consist merely of members of the Cabinet. They are committees *set up by* the Cabinet and contain other ministers and, when necessary, civil servants. The pattern of its committees no government will fully disclose because it would be foolish to expose the gray matter behind its public face to the probe of the Opposition.

There has been a steady increase in the powers and responsibilities of a prime minister. With the Queen's consent (which is formal) he appoints and may dismiss a minister—and the number of ministers increases. He is consulted about the appointment of the key men in the civil service, and their number is increasing. He has to settle disputes between the departments of government, and the number of departments is growing. He is responsible for seeing that the machine is running smoothly. He can advise the Queen when to exercise her prerogative of dissolution, which means that he decides when his team shall go to the country for the renewal or the ending of its power.

Neville Chamberlain who was prime minister in 1939 was inspired by a sincere, humane, and essentially practical conception of the social good. He had shown a mastery of the tough and technical problem of English local government, of health administration, and the problems of housing. Lloyd George once said of him that he was "a man of rigid competence, lost in an emergency or in creative tasks." When he became prime minister in 1937 he had been responsible for most of the social legislation since 1918 and had shown a mastery of the Conservative party machine, reorganizing its system of research and its central office. Churchill had shown what the office could become in the dread simplicities of war. In 1945 Clement Attlee was to embody for the Labour movement the virtue of respectability. He had the Victorian asset of character—in the sense of a combination of determination, generosity, diligence, and integrity. He showed in office that he could be crisp and ruthless where policy was concerned and where a colleague did not match up to his responsibilities. He totally refused to participate in any personal intrigues. He had seen the needs of the needy, the poverty of the poor, and the lack of opportunity of the many. He was able to secure that the elements of social justice, outlined as early as 1900, were provided when the knowledge and the institutional machinery were ready to provide them—as they were after 1945. Harold Macmillan, like Mr. Attlee, was a survivor of World War I. Educated at Eton and Balliol, his grandfather had been forced to leave Scotland on foot to seek his fortune in England, Macmillan was forty-six and had been in the Commons for fourteen years before, in 1940, he was given junior office in the wartime coalition. In the 1930's he had been a rebel in his party. He had advocated a wide extension of social enterprise and attacked the Munich settlement. Before he became prime minister in 1957 he had had wide experience as minister resident in Northwest Africa (1942), minister of Housing and Local Government (1951), minister of Defense (1954–55), Foreign secretary (1955), and chancellor of the Exchequer.

Since 1945 some of the prime minister's tasks have been simplified. In the Cabinet office he has almost a department of his own able to tell him what he might wish to know so far as that knowledge can be found within the machinery of government. The Ministers of the Crown (Transfer of Functions) Act, 1946, allowing functions to be transferred from one minister to another by Order in Council has simplified the task of distributing the functions of government in a period when the functions of government are always growing wider and more protean. In three fields since 1945 there has been a strengthening of the machinery of government: defense, economics, and scientific research. During the war itself Churchill, because he was prime minister, had been able to deal easily and smoothly with the three service departments—War, Air, and Admiralty. This brilliant improvisation does not hide the fact that in 1939 Britain was not ready for war. There was no part of the government responsible for the development of a unified defense policy. After 1945 it was decided that there should be a minister with the means and the authority to do so. The Ministry of Defense Act, 1946, said that there should be a Minister for Defense "in charge of the formulation and general application of a unified policy relating to the armed forces of the Crown as a whole and their requirements."

In the demographic and economic knowledge which a modern government needs, Britain in 1939 was weaker than she should have been. In World War II Churchill had to improvise his own statistical machine. In 1945 the Labour party realized that industrial efficiency would require the government to know more about the economic facts of national life than it did. The Cabinet Office was given a Central Statistical Office and an Economic Section. A minister for Economic Affairs with a central economic planning staff was appointed in 1947. A chief planning officer was to supervise an interdepartmental planning staff which would prepare a long-term plan for the country's manpower and resources. The machinery was later put into the hands of the Treasury. The Treasury method of co-ordination—discussion of departmental plans in order to arrive at agreed adjustments—was extended from the financial affairs of the government to the consideration of the economic life of the country. The government economic survey of 1947 was the first attempt by a British government, and perhaps of any government, to show the nation's needs and resources for all to see and criticize. The government does not withhold vital information merely because it might encourage its political opponents. The veil of money is not used to hide the economic facts of life. The Treasury is not merely a finance department; it is also a planning department.

The Treasury stands at the center of things. Its new planning functions have been grafted on a more ancient stock. The existence of the regular traditional framework of business through which the Treasury officials have a detailed knowledge of the work of other departments throughout the year does help its planning functions. But the Economic section of the Treasury cannot enter fully and intimately into every aspect of economic policy. It is too small to extend the frontiers of knowledge or for the profound study of long-term policy issues.[9]

In 1946 the Treasury was given a general statutory power to issue to the Bank of England such directions "as, after consultation with the Governor they think necessary in the public interest." This was little more than a change of form. The practice of collaboration with the central government and of deference to its requirements in critical issues of monetary policy had long been established. In 1957 the government set up an independent Council on Prices, Productivity, and Income. It was hoped that authoritative reports from time to time by an impartial body, free to survey the country's general economic condition and tell the public what it really thought, would help in the fight against inflation. Basic economic principles, economists assure us, are simple. But their relevance to a country's welfare can only be brought home with the exercise of considerable analytical powers. One may say that in economics as in geometry one begins with a point and a line. The point is that we all want more. The line is the limitation of available resources. The public can see the point. It needs some help if it is to toe the line.

Before 1914 scientists worked in isolated groups or as individuals with little or no assistance from the state. In this century there has been a revolution in their standing in Britain as in other countries. The lord president of the Council has been made minister for Science and is responsible for the general oversight of government scientific organization for civil purposes. In 1947 an Advisory Council on scientific policy was appointed to advise him in the exercise of his responsibilities for scientific policy. The office of the lord president of the Council is one of the most interesting in the modern British constitution. In the past, to appoint a committee of the Privy Council was one way of developing a new field of government work—the Board of Trade and the Ministry of Education began in that way. Before 1939 the lord president of the Council was often one of the prime minister's most sturdy political colleagues, acting as leader of the House. It is an interesting example of the tough empiricism of the British system of government that it should be the lord president of the Council, whose political functions have been so important, who should become the minister mainly responsible for the government's relations with the natural sciences and the place of science in the development of industry. In World War II professional experts of the army, navy, and air force were assimilated into the framework and traditions of the government. Since 1945 economists and natural scientists have been similarly assimilated. The system is tough, flexible, and, given Britain's limited resources, very efficient.

Even before 1914 a collection of small and almost unrelated staffs had been made into a unified civil service based on common methods of recruitment. The Treasury has been the department most concerned with the structure and well-being of the bureaucracy which, like any modern state, Britain must have. Between 1918 and 1939 the Treasury was criticized because it had made little systematic study of departmental organization and administrative techniques. The general layout of departments and the distribution of responsibility were not periodically overhauled or systematically reviewed. In 1939 it was only just able to cope with the problems of reorganization and expansion which emerged. During the war years the staff of permanent officials was supplemented by a variety of academic persons and businessmen. The top grade—the administrative class—which in 1939 consisted of just over 2000, of whom fifty were women, in 1945 had nearly 5000, of whom 900 were women. After the war the development of welfare services and the administrative problems created by the need for research and the responsibilities which new knowledge brings involved a transformation of the machinery of government and required the solution of administrative and political issues of the greatest delicacy.

The scope of government has so increased that public authorities have now some 40 per cent of all private incomes passing through their accounts. An analysis of the number of people in government service was made by Moses Abramovitz and Vera Eliasberg in their *Growth of Public Employment in Great Britain* (1957). In 1901 out of a total of about 16,000,000 working population, 958,000 or 5.8 per cent were employed by governmental authorities, including the armed forces and local government. By 1950 the proportion had become nearly 14 per cent. If the employees of the nationalized industries were included it was 24 per cent. This would cover what economists call the "public sector." A better indication of the scope of the government's problem is to take the central administration—excluding the industrial government employees, the Post Office, and the nationalized industries. In 1902 there were 28,000 members of this group; in 1955 there were 387,000, established and otherwise. This meant that there had been a rise from less than 0.2 per cent to nearly 2 per cent of the working population. In the mid-1950's some 29 per cent of income of all types was taken in tax. Between 1918 and 1939 housing and health service grew considerably. Since 1945 family allowances, child care, and the national health services have been established. Educational expenditure has risen both absolutely and as a proportion of the national income. In 1921 it took some 1 per cent; in 1938, 2.25 per cent; in 1955, 3.5 per cent; and in 1960, just under 4.5 per cent. The 1950's were an age of educational reform in Britain more far reaching than any since compulsory education began after 1870. The increase has been most important in the universities. In 1911 no university student received aid from the central government, and only 1400 received grants from local authorities. In 1950 nearly 3000 had aid from the Ministry of Education and over 34,000 from local authorities. The student population in the universities was about 48,000 before the 1939 war and 100,000 in 1958.[10]

In round figures it can be said that governmental organization's share of the working population is nearly three times as great as in the 1900's, and its share of national resources is at least four times as great. Figures for the United States show a similar movement—total government employment in 1950 was just over 12 per cent of the working population compared with the British 14 per cent.[11]

In Britain the current expenditure on social services as compared with the total of private income (personal income plus undistributed business profits) is about 12 per cent. The social grants as compared with the total of personal incomes (the amount by which individuals are dependent on the welfare state for money income) is about 7 per cent.[12]

The Representation of the People Act, 1948, completed the acceptance of the principle, implicit in the Reform Act of 1832, that every citizen, man or woman, should have one vote and only one vote. Universal suffrage, the increased scope of government, and the ever-more subtle web of communications have given political parties problems of organization. They must keep fully trained party workers in every constituency ready to fight a general election when it shall occur. And in Britain elections for the central government do not come with the regularity of the calendar but with the irregularity of thunderstorms. Political thunderbolts may come out of a blue sky. Dissolution—the appeal of the government to the country—may come at any time. The system of single member constituencies, mercifully, usually gives a clear majority which can support a stable government. In theory a system of single member constituencies could give a majority in the House of Commons to the party which had received only a minority of the votes. In fact this has occurred only once —in 1951 when the Conservatives received 0.8 per cent smaller vote than their opponents. Only once since 1880 has a party or parties supporting the government received more than 60 per cent of the votes—in 1931. The task of the party organization in an election is to bring out the con-verted voters and not to win over voters from the other side. The opinions of voters, so far as they can be discovered by the methods of enquiry now available, are the result of what they vaguely remember about the past and not of what is happening at the time. It is the image of a party created over the years and not the last pamphlet or the current newspaper, radio, or television output that guides their votes. Insofar as there is any "swing of the pendulum" it will be the effect of the new voters who are just of age or of those who do not usually vote: not the "floating voter" but the voter who has temporarily come to the surface.[13] The Labour party, which is only as old as this century, won a clear majority for the first time in 1945. Mr. Churchill was defeated and Mr. Attlee became prime minister. The Labour party was better prepared for the election than was its rival. It had held annual party conferences throughout the war. The Conservatives and Liberals had let their constituency organiza-tions run down. More important was the fact that the Labour party pro-gram seemed to offer the realization of the hopes of justice, peace, and plenty which had steadied many in the stress of war:

Peace is come and wars are over,
Welcome you and welcome all

Labour, which had supported the Conservatives and Mr. Churchill in the fight against dictatorships, would now show what free men could really do. The prewar aims of social justice would be achieved by the well-tried means which had won the war. The resources of the country would be used in the interest of the British people as a whole. In fact, it was able to complete the main lines of a welfare state started in 1906. The war had accustomed people to a much higher level of taxation than they had known before. It had improved administrative techniques as well as fostered advances in medicine, nutrition, and education. There had been a time when the British people had been threatened by every-thing that Hitler might have considered fit for the most deadly enemy of his Third Reich, which was to last a thousand years. The organization of modern war and the necessities of large-scale dispersal of population to avoid the dangers of bombing had partly lowered the class barriers in

British life. The welfare state would in some shape or form have been completed by any party. Provided that the skill of the economists could so guide the policies of governments that there should be no disastrous economic collapse following the transition from war to peace, the provision of a national minimum of the basic essentials for all citizens, insurance against sickness and unemployment, and an educational policy to mobilize what gray matter the nation had to meet the problems of the industrial revolutions thronging the horizon of the future were certain to be made. The new social services were introduced and developed by the Labour party with promptness and skill.

The hand of Labour was not so sure in the problems of industrial reconstruction. The idea and the techniques of nationalized industries had been discussed since the beginning of the century. At one time it was considered that the basic British industries were in the nature of separate political empires in which it was intolerable that there should not be a system of popular control. Nationalization was, as R. H. Tawney suggested, merely a question of constitution making. After 1945 the Labour party was to discover that the selection of industries for nationalization because they are basic, in need of reorganization, or with a tendency to monopoly would be frustrating. The forces of the market would be no respecter of the constitutions they might devise. There were other more subtle methods of securing the vitality of the nation's economic life.

In 1946 the Bank of England was brought formally under government control, though the formal statement may have added little to the actual position. Nationalization came in 1947 for coal and civil aviation, the railroads, canal and mainland waterways, some parts of the haulage industry, and the chain of hotels and restaurants owned by the railroads, and in 1948 for gas. The place of steel between the private and the public sector was to remain in dispute. The problems involved had been debated at every level from street corner to the most exclusive economic club for over half a century. There had been endless official enquiries into the technical minutiae of the industries concerned. The device used—of the public corporation—was developed in the first decades of this century. It was hoped that an industry might be controlled by it in the public interest while being immune from the day to day parliamentary criticism which an ordinary government department must face. The industries concerned —coal mining, inland transport, gas supply, electricity generation and supply, and civil air transport—were to be free from the direct executive control of ministers but subject to their influence or final decision on matters of basic policy.

There is a seeming paradox in a two-party system. Each party would seem to claim that it is the way and the life of the community. Each party's program implies the elimination of the other, yet each is an adaptation and extension of the other's. In Britain the underlying unity beneath the party differences has been nourished by some obvious realities in a world of technological innovations. When every day some spade becomes an automatic shovel, no party can hope for power which cannot promise a rising standard of living. But this will depend on the skill with which a government can prevent excessive unemployment and on the social harm which may be caused by inflation. Unless a party is prepared to substitute administrative controls and political direction for the working of freely operating economic forces the state will continue to operate within fairly clear limits. During World War II a manpower budget was the principal instrument of domestic planning. In peacetime people will not put up with the direction and control of labor; nor will they accept the central control of relative incomes.[14]

Before 1914 the nascent Labour party had two main appeals: while it is the things of the spirit that matter, it is the things of the body that are most urgently, unintermittently, and ruthlessly necessary. Man does not live by bread alone; but he cannot live without it. It seemed, too, that there was a latent plenty which could be made actual by the abolition of certain inherited privileges. It was also unjust that there should be advantages and disabilities which had their source, not in differences of personal quality, but in disparities of wealth, opportunity, social position, and economic power. Man may want but little here below nor want that little long, but that is no reason why he should not have a fair share of what is going.

The Conservatives for their part have been concerned to show that the institutions by which we live are a late birth of time; that the state is a partnership of the living with the dead and those yet to be born; that what you would do, must be done from the place where you stand, and with the institutional tools that you now understand. These truisms of Edmund Burke are no less true of the subtle web of interdependence spun by the spinning wheel of science than they were of the wider and looser net of an agrarian and preindustrial society. The Conservative has an insight into the technical processes of contemporary reforms. Guilty of the sin of property he knows how difficult it is to be good. He knows that any incarnation of ideas in institutions involves the dangerous adventure of giving birth. He knows that privilege cannot be shed merely by the willing. Because we live under the limitations of nature—our means are always scarce however virtuous our ends—and because we have the diversity of talents and desires that our humanity implies there must always be a hierarchy in our arrangements. A chain of command must involve privilege. In a free society the patterns of responsibility and of privilege must often be confused.

Experience of two world wars has shown the scope and the limitations of the techniques which economists can put at the service of the state. The two major parties—Conservative and Labour—know that there are no simple levers of power to be seized. There is no open sesame a political Aladdin can use to open the cave of peace and plenty.

In 1945 the Labour party could stimulate the intellectual resources and the moral feelings of the nation. Some modification of the naive individualism which had survived from the nineteenth century was needed. It was possible to abolish the kind of poverty which made it impossible for the poor to care for themselves or to lead their children into citizenship. But many of the controls which it had in mind were found to be cumbersome, unpopular, and unnecessary. In a considered statement of their principles in 1952, *Socialism: A New Statement of Principles,* we find it said: "For European Socialists in the nineteenth century the position seemed simple. Capitalism was to be overthrown; something known as Socialism would naturally replace it. To-day we know that this is a myth. There are no distinct and opposing systems, only an infinite series of gradations." The 1918 formula of "the common ownership of the means of production" is dead as the dodo. "The equality of subordination to the common interest," said to be fundamental to modern socialism, is a piece of mysticism. The electorate would now reject any party pledged to widespread nationalization. The diagnosis of former evils that underlay this panacea of public ownership was found to be false. It is not true that the private ownership of capital will make it impossible to remedy the inequalities in distribution or the vicissitudes of an industrial society. The high level of employment in the postwar years was not secured by nationalization. Looking back, it is seen that the postwar Labour government was completing a period of social reform which began in 1906 and not opening a new epoch.

The Labour party has in fact been showing all the symptoms of an agonizing reappraisal. The issue is whether the state shall operate through the price mechanism or try to replace it. Shall there be planning by inducement or planning by direction? In the opinion of some the state can do all the planning it may want by controlling the market which controls the entrepreneur. A healthy price mechanism can make industry responsible in a way that parliamentary government could never do. The state has no need to dig and plant the New Jerusalem—it need only control the weather. Like Plato's Guardians it will see that justice is done by its insight into the mathematical relations a body politic involves. To prevent the concentration of power in the hands of *either* industrial management *or* a state bureaucracy will require a close analysis of how responsibility may be distributed so that freedom of choice is enlarged. New Labour is Old Liberal armed with modern analytical techniques.

The outcome of the debate we do not know. It is even possible that the Labour party may never again secure a clear majority. But it is essential to the British system of Cabinet government that there should be an alternative government. How this will in the future be provided we do not know. The class divisions are not the same as they were when the Labour party was first formed. The nature of the free market of the economist's analysis was only dimly understood. The full impact of world competition on the basic British industries—coal, cotton, iron, and shipping—had not been revealed. The pressure of the great trade unions could then further the improvement of the market for labor and eliminate the privileges hampering the British industrial potentials. The Labour party's passion for equality helped to secure the health and educational services which set a people free.

The British people like any other is divided into groups with distinctive ways of life. The members of these groups are aware of the divisions and agree in ranking some as carrying more prestige than others. The company director, the research scientist, the member of Parliament, the clergyman, the works manager, and the film actor are recognized by all classes as middle class. The journalist, the elementary school teacher, the minor civil servant, the small shopkeeper, the factory foreman, the electrician, and the shop assistant are recognized as upper working class. The fitter, carpenter, coal miner, bricklayer, lorry driver, and railways porter are to themselves and others working class. The groups are recognized by their members as forming a hierarchy of prestige—with the middle, lower middle, and working class in that order of prestige.

It is possible that these cleavages may deepen. The hierarchy produced by the slow operation of the forces of change in the all but recent past may be replaced by new patterns based upon educational differences working on our growing knowledge of the genetical composition and intellectual aptitudes of the people. On the one hand, governments are concerned with the near mathematical techniques which are needed to keep the economy purring along the road to plenty—avoiding the hazards of inflations and the potholes of depression. On the other, governments are reaching down into the very genetical composition of the people.

These problems are not peculiar to the British people. In facing her share of them she has had and still has some advantage. Britain is a small island. The population is so closely interdependent that there has been little economic agitation on a regional basis. Political parties have not merely to determine what shall be done about basic national policy. They have also to act as brokers between diverse interests. The homogeneity of British economic life has made this comparatively easy to do. There have been no irreconcilable minorities since the Jacobites of the eighteenth century and the Irish before 1914. Since the Southern Irish went, British politics has been free from the disrupting passions of national minorities and religious rancors. The sting has been taken out of religious controversy since the Education Act, 1902, took religion out of education. If the Roman Catholic vote still goes mainly to Labour it is not from any sectarian allegiance but because most Roman Catholics are working class. Candidates without religious beliefs usually keep quiet about them. For the most part religious issues are dead in politics. There are diversities of interest and thought within both the Conservative and the Labour parties. Each can only retain its unity by its leaders' appeal to reason rather than to passion.

CHAPTER XXI

British Thought, 1870-1960

The last hundred years has been the first period in human history in which the life of each new generation has differed essentially from the last. The analogy between life in eighteenth-century Europe and life in the time of Caesar was very close. But the eighteenth century had the hope that the light of reason would dispel the darkness of superstition and that a well-bred Augustan peace would be diffused from China to Peru. Its philosophers had some doubt about the power of reason entirely to control the passions dividing mankind. From the publication of *The Wealth of Nations* and the American Declaration of Independence in 1776 to the publication of the *Origin of Species* in 1859 and the American Civil War, there had been a troubled debate between the rationalists, with their hopes for the future, and the romantics, with their feeling of awe for, and dependence on, the past. Neither had foreseen how in the last quarter of the nineteenth century the incarnation of new knowledge in material things would so entirely transform the human situation. It was not merely that there were new inventions. These had been made before: the invention of agriculture, of writing, of the steam engine. In these the process had been slow, unconscious, and unexpected. But in the late nineteenth century the great change, as Whitehead has said, was the invention of the method of invention. The process of change became quick, conscious, and expected.[1] The gap was narrowed between the scientific idea and the goods and services it made possible. Many new professional groups made their appearance, who saw to it that advances on the frontiers of speculation and research were used in the interior homelands where common men must live. It was as though the Guardians of Plato's *Republic* had used their mathematical studies to transform the craft of every citizen. The world was faced with a self-evolving system which it could not stop. The corridors of power were lined with laboratory doors. Every government became a sorcerer's apprentice. A terrible new power had been born.

In the first half of the twentieth century the harvest of four centuries of modern science changed the aspect and outlook of our civilization as well as our daily lives and habits of thought. It was the fourth revolution of the modern world. The first had been the publication of Newton's *Principia,* 1687; the second Lavoisier's *Chemistry,* 1789; the third Darwin's *Origin of Species,* 1859, establishing the homogeneity of man, beast, and nature, which hitherto all Western religions had implicitly denied and only a few philosophers had ineffectually affirmed. The fourth began with the discovery of Madame Curie and Sir J. J. Thomson that atoms were composite and that some of them were unstable and disintegrating at measurable rates.[2] This new conception of matter meant that nature was not a dance of particles to their laws enslaved, but a source of energy and activity, so ordered that, as Whitehead prophetically put it, any local activity shakes the whole universe. Hume in the eighteenth century had said that the world was more like a turnip than it was like a watch; it was now known to be more like a thought.

In 1897 Marconi sent a message by wireless telegraphy a distance of eighteen miles; in 1901 signals were successfully passed across the Atlantic; in 1961 radio pulses were "bounced" off the planet Venus. In the 1920's radio broadcasting became general. Music was "mantled in light's velocity." In Britain, John Reith, the first director of the B.B.C., was a new Caxton, who within a year established the basic features of British broadcasting. In 1936 came television; its birthday in Britain was its birthday in the world.

In 1919 Rutherford, the first of the modern alchemists, succeeded in transmuting certain light elements into hydrogen by bombarding them with alpha particles emitted in the disintegration of radium. Within three years after Hahn and Strassman in Germany had achieved atomic fission, American, British, and Canadian physicists were at work on what became the first atomic bomb on Hiroshima, 1945.

In 1903 the first airplane was flown 284 yards by the Wright brothers. In 1909 Blériot flew across the Straits of Dover. In 1919 Alcock and Brown flew the Atlantic from west to east. In 1947 an airplane flew faster than the speed of sound.

The preparation of new drugs with the property of being deadly to bacteria and other organisms of diseases infecting the higher animals, while harmless to their hosts, led to the revolution in medicine which has made the life expectancy of a male at birth sixty-eight years and of a woman seventy-four. The catalogue could be endless. Want and pain and fear were dissolving like mists before the new knowledge. A golden age of plenty was possible. The dreams of eighteenth-century rationalists had been made into blueprints.

The new power over nature was ethically neutral. It could and has been used in the wrong direction. It has changed utterly every detail of man's conception of himself and has made his cosmos as variable as his mind. It has meant that the twentieth century has been one of almost unbelievable intellectual glory and also of unspeakable degradation. Prometheus has brought down a new fire from Heaven, but it has been received by a tower of Babel. The world has been made physically one, but the partial unities, political and cultural, the ages' slow-wrought gains, have been tossed, disrupted, and tempted by the new powers. The powers which poets gave to giants and heroes are in the hands of common men. Every Lilliputian has the voice of a Stentor and can bend an Ulysses bow.

The most optimistic comment that has been made is that "it is the business of the future to be dangerous and it is among the merits of science that it equips the future for its duties." Civilization should not be confused with security. If there is a degree of instability inconsistent with civilization, on the whole the great ages have been unstable ages. If instability is the price of greatness we shall pay in full. We shall not be bored to death.

The platitudes about the terrors of our time have a clear and precise relevance to the work of the English poets, novelists, and philosophers who have sometimes shaped and always mirrored the life of their times.

We may glance first at the great philosophical debates which have taken place. It is as true today as it was in ancient Greece or medieval Christendom that in its philosophies the inner nerves of our world are laid bare.

F. H. Bradley, the greatest English philosopher since Hume, had as T. S. Eliot has written, "intense addiction to an intellectual passion." [3] In the 1870's and the 1880's Bradley was, with Matthew Arnold, on the side of a European and ripened and wise philosophy against an insular and immature and cranky one. In his work one can see mirrored the inner spirit of the vigorous and doomed pre-1914 English world. When he went to Merton College, Oxford, the destruction of English Protestantism by scholarship had begun. Scholars were asking questions about Moses and about Christ which hitherto had been asked only about Homer and about Livy. What Homer had been to the Greeks the Bible was to the British. What Plato had said about the inadequacies of Homer as a guide to social and political life for Athens had now to be said about the Bible for the middle class. In Bradley we can see the three great issues which formed the climate of English thought from 1870 to 1914 phrased and bared with deadly precision: the intellectual and moral inadequacy of Christianity as the British understood that religion, the need to assimilate the Darwinian perspective about the life of man, the confusions in the dominant utilitarian philosophy and its dangers as a political blueprint. The British enjoyed a vigorous way of life; in one sense they were, in their political maturity, the ancient Greeks of the modern world. But, unlike the Greeks, they had barely begun to analyze the real nature of their power. Bradley did his best, but that power had passed away before his example was seriously followed.

First the religious question. J. S. Mill had written that "the whole of the prevalent metaphysics of the present century is one tissue of suborned evidence in favour of religion." [4] The authors of *Essays and Reviews,* among them a youthful version of the great Jowett of later Balliol fame, had been denounced as the seven against Christ for their modest exercise in Biblical scholarship. To this debate Bradley contributed a pamphlet, *The Presupposition of Critical History,* in which, without a direct mention of the Bible, he restated the agnosticism of Hume: "History is a matter of inference ... every inference rests on a presupposition ... this presupposition is formed by present experience ... an inference is justified only on the assumption of the uniformity of nature ... How then can we accept as the real past of our own real world this riddle of an outer sphere, fallen down among us from heaven and written in a foreign tongue. Critical history assumes that the world is one. How can we affirm the existence in past times of events the effects of causes which confessedly are without analogy in the world in which we live." [5] In his great work *Appearance and Reality* (1893) he was to write: "In England irrelevant appeals to practical results are allowed to make themselves heard ... that a man should treat of God and religion merely to understand them, and apart from the influence of some other consideration and inducement is to many of us in part unintelligible and in part also shocking." One ought not to "trifle indecently with a subject which deserves some respect." [6] If we do take religion seriously then we have to meet the criticism that in religion we have the contradiction that "the whole is at once to be actually good and at the same time is to make itself good." The religious man may "dream his life away or be forced into action by chance desire and hallow every practice, however vile, by an empty spirit of devotion." "He may become an anchorite or he may lead a crusade." [7]

Linked with Bradley's criticism of the English religious climate was his attitude to the Darwinian controversy. That our rational life should have had a bestial origin was no invalidation of its present values. That a modern mathematician may have had an animal predecessor who could not count does not invalidate the former's theory of numbers. Awareness of our roots in nature is merely one example of the burden that knowledge brings. What the new knowledge might do was to help to Hellenize the English Philistine. The latter's ordinary moral creed was based on no rational principle. "The moral code of Christianity is accepted in part and in part rejected practically by all save a few fanatics. But we do not realize how in its very principle the Christian ideal is false." Referring perhaps to Newman, Bradley wrote, "The belief that human life is sacred is largely Christian. The individual in the next world has an infinite value; the things of this world, our human ends and interests, are all alike counted worthless and the rights and duties founded on those interests of course bodily disappear. . . . But once admit that life in this world is an end in itself and the pure doctrine is at once uprooted. Individuals now have unequal worth. The community is its own providence and therefore against its rights, the individual is not sacred. . . . Only before God are men equal; before men they are not and the development of the best is a good thing." [8]

If this should be mistaken for a cloud, no bigger than a man's hand, of that totalitarian darkness which has since covered our skies, the mistake will be corrected if we consider the other theme of Bradley's work —the criticism of the prevalent utilitarian theory and the failure to analyze the real nature of a political order which it involved. In his criticism of laissez faire and the presuppositions of the liberal theory of the state, Bradley was only one of many critics whose work, had it been taken more seriously, might have prevented the development of the religion of Marx-Leninism. It was J. M. Keynes who said that Communism is the *reductio ad absurdum* of Benthamism. It was Bradley who wrote: "Deduced by men of practical good sense the conclusions of the hedonistic art of life would never seriously conflict with common morality. But what is to happen if men with no sense or hold on real life but gifted with a logical faculty begin systematically to deduce from this slippery principle" the principle that we should seek the greatest happiness of the greatest number.

The technical skill and the practical wisdom of the classical economists from Adam Smith to the present day have deserved well of humanity. We do not live by bread alone but also by the curves and tables of our economists. There has often been some confusion in their minds about the relation between the economic order they were analyzing and the social order in which they lived. We know from the careful study of the history of economic thought by many generations of scholars how right were contemporary critics to fear the abstractions of the classical economists. They did not seriously analyze the character of the political order in which the economic forces they were analyzing had to work.

It may be, as Alfred Marshall suggested, that this was because a strong rationalist and a priori infusion had entered classical political economy, partly from French sources and partly from Ricardo.[9] Whatever the cause, in the nineteenth century a popular type of liberalism quieted ethical doubts about economic processes and obviated a sustained effort to think about social problems. J. S. Mill did not solve the problem because he inserted institutional criticisms into the liberal doctrine without seeing their full implications. With Mill production and exchange were to be left to natural law while welfare was to be increased by distributional reforms. The questions raised by the German historical school about the influence of civil and political institutions, custom, and historical tradition on the economic life of men were not fully explored. "There is some justice in the charge," wrote Marshall, "that the English economists neglected to enquire with sufficient care whether a greater range might not be given to collective as opposed to individual action in social and economic affairs. . . . Their most vital fault was that they did not see how liable to change are the habits and institutions of industry. . . . In particular they did not see that the poverty of the poor was the chief cause of that weakness and inefficiency which is the cause of their poverty." [10]

The English, who considered that they were free both from the abstract a priori thinking of the French economists and the cloudy historical determinism of the Germans, had to accept the evidence of their own empirical method that by 1870 there was little chance that the functions of the state would be reduced to smaller and smaller compass. Arnold Toynbee wrote in his *Lectures on the Industrial Revolution:* "Competition we now recognise to be a thing neither good nor bad; we look upon it as resembling a great physical force which cannot be destroyed, but maybe controlled and modified . . . the old economist thought competition good in itself. We think it neither good nor evil, but seek to analyse it." W. S. Jevons (1835–82), who had so clairvoyant an understanding of the fleeting nature of British industrial supremacy and who foresaw the incalculable economic potential of the metallurgical industry on the banks of the Ohio, said that "we must neither maximise the functions of government at the beck of quasi-military officials, nor minimise them according to the theories of the very best philosophers." [11] He had a vision that social progress would bring a diminution of social services as self-reliance and independence increased. But in the 1870's and 1880's Henry Sidgwick in Cambridge, who revived and restated the tradition of Hume and J. S. Mill, was prepared to regard the tide of socialist legislation as inevitable: "Of what is most important to know, we as yet, know much less than most people suppose." He saw that "actual human beings will not permanently acquiesce in a social order that common moral opinion condemns as unjust." But he considered that socialist legislation would always be a supplementary and subordinated element in a system mainly individualistic.

In P. H. Wicksteed we sense the presence of a sane and prophetic spirit. He was a born economist because he had a delight in abstract theory, close touch with concrete things, strong common sense, and an overwhelming moral sympathy. The translator of Aristotle's *Physics* and of Dante's *Divine Comedy,* a disciple of Jevons, influenced by Comte and Ruskin, a Unitarian minister, Wicksteed was well equipped to consider the vital question of the relation of the technique of economic analysis to the whole social order in its greatness and its misery. He was one of the most cogent critics of Marx's labor theory of value, rescuing even the flamboyant Bernard Shaw from that morass. But he was also quite clear that whatever the importance of the forces of the market for securing an increase of production, individuals could not be left to live on what they individually could earn in a competitive market. In the jargon of the day the marginal net product of the individual laborer would not necessarily be enough to support him as a citizen and the father of a family. "The belief has laid hold of men, whether for weal or woe, that intolerable social hardship and wrong are the issue of our present civilisation, and that society, by its corporative and collective action, must and can in large measure, make the crooked straight." [12] The lives of the masses, he wrote, are to be "regarded as ends rather than as means ... there is a life worth living, intrinsically accessible to all, and the human race is not born for the few." The life worth living which is intrinsically accessible to all was *"more* worth living than the life now secured for the happy few at the cost of the many." "The things that are most important and the things that are most necessary are not the same. . . . It is the things of the spirit that matter, but it is the things of the body that are most urgently, unintermittently and ruthlessly necessary. . . . the higher matters most, but the lower is the most necessary. I may have something to eat without being a saint, a poet, an artist a lover or a friend; but I cannot be a saint, a poet, an artist a lover or a friend unless I have recently had something to eat." [13] The case for a guaranteed minimum standard of living for every citizen was never more cogently put. It may seem platitudinous now, when the scale of living guaranteed to the unemployed, the aged, and the sick would make the mouths water of those who lived on the rations of World War II, but Wicksteed's analysis has to be set against the conditions of the London poor in the late nineteenth century and against that Edwardian society which, as Osbert Sitwell and Harold Nicolson have so elegantly shown, made poems drowsier, pictures bigger, summers hotter, and meals heavier than ever before.

The implications of the debate about laissez faire were far-reaching. Gunnar Myrdal has pointed out that the crucial issue for classical liberalism was the justification of the existing legal institutions. Property is an historical category. The liberals tacitly assumed that the pattern of property made by the past was good both for production and for distribution. When it was clear that this was not necessarily so, modern economics was born, because it became necessary to consider the full implications of deliberate intervention in either the productive or the distributive process.

The weakness of the classical laissez-faire tradition was not merely that it did not consider seriously the problem of poverty, it was also a failure in international politics because it did not create institutions which could counterbalance the power of the national state. While it was laissez faire about the internal distribution of goods and services, it was anarchical in its conception of interstate relations. It assumed that if governments had limited functions because of the harmony among the competitive interests of their individual citizens, war would not be likely because governments would not have the resources to wage it and should they ever be so foolish as to do so, they would find that it did not pay.

It is not unreasonable to have spent so long on the shortcomings of the great liberal tradition of the nineteenth century. If in the development of mathematical physics we find the roots of the balance of terror in which we live, it is in the work of the modern economist that one finds the gyroscope of the social order we still possess. The economist is to the social order what the physicist is to the material world. It is a difference about economic analysis which has riven the modern world as once it was disputes about the Logos which divided the medieval. Should Western civilization ever follow into oblivion the empires of the past one cause at least will lie in some failure in economic insight and analysis, for, as Wicksteed saw, economic analysis is a condition of our mortality— the entire life, whether of an individual or of a community, is a constant problem in the allocation of the talent or the span of years granted.

There was a more subtle and even more important question than the limitations of the analysis of the Victorian pattern of economic individualism. Bradley considered that the individualism of the utilitarians was responsible for the failure of the English before 1914 to understand the real nature of the civilization by which they lived. In this he was supported—with varying overtones—by T. H. Green and Bosanquet. To Bradley the Benthamite fallacy was its assumption that a community was the sum of its parts and that the individual would not perish if every form of community were destroyed. Of this Bradley said that it was mere fancy. "What we call an individual man is what he is because of and by virtue of community, and communities can be regarded only as the one in the many. The individual is what he is because he is a born and educated social being, and a member of an individual social organism . . . If we take this world away we take him away." [14] In Bradley the analysis of the nature of a human community is a restatement of the Platonic view that the social order is a moral order of which the individual members are aware of one another's identity and difference and of their interdependence in the making and the sharing of a common good. In Bradley the restatement of the Greek analysis of the community as a moral organism is made with a sceptical detachment and empiricism derived from Hume, with a sense of the past given by historical scholarship in the nineteenth century, and with a hope of development suggested by the evidence of the rise of human civilization from bestial roots.

The political implications of the distinction between the conception of the community as a collection and the community as a moral organism were far-reaching. They still lie at the heart of our present discontents. Bradley's point was that it is deadly to talk of self-determination and of self-government when we have not critically considered what we can mean by a self. How burning may be the sense of self we may know from a contemporary of Bradley's, Gerard M. Hopkins, who wrote: "When I consider myself being my consciousness and feeling of myself, that taste of myself, of I and Me above all and in all things, which is more distinctive than the taste of ale or alum, more distinctive than the smell of walnut leaf or camphor and incommunicable by any means to another man . . . Nothing explains or resembles it, except in so far as this, that other men to themselves have the same feeling." [15] So can a poet transmute a philosopher's statement that society "involves a reciprocal recognition of identity and difference."

Bradley with his passion for Shakespeare would have agreed. But under the scrutiny of his Humean analysis the self is almost dissolved: "Infancy and old age, disease and madness, bring new features while others are borne away. It is hard indeed to fix any limit to the self's mutability . . . This creature, lost in illusions, bereft of memory, transformed in mood, with diseased feelings enthroned in the very heart of his being

—is this still one self with what we knew?" Assert if you like that there is still a point untouched, a spot which has never been invaded. But is this bare remnant really the self? If the self had been narrowed to a point which does not change, that point is less than the real self. But anything wider has a 'complexion' which shifts to strange effects and therefore cannot be oneself.[16]

This is the analysis of Hume touched with the passion of Swift. It led him to one of the great English statements of what a social order implies. "It is obvious that I and you, this man and the other man, are finite beings. We are not one another; more or less we must limit each other's sphere . . . I must progress because I have another which is to be, and yet never is quite myself. I find myself by being not merely one of a collection, but by being a member in a whole. In this whole or moral organism the members are aware of themselves and aware of themselves as members." The world in fact is such that men can and do make the same intellectual construction. "We are convinced that we have understood, and again are ourselves understood." "In fact," he added, "the higher we mount from the facts of sense, and the wider our principles have become, the more nearly we approach identity . . . it is for example more likely that we share our general morality with another man, than that we both have the same tastes in common." [17] Then comes a touch of Augustinian realism: "Even in an imaginary society evils remain. . . . Finite beings are physically subject to accident; and the members of an organism must of necessity be sacrificed more or less to the whole. For they must more or less be made special in their function, and that means rendered to some extent onesided and narrow, and if so, the harmony of their individual being must inevitably in some degree suffer." [18]

Bradley was the most original and independent thinker of the philosophers who dominated British intellectual life before 1914. Their inspiration was as much Kant as Hegel, and, even more, was it Plato and Aristotle. Philosophy was then a timeless debate between men of genius in which Plato answered Hume and Russell criticized Aristotle. This idealist school was as much American as English. Josiah Royce at Harvard was one of its most distinguished exponents. It was not seriously attacked until in the 1920's the revolutionary works of Russell, *Principles of Mathematics,* and Moore's *Principia Ethica* and the *Refutation of Idealism,* which were to overturn the English-speaking philosophical world, made their full influence felt. Bergson and William James had prepared the way before them. The 1920–30 decade of realism in British philosophy passed after 1930 into an era of analytical empiricism or logical positivism, bred of realism as Death was born of

Sin. The new school held that they were in the great English-speaking empirical tradition, which, since the seventeenth century, had been the most striking English and American contribution to Western thought and culture. From this tradition the influence of the idealists from 1880 to 1920 had been an unfortunate aberration. The idealists, for their part, considered that they were in the great European Platonic tradition, of which the empiricism of Hume and his successors was a narrow and insular perversion. They would say that had they been understood there need have been no strange death of liberalism. Their opponents would say liberalism need never die provided that empiricism is understood.

In 1903 Moore in his *Refutation of Idealism* advanced the theory that what is known is independent of the knowing mind. Bradley had said —and it was central to the idealist position—that "the so called brute facts were half thought out theory, a scheme of terms and relations brought into being by the destruction of a felt whole." Show him a fact and he would prove it to be a theory. Moore and the realists held that in knowledge the facts were directly present to us and that the knowing of them did not change them. The claim that the mind has a direct access to reality meant a claim to have direct access to some very queer fish indeed. When one understands a statement which one neither believes nor disbelieves, what is it one really knows? The realists were soon moving in a realm of reals neither mental nor physical and stranger than any Platonic world of forms. The external world retreated behind a veil or screen of sense data. Persons and things slid away from their scrupulous and exact analysis. Their great principle that nothing is affected by being known was, if true, as true of human action as of anything else. Moral philosophy as a theory of moral action could make no difference to moral practice. Students were told, R. G. Collingwood said, that no philosopher could give them any ideals to live for. Guidance in the problems of life was not to be found from thinkers or from thinking. "If the realists," he wrote, "had wanted to train up a generation of Englishmen and Englishwomen expressly as the potential dupe of every adventurer in morals or politics, commerce or religion . . . no better way of doing it could have been discovered." [19] Political theory they destroyed by denying the conception of a "common good," the fundamental idea of all social life, and by insisting that all goods were private.

The realists held that the proper job of the philosopher was not to consider the general nature of things, but to state clearly what common sense and science in fact believed. He had not to speculate but to clarify. But the effort to be really clear destroyed the realist school itself and led to the new school of logical positivism. This denounced most traditional philosophy and gutted all British philosophy except Hume. It denied that it was possible to come to know anything merely by speculation or that it was possible to synthesize the results of the special sciences or to offer any hierarchy of values. It had been the claim of the idealists that we were entitled to satisfy our instinctive longing to reflect, that "the world and our share in it is a natural object of thought." Bradley had written, "unless we have a criterion which only metaphysics can give we can say nothing about the comparative meaning and place in the world owned by art, science, religion, social life, and morality." [20]

The new school distinguished between statements which say something about the world because they can be confirmed by experience, for example, the whole field of natural science; statements of meaning which are not descriptions but are either tautological or prescriptions about the use of words, such as, that a bishop in chess cannot make the same move as a rook or that hearts in this game are trumps; and statements of value which give no facts and state no logical necessities, but are either mere exclamations, for example, "how horrid!" or attempts to influence another person by calling his attention to certain natural features in a situation, such as, "you have your foot on my face." The cloud-capped pinnacles of traditional philosophy from Plato to Bradley were based on ambiguities in language.

Common speech being a part of the organism is not less complicated than the heart. It was not surprising the logic of language, like the circulation of the blood, should have been a late discovery of time. Once we saw that language had disguised our thoughts, as our clothes had covered our nakedness, we would see that the deepest problems of philosophy were really no problems at all. The job of the philosopher was to search out the ways in which language was misleading us about the structure of facts. In the case of morals one could attempt to show what people are doing when they make moral judgments, but it would be idle to suggest what moral judgments they are to make. In fact it was soon seen that while the new school might stigmatize the work of traditional philosophy as the giving of meaningless answers to pseudoquestions, it was, under the name of analysis, doing what under the name of philosophy has always been done. They were interpreting our experience to the best of their ability.

If one looks at the climate of thought from Bradley at the height of his powers to the full rigors of the modern analytical school one detects a certain similarity. Bradley had said, and all the great philosophers would have agreed with him, that (1) it was not possible to refrain from reflection about the nature of the world and of our place in it. It was simply a question of whether or not we were to follow the argument as far as it would go or to stop at some arbitrary point suggested by custom, by religion, or by self-interest; (2) it was not the function of the philosopher to anticipate the discoveries of particular sciences or to guess the course of history, but it was not unreasonable from time to time to give system to the results of the natural sciences and to arrange them on what seemed to be a principle of worth; (3) by nourishing a true scepticism which is "the attempt to become aware of and to doubt all preconceptions," philosophy will protect us against the false scepticism by which all beliefs come to be mere opinion:

> Ask what is reasonable.   See how time and clime,
> Conform the mind more than body in the environment.
> What then and there was reason, is here and now absurd,
> What I now chance to approve may be or become to others
>   strange and unpalatable

and against dogmatic superstition whether of an orthodox theology or commonplace materialism.

In the case of politics if we do not face the problem of the nature of our partial unities we may oscillate between the dangers of an abstract general will or a meaningless aggregate of separate desires—the sovereignty of the people or the will of the majority. The need for political philosophy comes from the fact that we have a unity which we do not fully understand and that we are divided we do not know precisely how. The philosophical idealist had seen the danger latent in the formulas of the utilitarians, the naive determinism of the positivists, and the uncritical assumptions of popular religion.

From all this the philosophers, who, since 1920, have destroyed the influence of the idealist school which flourished from 1880 to 1920, have not been far away. Moore said in 1910 that the most important thing which philosophers have tried to do is to give a general description of the *whole* of the universe, and he did not consider this to be in principle vicious or impossible. With Bradley they would have agreed that the function of philosophy is to keep out of our lives what we really do not understand. The function of philosophy is to sterilize the mind against the infection of monstrous beliefs and fantastic superstitions. The new movement after 1920 had, as part of its task, "to free the spirit from the tyranny of words by exposing the delusions which arise almost inevitably through the use of a word language." The poet may say "all sounds, all colours . . . evoke indefinite and yet precise emotions, or, as I prefer to think, call down among us certain disembodied powers whose footsteps over our hearts we call emotion." [21] The philosopher will say, when a sceptic struggles to express himself he seems to be talking non-sense because he has to use a language which is not fit for his purpose. His problems are not spurious. He has to contemplate things through the prism of language. But he may have a vision—a piercing of the dead crust of tradition and convention, a new and broader way of looking at things.[22]

A. N. Whitehead has in the first half of the twentieth century combined a philosophical criticism of abstractions with an insight into the spirit of the natural sciences. He saw that the literature of the nineteenth century in England witnessed a discord between the aesthetic intuitions of mankind and the theory of the mechanism of nature. The world was a dance of particles of which the nature was unknown and the pattern imposed was easy to understand but very difficult to believe. The doctrine of minds as independent substances somehow attached to colonies of particles, had involved private worlds of experience and also private worlds of morals. It had meant a habit of ignoring the intrinsic worth of one's environment, for example, aesthetic beauty. It had meant a celibacy of the intellect divorced from the concrete contemplation of the complete facts. It meant that the specialist functions of the community were performed better while the general direction lacked vision.

The concern of the philosophers was echoed in the poet T. S. Eliot's *The Sacred Wood:* "When there is so much to be known, where there are so many fields of knowledge in which the same words are used with different meanings, when every one knows a little about a great many things, it becomes increasingly difficult for any one to know whether he knows what he is talking about or not. And when we do not know, or when we do not know enough we tend always to substitute emotion for thoughts." [23] The result in political theory, Eliot said, was that its real data were "impersonal forces which may have originated in the conflict and combination of human wills, but have come to supercede them ... Being occupied with humanity only in the mass, it tends to separate itself from ethics; being occupied only with the recent period of history during which humanity can most easily be shown to have been ruled by impersonal forces, it reduces the proper study of mankind to the last two or three hundred years of man. It too often inculcates a belief in the future inflexibly determined and at the same time in a future which we are wholly free to shape as we like." [24]

If one had to say what was the most characteristic temper of British thought in the first half of this century, it would be the thirst for a philosophy of life and the failure to find one. Before it had been realized that the political, economic, and cultural supremacy of Europe, which had been steadily growing since about 1500, had been lost in little more than a generation, and the anxious quest had begun for some political means of recovering the lost unity of Europe as the only defense against the menace of alien cultures, the need for a philosophy had been felt by every man of letters sensitive to the climate of his time. It was G. K. Chesterton who wrote: "The best reason for a revival of philosophy is that unless a man has a philosophy certain horrible things will happen to him. He will be practical; he will be progressive; he will cultivate efficiency; he will trust in evolution; he will do the work which lies nearest; he will devote himself to deeds not words . . . a man who refuses to have his own philosophy . . . will only have the used scraps of somebody else's philosophy." And a far greater philosopher than Chesterton, and one who had a complete detachment from the Christian tradition, whether Catholic or Protestant, J. M. McTaggart, wrote that it would depend upon our metaphysics, or view of the ultimate nature of reality "whether we can regard the troubles of the present, and the uncertainties of the future, with the feeling of a mouse towards a cat, or of a child towards its father." [25] He was afraid that, as the study of metaphysics was only open to those who had a certain amount of natural and acquired fitness for it, "the number of people who will be left between the rapidly diminishing help of revelation and the possible increasing help of metaphysics seems likely to be unpleasantly large." [26] Because, as C. S. Lewis had noted, the most important change in Europe in the last hundred years has been its dechristianization, and because, in our age, the destiny of man has been for the first time posed as a political problem, the great literature has been about political philosophy, and most so when, on the surface, it was seemingly least political. The novels and poems of the age of E. M. Forster and T. S. Eliot, of D. H. Lawrence and W. H. Auden, of James Joyce and Virginia Woolf have been even more political than were Shakespeare and Swift.

In Wyndham Lewis we have had one of the great political satirists in the English language. If he was not so controlled as Swift; if his weapon was not a deadly literalness, but comic overemphasis it was because he had far more to disturb him. Swift had only to consider the comedy of man against nature; he had not to face the horrors of man controlling the inner forces of nature. In *The Art of Being Ruled,* Wyndham Lewis wrote: "It is because our lives are so attached to and involved with the evolution of our machines that we have grown to see and feel everything in revolutionary terms, just as once the natural mood was conservative. We instinctively repose on the future rather than on the past, though this may not yet be generally realized. Instead of the static circle of the rotation of crops, or the infinitely slow progress of handiwork, we are in the midst of the frenzied evolutionary war of the machines." [27] In his last book *The Human Age* he stated his anguish and despair for the fate of mankind in one of the great prose works of our age.

Of the seeming disjointedness and the wealth of literary borrowing of T. S. Eliot's *The Waste Land,* F. R. Leavis wrote that it reflected the present state of civilization. "The traditions and cultures have mingled, and the historical imagination makes the past contemporary; no one civilisation can digest so great a variety of materials, and the result is a breakdown of forms and the irrevocable loss of that sense of absoluteness which seems necessary to a robust culture." The rapid changes of a Machine Age cause a breach of continuity and uproot life. "We are witnessing today . . . the final uprooting of the immemorial ways of life, of life rooted in the soil." [28] If T. S. Eliot was to shore the ruins with fragments of the past, Yeats was "to create a whole cosmology out of pre-Christian myth, to come out openly for the pagan conception of the recurrent cycle as against the Christian liberal humanist conception of historical development as an irreversible process." [29] Yeats in his own words "made a new religion, almost an infallible church of poetic tradition, of a fardel of stories, and personages, and of emotions, inseparable from their first expression, passed on from generation to generation by poets and painters with some help from philosophers and theologians." [30]

That Yeats—the greatest poet of his time—should have made a new religion and T. S. Eliot, a great poet and our greatest critic since Coleridge, should have shored his ruins with fragments are symptoms of the strain, if not the sickness, which new knowledge has caused in the last hundred years. In Britain the tension between the insularity of her Protestant culture and the universal quality of her language—the speech that Shakespeare used and the working tool of a most philistine people—has increased the strain. It has a wider significance than a cause or symptom of the fall of the British empire; it is a symptom of the sickness of the West.

The influence of the new knowledge operates in many ways; it brings wider power and more onerous responsibilities—that is the political problem; it creates a tension between the unity which it implies and the existing unities political and cultural which it tends to destroy. E. M. Forster, whose *Passage to India* F. R. Leavis has called "a classic of the liberal spirit," has said that he may have stopped writing novels because the social aspect of the world has changed so much that although he can think about the new world he cannot put it into fiction. The nineteenth century he says had emphasized progress; the early twentieth century, while not rejecting progress, felt itself more realistic if it approached progress through problems. "The problems lay about like sheets torn out of Euclid, all waiting to be solved, and disposed of with impeccable clarity." [31] But in the 1920's it was realized that the so-called solutions "were hydras who produced more heads than had been decapitated." One had to turn "to curiosity, to pleasure, and to compassion, the shaky tripod upon which indeed any future civilisation will have to rest." [32] But a tripod must have a world on which to stand. Art for art's sake is a profound phrase which indicates that art is a self-contained harmony. "It is valuable because it has to do with order, and creates little worlds of its own, possessing internal harmony in the bosom of this disordered planet." [33] But between the microcosm of the artist, however harmonious, and the unknowable cosmos, there must be some ordered arrangement of matter, mind, and passion. The poet must live in some polis even though it is not Greek. It is for this reason that in the Western world the democratic principle as the political concomitant of the scientific spirit has an almost religious authority. If the voice of the people properly understood is not the voice of God then there is no God. The political order is a necessary condition of every art.

There can be no doubt that the democratic system of government is one of the triumphs of the human spirit. The British constitution has, like the Greek polis, the qualities of a great communal work of art. But the polis did not adapt itself to Alexander, and it is not obvious that the British constitution and similar subtle democratic forms can be adapted to the changes which are thronging round and through it, born of the mating of thought and matter modern science means. Poets and critics and novelists show their unease in the presence of forces which are changing the conditions on which their art depends.

In the nineteenth century the discussion of politics was dominated by two themes which sometimes subtly interwove and sometimes crudely clashed—the universal order of the economic world and the local, historically determined order of the nation state, which was the Greek polis writ large, freed from slavery, with every citizen an immortal soul. After 1870 these themes were twisted, knotted, and nearly broken by the new knowledge we have discussed. In particular, the extension of scientific method to the study of history meant that the past was opened, and men could see past the Garden of Eden into abysses of time swarming with men like themselves and civilizations which had been long and subtle before they passed away. For a time—under the influence of a naive positivist theory of social change—if the past were open the future was closed. We were on our way. It has been the task of competent philosophers from Bradley through Sidgwick and, in this decade, K. Popper to remove this delusion of determinism. The future is open because we do not know what we may come to know, and a new idea makes possible a future before undreamed.

The effect of the new knowledge on the writer has been put by Virginia Woolf: "The mind is full of monstrous, hybrid, unmanageable emotions; that the age of the earth is 3,000,000,000 years; that human life lasts but a second; that the capacity of the human mind is nevertheless boundless; that life is infinitely adorable but disgusting; that science and religion have between them destroyed belief; that all bonds of union seem broken, yet some control must exist. It is in this atmosphere of doubt and conflict that writers have now to create." [34] Writers have been driven to create their own worlds. They lack the strength which comes from feeling their world is a microcosm of a cosmos they and their readers know. Shakespeare's world was a humanist world and reason and passion could fill its space. Its planets sang, and its stars were moved by love. Its backroom boys were mere apothecaries and astrologers. It was a very different world from

> this stupid world where
> Gadgets are gods and we go on talking,
> Many about much, but remain alone.

In Shakespeare's world the questions were more searching than the answers. In the modern world the question may be trivial and the answers embarrassingly precise to x decimal places. The poet and the novelist have had to adapt themselves to this terrible and mysterious and everchanging cosmos.

The writer has certain advantages. All the past tends, with growing scholarship, to become contemporary. As T. S. Eliot had put it, we do not seek factual knowledge of a poet's period in order to project ourselves into his age, but "rather to divest ourselves of the limitations of our own age, and the poet, whose work we are reading, of the limitations of his age, in order to get the direct experience of the immediate contact with his poetry." [35] If the past can be made present in this way the mystery of personality has been made deeper. We carry our past in the structure of our mind.

> 'O the mind, mind has mountains cliffs of fall
> Frightful, sheer, no-man-fathomed,

so the poet G. M. Hopkins felt the depths that Freud was to measure. For writers it has meant a wholly new insight into the place of sex in civilization. In the past, civilizations have had phallic symbols which they worshipped. In our own, an attempt has been made to understand sex with the seriousness that the Greek gave to the study of thought. It has been a profound influence in the English novel. It is the more noticeable because the weight of the Victorian and Edwardian taboo had been so heavy. The evidence for this is not to be denied. The problem was clearly stated by Henry James in *The Future of the Novel* in 1899: "While society was frank, was free about the incidents and accidents of the human constitution, the novel took the same robust ease as society." [36] But later "there came into being a mistrust of any but the most guarded treatment of the great relations between men and women, the constant world renewal, which was the conspicuous sign that whatever the prose picture of life was prepared to take upon itself, it was not prepared to take upon itself not to be superficial." [37] He noted "the revolution taking place in the position and outlook of women," and added: "It is the opinion of some observers that when women do obtain a free hand they will not repay their long debt to the precautionary attitude of men by unlimited consideration for the natural delicacy of the latter." [38] In George Eliot there had been intimations of a revolt against the barriers imposed by convention—she does so wish to discuss female sexual desire in *Middlemarch*. Virginia Woolf was to note in her *Room of One's Own* how the woman writer would be hampered by taboos she could not break. Dorothy Richardson in *Pilgrimage* was to use the technique of the interior monologue to do for women what, in Hamlet, Shakespeare had done for men. But although H. G. Wells was her raw material for the masculine pole of her novel the sexual analysis is delicate and shy. Only in Joyce's *Ulysses* has female desire and reverie been given the full recognition that one is sure George Eliot would have admired.

There is a somatic soil in which the mind is rooted, and there is no greater diversity in unity than the sexual differentiation of the human psyche. Shakespeare's Beatrice said that a star danced when she was born. A modern poet, W. H. Auden, is troubled by a more earthly conjunction:

> ... Let slight infection,
>   Disturb a trifle some tiny gland,
>   And Caustic Keith grows kind and silly,
>   Or Dainty Daisy dirties herself ...

The sense of our deep involvement with nature, the root of all great poetry, has in this century been enriched by the growth of biological science:

> The force that through the green fuse drives the flowers
> Drives my green age; that blasts the roots of trees
> Is my destroyer.

F. R. Leavis had written: ". . . our time, in literature, may fairly be called the age of D. H. Lawrence and T.S. Eliot." [39] They dominated the age in creative pre-eminence. Eliot mirrored the waste land of a culture which seemed unable to bear the burden which knowledge brings. He had said himself: "We can assert with some confidence that our own period is one of decline; that the standards of culture are lower than they were fifty years ago; and that the evidence of the decline are visible in every department of human activity." [40] The strength of Lawrence was that, a miner's son born in the 1880's, he knew the working class from inside and, gifted as he was, could get to know life at other social levels. He knew too "in intimate experience and confrontation, the interpenetration of the old agricultural English with the industrial; the contrast of the organic forms and rhythms and the old beauty of human adaptation with what had supervened." His greatness came from his intelligence—"that generalizing power which never leaves the concrete—the power . . . of exposing the movement of civilization in the malady of the individual psyche." [41]

NOTES

NOTES TO CHAPTER I

1. T. S. Ashton, *An Economic History of England: The 18th Century* (1955), p. 1.
2. David Ogg, *England in the Reigns of James II and William III* (1955), p. 115.
3. *Ibid.*, p. 134.
4. B. Mandeville, *The Fable of the Bees* (2d ed.; 1723), p. 342.
5. Ogg, *op. cit.*, p. 293.
6. Mandeville, *op. cit.*, p. 211.
7. Ashton, *op. cit.*, pp. 31–33.
8. Ogg, *op. cit.*, pp. 116–19.
9. *The New Cambridge Modern History*, vol. VII (1957), p. 30.
10. Ashton, *op. cit.*, pp. 95–97.
11. Mandeville, *The Fable of the Bees*, Part II (1729), p. 336.
12. David Hume, *Dialogues Concerning Natural Religion* (1779), p. 25.
13. Mandeville, *The Fable of the Bees* (2d ed.; 1723) p. 86.
14. Ashton, *op. cit.*, p. 24.
15. Charles Wilson, *Mercantilism* (1958), p. 26.
16. *Ibid.*, p. 5.

NOTES TO CHAPTER II

1. *The Eighteenth Century Constitution* (Documents and Commentary). Compiled and introduced by E. N. Williams (1960), p. 2.
2. *Ibid.*, p. 26; D. Ogg, *England in the Reigns of James II and William III* (1955), pp. 211, 244.
3. Richard Pares, *The Historian's Business* (1961), chap. VII, and George S. Pryde, "Marriage of Convenience," *The Times*, Jan. 5, 1957.
4. Swift, *Political Tracts*, vol. 2 (1738), pp. 132–33.
5. Addison, *The Freeholder*, No. 22.
6. Ogg, *op. cit.*, p. 507.
7. *Ibid.*, p. 243.
8. B. Mandeville, *Free Thoughts on Religion, the Church, and National Happiness* (1720), p. 304.
9. *Ibid.*, pp. 314–15.
10. John Locke, *The Second Treatise of Civil Government*, chap. XIII, §157.
11. Ogg, *op. cit.*, p. 131.
12. *Ibid.*, p. 72, citing *State Trials*, XIV, 632.
13. J. H. Plumb, *Sir Robert Walpole* (1956), vol. 2, p. 240.
14. *Ibid.*, p. 19.
15. *Ibid.*, p. 73.

16. *Ibid.,* p. 80 and note. "The Walpole system was in fact a logical solution to the constitutional problem of the age . . ." W. R. Brock, *The New Cambridge Modern History,* vol. VII (1957), p. 253.

17. *Ibid.,* pp. 233, 325.

18. Erich Eyck, *Pitt versus Fox* (1950), p. 34.

19. *The New Cambridge Modern History,* vol. VII, p. 255.

NOTES TO CHAPTER III

1. On Britain's seven wars with France between 1689 and 1815 see Lord Strang, *Britain in World Affairs* (New York: Praeger, 1961), p. 63.

2. *Ibid.,* p. 53.

3. Mandeville, *Fable of the Bees* (2d ed.; 1723), pp. 204–5.

4. On the monetary preoccupations of mercantilism see Charles Wilson, *Mercantilism* (1958), p. 18.

5. The State Paper written by Sir Eyre Crowe on January 1, 1907, reproduced what were virtually Canning's ideas on foreign policy eighty years before. H. Temperley and L. M. Penson, *Foundations of British Foreign Policy* (1938), p. xxvii.

6. Strang, *op. cit.,* p. 63.

7. *The New Cambridge Modern History,* vol. VII (1957), chap. VIII, p. 175.

8. *Ibid.,* p. 174.

9. Charles Davenant, *An Essay upon the Balance of Power* (1701), pp. 72–73.

10. *The New Cambridge Modern History,* vol. V (1961), chap. XX, p. 475.

11. *The New Cambridge Modern History,* vol. VII, chap. XX, p. 465.

12. R. Pares, *The Historian's Business* (1961), chap. X, "American Versus Continental Warfare," p. 154.

13. *The New Cambridge Modern History,* vol. VII, pp. 536–37.

NOTES TO CHAPTER IV

1. B. Mandeville, *Fable of the Bees,* Part II (1729), p. 152.

2. J. Steven Watson, *The Reign of George III 1760–1815* (1960), p. 517. See H. J. Habakkuk, "English Population in the 18th Century," *Economic History Review,* 2d series, vi (1953–54), pp. 117–33.

3. Steven Watson, *op. cit.,* pp. 10–11.

4. T. S. Ashton, *An Economic History of England: The 18th Century* (1955), p. 16.

5. *Ibid.,* p. 125.

6. *Ibid.,* p. 74.

7. *Ibid.,* p. 140.

8. *Ibid.,* p. 47.

9. Steven Watson, *op. cit.,* p. 507.

10. Ashton, *op. cit.,* p. 183.

11. Joseph Schumpeter, *Two Essays: Imperialism; Social Classes* (Meridian Books, 1955), p. 18.

12. Steven Watson, *op. cit.,* pp. 20–22.
13. Elie Halévy, *A History of the English People in 1815* (1949), Book II, chap. 3 (p. 153 of Pelican edition).

NOTES TO CHAPTER V

1. Richard Pares, *King George III and the Politicians* (1953), p. 33.
2. *Ibid.,* p. 195.
3. *Ibid.,* p. 43.
4. *Ibid.,* p. 43.
5. Sir Lewis Namier, *Personalities and Powers, Essay on George III* (1955).
6. Pares, *op. cit.,* p. 75.
7. *Ibid.,* p. 78.
8. E. N. Williams, *The Eighteenth Century Constitution* (1960), p. 189
9. Pares, *op. cit.,* pp. 88–89.
10. John W. Derry, *William Pitt* (1962), chap. 3.
11. *Ibid.,* chap. 3.
12. W. K. Hancock and M. M. Gowing, *British War Economy* (1949), p. 13.
13. J. Steven Watson, *The Reign of George III 1760–1815,* pp. 388–89.
14. Edward Porritt, *The Unreformed House of Commons* (1903), vol. 2, p. 528.

NOTES TO CHAPTER VI

1. J. H. Plumb, *The First Four Georges* (1956), p. 106.
2. J. R. Alden, *The American Revolution* (1954), pp. 4–5.
3. Richard Price, *Observations on the Nature of Civil Liberty* (7th ed.; 1776), p. 15.
4. A. Sorel, *Europe and the French Revolution,* pp. 340–41, quoted by Lord Strang in *Britain in World Affairs* (1961), p. 90.
5. C. A. M. Dupuis, *Le Principe d'équilibre et concert européen,* pp. 41–42, quoted by Strang, *op. cit.,* p. 94.

NOTES TO CHAPTER VII

1. A. N. Whitehead, *Science and the Modern World* (1936), p. 104.
2. A. O. Lovejoy, *The Great Chain of Being* (1936).
3. C. D. Broad, *Ethics and the History of Philosophy* (1952), pp. 29–48. and cf. George Santayana, *Five Essays* (1933), p. 3.
4. H. A. Prichard, *Knowledge and Perception* (1950), p. 106.
5. *Ibid.,* p. 107.
6. *Ibid.,* p. 156.
7. David Hume, *Dialogues Concerning Natural Religion* (1779), p. 119.
8. Prichard, *op. cit.,* p. 175.
9. *Ibid.,* p. 199.
10. B. Mandeville, *Fable of the Bees,* ed. F. B. Kaye, 2 vols. (1924), Introduction.

11.   Jacob Viner, *Adam Smith 1776–1926* (1926), chap. 5.

12.   Gunnar Myrdal, *The Political Element in the Development of Economic Theory* (1953), p. 106.

13.   Samuel H. Monk, "The Pride of Lemuel Gulliver," *The Sewanee Review*, Winter 1955, pp. 48–71; reprinted in *Eighteenth-Century English Literature*, ed. by James L. Clifford (1959).

14.   J. M. Keynes, *Two Memoirs* (1949), p. 99.

NOTES TO CHAPTER VIII

1.   J. D. Chambers, *The Workshop of the World* (1961), p. 44.

2.   *Samuel Report on the Coal Industry* (1926).

3.   Quoted in Lord Strang, *Britain in World Affairs* (1961), pp. 132–33.

4.   H. J. Habakkuk, "A Powerful Agent of Social Change," *The Listener*, Dec. 22, 1955.

NOTES TO CHAPTER IX

1.   J. H. Plumb, *The First Four Georges* (1956), p. 162.

2.   Asa Briggs, *The Age of Improvement* (1959), pp. 184–85.

3.   W. R. Brock, *Lord Liverpool and Liberal Toryism 1820 to 1827* (1941), p. 34.

4.   Sir William Holdsworth, *A History of English Law*, vol. XIII (1952), p. 182.

5.   H. W. C. Davis, *The Age of Grey and Peel* (1929), p. 142.

6.   Holdsworth, *op. cit.*, p. 211.

7.   Briggs, *op. cit.*, p. 215.

8.   H. W. V. Temperley, *Foreign Policy of Canning* (1925), pp. 448–49.

9.   H. Temperley, in *Cambridge Modern History*, vol. X, p. 584.

10.   *Ibid.*, p. 591.

11.   Briggs, *op. cit.*, p. 228, quoting C. R. M. F. Cruttwell, *Wellington* (1936), p. 101.

12.   Plumb, *op. cit.*, pp. 158–59, quoting Roger Fulford, *George IV* (2d ed.; 1949), p. 222.

13.   *Ibid.*

14.   Norman Gash, *Politics in the Age of Peel* (1953), chap. I, "The Principles of the Reform Act."

15.   Frank Eyck, "Fresh Light on the Constitutional Monarchy," *The Listener*, June 20, 1957.

16.   J. Brooke, *The Chatham Administration 1766–68* (1956).

17.   Gash, *op. cit.*, p. 400, quoting Disraeli's *Coningsby*.

18.   Norman McCord, *The Anti-Corn Law League 1838–1846* (1958), p. 53.

19.   *Ibid.*, pp. 181–208.

20.   T. Layton and G. Crowther, *An Introduction to the Study of Prices* (2d ed.; 1935), p. 78; and see T. H. Marshall, "The Population of England and Wales from the Industrial Revolution to the World War," in E. M. Carus-Wilson (ed.), *Essays in Economic History* (1954), p. 343.

NOTES TO CHAPTER X

1. Lord Strang, *Britain in World Affairs* (1961), p. 158.
2. *Cabinet Memorandum of 26 December 1813; on Instructions for Peace-Making.* H. Temperley and L. M. Penson, *Foundations of British Foreign Policy* (1938), Document 4, p. 31.
3. Strang, *op. cit.,* p. 161.
4. Elie Kedourie, *Nationalism* (1960), pp. 77–79.
5. Sir Lewis Namier, *Basic Factors in Nineteenth Century European History* (1953), p. 2.
6. *Ibid.,* p. 2.
7. *Ibid.,* p. 3.
8. Temperley and Penson, *op. cit.,* Document 44, p. 174.
9. Richard Pares, *The Historian's Business* (1961), chap. V, "The Economic Factors in the History of the Empire," p. 65.
10. Temperley and Penson, *op. cit.,* p. 47, introduction to Document 6.
11. *Ibid.,* p. 54.
12. *Ibid.,* p. 86, Document 11. *Canning on Constitutions and Constitutionalism,* December 4, 1824.
13. *Ibid.,* p. 88, preface to Documents on Palmerston and Belgium, 1831–37.
14. C. K. Webster, *The Foreign Policy of Palmerston, 1830–1841* (1951), vol. 1, p. 397.
15. Temperley and Penson, *op. cit.,* p. 123.
16. *Ibid.,* Document 33. *Palmerston Instructs Nicholas I in the Obligations of the British Constitution,* January 11, 1841, pp. 135–38.
17. *The New Cambridge Modern History,* vol. X, p. 469.
18. *Ibid.,* pp. 267–68.
19. *Ibid.,* p. 270.
20. Temperley and Penson, *op. cit.,* Document 123. *Gladstone's Principles,* pp. 317–18.

NOTES TO CHAPTER XI

1. G. C. Allen, *British Industries and Their Organisation* (1951), p. 105.
2. W. Ashworth, *An Economic History of England 1870–1939* (1960), p. 42.
3. *Ibid.,* p. 237.
4. *Ibid.,* p. 254.
5. *Ibid.,* p. 161.
6. Allen, *op. cit.,* p. 52.
7. Ashworth, *op. cit.,* p. 12.
8. *Ibid.,* pp. 80–81.
9. H. W. Macrosty, *The Trust Movement in British Industry,* p. 337.
10. Ashworth, *op. cit.,* p. 49.
11. *Ibid.,* p. 191.
12. *Ibid.* p. 191.
13. *Ibid.,* p. 244.

NOTES TO CHAPTER XII

1. H. J. Hanham, *Elections and Party Management: Politics in the Time of Disraeli and Gladstone* (1959), an excellent analysis of boroughs, registers, carpetbaggers, and landlords and lodgers.
2. *Ibid.*
3. *Ibid.*
4. *Ibid.*
5. *Ibid.*
6. *Ibid.*
7. K. B. Smellie, *A Hundred Years of English Government* (1937), p. 141.
8. Balfour succeeded to the two offices of prime minister and leader without any opposition within the party. R. T. McKenzie, *British Political Parties* (1955), p. 27.
9. "Labour Party History," *Times Literary Supplement,* Mar. 10, 1950.
10. W. Beveridge, *Unemployment* (1908). A study of the unorganized condition of the labor market.
11. For a brief statement of the legal status of trade unions see chap. VIII of *Agenda for a Free Society* (Institute of Economic Affairs, 1961).

NOTES TO CHAPTER XIII

1. Lord Strang, *Britain in World Affairs* (1961), p. 373.
2. H. Temperley and L. Penson, *Foundations of British Foreign Policy* (1938), Document 164. Granville explains his attitude to the bombardment of Alexandria, July 12, 1882, pp. 420–21.
3. Strang, *op. cit.,* p. 165.
4. Temperley and Penson, *op. cit.,* Document 149. Gladstone stated his principles of foreign policy, November 27, 1879, pp. 391–94.
5. *Ibid.,* Document 200. Memorandum by the Marquis of Salisbury, May 29, 1901, pp. 518–20.
6. *The Cambridge History of the British Empire,* vol. III (1959), chap. XIII.
7. *Ibid.,* p. 114.
8. *Ibid.,* p. 134.
9. *Ibid.,* p. 167.
10. For detailed case, see R. Robinson and J. Gallagher, with Alice Denny, *Africa and the Victorians* (1961).
11. Lady G. Cecil, *Life of Lord Salisbury,* vol. 4, chap. 8–11, on the partition of Africa. House of Lords speech July 10, 1890, pp. 225–26.
12. Temperley and Penson, *op. cit.* Document 200, Memorandum by the Marquis of Salisbury, May 29, 1901, pp. 518–20.
13. H. V. Hodson, *Twentieth Century Empire* (1948).

NOTES TO CHAPTER XIV

1. J. S. Mill, "Coleridge," in *Dissertations and Discussions,* 3 vols. (2d ed.; 1867). There is a useful edition of J. S. Mill, *Bentham and Coleridge* (1956), ed. by F. R. Leavis.
2. A. N. Whitehead, *Science and the Modern World* (1936), chap. V, "The Romantic Reaction."
3. D. W. Harding, "William Blake," *The Pelican Guide to English Literature,* ed. Boris Ford, vol. 5, p. 79.
4. E. Heller, *The Disinherited Mind* (Pelican edition, 1961), p. 29.
5. Mill, *op. cit.*
6. J. R. Sutherland, *A Preface to Eighteenth-Century Poetry* (1948), p. 11.
7. Heller, *op. cit.,* p. 243.
8. Sutherland, *op. cit.,* p. 35.
9. R. O. C. Winkler, "Wordsworth's Poetry," *Pelican Guide to English Literature,* ed. Boris Ford, vol. 5 (1957), p. 161.
10. *Ibid.,* p. 169.
11. Martin Green, "A Year of Science," *The Listener,* Dec. 21, 1961.
12. L. E. Salingar, "Coleridge: Poet and Philosopher," *Pelican Guide to English Literature,* vol. 5, p. 200.
13. *Ibid.,* p. 186.
14. D. E. James, "Kant's Influence on Wordsworth and Coleridge," *The Listener,* Aug. 31, 1950.
15. William Walsh, "John Keats," *Pelican Guide to English Literature,* vol. 5, p. 230.
16. Carlyle to Emerson, Aug. 5, 1844; *Correspondence of Carlyle and Emerson,* vol. 2 (1883), p. 66.
17. F. Temple, "The Education of the World," *Essays and Reviews* (1860), p. 2.
18. T. S. Eliot, *Essays Ancient and Modern* (1936), p. 187.
19. A. and E. M. Sidgwick, *H. Sidgwick, A Memoir* (1906), p. 541.
20. Huxley to Tyndall, Oct. 15, 1892, *Huxley, Life and Letters* (1900), vol. III, p. 270.
21. "Laurel and Rue," *Times Literary Supplement,* Aug. 12, 1949.
22. "The Carlylean Vision," *Times Literary Supplement,* Feb. 13, 1956.
23. "Pablo Picasso," *Times Literary Supplement,* Dec. 22, 1961.
24. G. D. Klingopulos, "Notes on the Victorian Scene," *Pelican Guide to English Literature,* vol. 6, p. 22.
25. J. Y. T. Greig in *The Listener,* Sept. 15, 1949.
26. Humphry House, *The Dickens World* (Oxford Paperback, 1960), p. 145.
27. *Ibid.,* p. 151.
28. *Ibid.,* p. 152.
29. *Ibid.,* p. 180.
30. *Ibid.,* p. 215.
31. *Ibid.,* p. 217.

32. S. T. Coleridge, *Constitution of Church and State* (1830), pp. 23–24.
33. W. Bagehot, *The English Constitution* (1867).
34. Tom Paine. More simply "Society is produced by our wants, and Government by our wickedness" (First § of *Common Sense*).
35. Mill, *op. cit.*
36. Mark Pattison, "Tendencies of Religious Thought in England, 1688–1750," *Essays and Reviews* (1860), p. 257.
37. Klingopulos, *op. cit.*, vol. 6, p. 52.
38. Matthew Arnold, *Mixed Essays* (1874).
39. Gertrude Himmelfarb, *Darwin and the Darwinian Revolution* (1959), p. 196.
40. C. D. Darlington, "The Natural History of Man," *The Listener,* July 31, 1958.

NOTES TO CHAPTER XV

1. *The New Cambridge Modern History,* vol. XII (1960), p. 257.
2. C. E. Montague, *Disenchantment* (1922), p. 45.
3. *The New Cambridge Modern History,* vol. XII, p. 359.
4. Montague, *op. cit.,* p. 44.
5. *Cambridge History of the British Empire,* vol. III, p. 607.
6. Montague, *op. cit.,* p. 3.
7. *Ibid.,* p. 80.
8. *Ibid.,* pp. 30–31.
9. *Ibid.,* p. 3.
10. Lord Strang, *Britain in World Affairs* (1961), p. 312.
11. *Times Literary Supplement,* April 4, 1958.

NOTES TO CHAPTER XVI

1. Bernard Shaw, *What I Really Wrote about the War* (1931), chap. X, "Joy Riding at the Front," p. 240.
2. J. M. Keynes, *Essays in Biography* (1951).
3. *The Political Quarterly,* Oct.–Dec., 1952, p. 387.
4. Sir Ivor Jennings, *Party Politics* (1960), vol. I.
5. *Britain's Industrial Future* (1928), p. 85.
6. R. Bassett, *Nineteen Thirty-One* (1958), Introduction.

NOTES TO CHAPTER XVII

1. J. M. Keynes, *The Economic Consequences of the Peace* (1919).
2. *Ibid.,* p. 1.
3. *Chase Economic Bulletin,* March 14, 1960. Quoted in *New Cambridge Modern History,* vol. XII (1960).
4. W. Ashworth, *An Economic History of England 1870 to 1939* (1960), p. 288.
5. *Ibid.,* pp. 414–15.

6. Richard Stone, director of the Department of Applied Economics, Cambridge. *The Times,* Feb. 25, 1954.
7. *Salient Features of the World Economic Situation, 1945–47,* Economic Report, Department of Economic Affairs, United Nations (Jan. 1948), p. 243. Quoted *New Cambridge Modern History,* vol. XII, p. 49.
8. Dunning and Thomas, *British Industry* (1960), p. 19.
9. Hubert Henderson, *The Inter-War Years* (1955), pp. 92–93.
10. W. Arthur Lewis, *Economic Survey 1919–1939* (1949), chap. 5.

NOTES TO CHAPTER XVIII

1. H. E. Bates, Review of *The Battle of Britain* by Ed Bishop, *The Listener,* Sept. 8, 1960.
2. John Strachey, *Post D* (1941).
3. C. K. Webster and Noble Frankland, *The Strategic Air Offensive Against Germany 1939–1945,* 4 vols. (1961), vol. III, p. 288.
4. *The Listener,* Nov. 6, 1958.
5. *The Times,* July 25, 1959.
6. C. M. Woodhouse, *British Foreign Policy since the Second World War* (1961), p. 225.
7. L. Robbins, "Towards the Atlantic Community," *Lloyd's Bank Review,* July 1950.
8. W. Churchill, *The Second World War* (1954), vol. VI, p. 433.
9. J. Strachey, *The End of Empire* (1959), p. 145.
10. Woodhouse, *op. cit.,* p. 235.
11. *Ibid.,* p. 135.
12. *Materials Policy Commission,* 1952.
13. Woodhouse, *op. cit.,* pp. 227–29.
14. *Ibid.,* p. 229.
15. *Ibid.,* p. 232.

NOTES TO CHAPTER XIX

1. *The Sterling Area: An American Analysis. Economic Cooperation Administration Special Mission to the United Kingdom* (1951), p. 151.
2. Richard N. Gardner, *Sterling Dollar Diplomacy* (1957).
3. *The Economist,* July 15, 1961.
4. L. Robbins, *Lloyd's Bank Review,* April 1958.
5. B. Roberts, *Lloyd's Bank Review,* April 1957.
6. L. Robbins, *op. cit.,* April 1958.
7. Cmnd. 9725, para. 25.
8. *Lloyd's Bank Review,* Oct. 1957.
9. Graham Hutton, *Lloyd's Bank Review,* July 1961.
10. *Economic Survey,* Cmnd. 1334, para. 23.
11. *Ibid.*
12. Hutton, *op. cit.*

NOTES TO CHAPTER XX

1.   A. N. Whitehead, *Science and the Modern World* (1936).
2.   C. R. Attlee, *As it Happened* (1954). A classic of meiosis. Marx has no mention in it.
3.   Winston S. Churchill, *My Early Years* (1930; new ed. 1947), p. 90. Quoted *New Cambridge Modern History,* vol. XII (1960), p. 58.
4.   P. H. Wicksteed, in *The New Party* (1894).
5.   Whitehead, *op. cit.*
6.   A. L. Lewis, *Principles of Economic Planning* (1949), p. 10.
7.   *Lloyd's Bank Review,* July 1958.
8.   P. E. P., *The Growth of Government,* Dec. 1957.
9.   *Lloyd's Bank Review,* April 1957.
10. *London and Cambridge Economic Bulletin,* Sept. 1960.
11. P. E. P., *op. cit.*
12. *Lloyd's Bank Review,* July 1958.
13. *Times Literary Supplement,* Oct. 1, 1960.
14. *Lloyd's Bank Review,* July 1956.

NOTES TO CHAPTER XXI

1.   A. N. Whitehead, *Science and the Modern World* (1936), chap. VI, "The Nineteenth Century."
2.   *The New Cambridge Modern History,* vol. XII (1960), "Science and Technology," pp. 100–101.
3.   T. S. Eliot, *For Lancelot Andrewes,* p. 70.
4.   J. S. Mill's *Three Essays on Religion* (1874) should be compared with Hume's.
5.   Published 1874. Reprinted in *Collected Essays,* 2 vols. (1935), vol. I, p. 45.
6.   *Appearance and Reality* (1893; 2d ed., 1897), pp. 452–53.
7.   *Ibid.,* p. 444.
8.   *Collected Essays* (1935), vol. I, chap. VIII, "The Limits of Individual and National Self Sacrifice."
9.   A. Marshall, *Memorials* (1925), p. 153.
10. For the intellectual difficulties of nineteenth-century economists see T. W. Hutchinson, *A Review of Economic Doctrines 1870–1929* (1953).
11. W. S. Jevons, quoted in Hutchinson, *op. cit.,* p. 49.
12. P. H. Wicksteed, in *The New Party* (1894), ed. Andrew Reid, pp. 240–41.
13. *Ibid.*
14. F. H. Bradley, *Ethical Studies* (1927).
15. G. M. Hopkins, *A Selection of His Poems and Prose,* by W. H. Gardner (Penguin Poets, 1953), pp. 147–48.
16. F. H. Bradley, *Appearance and Reality* (1920 ed.), pp. 80–81.
17. For a critical study see chap. 6 of R. Wollheim, *F. H. Bradley* (1959).
18. *Appearance and Reality,* pp. 421–22.

19. R. G. Collingwood, *Autobiography* (1939), pp. 48–49.
20. *Appearance and Reality,* Introduction.
21. W. B. Yeats.
22. F. Waismann, "How I See Philosophy," *Contemporary British Philosophy,* 3d series, ed. H. D. Lewis (1956), p. 483.
23. T. S. Eliot, *The Sacred Wood* (1920; University Paperback edition, 1960), p. 10.
24. T. S. Eliot, *Notes Towards the Definition of Culture* (1948), pp. 88–89.
25. J. M. McTaggart, *Some Dogmas of Religion* (1906), § 26, p. 32.
26. *Ibid.*
27. Wyndham Lewis, *The Art of Being Ruled* (1926), p. 11.
28. F. R. Leavis, *New Bearings in English Poetry* (Ann Arbor Paperbacks, 1960), p. 91.
29. W. H. Auden, Preface to vol. 4, *Poets of the English Language* (1952).
30. W. B. Yeats.
31. *The Listener,* May 22, 1958.
32. *Ibid.*
33. E. M. Forster, *Two Cheers for Democracy* (1951), pp. 70–71.
34. Virginia Woolf, *Granite and Rainbow* (1958), p. 12.
35. *Poetry and Poets* (1957), p. 117.
36. *Future of the Novel* (1899), p. 56.
37. *Ibid.*
38. Cf. the early tale "At Isella" (1871) reprinted in *The Complete Tales of Henry James,* ed. Leon Edel (1962), vol. 2, p. 330. Women in America "live more in the broad daylight of life. They make their own laws."
39. F. R. Leavis, *D. H. Lawrence* (1955), p. 303.
40. Eliot, *Notes Towards the Definition of Culture* (1948), pp. 18–19.
41. Leavis, *op. cit.,* pp. 234–35.

SUGGESTED READINGS

In the list of books which follows I have included (1) the books I have plundered for my text; (2) books of value for the history of Britain in this period, even though I may not have used them as I should; and (3) books that will help the student with special problems.

CHAPTER I

The best short study of English economic history in this period is T. S. Ashton, *An Economic History of England: The 18th Century* (1955). The student will want to consult: T. S. Ashton, *Economic Fluctuations in England 1700–1800* (1959). J. H. Clapham's *A Concise Economic History of England from the Earliest Times to 1750* is useful. David Ogg's *England in the Reign of James II and William III* (1955) is full and thorough. There is a brief general survey by J. H. Plumb, *England in the Eighteenth Century*. H. J. Habbakuk, "English Landownership, 1680–1740," *Economic History Review* (1939–40), is important for the student.

CHAPTER II

In vol. X of Sir William Holdsworth's *A History of English Law,* chap. 1 is a masterly brief survey of the period. Buried in this vast work it is a treasure for the student. E. N. Williams' *The Eighteenth Century Constitution* (1960) has a selection of key documents and a clear commentary. Mark Thomson's *A Constitutional History of England, 1642–1801* (1938) is a good textbook. J. H. Plumb's *The First Four Georges* (1956) is the constitution without tears and diplomatic history with wit. Lord Hervey's *Memoirs of the Reign of George II,* ed. Romney Sedgwick, 3 vols. (1931) is monarchy unveiled. Basil Williams' *The Whig Supremacy 1714–60* (1939) is comprehensive. There is a wealth of special studies: C. B. Realey, *The Early Opposition to Sir Robert Walpole 1720–27* (1931); R. Walcott, *English Politics in the Early Eighteenth Century* (1956); J. B. Owen, *The Rise of the Pelhams;* and vol. 1 of the new life of *Sir Robert Walpole* by J. H. Plumb (1960).

CHAPTER III

There is an excellent general survey of Britain's foreign policy in Lord Strang, *Britain in World Affairs* (1961). This is a survey of the fluctuations in the power and influence of Britain from Henry VIII to Elizabeth II. There is an American edition.

There is a full bibliography of England's imperial expansion in vol. I of the *Cambridge History of the British Empire.* Richard Pares, *The*

Historian's Business has in chap. X a study of American versus continental warfare 1739–63, and in chap. V a sketch of the economic factors in the history of the Empire. Kate Hotblack, *Chatham's Colonial Policy* (1917) is most important. *The New Cambridge Modern History,* vol. VII (1957), has useful chapters on the War of the Austrian Succession (chap. XVIII); the Diplomatic Revolution (chap. XIX); the Seven Years War (chap. XX); Rivalries in America (chap. XXII); and Rivalries in India (chap. XXIII).

CHAPTER IV

There is a brief luminous study of the industrial revolution by T. S. Ashton, *The Industrial Revolution* (1948). Other general studies are: Sir G. N. Clark, *The Idea of the Industrial Revolution* (1953); Asa Briggs, *The Age of Improvement* (1959); A. Redford, *The Economic History of England, 1760–1860* (1931); G. M. Trevelyan, *Social History of England* (1946), chap. X–XVI. Important special studies are T. S. Ashton, *Iron and Steel in the Industrial Revolution* (2d ed. 1951); T. S. Ashton and J. Sykes, *The Coal Industry of the Eighteenth Century* (1929); Lord Ernle (Prothero), *English Farming Past and Present* (1912; revised 1927); R. A. C. Parker, *Enclosures in the Eighteenth Century* (1960), a pamphlet published for the Historical Association; H. J. Habbakuk, "English Population in the Eighteenth Century," *The Economic History Review,* 2d series, VI (1953).

CHAPTER V

There is an excellent chapter on the political and constitutional developments in vol. XIII of W. S. Holdsworth, *History of English Law.* L. B. Namier, *The Structure of Politics at the Accession of George III* (1929) and *England in the Age of the American Revolution* (1930) are essential. Special studies: H. Butterfield, *George III, North, and the Politicians* (reprinted as chap. VIII of *The Historian's Business* (1961); J. Brooke, *The Chatham Administration, 1766–68* (1956); A. Aspinall, *The Cabinet Council, 1783–1835* (*Proceedings of the British Academy,* vol. 38, 1952); E. and A. G. Porritt, *The Unreformed House of Commons* (1903); A. and B. Webb, *English Local Government,* 7 vols. (1906–27). In chap. 5 and 6 of vol. 4 the essential changes between 1689 and 1832 are summarized. J. Steven Watson, *The Reign of George III* (1960) is the most recent general survey. In L. B. Namier, *Personalities and Powers* there is an essay on the character of George III. John W. Derry has an excellent brief life of *William Pitt* (1962).

CHAPTER VI

J. C. Miller, *Origins of the American Revolution* (1945). W. L. Mathieson, *England in Transition, 1789–1832* (1920). *The Cambridge History of the British Empire,* vol. II (1940). H. Temperley, *Life of Can-*

ning (1905). C. K. Webster, *The Foreign Policy of Castlereagh, 1812–1822* (1931–34). John Strachey, *The End of Empire* (1959). Edward Thompson and G. T. Garratt, *The Rise and Fulfilment of British Rule in India* (1934). Lord Strang, *Britain in World Affairs* (1961).

CHAPTER VII

The Age of Reason has, as one might expect, a fascination for the modern world. Basil Willey, *The Eighteenth Century Background* (1946) is a useful introduction to the English intellectual climate. Sir Leslie Stephen, *History of English Thought in the Eighteenth Century* (1902) is comprehensive if not comprehending. E. Cassirer, *Philosophy of the Enlightenment* (1951) is wide and deep. A. Wolf, *A History of Science, Technology and Philosophy in the Eighteenth Century* (1938) is useful. A. N. Whitehead, *Science and the Modern World* (1926) is a good introduction. Carl Becker, *The Heavenly City of the Eighteenth Century Philosophers* (1932) and Louis I. Bredvold, *The Brave New World of the Enlightenment* (1961) will give the student the introduction he needs. There is an excellent collection of modern essays in criticism in James L. Clifford, *Eighteenth Century English Literature* (1959). Useful, too, is H. V. D. Dyson and J. Butt, *Augustans and Romantics, 1689–1830* (rev. ed. 1951). The student will want to use P. Laslett's edition of Locke's *Two Treatises of Government;* F. B. Kaye's edition of B. Mandeville, *The Fable of the Bees* (1924); the introduction by Maynard Mack to vol. III of the Twickenham Edition of Alexander Pope (*Essay on Man*); A. O. Lovejoy, *The Great Chain of Being* (1936); A. O. Lovejoy, "The Meaning of Romanticism," *Journal of the History of Ideas* (1941); Irvin Ehrenpreis, *The Personality of Jonathan Swift* (1958); A. Beljame, *Men of Letters and the English Public* (1881 Paris; translated by E. O. Lorrimer, 1938); E. A. Burtt, *The Metaphysical Foundations of Modern Physical Science* (1925); M. H. Nicolson, *The Microscope and English Imagination* (1935); D. Bush, *Science and English Poetry;* H. Butterfield, *The Origins of Modern Science* (1942); Jacob Viner, "Adam Smith and Laissez-Faire," chap. 5, *Adam Smith, 1776–1926* (1926).

CHAPTER VIII

J. D. Chambers' *The Workshop of the World* is a clear brief study of British economic history from 1820 to 1880; also Sir John Clapham, *The Economic History of Modern Britain*, vol. 1, *The Railway Age;* vol. 2, *The Age of Free Trade and Steel.* There is a bibliographical essay in *The Victorian Origins of the British Welfare State*, by D. Roberts (1960). Elie Halévy, *The History of the English People*, vols. I–IV; A. D. Gayer, W. W. Rostow, and A. J. Schwarz, *The Growth and Fluctuations of the British Economy*, 2 vols. (1953). E. M. Young and W. D. Hancock, *English Historical Documents 1833–1874*, vol. III (1) (1956). There is an important comment on the historiography of the period in T. S. Ashton, "The Treatment of Capitalism by the Historians," *Capitalism and the Historians,* ed. F. A. Hayek (1954). Underlying economic trends are discussed in W. W. Rostow, *The British Economy in the Nineteenth Century* (1948) and *Stages of Economic Growth* (1959). W. T. Layton and G. Crowther's *An Introduction to the Study of Prices* (1938) introduces the student of history to the economic facts of nineteenth-century British life. A. H. Imlah, *The Economic Factor in the Pax Britannica* (1958); G. J. Jones and A. G. Pool, *A Hundred Years of Economic Development in Great Britain* (1940); B. C. Hunt, *The Development of the Business Corporation in England, 1870–1914.*

The New Cambridge Modern History has in vol. X in chap. II an article on "Economic Change and Growth" by Herbert Heaton, and in chap. III on "The Scientific Movement and Its Influence on Thought and Material Development" by A. R. Hall.

CHAPTER IX

There is a good general survey in E. L. Woodward, *The Age of Reform, 1815–1870* (1938). W. L. Mathieson's *England in Transition* is useful for the period 1789–1832. G. M. Young, *Victorian England* (1936), and G. M. Young, ed., *Early Victorian England,* give the spirit of the age. There is a cloud of special studies: J. A. Thomas, *The House of Commons, 1832–1901* (1939); H. W. C. Davis, *The Age of Grey and Peel;* N. Gash, *Politics in the Age of Peel;* J. R. M. Butler, *The Passing of the Great Reform Bill* (1914); H. Wickwar, *The Struggle for the Freedom of the Press, 1819–1832;* Norman McCord, *The Anti-Corn Law League, 1838–1846* (1958); A. R. Schoyen, *The Chartist Challenge* (1959); H. J. Hanham, *Elections and Party Management; Politics in the Time of Disraeli and Gladstone* (1959); J. L. Hammond, *Gladstone and the Irish Nation* (1938). Charles Seymour, *Electoral Reform in England and Wales, 1832–1885,* unravels that tedious, technical, but vital matter.

CHAPTER X

Lord Strang, *Britain in World Affairs* (1961). In vol. X of *The New Cambridge Modern History,* chap. X by Gordon Craig on "The System of Alliances and the Balance of Power"; chap. XIII by David Thomson on "The United Kingdom and its World-wide Interests"; chap. XVI by C. W. Crawley on "The Mediterranean." These chapters give a useful sketch of the European scene in British eyes before 1870. There is the selection of documents: *Foundations of British Foreign Policy,* from Pitt (1792) to Salisbury (1902), ed. by H. Temperley and Lillian M. Penson (1938); Ronald Robinson and John Gallagher with Alice Denny, *Africa and the Victorians* (1962); H. S. Ferns, *Britain and Argentina in the Nineteenth Century* (1961).

CHAPTER XI

William Ashworth, *An Economic History of England 1870–1939* (1960) is a recent survey of the field in the light of modern research. Important special studies are: L. H. Jenks, *The Migration of British Capital to 1875* (1927): H. Feis, *Europe, The World's Banker, 1870–1914;* A. K. Cairncross, *Home and Foreign Investment, 1870–1913* (1953); C. J. Fuchs, *The Trade Policy of Great Britain and her Colonies since 1860;* R. L. S. Hoffman, *Great Britain and the German Trade Rivalry, 1875–1914;* J. Caird, *The Landed Interest and the Supply of Food;* W. S. Jevons, *The Coal Question;* W. Bagehot, *Lombard Street;* B. Mallet, *British Budgets, 1887–1912;* A. L. Bowley, *Wages and Income in the United Kingdom since 1860* (1937).

CHAPTER XII

R. C. K. Ensor, *England 1870–1914* (1935) is one of the best general surveys. D. L. Keir, *Constitutional History of Modern Britain* is a good textbook. It can be supplemented by A. V. Dicey, *Law of the Constitution* (the 9th ed., 1939 has a useful introduction by E. C. S. Wade); A. V. Dicey, *Law and Opinion in England During the Nineteenth Century;* R. F. Hardie, *Political Influence of Queen Victoria* (1938); *Queen Victoria Letters, 1837–1861* (3 vols.), *1862–1901* (6 vols.); Harold Nicolson, *King George V* (1952); R. Bassett, *The Essentials of Parliamentary Democracy;* Roy Jenkins, *Mr. Balfour's Poodle*—a study of the constitutional crisis of 1909–11. For the political parties there are R. T. Mackenzie, *British Political Parties* (1955); H. Pelling, *Origins of the Labour Party* (1954); F. Bealey and H. Pelling, *Labour and Politics, 1900–06* (1954); S. Maccoby, *English Radicalism 1832–1914* (1935–53); Graham Wallas, *Human Nature in Politics* (1908). Some of the important biographies are J. Morley, *Gladstone* (1903), which may be supplemented by Philip Magnus, *Gladstone* (1954); J. L. Hammond, *Gladstone and the Irish Nation* (1938); W. F. Monypenny and G. E. Buckle, *Life of Disraeli* (1910–20); S. Gwynn and G. Tuckwell, *Life of Sir Charles Dilke* (1916); Bernard Holland, *Life of the Duke of Devonshire;* Lady Gwendolen Cecil, *Life of Robert, Marquis of Salisbury;* the Marquis of Crewe, *Lord Rosebery;* A. G. Gardiner, *Life of Sir William Harcourt;* J. A. Spender's *Life of Campbell Bannerman* (1923); James L. Garvin, *Life of Joseph Chamberlain;* the Earl of Ronaldshay, *Life of Lord Curzon;* J. A. Spender and Cyril Asquith, *Life of Lord Oxford and Asquith;* Lucy Masterman, *C. F. G. Masterman* (1939); A. L. Kennedy, *Salisbury* (1953).

R. Coupland, *Welsh and Scottish Nationalism* (1954) is useful. C. C. O'Brien, *Parnell and His Party* (1957), and F. S. L. Lyons, *Irish Parliamentary Party, 1890–1910* (1951), are two important recent studies. E. Halévy, *History of the English People: Epilogue,* 2 vols. (1934), covers the period from 1895–1915 with detachment and precision.

CHAPTER XIII

The Cambridge History of the British Empire, vol. III, *The Empire-Commonwealth,* ed. by E. H. Benians, Sir James Butler, and C. E. Carrington has a full bibliography on the period 1870–1919. *The New Cambridge Modern History,* vol. XII, *The Era of Violence 1898–1945,* has no bibliography, but chap. IV, "The Western Question in Asia and North Africa, 1900–1945," chap. XI, "International Relations, 1900–1912," and chap. XII, "The Approach of the War of 1914" are useful. R. L. Schulyer, *Parliament and the British Empire* (1929) is a brief introduction to the constitutional development of the Empire. There is a good collection of documents in A. B. Keith, *Speeches and Documents on the British Dominions, 1918–1931.* G. M. Trevelyan's *Grey of Falloden* (1937) is important for the coming of the war of 1914. E. L. Woodward, *Great Britain and the German Navy* (1934). Lord Strang, *Britain in World Affairs,* and the H. Temperley and L. M. Penson documents are guiding threads.

CHAPTER XIV

Only a glimpse can be given of the riches to be found. The selection is inevitably very personal. A. V. Dicey, *Lectures on the Relation Between Law and Public Opinion in England During the Nineteenth Century* (reprinted 1948) is a good introduction to the strange nineteenth-century English world. Brief and cogent is the preface by F. R. Leavis to J. S. Mill's essays on *Bentham and Coleridge* (1950), in an edition Leavis prepared because he considered that the student would find in them a good introduction to the nineteenth century. From that brief introduction one can go to F. R. Leavis, *Revaluation* (1949) and *The Great Tradition* (1950). W. H. Auden, *The Enchafed Flood* (1951), is a study of romanticism. J. Heath-Stubbs, *The Darkling Plain* (1950), and G. Hough, *The Last Romantics* (1949), continue the story. Basil Willey's *Nineteenth Century Studies* (1949) and *More Nineteenth Century Studies* (1956) take one from Coleridge to Morley. A. N. Whitehead, *Science and the Modern World* (1936); C. A. Singer, *A Short History of Science in the Nineteenth Century* (1941); C. C. J. Webb, *A Study in Religious Thought in England from 1850* (1933); Sir Leslie Stephen, *The English Utilitarians* (1900, reprinted 1950); C. Brinton, *English Political Thought in the Nineteenth Century* (1949); G. H. Mead, *Movement of Thought in the Nineteenth Century* (1936); B. E. Lippincott, *Victorian Critics of Democracy* (1938); all these and many more throw varied lights on the period. Some special studies may be mentioned: J. H. Muirhead, *Coleridge as Philosopher* (1930); Sir Herbert Read, *Coleridge as Critic* (1949); I. A. Richards, *Coleridge on Imagination* (1934); L. Trilling, *Matthew Arnold* (rev. ed. 1949); F. R. Leavis, "Arnold as Critic," *Scrutiny* (1938); T. S. Eliot on F. H. Bradley in *For Lancelot Andrewes* (1928); F. H. Bradley's seven-page introduction to his *Appearance and Reality* (1893); his *The Presuppositions of Critical History* (1874), and *Mr. Sidgwick's Hedonism* (1877, reprinted in *Collected Essays,* vol. 1, 1935); Edmund Wilson on Dickens in *The Wound and the Bow* (1952). Humphrey House, *The Dickens World* (1941); R. G. Collingwood, *Ruskin's Philosophy* (1922); W. H. Auden, *Tennyson: A Selection and Introduction* (1946); F. R. Leavis, "Gerard Manley Hopkins," "The Letters of Gerard Manley Hopkins," in *The Common Pursuit* (1952).

On the vital theme of the relation between political and economic institutions Lionel Robbins, *The Theory of Economic Policy* (1952); Gunnar Myrdal,' *The Political Element in the Development of Economic Theory* (1929, English ed. 1953); W. Bagehot, *Economic Studies* (1880); William S. Jevons, *The State in Relation to Labour* (1882).

CHAPTER XV

Vol. 3, *Cambridge History of the British Empire,* chap. XVI, "The Empire at War, 1914–18," by C. E. Carrington; vol. XII, *The New Cambridge Modern History: The Era of Violence,* chap. XII, "The War of 1914–18," by C. T. Atkinson. Liddell Hart, *The Real War* (1930) and *The War in Outline* (1936); Cyril Falls, *The First World War;* P. H. Reynolds, *British Foreign Policy in the Inter-War Years* (1954); J. Ehrman, *Cabinet Government and War 1890–1940* (1958).

CHAPTER XVI

The Haldane Report on *Machinery of Government* (Cd 9230, 1918). Gilbert Campion *et al, British Government since 1918* (1950). D. E. Butler, *Electoral System in Britain, 1918–51* (1953). C. L. Mowat, *Britain Between the Wars* (1955). R. W. Lyman, *The First Labour Government* (1957). Roger Fulford, *Votes for Women.* R. Bassett, *Nineteen Thirty-One: Political Crisis* (1958). Harold Nicolson, *King George V* (1952). J. W. Wheeler-Bennett, *King George VI* (1959). Robert Blake, *The Unknown Prime Minister: Bonar Law* (1955). Keith Feiling, *Life of Neville Chamberlain* (1946). R. F. Harrod, *Life of J. M. Keynes.*

CHAPTER XVII

G. C. Allen, *British Industries* (1935). A. Plummer, *New British Industries of the Twentieth Century* (1937). G. P. Jones and A. G. Pool, *A Hundred Years of Economic Development in Great Britain* (1940). *Britain's Industrial Future,* the Liberal Industrial Report of 1928. J. M. Keynes, *The End of Laissez-Faire* (1926). Lionel Robbins, *The Great Depression* (1934). E. H. Phelps Brown, *Growth of British Industrial Relations* (1959). Mark Abrams, *Condition of the British People, 1911–45* (1945). A. M. Carr Saunders and D. C. Jones, *A Survey of the Social Structure of England and Wales* (1927). D. C. Marsh,

> *Changing Social Structure of England and Wales, 1871–1951* (1958).
> W. A. Lewis, *Economic Survey, 1919–1939* (1949).

CHAPTER XVIII

Winston Churchill has written the history of World War II, *Second World War,* 6 vols. (1948–54). Vol. VI of *The History of the Second World War* by John Ehrman (1956) is called *Grand Strategy* and chap. X has an analysis of the central organization. There are short histories: J. F. C. Fuller, *The Second World War* (1948); Cyril Falls, *The Second World War* (1948). In E. J. Passant, *A Short History of Germany 1815–1945* (1959) there is an excellent brief summary of Germany's war effort in chap. IV by D. C. Watt. Sir Llewellyn Woodward, *British Foreign Policy in the Second World War* (1962) is the record compiled from British archives (1962). C. M. Woodhouse, *British Foreign Policy since the Second World War* (1961). J. D. B. Miller, *The Commonwealth in the World* (1958). John Strachey, *The End of Empire*. Lord Strang, *Britain in World Affairs* (1961).

CHAPTER XIX

W. K. Hancock and M. M. Gowing, *British War Economy* (1949) records the mobilization of economic resources, 1939–45. The authors had free access to official documents. Richard M. Titmuss' *Problems of Social Policy* (1950) examines the changes forced upon society and the machinery of government by the demands of war; see also his *Essays on 'The Welfare State'* (1958). *The Sterling Area* (1951) is an American analysis prepared by the Economic Cooperation Administration Special Mission to the United Kingdom. A. Shonfield, *British Economic Policy since the War* (1958). F. C. C. Benham, *Great Britain under Protection*. J. H. Dunning and C. J. Thomas, *British Industry* (1961); G. C. Allen, *British Industries and Their Organisation* (4th ed. 1949); P. Sargant Florence, *Industry and the State* (1957); B. C. Roberts, *Trade Unions in a Free Society* (2d ed. 1962); A. E. Kahn, *Great Britain in the World Economy* (1946); U. W. Kitzinger, *The Challenge of the Common Market* (1961). James E. Meade, *U.K., Commonwealth and Common Market* (Institute of Economic Affairs 1962); Mark Abrams' *Social Surveys and Social Action* (1951) examines the source of our knowledge of social life. Brinley Thomas, *The Welsh Economy* (1962); George S. Pryde, *Scotland from 1603 to the Present Day* (1962).

CHAPTER XX

W. I. Jennings, *Cabinet Government* (new ed. 1959); D. N. Chester and F. M. G. Willson, *Organisation of British Central Government 1914–56* (1957); L. S. Amery, *Thoughts on the Constitution* (1947); W. Harrison, *Government of Britain;* Herbert Morrison, *Government and Parliament.* There are many other general studies of the British postwar system of government. Some special studies of interest are: D. E. Butler, *Electoral System in Britain, 1918–51* (1953); D. E. Butler and Richard Rose, *The British General Election of 1959;* E. Watkins, *The Cautious Revolution* (1951) for the Labour government, 1945–51; Samuel H. Beer, *Treasury Control* (1956); C. H. Sisson, *The Spirit of British Administration* (1959); A. H. Hanson, *Parliament and Public Ownership* (1961); *The Citizen and the Administration* (1961), a report (British Section of the International Commission of Jurists) on the redress of grievances. *Report of the Committee on the Management and Control of Research and Development* (H.M.S.O., 1961)— chap. 11 describes the general organization of government science. Francis Williams' *Dangerous Estate* is an anatomy of newspapers (1957).

CHAPTER XXI

Lowes Dickinson's *A Modern Symposium* is a pleasant introduction to the English intellectual climate before 1914. The sterner things: F. H. Bradley's Introduction to his *Appearance and Reality* (1893), already mentioned; G. E. Moore, *Philosophical Studies* (1922), chap. 1, "The Refutation of Idealism," and chap. X, "The Nature of Moral Philosophy"; J. McT. Ellis McTaggart, *Some Dogmas of Religion* (1906). In *British Philosophy in the Mid-Century,* ed. C. H. Mace (1957), C. D. Broad outlines the historical background of Cambridge philosophy, and in *Contemporary British Philosophy* (3d series, 1956) H. J. Paton gives a sketch of fifty years of philosophy. In *Horizon,* H. H. Price has a neat summary of British philosophy between the wars (Jan. 1949, vol. XIX, no. 109). G. J. Warnock, *English Philosophy since 1900* (1958).

Some particular themes may be of interest: Graham Wallas, *Human Nature in Politics* (1920); George Santayana, *Soliloquies in England;* A. N. Whitehead, *The Aims of Education* (1929) and *Adventures of Ideas* (1931); T. E. Hulme, *Speculations* (1924); T. S. Eliot, *Notes Towards the Definition of Culture* (1948) and *The Idea of a Christian Society* (1939); Gilbert Ryle, *The Concept of Mind* (1949); K. Popper, *The Open Society* (1945) and *The Poverty of Historicism* (1958).

SOVEREIGNS OF GREAT BRITAIN
(FROM 1689)

Name	Dynasty or House	Reign
William III and Mary	Stuart	1689–1702
Anne	Stuart	1702–1714
George I	Hanover	1714–1727
George II	Hanover	1727–1760
George III	Hanover	1760–1820
George IV	Hanover	1820–1830
William IV	Hanover	1830–1837
Victoria	Hanover	1837–1901
Edward VII	Saxe-Coburg	1901–1910
George V	Windsor	1910–1936
Edward VIII	Windsor	1936
George VI	Windsor	1936–1952
Elizabeth II	Windsor	1952–

PRIME MINISTERS OF GREAT BRITAIN
(FROM 1700)

Sidney Godolphin, Earl of Godolphin	1702–1710
Robert Harley, Earl of Oxford	1710–1714
Charles Talbot, Duke of Shrewsbury	1714
Charles Montagu, Earl of Halifax	1714–1715
Charles Howard, Earl of Carlisle	1715
Robert Walpole, Earl of Orford	1715–1717
James Stanhope, Earl of Stanhope	1717–1718
Charles Spencer, Earl of Sunderland	1718–1721
Robert Walpole, Earl of Orford	1721–1742
Spencer Compton, Earl of Wilmington	1742–1743
Henry Pelham	1743–1754
Thomas Pelham-Holles, Duke of Newcastle	1754–1756
William Cavendish, Duke of Devonshire	1756–1757
Thomas Pelham-Holles, Duke of Newcastle	1757–1762
John Stuart, Earl of Bute	1762–1763
George Grenville	1763–1765
Charles Watson-Wentworth, Marquis of Rockingham	1765–1766
William Pitt, Earl of Chatham	1766–1768
Augustus Henry Fitzroy, Duke of Grafton	1768–1770
Frederick North, Earl of Guilford	1770–1782
Charles Watson-Wentworth, Marquis of Rockington	1782
William Petty, Earl of Shelburne, Marquis of Lansdowne	1782–1783
William Cavendish Bentinck, Duke of Portland	1783
William Pitt (son of Earl of Chatham)	1783–1801
Henry Addington, Viscount Sidmouth	1801–1804
William Pitt (son of Earl of Chatham)	1804–1806
William Wyndham Grenville, Baron Grenville	1806–1807
William Cavendish Bentinck, Duke of Portland	1807–1809
Spencer Perceval	1809–1812
Robert Banks Jenkinson, Earl of Liverpool	1812–1827
George Canning	1827
Frederick John Robinson, Viscount Goderich, Earl of Ripon	1827–1828
Arthur Wellesley, Duke of Wellington	1828–1830
Charles Grey, Earl Grey	1830–1834
William Lamb, Viscount Melbourne	1834
Robert Peel	1834–1835
William Lamb, Viscount Melbourne	1835–1841
Robert Peel	1841–1846

List of Prime Ministers (*Continued*)

John Russell, Earl Russell	1846–1852
Edward Smith Stanley, Earl of Derby	1852
George Hamilton Gordon, Earl of Aberdeen	1852–1855
Henry John Temple, Viscount Palmerston	1855–1858
Edward Smith Stanley, Earl of Derby	1858–1859
Henry John Temple, Viscount Palmerston	1859–1865
John Russell, Earl Russell	1865–1866
Edward Smith Stanley, Earl of Derby	1866–1868
Benjamin Disraeli, Earl of Beaconsfield	1868
William Ewart Gladstone	1868–1874
Benjamin Disraeli, Earl of Beaconsfield	1874–1880
William Ewart Gladstone	1880–1885
Robert A. T. Gascoyne-Cecil, Marquis of Salisbury	1885–1886
William Ewart Gladstone	1886
Robert A. T. Gascoyne-Cecil, Marquis of Salisbury	1886–1892
William Ewart Gladstone	1892–1894
Archibald Philip Primrose, Earl of Rosebery	1894–1895
Robert A. T. Gascoyne-Cecil, Marquis of Salisbury	1895–1902
Arthur James Balfour, Earl Balfour	1902–1905
Henry Campbell-Bannerman	1905–1908
Herbert Henry Asquith, Earl of Oxford and Asquith	1908–1916
David Lloyd George	1916–1922
Andrew Bonar Law	1922–1923
Stanley Baldwin	1923–1924
James Ramsay MacDonald	1924
Stanley Baldwin	1924–1929
James Ramsay MacDonald	1929–1935
Stanley Baldwin, Earl Baldwin of Bewdley	1935–1937
Neville Chamberlain	1937–1940
Winston Spencer Churchill	1940–1945
Clement Richard Attlee	1945–1951
Winston Spencer Churchill	1951–1955
Anthony Eden	1955–1957
Harold MacMillan	1957–